News Reporting and

News Reporting and Writing

Melvin Mencher
Columbia University

Third Edition

wcb
Wm. C. Brown Publishers
Dubuque, Iowa

Book Team
Judith A. Clayton *Senior Developmental Editor*
Lynne Niznik *Assistant Developmental Editor*
Moira Urich *Production Editor*
Mavis M. Oeth *Permissions Editor*

wcb group

Wm. C. Brown *Chairman of the Board*
Mark C. Falb *President and Chief Executive Officer*

wcb

Wm. C. Brown Publishers, College Division
Lawrence E. Cremer *President*
James L. Romig *Vice-President, Product Development*
David Wm. Smith *Vice President, Marketing*
David A. Corona *Vice-President, Production and Design*
E. F. Jogerst *Vice-President, Cost Analyst*
Marcia H. Stout *Marketing Manager*
Linda M. Galarowicz *Director of Marketing Research*
Marilyn A. Phelps *Manager of Design*
William A. Moss *Production Editorial Manager*

Cover Photos: (top row, left to right:) Don Fontaine, Curt Hudson, Judith Siewert; (middle row, left to right:) New York Racing Authority, Robert Ortega, Frank Anderson; (bottom row, left to right:) Michel duCille, Joe Munson, Stewart Bowman.

Library of Congress Catalog Card Number: 83–71321

ISBN 0–697–04361–4

2–04361–01

Printed in the United States of America

Credits

Albuquerque Journal: News story on pp. 288–89. Used with permission. ■ *Anniston* (Ala.) *Star:* News story on p. 9, excerpt from news story on p. 563, news story on p. 661. Used with permission. ■ *APF Reporter:* Excerpt from news story on p. 633. Used with permission. ■ *Associated Press:* News stories on pp. 34–41, 269. Excerpts from news stories on pp. 569, 644. News stories on pp. 32, 76–77, 107 in the *Instructor's Manual.* News stories on pp. 76–77, 77, 78 of the *Workbook.* Used with permission. ■ Atlanta *Constitution:* Quotes and picture on p. 58, news story on p. 625. Used with permission. ■ *Atlantic Monthly:* Excerpt on p. 495 from the article "Let Us Now Praise Famous Writers," copyright © 1970; and excerpt on p. 495 from "Whatever Happened to Sam Spade," copyright © 1975 by the Atlantic Monthly Company, Boston. Reprinted with permission. ■ *Avalanche-Journal:* Letter to the editor excerpt on pp. 534–35. Used with permission. ■ (Baltimore) *Evening Sun:* Excerpts from news story on pp. 213–14. Used with permission. ■ *Berkshire Eagle:* Excerpt from obituary column on p. 540; excerpt from news story on p. 582; news story on p. 626. Used with permission. ■ *Bucks County Courier Times:* Excerpt from news stories on pp. 570, 668. Excerpts from news stories on p. 113; news story on pp. 114–15 of the *Instructor's Manual.* Used with permission. ■ *Buffalo Evening News:* Excerpt from news stories on pp. 218, 574. Excerpt from news story on p. 97 of the *Workbook.* Used with permission. ■ *Bulletin* (Bend, Ore.): Page of newspaper on p. 466. Excerpt from news story on p. 92 of the *Instructor's Manual.* Used with permission. ■ *Canadian Broadcasting Corporation:* Excerpt of a talk given by John R. Hunt reproduced on pp. 138–39 of the *Workbook.* Used with permission. ■ *Charlotte* (N.C.) *Observer:* News story on p. 123, excerpts from news stories on pp. 205, 206. Used with permission. ■ *Clear Creek* (Colo.) *Courant:* Excerpt from obituary on p. 533. Excerpt from news story on p. 35 of the *Instructor's Manual.* Used with permission. ■ *Columbia Journalism Review:* News story on p. 385. Used with permission. ■ *Columbus Enquirer:* Excerpt from news story on p. 194 of the *Workbook.* Used with permission. ■ *Daily News:* News stories on pp. 25, 48, 129; part of front page on p. 193; excerpt from news story on p. 504. News story on p. 39 of the *Instructor's Manual.* Used with permission. ■ *Daily Register* (Shrewsbury, N.J.): Excerpt from news story on p. 671. Used with permission. ■ *Denver Post:* Excerpt from news story on p. 582. Used with permission. ■ *Detroit News:* Excerpt from news story on p. 217. Used with permission. ■ *Editor & Publisher:* Article on p. 315, copyright © by Editor & Publisher Co., Inc. Reprinted with permission. Excerpt from news story on p. 74 of *Instructor's Manual.* Reprinted with permission. ■ *Esquire Magazine:* Excerpt on p. 184 from "On Chuck Hughes Dying Young," copyright © 1972 by Esquire, Inc. Reprinted with permission. ■ *Greenville* (S.C.) *News:* Excerpt from news

Washington Star Syndicate: Remarks by James J. Kilpatrick on acceptance of an award, reproduced on pp. 131–34 of the *Workbook.* Used with permission. ■ West Publishing Co: Court terms on pp. 589–90 based on definitions in *Black's Law Dictionary,* revised fourth edition, 1968. Definitions of court terms on p. 96 of the *Instructor's Manual* from the *Law Dictionary for Non-Lawyers* by Daniel Oran, 1975. Both books are published by West Publishing Co., St. Paul, Minn., and the material is reprinted with the permission of the publisher. ■ Walter B. Wriston: A speech given by Walter B. Wriston reproduced on pp. 136–38 of the *Workbook.* Used with permission.

Photographs

Unit Opening Photographs: Unit One: Curt Hudson; Unit Two: Michel duCille; Unit Three: Jim Peppler; Unit Four: Don Fontaine; Unit Five: Stewart Bowman; Unit Six: Bill Fitz-Patrick; Unit Seven: Jeff Widener.

Text: Frank Anderson: p. 250; Associated Press: p. 402; Don Black: p. 403; Stewart Bowman: pp. 405–6; Steve Campbell: pp. 209, 211; Linda Cataffo: p. 294; Andy Dickerman: p. 463; Michel duCille: p. 101 (top); Jim Eichenberger: p. 126; Heidi Evans: p. 673; Bruce Gilbert: p. 323; Chris Hardy: p. 685; John McDonnell: p. 487; Melvin Mencher: p. 595; *The Miami Herald:* p. 407; Eddie Motes: p. 8; Joe Munson: p. 282; Yo Nagaya: p. 594; New York Racing Authority: pp. 616–17; *The New York Times:* p. 284; Edward Nold: p. 545; Michael Patrick: p. 598; Robert J. Pavuchak: p. 604; Randy Piland: p. 550; Jack Rendulich: p. 457; Charles Ruppmann: p. 24; Judith Siewert: pp. 233, 245; Mark B. Sluder: p. 84; David Swan: p. 467; Rich Turner: pp. 101 (bottom), 474; United Press International: pp. 13, 498; Miriam Wieder: p. 692; Frank Woodruff: p. 264.

Contents

Part Three: Writing the Story 67

Part Six: Reporting the Spoken Word 449

Part Seven: A Reporter's Checklist 515

Preface

News Reporting and Writing, Third Edition, has a simple purpose. It proposes to teach the beginner how to become a reporter. But learning to report accurately and to write precisely and vigorously is no simple task. The young man or woman who would join the ranks of reporters must learn and then put into practice principles and concepts that have been developed over the years by men and women who understood that truth is elusive and that its pursuit and capture on paper require mastery of a demanding discipline.

To illustrate these principles, we will spend a lot of time with truth-seekers— another way of describing journalists—on newspapers and broadcast stations as they go about their work. We will accompany a young reporter as she conducts her first interview, and we will watch an experienced reporter cover a racial confrontation. We will be able to overhear a reporter's thinking as she ponders the lead to a story about a city council meeting.

We will join wire service reporters covering a West Coast trip of the president when a young woman breaks out of the crowd, pulls a .45 caliber pistol from her leg holster and tries to point it at the president. We will sit in the press box with reporters covering high school football and major league baseball games. At dawn, we will join a police reporter as he begins his rounds.

We will eavesdrop on a reporter as he struggles with his lead, watch him labor over his story until "little beads of blood form on his forehead," as the sportswriter Red Smith described the agony of the reporter's search for the words that will accurately portray the event. And we will share in the reporter's joy when the story is finished and is given a byline and placed on page one.

In other words, we will be concerned with the processes of reporting and writing—the ways in which reporters gather facts from sources and from their observations, how they check and verify these, and how they put them together in news stories.

The reporters we will be watching work for small newspapers in Iowa and Oregon, and they are on the staffs of metropolitan dailies in Chicago and New York. One reporter writes for a network television station in New York; another covers events for a television station in Columbus, Ohio. We will watch a young woman write news stories for TelePress, a cable news channel in Lexington, Ky. We will see how general assignment reporters and the men and women assigned to cover politics, sports, the police, city hall, education and other beats do their jobs.

Wherever they are, however they go about their work, and whatever their assignment, reporters have much in common. Covering a Rotary Club luncheon speech or the president's State of the Union address, the journalist uses the same basic processes. The general assignment reporter in a town of 25,000 and the AP's White House correspondent share a way of thinking, a set of techniques and an approach to journalism. Once learned, these enable the reporter to discover and to communicate information that all of us need in order to solve our problems and to get along with one another.

We will see that these journalists also share an ethic that directs and gives meaning to their work. Northrop Frye in an essay in *The Morality of Scholarship* (Ithaca, N.Y.: Cornell University Press, 1967, p. 4) could be discussing one aspect of journalistic morality in this passage: "The persistence of keeping the mind in a state of disciplined sanity, the courage of facing results that may deny or contradict everything that one had hoped to achieve—these are obviously moral qualities, if the phrase means anything at all."

Mary McGrory, the Washington columnist, described another aspect of the journalist's approach to his or her work in comments she made after interviewing 45 journalists who had applied for Nieman Fellowships at Harvard. She said she found these journalists to have "a great deal of commitment and compassion." Most had one trait in common, she said. "They knew a great deal about what they were doing. They did not think it enough."

The journalists I know—my former colleagues and students, from whom I have shamelessly taken time and borrowed ideas—would shrink at being described as moralists. Yet they are tireless in pursuit of a story and are dedicated to their work. Most of them also have an abiding suspicion of power.

Although adversary journalism is often criticized and sometimes ignored, it is as old as the Republic. In our third century as a nation, we must remember that today's journalists are descended from a colonial press described by historian Robert A. Rutland as "obstreperous newspapers (that) signalled the rise of a new kind of journalism in America that would not truckle long to any officialdom."

The journalist knows that democracy is healthiest when the public is kept informed about the activities of captains of industry and chieftains in public office. Only with adequate information can people check those in power. Repression and ignorance are the consequences of unchecked power. Walt Whitman, journalist and poet, described the fragility of democracy and its source of strength this way: "There is no week nor day nor hour when tyranny may not enter upon this country, if the people lose their supreme confidence in themselves—and lose their roughness and spirit of defiance."

Confident, rough and defiant—these are apt descriptions of the journalist. The journalist is also skeptical, independent, and sensitive but tough-skinned. An accomplished professional, the journalist is forever the student, reading, observing, always honing his or her talent and enlarging his or her mind.

For the third edition of *News Reporting and Writing* another area of reporting was added—business and economics journalism—and significant additions were made to most chapters. Newspapers and broadcast stations have been giving increasing space and time to the economy, and many schools and departments of journalism are responding by adding instruction in business journalism. All reporters should have some knowledge of how business and the economy work.

The third edition also reflects the increasing necessity that journalists be able to understand and to use figures, charts and data of various kinds. Government, social and physical scientists and special interests churn out material of this sort daily, and the reporter who can turn the information into news stories is prized. I have added data from a variety of sources. Students are encouraged to localize the material.

Learning how to handle this information is an excellent way for the beginning journalist to be introduced to the art of enterprising copy. Editors want self-starters, men and women who can spot stories on their own.

In chapter 8, already long, I have felt it necessary to add material about writing for electronic news delivery, the cable news channels that present written text and graphics on the screen. Many newspapers are hiring writers to rewrite their wire and local copy for local cable news programs. Journalists should know something about this field.

The suspicion and hostility that the press has experienced in recent years is noted. People are distressed by some of our excesses in the pursuit of news, and they seem angered by our persistence in refusing to allow any person or power other than the journalist to decide what shall be reported, published or broadcast.

The ever-shifting area of journalism and the law has been brought up to date. In the few years between the second and third editions, the courts have issued several restrictive rulings. They have refused to heed the warnings of journalists and others that infringements on access to information strike at the heart of democracy, which functions best when people know what is going on.

The chapter on taste had to be expanded because of the increasing use of questionable pictures. Death, brutality, horror and sexually provocative scenes are the daily fare of newspapers, and with the expansion of cable television, vast new areas of visual usage have been opened up. Guidelines in the use of pictures are essential.

The press will be hard-put through the rest of the 1980s to maintain its traditional independence and freedom of action. The task will be made easier if journalists look to this tradition. Albert Camus, the French journalist and author, was sustained by that sense of his calling during the Nazi occupation of France when he wrote from the underground. Accepting the Nobel Prize for literature in 1957, Camus said: "Whatever our personal frailties may be, the nobility of our calling will always be rooted in two commitments difficult to observe: refusal to lie about what we know and resistance to oppression."

In much of what the journalist does, there is an awareness of the relevance of his or her work to human needs and purposes, for the reporter knows that news is reality to most people. The reporter is interested in ideas, but avoids the sin of making the concrete abstract.

Journalism "is something more than a craft, something other than an industry, something between an art and a ministry," says Wickham Steed, an editor of *The Times* of London. "Journalists proper are unofficial public servants whose purpose is to serve the community."

My model for this amalgam of artist, sentry, public servant and town crier is Ralph M. Blagden, who taught a generation of journalists their duty and introduced them to the power and splendor of their native language. Ralph's classrooms were the newsrooms of newspapers from New Hampshire to California, where he worked as reporter and editor.

Ralph was my competitor as a state capitol correspondent, and never was there such a mismatch. As a beginning reporter, I was steeped in the necessity to report what people said and to stop there. Ralph generously took the youngster in hand and showed the beginner that a good reporter never settles for the surface of the news, that the compelling commandment of the journalist is to dig out the truth. He refused to make reporting divisible: All good reporting is investigative reporting, he insisted. The good reporter investigates the situation by verifying assertions and statements.

Long before investigative reporting became the fashion, Ralph was digging out documents and records to disclose the truth of official activities. His background in St. Louis journalism was in the tradition of Joseph Pulitzer and that great publisher's crusading editor, O. K. Bovard. Those of us who were fortunate to work with and to compete against Ralph feel ourselves to be members of a journalistic family whose roots are firmly embedded in a noble tradition.

Benjamin C. Bradlee, executive editor of *The Washington Post,* says of Blagden:

"Ralph taught me to be dissatisfied with answers and to be exhaustive in questions. He taught me to stand up against powers that be. He taught me to spot bullies and resist them. He taught me about patience and round-the-clock work. He taught me about ideals and freedom and rights—all of this with his own mixture of wit and sarcasm and articulate grace. He could also throw a stone farther than I could, which annoys me to this day."

Bradlee, who directed the *Post's* coverage of the Watergate story that earned his newspaper a Pulitzer Prize for meritorious public service in 1973, recalls his first story for Blagden when he was a young reporter.

"It had to do with the post-war housing mess, and he made me rewrite it 16 times. I've never done that to a reporter, but I suspect I should have. In all the investigative reporting I did for Ralph, he always wanted to know as much as I did about the story, and always shared his insights and suggestions. He had a great dollop of righteous indignation, which I learned to admire enormously.

"And of course he wrote it with style and punch and clarity."

I recall the first story I covered with Ralph. He had heard that patients in a state hospital for the mentally ill were being mistreated. Some had mysteriously died. We interviewed doctors, nurses, attendants and former patients, and we walked through the wards and corridors of the institution. I learned that second-hand accounts are just the starting point, that direct observation and other techniques of verification are essential, and when we wrote the story I learned the power of the simple declarative sentence. I also learned that journalists can be useful members of society, for after the story appeared and both of us had moved on, the state built a modern hospital to replace that aging snake pit.

Acknowledgments

News Reporting and Writing was written in the belief that the morality of journalism is as essential as the craft, and that it, too, can be taught, as it was by Ralph L. Crosman and A. Gayle Waldrop at the University of Colorado. Theirs was a journalism of commitment, compassion and conscience. Those of us who studied with them are forever in their debt.

I am also indebted to my former newsroom colleagues and to my students. They have all contributed to this book, some indirectly, like gentle George Baldwin, my first city editor, and some directly, like Berkley Hudson, one of my former students, whose work is included here. I learned from the young woman who stormed out of my classroom when I said I would not assign her to a certain story because I worried about her safety, and I learned from the copy editor many years ago who had worn down a pencil putting black lines through my copy. "Just tell us what the guy did," he told me. "Let the reader draw the conclusions."

I want to especially thank two of my former students, Marcia Chambers of *The New York Times* and Fred L. Zimmerman of *The Wall Street Journal*. Their contributions, as will be seen, are numerous. Chambers gave valuable advice in several areas of reporting, and Zimmerman read the original manuscript, rescuing major portions from ambiguity and prolixity.

For this third edition, John D. Mitchell of Syracuse University provided detailed suggestions.

Ted Billy of the University of Delaware, Frederick R. Blevins of Ball State University, Dorothy Bowles of the University of Kansas, Bruce Garrison of the University of Maine, and Mary Connelly Graff of Temple University, read the manuscript for the third edition and made helpful suggestions.

Wade Doares, the head librarian in the journalism library at Columbia University, tracked down clippings and quotes with the generosity and good spirit I have found among librarians who work with journalists. I single out Wade Doares, but I thank all the librarians who have helped me.

Jonathan Beard caught errors and repetitions in the proof and compiled the index.

Journalists are sojourners, and many of those who shared in the preparation of the first two editions have moved on to other jobs. In this third edition, I am listing the places from which they dispatched material and suggestions for the three editions.

The following list acknowledges many of the persons who shared in the preparation of this book, but only I bear the responsibility for *News Reporting and Writing:*

Marjorie Arnold
The Fresno (Calif.) *Bee*

Brian Barrett
Office of the New York County District Attorney

Frank Barrows
The Charlotte (N.C.) *Observer*

Professor Barbara Belford
Columbia University

Joan Bieder
Columbia University

Mervin Block
Freelance broadcast writer

Stewart Bowman
The Louisville Courier-Journal

Professor Warren Burkett
University of Texas, Austin

Art Carey
Bucks County Courier Times, Levittown, Pa. and *The Philadelphia Inquirer*

Larry Carroll
The Fresno (Calif.) *Bee*

Frances Cerra
The New York Times

Jean E. Collins
Core Communications

Kenneth Conboy
Office of the New York County District Attorney and Deputy Police Commissioner, New York City

Patricia Conboy
Associate Editor, Corporate Communications
The Continental Group, Inc.

Claude Cookman
The Miami Herald

Jonathan Dedmon
Rocky Mountain News, Denver, Colorado

Stuart Dim
Managing Editor, *The Charlotte* (N.C.) *Observer* and *Newsday*

Robert A. Dubill
Executive Editor, Gannett News Service

Charlotte Evans
The Bergen Record and *The New York Times*

Carol Falk
The Wall Street Journal

Ellen Fleysher
WCBS-TV, New York, N.Y.

Robert Frazier
Eugene (Ore.) *Register-Guard*

Joseph Galloway
United Press International

Steve Gettinger
Corrections Magazine

Mary Ann Giordano
Daily News, New York City

J. J. Gonzalez
WCBS-TV, New York, N.Y.

Joel M. Gora
American Civil Liberties Union

Professor Dean M. Gottehrer
University of Alaska

Sally Grimes
The Philadelphia *Bulletin* and the University of Massachusetts at Amherst

Susan Hands
The Charlotte (N.C.) *Observer*

Donna Hanover
WTVN-TV, Columbus, Ohio

Michael Hiltzik
Courier-Express, Buffalo, N.Y.

Thomas H. Jones
Night city editor, the *Chicago Sun-Times*

Harry Jupiter
San Francisco *Chronicle*

E. W. Kenworthy
Washington Bureau, *The New York Times*

Professor Penn T. Kimball
Columbia University

Eric Lawlor
The Houston Chronicle

Lynn Ludlow
San Francisco *Examiner*

Tony Mauro
Gloucester (Mass.) *Times* and Gannett
News Service

John McCormally
Editor and publisher, *The Hawk Eye,*
Burlington, Iowa

Frank McCulloch
Executive Editor, *The Sacramento Bee*

Julie McDonnell
The Register, Shrewsbury, N.J.

Bill Mertens
The Hawk Eye

Professor Alan Miller
University of Maine at Orono

Dick Oliver
City editor, *Daily News*

Sydney Penner
Assistant city editor, *Daily News*

Merrill Perlman
The New York Times

Paul Peterzell
Independent-Journal, San Rafael, Calif.

Professor L. D. Pinkham
Director, Journalistic Studies, University of
Massachusetts at Amherst

Francis Pollock
Director of public information, Federal Trade
Commission

Lew Powell,
The Charlotte (N.C.) *Observer*

Ron Rapoport
Los Angeles Times and the *Chicago Sun-Times*

Richard C. Reid
Minneapolis Tribune

Elizabeth Rhodes
The Charlotte (N.C.) *Observer* and *Seattle
Times*

Professor Ronald Robinson
Augustana College, Sioux Falls, S.D.

Mort Saltzman
The Sacramento Bee

Professor A. M. Sanderson
University of South Florida, Tampa, Fla.

Sydney Schanberg
The New York Times

John Schultz
Columbia University

Donna Shalala
Teachers College, Columbia University, New
York City and Hunter College

Eleanor Singer
Editor of the *Public Opinion Quarterly*

H. L. Stevenson
Editor-in-chief, UPI

Professor Herbert Strentz
Dean, School of Journalism, Drake
University, Des Moines, Iowa

Mike Sweet
The Hawk Eye

Jeffrey A. Tannenbaum
The Wall Street Journal

Jim Toland
San Francisco *Chronicle*

Kurt van der Dussens
Vincennes (Ind.) *Sun-Commercial*

Mary Voboril
The Miami Herald

Douglas L. Watson
The Washington Post

Howard Weinberg
Senior producer, Bill Moyers' Journal,
Channel 13, WNET-TV, New York City

Ken Wilson
San Francisco *Chronicle*

The Reporter at Work

On the Job

Watching reporters at work, we see that they are:
- Hard working
- Enterprising
- Curious
- Calm under pressure
- Knowledgeable
- Compassionate
- Courageous

Reporters are followed from assignment to reporting and writing for print and broadcast. Journalism is a group enterprise.

```
*AP40--To city editor: Information police
headquarters has a report of an explosion in a
telephone company office at Broadway and 215th
street.

    This office covering.
      The AP
    DF1213PED
```

Brentwood Parent-Teacher Association discusses raising teachers' salaries
  $2,000 a year.
United Nations considers sending troops into Middle East.
Springfield City Council candidate opposes city park and recreation bond
  issue.
Billy Harms leads at half-way point in Indianapolis 500.
Five governors argue about water rights at interstate water compact
  commission meeting.

    Few people see these events. But everyone will be able to read, see or hear
about them this evening or tomorrow morning because a reporter is covering the
news as it develops. The reporter is the link between the event and the reader, viewer
or listener. The public sees the UN debate through a reporter's eyes, hears the candidate's speech through a reporter's ears.

Even when people witness events, direct observation is insufficient. They want to savor the experience again and to have details they may have missed. A good news story also will provide interpretations and explanations. Readers want to know how the proposed salary scale for teachers will affect the property tax, whether the mayor opposes the bond issue, the race driver's winning strategy.

A tacit agreement exists between the reporter and the public. The reporter does his or her best to give the reader, viewer and listener the truth of the event, and the public presumes that the reporter's account is honestly and fully reported and is accurately written. This agreement is important, for people act on what they read and hear:

> The last paragraph of the story on the Brentwood Parent-Teacher Association meeting says parents are invited to a dinner Thursday at the local high school. A Brentwood couple decides to attend.
>
> The Friends of Peace in the Middle East lines up pickets for a march on the UN during its debate. A high school student in Peoria and a retired postman in Tacoma write letters to their congressmen urging action by the United States.
>
> A mother of three, angered by the candidate's position on the park and recreation program, calls friends and asks them to vote against him.
>
> Texas cattlemen wire their governor to turn down the Colorado governor's proposal for water allotments.

Behind these news stories is a man or woman sitting alone at a typewriter or a video display terminal pecking out an account of what has happened. Let us look at some reporters and watch them cover the news.

An Announcement and a Fire

We are in the newsroom of a midwestern newspaper with a circulation of 25,000. The telephone on the city editor's desk rings and after listening for a moment, the city editor calls to a young reporter.

"Bob, the publicity director of the Lions Club has a story."

The caller tells the reporter his club intends to donate some equipment to a city playground next Saturday at 10 a.m. The reporter asks if there will be a ceremony.

"Yes," the man replies. "We hope to have the governor there. Hope you can make it, too."

The reporter calls the governor's press secretary to verify the governor's visit and spins some copy paper into his typewriter. In 15 minutes, he has written a short piece, putting the governor in the lead. Before handing his copy to the city editor, he again checks the date, time and location of the ceremony against his notes.

A few minutes later, he is told to cover a fire and take along a photographer.

An hour later, Bob returns to the newsroom.

"It was a small fire, about $7,500 in damages, but there's some good human interest in it," he tells the city editor.

"Don't tell me you've got three columns on a three paragraph fire, Bob," the city editor replies. "What's it about?"

Without looking at his notes, he answers:

"The story isn't the fire but the background. I found out the family bought the house a few months ago, had just remodeled it, and this week the wife went to work to help pay for it. She leaves their 10-year-old boy home with his 12-year-old brother for a few hours every day.

"Well, the 12-year-old wanted to make some money cutting grass. He knows they're short of money. He was filling the lawn mower in the garage with gasoline when the tank tipped over against the water heater. Woosh. Lucky he wasn't hurt."

The city editor thinks a moment.

"Got any good quotes from the older boy?" he asks.

"Yes."

"Well, it sounds as though it's worth more than a couple of paragraphs. But don't make it a chapter in a book, Bob."

At his typewriter, Bob pauses before writing. He can start his story like most accounts of fires he has read:

A fire of accidental origin caused $7,500 in damages to a dwelling at 1315 New Hampshire St. today.
No one was injured in the blaze that began in the garage when the 12-year-old son of the owners, Mr. and Mrs. Earl Ruman . . .

But he tears that out of the typewriter. This is not the way he described the fire to the editor, he recalls. Then he remembers advice he was given by an experienced fellow reporter: "Every story demands to be told a certain way. Don't impose a form or style on it. The way you write it has to flow from the nature of the event."

The nature of his story was the youngster's good intentions gone awry. So he starts again:

Two months ago, Mr. and Mrs. Earl Ruman moved into a three bedroom house at 1315 New Hampshire St. It was their dream house.
After years of skimping and saving . . .

He stops again. At this rate, he will write the book his editor warned him against. Although he does want a dramatic story—one that will build to a climax—he cannot take forever to develop the point. Readers will drift away.

The youngster is the heart of the tragedy, he reasons, and the boy must go into the lead. Another ball of copy paper flies into the wastebasket. He tries again:

Teddy Ruman knew his father and mother had skimped and saved to put aside enough money to buy their dream house at 1315 New Hampshire St.
This morning, he decided to help, too. But his well-intentioned efforts turned to tragedy.
The 12-year-old . . .

That seems to be more like it. In 40 minutes, he has the story in good shape, he thinks.

The city editor reads through the copy.

"Yes, it's a sad story," he tells his cub reporter. "Be sadder still if they didn't have insurance to cover their loss."

Bob wheels around and makes for the telephone on his desk. He remembers another bit of advice:

"Don't leave unanswered any questions the reader may have. Don't leave any holes in your story."

A Daring Rescue

Some 1,500 miles to the west, we are in Yosemite National Park.

Harry Jupiter, a young reporter from the Fresno Associated Press bureau, leans over a ledge on his stomach, his feet grasped firmly by a park ranger. Several hundred feet below in a tiny pocket of rock is a 17-year-old climber who had found himself stymied while working his way up the face of an almost sheer cliff.

It is morning and the youth had been squatting—knees half bent, back against the wall—on an 18-inch ledge since last night. Had he fallen asleep or tried to change his position, he would have plummeted 1,500 feet to the floor of the valley.

Jupiter is watching park rangers prepare to rescue the youth. It is a complicated and daring operation. A group of seven rangers descends from the top of Glacier Point to the farthest they can reach on foot. From this ledge, four rangers are lowered by rope to the next ledge. At this point, the rescue party splits again and two men are lowered to a third ledge. From here, a sheer granite wall drops below them for some 500 feet. About a third of the way down on a small niche in the rock squats the object of this daring and dangerous rescue.

Lowering the rope to the youth, the two rangers begin the long and hazardous job of pulling him and then themselves back to the top.

Jupiter has been watching, taking notes and obtaining information from rangers overseeing the operation. As soon as the youth is hauled up from his precarious perch to the bottom ledge, Jupiter leaves for a telephone to call in a fresh lead to the continuing story. He tells his office that the youth has been reached and hauled part-way, but there is still a long way to go. It will take hours.

The AP rewriteman tells Jupiter that some newspapers and TV stations are now stating that the youth has been rescued. Jupiter refuses to change his story. He tells the rewriteman that the rescue is a long way from completion and that the youth and four rangers still must be raised by rope a few hundred feet. Anything can happen.

Then Jupiter returns to his ledge.

It is midafternoon and the rescue party still is not out of danger when Jupiter makes another call to the San Francisco office to dictate a new lead to his story.

"Harry, you can't be right this time," the news editor tells him. One of the San Francisco newspapers has a story in print about the youth's rescue and describes him as being in the park hospital.

Jupiter assures his editor he has not been drinking and that the group is still making the long climb up.

"Here's some color on the rescue," he tells the editor. He reads his notes on the reactions of the hundreds of spectators. He describes the feelings of the rangers' wives and children nervously watching the rescue.

Then he goes back to the ledge to wait for the group. At last they stagger up. Jupiter dashes to meet them. He discovers that one of the rangers is carrying a camera. While the ranger is catching his breath, Jupiter asks him if he had used his camera during the rescue. He replies that he had. Jupiter tells the ranger he would like to use the pictures, and if the ranger will turn over the film to the AP, it will develop the film and return it quickly. (The photos turned out to be spectacular and were used in papers around the country.)

Jupiter approaches the youth and asks him about his feelings during the long hours on the ledge. The youngster replies that he was never worried. Lagging behind the main group, Jupiter chats with one of the rangers in the rescue party who tells him, "Boy, was this kid arrogant. He gave us plenty of trouble on the way back up and almost got us killed a couple of times. And you know something, he hasn't so much as said, 'Thanks.' "

Enterprise

Chicago Daily News reporter Raymond R. Coffey has been sent to cover a student riot on the University of Mississippi campus in Oxford, Miss. Coffey can hear the shouts of the students on the campus, but the police tell the reporters they cannot enter. The reporters try another entrance, then another, five in all, and each is blocked by state highway patrolmen.

There is a story behind those walls, and Coffey intends to dig it out.

"Back in my hotel room, I took off my suit," he said later, "put on khaki pants, rolled up the sleeves of my blue shirt, and left the collar open. I left my notebook with other reporters and stuffed a few pieces of paper and a pencil into a pocket."

Disguised as a student, he slipped into the campus and gathered material for his story.

A Feature

During the 1980 Carter-Reagan presidential campaign, *The Anniston Star,* a 32,000 circulation daily newspaper in Alabama, decided to do a series on people and politics. For the first article, the paper assigned R. Robin McDonald, a new reporter on the staff.

"It was my third day on the job," McDonald said, "my second in Clay County. My first day in the county I had spied two old men on the courthouse steps, but when I had gone back later to talk with them, they had disappeared."

McDonald learned that they had been watching the political scene from their courthouse vantage point for more than a decade. He decided to interview them for his story.

The Regulars. From their seats in the Clay County Courthouse, these old-timers have observed local politics for more than a decade.

"I found them the second day, ensconsed in the old chairs in the courthouse rotunda. I first asked for directions to an office located in another building below the courthouse, just to break the ice. I left briefly to go to the building, though I already knew the person I wanted to see was out. Then I came back to talk.

"I volunteered the information that the man who I was ostensibly looking for wasn't in, told them it was my second day in the county, my first week in Alabama and I wanted to know about the county. I didn't mention the story at all. I pulled up a chair and we talked county, family (most of my relatives are from Georgia) and gradually drifted into politics. I didn't pull out a notebook, didn't take notes. We talked for about three or four hours. Then I left, telling them I would see them Monday. And I mentioned I might want to do a story on them, if they didn't mind.

"I went back to the *Star* where I typed like crazy, putting impressions, phrases, bits of conversation, anything I could remember on paper. I went back on Monday and we talked again, this time more directly about politics and how it had shaped their lives. By that time I had built a trust—something necessary for the kind of story I wanted. I then set up official interviews for the following day. Again, I returned to the *Star* and typed up what I had remembered.

"On Tuesday, I simply could ask them in the interview, 'Tell me about . . .' or say, 'Remember when you told me about . . .' and thus get some direct quotes. By that time, I had the background, knew the stories and knew what I wanted in them. I had a flavor, an atmosphere. And I had the old men's trust. So they talked more freely than I think they normally would have to a newcomer and a reporter.

"Then I came back, wrote the stories, using my notes. By that time, I had had a chance as well to talk with the old men's cronies, hear their stories, and watch them move around the courthouse.

"It took longer than one might normally spend on a feature story, but I think it was better for it."

McDonald decided to give each of the old timers a separate piece. Here is how his story about Jack Crawford begins:

ASHLAND—Jack Crawford's been sitting in the rotunda of the Clay County Courthouse for 17 years, and he spots a new face like a bird dog on point. There's no one more delighted than Jack to hook a stranger and talk about Clay County, people and politics—as long as the politics are Democratic.

Crawford, at 75, is proud to say he's a lifelong Democrat. The one time he didn't vote the Democratic ticket, in 1928 when Al Smith ran against Republican Herbert Hoover, he just didn't vote. . . .

McDonald reaches the news peg in the fifth paragraph:

He believes the president is a good man, and he's pretty certain Carter will carry Alabama in two weeks. But he's not so sure that a Democrat will win the presidency this time around. But he's going to vote anyway, and his man is Jimmy Carter.

Here is the beginning of the piece about Mike Carter:

ASHLAND—Eighty-one-year-old Mike Carter's clear blue eyes and angel smile disguise a spirit of pure devilment. He's Jack Crawford's best friend and for years, he too, has staked out a broken-back, red leather chair in the rotunda of the Clay County Courthouse.

The two of them sit on each side of the main hall, just like watchdogs at the gates of Hades. "We know everybody's business that comes through the courthouse," Carter said recently. "And if we don't, we find out."

Carter, like his cohort Crawford, is always eager to listen to people talking politics.

He's more reticent when it comes to voicing his own opinions on the subject, except to proclaim proudly that the blood in his veins is pure Southern Democrat.

He's voting for President Carter for that reason, but this election doesn't stir his emotions as much as earlier ones. It's not that he's not interested. The stakes to him just don't seem as high as they once might have been. "I am," he said, "living better than I ever did in my life."

Localizing a Wire Story

In a newsroom in upstate New York, the news editor tears a story off a long section of wire service copy and calls out:

"Hey, Anne. Here's a short piece on Bemelmans' death."

He shows the news story to a reporter. It is about the death of humorist and artist Ludwig Bemelmans in New York City.

"He's the author of those books I read my children," the news editor says. "He was in the service around here in World War I, they say. Wasn't the main character named Madeline?" he asks the reporter.

"That's right. I remember my sister reading them to me when I was a kid," she answers. "I'll never forget those first two lines."

In an old house in Paris that was covered with vines
Lived twelve little girls in two straight lines.

"Yes, that's it," says the news editor.

"I'll bet a lot of our readers know the Madeline books. It's a slow day for local news. Why don't we localize the story?"

She takes the copy to the city editor, who agrees to localizing the wire story. "See what you can do, give me a couple of pages of copy," he tells her.

For her rewrite, Anne needs more information and goes to *Who's Who*. Then she verifies her memory of the first few lines of the book by calling the city library and asking for the children's department. The librarian says that Bemelmans also illustrated his books.

"Are the books still popular?"

"Oh, yes," the librarian replies. "They are always in demand, almost as much as Winnie the Pooh books. I think parents like them as much as the children."

Anne verifies from the newspaper library the news editor's recollection about Bemelmans having been stationed at a nearby army camp.

Finally, she is ready to write. She lines up her notes and the wire service story on her desk.

The news, of course, is the death of Bemelmans. But Anne wants to put a local angle into the lead. She can say that Bemelmans was stationed nearby. But that was a long time ago. Also, it reminds her of a parody on localizing news that she read somewhere. It ran something like this, she recalls, "Winston Churchill, whose train stopped near here en route to his famous speech at Fulton, Mo., died today in London."

No, it would be best to stress the books he wrote that local people read.

She writes:

```
The author of the Madeline books, Ludwig Bemelmans, died
in New York City yesterday . . .
```

But she does not like the beginning and she tears it out of the typewriter before she has finished the lead. She tries again:

```
     The author of the Madeline books, beloved by children
here and everywhere, died yesterday in New York City . . .
```

Yes. That is closer. But she has neglected the parents. Another try:

```
     The author of the Madeline books, read and loved by
parents and children here and everywhere, died yesterday in
New York City. Ludwig Bemelmans was 64 years old.
```

We take leave of Anne as she slowly rereads her lead, a corner of her eye on the clock. Pleased with her handiwork, she steps up her pace, for she has only 40 minutes before she has to cover a meeting of the city zoning commission.

TV Covers a Fire

It is Christmas day, and in the newsroom of a New York City television station a teletype is clicking off a story about a fire in a small town in New Jersey. The Associated Press (AP) reports that while the family was asleep, a fire broke out and flames raced through the house. Four died. Only two boys escaped.

The news editor scans the story and tells a reporter, "Elaine, take this one on."

On the way to New Jersey, the reporter and the crew discuss the wire story. Elaine thinks of the questions she will ask, the locations in which the film will be shot.

"When I go out on an assignment I am conscious of the need for film," she said later. "I look for things that have an immediate impact, because I have a short time to tell the story—maybe two and a half minutes.

"So I look for the strongest statement in a talk, the most emotionally appealing part of a running story. When I arrive at a story, I want to be the first one to interview the eyewitness, so that the person is still experiencing the event. The emotional facts have to tell the story."

In New Jersey, she learns from the fire chief that the surviving youngsters had run to a neighbor's house during the fire. As crews from competing stations are arriving, she and her crew approach the neighbor's house through the back yard to avoid being spotted.

"When I spoke to the woman next door, I asked her what happened when the boys burst into her home. She became tense and distraught as she described one boy's face, burned and blackened by the fire," Elaine said.

Although television reporters often conduct pre-interviews for background and to put subjects at ease, the camera began to roll as the neighbor relived the early morning tragedy.

"On a breaking story, a broadcast journalist usually asks fewer questions than the print journalist," Elaine said. "On this story all I needed to ask the neighbor was two or three questions and let her tell the story.

"I never ask for a yes or no reply since a person answering that kind of question can't become too emotional. But I don't believe the reporter's questions should necessarily be in the film.

"After I asked her about what had happened, I asked her what life would be like without the family next door. Her husband replied, 'I don't want to seem dramatic, but you couldn't have asked for better neighbors.' "

Elaine then sought out the fire chief for background.

On the return drive, Elaine structured the script in her mind. She had film of the fire scenes and sound-film interviews of the neighbor and the fire chief. She worked the script around the most dramatic parts of the film. She would end the report with the interview of the fire chief warning of the dangers of home fires.

Back in the newsroom Elaine wrote her copy while the film was being developed. Then she edited it to the film selected for use.

"I looked at the competition that night," she said. "By the time they got to the neighbor's house, her story had lost its drama. She had become accustomed to talking about it."

Elaine, who worked for newspapers before switching to reporting for television, said that she found similarities between print and broadcast journalism and significant differences. The print journalist is word-oriented.

"Without pictures, the TV journalist has no story," Elaine said.

The newspaper reporter may complain that space limitations confine him, but the broadcast journalist works in a far more constricted dimension. The news on a 30-minute newscast would not fill the front page of a standard-size newspaper. The print reporter may be given half a column, about 350 words, for a story that the broadcast journalist would be allowed at most a minute, more likely less—five to six sentences.

"On some of the stories I cover," Elaine said, "I watch what we did and wish it was a 70-second minute."

Covering Watergate on Deadline

It is April 29, 1974, a few minutes after 9 p.m. in the Washington bureau of *The Wall Street Journal*. On a television set in the office, President Richard M. Nixon is describing his activities following the break-in at the Democratic headquarters in the Watergate apartment complex. Nixon had denied that he agreed to pay the burglars to keep them from revealing who had hired them. Pointing to a large stack of notebooks next to him, the president says he is turning over to the House Judiciary Committee transcripts of tape recorded conversations he had with his advisers following the break-in.

As the president finishes speaking, *Journal* staffers are writing furiously. The normal deadline for the late edition was some 15 minutes ago and they have only about 20 minutes until the presses roll.

It is clear to those handling the story that when the transcripts are made available—probably the next day—there will be another tense scene. No one reporter will be able to go through the massive amount of material for a story before the deadline. Even with several reporters at work it will be difficult.

One of those working on the story is Carol Falk, a general assignment reporter in the bureau. She recalled later that she had assumed that Nixon had probably quoted the most damaging sections from the transcripts in his television address in order to disarm his critics, who were gaining support for impeachment.

The president's 50-page summary of the transcripts is released the next morning at about 10:30 and Falk finds nothing beyond what the president has said the night before on television.

"At this point," she recalled later, "I was operating on the theory that the president might really have turned it around and releasing the transcripts could be a big plus for him."

The bureau's deadline for the first edition is 6 p.m. Unless reporters can obtain material quickly from the transcripts sent to members of the House Judiciary Committee, the early story will have to be based on the president's version of the tapes and his summary.

Awaiting the release of the full transcripts of the tapes—and hoping they will be released to the press before her deadline—Falk decides to pinpoint the key dates

Nixon Addresses the Nation on Watergate. President Nixon has just told the nation in a television address that he is turning over transcripts about the Watergate scandal to the House Judiciary Committee. Referring to the material, stacked on a desk next to him, he said it will describe his conversations with his advisers following the Watergate break-in. The material will "tell it all," he said.

by going through a copy of a Watergate chronology. When the transcripts become available, these dates will be the first sections she will examine. Of these dates, March 21, 1973, is one of the most important. On that day, the president met with John Dean and H. R. Haldeman, his close advisers, and ostensibly discussed payments—"hush money"—to the men who had been arrested in connection with the Watergate break-in.

Later in the day, with the deadline ever nearer, the press associations began to run stories quoting sources who had seen material in the March 21 transcripts—and the story seemed to be changing shape.

"Our theory about the news in the transcripts began to shift," Falk says.

The material coming in, apparently from some members of the House Judiciary Committee, indicated the president's speech and summary were highly selective and did not reflect the material in the transcripts.

"I began to work on a first edition story based on the president's summary and the contrast with the more damaging reports coming out on the Hill," she says. "I was barely into the second graf [paragraph] when we got our own copy of the transcript from the White House at around 3:30 p.m."

Falk tore out the March 21 section and a colleague and the bureau chief took the rest of the transcript. She spent almost an hour checking the March 21 transcript against the president's speech and his summary to see whether they agreed. She decided that the transcript did not fully corroborate the president's version, and that conclusion went into her lead. By 4:30 p.m., she had half a page done. As she turned out her copy, the bureau chief and another reporter were sending material to the desk also. There, the work of the three was stitched together into a single story.

The bureau decided to run long stretches from the transcripts to allow readers to draw their own conclusions, and to forestall any accusations of out-of-context quotes.

The story, published May 1, 1974, began this way:

WASHINGTON—The transcripts of President Nixon's Watergate conversations aren't nearly as clear a portrayal of his innocence as the White House is trying to tell the American people they are.

Although Mr. Nixon conceded that the material would prove embarrassing and ambiguous, the full transcript of one controversial meeting—that of March 21, 1973—includes numerous damaging statements that weren't foreshadowed in the president's confident television presentation Monday night.

For instance, while Mr. Nixon said in his speech that his clear intention at the end of the March 21 meeting was that further payments of hush money to Watergate defendant E. Howard

Hunt shouldn't be made, the edited transcript shows him looking favorably on that option very near the end of the session. On page 67 of the 79-page account of that meeting among the President, White House Counsel John Dean and Chief of Staff H. R. Haldeman the following exchange begins, referring to Hunt's demand for money:

President: Would you agree that that's the prime thing, that you damn well better get that done?

Mr. Dean: Obviously, he ought to be given some signal anyway.

President: (expletive deleted) Get it. In a way that—who is going to talk to him; Colson? He is the one who is supposed to know him.

Falk and the others continued to read the transcripts over the next few days, writing stories based on other aspects of the White House conversations. She would decide on a theme and then she and her colleagues would search out the quotes to document and amplify it. The bureau's final story, six days after the first, tried to sum up "the things the transcripts didn't tell."

Looking back a few weeks later, Falk said she approached her coverage of this aspect of Watergate with a question:

"Does it help or hurt Richard Nixon's chances of staying in office? That's the 'bottom line,' as the White House would say."

She added, "Often reporters haven't much idea of what the event is going to be until we get to the scene. But as I'm listening to a hearing, courtroom arguments, a press conference or whatever, I constantly say to myself, 'What does this really mean in broad terms—what's the significance to our readers?' Often I find that the quick headline I think up to file for our wire service, or even the flip response I give to a colleague back at the office who asks, 'What happened today?', will form a lead with just a little polishing."

An Investigative Reporter at Work

A few weeks after Cammy Wilson has taken a reporting job with the *Minneapolis Tribune,* her city editor has an idea for a feature story: Spend a day with a woman in a wheelchair to see how handicapped persons get around in the city. Wilson accompanies the woman as she goes about her chores, does some shopping and has lunch. At the end of the day, the woman remarks to Wilson, "Isn't it awful how much we have to pay to be taken to the doctor." How much? Wilson asks her. "Forty to fifty dollars," she replies.

Wilson senses there is a story here of greater impact than the feature she was assigned to write. She asks the woman if she has a receipt for a trip to the doctor. The woman does. With the name of the firm, Wilson begins to ask questions.

By the time she has finished with her questions, Wilson has a major scandal laid out: The transportation of the disabled is a multi-million dollar operation in which the poor, the elderly and the handicapped are being billed $40 to $120 for a round trip to a medical facility. Companies are billing persons at an individual rate even when they take groups from a nursing home or a senior citizen center to a clinic.

Her stories interest the Health, Education, and Welfare Department in Washington D.C., and, since Medicaid money is involved, HEW investigates. The Minnesota legislature holds hearings and enacts several laws to regulate the transportation firms.

A couple of weeks after these stories appear, Wilson is house hunting. In one house, she notices that every item is for sale. From worn-out wash cloths to underwear, everything has a price tag. "Has the owner died?," she asks the realtor. "No," he says, "the owner is in a nursing home." "Why is he selling?" "He's not selling it. The conservator is," the realtor replies.

Once again, Wilson thinks she has a story. In checking it out, she learns that the owner, Ludvig Hagen, 86, suffered a fall and was taken to a nursing home to recover. While there, the church that he had named in his will marked the house and all of Hagen's possessions for sale. Wilson begins her story this way:

> "4415 17th Ave. S."
> "4415 17th Ave. S."
> The old man in his wheelchair re-peated the address, tears beginning to well.
> "I don't have to sell my house. It's paid for."
> But his house is for sale. It and all his possessions are part of an estate valued at $140,000. . . .

As a result of the story, the county attorney's office launched an investigation, and the community examined the issue of home care versus nursing home care.

This story begot still another investigation, this one into the area of probate, the handling of wills and estates by the courts. Wilson learned that the county probate court had appointed a management firm to handle the estates of various persons and that the firm had sold houses owned by these persons for well under the market price to the same buyer, who within six months re-sold the houses for 50–100 percent more than the purchase price.

A Press Release That Needs Backgrounding

In the newsroom of a daily newspaper in Maryland, the city editor calls the education reporter over to his desk.

"Dick, here's something pretty important. The overnight man took these notes from a fellow who said he is the publicity chairman of an organization called the Black Parents Association. See if the outfit amounts to anything, and if it does, let's have some comments. Write it down the middle. It's a touchy issue."

The notes read as follows:

> The Association has just sent a complaint to the state board of education. We are disturbed by the use of certain books our children are being given in the city's schools and school libraries.
> Some of this reading gives the children--black or white-- a stereotyped view of minority people. At a time when we are in danger of becoming two societies, every effort must be made to understand each other. Some of the books our children are being asked to read do not accomplish this. They portray black people as ignorant, lacking in culture, child-like, sexually loose, etc.

We are asking that certain books be removed from the
library and the classroom--Huck Finn, Manchild in the
Promised Land and Down These Mean Streets. We intend to add
to the list.

"The picture of Jim in the Twain book is that of the
stereotyped black man of slave days," says James Alberts,
Association president. "Impressionable children are led to
think of black people as senseless, head-scratching, comic
figures. We object to that portrayal of Nigger Jim."

Alberts said that in 1957 the Finn book was banned from
elementary and junior high schools in New York City by the
city board at the request of the NAACP. Later, he said,
black students at Brandeis University picketed a school
near the university that used the book.

"If it is to be read, it should be read at home under the
direction of their parents," Alberts said.

The group met in Freedom Hall of the Mt. Zion Baptist
Church tonight.

The reporter goes to his newspaper's morgue (library) to see if there are any
clips about the Association. He also looks up the names of the books in case they
have been in the news. He finds that the Association was formed in 1955, a year
after the U.S. Supreme Court ruling on school desegregation and has taken an active
interest in local school affairs. He finds nothing on the books in the morgue but he
has the feeling that he has seen or heard something about one of them.

He telephones the president of the Association to authenticate the release and
to ask if any particular incident provoked the action. The president tells him a parent
brought up the issue at a meeting last month. The reporter asks for the name of the
parent, but the president has forgotten it.

Dick knows that he should obtain reaction from the schools. He looks up the
telephone numbers of the city school superintendent, some high school principals
and the head of the board of education.

If he has time, he thinks he will try to go over to a high school for some quotes
from students. It would be appropriate to interview black students, he decides. But
that may have to wait for the next day for a folo (a follow-up story).

As Dick goes through his notes he recalls an argument he overheard a few
years ago when he was a copy boy on a newspaper. An editor ordered a reporter
to cut a story in half and the reporter had refused. "There are some stories that
shouldn't be cut," the reporter had told the editor. He went on to say that on public
issues the public must be completely informed. It was, he said, the task of journalism
to give people information so they could feed back to officials their sentiments and
opinions. This story, Dick decides, is one like that. The school board will want public
reaction, Dick reasons.

He rereads the release. Many readers will know *Huckleberry Finn*, but what
about the other books? He will have to find out something about them.

On the Job   17

No matter how well some persons may know *Huckleberry Finn,* he had better give the author's name and tell something of the plot of this book, too. He remembers that when he took a course in American literature, one of his textbooks described *Huckleberry Finn* as the greatest of all American novels. Maybe he will have to work that in to give the story some balance. He read the book for the course and remembers Jim as a man of dignity. But his reactions certainly are not those a black high school student might have, he concedes. Yes, he will have to talk to students and their parents, also.

Dick looks under "Twain" in the encyclopedia and to his surprise he finds that the book is properly titled, *The Adventures of Huckleberry Finn.* He had better check the other titles.

Dick looks out the window. He admits to himself he does not like what the Association is doing. It is too close to censorship, he muses. After all, Mark Twain is a great writer. And people are always objecting to authors: Hemingway, Salinger, Vonnegut, Steinbeck. But Mark Twain? Can a great writer be prejudiced? There's a running debate about Shakespeare's *Merchant of Venice* and Dickens' *Oliver Twist.* In fact, he recalls, he had read an article asserting that Shylock is an anti-Semitic stereotype. Well, maybe the Association has a point about Jim, he thinks.

Suddenly, he recalls having read somewhere a reference to one of the books in connection with a censorship case. It might have been an interview with the author. Something about the book's being obscene, he thinks. Then he remembers another article he had read in a magazine—was it *The Nation?*—about a violent controversy in West Virginia about books that parents charged were anti-American and anti-religious. The more he thinks, the more he realizes this is no isolated phenomenon. He asks another reporter if she recalls reading about book censorship recently. She replies that she, too, read about a book banning, this one in Long Island, N.Y.

"It was about *Black Boy,* I think, and some books supposed to be anti-Semitic. It was in 1976, I think," she says.

Dick decides to take these one at a time. As he recalls, the first book banning he was thinking of occurred in Maryland. He decides to consult *The New York Times Index,* which his newspaper receives. First, he looks under "Obscenity," then "Pornography." There are no helpful entries, but there is a note suggesting the reader check "Books—Censorship." The third entry turns out to be what Dick is looking for. Under it, he begins to read:

> Baltimore, Md, School Board is expected to reconsider shortly Nov 29 decision to ban C Brown's book about life in Harlem, *Manchild in the Promised Land*
> . . .

The entry goes on to describe the school board action. Dick decides he would like to see the original story. He also continues to search subsequent volumes of the *Index* for a story about the board's action. Did it reconsider the ban? The *Index* has no further information, and he decides he will have to call Baltimore.

His research turns up similar incidents in Wisconsin, Texas and Oregon. An article in *The Reader's Digest* quotes the American Library Association as reporting that there were three times as many incidents of censorship in schools between 1975 and 1979 than in the preceding ten years. Since 1980, the Association says, the rate tripled again with more than 1,000 reported attempts to ban or restrict books in public schools.

He also discovers there was a U.S. Supreme Court decision in the Long Island book banning. The decision supported the students who had appealed the censorship.

He again checks *The New York Times Index* under "Books—Censorship" and finds this entry in 1982:

SupCt rules that 1st Amendment guarantees of freedom of speech limits discretion of public school officials to remove books they consider offensive from school libraries. . . .

Dick finds the story from the *Times* microfilms in the newspaper library. The school board of the Island Trees Union Free School District removed nine books from the shelves of junior and senior high schools on the grounds they were "anti-American, anti-Christian, anti-Semitic and just plain filthy." *Down These Mean Streets* was one of the banned books.

The Supreme Court ruled that the students could try to prove their case in the federal court. Faced with the Court's limitation on its powers, the Island Trees school board decided to rescind the book banning rather than go through with a trial in which it would have to defend its action.

Another entry in the *Index* sends him to a *Times* story that lists in order the most frequently censored books from 1977 to 1982:

Go Ask Alice, a diary of a teen-age girl who fell into drug use and committed suicide. The author is anonymous, supposedly the parents of the girl.
The Catcher in the Rye by J. D. Salinger, long on the list.
Our Bodies, Ourselves by the Boston Women's Health Collective.
Forever by Judy Blume.
Of Mice and Men by John Steinbeck.
A Hero Ain't Nothing but a Sandwich by Alice Childress.
My Darling, My Hamburger by Paul Zindel.
Slaughterhouse Five by Kurt Vonnegut.
The Grapes of Wrath by John Steinbeck.
The Adventures of Huckleberry Finn by Mark Twain.

No doubt he will have much more information than he can use, but he would prefer to be thorough. Anyway, it is possible that interesting and significant material will turn up in the checking.

The telephone call to Baltimore reveals that the board rescinded its action to ban the book after a public hearing in December. Dick thinks he will put that into his story.

Dick decides he will have to handle the rest of the story by telephone. There are too many people to reach in person. He makes about a dozen calls and an hour before his first deadline he decides he had better start writing. He will base his story on the parents' request:

```
   A local school group, the Black Parents Association, has
asked the city school system to remove three books from high
school libraries because they allegedly present a
stereotyped view of blacks.
```

Too long, he thinks. Dull. Also, he does not like too many commas in a lead. A comma makes the reader pause. Maybe he should try a more dramatic lead:

```
   Huckleberry Finn should be banned from high school
libraries, a local black parents organization urged today.
```

Too sensational for this kind of story, he thinks, and discards this lead. Another couple of tries, and he hits on something he likes:

```
   A local black parents organization has charged that the
city school system uses books that debase blacks and other
minorities.
   The organization, the Black Parents Association, asked
that the State Board of Education order three books removed
from Freeport school libraries and classrooms. The group
charged that the books present a "stereotyped view of
minority people." The books are: "The Adventures of
Huckleberry Finn" by Mark Twain, "Manchild in the Promised
Land" by Claude Brown, and "Down These Mean Streets" by Piri
Thomas.
   The Association, which took the action at a meeting last
night in the Mt. Zion Baptist Church, said it intends to add
other books to the three it named.
```

Looking this over, Dick realizes he will need to quote extensively from the statement the organization called in so that readers have the full flavor of the group's anger.

"Too bad," he says, half-aloud, "we didn't have a reporter there." Then he would have something to work with—the sense of outrage, possibly the rebuttals of others. He puts the luxury of speculation aside and settles down to more writing.

After he has written his story, Dick decides to drive to the nearest high school. He knows that there is a luncheonette near the school where the students hang out. He sits at the counter and orders a pizza and a soft drink. Around him, the students are talking about a basketball game. Gradually, Dick eases into the conversation. He remarks that the team will have its work cut out for it next week. The students agree.

In a short time, he is chatting easily with three boys. He slowly turns the conversation from sports to school work and asks them about the books they read for English classes. He asks if any one has been assigned *Huckleberry Finn*. One student says he has read the book on his own.

Dick decides that this is the time to identify himself. He realizes that some students may posture once they realize he is a reporter, but he prefers to be open with his sources.

He asks the student for his reaction to the book, and then tells him about the Association's action. One of the boys calls over some other students in a booth nearby, and soon several students, both black and white, are chatting with Dick. He lets them talk. He does not take out his notebook. He wants them to speak freely. He trusts his memory for this part of the discussion.

One youngster ventures an opinion. "Maybe there are some bad things in those books. But maybe censorship is worse."

The others nod in agreement, Dick takes out his pad.

"That's interesting," he says. "Mind if I jot that down here?"

The others go on talking, and Dick quickly notes what he has stored in his memory as he also tries to keep up with the running conversation.

He asks some of the students for their names. He would like to use them in his piece, he says. Some readers, Dick knows, will distrust the vague attribution to "a student." It is always best to have names in a controversial story.

Back in the newsroom, Dick tells his editor about his chat with the students. The editor suggests Dick use the material as the basis for a Sunday interpretative piece. He and Dick discuss other persons to interview.

"Maybe you'd better talk to some of the people over at the university," the editor suggests. "We ought to have a rounded picture. They can tell us about literature and efforts to condemn or censor important works."

The Qualities of a Reporter

We have watched nine reporters at work, beginners and veterans, members of small and large staffs. Different as they appear at first glance, they share certain characteristics, and there are many similarities in the way they handled their assignments.

One of the characteristics we notice is the reporter's attitude. He or she is curious. The reporter wants to know what is happening—firsthand. Coffey would not accept the version of officials about the demonstrations on the campus. He had to go in, and he did.

The reporter wants to know what happened yesterday and today, and he tries to learn from sources what they think will happen tomorrow. He wants to know why it happened and how.

The reporter has an eye for precise detail. Journalism can be defined as the practice of the art of the specific. *The Wall Street Journal's* May 1, 1974, Watergate story quotes from "page 67 of the 79-page account," and it goes on to give the exact quotation.

Some observers might say that journalists are courageous in pursuit of the news, although many reporters would shrug off this description. Yet, reporters have died covering wars and disasters, and every journalist worthy of his or her job is familiar with harassment. A reporter needs some courage to refuse the official version and to ask questions that seem to challenge an official's probity. Reporters question authority, and those in command often dislike being questioned.

The reporter needs courage to face facts and the results of reporting that contradict his or her own beliefs. The reporter who covered the Black Parents Association's condemnation of *Huckleberry Finn* had to question his assumptions about discrimination and censorship.

The reporter requires courage to stand by a conviction in the face of pressure from competitive news agencies. Jupiter, knowing that perilous work still lay ahead, refused to go along with the competition's assertion that the youth had been rescued.

The reporter must be aggressive in gathering the facts. Sometimes this task may involve viewing events that would turn away the squeamish. It may mean interviewing the victims of personal tragedy. The reporter has to know where to draw the line between exploitation and legitimate public interest.

The journalist has a commitment to truth that encompasses the correct spelling of a name and the refusal to accept unproven assertions—no matter how prestigious the authority or expert who makes them.

The reporter digs into every assignment. The digging may be as simple as checking to see whether the governor intends to attend the local ceremony or as complex as talking to youngsters about their feelings.

Stanley Walker, one of the great city editors, was once asked, "What makes a good reporter?"

"The answer is easy," he replied, with a slight show of a smile around his eyes. "He knows everything. He is aware not only of what goes on in the world today, but his brain is a repository of the accumulated wisdom of the ages." Walker, a Texan who helped make *The New York Herald Tribune* into a writer's newspaper, continued: "He hates lies and meanness and sham, but keeps his temper. He is loyal to his paper and to what he looks upon as his profession; whether it is a profession, or merely a craft, he resents attempts to debase it."

"The job of the reporter is to get all the facts on an assignment," says a southern editor. "This is his life."

The editor of an Oregon newspaper describes the reporter he wants on his staff, "The kind of reporter I look for is a fast writer who can turn out bright leads, knows how to use quotes, knows what he or she is writing about, can explain the why behind the actions of the group or individual he or she is covering, and is attentive to the need for brevity and accuracy."

Such diligence involves hard work—physically, emotionally and intellectually—and the rewards, particularly for the beginner, are not always immediate and abundant. But most reporters are sustained by the pleasure of creating meaning out of chaos, and by the sheer joy of reporting and writing about events that people are talking about.

For some, the work is too hard, as one beginning journalist reports: "In the past days, I've filed stories on a pilot who crashed his plane into a swimming pool, a woman who was killed by a truck tire that rolled one-half mile and struck her on the head, and a race riot in South Boston . . . I find I begin to wonder what I'm doing here. I'm only 20, and I'm working until midnight on Sunday."

The young reporter, a summer intern on a Boston newspaper, was delighted when he was able to return to the comfort of school life. Journalism, he said, was hardly the "glamorous world" he had imagined.

The excitement and varied experiences of journalism had the opposite effect on another summer intern, Richard E. Gordon of the University of Pennsylvania. At *The Pittsburgh Press,* Gordon handled feature assignments, covered a convention of the Jehovah's Witnesses, and was sent to city hall to help one of the regular staffers. He emerged at summer's end convinced that journalism was his calling.

At city hall, Gordon displayed one of the most important qualities of the good reporter—enterprise. Editors like what they call the self-starter, the reporter who can generate story ideas. Cammy Wilson's stories in Minneapolis are examples of enterprise.

"Things got slow one day at city hall," Gordon recalls. "So I started skimming through minutes of city council meetings. I noticed that at almost every meeting the council had to adopt a resolution to pay some resident for damage to his car or house. I decided to check into it."

The result of his check was a two-column headline over an 18-inch story and a byline. Here is how Gordon began his piece:

The driver of the city refuse truck might have hesitated as he turned down a narrow one-way street in the city's Allentown section on a cold day last February.

But, though the street was icy, he drove ahead. The truck skidded, crashed into a row of parked cars and damaged two of them.

The two car owners who filed claims to recover the costs of repairing the damages became part of a rising tide of liability claims filed against the city in recent years. . . .

Journalists live in a world of confusion and complexity. Nevertheless, they manage through enterprise, wit, energy and intelligence to discern the truth of the event and to shape their understanding into a form comprehensible to the ordinary citizen. The task ahead of us in this book is to open the reporter's mind to this task and to assist the young journalist to find a personal credo to work by. A reporter who worked her way from small newspapers in New Mexico, Pennsylvania and New Jersey to the AP and then to *The New York Times* says her motto is: "Keep cool but care." This philosophy seems to describe the reporters we have been watching.

The *Daily News* City Desk.
City Editor Dick Oliver reads through the story about the funeral service for a Metropolitan Opera singer. To his left is assistant editor, Sydney Penner.

In the Newsroom: The News Flow

Before we dig into the business of reporting and writing, let us see how the reporter fits into the newsroom operation.

We could visit any one of the thousands of newspaper and broadcast station newsrooms of various sizes. But whatever the size of the staff we will find similarities in how assignments are made, how the stories are covered and how they are processed in the newsroom. Our trip takes us to the newsroom of the *Daily News* in New York City. It has the second largest daily circulation in the United States, some 1.5 million. We are at the city desk and the telephone is ringing. An assistant editor takes the call and turns to the city editor, Dick Oliver.

"This fellow says the governor's daughter is going to get a marriage license at 2:30. Maybe we ought to get a picture," he suggests.

Oliver is not enthusiastic.

"We had her announcement a few weeks ago," Oliver says. But he decides they may as well take it. Nothing better may turn up for inside pages. (Nothing does, and the picture will run on page three.)

A courthouse reporter calls Oliver about a suit the reporter thinks will make a good story. A twenty-one-year-old woman has won $925,000 from a car-rental company. Oliver gives him the go-ahead and tells the reporter to slug the story "Suit."

Tucker's Last Song Played at the Met

By ROGER WETHERINGTON

"Richard's song was ended in mid-course." Those were among the words of farewell to Richard Tucker yesterday at a moving funeral service in the Metropolitan Opera House. As thousands of mourners look on, Tucker was eulogized as not only a great artist, but a good man.

A son of immigrant parents, he was described as devoted to his family and a devout Jew, a man who, originally aspired only to be a cantor. But he also became the "Brooklyn Caruso," one of the most famed, durable and beloved of Met stars.

His name was almost synonymous with the house.

Rabbi Alvin I, Kleinerman of the Park Synagogue in Chicago, where Tucker appeared as cantor every year during the High Holy Days, said Tucker had considered his voice a gift from God and he "dedicated it to the Lord."

Rabbi Bordecai Waxman of Temple Israel in Great Neck, L.I., where Tucker worshipped, said the tenor's greatest "moments of song" were not those heard at the Met but those he chanted at the bar mitzvahs of his three sons, now grown. "He poured his heart into those moments when he inducted his children into the Jewish tradition."

The home he shared with Sara, his wife of nearly 35 years, "was rich in Jewish tradition and observance," the rabbi said. "The melodies of the synagogue rang in his ears. Richard's song was ended in mid-course," but "it lives on in many hearts."

Cardinal Cooke, a friend of Tucker's, called him "a man of great religious spirit and deep personal faith in God," a "prayerful man."

Herman Malamood, a cantor and a tenor with the New York City Opera, brought the service to an end in singing the prayer for the dead, "El Mole Rahamim," and the Met's great gold curtain closed slowly on Tucker for the last time.

Tucker, 60, died Wednesday, apparently of a heart attack while on a concert tour in Kalamazoo, Mich.

Met spokesmen originally said that they believed his funeral was th efirst held by the Met in its 91-year history. But a check of the archives yesterday showed that services for Leopold Damrosch, the conductor, were hled at the old Met on Broadway at 39th St. in 1885; and services for Heinrich Conried, a Met general manager, were held there in 1908.

News photo by Jim Hughes

Soprano Leontyne Price leaves Met after services for Tucker.

(The slug is important, for this is the story's identifying mark for everyone, from reporter to editor to the mechanical department.) Usually, the desk will tell a reporter how long the piece should run, but Oliver knows that his courthouse man, an experienced reporter, will hold it to three or three and one-half pages of copy—450 to 500 words.

At 2:45 p.m., a reporter turns in a story about the funeral of Richard Tucker, an opera singer who died in Michigan while on tour. He was one of the world's leading tenors, and the funeral was held in the New York City Metropolitan Opera House. Sydney Penner, Oliver's assistant who reads through all local copy, looks it over for major errors. On the fourth take (page), he spots what he thinks is a mistake in a name. He tells the reporter to check whether the first name of a conductor in the story is Leopold—not Walter, as the copy has it. While the reporter makes his call, Penner is pencilling "Leopold" in. The reporter verifies Penner's recollection.

When Penner finishes his quick but thorough reading of the Tucker piece, the copy goes to the news desk where the news editor determines where it will be placed in the paper and the size of and type for the headline. Tucker was well known and at the editorial conference the story had been scheduled for good play. The news editor indicates on the copy that the piece, slugged "Tucker," is slated for page five. The story then moves to the copy desk where it is closely edited to fit the space and the headline is written.

The next story Penner picks out of the basket on his desk makes him frown. He looks up from the copy and calls over the reporter who wrote it. He points to the story.

"Are you sure you checked the spelling of this name?" he asks. "You should have. It's wrong."

Defensively, the reporter replies, "But if I'm not sure how it's spelled how could I look it up?"

Penner, a courteous, soft-spoken editor, says nothing. Later, when the copy flow eases, he remarks that he reads the copy of some reporters closely and only scans the stories of others.

"You can spot the good reporters and the weak ones early," he says. "Sometimes you can tell on the first piece of copy they hand in."

Early in the day, the city desk had made up a schedule of stories the local staff would work on (see fig. 1.1). One of these, a murder, had broken the day before in the *New York Post*. The *Post* story began:

> A 22-year-old American Airlines employee was slain by one of three holdup men in her Bronx apartment early today while her husband, bound hand and foot, lay helplessly in another room.

Oliver had instructed a reporter in the Bronx to dig into the story. He told a rewriteman in the newsroom to handle the copy as it came in. The story was slugged "Slay."

The *News* learns that the victim was a stewardess, which gives the slaying what journalists describe as "class." The death of someone with a glamorous or out-of-the-ordinary job is assumed to perk up reader interest.

The *News* picks up a few other facts the *Post* did not have. The police report that the gunmen had asked for $25,000 and that the woman was slain with a shot from a pistol that was placed against her head. Oliver instructs the rewriteman to double check the names, and it is learned that the victim's name was Gwendolyn Clarke, not Gwendolin Clark. First reports of victims' names frequently are garbled. Also, she was 27, not 22.

The rewriteman, Arthur Mulligan, asks if there are any pictures of the victim. Told there is nothing available yet, he asks, "Was she pretty?"

One of the deskmen looks up from his copy and replies, "There are no ugly stewardesses." Mulligan is not convinced.

"I have a theory on this one," he tells Oliver. Again the deskman looks up. "Take it easy," he tells Mulligan. "Remember your theory on the Rainslayer?" (After three holdup victims were murdered during nighttime rainstorms several months before, Mulligan had theorized the killer was the "Roving Rainstorm Robber," who preyed on people when their heads were bent under umbrellas. It was not.)

CAREY—Names Joe Hynes and Morris Abrams as special
    nursing home prosecutor and Moreland Commissioner,
    respectively.

PROFILES—of Hynes and Abrams.

NURSE—Nearly half of the 175 nursing homes in city
    could face cutoff of federal funds, according to
    list made available to us.

BERGMAN—files libel suit against Times, Stein et al
    for $1 million.

SLAY—Robbers invade home, slay wife, bind hubby and
    escape with car.

SUIT—Good reader on young woman, blinded and severely
    hurt in car crash in France, living off welfare's
    $154 Month, wins $925,000.

ETHICS—Board rules Lindsay can't appear before city
    agencies for at least 2 years, but Goldin's wife
    can hold $13G museum job.

JOBS—On deadline, city submits proposal for $46.7M in
    fed job funds.

UN—Ralph Bunche Institute report finds incompetence,
    cronyism and nepotism in the folks who work for
    our world body.

TUCKER—Services for the famed tenor held at the Met.

ABORT—Morgy OK's abortion for woman in her 28th week,
    2 weeks late.

AUDIT—Levitt report says city isn't even close to
    coping with fraud in the welfare department,
    citing huge jump in fraudulent checks.

CIVIL—Service News column.

BRIEFS—Etc.

Figure 1.1 City Desk Schedule. This list of stories is made up early in the day by the city editor and is submitted to the managing editor at the early-afternoon news conference at which the various editors discuss the stories in hand and anticipated. This discussion gives the managing editor the information he needs to decide on major play in the morning newspaper.

Mulligan says, "My theory is that it was narcotics. Must be. Who has $25,000 sitting around the house? The guy has no job and drives a new Lincoln Continental. She'd just come in from a run, too."

It makes sense, Oliver agrees and calls his Manhattan police headquarters man to check out the narcotics possibility.

It is 3:40 p.m. and "Slay" has not yet taken shape. The reporters have not called in. At the news conference, Oliver had suggested that "Slay" might be page one material, and the managing editor gave the story the green light. (Murders are given good play in the *News*. The day before, a knife-slaying in New Jersey was displayed on page one of the *News*, whereas *The New York Times*—the *News*'s morning competition—played the story on page 39.)

It is now 4 p.m.—an hour before the copy should be off the city desk—and the activity in the newsroom picks up. Reporters are typing faster, copy is moving to the various desks in greater volume, and the tension increases. Oliver would like to have all his copy in the hands of the news editor by 5 p.m., but on big stories he can hold until 6 o'clock for the first edition.

At 4:30 p.m., the police reporter in Manhattan headquarters calls in with additional information on "Slay." He reports that the narcotics bureau is looking into the possibility that drugs were involved. Mulligan has enough information to go to work on the story.

Ten minutes later, the picture editor relays information from the police radio, which has been crackling with calls all day.

"The police think they've spotted a suspect in that bank holdup where the cop was killed," he says. "They're stopping the subways around 42nd Street and Eighth Avenue."

This could be a good story—a chase for a cop-killer through the New York subway system during the rush hour. But the desk takes the information calmly. Rather than send someone out looking for the police, the desk calls the Manhattan police reporter—a busy man today—and asks him to pinpoint the search area. He had already started to do so.

At 4:58, Mulligan has the first two takes of "Slay" on the city desk. Oliver goes through them, changes a couple of words, eliminates a few others. It now reads:

```
    Bronx homicide police were puzzled yesterday by
circumstances surrounding the murder of a 27-year-old
American Airlines stewardess who was shot in the head by one
of three men who burst in on her and her husband shortly
after midnight in the couple's apartment.
```

After describing the demands of the three men, the details of the slaying, and giving the address of the victim and the means by which the men got away, the story refers to "speculation by the police that the shooting involved narcotics. . . ."

At 5:01, the police radio carries the information that a man has been picked up in the subway for questioning. Later, he is released. No one is ruffled by the collapse of the story about the search for a cop-killer.

At 5:07, the third take of "Slay" is on Oliver's desk. He looks it over and sends it on its way.

At 5:15, the Manhattan police reporter calls Mulligan and says that the police think there may be a link between the murder of the stewardess and the slayings of two men whose bodies were discovered in the Bronx. One of the victims was stuffed into a steamer trunk, the other was put into a wooden box. An insert is written for "Slay," and a short piece that had been written about the bodies and slugged "Trunk," is killed.

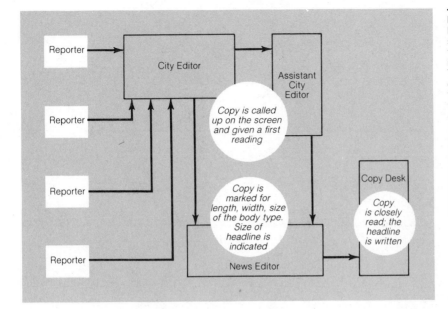

Figure 1.2 The Copy Flow. Reporters keyboard their stories on video display terminals, and they are stored in the computer or on a disc. The copy is called up by the city desk where it is given a first reading on the screen by the city editor or the assistant city editor. On small newspapers, the city desk will also determine the length of the story, size of type and headline size. This task is done on large newspapers by the news desk. The copy then is called up by the copy desk for close editing and writing the headline.

The next day, Saturday, a general assignment reporter, Daniel O'Grady, was assigned to check out the narcotics angle and to do a roundup. Police confirmed Mulligan's theory about narcotics, and the lead in Sunday's newspaper read:

> A gangland war for control of the lucrative narcotics trade in Harlem and the Bronx reportedly has left six dead in the last two months, including an American Airlines stewardess who, police believe, may have smuggled drugs from the Caribbean for one faction of the all-black mob.

Although work on a metropolitan daily probably will not be the first newspaper job a journalism student lands, even much smaller newspapers operate as the *News* did on this day: Assignments are made, reporters cover them and also develop their own stories, copy is turned in under deadline pressure in time to be edited and placed in the newspaper.

A good reporter knows how the newsroom functions and what its requirements are. The reporter is aware of the deadline and operates within its iron grip—a good reporter never misses a deadline. Nor will the reporter give any but his or her best efforts in reporting and writing a story, no matter how inconsequential it may seem.

The Basics

2

2 Basic Components of a News Story

News stories are:

- Accurate. All information is verified before it is used.
- Properly attributed. The story quotes competent sources.
- Balanced and fair. All sides in a controversy are given.
- Objective. The news writer does not inject his or her feelings or opinions.
- Brief. The news story gets to the point quickly.

If we were to generalize about the job of the journalist from the work of the reporters we have been watching we might conclude that he or she:

1. Attempts to report accurately the truth or reality of the event by
   A. Direct observation.
   B. Seeking out authoritative, knowledgeable and reliable human sources and relevant and reliable physical sources that can provide information about the event and its causes and consequences.
2. Tries to write an interesting, timely, and clear story by making sure it is succinctly and colorfully told. The reporter uses quotations, anecdotes, examples and human interest to make the story vivid.

If journalism needs rules, these points would be the basis of their formulation.
Underlying and directing the application of these rules or guidelines is the reporter's imperative: The story must be accurate.

Accuracy

The highest praise A. J. Liebling, a master reporter for newspapers and *The New Yorker* magazine, could pay a colleague was, "He is a careful reporter," by which Liebling meant that the reporter took great care to be accurate. Although the reporter works under severe space and time limitations, he or she is never too pressed or rushed to pass on to the reader or listener dubious, much less incorrect, material. A reporter will make every effort to check the accuracy of information through verification and documentation.

Liebling would have appreciated the work of the staff of the *Harvard Magazine* in checking a supposed fact. The magazine had received a wire service photo of the U.S. ambassador conferring with the Chinese vice premier at a party marking the beginning of formal ties between the two countries. The caption identified the interpreter in the picture as Chi Chou-Chou. But the magazine editor had a feeling the man was Chi Chao-chu, a member of the Harvard College class of 1952. He asked for verification. That set in motion a series of long-distance calls. Four hours later, at 1:10 a.m., verification came through: The interpreter was indeed Chi Chao-chu. Cost: $10.20 for three minutes. Avoided: The unforgivable error in journalism—misspelling a person's name.

As we can see from the summary of the reporter's job, the reporter tries to observe the event he or she is called upon to report. The reporter knows that although many people are willing, even anxious, to help, a story based on the reporter's first-hand observation is superior to one based on second-hand or third-hand information. Observation is also the journalist's way of verifying information and assumptions that seem to have the ring of truth.

As Bertrand Russell, the British philosopher, advised students:

Make the observation yourself. Aristotle could have avoided the mistake of thinking that women have fewer teeth than men by the simple device of asking Mrs. Aristotle to keep her mouth open while he counted. Thinking you know, when in fact you don't, is a fatal mistake to which we are all prone.

Despite the air of certainty in the tone of news stories, a close reading reveals that many are not based on the reporter's direct observation. The reporter rarely sees the burglar breaking in, the policy being drafted, the automobile hitting the telephone pole. The reporter obtains information about these events from authoritative sources such as documents and records (police files for the burglary and the accident) and from individuals (policy makers and participants at meetings).

News Filters   When the reporter bases his or her story on direct observation, the story can be said to be a firsthand account. But when the reporter is not on the scene and information is obtained from those present, the reporter's story is a secondhand account. It has been filtered through the source once and then is filtered a second time by the reporter who selects and emphasizes some material and condenses other details.

Although the reporter seeks eyewitnesses and participants, some important stories are based on accounts that have been filtered twice before reaching the reporter. For example: An official agency holds a meeting at which the participants are sworn to secrecy. The reporter learns that one of those attending the meeting described it to a member of his staff, who happens to be a good source of news for the reporter. The reporter manages to obtain the staff member's account of the executive's account of what occurred.

News Filters. Firsthand Account. The story is based on direct observation of the event by the reporter.

News Filters. Secondhand Account. The story is based on the account passed on by a participant eyewitness.

News Filters. Thirdhand Account. The story is based on information supplied by a source who was told by a participant.

BULLETIN
2d LEAD FERGUSON
STATE PRISON, TRENTON, N.J. March 31-(UP)-The
State of New Jersey, which spent $1,200,000 to
capture and convict Bruno Richard Hauptmann,
executed him tonight with a penny's worth of
electricity.

Before his body ever hung loose and heavy
against the straps of the electric chair,
officials collected from witnesses a dozen
affidavits, swearing that Hauptmann had died in
the place, time and manner prescribed by law.
Then they closed their four-year file on the
murder of Charles A. Lindbergh, Jr.

Hauptmann died without confessing.

Not a word passed his lips as he entered the
electrocution chamber and he needed no assistance
when he sat down in the chair. . . .

AOSS
R A
PM-SHUTTLE 2NDLD-PICKUP THGRAF11-6
BY AL ROSSITER JR.
UPI SCIENCE EDITOR
CAPE CANAVERAL, Fla. (UPI)--A faulty regulator
allowed fuel tank pressure to come close to
bursting a safety disc in the space shuttle
Columbia, but engineers caught it in time and
pressed on today toward launch Thursday with two
satellites aboard.

Had the disc ruptured, a lengthy delay would
have been necessary to repair the fuel system for
14 of the ship's 28 rear control jets, project
engineer Gene Thomas said.

"The guys were sharp enough to catch it,"
Thomas said.

Thomas said he was "90 percent certain" project
officials would clear Columbia for launch with
the faulty regulator even though it meant the
ship would be taking off without a backup system
in part of its control jet system.

Thomas said the helium which pressurizes the
fuel tank reached 320 pounds per square inch--
just 10 pounds short of the pressure needed to
burst a safety disc. The disc is designed to
relieve pressure to prevent serious damage, just
as a freeze plug in a car engine is designed to
let go to avoid serious damage from a frozen
engine block.

FBI agents have established that the Watergate bugging incident stemmed from a massive campaign of political spying and sabotage conducted on behalf of President Nixon's re-election and directed by officials of the White House and the Committee for the Re-election of the President.

The activities, according to information in FBI and Department of Justice files, were aimed at all the major Democratic presidential contenders and—since 1971—represented a basic strategy of the Nixon re-election effort.

During their Watergate investigation federal agents established that hundreds of thousands of dollars in Nixon campaign contributions had been set aside to pay for an extensive undercover campaign aimed at discrediting individual and Democratic presidential candidates and disrupting their campaigns. . . .

–*The Washington Post*

Thirdhand Account.
The reporters handling Watergate for *The Washington Post,* Carl Bernstein and Bob Woodward, based this story "on strains of evidence, statements from numerous sources, deduction, a partial understanding of what the White House was doing, the reporters' familiarity with the 'switchblade mentality' of the President's men and disparate pieces of information the reporters had been accumulating for months," they write in their book, *All the President's Men* (New York City: Simon and Schuster, 1974) pp. 142–144.

Attribution

The further the reporter is from direct observation, the more dubious he or she is about the accuracy of the report. Accurate and comprehensive direct observation is difficult enough. After the information has been filtered once or twice, only the most foolhardy journalist would stake his reputation on the accuracy of the report. To make clear to the reader that secondhand and thirdhand accounts are not based on the reporter's direct observation of the event, the reporter usually attributes the information about the event to a source.

Here are the first two paragraphs from a story in *The Detroit News*:

For six minutes, a Detroit police operator listened on the telephone as 24 bullets were fired into the bodies of an East Side couple.

But, according to the police, the civilian mistook the shots for "someone hammering or building something" and dispatched the call as a routine burglary.

The lead may give the reader the impression the reporter was at the operator's elbow. But the second paragraph attributes the information to the police.

Attribution actually refers to two concepts:

1. *Statements* are attributed to the person making them.
2. *Information* about the events not witnessed by the reporter is usually attributed to the source of the information.

Here is a story that contains both types of attribution:

(1) Mayor Stanley Kretchmer said yesterday the city probably could balance its budget this year and next without laying off any workers.

(1) The decision, he said, "depends on a number of factors—the passage of a new tax package, the cooperation of municipal labor unions, general prosperity that keeps revenues high."

(2) At a meeting last week, the mayor told department heads they should consider the possibility of layoffs of about 10 percent of their work force, according to city officials who attended the meeting.

In the following, the first type of attribution is used. All statements are attributed to those making them.

Wayward Car Finds Home

Michael Sellars, 16, was sleeping on the living room floor of his South Side home at about 2:45 a.m. Wednesday when a car crashed through a picture window.

"This big light was in my eyes," he said after receiving a few stitches to close a cut on the back of his head caused by either the car's bumper or flying debris. . . .

Michael's father, Donald, 42, said the accident also woke up the rest of the family in their bedrooms—his wife, Barbara, 37, and his other son, Bobby, 12. . . .

"Bobby said the crash sounded like an atomic bomb," said Donald Sellars.

Michael said: "The driver got out of the car and asked if everybody was okay. . . ."

—The Milwaukee Journal

Attribution of Information

Just as no reporter from *The Detroit News* was with the police operator when the call came in, so no member of *The Milwaukee Journal* news staff was sleeping over at the Sellars' home the night the car dropped in. The car's intrusion falls under the category of information not witnessed by the reporter. But it is stated as fact, without attribution. This point takes us to an imprecise area of journalism in which the reporter's guideposts are the policy of the publication or station and his feeling about the particular story.

Generally, we attribute police stories to the police. Although the reporter may take the information from a police record, the document does not necessarily attest to the truth of the information, only that some source—the police, a victim, the suspect, a witness—said that such-and-such occurred. The reporter will usually attribute the information to this source.

At the Sellars' home, the broken glass, the gap in the house the picture window once occupied, and the presence of the battered automobile would attest to the truth of the fact that an accident had occurred. So would the assertions of the family.

Some news organizations like the AP demand rigid adherence to the following policy: Always attribute what you do not see unless it is common knowledge.

Let us examine several AP stories to see how this policy is carried out. Here are three randomly selected news stories that ran one Friday shortly before noon on a regional wire. Under each story is the speculation of an experienced reporter about the reasons attribution was or was not used. (Her direct quotes are in parentheses.)

Most of the stories appear to be rewrites, shortened versions of stories covered by newspaper reporters. Even if we tracked the pieces to their origins we would discover that most of them came from statements given to the newspapers and from telephone calls made by reporters, not from direct observation.

Here are the stories and her comments paragraph by paragraph:

```
Y165
    d vvyyxwyyf
YMCA
(1) NEW YORK AP--Dr. Jesse L. Steinfeld, former
Surgeon General of the U.S. Public Health
Service, has been appointed chairman of the
National YMCA Health and Physical Education
Advisory Council.
(2) Steinfeld is presently professor of medicine
at the University of California at Irvine,
Calif., and chief of medical services for the
Veterans Hospital in Long Beach, Calif.
(3) The advisory council will play an important
role in the setting of future directions of the
Y's nationwide programs, national board chairman
Stanley Enlund said today in announcing
Steinfeld's appointment to the non-salaried post.

1113aED 03-26
```

YMCA:

(1) There is no need for attribution of the appointment because the action is obviously on the record.

(2) Steinfeld's background is taken from records and needs no attribution.

(3) The role of the council is an opinion offered by the chairman of the board and must be attributed to him.

y167
    d vvyyxeeev
HOTEL FIRE
(1) BRANFORD, Conn. AP--The Waverly Hotel,
popular earlier in the century, was destroyed by
a two-alarm fire today.
(2) The roof collapsed into the heart of the
building. At daylight the burned-out hotel was
still smouldering.
(3) Myrtle Braxton, 73, who lived alone in the
massive three-story building, was reported in
fair condition at Yale-New Haven Hospital
suffering from smoke inhalation.
(4) Officials said the fire was reported by Mrs.
Braxton at 3:41 a.m. They said it apparently
started in the kitchen area where Mrs. Braxton
was living after having closed off most of the
rest of the building. She was living there
without central heating or electricity, officials
said.
(5) A neighbor said that a large number of
antiques on the third floor were destroyed. Also
lost was a huge ship's wheel from a sailing ship,
a centerpiece in the dining room.
(6) The bank that holds the mortgage said the
land and hotel were worth $40,000 to $50,000.

1124aED 03-26

Hotel Fire:

(1)(2) The condition of the hotel is a physical fact about which the reporter
has no doubt.

(3) The attribution is implied here as coming from the hospital.

(4) "Officials," presumably fire department officials, are cited as the authority
because only they could have known this. In the second sentence, the cause is attributed. ("Always attribute the cause of a fire.")

(5)(6) Attribution gives the information credibility.

y171
    d veeevv
CPEC
(1) HARTFORD, Conn. AP--The Connecticut Public
Expenditure Council, a private fiscal watchdog,
said today that Gov. Ella Grasso's proposed
$1.43-billion budget would spend more than the
state's economy could afford.

(2) The new governor has proposed what she calls
an austerity budget for the coming fiscal year.
(3) But the watchdog group said that state
spending must be cut beyond the Grasso
recommendation. It also recommended a state
constitutional amendment requiring the budget to
be in balance at all times.
(4) There is an estimated deficit of about $90
million in the current Connecticut budget.
Governor Grasso wants to pay off the deficit with
some short-term borrowing, but the Expenditure
Council says the deficit should be paid off in
next year's budget "to protect the state's
financial credibility."
(5) The council is supported by the business
community.
1146aED 03-26

CPEC:

(1) A charge, allegation, or opinion is always attributed, usually at the beginning of the lead. Here, the Council is immediately identified as the source of the allegation.

(2) Background information that need not be attributed since it is part of the record.

(3) Attribution to the source of the material.

(4)(5) Background needing no attribution. ("The last graf is the reporter's attempt to give the reader the why of the Council's opposition—it's a taxpayer's group that likes austerity budgets because it means lower taxes. Nice touch.")

"You identify the source of the information in your story," the reporter commented after going through the AP stories, "so that if it isn't true then the paper isn't blamed for the mistake, unless your reporting is bad and you misquoted someone, or didn't read the record carefully.

"If you don't identify the source the reader is going to assume that we stand behind the statements because we know they are true.

"My first editor would tell me to give him the source all the time, a person, an organization. If it's impossible to use the source's name, then he wanted it 'spokesman, an official, an official source,' or something similar, although he didn't like that as much as a name."

Identification also helps the reader or listener know something about the source. Personal data is often included, such as the source's name, title (if any), age, address, occupation, education, and possibly race, religion and ethnicity. Use only those identifying characteristics that are relevant to the story.

Look at the following story that came in over the wire:

```
SX22B
   LOMA LINDA, Calif., July 16--Leave the teen-age
drinking problem to the teenager and it will be
solved, says a specialist in classroom
instruction on alcohol.
   Mrs. Viola Eldon, Fresno, Calif., a specialist
in alcoholic instruction, yesterday told the
ninth annual Institute of Scientific Studies on
the Prevention of Alcoholism the teenager is fed
up with the ways adults 'beat about the bush.'
   xxxx
```

It would have helped the reader to know that the "specialist" was also the state director of scientific temperance instruction for the Women's Christian Temperance Union. It is important to include any of the source's affiliations that are relevant to the subject.

Attribution may not be necessary, however, when the reporter is certain of the truth or accuracy of the source of the material. For official bodies—the police, fire, health, welfare and similar agencies—that have a reputation for accuracy, attribution may be unnecessary, particularly in the lead. The attribution usually is inserted unobtrusively in the story. Here are two leads with unnecessary attribution:

```
   Tomorrow will be sunny and warm, John Connors of the Mt.
Pleasant Weather Bureau said today.
```

```
   Columbia University will receive $4,250,000 in Atomic
Energy Commission funds for research in atomic particles,
President Michael Sovern announced today.
```

These stories are of no great significance, and minimal damage would be done by an error. Important stories should always carry attribution. When 1,000 guards, deputies and state troopers stormed the Attica Correctional Facility in upstate New York in 1971 to quell a rebellion, many of the news accounts stated flatly that the convicts had slashed the throats of some of the hostages. Some stories also reported as fact that one of the hostages had been castrated. No sources were given for the reports.

A medical examiner later disclosed that most of the deaths of the 11 hostages and 32 prisoners had been caused by rifle and shotgun fire from the lawmen who stormed the penitentiary. Two months later, an official of the State Correctional Services told a Congressional investigating committee that he had been the source of the misinformation.

The Attica incident embarrassed the press corps. Mistakes were made by *The New York Times*, veteran network television reporters, and others. In their post-mortems to determine how they had made such a blunder, the journalists agreed that to some extent they had been swept up by the hostility against the prisoners that developed during the four-day insurrection, and that when an official gave them the information about throat slashings it seemed to confirm many rumors about convict violence. Some of the convicts had been seen holding knives to the throats of their hostages.

Most of the time, reporters do drop attribution from stories of such certainty that there is little danger of their backfiring. But when an unattributed story happens to go wrong, the reporter learns an unforgettable lesson. Here is an account of an unattributed story from the AP newsletter:

This was a UPI lead from Fortaleza, Brazil on Friday: "The huge Oros dam broke tonight and sent millions of tons of water cascading down on five towns in the Jaguariba River valley. The dam crumbled under pressures of flood waters at 7:03 p.m. EST. . . ." A cleancut lead, uncluttered by attribution, but— the dam had NOT broken. . . . In a later rowback, UPI said the "original reports" came from two domestic news agencies and a correspondent at the scene, and had been broadcast by Bra- zilian radio stations. With rumors so widespread, how come AP didn't fall for them? We quote Ed Butler of Rio de Janeiro: "It was a case of AP keeping its shirt on and relying on our man at the scene, Aloisio Bonavides, whose reports had been exceedingly accurate and prompt. At the bureau, we checked government sources and they had heard nothing". . . . Part of the dam did give way on Sunday; no loss of life, no injuries.

Remember: Matters of accepted, common knowledge and events witnessed by the reporter need not be attributed. Attribution is used:

1. To give strength and credibility to material.
2. When opinions are offered, or controversial statements are made.
3. When a reporter is unsure of the accuracy of the information. (A frequent admonition of the city editor is, "Hang this on someone. We can't be responsible for saying this.")
4. When inferences, conclusions, generalizations are made.

Attributing secondhand and thirdhand accounts to their sources does not absolve the reporter of responsibility for libelous statements in the story. A reporter for a Florida newspaper reported that a county employee smoked marijuana, and the worker brought a libel case. "The reporter's own testimony indicated she had relied on second- and thirdhand accounts when writing the story," *Editor & Publisher* reported. A jury awarded the employee $70,000. (See chapter 14 for further discussion of libel.)

Warning

Types of Attribution

When the source of information for a story says nothing about being quoted, the reporter can presume that the information is on the record. Sometimes sources do not want to be named. White House reporters were so unsure of the nature of some of their briefings—whether statements could be attributed to sources—that the press secretary to President Ford, J. F. terHorst, issued these guidelines to four types of attribution:

- *On the Record:* All statements are directly quotable and attributable, by name and title, to the person who is making the statement.
- *On Background:* All statements are directly quotable, but they cannot be attributed by name or specific title to the person commenting. The type of attribution to be used should be spelled out in advance: A White House official, an Administration spokesman, a government lawyer or whatever.
- *On Deep Background:* Anything that is said in the interview is usable but not in direct quotation and not for attribution. The reporter writes it on his own, without saying it comes from any government department or official.*
- *Off the Record:* Information given "off the record" is for the reporter's knowledge only and is not to be printed or made public in any way. The information also is not to be taken to another source in hopes of getting official confirmation. This form is mainly used to prevent reporters from speculating along inaccurate lines.

*Note: Reporters generally dislike this form of attribution and it should be used only in the most delicate circumstances and for urgent news. Too often, government officials use "deep background" to plant or leak stories, or to get the reporter to stick his neck out when the official has only part of the information.

These were terHorst's guidelines for White House reporters. Most sources are not so specific. An "on the record" interview may also have attached to it the proviso that although the information can be used, the source cannot be quoted by name. Some sources who give material "off the record" permit reporters to use the information on their own authority or to use it if it can be obtained elsewhere and attributed to the second source. Generally, reporters presume everything is on the record for attribution. When a source does put restrictions on the material, it is best to find out precisely what the limitation is.

Some reporters refuse to accept material with the condition that there is an absolute restriction, such as terHorst's "Off the Record," and almost none of them like it. In a poll of news bureau chiefs in Washington, Courtney Sheldon, chief of the Washington bureau of *The Christian Science Monitor,* found that 19 of 24 chiefs contend that White House officials take advantage of background briefings. Sheldon said the bureau chiefs agreed generally:

They do not feel bound by briefing rules on off-the-record information at conferences they do not attend.
They feel perfectly free to identify a briefer at any conference they do not attend but learn about later.
The handicaps of off-the-record and anonymous background briefings could, on occasion, be lessened by interpretative, balanced reporting.

The general feeling was that background briefings should be abolished. But the bureau chiefs said they had to attend them or else be at a disadvantage competitively. The chiefs worry, as do all reporters, that the public suffers when officials can escape accountability.

"All administrations now put out propaganda in the guise of information through background or off-the-record briefings," says Richard Dudman of the *St. Louis Post-Dispatch*.

James Anderson, the state department correspondent for UPI, says that backgrounders are "inherently undemocratic . . . full of dangers." Still, he says, because of them he knows more about the workings of U.S. foreign policy than he otherwise would.

In adding up the pluses and minuses, the reporter who accepts material with the promise of anonymity for the source or absolute off-the-record status for the information realizes that he is trading the public's right to know for his or her access to information. It is a calculated risk.

Ralph Blagden says that the only promise he ever made was that neither the name of the source or any identifying information about the source would be used in a story. "Most people who give off-the-record information want the information out," he says. "I frequently let the person go off-the-record with the conviction I could get the material from files and records or other sources. I got some of my best stories by following up off-the-record information, which I used as leads.

"I rarely found a lead that could not be developed from other sources without leading in any way to my informant. But I would never let a source go off-the-record retroactively."

Trial Balloons

Background and off-the-record information pose problems for the conscientious reporter because he or she knows that backgrounders are used to float trial balloons. These stories are designed by the source to test public reaction without subjecting the source to responsibility for the statements. Reporters, eager to obtain news of importance and sometimes motivated by the desire for exclusives, may become the conduits for misleading or self-serving information.

When Vice President Spiro Agnew was facing prosecution for accepting bribes, *The New York Times* ran an exclusive, page one story about Agnew that began: "Vice President Agnew has made up his mind about the next phase of what he calls his 'nightmare.' " After this sympathetic picture of a suffering political leader, the story asserted that Agnew would not resign, would fight for exoneration in the courts and would press his request for a hearing by the House of Representatives. No source was given for the information in the story, but it was clear Agnew was the source. The story carried such statements as: "Mr. Agnew decided . . . He does not intend . . . He resents . . ." These comments also gave the story the semblance of veracity and a ring of certainty.

The story also made assertions that later turned out to be dubious, even false. Attributed to Agnew, the comments would have been his responsibility. Stated as they were, the remarks became the newspaper's burden.

Agnew's purpose in granting the interview—many Washington reporters were convinced—was to warn the Justice Department and the president that unless he were treated with some leniency he would cause political problems. His lawyers had been dickering with the Justice Department over some kind of arrangement that would enable Agnew to escape prosecution, trial and a possible jail sentence. His lawyer let it be known that Agnew did not want to involve the nation in "a lengthy, bloody, and convulsive battle." At the time, the president was in danger of impeachment and Agnew was in line for the presidency. Agnew had bargaining power, and he used it, reporters believed. The bargaining—behind closed doors and through the agency of the press—was successful. Within two weeks of the story in the *Times*, Agnew resigned and pleaded no contest to a charge of federal income tax evasion. He was not sent to prison. One of the federal attorneys assigned to the case, James R. Thompson, later to become governor of Illinois, said after seeing the government's case against Agnew, "I've never seen a stronger case of bribery and extortion. If it had gone to trial, I'm sure he would have been sent to jail. He was simply a crook."

During the last months of the Nixon presidency, when it became clear the White House had been directly involved in covering up the break-in at Democratic headquarters in Washington, several aides sought to work out deals for themselves with investigators. The press became a willing ally in their machinations. Stories that were fed to reporters and used by them—without attribution—implicated other aides and party workers. One purpose was to convince the investigators that the aides and officials had enough information to make it worthwhile for the prosecutors to grant them immunity or to lessen the charges against them in return for their testimony against the higher-ups. Lawyers also leaked information that furthered their clients' ends.

In all this, it was clear that the public was not well served. When a reporter attributes assertions to a source, the reader can assess the accuracy and truth of the information on the basis of the general reliability of the source and his or her stake in the information. Stories without attribution seem to have greater truth, for the reader usually believes the reporter stands behind the information. When "a White House official," "authoritative sources" and "high officials" are used in lieu of a named source, trust also is generated in the reader.

The lesson for reporters is clear: Avoid background and deep background commitments whenever possible.

Not-for-Attribution Backgrounders: Pros and Cons

The backgrounders are in effect full-blown news conferences, with one major difference. The official conducting the news conference cannot be identified and thus is not directly responsible for what he said . . .

Benjamin C. Bradlee, executive editor of *The Washington Post,* contended that "by accepting unattributed information, we are allowing ourselves to be used by the government. . . ."

A. M. Rosenthal, managing editor of *The New York Times,* was also critical of the background sessions. He said such sessions were justifiable at times, but added that "the press had allowed this to go much too far."

"The backgrounder has become a way of life and often becomes an obstacle in the way of the flow of full information," Mr. Rosenthal said.

Mr. Bradlee and other newsmen noted that such sessions were sometimes used for Administration propaganda, to float trial balloons and even to inform government officials indirectly that they were in disfavor and should resign before being dismissed.

Defenders of the backgrounders, including Herbert G. Klein, the Nixon Administration's Director of Communications, and some newsmen, contend that officials are less inhibited and more likely to be frank in such sessions.

"Reporters can get more information on an informal basis," said Mr. Klein in a telephone interview. "The more important thing is to get the people the information. They don't care about who is giving the information."

–The New York Times

Verification

Attributing material to a source does not prove its truth. All a reporter does when attributing information is to place responsibility for it with the source named in the story. Attribution says only: It is true that the source said this.

The reporter who cares about truth is reluctant to settle for this half-step but often is prevented from moving on by deadline pressures and the difficulty in verifying material. If a reporter tried to check out every piece of information, most stories would never be written. There are, of course, certain routine verifications a reporter must make:

- Names, addresses and telephone numbers are checked in the newspaper's library, the telephone directory and the city directory.
- Background information is taken from clips in the morgue.

This kind of verification is essential to the reporter's work. Without doing it, he or she would not last long on the job. Yet error, inaccuracy and fanciful tales creep into the news daily. Some years ago, when Judy Garland died, her death was noted in the Lyons Den, a syndicated column by Leonard Lyons, as follows:

Her end was inevitable, from the day in Chicago's Oriental Theater when George Jessel was to introduce the child singer, Frances Gumm. His tongue resisted the clumsy sound, "Frances Gumm." He suddenly thought of the message he'd just sent to Judith Anderson, who was opening in a Broadway play:

"Dear Judy, may this new play add another garland to your Broadway career."

Jessel therefore blurted the name, "Judy Garland." Then he turned to the child singer waiting in the wings and told her: "Judy Garland . . . That's you, honey."

Even a columnist should tell truths. Had Mr. Lyons sought to check the anecdote he might have learned the truth, that Garland was her mother's maiden name. But that, to be sure, would have ruined his little tale. As it was, he proved the contention of the press critic who observed: "Newspapers never let the facts get in the way of a good story."

Causes of Errors

The veteran reporter knows that errors cannot always be avoided. Here are some of the causes of errors:

Sources Make Mistakes.
The sources for this story apparently took as truth an aritcle about Rudd that had appeared in the *National Lampoon*, entitled "I Am A Prisoner in a Cuban Homo Farm: An Open, Uncensored Letter from Mark Rudd." The newspaper corrected its story the next day.

- Sources can be mistaken. (See news story, "Cuba Has Jailed Mark Rudd . . .")
- Sometimes even the source does not know the truth. When President Nixon was under attack during the Watergate period, he told his party's leader in the Senate, Hugh Scott, "Hugh, I have nothing to hide." Scott relayed to the press his belief that Nixon was above suspicion. Yet seven hours later, the president told an aide that the administration had to fight to retain executive privilege—the right to maintain secrecy of presidential records—because there was plenty to hide.

Cuba Has Jailed Mark Rudd, a Lawyer Says

By SAM ROBERTS

Mark Rudd, the 28-year-old radical still sought for questioning about bombings here and elsewhere across the country, has been jailed by Cuba's regime, an international lawyer said yesterday.

The lawyer, Luis Kutner, said in a telephone interview that he had "no doubt" about the fate of Rudd, a former Columbia University student leader. Kutner said he had had discussions with friends of Rudd, who was said to have smuggled out of Cuba written appeals for help.

According to Kutner, these letters say that Rudd was mistakingly placed in a camp for the rehabilitation of homosexuals after he had been arrested while applying an ointment to cure chapped lips.

The lawyer, who has handled a variety of prominent clients in international law, said he was attempting to make contact with the Cuban authorities to verify Rudd's arrest record and conditions in the prison camp.

Police Here Want Him

Law enforcement officials here said Rudd, from New Jersey, was still being sought on a federal fugitive warrant and on a marijuana-possession charge filed in Buffalo.

The police here also want to question him in connection with a series of bombings — of public and corporate buildings — including Police Headquarters, in mid-1970 — for which the Weather Underground has claimed responsibility.

His former lawyer, Gerald Lefcourt, said yesterday that he last saw Rudd shortly before the issuance of a bench warrant for Rudd's arrest in 1970 for his failure to appear for a trial stemming from the 1968 Columbia riots.

Lefcourt said he had received no indication that Rudd — of others sought for questioning in connection with the Greenwich Village "bomb factory" explosion in 1970 and other blasts — had left the country.

Shortly before he was chosen president of the Columbia chapter of Students for a Democratic Society, Rudd used some saving to pay for a trip to Cuba in 1968. He was said to have returned more enthusiastic than ever about the Castro regime.

Investigators here said that they had no reason to discount the possibility that Rudd had later returned to Cuba, but that hey had no hard evidence to confirm this.

Kutner said he had been approached by people who told him that "Mark is protesting about being sodomized." He said these people were "pretty logical and not hysterical at all."

Mark Rudd
Still sought in bombings

- Authorities may have an interest in relating ambiguous, misleading, even erroneous information.
- Even the verifying information can be wrong. Newspaper files sometimes perpetuate an original error. Data and records can be tampered with.

Many matters cannot be verified. Opinions, conclusions, inferences, generalizations—these often resist the tests of truth. In this case, all the reporter can do is to determine that the statements attributed to those making them were indeed made.

The reporter can verify the statement: "The mayor submitted a $1.5 million budget to the city council today." All the reporter needs to do is examine the minutes of the meeting or the budget if he did not attend the council meeting. But he cannot verify the truth of the statement: "The budget is too high (or low)." A city councilman might have indeed stated that he would oppose the budget because it was too large, whereas the head of the Municipal League might have declared her organization's distress at the "paltry budget that endangers health and welfare projects." We can determine whether the statements were made, but we cannot determine the truth or falsity of the statements themselves, that is, whether the budget is too high or too low. These statements are opinions, judgments.

Despite these obstacles, reporters are obligated to verify their stories whenever possible. Yet squadrons of journalists on scores of papers never bother to go beyond routine checks.

Good reporters learn to discriminate between reliable and unreliable sources and to check material from the latter. Some reporters also develop, or are born with, a sixth sense that allows them to perceive warning flags in some statements and materials. These signals warn the reporter to seek verification. Verification is not the use of another opinion or a countercharge to balance the version of one source with that of another on controversial issues. Journalists should offer several views on controversial matters, and they should seek out the victims of charges. But that is balance, not verification.

When a minister charged that a magazine in use in a public school system in California was Communist-inspired, a *Fresno Bee* reporter sought to balance the charge with a reply from school officials. He also sought to verify the allegation by doing some checking on his own to determine whether the publication had ever been listed as subversive. The reporter examined several publications that listed so-called subversive oganizations and individuals. He could not find the magazine listed.

Here is how he began his story:

Rev. August Brustat, a Lutheran minister, has charged the "Scholastic" magazine, which is used in some Fresno schools, with carrying the Communist line to students. But a librarian in Fresno County Free Library and a school official said they can find no evidence the magazine is subversive.

Then he went on to state that no record could be found anywhere that the magazine had been declared subversive.

Although checking charges of subversion is more dramatic than verifying a name and address or confirming a councilman's recollection that the property tax five years ago was $28 per $1,000, the process is the same. It is impossible to over-emphasize this reporting rule: Whenever possible, the reporter should seek to verify the information—to get the truth of the fact—himself or herself.

However, on some occasions, adequate verification is impossible even when data and records exist. When reporters are out on a story and under the pressure of a deadline, verification is a difficult task. Political campaigns are especially troublesome because candidates sometimes make serious charges or issue complex statements to reporters who are hundreds of miles away from their files.

Verifying
Political Charges

During the 1964 presidential campaign, Senator Barry Goldwater, the Republican presidential candidate, frequently attacked the Democratic vice-presidential candidate, Hubert H. Humphrey. One of Senator Goldwater's themes was that Humphrey had an affinity for "socialism."

During Goldwater's swing through Texas in October, he enumerated several positions of the Americans for Democratic Action (ADA), a small liberal organization of which Humphrey was a founder and member. In talks in Austin and Corpus Christi, Goldwater said the ADA "wants to do away with the Internal Security Act and the Communist Control Act." He associated Humphrey with these positions.

Goldwater said, "I haven't heard Mr. Humphrey deny that he would not back his organization on admitting Red China to the United Nations or recognize trading with Red China. . . . At one time, he suggested the United States turning over to the United Nations our entire stockpile of nuclear weapons."

Some of the reporters with the Goldwater campaign quoted Goldwater's assertions. An AP story from Austin included this sentence: "Goldwater also charged Humphrey favored admission of Red China to the United Nations, and giving the U.S. stockpile to the U.N."

If we compare what Goldwater said with the sentence from the AP story, we see that the AP's reference to China is not accurate. Goldwater may have hoped his listeners, including the press, would conclude Humphrey favored Mainland China's admission to the U.N. But he carefully skirted making such an assertion.

Clearly, Goldwater sought to brand Humphrey as a radical who was unfit for national office. The journalists covering the Goldwater campaign were aware of Goldwater's intentions and attempted to be careful about such volatile charges. But covering whistle-stop tours is difficult. In this trip through Texas, reporters later recalled, Goldwater levelled a barrage of charges, sometimes without giving reporters advance copies of his speeches, so that the press corps had time only to listen and dash to the telephone or typewriter. Even bland fare takes time to digest, and the Goldwater charges were hardly the usual fare. Despite their inflammatory nature, the allegations Goldwater was making were often passed on in unverified, unchecked form.

Recalling Goldwater's appearance in Austin, E. W. Kenworthy of *The New York Times,* one of the reporters on the tour, said he was worried as soon as he walked into the auditorium in Austin. "I knew there was going to be trouble covering the story," Kenworthy said. "He talked fast. The din was terrific. It was impossible—at least for me with no shorthand—to get complete sentences."

The speech was so loaded with allegations, Kenworthy said, that he decided he had to be certain of accurate quotes. Unlike the wire service reporters who had to file their stories as soon as possible, Kenworthy could wait. On the press plane, he checked his notes with other reporters, and when he found many of the quotes did not match, he decided to wait until he could obtain a transcript of the Austin talk.

Kenworthy also took time to check the truth of Goldwater's references to Humphrey. He was more fortunate than other correspondents because he had been covering Humphrey's activities for a year and a half and knew in general Humphrey's positions on many issues.

"Second, I had been on Humphrey's campaign plane for three weeks," he said. "Time and again he had been asked about the ADA, whether he agreed with all of its positions. Specifically, he had been asked about Communist China, about recognition of the Castro regime, about denial of passports to Cuba, etc."

Also, a fellow reporter had with him on the plane out of Austin the *Congressional Quarterly's* compendium of quotes by Lyndon Johnson and Humphrey on a wide variety of subjects and their votes. This source, and Kenworthy's own material that he toted in his briefcase, enabled him to refer to Humphrey's positions on the issues that Goldwater had raised.

In his story, Kenworthy reported Goldwater's assertions and followed them with contradictory information based on his own knowledge and on background material.

Four other reporters who were with Goldwater on that Texas swing were asked how they handled the flurry of charges. They all confessed they had tremendous problems.

Jack Wilson, a Washington correspondent for *The Des Moines Register and Tribune,* said his early deadline meant he had to write under pressure. He wrote Goldwater's allegation about Humphrey and Mainland China, he said, "without trying to get into the question of whether it was true or false.

"I did not know Humphrey's feelings about admitting Red China in enough detail to feel free to say Goldwater was misrepresenting them. There was no way to check. Under the circumstances, I would always write the bare facts and trust the desk to put in the explanation if it seemed necessary."

On a previous story that Wilson had covered about a Goldwater attack on President Johnson, Wilson had precise information about the subject to which Goldwater was referring. Consequently, he said he was able to check Goldwater's assertions. They were false, and Wilson wrote a paragraph in which he explained that Johnson had not said what Goldwater had charged he had said.

Wilson, along with the other reporters, said that it is the reporter's job to verify material.

"But reporters seldom work under ideal conditions, and they must rely on the desk to back them up," he said.

Wilson, in a letter to the author, recalled discussions among the reporters about their Goldwater coverage:

Boiled down, it amounted to a fairly general feeling that we could not give an accurate picture of the campaign within the limits of what you might call straight news reporting. We could not, without "editorializing," tell the readers that Goldwater was not getting a strong reaction from the crowds, that he was in some cases boring them.

We couldn't say that some of what he said didn't make sense, in terms of being bad logic expressed in sentences that didn't say anything.

In one of the more blatant cases, when he blamed the fall of Khrushchev on our shipments of wheat, I was able to show indirectly that he was talking nonsense by simply quoting the entire passage verbatim out of the transcript. Even here I probably was taking liberties that would not be allowed a wire service, and even with this additional freedom I didn't feel I had the right to underline the nonsense by saying it was nonsense.

And of course transcripts aren't always available, and the syntax was usually so involved that it would be idiocy to trust longhand notes.

A few newspapers have recognized these difficulties and have adopted specific policies to cope with them. A spokesman for The Louisville Courier-Journal described his paper's policy as follows:

If the truth is readily available, we will put it right in the same story in brackets. If one man misquotes another and we know it is a misquote, we'll put the correct quotation in brackets. We try to correct as we go along, and if it is not readily available, we'll dig. That is sometimes a difficult process because the news breaks fast and many lies carry over before you can catch up with them.

The reporting limitations that Wilson chafed under were exploited by politicians, public officials and others. During the 1960s and early 1970s, it became obvious that lying and shading the truth, manipulation of public opinion and withholding information were conscious policies of some public officials and others seeking to influence the ideas, the votes and the buying habits of the public. Although the experience of the press with Senator Joseph McCarthy in the early 1950s should have proved to the press that attribution without verification is inadequate journalism, it did not. The Vietnam War helped to hammer the point home again.

A Vietnam War Story

In a war, the press is partially dependent on official communiqués since so much goes on beyond the reporter's range. When a reporter tries to verify what he is told by military press officers, independent checking can be made difficult.

Nevertheless, some reporters managed to describe the realities of Vietnam, and their versions sometimes differed sharply with those of the Pentagon and the White House.

In August, 1973, the United States announced its planes had accidentally bombed the Cambodian village of Neak Luong. The U.S. Embassy told correspondents that the damage was minimal. Sydney H. Schanberg, a *New York Times* correspondent, decided to see for himself and sought air transportation to the village, 38 miles from Phnom Penh, where Schanberg was based. The Embassy intervened to keep him from flying there, but Schanberg managed to find a boat.

Schanberg stayed in Neak Luong a day and night, interviewing villagers and taking pictures. When local authorities learned he had been gathering material, they put him in confinement overnight.

Here is how Schanberg's story begins:

> The destruction in this town from the accidental bombing on Monday is extensive.
>
> Big chunks of the center of town have been demolished, including two-story concrete buildings reinforced with steel. Clusters of wood and thatch huts where soldiers lived with their families have been erased, so that the compounds where they once stood look like empty fields strewn with rubble.

Schanberg then quotes the air attaché at the Embassy as saying, "I saw one stick of bombs go through the town, but it was no great disaster." Schanberg goes on to point out that there were almost 400 casualties, and he takes the reader through the village:

> The atmosphere in Neak Luong, on the east bank of the Mekong River 38 miles southeast of Phnom Penh is silent and sad—bewildered at being bombed by an ally. Everyone has lost either relatives or friends; in some cases entire large families were wiped out.
>
> Yesterday afternoon a soldier could be seen sobbing uncontrollably on the riverbank. "All my family is dead! Take my picture, take my picture! Let the Americans see me!"
>
> His name is Keo Chan and his wife and 10 of his children were killed. All he has left is the youngest—an 8-month-old son. The 48-year-old soldier escaped death because he was on sentry duty a few miles away when the bombs fell.
>
> The bombs went down right in the middle of this town from north to south as it lay sleeping shortly after 4:30 a.m. Over 30 craters can be seen on a line nearly a mile long, and people reported others in jungle areas outside the town that this correspondent could not reach.

The story states that a third of the village hospital was demolished and then quotes the Air Force spokesman as saying there was a "little bit of damage to the northeast corner of the hospital" and some "structural cracks" in a wall. Schanberg is like a bulldog that refuses to let his quarry go.

Although the attaché had described a compound for Cambodian Marines that had been destroyed as consisting of "hootches," the *Times* reporter points out that the Cambodians lived with their families in these shacks.

A woman's scalp sways on a clump of tall grass. A bloody pillow here, a shred of a sarong caught on a barbed wire there. A large bloodstain on the brown earth. A pair of infant's rubber sandals among some unexploded military shells.

The colonel is quoted as saying about the reactions of the townspeople, "They were sad, but they understand that this is war and that in war these things happen." Schanberg goes on:

"I do not understand why it happens," said Chea Salan, a 21-year-old soldier who lost relatives and army buddies. "Before, every time we saw the planes coming we were happy because we knew the planes came to help us. Now I have lost heart."

When the U.S. Embassy learned Schanberg was in Neak Luong, it flew in five foreign journalists who stayed 30 minutes to view the damage and then were returned to Phnom Penh to brief other reporters.

Schanberg's story demonstrates how the rules that guide the reporter can be used with consummate craftsmanship:

- *Verification*—Assertions are checked against the reporter's observations.
- *Dramatization*—Interviews with those involved personalize the event.
- *Truthfulness*—The detailed and specific observations give a reader the sense of the truth as well as the accuracy of the report.
- *Balance*—Both views, the military's and that of the victims, are presented.

Schanberg won a 1975 Pulitzer Prize and the Sigma Delta Chi Award for foreign correspondence in his coverage of Cambodia.

Covering the President

Corresponding to the shift in Vietnam War coverage was a parallel change in the reporting of the presidency. Gradually, journalists learned they were being lied to systematically by President Nixon.

Any reporter who had read the history of White House correspondence would have known that this was not new. From the time Theodore Roosevelt set up the White House Press Room, presidents have sought to manipulate the press. At times, hard pressed for copy, reporters went along with the stage-managing, such as the selling of Calvin Coolidge as the "Sage from Vermont." Coolidge's sagacity consisted of utterances such as, "Civilization depends not only upon the knowledge of the people but upon the use they make of it . . . . The nation with the greatest moral power will win . . . . What we need is thrift and industry . . . . Let everybody keep at work . . . The man who builds a factory builds a temple, the man who works there worships there, and to each is due not scorn and blame but reverence and praise. . . ."

Herbert Hoover was less successful with the press. As he became more remote and more manipulative—even falsifying data and issuing intentionally misleading statements—the press stiffened. Although correspondents had gone along with censorship in the Hoover administration, they became angry and hostile toward its end. Not until the presidency of Richard M. Nixon did the normal press/presidential tension again become that strained.

The press's anger with Nixon stemmed from causes similar to those that aroused reporters in the Hoover era—remoteness of the president and manipulation of information. In 1969, the first year of Nixon's term, he held 11 news conferences. In 1964, Lyndon B. Johnson's first year in office, Johnson held 27. In 1961, John F. Kennedy's first year, Kennedy held 20.

This was not to say Nixon was absent from the television screen. His appearances—for announcements and explanations of national and foreign policy—were frequent. But these appearances were carefully planned and artfully staged. They were more sophisticated than Hoover's reading an announcement and then distributing mimeographed sheets. But the effect was the same—no searching questions from the press, no give and take.

Turner Catledge, former executive editor of *The New York Times,* in commenting on Nixon's attitude toward the press, wrote:

> He seems to think that the press should be a kind of soulless transmission belt, passing along without question or explanation anything he chooses to feed into it. . . .
>
> In theory, our national leaders have wanted and now want a free and independent press as a check on government, but in fact they have not wanted anything of the kind.

A few broadcast and print journalists worried about their inability to serve as the public's representative by asking questions and engaging in a dialogue with the president. They sought to cope with the situation through interpretive reporting, but these efforts worsened relations between the White House and the press, particularly the networks. Documents from the Nixon period reveal that the White House sought to array presidential power to silence television. Eric Sevareid, a network commentator, said he was convinced there was a calculated campaign "to impugn in advance the credibility of those who reported and tried to explain the facts."

Some journalists refused to accept Nixon's contention—first made in a statement to the press in 1962 after his loss in the California governor's race—that the job of the press is "to write what I say." These journalists believed their job was to report what was said and also to verify the truth of the assertions, to explain them and to put them into perspective. The president was particularly annoyed by network television reporters and commentators. This annoyance marked a considerable change from his attitude toward television in 1962 when he condemned newspapers and praised television:

> I think that it's time that our great newspapers have at least the same objectivity, the same fullness of coverage, that television has. And I can only say thank God for television and radio for keeping the newspapers a little more honest.

But television matured in the decade from 1962 to 1972, dropping the mindless objectivity that Elmer Davis had warned against in the early 1950s. Television journalists realized that the president was using them and the medium, and they sought to dig deeper into the presidency and then the Watergate morass.

The president became a man on the run, as revelation overtook cover-up and falsehood until the country rid itself of the men that even the temperate *New York Times* columnist James Reston was moved to describe as "the White House gang."

The Lessons of Watergate

As important a victory as the Watergate disclosures were for an adversary press, the episode proved the press's vulnerability. Had it not been for two young reporters, Carl Bernstein and Bob Woodward, and a few others among the hundreds in Washington, the White House comment that the break-in was a "third-rate burglary" might have ended the matter. The work of these reporters reminded their colleagues that journalism pivots on the sturdy legs and the skepticism of the reporters who seek verifying material by climbing the stairs, knocking on doors and digging through records.

"It is this personal and independent examination of the event, the verification that gives journalism its credibility over other institutions that make claims to truth telling," wrote two sociologists, Joseph Bensman and Robert Lilienfeld, in assessing journalism in their book, *Craft and Consciousness* (New York: John Wiley & Sons, 1973).

Verification presumes an active, not a passive, role. The journalist intrudes. He seeks out the truth of the so-called facts. During a demonstration over black studies at the University of Wisconsin in 1969, the chancellor, H. Edwin Young, stated that the radicals were taking advantage of the situation. At a press conference, *The New York Times* reported that Young "repeated his contention that revolutionary groups had sought to capitalize on the strike. He offered no proof." In four words, the reporter told his readers that Young failed to support his accusations to reporters seeking verification of his allegation.

The Student Press

The student press preceded most of the commercial press in seeking verification of assertions by authorities, perhaps because the lapses of the press in covering Senator Joseph McCarthy's self-styled crusade against subversion and treason in the 1950s indelibly impressed the academic community. In the late 1950s, when a student at the University of Kansas told a friend that he suspected the university kept separate lists of available housing in the community for students, one for white students, the other for non-whites, the friend told a reporter for the university *Daily Kansan*. The reporter then called the official in charge of the housing office, who denied two lists existed. But the allegation seemed to have the ring of truth, and the reporter decided to dig into the situation.

He asked black students and white students using the housing service for the addresses they were given. There were two lists. The reporter pieced together additional information and determined that some homeowners in the college town had told the university they would list their vacancies with the school only if they were guaranteed white students. The university cooperated, and the two lists resulted.

The story the student newspaper published caused considerable controversy. Several students protested in letters to the *Daily Kansan* that the newspaper had no right to check into the affairs of the university. In an editorial, the newspaper defended its prying on the ground that all students were entitled to equal treatment and added that by calling attention to the situation it might be changed before more drastic actions were taken by the offended groups. Although several student groups sought to change university policy on racial matters, it was not altered until several years later in the mid-1960s after campus demonstrations that included a sit-in in the administration building.

A young reporter, new to the courthouse beat, learned that one of the criminal court judges had placed a man with a long criminal record on probation. Despite the seriousness of his latest crime, an armed robbery, the defendant was not sentenced to prison. The reporter, conscious of the community's anger at the growing crime rate, dug into the story. He obtained the details of the defendant's criminal record from a source in the police department. He spoke to the district attorney who prosecuted the case to find out why he had agreed to a reduction in the charge from a major to a minor felony.

Balance and Fairness

The piece he handed in the following week was heavy on factual detail, and the reporter was proud of his work. However, he had one hole—a big one—which the city editor spotted immediately.

"Where's the judge in this?" he asked the reporter. "Didn't you ask him why he did it? Around here we give both sides, always."

The story made the judge appear incompetent or careless, whereas he may have had a valid reason for not sending the criminal to prison. He should have been asked why.

Although readers and listeners often tell pollsters they do not believe what they read in the newspapers and what they hear on their radio and television stations, most people are influenced by the news media. In recent years, the journalist has been made even more aware of this power because of the intensification of competition for the rewards of public office and the marketplace. The politician and the businessperson know that a story that echoes their assertions can sell a candidate, a policy, a piece of merchandise or damage an opponent or competitor. Journalists have coped with these pressures by attributing and verifying material and by balancing assertions and allegations from sources.

THE ATLANTA CONSTITUTION, Fri., May 3, 1974

SON WORKS FOR FIRM SUBMITTING BID

State Senator Pushes Computers

SALESMAN'S FATHER
Sen. J. Ebb Duncan

'I have not been in state government long, but it seems most unusual to me that a state senator accompanies a marketing representative on a sales visit.'

—Bill Oliver

'It is not news to me that my son works for Univac. I made a statement that my son works for Univac before a joint meeting of the House and Senate Appropriations committees, the public, and the press.'

—Sen. J. Ebb Duncan

For instance, a council member says that businesses will be driven from downtown into suburban shopping malls unless property taxes are lowered. If the reporter can find a spokesperson who justifies the present rate, he or she will do so in order to balance the council member's position. During political campaigns, editors try to balance—in some cases down to the second of air time or the inch of copy—candidate A and opponent B.

Balance is important. But some journalists contend that balance does not mean they must station themselves precisely at the midpoint of an issue. If candidate A makes an important speech today, the speech may be worth page one play. If, on the same day, opponent B repeats what he said yesterday or utters nonsense, the newspaper or station is under no obligation to balance something with nothing. A journalism of absolute balance can add up to zero. Balance is a moral commitment and cannot be measured by the stopwatch or the ruler.

The same common sense should be applied to matters that require fair play. Should candidate A make a serious accusation against opponent B, fairness requires that a reporter seek out B for a reply. The targets of charges and accusations should always be given their say, and the reply should be placed as closely to the allegation as possible.

When a state official told the Atlanta *Constitution* that a state senator had been pressuring the state to do business with a computer company that employed the senator's son as a salesman, the charge was the subject of the lead. Three additional paragraphs elaborated the allegation. The fourth and fifth contained the senator's reply:

Denying any conflict of interest in the matter, Duncan said these contacts were an effort by him to keep the state from wasting millions of dollars on more expensive IBM computers.

He admitted that he became interested in state government's computer business through his son but insisted he was only trying to save the state money as a member of the Senate Appropriations Committee. . . .

Fairness

Reporters and editors of the *Post* are committed to fairness. While arguments about objectivity are endless, the concept of fairness is something that editors and reporters can easily understand and pursue. Fairness results from a few simple practices:

- No story is fair if it omits facts of major importance or significance. So fairness includes completeness.
- No story is fair if it includes essentially irrelevant information at the expense of significant facts. So fairness includes relevance.
- No story is fair if it consciously or unconsciously misleads or even deceives the reader. So fairness includes honesty—leveling with the reader.
- No story is fair if reporters hide their biases or emotions behind such subtly pejorative words as "refused," "despite," "admit" and "massive." So fairness requires straightforwardness ahead of flashiness.

Reporters and editors should routinely ask themselves at the end of every story: "Have I been as fair as I can be?"

–The Washington Post, Desk Book on Style

When the government of Juan D. Bosch was overthrown in the Dominican Republic in the 1960s, the military was quoted in the second paragraph of one news story as describing the deposed government as "corrupt and pro-Communist." Eleven paragraphs later, the reporter wrote, "Charges that the ousted president was sympathetic to Communism run directly counter to the Kennedy administration's conviction that Dr. Bosch was a democratic leader opposed to Communism." That paragraph came so deep in the story that it was continued on the inside pages of many newspapers that began the story on page one. Not every reader saw the continuation.

When charges are made for which there is no documentation, the reporter is required to say so high in the story. In a wire service piece from South Africa, the *Sunday-Express* of Johannesburg was quoted as saying that the South African government secretly contributed $3.9 million to President Ford's unsuccessful re-election campaign. In addition to carrying a denial from Ford's general counsel, the story stated in the second paragraph that the charges had been made "without supporting evidence." That statement was the reporter's, acting in the interest of fair play. He was not saying the charges were untrue, but that they had been made without accompanying proof of their truth.

When Emotions Get in the Way

Lack of balance and the absence of fairness are often inadvertent. Since writing is as much an act of the unconscious as it is the conscious use of controlled and disciplined intelligence, the feelings of reporters crop up now and then.

In describing an official the reporter dislikes, a reporter might find himself writing, "C. Harrison Gold, an ambitious young politician, said today. . . ."

Or, writing about an official the reporter admires, that reporter might write, "Gerald Silver, the dynamic young state controller, said today. . . ."

It is all right for a young man or woman to be "ambitious," but when the word is used to describe a politician, it can have a negative connotation. On the other hand, the "dynamic" politician conjures up an image of a young man hard at work serving the public. Maybe the reporter is accurate in these perceptions. Maybe not. The reporter lets the reader conclude by writing what the politician says and does.

Here is a press association story in which the reporter's feelings about East Germany emerge in the choice of adjectives and adverbs:

```
LEAD EAST GERMANY
    BERLIN, Oct. 7--East Germans dutifully trooped
to the polls today to cast ballots in a no-
contest election.
    The candidates for local and country government
posts all were approved by the communist-
controlled "national front."
    Results of the election were to be announced
early this week.
    For the first time ever the single-list ballots
contained more names than offices to be filled,
so that voters could scratch candidates they did
not favor.
    However, the ruling Socialist Unity (Communist)
party was assured of overall majorities no matter
which candidates were successful. The regime's
slick propaganda apparatus encouraged voters
simply to pick up their ballots and put them in
boxes without using the curtained polling booths.
    The Communists used well-oiled propaganda
techniques to create an atmosphere of excitement
and significance for the voting.
    Bands of heavily-indoctrinated youngsters
paraded through the city streets at 6 a.m.
blowing horns to wake their elders to go to the
polls. The streets were strung with red banners
proclaiming "trust in our candidates" and "our
voice for the nation of peace."
```

Goateed Walter Ulbricht and his wife Lotte were
handed bouquets of carnations and red roses as
they ceremoniously cast their votes at a polling
station in a walled and guarded section of East
Berlin.

HZ 568 PED

This approach to foreign news is sometimes referred to as "nationalism in the news." Professor Lawrence D. Pinkham of the University of Massachusetts describes it as "patriotic prose." In this wire service story, the reporter was so affected by his dislike for East Germany that he lost sight of the lead. The fourth paragraph indicates that this election was an exception to prior balloting procedures in East Germany.

One of the best preventives for imbalance and lack of fairness is the advice a senior copy editor gave a young reporter. Peering up from his desk where he was slashing the young man's work vigorously, he said, "Eschew adjectives."

Danger exists any time a reporter departs from the recital of observed fact. Similes and metaphors can cause trouble because their use sometimes leads the reporter to inject his or her feelings into a piece. One reporter wrote, "Looking as though he would be more comfortable in a scarlet bowling shirt than in the delicately plaid business suit he wore, State Assemblyman Louis Montano faced tenants from the end of a long table." The imagery ran away from the reporter's good sense and decency. The sentence implies that the legislator was more suited to bowling than lawmaking. Montano, like others written about by the press in disparaging ways, has little rejoinder. He could write a letter to the editor. But the damage has been done. The reporter has to keep in mind his enormous power to harm.

Fairness and Balance for Broadcasting

The print journalist is morally bound to balance and fairness, but the First Amendment gives him the freedom to be as irresponsible as he wishes. Not so the broadcast journalist who is bound by legal requirements set by the Federal Communications Commission (FCC). The fairness doctrine requires broadcasters to meet standards of "fairness" and "balance" in their programming. The reasoning behind this requirement is that the limited number of stations on the public airwaves—unlike the unlimited possibilities for newspapers and magazines—must present competing views and ideas about issues that affect the public.

The FCC also requires broadcasters to give a "right of reply" to the subjects of personal attack on radio and television.

Unless the broadcaster gives both sides of an issue and grants a person the right to reply within seven days of the attack, the station is subject to a fine. Persistent or serious violations can be cause for the revocation of the station's license.

The constitutionality of these requirements has been attacked by some broadcasters who contend that the regulations are inconsistent with the First Amendment. As the Supreme Court has established the constitutionality of the regulations, broadcast journalists should be aware that they are required to present opposing and contrasting points of view on stories about controversial issues.

Objectivity   Unfair and unbalanced journalism might be described as failures in objectivity. When journalists talk about objectivity, they mean that the news should be free of the reporter's opinion or feelings, that it should contain facts. News is objective when it can be checked against some kind of record—the text of a speech, the minutes of a meeting, a police report, a purchase voucher, a payroll, unemployment data, or vital statistics. An objective report contains material that everyone would agree is true. The verification of the material is so convincing that there can be no argument about its truth. The reporting of facts that can be verified is the mainstay of journalism in the United States.

If the reader wants to weep or laugh, write an angry letter to a congressman or send money to the Red Cross for tornado victims, that is his or her business. The reporter is content to lay out the facts.

In a culture infatuated with supposedly neutral science and technology, objective journalism was the standard into the 1950s. Then, social and political problems that had been proliferating since the end of World War II began to cause cleavages in society, and reporters found their methodology—objective reporting—inadequate. Journalists also were concerned about the attention they had given Joseph McCarthy, the Wisconsin senator whose charges of Communist conspiracies had been given front-page play over the country. Their tortured self-analysis led them to assume collective responsibility for the senator's power. They realized it was not enough to report what McCarthy had said—which was objective reporting.

Objective journalism can be limiting. It encourages passivity. The reporter waits for the events to develop, the authority to speak out. It does not venture into areas that are not discernible or not measurable. It does not seek the depths of the iceberg, but settles for the observable tip. That kind of journalism, with little predictive capacity, is unable to fulfill journalism's role of supplying the public with information on which to base decisions.

Objective journalists reported the announcement of policies and programs, but infrequently examined their consequences among those affected. The monitoring was left to the bureaucracy, taxpayer organizations, other special interest groups and a few journalists. Objective journalism failed to alert the public to the problems of poverty, racism, inequality and the domestic consequences of the Cold War. It seemed to be committed to institutions rather than to people and to have a built-in bias toward established authority, presumed to be rational, disinterested and responsive.

Elmer Davis, a courageous radio journalist, pointed to the limitations of objective journalism in the 1950s. He described the frustrations of reporters who knew officials were lying, but were unable flatly to assert that knowledge in their stories.

Davis advised journalists that they had to walk a tightrope between irresponsible objectivity and subjectivity. He said bare facts were not enough.

Another broadcast journalist, Edward R. Murrow, moved from radio to television where he pioneered in-depth reporting. He sought to make journalism more than a bulletin board with news for the middle class. In his work in the 1950s, Murrow demonstrated passion and conviction along with curiosity and journalistic discipline. His work completely changed television journalism and its present form is a tribute to his success.

At that time, journalists—with their unique non-partisan perspective, and their commitment to democratic values, accurate observation and truth—began to see how they could provide insights for the public and for policy makers. But to do so more effectively, they knew they had to change some of their traditional practices. Underlying their conviction that change was needed was their assumption that journalists are publicly useful men and women.

The Commission on Freedom of the Press in the late 1940s (see *A Free and Responsible Press. A General Report on Mass Communications: Newspapers, Radio, Motion Pictures, Magazines, and Books,* Chicago: The University of Chicago Press, 1947, pp. 21–22) had told journalists that they are most useful when they give "a truthful, comprehensive, and intelligent account of the day's events in a context which gives them meaning. . . . It is no longer enough to report *fact* truthfully. It is now necessary to report the *truth about the fact*."

With the guidance of a Davis, a Murrow, and with the perceptions of the Commission of the Freedom of the Press, journalists began finding ways to work themselves away from the constrictions that the Commission had said impeded truth-telling. One of their responses was a shift from the geographic beat to the topical beat, which resulted in a change in emphasis from the breaking news story to thematic coverage. For instance, instead of emphasizing crime reporting, a journalist might examine the problems of law enforcement. Rather than wait for events to occur, reporters began seeking out causes. Viewing the urban crisis as having its roots in the problems of race and class, journalists began digging into official releases and statements by authorities. Learning about the previously invisible worlds of blacks, the Spanish-speaking, youth and women, journalists were forced to make analyses of their own, to put their intelligence as well as their craft to work.

Journalists who took time to study their craft understood that they could apply the great strengths of objective journalism to the digging journalism they were engaged in. The two kinds of objectivity—the one that takes assertions at face value as news, and the other that digs into the background of the assertions and applies tests of objectivity to the findings—were demonstrated in the coverage of Watergate and in the coverage of the Vietnam War like that of Sydney H. Schanberg.

Objectivity is still the reporter's basic state of mind as he or she approaches a story. But today the journalist relies less on authority and is less passive. The contemporary reporter has emerged as less the stenographer, more the fully-functioning man or woman of critical intelligence.

Basic Components of a News Story 63

Brevity   In our generalization about the reporter's job at the outset of this chapter, we pointed out that the news story is succinct. The tersely told story is admired by editors and by busy readers and listeners. Here is a two-paragraph story that says a great deal although it contains only four sentences:

> JOHANNESBURG, South Africa, Nov. 8—The bodies of 60 victims of an accidental dynamite explosion a mile and a half down a gold mine 100 miles southwest of Johannesburg were brought to the surface today.
>
> Of the dead, 58 were Basuto tribesmen from Lesotho, chosen for the dangerous job of shaft-sinking, or blasting a way down to the gold-bearing reef. The two others were white supervisors. The black Africans will be buried in a communal grave tomorrow.
>
> *—The New York Times*

All creative activities are based on the art of omission. In architecture, the twentieth century has been marked by structures that follow the dictum: Less is more. Economy of expression is the hallmark of the artist.

When Beethoven was struggling with the music to his only opera, *Fidelio,* he realized that the leisurely pace of the music did not meet the demands of the theater, and for years he pared down his work. David Hamilton, the music critic, describes Beethoven's efforts as a "ruthless piece of self criticism . . . Beethoven expunged balancing phrases, trimmed decorative expansions, excised anything that did not move forward, eventually achieving the terse urgency that now marks the opera's crucial scenes."

In eliminating large sections of his music, Beethoven rejected three overtures he had written. One, "Leonore No. 3," became one of the most popular pieces in the orchestral repertory. Despite its obvious beauty and power, Beethoven found it unsuited to his opera—a decision reporters entranced with their own writing might emulate.

Joseph G. Herzberg, an editor on several New York City newspapers said: "Newspapering is knowing what to leave out and condensing the rest."

Too often, beat reporters and specialists write more than they need to because they forget they are writing for general readers, not for their sources. The reporter covering new transplant technology for a newspaper cannot go into the kind of detail that a reporter for the *Journal of the American Medical Association* must report in his story. The newspaper reporter would lose his reader.

But stories can be too brief. A copy editor can always remove excess material. He cannot add essential detail and background that an overly brief report ignores.

The way out of the dilemma of being brief but not writing telegrams is through Herzberg's advice, which can be summed up in one word—selectivity. Brevity is a function of selectivity—knowing what to leave out. The ability to select essential facts from the welter of material that the reporter gathers comes with experience.

A natural tension exists between the editor and the reporter over the issue of brevity. The desk, confronted with ever-decreasing space and time, wants shorter stories. The reporter, excited by the event and driven by a compulsion to tell the full story, wants more time and more space.

Some editors contend that if Genesis can describe the creation of the world in a thousand words then no reporter needs any more than four pages of copy for any event of human dimension. But some events are so complex than any report but an extended account would be incomplete. Important stories often require scenesetting and background that consume time and space. The guide for the length of stories is: Make it brief but complete.

Selectivity

In the mid-1970s, the Iowa Daily Press Association conducted a study of the 40 daily newspapers in the state. In one phase of the study, the executives of the newspapers and journalism instructors at the state's three journalism schools were asked to rank certain characteristics considered most important for beginning reporters. Both groups agreed that the most important skill the beginner should have is the ability to write clearly and interestingly.

Clear prose follows comprehension. That is, the reporter must be able to understand the event before he or she can explain it clearly and succinctly. Clarity follows analysis. No reporter can successfully handle a story without putting his or her intelligence to work first, and then applying the art and skill of writing to the conclusions that have been reached.

Clarity usually relies on simplicity of expression, which generally means short sentences, short words, coherence, and logical order. We shall be looking at these in detail in chapter seven.

Clarity

The job of the reporter can be justified on two counts. First, he or she is necessary to a society in which people cannot witness most events. Second, the reporter is essential because the world has become so complex that even when people do witness an event they are unsure of what they have experienced, how it fits into the sequence of events that preceded it and what its consequences may be. Thus, the task of the reporter is to report and to explain.

To meet these needs and to make certain the report is read, the journalist must recount events accurately and thoroughly and in ways that substitute for the drama of the personal encounter. That is, the reporter must bring these events to life in the telling.

Human Interest

One of the ways the journalist does this is to tell the story in human terms. Reporters personalize and dramatize the news by seeking out the persons involved in the event. Dorothy Flanders Strange of Northern Illinois University says that in all news events some kind of human action occurs. "Either people perform the action, or the action demands human reaction," she says. This action-reaction concept indicates that news is the story of human reality. "Human interest is not something to be added after one has the news," Strange says. Human interest is the essential ingredient of news.

A change in city zoning regulations is made dramatic by pointing out that now low-income families can move into an area that had been effectively sealed off to them by the previous two-acre zoning rule. A factory shutdown is personalized by talking to workers who must line up at the unemployment office instead of at a workbench.

When *The Wall Street Journal* published one of its stories about the payment abroad of bribes by large U.S. firms seeking foreign business, it began its piece this way:

> WOODCLIFF LAKE, N.J.—William Wearly, chairman of Ingersoll-Rand Co., leans back in his chair and professes confidently that the company hasn't been involved in any bribe payments.
>
> "We haven't been in a position where we would have to decide on bribes. I don't think many companies have had that sort of proposition put to them. We haven't."

Then the reporter, Lindley H. Clark, Jr., went into detail about the attempts by this and other firms to avoid paying bribes.

In the same issue, a story about chemicals polluting the Hudson River and ruining the fishing industry, by Barry Newman, begins:

> GRASSY POINT, N.Y.—In the gray-shingled shack at water's edge, four fishermen sit playing cards around an old kitchen table, ignoring the ebb tide laden with the spring run of shad. The wall is hung with foul-weather gear; rubber boots are piled in the corner. On the refrigerator door somebody has taped up a newspaper clipping about the awful chemical in the fish of the Hudson River.
>
> "I do my fishing from the window here," an old man says, looking off to the quiet hills on the east bank, three miles across the river from this small valley town.
>
> "No nets for me this year," another man says. "No pay," says the third. And the fourth: "A lot of trouble, this."

Writing the Story

3

What Is News?

Preview   Reporters have established a set of news values to help them determine the newsworthiness of events. The values are:

- Impact or importance.
- Timeliness of the event.
- Prominence of the people involved in the event.
- Proximity, the closeness of the event to readers and listeners.
- Conflict.
- Unusual, bizarre.
- Currency, the interest people have in the situation.

We have discussed several essentials of journalism—accuracy, attribution, verification, balance and fairness, objectivity, brevity, clarity and human interest. These elements are the reporter's guides to reporting and writing the story. But what guides the reporter to the events worth reporting? Among the cascade of events the reporter encounters in a work day, which should be singled out for attention?

How does the courthouse reporter leafing through a dozen civil complaints filed in the district court know how to choose the newsworthy document? How does the police reporter determine which of the score of arrests is noteworthy? After determining that an event or idea is worth reporting, how does the reporter decide whether to write two paragraphs or seven? How does the broadcast journalist know a story is worth 60 seconds at the start of the 6 p.m. newscast or 10 seconds toward the end? If journalism can be described as the art of selection, then what guidelines can the journalist use in practicing selectivity?

A simple answer to our questions is that news is what newspapers print in their news columns and what stations broadcast on their news programs. If we go back to the beginning of formal news communication we learn that what we read, see and hear today is not much different from the material in the daily bulletins posted in the Roman Forum and what was later printed in gazettes and newsbooks.

Some Answers, Past and Present

Realizing that Roman citizens needed to know about official decisions that affected them, Julius Caesar posted reports of government activities in the *Acta Diurna*. In China, the T'ang dynasty (618–906 A.D.) published a gazette—handwritten or printed by wood block—to inform court officials of its activities. The more immediate predecessor of the newspaper was the handwritten newsletter, containing political and economic information, that circulated among merchants in early sixteenth century Europe.

The first printed newsbook, published in 1513 and titled "The trewe encounter," was an account of the Battle of Flodden Field. The Anglo-Scottish wars of the 1540s provided printers with material for more newsbooks.

During the seventeenth century, news sheets spread to the business centers of Europe, reporting news of commerce.

To this day, much of our news is about the actions of government and business, and our journalism continues to stress the drama of war and other calamities. In this country, as historian Bernard Weisberger has pointed out, the newspaper "served as a handmaiden of commerce by emphasizing news of trade and business."

A major difference between these old information carriers and modern journalism is that the news media—newspapers, television, and radio stations—aim at such a diverse audience that many different kinds of news are in a single issue or newscast. Editors look for a balanced news report to appeal to a wide audience, for survival of the newspaper or station depends upon holding the mass audience.

Day and Bennett

The newspaper editors of the nineteenth century understood the need to appeal to a large audience, and their acumen led to definitions of news that hold to this day. The papers in the large cities—New York, Boston, Chicago, St. Louis, Philadelphia, New Orleans—were printing news for the newly literate reader. One of the first penny papers—inexpensive enough for the working man—contained the ingredients of popular journalism. In 1833, the first issue of Benjamin H. Day's *New York Sun* included a summary of police court cases and stories about fires, burglaries and a suicide. Other stories contained humor and human interest.

Several years later, James Gordon Bennett—described by historian Samuel Eliot Morison as the father of American yellow journalism—used the recently developed telegraph to give the readers of his *Herald* commercial and political news to go along with his reports of the everyday life of New York City, its sins and scandals. His formula of news for "the merchant and man of learning, as well as the mechanic and man of labor" guides many editors today.

Pulitzer

Day and Bennett followed the tastes and appetites of their readers, but they also directed and taught their readers by publishing stories they deemed important. This blend of entertainment, information and public service was stressed by Joseph Pulitzer, who owned newspapers in St. Louis and New York. He, too, gave his readers what he thought they wanted—sensational news and features. But Pulitzer was not content with entertainment. He also used his news staff for his campaigns to curb business monopolies and to seek heavy taxes on income and inheritance. In 1883, Pulitzer charged the staff of his New York *World* with this command:

> Always fight for progress and reform, never tolerate injustice or corruption, always fight demagogues of all parties, never belong to any party, always oppose privileged classes and public plunderers, never lack sympathy with the poor, always remain devoted to the public welfare, never be satisfied with merely printing news, always be drastically independent, never be afraid to attack wrong, whether by predatory plutocracy or predatory poverty.

Today's Editors

Modern editors overseeing newsrooms humming with video terminals and cathode-ray tubes use many of these nineteenth century concepts of news. If asked, they would also agree with the definition of news offered by Charles A. Dana, who ran the *New York Sun* from 1869 to 1897. Dana said news is "anything that interests a large part of the community and has never been brought to its attention before."

One of Dana's editors contributed the classic comment, "If a dog bites a man, it's not news. If a man bites a dog, it's news."

Another enduring definition of news was offered by Stanley Walker, a Texan gone East to success as city editor of *The New York Herald Tribune* in the early 1930s. He said news was based on the three W's, "women, wampum, and wrongdoing." By this he meant that news was concerned with sex, money and crime—the topics people (males, to be sure) secretly desired to hear about.

For the mass media today, Walker's definition holds true. But their stories about women and sex are likely to be concerned with patterns of divorce, sexual liberation and feminism; stories about money will include analyses of the local economy and of the community's tax structure; and crime stories will include opinions on the age at which a juvenile should be treated as an adult offender, as well as an account of the slaying of a suburban housewife.

Definitions of news reflect the period in which they are made. In the mid-1970s the United States had been through three crises: A war in Vietnam that wound down with guilt and defeat for many Americans; the Watergate scandals, and the realization that some political, social, and economic experiments of the 1950s and 1960s that had been hailed as solutions to international conflict, racial tension and unemployment had failed. Millions of men and women were out of work. Crime was increasing. People had lost confidence in their leaders.

It was not surprising, then, to see a shift in the criteria used to determine the news. Av Westin, the executive producer of the American Broadcasting Company's Evening News program, said Americans want their news to answer the following questions: Is the world safe? Are my home and family safe? If they are safe, then what has happened in the last 24 hours to make them better off?

As unemployment and prices rose, economic issues became more important on the Evening News. Westin said that these concerns shifted the meaning of the second question to include: Is my pocketbook safe?

Another trend developed in the late 1970s and carried into the following decade. The UPI's 1978 survey of its daily newspaper subscribers found that editors not only wanted more pocketbook stories but escape as well. Reflecting the interests of their readers, the editors asked for more entertainment in the form of copy about life-styles, leisure subjects and people.

With the election of Ronald Reagan, new economic policies were adopted and considerable controversy developed. News centered on interest rates, unemployment and other economic issues.

The importance of these criteria and guidelines used by editors and producers should not be underestimated. Westin's news judgment directly affected what 11 million persons knew about the day's events. The majority of the Evening News viewers would not read, or would only glance at, a newspaper the next day. Their knowledge of what was happening was confined to the 15 or 20 stories that Westin was able to cram into the 22 minutes of news allotted for the half-hour program.

The UPI's decisions about what events to staff and what news to put on its wires is equally important. The UPI has 1,150 daily newspaper clients in the United States whose circulation is some 271 million a week. The UPI also has 3,700 broadcast clients in the country.

Reporters follow the guidelines of their editors and publishers, who generally agree on the major components of news. Reporters also form agreements among themselves on what constitutes news. Thus, at any given time, news in the mass media is similar. The differences occur in the writing and the presentation. Except for the news of local events, the 11 p.m. television newscast in Kansas City and the morning newspaper in Houston will not be appreciably different in their selection and emphasis of national and international news.

Summing up these definitions of news, two general guidelines emerge:

- News is information about a break from the normal flow of events, an interruption in the expected.
- News is information people need in order to make rational decisions about their lives.

As we have seen, the successful editors, at least those who dominate the history of United States journalism, managed to blend these two definitions in their newspapers. But how does a reporter or editor determine what events are so unusual and what information is so necessary that the public should be informed of them?

News Values

The following seven factors determine the newsworthiness of events and ideas:

Impact: Events that are likely to affect many people. Here, journalists talk about significance, importance, the kinds of information that interest people or that journalists decide the people need to know to be informed. A postal workers' strike will be covered in detail because everyone is affected by the delivery of mail. A campaign for Congress will receive attention in the candidate's district, since journalists consider it essential that voters know the candidates' positions before voting.

Some news that has considerable impact in one community may be unimportant in another. To residents in Milwaukee, a November cold snap has little impact because cold weather is hardly an interruption in the expected in that month. But

Cool snap is downright frosty but highs in 70s are forecast

By DICK BOTHWELL
St. Petersburg Times Staff Writer

A November chill settled over the Suncoast Thursday, and weathermen predicted spotty frost for this morning.

But warmer weather is on the way.

Temperatures in the low to middle 40s were predicted for today, with the upper 30s in store for colder locations, the National Weather Service said.

In North Florida, a cold front Wednesday brought minimums in the lower 40s, about 25 degrees colder than Tuesday morning. Spotty frost is expected there early today in colder locations.

The invasion of cool air was described by J. Thundersquall Drip, Times oracle, as "exceptionally uncommon."

"What we have here," he said Thursday evening,

"is yer temperature inversion, in which readings were running maybe eight degrees above normal — like Tuesday's 66 low, 87 high.

"All of a sudden, the cold front sweeps this away and zaps us with below-normal readings, which means a drop of maybe 20 degrees in two days, see?

"The whole trouble is, Floridians just are not geared for extreme changes like this. Therefore, it seems a lot colder than it really is ."

when 40-degree weather was forecast for St. Petersburg, Fla., many of whose residents had fled northern winters, it was front page news under a large headline. (See news story "Cool snap . . . forecast.")

Timeliness: Events that are immediate, recent. The daily newspaper and the hourly newscast seek to keep readers and listeners abreast of events, to give the public a sense of immediacy and of participation. Thus, broadcast news is written in the present tense, and most leads on newspaper stories contain the word "today." No matter how significant the event, how important the people involved, news value diminishes with time. André Gide, the French novelist, acknowledged the importance of timeliness to the journalist in his definition of journalism: "Everything that will be less interesting tomorrow than today."

The drive to be first with the most recent news is especially strong in competitive situations—among the press associations and in cities with more than one newspaper or broadcast station. The communication media are commercial enterprises. They sell space and time on the basis of their ability to reach people quickly with a highly perishable commodity. The marketplace rewards a fast news carrier. Although newspapers place less emphasis on speed than do the electronic media, a newspaper that offers its readers rehashed news much of the time will not survive. Radio, which was being prepared for its funeral when television captured a large segment of the listening audience, staged a comeback with the all-day, all-news stations.

But keeping up-to-the-minute with news is not enough. Newspapers and television stations offer analyses and interpretations of the news almost as quickly as events break in the news columns. This practice has led some media critics to condemn these efforts as "instant depth."

Timeliness is important in a democracy. People need to know about the activities of their officials as soon as possible so they can assess the directions local and national officials are taking. Told where they are being led, citizens have an opportunity to react before actions become irreversible. In extreme cases, the public can rid itself of an inefficient or corrupt official. For their part, officials also want quick distribution of information so that they can have feedback from the public. This interaction is one of the reasons the Constitution protects the press. Without the give-and-take of ideas, democracy could not work.

What Is News? 73

Prominence: Events involving well-known persons or institutions. When the president trips disembarking from an airplane, it is front-page news; when a city councilman missteps, it is not worth a line of type. A local banker's embezzlement is more newsworthy than a clerk's thievery, even when the clerk has stolen more. Names make news, goes the old journalistic adage, even when the event is of little consequence. And so the fishing exploits of Calvin Coolidge and the religious ruminations of the Beatles were chronicled.

In 1884, an American poet, Eugene Field, was moved by the journalism of personalities, and wrote:

> Now the Ahkoond of Swat is a vague sort of man
> Who lives in a country far over the sea;
> Pray tell me, good reader, if tell me you can,
> What's the Ahkoond of Swat to you folks or me?

Obviously, the answer to Field's question is, not much. Mere prominence should be insufficient to justify the attention of the press. Reporters must ask whether the individual's words and actions are being given attention because of what is said and the individual's competence to say it or because of the person's notoriety. Billy Graham's assessment of international affairs may be worth a paragraph or two, but the comments of the secretary general of the United Nations would be worth a dozen paragraphs.

Dick Harwood, ombudsman for *The Washington Post,* commenting on the coverage of the president's part in a Congressional campaign, discussed the journalistic yearning for important persons.

> We salivated over the Republicans last fall for one reason only—the president was out campaigning for them. No matter that he had very little to say that was significant or unpredictable at the whistlestops along the way. No matter that he *did* very little beyond waving at crowds. No matter that there was little or no evidence that what he said or did affected a single vote, the mere fact that he was out there was page one news in *The Washington Post.* What he was doing was "important," we told ourselves, because presidents are "important" men. That kind of circular reasoning frequently affects our news judgments. . . . It says something about our sense of values and about our perspectives on the world. . . .

Proximity: Events in the circulation or broadcast area. People are interested in, and affected by, activities close at hand. A city ordinance to require licensing of dogs in Memphis, Tenn., would be of great interest to that city's residents, of some interest to Nashville, Tenn., residents, and of almost no interest to dog owners in Butte, Mont.

Journalists recognize the need of readers and listeners to know what is going on around them. If 42 people die in an airplane crash in the Andes and one of the passengers is a resident of Little Rock, the news story in Little Rock will emphasize the death of the local resident. This process is known as *localizing* the news. (See "Local Emphasis," front page.)

NCAA: Kentucky meets Louisville - B1

THE THORN BIRDS

Critic gives high marks - C1

EPA firings - A2

The Times-News

25¢

78th year, No. 84   Twin Falls, Idaho   Friday, March 25, 1983

Twin Falls officer shot in the back

By KELLY EVERITT
Times-News writer

FILER — Bob Gauthier, 29, a deputy sheriff with the Twin Falls County sheriff's office, was shot in the back with a shotgun Thursday evening while responding to a family dispute in Filer.

A Filer police officer, who had served as backup on the call, returned the fire, wounding Gauthier's alleged assailant, Fred Miller, age unknown, of 901 Stevens St., Filer.

Gauthier was listed in serious condition at Magic Valley Regional Medical Center late Thursday night. Miller was listed in critical condition.

According to Sheriff Jim Munn, Gauthier was making a "second call" at about 6:30 p.m., on what was apparently a family dispute at the Miller home, which is located in a mobile-home park on the west edge of Filer.

One eyewitness to the shooting, who asked not to be identified, said that she saw Gauthier go to the door of the mobile home and apparently identify himself.

"I saw him, Mr. Miller, close the door and then open it again right away. The officer was standing at the door (at that time), but he must have seen the weapon or something, because it looked like he started to move to the front of the trailer — to get out of the way, I guess.

"Then I heard a shot. It sounded like a shotgun, I'm not sure, and he (Gauthier) went down. Then, I heard two or three other shots. I guess from the Filer officer. At least that's what I was told (by police). I thought at first they came from inside the trailer, but the first shot startled me so much I couldn't see for sure."

According to county Prosecutor Harry DeHaan, the Filer officer, who was not identified and reportedly was "considerably shook up" over the incident, fired three shots at Miller.

"The suspect appeared to be attempting to pump a second round into the shotgun to take a second shot at the officer," DeHaan said. "In my opinion, the Filer officer saved Gauthier's life by promptly returning fire, as he is supposed to do. A second shot would have killed Gauthier."

Twin Falls police Chief Tom Qualls said Miller was hit twice as he stood in the partially closed doorway of his home.

Munn has turned the investigation over to Qualls, which is standard procedure whenever an officer in his department is involved in any incident, he said.

Three bullet holes could be seen in the aluminum door of the Miller home. Qualls said Gauthier apparently was shot with a 12-gauge shotgun at a range of six to 10 feet from the door of the mobile home. According to the eyewitness, the backup officer's return fire came

See SHOOTING on Page A2

Sheriff James Munn holds a rope cordoning off the crime scene as Fred Miller, suspected in the shooting of a deputy sheriff, is placed in an ambulance.

Jobs Bill: Passed, signed, now law

By IRA R. ALLEN
United Press International

WASHINGTON — President Reagan Thursday night signed a $4.6 billion package of new jobs and recession relief into law, apparently in time to keep benefits flowing to thousands of unemployed people, a White House spokesman said.

Spokesman Mort Allin said the legislation reached the president's desk between 9:30 p.m. and 10 p.m. EST, "and he signed it shortly thereafter."

About 2 million jobless nationwide depended on Reagan's signature by Thursday to continue getting benefits attached to the legislation. But White House spokesman Larry Speakes said earlier in the day signing would not occur until Friday.

In addition to public works construction projects and social programs that might provide up to a half-million jobs — and $50 million in humanitarian aid — the bill contains $5 billion in fresh money for the federal fund that lends money to states to pay their unemployment compensation claims.

The fund ran dry Tuesday, and 25 states and three other jurisdictions scrambled to shift other funds around to meet the claims of the estimated 2 million people that might be affected.

Four states stopped sending out checks. Missouri held up checks for 32,000 recipients Thursday; West Virginia sent 4,000 checks before it ran out of money and held up payments to 6,500; Colorado delayed checks to 5,000 to 6,000 recipients, and New Mexico did not pay 502 on time.

It normally takes several hours for the legislative paperwork to be dispatched the mile from Capitol Hill to the White House, and presidential aides usually examine the bill in detail before the president signs.

Spokesman Jack Hashian said Thursday the Labor Department sent telegrams to the states telling them they can count on getting more money and in the meantime they could take a "prudent risk" by sending checks backed by other state funds. But the federal government would not reimburse interest, he said.

"The best we can say is, 'Okay, states, you can take a prudent risk and advance the death, but we can't give you the money until the president signs,'" he said.

The final version of the jobs bill got approval from the Senate Tuesday, but the House did not give its final O.K. until nearly noon Thursday.

About $2 billion in the bill is aimed at states and localities with the highest rates of unemployment under a complex distribution formula that held up final approval for two days as House and Senate negotiators argued over how much should go to states and how much to cities and counties.

The compromise would funnel $1.25 billion to the localities and $825 million to the states.

Passage also had been delayed in the Senate by a fight over an unrelated move to repeal tax withholding of dividends and interest.

The biggest single block of money in the bill, $1 billion, is for community development grants, money for states and cities to use on public works programs, half of which can be used for public service jobs, aiding women shut out from the heavy construction tilt elsewhere in the bill.

Road was tough, but Barney Clark trod it successfully

By DUSTON HARVEY
United Press International

SALT LAKE CITY — Dr. Barney Clark accomplished "his goal, his mission" before his death by proving the permanent artificial heart worked and that made the 112-day ordeal worthwhile, his surgeons said Thursday.

Clark, 62, a humorous, golf-playing dentist with a zest for life, died of collapse of his blood circulation system and "multiple organ failure."

The medical team determined "he was essentially dead and thus courageous man's heart was turned off," said Dr. William DeVries, chief of the surgical team that implanted the heart on Dec. 2, 1982.

"The heart could not support the rest of the body and it (the body) died," said DeVries, who told a news briefing the circulatory collapse and organ failure were triggered by antibiotics used to fight pneumonia.

Clark had lived for 111 days, 12 hours and 55 minutes with the implanted heart — long enough to celebrate Christmas with his family

and his 62nd birthday with them and the staff at the University of Utah Medical Center. He was conscious and communicated with his doctors on the morning of his death, informing them he was in no pain, DeVries said.

On Saturday, Clark told doctors he was very pleased with the heart's success, said Dr. Lyle Joyce, one of his heart surgeons, who called the patient "a very dear friend."

"He realized the tough road he had been through and was happy he had taken that route," Joyce said.

Dr. Chase Peterson, the university's medical vice president, said Clark "accomplished what he set out to accomplish" and would have been satisfied if he had only shown the heart could be implanted successfully.

"But he proved that an artificial heart could work in man for 112 days, for 2,998 hours, for 12,912,400 beats," said Peterson. "And he also proved that courage and good humor and love of wife and children are sustained by an artificial heart."

Clark's unfulfilled hopes of leaving the hospital and to play golf again with a portable air compressor pumping his heart "were extra," said Peterson.

DeVries said a second artificial heart and its support equipment were ready to go, but data from Clark first must be analyzed and an ethics review committee must assess risks-versus-benefits before the school performs another implant.

Nonetheless, Peterson said: "We expect to proceed on with this research."

Peterson said the cost of the 112 days of additional life was "nothing to the patient," with private donors picking up a hospital bill he estimated at $150,000 to $200,000.

That didn't include the $2.4 million spent in the past two decades developing the Jarvik-7.

In explaining the cause of Clark's death, DeVries said the patient's body shut down in "a spiraling downhill course" that started on March 3 when the medical pioneer threw up, inhaled vomit and contracted aspiration pneumonia.

Antibiotics used to fight the pneumonia killed protective bacteria in the colon, allowing a staph infection to ultimately weaken the entire body, DeVries explained.

"His colon failed," DeVries said. "Then his kidneys failed ... Then his lungs failed. Then his brain failed and, lastly, when the key was turned off, his heart failed."

William DeVries and Chase Peterson discuss patient's death

Vocational budget very costly to CSI

By BRUCE HAMMOND
Times-News writer

BOISE — Passing by only one vote, a vocational education budget — that College of Southern Idaho officials say will cause the loss of five teachers and two programs — cleared the House on Thursday.

"This appropriation level is $210,900 down from the original appropriation we received this year," said Orville Bradley, CSI's vocational director. "At that level, we'll have 11 positions, including five teachers."

Programs targeted for elimination under the proposed budget are plant maintenance and auto-parts-counter courses.

The appropriation calls for a statewide allocation to vocational education programs of $16.5 million. About $1.8 million of that would go to CSI — amounting to almost a third of the college's operating budget.

Opponents say this is too little funding for a program that can retrain laid-off workers, allowing them

See FUNDING on Page A3

Override measure passed by voters

By HARRIET GUTHERTZ
Times-News writer

HAILEY — Blaine County voters gave the school district a narrow victory Thursday, passing a $906,000 override levy, with 53 percent of the voters casting "yes" ballots.

With all four polling places counted, the final tally was 1,427 "yes" and 1,140 "no."

The measure passed in Ketchum with no problem, gaining 639 votes for

passage, vs. 206 against. Hailey voters were a little more hesitant; they approved of the override by a 511-430 margin.

Carey and Bellevue citizens, however, said "no" to a tax increase. In Carey, 141 voters supported the measure, but 144 did not. Only 132 Bellevue voters were for the levy, vs. 356 opposing votes.

Superintendent Richard Jones said he was "extremely pleased and ap-

See OVERRIDE on Page A3

People also feel close to events and individuals with whom they have emotional ties. Newspapers and stations in communities with large Catholic or Jewish populations will give considerable space and time to news from the Vatican or the Middle East. When Duke Ellington, the composer and bandleader, became critically ill, the story was given lead play on page one of the *Amsterdam News,* a weekly in New York City with a predominantly black readership.

Economic interests can bridge distances, also. As the ownership of common stocks became more widespread in the United States, the annual report of the American Telephone & Telegraph Company became almost as important in the shoptalk of Jackson, Miss., businessmen as the state's annual cotton yield. Every major newspaper had to make room for the daily closing prices of the New York Stock Exchange. A newspaper in Mankato, Minn., will devote staff time and news space to the weather, crop reports and the livestock and grain markets. If the newspaper in an agricultural area has a correspondent in Washington, much of his time will be devoted to covering the Department of Agriculture and the committees dealing with farm matters.

Conflict: Events that reflect clashes between people or institutions. Strife, antagonism and confrontation have been the building blocks of stories since people drew pictures of the hunt on the walls of their caves. Man's struggles with himself and his gods, a Hamlet or a Prometheus, are the essentials of drama. The contemporary counterparts are visible to the journalist whose eye is trained to see the dramatic—an official who must decide whether a proposed highway should go through the homes of a dozen families, a parents' movement that seeks changes in the curriculum that school authorities have adopted.

Although critics of the press condemn what they consider to be an over-emphasis on conflict, the advance of civilization can be seen as an adventure in conflict and turmoil.

The Bizarre: Events that deviate sharply from the expected and the experiences of everyday life. The damage suit filed by an Albuquerque couple because the club they had rented for their wedding reception was occupied when they and their 200 guests arrived stands out from the dozen other suits filed that day.

To some, the election of a woman as governor of Connecticut in 1974 was more than merely unusual. Never mind the fact that a woman was elected governor of Wyoming as far back as 1925. To Easterners, a woman in the statehouse was so unusual that editors gave it considerable space and time. In 1970, when an all-white jury awarded a black man $70,000 in damages, the racial angle was played up in the wire service story:

Police Victim Gets $70,000

CHICAGO, June 17—An all-white jury awarded $70,000 in damages yesterday to a black man who said that two policemen had violated his civil rights by beating him after they stopped him on a traffic charge. . . .

Nowadays, it is not unusual in most parts of the country for a white jury to make awards to black plaintiffs, and such a story would probably not be put on the transcontinental wires of the press associations.

A story that merited the attention of a press association only because of its bizarre nature surprised many staid newspaper readers a couple of decades ago when the unwritten rules about suggestive material were strict and unbending.

Despite the obvious purpose of the flagpole assignation, this story was given considerable play, even by conservative editors. Some editors may have seen in it one of life's oldest stories: Man and woman's triumph over adversity. (The name of the flagpole sitter has been changed.):

Flagpole Sitter Charged with Rape of 15-Year-Old

EL PASO, Tex., Oct. 22—William M. Jones, 33-year-old flagpole sitter, today faced charges of statutory rape of a 15-year-old girl atop a 62-foot flagpole.

According to the charges, the incident took place more than a month ago while Jones was spending 65 days on the pole as an advertising stunt.

His living quarters on the pole consisted of a four by five foot platform, covered by an awning which he could let down around himself at night.

There was no ladder and apparently the girl was raised to the platform by a rope Jones used to haul up food.

The incident came to light when a relative of the girl spotted Jones on the street Monday and beat him severely about the head. Charges were filed yesterday.

The girl signed a statement admitting that she consented to relations with Jones. However, in cases of statutory rape involving a minor, consent is not an issue.

Her parents said they knew she had been seeing Jones and ordered her to stay away from him.

Several months ago Jones was no-billed by a grand jury in a rape case involving a 19-year-old housemaid from Juarez, Mexico, just across the Rio Grande River from El Paso. A companion was given a 10-year sentence in the case.

Currency: Events and situations that are being talked about. Occasionally, a situation of long-standing will suddenly emerge and become newsworthy. As the historians might say, it is an idea whose time has come.

The poor have always been with us. But following the Depression it was not until President Kennedy read a book by Michael Harrington, *The Other America* (New York: Macmillan, 1962), that the welfare of millions of Americans living in poverty became newsworthy. By speaking about the welfare of these men, women and children, Kennedy made Americans examine their relationships with the poor in their communities. Newspapers assigned reporters to what some of them called the poverty beat. Health and welfare agencies suddenly were discovered by reporters. A few newspapers opened bureaus in ghetto areas.

In August, 1964, following race riots, Congress passed the Economic Opportunity Act in response to President Johnson's call for a "war on poverty." For the next decade, poverty and its ramifications in vast areas of American life were news. Then, in the mid-1970s, interest waned. And even the announcement by the leaders of the Roman Catholic Church in the United States in 1975 that there were some 40 million Americans living in poverty engendered little journalistic interest.

Newspapers and broadcast stations will sometimes make discoveries of their own and push them so that they become current. The depredations and violence of the young are a continuing fact of life, but not until the mid-1970s did some newspapers take an interest in such local problems as school vandalism and juvenile street crime. Suddenly, these newspapers discovered that broken windows and wanton destruction of school equipment were major cost items in the annual budget. In Washington, D.C., serious crime, most of it committed by late-adolescent males, rose 400 percent between 1960 and 1970.

When a newspaper decides that some facet of community or national life is worth intensive coverage as a public service, it may assign a reporter or a team of reporters to dig into the situation. The result, usually a number of stories, is called a campaign or a crusade. Much of this news has a steamroller effect and further news is developed because of the currency of the theme or issue.

Few events fall solely into one or another of the seven categories: Impact, timeliness, prominence, proximity, conflict, the bizarre, currency. The illness of Duke Ellington was newsworthy because of Ellington's prominence, and it received particular attention in newspapers with a black readership because of his proximity to these readers. Most newsworthy events are combinations of these guidelines.

Journalists and journalism teachers use a variety of terms to describe the news values. A study of many journalism textbooks by Professor Wallace B. Eberhard of the University of Georgia found that authors used 43 terms for news values. Professor John D. Mitchell at Syracuse University uses the term prominence to cover an event that affects a large number of people, and he says that conflict and the bizarre can be interpreted as forms of prominence.

Whatever terms are used, there does seem to be near-unanimous agreement on two components of news stories:

- Consequence—news that affects or is important to large numbers of people. (Impact, importance significance.)
- Interest—news that is unusual, strange, entertaining.

At least three-fourths of all stories journalists write fall into one or the other of these two categories.

These guidelines do not tell us that one of the most enduring stories is the timeless, undramatic tale of how man prevails. How we live now is a story few readers have ever been able to resist. Also, these guidelines do not tell us how news values change. Nor do they give us any hints about the realities of the newsroom—its pressures and its politics.

News Is Relative News obviously is a relative concept. It changes with geography, demography and time. A century ago, when 80 percent of the people in the United States made their living from agriculture, farm news was important. Today, with fewer than eight percent of the population so employed, farm news is important outside agricultural areas only when it affects the residents of cities. When the price of a chuck roast or a loaf of bread goes up, city dwellers read about it. At the turn of the century, fewer than 115,000 young men and women were in college. Now more than 50 times as many students attend college, and newspapers assign reporters to cover the colleges in their areas on a regular basis.

Even the so-called essential guidelines change. For years, human interest was considered one of the seven basic criteria to be used in assessing the news value of an event. Stories would be sought that had a high entertainment quotient. The feature story, with its focus on individuals and their foibles, was a fixture in almost every newspaper. This led to a wild assortment of trivia in the news, the journalistic equivalent of the carnival's two-headed boy and the bearded woman. Editors rebutted criticism with the argument that the newspaper had to take a carnival approach to news—to entice readers into the newspaper with the barker's pitch and then move them on to the important news.

Today, the emphasis is on finding the human element in all events, if possible. A budget story is personalized by showing the consequences of the new property tax to those affected by it—homeowners, apartment dwellers and the merchants who may have to raise their prices as taxes increase. Changes in the school curriculum are made interesting by describing what John and Jane will be reading in the third grade next fall. *The Wall Street Journal* has been influential in the trend toward personalizing the news. A typical *Journal* story will begin with several paragraphs about an individual—perplexed, hard-pressed, triumphant or defeated—and bring in the significance paragraph after personalizing the issue through the affected individual.

The personalizing of the news is the result of many forces at work on the newspaper. For many years, the magazines that published "inside" and—so it was claimed—true stories of the activities of actors, actresses, oil or shipping magnates and other well-known men and women were massive sellers. The newspapers that hewed to the dry, factual presentation of the events of the day barely held their own in the battle for advertising and readers. Those newspapers that emphasized the human interest story fared better, although they were described by their more respectable brethren as sensational.

With the coming of television as a competitor and the arrival of the age of intimacy—everyone is entitled to know what the president and his wife talk about in bed—newspapers joined the movement toward personalizing the news.

Pictures and Print

Watch the local evening news on television. Compare the placement and time given each news item in the broadcast with the play each receives in the newspaper. Clearly, some of the news that is emphasized on television is given routine treatment in the newspaper, and some newspaper stories receive slight mention in newscasts. Obviously, some news is better suited to the newspaper than to television, and television is better able to capture some events than the newspaper.

Television technology and the audience demand pictures; ideas are sometimes difficult to capture on film. Thus, the television newscast leans heavily on action. As Richard Salant, then president of Columbia Broadcasting System News, put it, "You see more fires on local television than you do in the newspapers because fires look better on television."

Unlike the newspaper reader, who can decide not to read some stories on the basis of the headline or the lead, the television viewer and radio listener must sit through the news items that distress or bore him, turn off the set or change the channel. The broadcast editor is thus faced with a potentially flighty audience and must be careful not to lose it with too much detail or too many complex ideas. Reporters for the electronic media understand the needs of radio and television and respond to them in their reporting, writing and editing.

Advertising and News Flow

In a newspaper, the space allotted for news usually depends on the amount of advertising that is sold. Unlike radio and television, which have nonexpandable five, 10, 15 or 30 minutes—minus commercials—for newcasts, a newspaper may run 32 pages one day and 48 the next, when department stores place their white-sale advertising. A story that would run half a column on a day when the news hole is tight would be given a full column when ample space is available.

On any given day, the news flow may be slow. That is, important stories simply may not be breaking. On days like these, events that would be ignored on busy news days are covered.

Some reporters are able to sell their stories better than others. They can convince their editors of the importance of their pieces, whereas a reporter who believes that a story speaks for itself may find his story cut or spiked.

Advertising Pressures

After a Connecticut newspaper had printed a front-page story about a kidnapping at a shopping center, the merchants at the center demanded a meeting with newspaper management. At the session, the merchants reminded the editor and publisher that the newspaper's survival depended on the economic health of local business but that such stories would drive shoppers elsewhere. The newspapermen replied that crime was always covered by the newspaper and that no individual or group could be given special treatment.

Such confrontations are infrequent, but when they do occur the response of the journalist is usually that advertiser intrusion in news policy is intolerable. Nevertheless, media managers are conscious of the feelings and needs of their advertisers, and this awareness affects news decisions. The recognition that advertising lubricates the media may mean that the newspaper or broadcast station will assign a new staff member to general assignment rather than to consumer reporting. The Connecticut editor who was criticized by his advertisers may put the next shopping center crime on page three instead of page one.

After *The Charleston Gazette* ran a series of articles indicating that local automobile dealers and garages were engaged in several dishonest practices, advertising by auto dealers declined. In his column, Don Marsh, the editor of the West Virginia daily newspaper, wrote frankly of the situation. No one in the advertising department had mentioned the series to anyone in the news department, Marsh wrote, quoting the advertising manager as saying, "I don't think they should. And anyway, they knew it wouldn't do any good."

Marsh then went on to name the companies that had stopped advertising and those that had continued to advertise.

"I find myself unable to get mad at those who aren't advertising," Marsh commented. "I suspect that if I were in their place I would ask myself why I should be giving money to an enterprise that appears to be willing to do me in." He said that he did not question the right of the advertisers "to boycott, if that's what they're doing.

"I do question their reason. Their action represents an attempt to economically silence their critic, to muscle him into subjection, without regard to the accuracy of his criticism."

Marsh admitted that advertising boycotts and threats can be and have been "an effective muzzler. Lose an account because of a story?—madness. Ask any publisher of a struggling paper whether he would prefer an exposé of a county official or the continued placement in his columns of the county's advertising. His answer is inevitable."

A newspaper is as independent as its finances permit, Marsh concluded. The *Gazette* is strong enough to be independent, he wrote. "Ask any car dealer."

But the pressure to please advertisers sometimes does lead to direct bottling-up of the news. *The Wall Street Journal* reported such a case in its April 12, 1976, issue.

The story has its origin in the seizure in 1971 of some 1.5 million cans of soup produced by Bon Vivant of Newark, N.J. The Federal Food and Drug Administration acted after a man died and his wife was paralyzed as the result of drinking the company's vichyssoise. The soup contained bacteria that cause botulism, a crippling and often fatal disease. But not all the cans were seized and destroyed. Years later, a University of Wyoming student spotted the cans on the shelf of a Laramie food store, and the city's environmental commissioner dashed over to pick them up. He turned them over to the state department of agriculture which issued a press release advising consumers that the soup had turned up and warning them not to eat it if they had any at home. The local newspaper ignored the story.

Only after the local radio stations and television stations in Cheyenne and Denver ran the story did the local newspaper print an item, on page three. The name of the store was not mentioned.

Asked what had happened to the story, the newspaper's managing editor is quoted in the *Journal* as answering:

"I think you could say this was one of those cases where the advertising department did have some influence over a news story. We're a small town and we have to react differently from the big cities. We can't just run out and say, 'My God, everybody, John Shuster's selling poison soup.' We didn't want to prejudice his business."

The advertising manager didn't want the story to run, said the managing editor. "So it didn't," he said.

At one of the local radio stations, the news director, Ralph Swain, who was also an instructor in journalism at the University of Wyoming, energetically dug into the story, identifying the store so that people who shopped there would be careful and "so we wouldn't cast suspicion on the other stores that hadn't sold Bon Vivant." Following his 6 p.m. newscast, the store cancelled its advertising with the station. According to the *Journal,* Swain said he was cautioned about future stories on the soup and that his reporting led to his dismissal.

Big city newspapers may not be as different in their solicitude for advertisers as the Laramie newspaper's managing editor thinks.

In 1974, the Chicago regional office of the Federal Trade Commission (FTC) accused Sears, Roebuck and Company of advertising low-priced products and then making them unattractive or unavailable and pressing the customer to buy higher-priced items.

This technique is called bait-and-switch selling. Sears denied the charges and in February, 1976, an FTC administrative law judge heard the case. After 11 days, Sears sought to negotiate a consent order, agreeing to stop some of its sales tactics.

In an article, "The Sins of Sears Are Not News in Chicago," in the July-August 1976 *Columbia Journalism Review,* Michael Hirsh reported that 18 former Sears employees from 13 states and 25 consumer witnesses from 11 states "gave evidence of dirty tricks that made Sears sound like the CREEP of the business world."

Hirsh reported that despite the hearing's potential impact: The *Chicago Tribune* carried only a four-paragraph item from the Dow-Jones News Service nearly a week after the hearing ended; the *Chicago Sun-Times* ran its first story on the seventh day of the hearing, and three after its conclusion; and *The Chicago Daily News* ran two stories.

Sears is the world's largest retailer and it employs 30,000 persons in Chicago and 417,000 nationally. It provides advertising revenues—$370 million in 1974—for countless newspapers, radio and TV stations.

Hirsh speculates on the coverage a murder might have received. "Suppose that the chairman of the board of a multi-billion dollar corporation was accused of murdering his wife. How would the press react?" Front-page stuff, says Hirsh.

"Yet how many Americans would be directly affected by that story?"

In 1982, a reporter for the *Trenton* (N.J.) *Times* was fired because he inserted background material into a press release his editor had told him to run without any changes. The press release was from a local advertiser. After the dismissal had led to a barrage of criticism of the newspaper, the publisher apologized in a signed editorial that stated, "It is not now, nor has it ever been, the policy of Albritton Communications Co. to allow the interests of our advertisers to influence the news or how the news is to be printed."

But the reporter was not rehired. A quarter of the reporting staff quit in disgust.

Elizabeth Whalen, the executive director of the American Council on Science and Health, was asked by *Harper's Bazaar,* the well-known fashion magazine, to write an article with the title, "Protect Your Man from Cancer." Whalen said that she "emphasized the contribution of tobacco to cancer of the lung, prostate, oral cavity and other sites." The article began with the link of smoking and cancer.

Jane Ogle, then an editor of the magazine, said that when the editor saw the article he told her, "Christ, Jane, I can't open this article with smoking." She said she moved the material to the end "so it wouldn't jump in the face of every cigarette advertiser."

Whalen said that only parts of her article were used and that she was told the cutting was based on her "frequent mention of tobacco and the fact that they (the magazine) ran three full-page cigarette ads each month."

Some newspapers do not succumb to the pressures of cigarette advertisers. *The Charlotte Observer* carried a 20-page special report titled, "Our Tobacco Dilemma." The state's farmers grow two-thirds of the tobacco used for cigarettes, and North Carolina workers manufacture more than half of the almost 700 billion cigarettes made in the United States each year. Tobacco, the state's leading cash crop, brings in $1 billion a year to growers.

Yet the *Observer* did not shrink from putting under the title of its special section this headline:

N.C.'s top crop; part of our lives but bad for health

On the front page next to a picture of a tobacco warehouse was a photograph of James McManus, 62, a former painter and paperhanger, a five-pack-a-day smoker. He was pictured with the tubes from his oxygen tank attached to his nose and mouth. "McManus speaks only with difficulty and needs an oxygen tank to survive," the paper states. He has "smoking-caused emphysema."

The tobacco industry outspends all other national advertisers in newspapers and is second to the transportation industry in magazine advertising. The Federal Trade Commission reported that in 1980, the tobacco industry spent $1.24 billion on advertising cigarettes, about $23.40 a smoker.

In a story on the consequences of this huge advertising budget, *The Wall Street Journal* reported that the financially weak publications are subject to pressure from the tobacco companies. When a reporter for the *Twin Cities Reader* in Minneapolis covered a press conference announcing the Kool Jazz Festival, sponsored by Brown & Williamson, he inserted a list of famous jazz artists who had died of lung cancer. The reporter was fired the next day.

But even the giants of publishing cater to the tobacco companies, the *Journal* stated. If a cigarette advertisement should run near an obituary or close to a story about the effects of tobacco on health, then the company is given a "make good," or free ad, the paper reported.

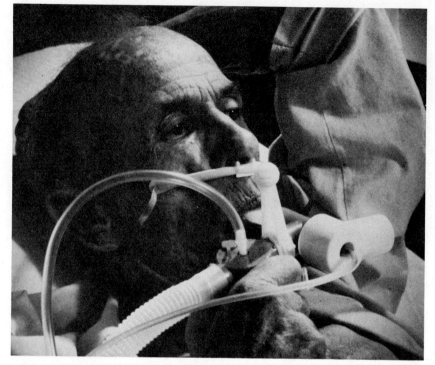

Five Packs a Day. Although *The Charlotte Observer* serves farmers who grow two-thirds of the tobacco used to make cigarettes, it ran this picture of a victim of "smoking-caused emphysema" in a section entitled, "Our Tobacco Dilemma."

Newsroom Politics and Ideology

The politics in the newsroom can affect the news. The power structure, which puts the reporter close to the bottom of the power hierarchy, places decision making in the hands of the editors, publishers and news managers who rarely see the events the reporter writes about. Yet they often have firm ideas about how stories should be written, and the reporter is tempted to go along to get along. Some publishers and station owners have pet projects—a favored charity, the downtown business mall—and these will be given special attention. Political and social cronies may be granted time and space disproportionate to their actual news value.

Ideology sometimes determines what is printed. Reporters and copy editors are proud of their independence, particularly of the distance they put between the newsroom and the editorial writer's alcove. But the ideological commitments of the newspaper sometimes seep into the newsroom and affect what is covered and its play.

When Fidel Castro had a swimming accident, the *El Paso Times* ran this headline.

Castro Narrowly Escapes Drowning
Too Bad! Too Bad! Too Bad! Too Bad!

These pressures work in two directions—what is used and what is tossed out. A publication or station can be assessed as much by its wastebasket as by its columns and newscasts, for the sins of omission are as serious as those of commission in journalism. Reporters and editors are affected by common assumptions and the tide of public opinion. As a consequence, the divergent idea or the unusual person may not be assessed with the same criteria applied to the accepted and the expected.

Some editors favor certain types of news—political stories, features, hard news—and give less attention to other kinds of news. The commitment of a newspaper to a large statehouse staff may mean a lot of news from the state capitol, even at the expense of important international news, because people on the payroll must be put to use.

The nature of the audience is an essential factor in determining what is covered and how events are reported. News directors of non-commercial television and radio stations lean heavily on analysis and venture into advocacy journalism, whereas the commercial stations with their mass audience stay close to so-called objective, event-oriented reporting. Reporters for special-interest magazines and alternative newspapers are less sensitive to the needs of the mass audience than are the reporters for daily newspapers.

The American Society of Newspaper Editors reported in 1982 that a readership study had shown that 79 percent of people 65–74 years old read newspapers nearly every day. The main interest of older people, the study found, is news—local, national and international. After news, they want to read about the best food buys, health and medicine. Obituaries are also a strong interest.

Reporters and editors learn to anticipate the responses of their audience to a subject. Sometimes, the guesswork leads to a disproportionate amount of news about what readers already know or want to hear confirmed and to oversimplification in writing. A steady diet of this kind of journalism can become a self-fulfilling prophecy, developing readers and listeners who suspect the different and fear the new.

The economics of stations and newspapers affects coverage. A small station may not have the resources to cover many events in the community. It may rely on sources other than its staff—publicity handouts and releases, the press associations, volunteers—and rewrite news from the city newspaper, which is usually able to muster more reporters than the local radio or television station. Short-handed news staffs rely on the telephone rather than on-the-scene coverage, a poor substitute.

Policies and traditions also determine how news is covered and what is reported. Many newspapers are satisfied with being publications of record. That is, they will cover the formal activities of their communities. The kind of journalism that results from this policy is described as event-oriented, since it leans heavily on meetings, speeches, accidents and disasters, crime and other overt activities. It is a denotative journalism, pointing to what has happened, and it is a fairly inexpensive and non-controversial journalism.

The Influence of Owners

The strong publisher determined to influence public policy through his or her newspaper has just about disappeared. But ownership still influences how news is covered and what is published. Without the spur of competition, the monopoly newspaper may become lazy, sitting back to await news rather than going out to dig it up. It may ignore what Benjamin C. Bradlee, executive editor of *The Washington Post,* describes as the "special responsibilities" of the monopoly newspaper: "to listen to the voiceless; to avoid any and all acts of arrogance; to face the public with politeness and candor."

The chain newspaper might be light on local news, which is expensive to gather, and heavy on wire news and syndicated material, which requires only editing. An anonymous home office concerned with the profits of the chain may direct the editor of the local newspaper to the bottom line on the ledger rather than to the local news hole figures. The editor may not be willing to run the story that would provoke local advertisers or the major employer in town.

The chains, which are swallowing newspapers at such a rapid rate that three of five newspapers are now within one of the 170 groups, contend that the financial strength of group ownership gives local editors greater resources to risk offending the local power structure. But Ben Bagdikian of the University of California, a press critic, disagrees with this optimistic view of chain ownership. He sees the ever-present need for profits precluding the development of quality journalism.

Because of the gradual and steady absorption of independent newspapers by the chains, Bagdikian is pessimistic about the development of any new, high-quality newspapers. At least, he says, these newspapers will not come out of the chains. "It takes five or six years or more of pouring money into a paper to make it really distinguished. No modern corporation is going to wait that long for good dividends.

"There's real danger that the number of distinguished papers will decline, because they're part of chains now, too, and the pressure is on them to produce dollars."

The Personal Element

Impersonal and objective as some journalists would like to make the determinants of news, journalism clearly is based on selection, and choice is a highly personal matter. It derives from factors such as the reporter's professional background, his or her education and the intangible influences of family and friends. Even more elusive are the decisions that have their origin in the arena where ambition and conscience battle.

Vague as these factors may be, the reporter must cope with them. Fortunately, the reporter's handiwork is tangible. Once the heat of reporting and writing has cooled, the reporter can examine the story. Then, alone or with a trusted friend or colleague, the reporter can try to pinpoint the reasons for decisions. This self-questioning—directed by some of the principles we have discussed in this chapter and those in chapter 16 where the morality of journalism is discussed—is part of the journalist's continuing education.

4

The Tools
of the Trade

Preview   Journalists use a variety of tools to do their job, from the simple mechanical devices that are necessary to reporting and writing to several complex techniques. The journalist must:

- Master the VDT, tape recorder.
- Understand how to use basic references.
- Know public-record laws.
- Feel at home using mathematics.
- Understand how the computer can help analyze information for stories.
- Be able to conduct and interpret a public opinion poll.

Journalists use several kinds of tools. There are the instruments with which they shape the raw material of their reporting—the pencils, pads, tape recorders, typewriters, video display terminals. There are the reporting devices—the telephone, reference materials and such analytic tools as mathematics and polling techniques. Then there is the special language the journalist uses to communicate with co-workers.

Learning the language is essential, as the apprentice electrician finds out the first day on the job when he is told to get a bucket of volts, or the chemistry student who is immortalized in the couplet:

Johnny was a chemist; Johnny is no more.
What Johnny thought was H_2O was H_2SO_4.

Hugh Mulligan, a long-time AP reporter, recalled what happened when a news editor did not know what a certain word in the journalist's special vocabulary meant:

The paper in Walsenburg, Colo., was going to press. In those days the PMs wire closed at 3 o'clock and they were anxious to know who won the Indianapolis 500. They messaged the AP bureau in Indianapolis and the bureau said they would send it to them by Western Union, which of course was "overheading," and the bureau message read: "Will overhead winner of Indianapolis 500."

And we had the famous headline: Will Overhead Wins Indianapolis 500. They even concocted a little story to go with it.

They said he was so far behind that his name didn't even appear in any of the previous stories.

A glossary of journalism terms is provided in the back of the book. When in doubt about any term, consult it. You may want to pencil in comments and additions.

The Tangible Tools

Unlike the reporter's vocabulary, the tangible tools are supplied by the employer. They include:

The typewriter, which used to be the reporter's daily companion but has been replaced by the video display terminal (VDT) in most newsrooms. The typewriter, however, remains the student's primary writing instrument.

The VDT is used on most newspapers. Reporters work at the keyboard of the VDT, which relays electric impulses to the computer. The story is visible on the video screen. Printouts can be made from the stored material.

A pad with a hard back like a stenographer's notebook is best for note-taking. The stiff backing makes jottings good and black, and the spiral binding keeps them in order.

The tape recorder is a necessity for the radio reporter, optional for the print reporter. The tape recorder is useful in covering speeches, formal interviews, symposia. It is an aid in stories requiring precise quotes, but it cannot substitute for the reporter's patterning—determining the placement of story ideas and the general construction of the piece. The broadcast journalist may not tape the voice of the source without asking permission.

The telephone is a basic tool of the trade. It allows reporters to gather information quickly under deadline pressure and to reach sources too far away for personal interviews. Some reporters have become experts at pulling information from reluctant sources by telephone. But beginning reporters should not become dependent on the telephone. It cannot substitute for the face-to-face interview.

Obtaining detailed information by telephone can sometimes be difficult because of the similarities of sound when names and other key information are spelled out. To cope with this, various phonetic alphabets have been adopted. The armed forces use A for Alpha, B for Bravo, etc. The alphabet in table 4.1 has been used by many telephone systems in training operators. It uses common first names for most of the letters.

Table 4.1 Phonetic Alphabet for Telephone Use

A—Alice	H—Harry	O—Olive	V—Victor
B—Bertha	I—Ida	P—Peter	W—William
C—Charles	J—James	Q—Quaker	X—X-Ray
D—David	K—Kate	R—Robert	Y—Young
E—Edward	L—Lewis	S—Samuel	Z—Zebra
F—Frank	M—Mary	T—Thomas	
G—George	N—Nellie	U—Utah	

Here are some suggestions for the development of sound newsroom work habits:

- Be punctual.
- Observe the deadlines, yours and others.
- Conform to office dress and appearance standards.
- Be courteous to sources and co-workers—colleagues, telephone operators, receptionists, janitors, interns.
- Adhere to the chain of command.
- Read the newspaper and watch and listen to news programs every day.
- Do not:
    Ask editors unnecessary questions.
    Break office conventions.
    Interrupt persons on deadline.
    Vanish from the office.
    Telephone family or friends from the office.
    Write memos explaining why you missed or blew a story.
    Complain about an assignment.

On the desk, every reporter has at least two volumes—a dictionary and the city telephone directory. Reporters should always verify a questionable spelling. The dictionary is also used to determine whether a word has the shade of meaning intended. Since editors conclude that a reporter who misspells is a lazy reporter—and some even have the notion that spelling ability and intelligence are synonymous—the reporter who ignores the dictionary is inviting disaster.

Some newspapers have cross-indexed directories, a listing of telephone numbers by address. This directory is invaluable on a late-breaking story when the reporter cannot go to the event and needs details from the scene.

A few reporters have a small library on or near their desks—a one-volume American history, an atlas, a thesaurus and a world almanac. If these are not within arm's reach, the reporter should know where they are kept in the newsroom.

Every reporter should know how to use these references:

- *The World Almanac.*
- *The Reader's Guide to Periodical Literature.*
- *The New York Times Index.*
- Bartlett's *Familiar Quotations*. Who penned: ''How do I love thee? Let me count the ways.''? Had *The Chicago Daily News* caption writer consulted Bartlett's, the newspaper might have been spared embarrassment one summer day. The quotation was used under a large page-one picture of a couple sitting on a statue of Shakespeare in a Chicago park—with attribution to William Shakespeare. (If you do not know the author, look it up.)
- *The National Zip Code & Post Office Directory*. For locating cities in states and for finding the ZIP code.

- City directory. Several firms produce directories, which are invaluable references for information about persons living in the community. A typical entry will have the following information: correct full name, occupation and employer, complete street address including apartment number, husband's or wife's name and initial, homeowner, whether the person is retired, whether husband and wife are employed, whether the person is a student. Most of the directory firms include a street directory so that the reporter can find the name of the person and his or her telephone number from a given address. Some directories are based on telephone numbers; given a number, the reporter can find the name of the telephone subscriber. The directory companies also make up a classified business directory that lists, at no charge, all businesses.
- U.S. General Accounting Office issues a *Monthly List of GAO Reports* that is useful for reporters needing background on a variety of topics, including social services, community development, national defense, energy, natural resources and environment and other topics. The GAO is a respected independent federal agency whose auditors and accountants make perceptive and comprehensive reports, including recommendations for improvements. The *Reports* are free. To be placed on the GAO mailing list for the Monthly List, write: U.S. General Accounting Office, Document Handling and Information Services Facility, P.O. Box 6015, Gaithersburg, Md., 20760.
- *Who's Who in America* contains biographical information about 72,000 living North Americans and is an essential source for basic information about leaders in social, economic, cultural and political affairs. Biographical information is supplied by the person listed. Other biographical directories are published by the same firm, Marquis Who's Who Inc., including regional directories and those based on the biographee's profession. For biographies of long-dead persons, the *Dictionary of American Biography* is useful. For persons who have died within the last several years, back volumes of *Who's Who* can be consulted or *Who Was Who* or back volumes of *Current Biography*.
- Source book and futures book. Every reporter keeps a current address book of names, titles, addresses and telephone numbers from his or her beat. A date book or date pad listing future assignments and appointments—called a futures book—is also necessary.
- Stylebook. The new reporter should have the newspaper's or station's stylebook handy.
- Maps. Some reporters keep in their desks or have quick access to the city map or street directory and a mass transit map. A Rand McNally road atlas for the U.S., Canada and Mexico can be useful.
- Grammar. Deep in a drawer and consulted on the sly by a few journalists is a grammar, high school or college variety. Some reporters never do learn how to punctuate the question in a quote within a quote or the possessive of Jones. Grammatical errors can be embarrassing.

However, no reporter should be crushed if now and then an error sneaks into copy. In pursuit of the elusive idea or phrase, words become pebbles on the path that can trip up the most careful writer. How else explain this error in *The New York Times,* surely one of the nation's most carefully edited newspapers?

> The contractors don't have people to inspect. And the textile manufacturers don't have people to inspect. *Who's* job is it?

The list of references is endless. Some reporters make a habit of browsing through the *Congressional Record,* the daily account of congressional debate and activity. *The Federal Register,* another federal daily publication, lists the actions of federal agencies, executive orders of the president and a variety of other actions. One area of special interest to journalists is the publication of petitions and forms of relief granted to special interests.

Government agencies have a variety of forms that groups and individuals file with them, and these can be useful in investigative work. When the Sun Newspapers of Omaha investigated Boys Town and found that despite pleas of poverty the non-profit organization had a $209 million portfolio, it relied heavily on the Form 990 that the institution filed with the Internal Revenue Service. Tax-exempt organizations file these forms that detail their financial situation.

To obtain Form 990, write the "Disclosure Officer" at the local IRS district office, giving the name of the organization and mention that the newspaper or station will be willing to pay for copying expenses. Private foundations are exempted from disclosure.

Census Data

Census data provide much more than the national head count. Since the Bureau of the Census breaks down its count into census tracts of around 4,000 persons, vast amounts of information of a social and economic nature are available to the local reporter. The population census provides data about where people live, their age, race, sex, education, occupations, income, marital status. There is information about how many married women are living with their husbands, how many households are headed by females, median and average family incomes. The housing census has information about the types of dwellings in which people live, their bathing facilities and plumbing.

The reporter who wants to track social change in his or her community will find census data essential. Working mothers, children in nursery school, shifts in family patterns and demographic changes—all this is available. Ray Jenkins of the *Montgomery* (Ala.) *Advertiser* used census data to prove that, contrary to prevailing opinion, the black migration out of the South in the 1960s had not only continued from the previous decade but had accelerated. He found that almost 228,000 blacks—many of them males from 15 to 35 years of age—had migrated in that decade, nearly a quarter of the state's black population.

Table 4.2 Census Counts

The Census Bureau makes a national population count every ten years. But it conducts other counts continuously. The Bureau takes more than 250 sample surveys a year to monitor trends in employment, population growth, fertility, living arrangements and marriage patterns.

Schedule of various censuses

	Periodicity	Last census
Population	10 year	1980
Housing	5 year	1980
Agriculture	5 year	1982
Business	5 year	1982
Construction industries	5 year	1982
Governments	5 year	1982
Manufacturers	5 year	1982
Mineral industries	5 year	1982
Transportation	5 year	1982

If a local reporter wants to do a story about the housing stock in the community, census data are rich in material. The reporter can find the number of houses that lack toilets, private baths and hot water. The number of persons living in housing units (density) can also be determined. By analyzing who lives in a representative's district, it is possible to indicate how he or she is most likely to vote or to determine the pressures exerted on the legislator on public housing, social security and other social issues.

Printed census reports are available at public and university libraries and at many local, state and federal agencies. An investment of about $100 will purchase all the reports for a state. More detailed information is stored on computer tapes, and this, too, is available. Colleges and universities often have the tapes. If not, the Bureau of the Census, U.S. Department of Commerce, can help in locating the nearest tape center.

Detailed information on what the Census covers can be obtained by writing: Public Information Office, Bureau of the Census, Washington, D.C., 20233.

Death and Disease Data

Some of the best-kept official records are those for disease and death. Doctors, clinics and hospitals are required to keep scrupulous records, and these are sent to city and county health offices, which relay them on to state and federal agencies.

Since this information has been carefully kept for many years, it can provide the journalist with an insight into community health standards and care. In fact, infant

Table 4.3 Infant Mortality Rates For Major Cities

City	Total	White	Black
Average (U.S.)	**12.6**	**11.0**	**21.4**
Baltimore	20.0	17.7	21.5
Boston	13.0	8.8	20.1
Chicago	13.4	9.9	26.9
Cleveland	23.4	16.5	30.2
Columbus, Ohio	12.0	10.1	17.0
Dallas	13.7	11.1	18.3
Detroit	21.2	11.5	25.3
Houston	13.3	12.2	16.6
Indianapolis	14.4	11.8	22.0
Jacksonville	14.6	11.2	21.9
Los Angeles	12.4	10.2	22.5
Memphis	17.7	12.5	21.2
Milwaukee	13.5	11.0	18.6
New Orleans	20.2	11.8	23.9
New York	15.0	13.5	19.1
Philadelphia	19.8	15.8	22.9
Phoenix	12.5	12.3	17.1
San Antonio	12.9	11.9	27.0
San Diego	12.0	10.8	23.2
San Francisco	11.1	12.3	14.7
San Jose	10.7	11.1	11.8
Washington, D.C.	25.0	17.8	26.7

The rate is calculated per 1,000 live births. Figures are for 1980 and are from the Mortality Statistics Branch, Division Vital Statistics, National Center for Health Statistics.

mortality rates are sometimes described as the measure of a society's degree of civilization. Reporters can compare their community's health care with that of cities of similar population.

Internal comparisons can also be made since most municipal health agencies break the city down into health districts. Middle-class districts can be compared with low-income districts, white with non-white. Age of mothers is also on record, and an enterprising reporter might find a relationship between teen-age pregnancy and infant mortality.

Table 4.4 Syphilis

States		Cities	
Average	**32.0**	**Average**	**73.2**
1. Louisiana	77.4	1. San Francisco	327.5
2. Georgia	74.1	2. Washington, D.C.	267.6
3. Texas	63.0	3. Atlanta	259.9*
4. Florida	59.2	4. New Orleans	220.3
5. Mississippi	47.5	5. Dallas	135.9*
6. New York	45.2	6. Newark	130.4
7. California	43.2	7. Houston	129.8*
8. South Carolina	40.9	8. Richmond	125.8
9. Maryland	39.3	9. Norfolk	115.8
10. Illinois	39.0	10. Chicago	113.0

Number of cases per 100,000 population.
*County data or equivalent.

VD   One reporter noticed a short wire story reporting that San Francisco had more cases of syphilis and Atlanta more cases of gonorrhea than any other cities and that the incidence of syphilis had increased 30 percent since 1977. The source was the Disease Control Center and the dateline was Atlanta, Ga.

To find out how his city ranked in these diseases (which local doctors had described as being at near-epidemic proportions), he wrote the Center for information. Tables 4.4 and 4.5 contain the 1981 figures that the Center released.

There are two excellent sources of information for health data. For figures on deaths such as infant mortality rates write:

Scientific and Technical Information Branch
Division of Operations
National Center for Health Statistics
3700 East-West Highway
Hyattsville, Maryland 20782
(Phone: 301 436–8500)

For morbidity reports on notifiable diseases—sexually transmitted diseases, tuberculosis, childhood diseases—write:

Disease Control Center
Atlanta, Georgia 30333
(Phone 404 329–3761)

Table 4.5 Gonorrhea

States		Cities	
Average	**435.2**	**Average**	**893.3**
1. Alaska	1,040.1	1. Atlanta	3,073.5*
2. Georgia	927.7	2. San Francisco	2,561.8
3. Nevada	805.6	3. Baltimore	2,393.3
4. South Carolina	771.9	4. Washington, D.C.	2,262.6
5. Maryland	689.3	5. Dayton	2,069.7
6. Tennessee	688.6	6. St. Louis	1,985.0
7. Delaware	662.9	7. Jersey City	1,937.7
8. Mississippi	638.4	8. Cincinnati	1,880.8
9. North Carolina	637.1	9. Cleveland	1,744.5
10. Alabama	628.9	10. Charlotte	1,712.3

Number of cases per 100,000 population.
*County data or equivalent.

Public Records

Reporters should know just what records are available to them on their beats. These are basic news sources for reporters. Among the many records usually accessible to the public are:

Assessment and tax records, deeds, property transfers.
Records dealing with licenses—restaurant, dog, liquor, tavern and the many other business and professional licenses.
City engineer's records—streets, alleys, property lines, highways.
City building permits, variances.
Automobile ownership.
Liquor license applications and recommendations for these.
Election returns.
Articles of incorporation. Some states do not require officers to file their names; most do. Partnerships.
Bills and vouchers for all governmental purchases. Copies of the checks (warrants) paid out for goods and services.
Minutes of city council, county commission meetings. All appropriations, budgets.
Most records in judicial area—indictments, trials, sentences, court transcripts.
Wills, receiverships, bankruptcies.
Most police records on a current basis. There are limits to arrest records.

Reporters sometimes discover that legitimate public records have for some reason been denied to the public and to reporters. A check of the law is helpful in opening them up. Half the states have "sunshine laws" that require records be available for public examination.

Freedom of Information Act

Access to one of the vast areas of information—federal records—had been limited until congress enacted the Freedom of Information Act in 1966. The act, and important amendments in 1975, unlocked uncounted millions of pages of federal documents for the public. The FOIA states that the public has the right to inspect any document of the executive branch that the federal government possesses, with nine exceptions. These exceptions prevent reporters, or anyone else, from examining income tax returns, secret documents vital to national defense or foreign policy, intra-agency letters and other sensitive material.

The 1975 amendments give the federal courts the power to review classified documents to make sure that they are properly classified, and they put a limit on the time an agency can take to reply to a request.

Increasingly, reporters are using the FOIA to examine such material as Justice Department activities, mortgage appraisal reports by the Federal Housing Administration, activities of the Federal Trade Commission and the work of the Central Intelligence Agency. One reporter, Jack Taylor, a veteran newsman with the *Daily Oklahoman* and *The Denver Post,* has used the act some 1,200 times. Taylor says that one way to cope with recalcitrant agencies is to threaten a suit to unlock the information.

Government officials have become increasingly unhappy with the FOIA, and in 1982 the Society of Professional Journalists criticized President Reagan for encouraging federal agencies to be more restrictive in their release of information under the act.

To use the act, it is best to find out which agency has the records sought. A guide is the *U.S. Government Manual,* which may be obtained from the Government Printing Office, Superintendent of Documents, Washington, D.C., 20402. Ask for Stock Number D22-003-00424-8. Requests usually should be sent to the Freedom of Information Officer of the agency. No reason need be given for the request for information, but it sometimes makes the request easier to handle if specific information is offered. Charges are usually nominal, but the request may limit the amount that the newspaper or station is willing to spend. The reporter may ask for charges in advance of any work by the agency.

The letter should state that the request is being made "under the provisions of the Freedom of Information Act, 5 U.S.C. 552."

State Laws

Most states have enacted open records and open meeting laws. Usually, these laws presume that everything is open with stipulated exceptions. Most denials of requests for records fall into these categories:

1. *Confidential records.* Those records that are exempted by federal or state law such as income tax returns, health and welfare files on individuals.
2. *Privacy.* Records that would allow an unwarranted invasion of an individual's privacy. (Officials have less right of privacy than private individuals.)
3. *Contract awards and collective bargaining negotiations.* Disclosure of present or imminent actions in these areas could impair developments.

4. *Trade secrets* that might injure a person or firm in a competitive situation.
5. *Records compiled for law enforcement agencies* that would impede a fair trial, endanger the life or safety of an agent or an informer.
6. *Inter-agency memoranda and intra-agency reports* except statistics, policies and instructions to the staff.
7. *Examinations and evaluations* that will be used again.

The states' open meetings laws exempt executive sessions that are concerned with collective bargaining, imminent legislation, the medical, financial or credit records of a person or corporation and any matters made confidential by state and federal law.

The UPI dispatch read:

Mathematics for the Reporter

> The average American who lives to the age of 70 consumes in that lifetime the equivalent of 150 cattle, 24,000 chickens, 225 lambs, 26 sheep, 310 hogs, 26 acres of grain and 50 acres of fruits and vegetables.

A Nevada newspaper reader who saw the story was puzzled. That seemed like a lot of meat to consume in a lifetime, he thought. He consulted his butcher who estimated the dressed weights of the various animals. They came up with a total of 222,695 pounds of meat. The reader wrote the UPI that he then did some figuring. He multiplied 70 years by 365 days to find the total number of days in the person's meat-eating lifetime. The figure was 25,500 days. He divided the total meat consumption of 222,695 pounds by the number of days. "That figures out to a whopping 8.7 pounds of meat a day," he wrote.

The UPI confessed in its newsletter to editors, "We've retired the reference work from which the item was gleaned for our daily wire opening feature."

All this is by way of pointing out that journalists, along with many others, have a tendency to accept figures without question. Figures not only awe people, they frighten many. But a knowledge of the basic arithmetical processes is essential for a reporter. The ability to handle figures is one of the most useful analytical tools a reporter can possess.

We live in an age of quantification. Everyone shoots figures at us. Take the police reporter. Looking over the annual report of the police department, he is awash in a sea of data. One figure seems to stand out. The number of arrests for violent crimes declined from 22,560 two years ago to 17,030 last year. That seems a sharp drop, he reasons, and he decides to make it the lead of his piece. He tells his city editor his plan, and the editor cautions him: "Don't give us the raw numbers in the lead."

The reporter knows what his editor wants, a percentage decrease. By subtracting 17,030 from 22,560, the reporter obtains the decline last year. He puts his subtraction over the original figure, 22,560, to obtain the percentage drop, almost 25 percent. Not only is the figure easier for the reader to grasp, it makes a good headline.

"An estimated 53 million Americans smoked 634 billion cigarettes in 1982," the story about a local anti-smoking measure said. The city editor looked up and called the reporter handling the story to the desk.

"Let's put this and a lot of the other figures into some understandable terms," he told the reporter. "In this case, why not follow the sentence with one that says, 'This means the average smoker lit up so many cigarettes a day.'"

Back at his desk, the reporter makes a few simple calculations: 634 billion cigarettes smoked a year ÷ 53 million smokers = 11,962 cigarettes per smoker a year.

We want average daily use, so we make the next calculation: 11,962 cigarettes a year ÷ 365 days = 32.77 cigarettes per smoker a day.

The reporter rounds that off to 33 and has a strong addition to his story. A reader can see someone crumpling up a pack and smoking half the way through a second pack for his daily smokes. This is more graphic than the millions and billions, which tend to depersonalize the story.

The Electronic Newsroom

Since 1970, when the first electronic editing terminal was placed in the newsroom of *Today* in Cocoa, Fla., hundreds of newspapers and the UPI and the AP have replaced reporters' typewriters and editors' pencils with video terminals. Some of the smaller newspapers have two or three terminals. *The* Baltimore *Sun* has more than 75, *The New York Times* more than 300.

The terminal is an electric typewriter keyboard with an 11-inch television screen that replaces copy paper. As the reporter types a story on the keyboard, the story appears on the screen and is recorded in a central computer, called a controller. All the terminals in the newsroom are wired to the controller, and copy stored there can be called back by reporters or editors. The reporter can make changes in copy as he or she types by moving the copy up and down with some of the keys and using other keys to erase letters and words. Copy editors also insert or delete material by using these keys. Paragraphs can be moved around with equal ease.

In completely electronic newspaper plants, the automatic typesetter now takes over. Photo-composition machines produce type on film for paste-up on pages from which a thin plate is made that is placed on the press. This process is known as cold type.

Most newspapers in the United States have converted to the electronic newsroom. Students who enter journalism today will find a newsroom completely different from the one in which their teachers and older colleagues worked for decades. Rex Smith, a reporter for *Newsday,* talks about the difference.

Large and Small.
Newsrooms over the country
have installed video display
terminals (VDTs) for their
reporters and editors. In the
top photo, reporter Itabari Njeri
goes over her story with an
editor in *The Miami Herald*
newsroom. In the bottom
photo, reporter Barbara
Serrano of *The Stockton*
(Calif.) Record looks over a
story she has just written.

"I started in newspaper work when every reporter's desk included a glue pot, and when the clatter of typewriters at deadline sounded like the L & N freight yards. That was just 10 years ago.

"Now one pot of rubber cement remains in the *Newsday* city room—a relic held by an old-timer who keeps it around just so he can take a nostalgic whiff of the stuff occasionally. Nor can you find black editing pencils here."

Smith says the atmosphere is almost as antiseptic as an insurance office.

"I hear the plastic clicking of keyboards as reporters work at their terminals, but never the rip of the typewriter carriage being thrown back in a rush to meet a deadline. I see editors peering into their screens, but none ever has a piece of copy in hand. It's all done by computer."

Not only does the computer enable the reporter to make inserts quickly and to move chunks of copy from one part of the story to another without cutting and pasting, it makes note-taking by telephone faster and more efficient. The VDT is so quiet that the caller's every word can be heard, and typing is much faster on the VDT keyboard, so the caller does not have to be asked to repeat something.

Newsday's computer also allows reporters to use the keyboard for mathematical figuring—it adds, subtract, multiplies and divides. When Smith wants the telephone number of a source, he types in a name, presses a button and the number comes up on the screen. Smith has stored names, addresses and phone numbers from his beat book in the computer.

Some reporters say that the computer has made for better stories, if for no other reason than that the computerization of the newsroom has speeded up the process of producing a newspaper enormously. A reporter has more time to write the story since deadlines can be moved back. The time-consuming process of setting stories in type is replaced by the reporter's own hand; by typing stories on the keyboard, the reporter has copy ready for editing and for photocomposition.

The computer is also used to help with complicated stories, often shortening the process by months.

Computer-Aided Stories

The computer is used to help pattern and analyze large quantities of information. It is especially helpful with polling data. In a presidential race, information from 1,300 people about their preference—along with their age, party, education, race, religion, address and other demographic data—is fed into a computer. The reporter can determine quickly how those over 45 say they would vote, the party loyalty factor, how those with a college education say they will vote and so on. Usually, such polls ask for information on specific issues—the person's feelings about abortion, the death penalty, a nuclear freeze. The computer will feed out information on what percentage of those against abortion on demand would favor the Democratic candidate, for example.

Newsday used the computer to help analyze which areas on Long Island had significantly higher arrest rates for driving while intoxicated and the conviction rates of different judges for the offense.

When the 1980 census data became available, *Newsday* fed demographic information into its computer and was able to show in a powerful story how black and Hispanic ghetto areas were growing in predominantly white sections of Long Island.

The Philadelphia Inquirer has used its computer to check the performance of judges, analyzing how judges treated white defendants and black defendants accused of the same offense, among other analyses.

In Florida, *The Miami Herald,* the Orlando *Sentinel Star* and the *St. Petersburg Times* joined to computerize all campaign contributions to Florida officials. Each time a politician seeking a statewide office reports a contribution—a requirement of Florida law—the contributor's name and amount goes into the data base in the Florida State University computer that the newspapers use. The computer checks the name of the campaign donor against the names of previous contributors, directors of Florida corporations, registered lobbyists, real estate brokers and others likely to be interested in a friend in the state capital.

"The politician who regulates banks in Florida (the comptroller) has received contributions from people connected with banks whom we would have failed to identify that way without the computer's help," said Patrick Riordan of the *Herald*.

"I wrote about a bank that had six of its nine directors and two of its officers make donations. That wasn't evident on the paper forms filed."

Many contributors, he found, cloaked their affiliations. But the computer turned up their relationships once the names were fed into it.

When the newly-elected Albany County treasurer told reporters she had discovered millions of dollars in uncollected taxes going back to 1900, the *Knickerbocker News* of Albany, N.Y., decided to investigate. However, the treasurer told the *News* she had been able to make only a visual inspection of the records because she had neither the time nor the staff to sift through the 8,700 hand-written cards on which the records were kept.

The *News* did not have the time, either. But unlike the treasurer, it did have a computer, and the executive editor told the reporters to use it to dig into what appeared to be a scandal.

First, the reporters made a list of delinquent taxpayers, the location of their property, how much they owed and other notations—in all, 11 different categories of information. They noted 97,000 separate pieces of information. Trying to find patterns among owners, the amounts they owed and the location of the property in this mountain of material would have taken months. Instead, the information was given to a key punch operator who placed it on IBM computer cards. A computer programmer then developed a program, and the cards were fed to the computer.

The result was enough information for a series of articles under the title, "Paper Millions, Albany County's Unpaid Taxes."

Robert G. Fichenberg, the executive editor of the *News,* who oversaw the project, said less than 120 hours was spent collecting and processing the information. Had the entire operation been done by hand, he estimated a team of six persons would have taken six months to do the job, since more than half a million additional notations were involved in patterning the material.

The computer has also made it possible to conduct meaningful surveys. By using a scientifically selected sample, an accurate idea of how people feel about an issue can be published. One editor said he switched to this scientific method after reading a headline:

State College Students
Favor Co-Ed Dorms

The story contained the opinions of 10 students. The college had an enrollment of 14,000.

The computer has changed political reporting permanently. No longer do political reporters put all their faith in their intuition and what insiders tell them. During the 1976 presidential campaign, the conventional political wisdom held that Jimmy Carter had aroused the opposition of Catholic voters by refusing to support a constitutional amendment prohibiting abortion. His opponent, Gerald Ford, had endorsed such an amendment, and this was considered a significant aid to the Republican presidential campaign.

Robert Reinhold of *The New York Times* showed this was all guesswork, and wrong at that. The opinions of the sample of voters that the *Times* fed into its computer indicated that most Catholics did not enthusiastically support such an amendment.

Since many governmental units now have computers, reporters have access to an enormous range of information. The police reporter can find out quickly the precincts with the highest percentage of violent crime and then obtain data on unemployment and welfare in the same areas. This information can then be fed into the newspaper computer to find correlations. Some officials will give reporters their computer printouts for use by the newspaper.

The federal government also makes computers, computer tapes and computer printouts available to reporters. The U.S. Census Bureau sells tapes at nominal cost.

The computer is being used on a number of newspapers to store the newspaper library. This allows a reporter who is working on a story about a candidate for mayor, for example, to call up on the VDT screen all the clips on the candidate.

For a more detailed description of the computer's role in writing stories, read "Plugged-in journalism" by Steve Weinberg in the November/December 1982 *Columbia Journalism Review*.

Home Information Retrieval

Computer terminals can be placed in the home as well. By 1990, it is estimated that one in four homes will have such terminals. Homes will then be electronic cottages, and people will be able to shop, bank and communicate without leaving their living rooms.

News, as well as other information, will be delivered on request in many homes by the end of the 1980s. The delivery of text and graphic messages on the computer monitors is the subject of experimentation in almost 100 areas around the world.

The users of such a system can call up on their home terminals a vast array of information—news, sports, stock market closings, travel conditions, weather, display advertising and more.

"We can update the information constantly so people don't have to wait for the traditional newspaper," says an official of the Videotex firm. Viewers would have access to 3,000 pages of information every 24 seconds on these systems.

The Systems

Videotex is described as "two-way interactivity." That is, the person using the modified television set or computer in the home can request news, weather information, sports results, or advertising from a central computer where information in the form of pages is stored and requests are processed. Videotex uses two-way cable or telephone lines.

Teletext is "one-way interactivity." With this system, the viewer uses a special decoder to intercept the pages he or she wants. The teletext system gives the appearance of interactivity, but it is actually a one-way transmission of data. Teletext uses over-the-air broadcasting or cable TV.

Cable news or **Cable text** is the system many newspapers and cable companies are using to send out news, sports, weather and stock market information to homes hooked into the cable. Costs to the companies are minimal. The channels offer written text, graphics and advertising on a regular schedule. News is often provided by newspapers and delivery by the cable station.

Jenkin Lloyd Jones Sr., publisher of *The Tulsa Tribune,* described the new role of the newspaper when he said that the newspaper's owners and workers must think of themselves as gatherers of news rather than as its printers.

A new kind of newswriter is necessary to the cable news operation, one who can compress stories into half to a fifth their original size. In its Viewdata operation, AP newswriters take 1,000 word stories and condense them to half or a quarter that length for cable viewers. In Lexington, Ky., TelePress uses stories that run about 45 words each.

Chapter 8 describes the writing techniques for this new field.

Public Opinion Polls

Midway through 1982, the news was about high interest rates, unemployment and the battle between Congress and the president. The political season was warming up also. Would the people support or repudiate the president in the congressional elections? A sophisticated technique—public opinion sampling—gave some indication of the answer.

In the past, the news derived from the taking of the public pulse was hardly convincing. Reporters would chat with political leaders, those supposedly perceptive insiders with delicate olfactory nerves attuned to the mildest of political winds, and a cross-section of voters might be interviewed. The result was a mood piece of no great significance.

Now, the science of polling and surveying gives the journalist a surer hand to reach into areas of coverage that had been handled with impressions and conjecture.

The well-designed poll can tell a reporter with a fair degree of accuracy not only what people think of a president's performance but also whether a proposed school bond issue is popular in a middle-class section of the community or what types of day care are favored by working mothers.

Realizing the value of polls and surveys, many newspapers and television stations are hiring pollsters and polling organizations. The reporter is still essential, for the poll can only supply the information. The reporter must make the poll into news. To do this, he or she must understand how polls work and their possibilities and limits.

The poll is a systematic way of finding out what people are thinking at a given time. It can provide a fairly accurate stop-action photo of a situation, and it does so in a far more reliable way than the standard journalistic interviewing techniques. This does not mean that all polling data given the journalist should be taken at face value. There are some inherent problems in polling, and there are pollsters whose purpose is to sell their clients. Reporters who understand polls know what to accept, what to discard. Reporters who are overwhelmed by data, who believe there is some mystery about figures, will be victimized by self-serving pollsters, just as they can be misled by any public relations gimmick.

Polls are "able to establish with great accuracy the extent to which an opinion is held, and they can successfully predict behavior over the short run," writes Sheldon S. Wolin of the Department of Politics at Princeton University. "Once the period is extended," he cautions, "the reliability of the findings diminishes rapidly."

There are hundreds of polling organizations and firms. The majority are local groups that conduct marketing surveys. The big firms—Gallup, Harris, Roper and others—handle commercial clients, too, but are best-known for their political polls and surveys which, although they are not too profitable, give the organizations considerable publicity. It is this political polling that so often finds its way into newspapers and news broadcasts. During a political campaign, as much as one-third to one-half of the news is about the public's reaction to a candidate or an issue. On election day, most Americans are tuned to their television sets to find out who is ahead and who is projected the winner. The networks lash their pollsters in the race to be first with the news of the winner during presidential elections. Unfortunately, the emphasis on calling the outcome rather than interpreting the data leads to the waste of huge amounts of fascinating material about how people are voting and why, whether some groups—blacks, Jews, Irish Catholics, Swedes, farmers, government employees—have switched their traditional allegiances.

As excited as readers and viewers are by the predictions and projections of the pollsters, editors were slow to accept polls. Businessmen were the first to use polls in order to test the market for their goods. George Gallup began to do political polling to authenticate his methods. If his methods were sound, Gallup reasoned, they would work on political contests, which had the great asset that polling data could be checked against tangible results.

The press has an insatiable appetite for polls—whatever the subject, however flimsy the material. Several years ago, the Gallup organization reported that its poll showed Nixon was the third most-admired man in the world in the opinion of Americans. A few days before, the Gallup Poll had issued one of its periodic confidence polls, and this one showed that 29 percent of the American public approved of Nixon's performance as president and 60 percent did not.

Asked to explain the paradox of a public admiring and disapproving of the same person, a Gallup official said that the president usually fares well—whoever he may be—in certain types of polls since his is the name that comes quickly to mind when people are asked for names.

This incident illustrates the importance of the wording of the questions asked by pollsters. Although reputable pollsters pretest their questions to make sure they test precisely what the pollster desires, ambiguities do creep in. Reporters should always examine the questions behind the polling data to make sure that they are clear and, in the case of polls conducted for private clients, to ascertain whether they are loaded.

Sometimes, polling on the same issue may lead to slightly different results because of the way questions are worded by several pollsters. The interpretation of words by pollsters may also be controversial. During the Nixon administration, the White House objected to the way the Harris organization evaluated its polls of Nixon's public rating. The Harris polls asked people to rate the president's performance as excellent, pretty good, fair and poor. It counted fair and poor replies as negative assessments. The White House complained that fair was a positive word.

Many of the smaller polling groups that are employed by politicians have a vested interest in their client, and their work should be carefully examined. The reporter should be especially wary of polling material leaked to the press. Rarely does the information meet the requirements of the checklist at the end of this section.

The reporter should always take his or her natural skepticism to polling data. But there is general agreement that polling is a social science that has managed to acquire respect as a profession. Although most attention—by journalists as well as the public—is focused on the horse-race aspects of election campaigns, the alert reporter will find ample material in the exit poll for significant articles about what people say are their reasons for their preferences and among what groups the candidates do well or poorly. In 1982, pollsters noticed what they called a "gender gap," the preference of women for Democratic candidates and the opposite tendency for men. Exit polling confirmed this.

In an exit poll, people are questioned when they leave voting places. In the 1980 Democratic presidential primary in New York, *The New York Times*/CBS News Poll interviewed voters after they left the polling booths to find out the reasons for their votes. The findings—that Jews, blacks and Hispanics strongly preferred Senator Edward M. Kennedy—underlined Kennedy's surprising triumph in the state. Voters, the poll determined, were casting ballots for Kennedy as a protest against President Carter's policies on inflation, the Middle East and aid to New York City. Jews voted 4–1 for Kennedy, and Catholics, who had been drifting away from the Massachusetts senator in earlier primaries, returned to the senator's campaign in large numbers. The poll found one in six New York Democrats endorsed Carter's handling of the economy compared to 40 percent in the Illinois primary the previous week and 30 percent nationwide.

Types of Polls

The first check a reporter should make of polling material is a determination of how the poll was conducted. There are a variety of ways to elicit information from the public, some of them unreliable, some less reliable than others.

The coupon poll is just about worthless. People are asked to clip, fill out and mail a coupon that appears in the newspaper. The results are distorted because the person who goes to all that trouble—including paying for postage—is usually someone with strong feelings about the subject and hardly representative of the general population.

The call-in poll, in which readers or viewers are asked to express their sentiments about an issue by telephoning the newspaper or station, is subject to the same criticism as the coupon poll. When the San Francisco *Chronicle* conducted a call-in poll on the death sentence late in 1979, it headlined the results on page one. Not surprisingly, three-fourths of those calling favored the death penalty. The newspaper did tell its readers that the poll had limited value. In the 12th paragraph of the story, the reporter wrote:

> The Chronicle Poll is not designed scientifically, for it does not use the standard sampling techniques that major opinion surveys use. It does, however, provide readers with an opportunity to express their opinions on topics of current interest.

The straw poll is no more reliable, although some newspapers have been using this technique for many years. A person is delegated to hand out ballots at one or more locations. People then drop their ballots into a box at the spot. It is difficult to keep the straw poll from being over-represented by the people in the one or two locations selected—usually supermarkets, factory gates and the like. The *Daily News,* which conducts straw polls for New York and national elections, uses a professional pollster to organize its straw locations.

The man-in-the-street poll is probably the most frequently used technique to gather opinions at the local level. Newspapers and stations without access to their own polling apparatus will send reporters out to interview persons about a candidate or an issue. Those who have had to do this kind of reporting know how badly it is done, how non-representative the persons interviewed may be. Reporters may seek out persons who look as though they can supply a quick answer, those who do not need to have the question explained to them. Reporters may stay away from those who are poorly dressed, members of minority groups, young people.

This kind of interviewing can be used so long as the story says precisely what it is—the opinions of a scattering of people. It is no more than that, no more scientific than astrology. There are no controls in this group. The reporter has no idea what kind of people are being interviewed. Usually, such polls over-sample the unemployed, the elderly and non-working women. The sample of people interviewed in this type of polling is known as a "non-probability sample," meaning that the conclusions cannot be generalized to the population at large.

A good poll, says Professor Penn T. Kimball of the Graduate School of Journalism at Columbia University, who was associated with the Harris organization, should be done at night and over weekends, not just during the day. Also, he says, it is best to poll persons in their homes rather than on the street.

"Quite often, reporters talk about New York problems to shopkeepers or taxi drivers who actually live in New Jersey or Long Island," he says. "The point is that a sound sample is based on home addresses from which flow census data, voting statistics and other vital information for interpreting the data."

Some polls are conducted in just this way, by home interviews, and they are usually more reliable than the catch-as-catch-can polling techniques of the straw poll or man-in-the-street interviews. Polling by telephone is done to save time and money, although many Americans do not have their own phones. There is some debate over the relative merits of the telephone poll vs. the door-to-door poll.

To reach its conclusions about how well adults around the country thought President Carter was handling his problems during his first term, The New York Times/CBS Poll spoke to 1,422 persons by telephone. At first glance, this seems madness. To pass off the opinions of fewer than 1,500 people as representative of more than 100 million seems folly. Yet if the sample is selected carefully, the questions properly put, the results stated fairly and completely, and the interpretations made with discernment, a sample of around 1,500 persons can reflect accurately the opinions of people across the country.

When the Gallup organization was hired to find out what New Yorkers thought of city government, it based its conclusions on interviews with 709 adults. This one-ten-thousandth of the city's population was the polling sample.

The Sample

Obviously, if a small group is to speak for the many, that group must be carefully chosen so that it is representative of the larger group. The key word here is representative.

If we want to know what people think of an incumbent governor, we can interview voters and non-voters. But if we want to know whether people will vote for him for reelection it is common sense to interview eligible voters, those who have registered. But we cannot stop there. If we went out in the daytime to supermarkets, laundromats and parks where young mothers gather with their children our sample would be skewed heavily toward women. That would be a non-representative sample since men constitute a large percentage of voters.

Samples are selected in a number of ways. The New York Times/CBS Poll sample of telephone exchanges was selected by a computer from a complete list of exchanges around the country. The exchanges were chosen in such a way that each region of the United States was represented in proportion to its population.

Once the exchanges were selected, the telephone numbers were formed by random digits. This guaranteed that unlisted as well as listed numbers would be included in the sample.

The making of this sample demonstrates how pollsters try to eliminate the human factor from the choice of those who will be interviewed. The concept of a good sample is that it should give everyone in the population we are trying to learn something about a chance of being included in our poll. This is what is meant by the term "random sample." To the average person, the word random usually means haphazard, without plan. Pollsters use it to mean that the sample guarantees that any of those in the larger population group have as good a chance as anyone else in that group to be polled.

Once the sample has been drawn, it is then weighted to adjust for sample variations. In the *Times*/CBS Poll of President Carter's popularity, the sample consisted of 445 persons who told the pollsters making the calls that they were Democrats, 482 who said they were Republicans and 495 who said they were independents. For the opinions of Republicans, the sample was adequate. But to reflect the opinions of the general population, using the breakdown in the sample would over-represent the Republicans. To reflect the proper proportion of party members in the voting population, the groups of voters were then weighted by party identification.

The poll also weighted the results to take account of household size and to adjust for variations in the sample relating to region, race, age, sex and education. This weighting was done in accordance with what is known of the characteristics of the adult population.

Professor Kimball says, "Pollsters check the data that have been gathered against base data that they know to be true: how many voted Republican in the last election, the proportion of men and women in the population, census figures on nationality, religion, income and so on. They then adjust their raw data to eliminate distortions from the norm. This is called 'weighting'—an attempt to eliminate errors of execution."

Despite our first inclination to think that the more persons interviewed the more accurate the results will be, the statistical truth is that it is not so much the quantity of persons counted as it is the quality of the sample to represent a true cross-section that determines the accuracy of the poll. After a critical mass of interviews has been conducted, little additional accuracy is achieved by huge quantities of additional interviews. Results based on a good sample successfully interviewed are adequate for most purposes. After all, polls say no more than at the time the poll was taken, this is what people say they would do, or this is what they say they are thinking.

The *Literary Digest* Disaster

You would think that a poll that asked the opinions of well over two million persons would be accurate. But the most disastrously wrong election prediction relied on 2,376,523 replies and was 20 percent off.

In 1936, the *Literary Digest* set out to forecast the presidential contest between Franklin D. Roosevelt and Alf Landon. The *Digest* selected names from telephone subscriber lists and automobile registration lists and mailed out straw ballots to 10 million persons on the lists.

This was a classic example of quantity over quality. The numbers were huge, but the persons selected were hardly a random sample of the voting population. The poll was taken during the height of the depression, when few persons could afford a car or a telephone. The sample thus was tipped toward persons who were likely to favor the conservative candidate, Landon, rather than the candidate who was campaigning for social and economic reforms, Roosevelt. This is just the result the *Digest* obtained: A Landon victory. Roosevelt easily swept into office, carrying every state but Maine and Vermont.

Although polling techniques have improved considerably since the *Literary Digest* disaster, polls are not—can never be—foolproof. In 1978, the final pre-election poll of the *Minneapolis Tribune,* which has a record for accuracy in its election polling, indicated that the Democratic candidates were doing much better than they actually did.

The *Tribune* had used a panel of voters for its three pre-election polls. A panel enables the pollster to ask the same persons over time for their opinions and is an excellent device for reporting how these persons are reacting to changing events. But in the *Tribune* poll, the replies in the third poll had shrunk to three-fifths of the original panel size, and as the panel shrank the reliability of the poll decreased. (See "Margin of Error.")

In Iowa in 1980, all the polls showed Democratic Sen. Dick Clark running ahead of his conservative challenger, Roger Jepsen. The respected Iowa Poll had Clark leading Jepsen by nine percentage points late in the campaign.

The result: Jepsen won with almost 52 percent of the vote. Clark's pollster, Peter Hart, an experienced pollster who had worked for the Harris and Oliver Quayle organizations, resurveyed Iowa voters to find out where he had gone wrong. His polls had indicated Clark was well ahead. His resurvey showed that 23 percent of the Clark voters in his poll had switched to Jepsen and that 10 percent of Clark's voters in his poll did not vote.

Hart said that he had found in his preelection polls that 40 percent of the declared Clark supporters were "weak" or not strongly committed. Of these, he later learned, 41 percent switched to Jepsen.

The lesson for journalists is to ask such questions of the pollster making political assessments as: Was the intensity of commitment measured? Have those who say they are leaning toward a candidate been counted in that candidate's tally? Have those who say they have not voted in past elections been included in the tally or tossed out? How have those who "don't know" been handled in making the final percentages? Was a panel used throughout the several polls, and how much did it shrink?

Their mistakes have taught journalists to be careful about their tendency to heed the demands of readers and listeners for winners and losers. A poll can only state what voters say they are thinking or say they would do at the time they are polled, and sometimes even then the races are too close to call from a statistically reliable vantage point.

Journalists should remember: Persons change their minds; polls cannot guarantee behavior will always be consistent with previous intentions.

Margin of Error

If a poll were to be made of everyone in a group that we want to learn something about, our conclusions would be completely reliable. But because of such practical considerations as time and cost, population samples must be used, and this leads to sampling error—the difference between what we would have learned from the entire group (called the *universe* in polling parlance) and what we found out from the sample.

The more persons interviewed, the smaller the margin of error. At a 95 percent confidence level—which means that in 95 of 100 surveys the data will be within the limits of margin of error stated—the error will be:

Number Interviewed	Margin of Error
50	± 14
200	± 7
600	± 4
1500	± 3
9600	± 1

If we wanted the maximum confidence (99 percent) and the minimum margin of error (plus or minus 1 percent), we would have to interview 16,590 persons. In national polls, a 95 percent confidence level with a 3 percent margin of error is usually accepted.

By the time a national pollster has conducted a number of polls on the same question, his cumulative totals sometimes approach the numbers that give maximum confidence and minimum margin of error.

The margin of error should be applied to all polling results so that they do not seem to be more exact than they are. Here is how the margin of error is applied:

With a 3 percent margin of error, a candidate's percentage can move up or down 3 percent, which is a 6 percent range or spread. Thus, polling results that are close cannot be said to favor one or the other of the candidates. With a 3 percent margin of error, any results that are separated by 6 percentage points or fewer are too close to call.

A poll that shows Jackson leading Torrance by 53–47 could actually be a nip-and-tuck race, 50–50 (subtracting 3 percent from Jackson; adding 3 percent to Torrance). Or it could be decisively for Jackson, 56–44 (adding 3 percent to Jackson and subtracting 3 percent from Torrance).

If the poll showed Jackson leading Torrance 52–48 with a 3 percent margin of error, the actual result might be Torrance ahead 51–49 (subtracting 3 percent from Jackson and adding 3 percent to Torrance).

Even these margins do not tell the full story. Five times out of 100 (the confidence level) our poll can be off target. Also, these are the lower limits of possible error. There are problems that exist beyond the statistical area, such as the human errors made during polling and the mistakes made in interpreting the results.

All stories about polls should include the margin of error, and any predictions about the results must be measured against the limits set by these statistical necessities. The reporter should tell the whole story, including what he or she does not know for sure.

Although editors and broadcast producers tend to be most interested in the top of the poll—who's ahead—most of the significant material in the poll usually is found in why the candidate is ahead or behind and how the candidate is faring with certain groups. This can make interesting and significant news. There may be a good story in the candidate who does well with a certain religious group and poorly with another because of his or her stand on abortion or prayer in schools.

Reputable pollsters know just how far they can take their data. But they are often under pressure to pick winners in election contests. When preelection polls indicate a 60–40 percent breakdown, a pollster feels at ease in choosing the winner. But when an editor, reflecting the desire of readers and listeners, asks for a choice in a 44–42 race with 14 percent undecided, then trouble lies ahead.

A Checklist for Polls

Reporters should satisfy themselves on each of the following points before making extensive use of any poll:

Date. When was the poll taken? Later polls are more accurate than earlier ones in political races as persons have less time to change their minds. Polls taken early in a campaign and released close to an election can be misleading. There is a natural delay in gathering data, writing it up and distributing it to the press. The reporter should work quickly and efficiently to keep the material from becoming dated.

Interviews. How many were made? How were they conducted? Face-to-face interviews at home are best; telephone polls are quicker and cheaper. Mail surveys achieve small returns and those answering may be non-representative.

Methods. Does the pollster divulge the methods used and allow reporters to see computer breakdowns that are the basis of the pollster's conclusions? How have those who ''don't know'' been handled in adding up the final percentages? What was the technique used to estimate those who are eligible to vote and those likely or unlikely to vote? How big is the subsample of groups that are being broken out for specific analysis?

Disclosure. What part of the data is disclosed and what part is not? If the data are released by sources other than the pollster, does the material have the approval of the pollster? Is the material self-serving? (''Politicians trying to influence the media will play fast and loose with otherwise reliable data,'' says Professor Kimball.)

Sample. Who were interviewed and how were they selected? Was a probability sample used? (Did everyone eligible have an equal likelihood of being interviewed?) If a probability sample was used, how was the list selected from which the sample was drawn? The population that was sampled should be made clear. A check should be made to make sure the poll claims no more than the persons in the sample are qualified to say.

Questions. Is the exact wording of all questions provided? Questions can be slanted to favor a predetermined result. (A national mail survey asking who voters favored for the Republican nomination for president in 1980 offered only the names of conservative candidates.) The questions may be unclear. Are the questions of the generally accepted type for the purpose? If not, were they pretested?

Interviewers. Who are they? Survey interviewers are supposed to be trained for the task. Campaign workers and reporters often are not. (Most reputable newspaper polls are conducted by professional organizations.)

Sponsor. Is it clear who paid for the poll and who made it? Polls made by candidates and political parties should be scrupulously examined.

Accuracy. Does the information include the error allowance or margin of error that will allow the results to be set within the actual limits of reliability? All polls should include this information, and the reporter should include it in the story. A pollster or a politician cannot claim that a 51–49 result is conclusive if the margin of error is the usual 3 percent in a national poll. Readers and listeners should know this. (See "Margin of Error.")

Saliency. Do opinions reflect subject matters of importance to respondents? Do respondents have enough information to understand the question?

Interpretation. What does the pollster or source distributing the results claim? Has the poll been fragmented in the interpretation so that only favorable results are used? Does the pollster or source claim more than the results indicate? Sometimes a segment of a poll will be used to assert that a certain part of the population favors a candidate when the actual sample of that part of the population is too small for the claims. The smaller the sample, the larger the margin of error.

Early Polls

Polls taken some time—a month or more—before an election say more about the state of the campaign at that precise moment than about the possible outcome. The closer to election day, the less time for voters to change their minds. But voters are often undecided even as they enter the voting booth.

The release of early polls by a candidate may be intended to influence the election. The press itself may accomplish the same result with its own early polling, although there is no clear evidence that the "bandwagon influence" is any more real than the "underdog influence." Certainly, the victory the newspapers and everyone else forecast for Thomas E. Dewey in 1948 turned out to be almost as sour a prediction as the Landon victory in 1936. One newspaper, The *Chicago Tribune,* went so far as to banner Dewey's victory across page one in an early edition. One of the most famous political photographs shows a beaming Harry Truman holding the *Tribune* the day after election.

Dubious as the actual effects of polls may be, there is no question that a strong start helps a candidate and that early polls showing strength can affect donations and press coverage. Cash tends to follow success. A potential donor may divert a contribution from what appears to be a losing cause. The press also takes cues from early polls. A third or fourth finisher in a preprimary poll will not be given as much coverage as the leaders. Thus, a self-fulfilling prophecy is brought about: The polls say Bettinger is trailing; we will not spend much time covering his primary campaign, which guarantees the public will know little of Bettinger. Without adequate press coverage, Bettinger cannot compete equally, and he loses.

Polls and surveys are useful additions to the standard reporting techniques. There is nothing magical, nothing fraudulent about polls. Used within the limits of their capabilities by discerning journalists, they extend the reporter's eyes and ears beyond the traditional interviewing process.

The polls that showed that many blacks understood Jimmy Carter in 1976 as the kind of southerner they could trust enabled reporters to write with conviction about Carter's chances with the black electorate. The stories were far more reliable than those quoting local and national politicians—the so-called black spokesmen.

Newspapers should describe how they conduct their polls. One way to do this is to run a short piece next to the main story explaining the polling methods used. Here is a piece that could serve as a model:

This poll is based on telephone interviews November 18 through 23 with 600 adults who live in the city.

The telephone numbers were chosen in such a way that all sections of the city were represented in proportion to population. Numbers were formed by random digits, thus permitting access to unlisted and listed numbers.

The results have been weighted to take account of household size, and to adjust for variations in the sample relating to race, sex, age and education.

In theory, it can be said that in 95 cases out of 100 the results based on this sample differ by no more than four percentage points in either direction than from what would have been obtained by interviewing all adults in the city.

The theoretical errors do not take into account a margin of additional error that could result from the several practical difficulties in taking any survey of public opinion.

Subgroups

Pollsters make groupings on the basis of religion, occupation, sex, region, race and income. The generalized assumption of the pollster is that persons with particular characteristics will vote in ways that differ significantly from the voting patterns usually evident among persons with other characteristics.

This has led to such generalities as: Jewish areas vote more Democratic than the overall average; Lutherans vote more Republican; factory workers vote more Democratic; farmers vote more Republican.

When such groups behave differently, change their normal voting proportions, there is a story in the shift and the reason for it.

However, journalists should be cautious about drawing conclusions from such data. The way a person votes is a reflection of a variety of influences. Also, patterns change as old ethnic neighborhoods break up or as workers become more affluent. As the culture becomes more diverse, it is increasingly difficult to establish a cause-and-effect relationship. Beware of single-cause explanations.

Polls, says Professor Kimball, suffer from the same problems as do the media: Competition, oversimplification, sensationalism, inadequate editors or reporters, a skeptical public. There is a good deal of hypocrisy connected with the use of polls. Politicians who use them, denounce them. Reporters who use them, conceal their use. And pollsters gamble to make a reputation or are too cautious for fear of losing a reputation.

News organizations understand the value of polls—that they add an important dimension to reporting. Increasing space and time will be given over to the results of polls and surveys, and reporters will have to be able to handle the data with intelligence and professional competence.

Preparing Copy   For students preparing stories on typewriters, use the copy editing symbols in figure 4.1 to correct copy.

Preparing Copy for Print on the Typewriter

A. Use copy paper, newsprint or some other non-glossy paper; triple space; leave adequate margins left and right.
B. Make a carbon of all your work. Retain the carbon.
C. In the upper left-hand corner of the first sheet of all assignments, place your name, slug of story, news source, and date. Thus:
   Goldstein
   PHA-attended
   2/25/84
D. Begin one-third down the first page. Write on one side of the paper only.
E. If the story consists of more than one page, write "more" at the bottom of the page, circle it. On the next page, place your name, "2", and slug at top left of the page. Thus: "Goldstein-2-PHA."
F. End each page with a paragraph, not in the middle of a sentence.
G. Do not correct mistakes by backspacing and writing over. Cross out and retype. Never write over. Use copyediting symbols to make changes.
H. Never divide words at the end of the line. Hit margin release and continue, or cross out and begin word anew on next line.
I. Keep copy clean. Re-type hard-to-read sections and paste over.
J. Do not write more than one story on each sheet of paper.
K. Follow the stylebook.
L. End stories with end mark: 30, # or END.
M. When finished, fold all pages together, in half, copy on the outside, reporter's name in the upper left.

Copy Editing Symbols

Action	Marked copy	Result
Spell out	The (PHA) is pushing for the extension, viewing	The Pittsfield Housing Authority is pushing . . .
Transpose	it as the final link in its urban road renewal	. . . urban renewal road
Begin new paragraph	network. If undertaken, the city is planning	network. / If undertaken, the city . . .
Delete letter	to work in conjunction with a neighbourhood	. . . a neighborhood
Restore marked-out or hard-to-read material	revitalization program for the three-block area that is ~~that is~~ affected.	that is affected.
Change to lower case	The State and Federal governments would pay	The state and federal governments would pay
Separate words	for the road work.	for the road work.
Abbreviate	The (Pittsfield Housing Authority) says that	The PHA says that
Insert	five houses would be taken by the projet with	. . . by the project with
Spell out	a possibility that as many as (8) more would	. . . eight more would
Delete material; close up	have to ~~eventually~~ come down.	have to come down.
Indent for paragraph	The finite takings involve buildings at 90	The finite takings . . .
Capitalize	summer st., 83 and 90 Union St., and 88 and 95	Summer St., 83 and 90 . . .
Run in, or bring copy together	Bradford St. Of the five, only one is a single-family home.	Bradford St. Of the five, only one is a single-family home.
Punctuation	The others are multiple family dwellings.	. . . multiple-family dwellings.

Figure 4.1

Many newspapers do not use typewriters and students should be prepared to handle the VDT.

Briefly, the terminal consists of a keyboard and screen. Raw copy is typed into the terminal on the keyboard. Before the story is typed, the reporter must "input" various typesetting parameters. The parameters are instructions on size of the type, line length, typeface and spacing.

Copy is typed into the machine continuously. The computer or the disk justifies lines automatically. When the reporter makes a mistake, the cursor is used—a movable block of white light that can be placed anywhere on the screen to make insertions, deletions and corrections.

As the story is typed, it can be read on the screen. When the reporter has a long story, the previous material is stored in the computer or disk and can be recalled for examination by the reporter's scrolling the story (moving the type up or down on the screen).

5 The Structure of the News Story

Preview   Planning precedes writing. Even while reporting their stories, reporters try to visualize what they will write, especially the beginning of the story, the lead.

News stories have a linear structure:

■ The beginning includes the most important material. It tells the reader what to expect.

■ The remainder of the story—the body—amplifies, buttresses and explains the beginning.

"First the idea. Then the words."

As the young reporter struggled with his story he recalled this advice that his city editor had given him the day before. He had written an obituary about a Denver banker in 45 minutes and had been proud of his speed. But the editor had said that the story was disorganized. Then, the editor had offered him the advice about writing. Remembering the editor's comment, the reporter pulled the story from his typewriter and read it carefully. Again, he concluded, he was writing without a firm idea of what he wanted to say and how it would fit together.

Suddenly, he was struck by what he had just told himself: "What do I want to say? Where do I put it?" No one, not even his city editor, had told him that. But that was the key to putting notes into some kind of structured shape.

- What do I want to say?
- Where should it go?

This reporter's discovery is made all the time by young journalists. Usually, it is followed by another revelation, that the news story form or structure is simple and that most stories fit into this structure:

- The lead.
- The material that explains and amplifies the lead.
- The necessary background.
- The secondary or less important material.

The city editor's advice about thinking before writing has been offered to generations of students. As an essay in the *Fifth Reader,* a grade school textbook of the 1880s, puts it: "In learning to write, our first rule is: *'Know what you want to say.'* " (The italics are those of the author of the essay, Edward Everett Hale, the Boston clergyman who wrote the short story, "The Man Without a Country.") Hale had a second rule: "*Say it.* That is, do not begin by saying something else which you think will lead up to what you want to say."

Every writer who has written about the writer's craft—whether journalist, poet, novelist or critic—has understood these first principles of writing. George Orwell, the British journalist and novelist who wrote *1984,* was concerned that the English language was being endangered by unclear thinking. In an essay, "Politics and the English Language," he wrote that the first question scrupulous writers ask themselves before writing is: "What am I trying to say?"

In *The Elements of Style* (third ed. New York: Macmillan Publishing Co., 1979, p. 15), the "little book" that generations of college English students have used, authors William Strunk Jr. and E.B. White begin their section on writing this way: "Choose a suitable design and hold to it." They continue: "A basic structural design underlies every kind of writing. . . . The first principle of composition, therefore, is to foresee or determine the shape of what is to come, and pursue that shape."

No reporter should start to write without a plan. Sometimes plans change. While writing, a reporter will develop new ideas, and the original plan has to be discarded. But even then a new plan should be substituted.

Essential as a plan would seem to be, many reporters write without thinking. As a result, their stories exhibit one of the most common faults of journalistic writing—disorganization or lack of focus. Henry Fairlie, a British journalist, calls this deficiency "shapelessness." He attributes it to "an intellectual inability, on the part both of the reporter and copy editor, to master the story." This mastery, Fairlie says, must come "before writing."

As one journalism teacher has been telling his students for two decades: "You can't write if you can't think." Ambrose Bierce, a newspaperman and author of *The Devil's Dictionary,* described good writing as "clear thinking made visible."

The Basic Idea

Almost all writing is based on an observation, an emotion or an opinion that the writer wants to communicate. This basic idea may come at the beginning of the piece as it usually does in a news story, or it may be tacked on at the end, as is a request for money for the flight home at Christmas in a student's letter to his or her parents. The basic idea is *always* there.

The news story has a beginning that sets out the theme and a body that elaborates and explains the theme. In the language of journalism, the story's theme—its most significant fact or facts—is stated in the lead. Thus, when reporters attempt to form an idea for stories, they search for the lead of the piece. Fairlie describes the importance of the lead this way: "Every journalist who has ever struggled with [a lead] knows why it can take so much effort. It is as important to him as to the reader.

Writing it concentrates the mind wonderfully, forcing him to decide what in the story is important, what he wants to emphasize, and can eventually give shape to the rest of the story as he writes it."

The hunt is not ended when the writer corners the lead, however. The reporter still has to identify material that explains, supports, buttresses and amplifies the lead before he or she can begin to write. Since most news events consist of more than the important action or actions singled out in the lead, the reporter also has to identify the secondary material that will have to be included.

Planning the Single-Element Story

A story that consists of one important action or is based on one major fact or idea is a single-element story. Also known as the single-incident story, it is the story handled most often by beginning reporters. The story requires:

- Lead.
- Explanatory and amplifying material.
- Background (if necessary).
- Secondary material (if any).

Let us take apart a single-element story to learn how it is structured:

Thieves Get 36 Batteries

Thieves who entered a Charlotte auto parts store stole 36 Delco batteries, police were told yesterday.

Crowell Erskine, 49, manager of the Piedmont Auto Exchange at 410 Atando Ave., told officers the store was broken into between 5 p.m. Tuesday and 8 a.m. Wednesday by knocking a hole in the rear wall of the one-story brick building.

Erskine said the batteries were valued at $539.18.

—*The Charlotte Observer*

Analyzing this short piece, paragraph by paragraph, we see the following:

1. The lead focuses on what the reporter concluded was the basic idea, the theft of a batch of batteries. He knows the reader opens the newspaper each day with the question: *What* happened today?
2. The reporter answers what he thinks will be the logical questions a reader of the lead might ask: *Where* did the break-in occur? *When* did it happen? *How* was it done? The answers to these questions explain and amplify the lead.
3. To round out the story, the reporter provides background that will answer other questions the reader might have. Here, the reporter knows the reader will want to be told the value of the goods stolen.

But let us suppose that the break-in occurred in the police department's property room at headquarters. Then the lead would emphasize *where* the theft occurred. If the theft took place in broad daylight while shoppers thronged the streets, this fact—*when* the theft occurred—would go into the lead.

Had the thief scaled a 15-foot wall to gain entry, *how* the theft was managed would be placed in the lead.

If the thief left a note in the store apologizing for his act and saying he needed the money to pay medical bills for his sick wife, *why* the theft occurred—according to the thief—would be put into the lead.

The most important element always forms the basic idea for the lead. To find that basic element, the reporter anticipates the questions the reader will ask, and then goes about answering them. These questions have been summarized as *who, what, when, where, why* and *how*—the Five Ws and an H.

Burying the Lead

A student was assigned to interview the chairman of the local United Way Campaign, which was in the middle of a fund drive. The reporter knew that the campaign issued weekly reports, and he thought that the mid-point of the drive might be a good time to check progress. Here is the story he turned in:

> The local United Way Campaign today issued its second weekly report in its current campaign to raise $750,000 for next year's activities.
>
> Tony Davis, the campaign chairman, said that donations in the first two weeks had exceeded last year's fund raising at a similar time.
>
> "We've collected $350,000, and that's about $25,000 ahead of last year," Davis said. "Thanks to the work of our downtown volunteers, the local merchants have been canvassed more thoroughly than ever before, and their gifts have been very generous."
>
> The month-long drive seeks funds for 28 local organizations, including the Big Brothers, Senior Citizens House, and a new program to aid crippled children.

The story is clear but it has a glaring fault: What should have been the idea for the lead was placed in the second paragraph. Now and then a reporter will intentionally delay the lead, usually for dramatic effect. This was no such instance. The story was faulty because the student journalist had failed to act on the key questions that our young reporter wrote as a reminder to himself: What do I want to say? Where does it go?

Obviously, the principal newsworthy fact the student reporter gleaned from his reporting was that the campaign was running ahead of last year's receipts. And since this is a straightforward news story, it should have gone in the lead. Given this advice by his instructor, the student returned to his typewriter and wrote another story. The first three paragraphs read:

> The United Way Campaign to raise $750,000 is running ahead of last year's drive at the mid-way point.
> Tony Davis, the campaign chairman, said today that in the first two weeks of the month-long fund drive $350,000 had been collected. That is $25,000 ahead of last year's collections at this time.
> "Thanks to the work of our downtown volunteers, the local merchants have been . . ."

The same set of facts was given to a reporting and writing class. Here are some of the leads that emerged:

> Tony Davis, the chairman of the United Way Campaign, reported today that the fund drive is running ahead of schedule.

> The United Way Campaign has collected $350,000, which is $25,000 ahead of last year's drive at this time.

> Local merchants were credited today with helping to push the United Way Campaign closer and faster toward its goal of $750,000.

In each of these leads, the basic idea is the same: Collections are ahead of last year. This was the most important element and it had to be the basis of the lead.

A TV Story

When five persons died at a fertilizer plant in Columbus, Ohio, the local newspaper and broadcast stations gave it saturation coverage. The next day, the story was still alive, and Donna Hanover of WTVN-TV in Columbus, who anchored the noon report, wrote this script. The single new element was the autopsy underway at the time of the newscast. Hanover also brings the story up-to-date with the condition of two critically injured firemen.

Notice that Hanover uses only two-thirds of the page. The left-hand third is used for technical instructions. The station ran silent film from the A roll—the projector running the film—as Hanover read the script. The film was of the scene of the accident.

Last-Minute Preparations.
Television reporter Donna Hanover goes over her news script with the cameraman before she anchors the local evening newscast.

```
INLAND PRODUCTS


Silf: 40
A roll
```

```
DH/dn              7/1/75 noon
Autopsies are underway at this
hour on five victims of poison
gas who died late yesterday
afternoon at Inland Products
corporation. Two firemen who
attempted rescues are still in
critical condition. The accident
apparently began when an
employee who was fixing a pump
fell 15 feet into a sludge pit
containing animal carcasses used
in making fertilizer. Three
other employees attempted
rescues, not realizing that
bacteria in the rotting
carcasses were apparently
producing deadly hydrogen
sulfide gas. The first fireman
into the pit also died from the
gas, which acts like carbon
monoxide, except that it kills
almost instantly. Inland
Products still refuses to
comment on the accident.
```

Wire service reporters are masters of the art of telling stories simply without sacrificing detail or meaning. Here is a single-element story whose simplicity has eloquence.

By Preston McGraw
United Press International

DALLAS, Tex, Oct. 5 (UPI)-House Speaker Sam Rayburn, 79, is dying of cancer. Hospital tests today showed there was no hope.

Rayburn was not told.

A surgeon took a sample of tissue from "Mr. Sam's" groin at Baylor University Medical Center today and found in it a "metastatic malignancy."

This meant that the cancer developed somewhere else--probably in Rayburn's pancreas--and that the cells have broken loose and spread the malignancy to other parts of his body.

"No further surgery is anticipated," a bulletin announcing his condition said. A spokesman for the hospital said the only surgery performed was what was necessary to get the tissue sample.

Asked how long Rayburn will live, Dr. Robert F. Short, Jr., in charge of his case, said: "There is no way of telling."

Rayburn was under sedation from the operation necessary to get the tissue sample when Dr. Short issued a short bulletin, announcing that he had cancer.

Rayburn's sisters, Mrs. W. A. Thomas of Dallas and Mrs. Robert Bartley of Bonham, Tex., have been with him since Monday, when he entered the hospital. A friend said they were "resigned to it."

Rayburn is at the end of a hall on the seventh floor of the hospital in room 729. A sitting room adjoins his room. His sisters remain in the sitting room most of the time. They have remained composed.

Three nurses, in addition to doctors, are attending Rayburn. A nurse accidentally left the door partly open for a moment and through it, Rayburn's head and left arm could be seen.

He was deathly pale and appeared to be asleep or unconscious. His arm was painfully thin and he was being given a blood transfusion. . . .

The story's one major element is Rep. Rayburn's impending death. As the reporter develops his story, he adds secondary information that he considers worth using but of lesser importance than the lead fact. The secondary material includes:

- The family's reactions.
- Possible successors.
- President's reaction.
- History of disease.
- Rayburn's background.
- Whether to tell Rayburn.
- Diagnosis, treatment.

The secondary material is not presented in haphazard order but in line with what the reporter thinks is the relative importance of this material.

Generalizing from this story, we can see that the single-element story can contain several facets but that only one is worthy of the lead. A story of this kind may have the following structure:

- Lead: Idea A.
- Explanatory material. Elaboration of Idea A.
- Secondary material. Sub-themes B, C, D, E.
- Background.
- Further elaboration of Idea A.

Go back over all these stories and see how large a cut can be made without eliminating essential material. The short stories could be cut after the lead or two paragraphs, and the two longer pieces could have been cut after a few paragraphs.

Multiple-element stories can be similarly edited because we write them the same way as the single-element story. The difference is that we place more than one basic idea high up in the story.

Planning the Multiple-Element Story

An event that has two or more major ideas or themes calls for a multiple-element story. The structure of the multiple-element story is:

- Lead: Idea A, Idea B.
- Explanatory material. Elaboration of Idea A, Idea B.
- Secondary material. Sub-themes C, D, E, F.
- Background.
- Further elaboration of Idea A, Idea B.

Every multiple-element story may not be structured precisely in this order, but these five components invariably are included in the multiple-element story.

Here are the first dozen paragraphs from an election story that appeared in the *Daily News*. Seemingly complex, the story has a simple structure that is based on the two major story ideas: A. Rejection of the bond issue; B. Republican control of the Legislature.

As you read the story, you might want to jot down how Ideas A and B are handled and what is done in each of the 12 paragraphs. Use the multiple-element story structure as a guide.

Gov. Hughes Loses Bonds & Legislature

by Joseph McNamara

(1) New Jersey Gov. Richard J. Hughes took a shellacking all around in yesterday's statewide election. The voters rejected the $750 million bond issue proposal on which he had hung much of his political prestige, and the Republicans gained control of both houses of the Legislature.

(2) Hughes, who had warned during the campaign that if the bond issue were defeated he would ask the Legislature in January for a state income tax and sales tax to meet the state's financial needs, announced early today that he "may have to do some rethinking" about the size of the need. And he made it clear that the "rethinking" would increase his estimate of the amount required.

(3) "I accept the verdict rendered by the people," he said in a written statement.

Behind from the Start

(4) The bond issue proposal, which was broken into two questions—one on institutions and the other on roads—trailed from the time the polls closed at 8 p.m. With the count in from 4,238 of the state's 4,533 districts, the tally early today was:

(5) Institutions: No. 868,586; Yes, 736,967.

(6) Highways: No. 866,204; Yes, 681,059.

(7) As a measure of Hughes' defeat, in the Democrats' Hudson County stronghold—where the Governor had hoped for a plurality of 150,000—he got only a 100,501 to 64,752 vote in favor of the institutional bonds and 93,654 to 66,099 in favor of the highway bonds.

(8) He had promised that if the bond issue were defeated, he would go before the Legislature in January and ask for a state income tax and a state sales tax to meet the state's obligations.

(9) Four other referendums had no great opposition, and passed easily. They were on voter residency requirements, a tax break on farm land and a change in exemptions from the ratables to the finished tax for both veterans and the elderly.

(10) The Republicans have controlled the State Senate for the last half century, and smashing victories yesterday in crucial Essex, Burlington and Camden Counties increased their majority—which had shrunk to a hairsbreadth 11–10—to two-thirds.

(11) Democrats swamped in the avalanche included Gov. Hughes' brother-in-law Sen. Edward J. Hulse of Burlington County. He was unseated by Republican Edwin B. Forsythe who ran up a convincing 6,000-vote majority.

(12) In populous Essex County, Republican C. Robert Sarcone defeated Democrat Elmer M. Matthews—who conceded shortly after 11 p.m. without waiting for the final count. And in Camden County, Republican Frederick J. Scholz unseated incumbent Joseph W. Cowgill. . . .

Breaking down the 12 paragraphs according to the two basic ideas of the event, we find:

(1) The lead paragraph contains a summary of the two elements in the first sentence. The second sentence refers to A and B.

(2–8) These seven paragraphs amplify, elaborate and buttress Idea A.

(9) This paragraph gives secondary information.

(10–12) These three paragraphs amplify Idea B.

The Three-Element Story

The following is an example of a story that begins with a three-element lead. The reporter would have singled out one element for the lead had she felt that one was the most important of the three. Correctly, she felt the three were of equal importance. Here is her story:

Study Links 3 Factors to Heart Ills
By Jane E. Brody

A new study conducted among 110,000 adult members of the Health Insurance Plan of Greater New York has once again demonstrated that smoking, an overweight condition and physical inactivity are associated with a greatly increased risk of death and disability from heart disease.

(A) The study, published yesterday in the June issue of The American Journal of Public Health, reported that men and women who smoke cigarettes face twice the risk of suffering a first heart attack as do non-smokers.

The annual incidence of first heart attacks among pipe and cigar smokers was also found to be higher than among non-smokers, but not as high as among cigarette smokers.

(B) Men who are "least active," both on and off the job, are twice as likely as "moderately active" men to suffer a first heart attack and four times as likely to suffer a fatal heart attack.

Men who were classified as "most active" showed no advantage in terms of heart attack rate over men considered "moderately active." The authors reported that other differences between active and inactive men, such as the amount they smoked, could not account for their different heart attack rates.

(C) The heavier men in the study had a 50 percent greater risk of suffering a first heart attack than the lighter-weight men. An increased risk was also found among women who had gained a lot of weight since age 25.

None of the differences in risk associated with weight could be explained on the basis of variations in smoking and exercise habits, the authors stated.

The incidence of heart attacks was also found to be higher among white men than among non-whites and among Jewish men than among white Protestants and Catholics. But the heart attack rate among Jewish women was not markedly different from that among non-Jewish women.

–The New York Times

The lead has a three-part theme: A study reports that smoking, overweight and physical inactivity are associated with heart disease. Brody then takes the three parts of the theme and elaborates each. First, smoking; next, inactivity; and third, overweight. (Notice that the order in the body of the story varies from that in the lead. It might have been better to have kept to the order in the lead.) The final paragraph introduces secondary material. Some reporters might have found a lead in the information Brody places in the last paragraph. Although most events have obvious leads, a number do not. News judgment is essential on multiple-element stories, and judgments differ. But in this case, Brody was on target. The last paragraph is secondary.

The story also illustrates another basic guideline for structuring a story: Put related material together.

Story Units

In organizing their stories, news writers move from one major theme to another in the order of the importance of the subjects or themes. The lead is elaborated first, and then the next-most-important theme is stated, and then elaborated and explained. The news writer does not hop from one theme to another, and then back to the first theme. The rule of thumb here is: Put everything about the same subject in the same place.

When his editor explained the rule to Dwight Macdonald, a journalist and critic, his first reaction was, "Obviously." His second, he said, was, "But why didn't it ever occur to me?" His third was, "It was one of those profound banalities 'everybody knows'—after they've been told. It was the climax of my journalistic education."

Only when an event is complex does the reporter return to subjects already elaborated and buttressed. This second elaboration usually is placed far down in the story, after all the major themes have been handled.

The Inverted Pyramid

We noticed that if any of the stories had to be cut for space there would have been no difficulty doing so because the important material was at the beginning, the less important at the end. This story structure—important elements at the beginning, less important at the end—has for decades been taught to students as the "inverted pyramid" form. The term is somewhat misleading. An inverted pyramid is an unbalanced monolith, a huge top teetering on a pin-point base. It is a monstrous image for journalists, for the top of a story should be deft and pointed. If the student can discard the picture of this inverted chunk and remember that all it means is that the most important material is usually placed at the beginning of the story and the less important material placed at the end, all is well.

However many elements it may include, the news story takes its shape from the requirements and limitations of the craft as measured by the clock—a silent but overwhelming presence—and finite time and space for copy. Given these realities, most stories must be written in such a way that they can be handled quickly and efficiently. If the 10 inches of available space suddenly shrinks to eight, there is no problem. The news story structure makes it possible with the slash of a pencil to cut the bottom two paragraphs.

If the only justification of the standard news story form were its utility to the people writing and editing the news, it would not have stood up over the years. The form has persisted because it meets the needs of media users. The readers of news usually want to know what happened as soon as the story begins to unfold. If it is interesting, they will pay attention. Otherwise, they turn elsewhere. People are too busy to tarry without reward.

Sometimes the pleasure may come from suspense, a holding of the breath until the climax is revealed deep in the story. When the reporter senses that this kind of structure is appropriate for the event, a delayed lead will be used.

News forms may be said to be utilitarian or pragmatic, in the tradition of the hustle and bustle of American life. But there is also an aesthetic component in the standard news form that its detractors sometimes fail to detect. If the expression "form follows function" implies beauty in the finished work, then the news story is a work of art, minor as it may be. The news story does meet the demands of art, that the work reveal a harmony of design.

Organizing Your Thoughts

It is easy enough to say that stories cannot be written without a well-thought-out plan, that unless the reporter's notes are structured before writing, the story will be a jumble of unrelated information. But how does a reporter go about putting his or her notes in order?

We can begin the answer by recalling from chapter 1 the advice of the city editor to the beginning reporter who covered a fire. The editor tried to tell the reporter that every story has its own necessities, that to be fully told each story requires the inclusion of certain facts. Once these essential facts are firmly in mind, the reporter makes a priority list: What fact comes first (the lead); what facts are next (the body)?

Story Necessities

Take any event and play the reporter's game. What are the necessary facts for an automobile accident story, a fire story, an obituary? Let us say an automobile hits a child. What must the story include? It will have to contain the child's name, age and address; the driver's name, age, address and occupation; the circumstances and location of the accident; the extent of the child's injuries; the action, if any, taken against the motorist. Any other necessities?

Given an assignment, the reporter has in mind a list of necessities for the story. The necessities guide the reporter's observations and direct the questions he or she will ask of sources.

Like a herd of cows in a field or apples in a bag, automobile accidents and obituaries have a basic similarity. Unless the reporter has the observational power to spot the differences, one accident story will be like another, one obituary like a dozen others. The reporter on the "automobile hits child" story tries to discern the unusual aspects of the event that should be given priority: Was the youngster playing? If so, was he or she running after a ball, playing hide-and-seek or jumping rope? Was the child looking for a dog, cat, younger brother? Was the child crossing the street to go to school? If seriously injured, how badly was he or she hurt? Will the youngster be able to walk normally?

Once the reporter has thought about the necessities of stories he or she is assigned and then seeks out the facts that differentiate this story from others like it, the story is on its way to being organized. The final step is to single out the important or unique element and then construct a lead around it. There is no simple formula for determining what should go into the lead. The criteria for news we developed in chapter 2 are helpful. Basically, news judgment is an exercise in logical thinking.

When a fire destroys a hotel worth $3 million and takes 14 lives, the reporter focuses the lead on the lives lost, not the destruction of the hotel, no matter how costly. The reporter reasons that a life cannot be equated with money. But if no one was killed or hurt in the fire, then the significance may well be that it was a costly structure, not a three-story hotel for transients that had seen better times. If there were no injuries and the hotel was an old landmark structure in a rundown part of the city, the lead might be that a landmark in town was destroyed by fire. Finally, if no one had been hurt and the hotel was a small, old building like three or four others in town, the fire would rate only two or three paragraphs, perhaps not even be used by a metropolitan daily newspaper.

Seen this way, the thinking process that underlies writing news stories is precisely the same as the thinking process that guides reporting. Reporting and writing are inextricably bound together.

Let us visualize a reporter assigned to the education beat who is told to check a report that public school teachers may not report for work next fall. When she was given the assignment, the reporter thought of several questions necessary to such a story:

Covering a Strike Threat

- Is the report true?
- How many teachers are involved?
- What are the reasons for the strike?
- When will the decision be made whether to strike?
- What are the responses of authorities to the threat?
- What plans are being made for the students should there be a strike?

The answers to these questions and other observations made during her reporting were the building blocks for the story. The reporter knew what her lead would be from the minute she received the assignment. If the report were true, the fact that teachers might strike next fall was big news. She had a simple formula for finding the lead: What do I know today that I did not know yesterday and that everyone would like to know?

These are the first few paragraphs of the story she might have written:

Teachers in all 15 public schools in the city today threatened to strike unless they are given a 12 percent wage increase in next year's contract.

Spokesmen for the local unit of the American Federation of Teachers, which represents 780 Freeport school teachers, said the strike threat will be presented to the City Board of Education at Thursday's negotiating session.

"Without a contract that contains pay levels reflecting the increased cost of living, we will not report for work in September," said Herbert Wechsler, the president of the local unit. "No contract, no work."

When the Thursday session led to no resolution of the issue, the reporter's story began this way:

> The possibility of a strike of public school teachers next September loomed larger today when six hours of contract talks failed to settle the wage issue.
>
> The teachers' union seeks a 12 percent pay increase over the current pay levels for next year's contract. The school board has offered 5 percent.
>
> The non-stop discussion between the union and the city school board failed to produce a settlement, said Herbert Wechsler, the president of the local unit of the American Federation of Teachers. The 780 public school teachers issued their strike threat Tuesday and presented it formally at today's session.
>
> Joseph Foremen, the state superintendent of education, who is attending the contract talks at the invitation of both sides, said:
>
> "The two groups are widely separated. We need a cooling-off period. Unless one side or the other makes some kind of concession, we may have no teachers in the schools Sept. 9. And a concession is the last thing on their minds now."

Four Planning Steps

Anyone who watched the education reporter in the newsroom as she worked on her story might conclude that writing news is not too difficult. She walked into the newsroom, put her notes on her desk and started to write. Occasionally, she looked at her notes. It seemed effortless.

Appearances are deceiving. A lot of logical, tough thinking went into the story. As a reporter of some 30 years' experience on a California newspaper put it to a beginner, "Those of us who survive work on our stories from the minute we get the assignment." The work the reporter was talking about takes the form of projecting at each level of reporting and writing the story as it will appear in its final form.

Reporters try to visualize their stories at these stages:

- Immediately on receiving the assignment.
- While gathering material at the event.
- Before writing.
- During writing.

It is time to examine the most important step in the writing process—creating the lead.

The Lead

Preview   The lead gives the reader an idea of the story to follow. There are only two types of leads:

■ Direct: This lead gives the reader or listener the most important aspect of the story at once. It is usually used on straight news stories.

■ Delayed: This lead entices the reader or listener into the story by hinting at its contents. It is most often used with feature stories.

In writing the lead, keep it under 35 words whenever possible and follow the subject-verb-object sentence structure for clarity.

The effective news story lead meets two requirements. It captures the essence of the event, and it cajoles the reader or listener into staying awhile. The first necessitates the use of disciplined intelligence. The second calls on the reporter's art or craftsmanship. For the writer, the proper lead helps to organize the story.

We slept last night in the enemy's camp.
—By a correspondent for the *Memphis Daily Appeal,* after the first day of the Civil War Battle of Shiloh.

Millionaire Harold F. McCormick today bought a poor man's youth.
—Carl Victor Little, UP, following McCormick's male gland transplant operation in the early twenties. UP's New York Office quickly killed the lead and sent out a sub (substitute lead).

The million-to-one shot came in. Hell froze over. A month of Sundays hit the calendar. Don Larsen today pitched a no-hit, no-run, no-man-reach-first game in a World Series.
—Shirley Povich, *The Washington Post* & *Times Herald,* on the perfect game the Yankee pitcher hurled against the Brooklyn Dodgers in 1956.

"I feel as if I had been pawed by dirty hands," said Martha Graham.
—Walter Terry, dance critic of *The New York Herald Tribune*, after two members of Congress denounced Graham's dancing as "erotic."

What price Glory? Two eyes, two legs, an arm—$12 a month.
—St. Clair McKelway, *Washington Herald,* in a story about a disabled World War I veteran living in poverty.

Snow, followed by small boys on sleds.
—H. Allen Smith, *New York World-Telegram,* the weather forecast.

These leads defy almost every canon decreed by those who prescribe standards of journalistic writing. The first lead violates the rule demanding the reporter's anonymity. The UP lead is in questionable taste. Povich's lead has four sentences and three clichés. Terry's lead is a quote lead, and McKelway's asks a question—both violations of the standards.

Yet, the leads are memorable.

They work because they meet the requirements of lead writing: They symbolize in graphic fashion the heart of the event, and they entice the reader to read on. Here are two leads from New York City newspapers that appeared the morning after the mayor announced his new budget. Which is the more enticing?

> Mayor Lindsay listed facilities for public safety yesterday as his top spending priority for next year, shifting from his pledge of a year ago to make clean streets his first objective in capital expenditures.
> *—The New York Times*

> Mayor Lindsay dropped his broom and picked up the nightstick yesterday, setting law enforcement facilities as the top priority in the city's construction plans for the coming fiscal year.
> *—Daily News*

The business of luring the reader into a story is hardly confined to journalistic writing. Andrew E. Svenson, the prolific author of many of the Nancy Drew, Bobbsey Twins and Hardy Boys juvenile books, once said that the trick in writing children's books is to set up danger, mystery and excitement on page one, and force the child to turn the page. He said he had written page one as many as 20 times.

Plato knew the importance of the first words of a written work. "The beginning is the most important part of the work," he wrote in *The Republic.*

Editors sometimes tell their staffers they want a "grabber" in the lead, something that will take hold of the readers or listeners and keep them pinned to the newspaper or the set.

The lead also serves the reporter. It enforces a structure on the piece. Once the reporter makes a decision as to which fact or facts will go into the lead, the story automatically takes shape. The lead material must quickly be amplified and buttressed. Secondary facts must be placed farther down in the story.

New Yorker writer John McPhee says, "The first part—the lead, the beginning—is the hardest part of all to write. I've often heard writers say that if you have written your lead you have 90 percent of the story." But that's not easy.

"You have tens of thousands of words to choose from, after all—and only one can start the story, then one after that, and so forth. . . . What will you choose?" McPhee asks.

There are many facts as well, and before the words can be selected, the facts must be sorted out. How does the reporter select the one or two facts for a lead from the abundance of material he or she has gathered?

Beginning reporters find lead writing their most troublesome task. A beginner looking over the six leads that begin this chapter might despair of ever becoming a journalist as he compares them with his handiwork. No need to worry. With practice, most journalists do learn to write good, better and then arresting leads. But first to the essentials.

The thinking process involved in lead writing often begins with the reporter's asking himself or herself:

Finding the Lead

1. *What* was unique or the most important or unusual thing that happened?
2. *Who* was involved—who did it or who said it?

After these questions have been answered, the reporter seeks words and a form that will give shape to the responses. This leads to three more questions:

3. Is a direct or a delayed lead best?
4. Is there a colorful word or dramatic phrase I want to work into the lead?
5. What is the subject, and what verb will best move the reader into the story?

The five questions are simple enough. The answers, however, can be so difficult that a reporter with years of experience may halt in the middle of a story, suddenly aware the story is going off in the wrong direction, that it has lost its focus. The reason is that the reporter failed to answer the first two questions properly. By moving in the direction set by the lead, the reporter had worked himself or herself into a corner far removed from the central point of the event.

Here is a lead a reporter wrote about a congressional race. He thought he had answered the first two questions. In a way, he had:

Backing Into the Lead

> Replies of Representative Ronald A. Sarasin and William R. Ratchford, candidates in the Fifth Congressional race, to a Connecticut League of Women Voters questionnaire were released today.

He did include *what* had happened and *who* was involved. But he did not make his answer to the first question sufficiently specific. What did they say in their replies? The reporter might have reached this answer in the story, had his editor let him continue. But the editor pointed out that voters want to know the opinions and positions of their candidates quickly in stories about politics. Such events do not lend themselves to delayed leads.

Reporters who write non-specific leads for events requiring direct leads are said to back into the story or to bury their leads, like the student who wrote a non-specific lead on the United Way Campaign in a previous chapter.

A better lead for the political story might have been:

Ronald A. Sarasin and William R. Ratchford, candidates for Congress in the Fifth District, agree that inflation is the major domestic issue facing the nation.

The next paragraph might have included the background information that the reporter had mistakenly put into his lead:

Their positions on the state of the economy and on other issues were released today by the Connecticut League of Women Voters. The League had sent its questionnaires to all major candidates for office.

The subsequent paragraphs would expand the lead and introduce other material from the replies of the congressional candidates and others.

Types of Leads

Beginning journalists often are offered lists of leads. They are told about the who, what, where, when, why and how leads; the anecdotal, clause, gag, shotgun and quote leads. And a score of others.

This categorizing may be useful for a research project, but the lists are of little use to the working reporter. No reporter looks at his or her notes and thinks, "Well, this looks like a *who* lead here. Or maybe it's a *what* lead."

What ran through the mind of the reporter who wrote this lead?

NORFOLK—Charley Greene has hit the roof in an effort to prove that he isn't 6 feet under.
　　　　　　　—The Virginian-Pilot
　　　　　　　(Norfolk, Va.)

Is that a *who* or a *what* lead? What is the difference and who cares? The reporter learned that a retired Navy warrant officer had not been receiving his retirement pay because the government thought him dead. The situation seemed humorous enough for feature handling. Then the reporter played with some words that would express the plight of a man caught in coils of red tape.

There are only two basic types of leads, direct and delayed. Let us examine both.

This type of lead is familiar to most reporters. It is the workhorse of journalism, the lead that is used on most stories. The direct lead focuses on the theme of the event in the first paragraph.

Direct Lead

Here are some direct leads:

A local couple was awarded $150,000 in damages yesterday in Butte County Court for the injuries they suffered in a traffic accident last March.

WASHINGTON (AP)—Abe Fortas, the immigrant cabinetmaker's son whose brilliant legal mind and alliance with President Johnson led to a Supreme Court career cut short by scandal, is dead at age 71.

Another in a series of snowstorms is expected to hit the Sierra today.

The delayed lead is most often used on soft news and features, the kinds of stories that are not about developing, running or fast-breaking events. The delayed lead usually seeks to set a scene or evoke a mood. Increasingly, the delayed lead is being used on all types of newspaper stories, not only on features, for the delayed lead offers the reporter much more latitude in writing. As editors demand better writing from their staffers and give them time to write well, the use of delayed leads has increased.

Delayed Lead

Here is a delayed lead on a feature about a man who runs a demolition company. It was written by AP Newsfeatures writer Sid Moddy:

Jack Loizeaux is a dentist of urban decay, a Mozart of dynamite, a guru of gravity. Like Joshua, he blows and the walls come tumbling down.

Notice that the reader does not know from this lead just what Jack Loizeaux does— the delayed lead does not reveal essential information to the reader.

Here is a delayed lead the UPI put on a news story that could have taken a direct lead—the passage by the House to extend daylight saving time two months:

WASHINGTON—The House wants to add a little daylight to the dark and dreary days of March and April.

Here is how an investigative reporter for the *Chicago Tribune* began a series of articles exposing corruption in Chicago's ambulance services:

> They are the misery merchants and
> they prowl the streets of our city 24 hours
> a day as profiteers of human suffer-
> ing. . . .

A Feature   A reporter for a large eastern newspaper was assigned to find out whether women served on the boards of the city's major firms. She found that although some of the nation's big industries had been naming women to their boards, most local companies—metal manufacturers, paint firms and others—had no women on theirs. The reporter began her story this way:

> The scene is the deeply-carpeted boardroom of one of the
> city's major industries.
>   Community leaders, an educator and business executives
> file into the room. They take their seats at a large, highly
> polished table and prepare for the business at hand.
>   All is ready for a meeting of the board of directors, and
> everything is in place.
>   The session looks like any other formal meeting, except
> for one aspect: It is an all-male affair. There are no women
> on the board.

The story begins leisurely. The first paragraph, which we usually consider to be the lead of the news story, tries to set a scene, as do the next three. The fifth paragraph states the theme:

> Although the city's population is more than half female,
> women constitute a small fraction of the boards of almost
> all the city's industries.

A direct lead could have been written from the information in the fifth paragraph:

> Few women serve on the boards of the city's major
> industries, a survey by this newspaper revealed today.

This lead would be acceptable to some editors. But it is not too imaginative. Also, it has a sense of immediacy that is inconsistent with the nature of the event being described. It is probable there have been no women on the city's boards of directors for some time, perhaps forever. The delayed lead is more appropriate than the direct lead.

Although the first paragraph of the story that employs the delayed lead might seem to violate our first rule—that the lead capture the essence of the event—the first paragraph is not haphazardly chosen. It must be consistent with the theme of the piece, and it must blend into the paragraph containing that theme. The first few paragraphs that precede the theme—an illustration, anecdote or quote—must set up the lead.

A News Feature

Given the opportunity, a reporter will try to featurize a straight news story by putting a delayed lead on it. At first glance, the death that police reporter Robert Popp of the San Francisco *Chronicle* saw in the police file seemed routine. But rewrite man George Williamson, copy editor Jim Toland and Popp turned it into a tragic tale. Here is their story:

Small Boy's Big Loss to Drugs

Johnny B., 6, awoke at a pre-dawn hour yesterday and saw his fully clothed mother lying on the floor next to the bed they shared in the Roy-Ann Hotel at 405 Valencia street.

Her nose was bleeding badly. Johnny got up, found some tissues, and wiped her face clean. Then he went back to sleep.

When he awoke again at 8:30 a.m., Anne B., 25, was still on the floor. Her face was covered by new blood.

Johnny dressed himself neatly—as usual—and groomed his Dutch boy haircut before going downstairs to tell the hotel clerk about his "sick" mother.

The coroner's office later determined that she had died from an overdose of an undetermined drug.

Johnny recounted that the night before, two men had visited the studio apartment in the Inner Mission District. He said he asked one man why he was using a rubber cord to make his arm veins bulge, and the man responded that he was taking a blood test.

The men left sometime after Johnny went to bed.

(The names in this story have been changed.)

Post script: Jim Toland had given students in his news writing class at San Francisco State University the facts taken from the police report. One student, curious to see if there is such a place as the Roy-Ann Hotel, drove by. She found the *Chronicle* had misspelled the name of the hotel. It was the Royan.

College Admissions

When Anthony Ramirez of *The Wall Street Journal* was ready to write his story about the admissions policies of selective colleges and universities, he decided that a delayed lead would be appropriate. In his first paragraph, he plunges the reader into the deliberations of a college admissions committee. Gradually, he works his way to the point of the piece in the fourth and fifth paragraphs:

DURHAM, N.C.–It's a sunlit Thursday morning, and around a long wooden table, a college admissions committee squints at thick books of computer printouts and argues about a black high-school senior with much promise but bad grades.

One of 12 children from a Detroit ghetto family, he wants to attend Duke University here, but his case perplexes admissions officials. Although they want to admit more blacks, this young man ranks in the bottom fifth of his class, and his scores are just average on the Scholastic Aptitude Test, which is said to measure college potential. "He's scary," mutters Edward Lingenheld, Duke's admissions director. Yet the Massachusetts prep school that the student is attending on an affirmative-action scholarship is one of the best private schools in the country. It backs him strongly, saying his character and leadership ability are outstanding.

Painstaking Process

After a few minutes of sharp debate, the committee, swayed mainly by the school's praise, decides to accept him. He is one of more than 6,800 high-school seniors who want to get into Duke's freshman class next fall. Only 1,000 will make it.

Every year, elite colleges and universities get tens of thousands of applications from anxious high schoolers throughout the nation—and launch a painstaking selection process that most other schools don't bother with. By mid-April, the colleges tell most of their applicants that they aren't getting in. Watching the admissions committee's deliberations here at Duke for a few days shows the sifting and sorting that lands some students in the college of their choice, and leaves others—often with almost identical grades and test scores—rejected.

Like other selective institutions, Duke wants a "diverse" student body. The reasoning is that a kind of gumbo of top students who are different, either in the lives they have led or the talents they possess, produces opportunities for learning that books don't provide. To admissions officers, getting the right mix requires the work of reasonable people trying to judge reasonably. To high schoolers and their parents, the process can often mean apprehension and mystery, followed by disappointment. . . .

News Magazines, the *Monitor* and the *Journal*

The delayed lead is a favorite of *Time, Newsweek, The Christian Science Monitor* and *The Wall Street Journal.* Since most of these publications are read after their readers have seen the news on television or read about it in their local newspapers, a different writing style must be used lest readers decide they cannot afford to pay twice for the same information.

The news magazines emphasize drama, interpretation, explanation and background in their stories. But many stories contain not much more information than the wire service stories that moved the day the event broke. The magazines just do a better job of writing and much of the dress-up is based on the delayed lead.

Here is the UPI lead on the verdict at a trial that attracted international interest:

> NEWPORT, R.I.—Claus von Bulow, the Danish aristocrat who married the American beauty heiress, was found guilty today of twice attempting to murder his wife by injecting her with insulin.
>
> A Superior Court jury of five married women, six married men and one bachelor chorused as of one voice, "We do!" when queried at 11:16 a.m. EST by the court clerk whether the verdict announced by their foreman was correct. . . .

Compare this with the beginning of the story that ran in an issue of *Time* dated 13 days after the verdict was returned:

> In the crowded Newport courtroom, spectators gasped. "My God!" cried one. "I don't believe it." The prosecutors seemed almost as surprised; they beamed and squeezed each other's hands in celebration. "By God, we've done it," whispered Rhode Island Assistant Attorney General Stephen Famiglietti. But as Jury Foreman Barbara Connett twice pronounced the verdict "Guilty," Claus von Bulow, 55, did not even flinch. . . .

Discovering the high readability of delayed leads, *The Wall Street Journal* made economic necessity into an asset. It puts delayed leads even on exclusive stories that could take a direct lead. The *Journal* has all but patented the human-interest lead in which a news event is personalized through the use of people affected by or involved in the event.

Notice how Janet Guyon of the *Journal* uses two human interest incidents to begin her story. The lead is in the third paragraph:

Paul Maccabee, an aggressive young reporter at the Twin Cities Reader in Minneapolis, was always alert to offbeat angles in his stories. So, when he covered a press conference announcing Brown & Williamson Tobacco Corp.'s annual Kool Jazz Festival last spring he inserted an unexpected twist: a list of jazz greats who had died of lung cancer. The next day he was fired.

Carol Wheeler, a free-lance writer for Savvy magazine in New York, was listed on the magazine's masthead until last May, when Savvy published her review of a book titled "The Ladykillers: Why Smoking Is a Feminist Issue." Miss Wheeler maintains that her name was subsequently striken from Savvy's masthead because its publisher feared offending tobacco-company advertisers.

Such incidents, while isolated, are cited by anti-smoking groups like the American Cancer Society as evidence of the tobacco industry's subtle yet powerful influence over what is—and is not—published about the hazards of smoking. Although tobacco companies aren't accused of heavy-handed direct pressure on editors and publishers, critics contend that smaller and weaker publications especially may engage in self-censorship when it comes to the smoking issue. The sheer weight of the cigarette advertising budget, critics say, is enough to make some magazines and newspapers tread lightly when covering the negative effects of smoking, toning down stories or ignoring the issue.

The Dangers

The *Journal's* narrative style has influenced papers across the country, but its news style sometimes has spread by contagion rather than by healthy example. The delayed lead requires a talented hand. Moreover, it cannot be used on just any story.

In an attempt to sell minor pieces to their editors, ambitious reporters use delayed leads on straight news stories. Some reporters play with delayed leads when they are unable to write a direct news lead. By taking the narrative or chronological approach or by focusing on an individual, they hope that the reader will somehow figure out just what the news point is.

Editors are aware of these tactics.

"We don't go for long scene setters," says Jerry Gold of *The New York Times*. In the Washington bureau of the *Times,* the working rule is that when a reporter uses a delayed lead the reporter must tell the reader what the story is about by the fourth paragraph. There is a similar rule-of-thumb at the *Journal.*

Some editors are so suspicious of the delayed lead they prohibit its use on any stories except profiles and features.

The Blind Lead　Delayed leads are risky. They can repel as well as attract. Here is a lead that has become a classic because of this duality:

> Unwise were the flies that plagued Keshoprasad Varma when he was shaving 10 years ago.
>
> *—AP*

It is a lead, an editorial in *Life* magazine said, that has "added a bijou to the great lead sentences in the museum of journalism. Curators will doubtless classify it with the blind, indirect or up-the-dark-stairs type of lead popular in the *New York Sun* in Frank Ward O'Malley's time. But in our opinion it transcends this category and belongs with those which convey just enough information to make further reading either impossible or absolutely necessary."

The story, by the way, was about a patent for a new fly trap.

To sum up: All leads are direct or delayed. Within these two categories are a variety of types of leads.

Single-Element, Multiple-Element and Summary Leads　Let us backtrack for a few minutes and look over the guidelines in this chapter to finding the lead. We said that the reporter usually asks himself or herself five questions. Look back at the first two. In answering the first two questions—what happened; who said it or did it?—the reply the reporter gives may be a single statement of fact. When that occurs, the lead that is based on the reply is said to be a single-element lead.

Single-Element Lead　This is the type of lead most often used.

> WASHINGTON (UPI)—The administration today demanded that a House committee studying U.S. intelligence activities return immediately all secret documents supplied under subpoena by the White House.
>
> *—UPI*

> Burlington police are to begin enforcement of the city's noise ordinance on a warning ticket basis for the next month.
>
> *—The Hawk Eye*
> (Burlington, Iowa)

Multiple-Element Lead　Sometimes the answer is more complicated. Two or more essential facts may emerge from the event that the reporter feels must be placed in the lead. In this case, the lead is a multiple-element or summary lead.

Two elements are included in this lead:

> WASHINGTON (AP) — The Supreme Court agreed Monday to decide the fate of a federal program against drug smuggling and heard arguments on whether presidents can be sued for money damages for violating the rights of Americans.

The lead in a previous chapter that put the three causes of heart disease in the lead is another example of the multiple-element lead.

Here is a variety of the multiple-element lead. The first three paragraphs constitute the lead:

The closing days of the run-up to Portugal's first elections since last year's coup have been marked by:
• A coming into the open of a breach between the Portuguese Roman Catholic Church and the radical leaders of the Armed Forces Movement (MFA) now running the country.

• A massive turnout Sunday in the Socialist Party's final big pre-election rally in Lisbon, said to be the biggest party rally in the capital since the MFA ousted the authoritarian right-wing regime of Marcello Caetano last April.
                        —*The Christian Science Monitor*

Roundups

A roundup is a story that joins two or more events with a common theme. They are often used for traffic accidents, weather, crime stories. When the events are in different cities and are wrapped up in one story, the story is known as an "undated roundup." Roundups often take multiple-element leads:

Torrential rains in Missouri and Kansas left five persons dead, hundreds homeless and crop losses of more than $1 million.

Teachers in 11 states walked picket lines yesterday for more money and other demands. Nearly one million children thus had an extended summer vacation or dawdled the hours away in understaffed schools.
New strikes idled teachers in Massachusetts, Pennsylvania, Illinois and Ohio. Settlements opened strikebound schools in Marion, Ind.; East Detroit, Mich., and Scituate, R.I.
The back-to-the-classroom moves were balanced by fresh walkouts. A United Press International count showed that at least 961,000 elementary and high school pupils were affected by strikes.
                        —*UPI*

Summary Lead

Multiple-element leads tend to run long. One device used to shorten these leads is to summarize the two or more elements in a single phrase and quickly expand it:

WASHINGTON — President Kennedy committed the full weight of the Federal Government at midnight last night to end Mississippi's defiance of the Union.
He called the state's National Guard into Federal service.
He sent troops of the United States Army to Memphis, Tenn., to stand in reserve if more forces were needed.
And he issued a proclamation calling on the Government and people of Mississippi to abandon what had become the most serious challenge to Federal authority since the Civil War. . . .
                        —*The New York Times*

Deciding on a Lead   Let us see how these types of leads are applied by listening to a reporter as she mulls over the notes she has taken at a city council meeting. Let us listen:

There were 13 items on the agenda. Well, which were the important ones? I'll circle them in my notes—

- General traffic program to route heavy trucks to Stanley Street and keep Main for lighter traffic.
- 56 stop signs to be bought.
- Paving program for Kentucky Street that will later fit into the bypass.
- OK'd contract to White Painting Co. to paint City Hall. $28,000.
- Hired consulting firm for traffic study.

Four of them seem to deal with traffic. Should I put them into a summary lead? Or should I pick out the traffic truck route or the traffic study? They seem equally important, so maybe I'll play with a summary lead. I'll drop the stop signs way down and then go into the painting contract.

She writes:

```
    The City Council today took three significant actions to
cope with the city's downtown traffic congestion.
    The Council:
    1. Approved the employment of Rande Associates, a
consulting firm from Burbank, Calif., to make a study of
traffic patterns.
    2. Called for bids on paving 12 blocks of Kentucky
Street, which is planned as part of a downtown bypass.
    3. Endorsed the city traffic department's proposal to
route heavy vehicles to Stanley Street before they enter
Main Street.
```

At this point, some doubts assail the city hall reporter. She remembers that the truck traffic issue has been argued for several months. Downtown merchants complained to the mayor about the truck traffic, and Stanley Street homeowners petitioned the Council to keep the trucks away. The local newspaper and radio station have editorialized about it. In her haste to structure a complicated story, her news judgment went awry, she thinks. She writes:

```
    The City Council today decided to route truck traffic to
Stanley Street and away from downtown Freeport.
```

The reporter is pleased with the lead she has written. But then more doubts. Maybe the over-all pattern is more important than the single item about Stanley Street. After all, she thinks, the Council's three major actions will affect more people than those involved in the Stanley Street situation. She decides that she needs some advice and she walks over to the city editor. She shows him both leads.

"That's a tough one," he tells her. "Sometimes you flip a coin. Why don't you use your first lead and move up the third item, the one on Stanley Street, and make it first? I like your conclusion in the lead that the actions were significant."

If we look closely at the two leads the city hall reporter prepared, we notice that the single-element lead about the routing of truck traffic to Stanley Street denotes a specific action the council took. The summary lead about the council taking three "significant" actions to "cope with" traffic congestion is, as the city editor remarked, the reporter's conclusion or interpretation. The *Daily News*'s summary lead on the New Jersey election also contains an interpretation, that the governor "took a shellacking all around in yesterday's statewide election."

Denotative and Interpretative Leads

We have just described two other types of leads that reporters consider before writing: 1. Denotative lead; 2. Interpretative or explanatory lead.

The denotative lead, which is almost stenographic in its adherence to fact, is most often used by press associations, daily newspapers and broadcasters since most news they handle is breaking or spot news. Interpretative or explanatory leads are used in news magazines, by columnists and by reporters doing news analyses to supplement breaking news stories. Sometimes a straight news story will be given an interpretative lead. The city hall reporter's use of the word "significant" was interpretative. Otherwise, the story was denotative.

Denotative

The University of Iowa has established an Undergraduate Advising Center to help students choose their major fields of study.

Interpretative

Teamsters Union Local 959 is fashioning an empire in Alaska, stretching across an ever-widening slice of life from the infant oil frontier to the heart of the state's major city.

The first lead, from the *Press-Citizen* in Iowa City, simply reports the availability of an organization to assist students. The second lead, which is from the *Anchorage Daily News,* is the interpretation by the newspaper's reporters, Howard Weaver and Bob Porterfield, of the impact of the Teamsters local on the state. The stories these reporters wrote about the union won the 1976 Pulitzer Prize for meritorious public service.

Usually, editors are reluctant to let reporters write as many interpretative pieces as reporters would like. As a result, reporters resort to a fairly simple device: They pin their interpretations on a source. They will seek out someone in authority willing to make their point. This turns an interpretative lead into a denotative lead.

For example, during the Vietnam War, reporters long in that country believed themselves as knowledgeable about the war as any authority. And they found officers with views similar to their own. The sources could not permit use of their names, and so, many stories quoted nameless colonels and majors. One correspondent quipped that if the U.S. Army actually had had that number of officers in the field, the United States would have won the war.

Leading a Non-Story

Let us watch a reporter who is having trouble with a story. He has just returned from a political debate and has written the following lead:

> To many of the voters in the civic auditorium last night, the debate between Freeport's mayoral candidates was a discourse between Tweedledum and Tweedledee.

Called to the city editor's desk, the reporter defends his lead. "Look, they really said nothing at all. Their disagreements on solving the traffic problem were insignificant," he tells his editor. "That's the real story."

The reporter, who covers city hall, then demonstrates to his editor's satisfaction that the differences were indeed of no real importance, that the discussion was largely puffery.

"OK," the editor tells the reporter. "You write what you think it means, but we'll put it on the editorial page as a signed column. In the news story for today, write it down the middle, but see if you can get some sources to assess the solutions. I agree that we can't mislead readers into thinking that the solutions of the candidates are important.

"If you can't get some comments today, give us a fairly straight story on the debate and we'll run a folo with comments tomorrow."

Satisfied, the reporter returns to his typewriter and carefully pecks out this lead:

> Freeport's mayoral candidates last night offered what they said were significant solutions to the city's downtown traffic problems.

The lead is hardly exciting. A more dramatic lead might have been written by stressing the conflicting solutions of the candidates. But the reporter decided—and the city editor agreed with his decision—that emphasizing the conflict in the candidates' positions would imply that their proposals were significant. In the reporter's judgment, they were not. He sought to suggest to the reader they were not by the use of the words "they said," which pins the claim of significance on the candidates.

The editor went along with the reporter's decision by allotting half a column to the story on an inside page, although it had been scheduled for a full column on page one.

If we look at this newsroom episode closely, we can sense something about the morality of journalism. Although reporters carry a "Front Page" image, they will not swap the family silver for a story. Nor will they inflate a story for a byline and page one play. However, no reporter can excuse a dull lead if a more dramatic one would better describe the event.

Good Reporting Equals Good Leads

Most weak leads are the result of poor writing. Almost as many are the consequence of inadequate reporting. Consider this lead:

> Barbara Elizabeth Foster, 19, St. Mary's University sophomore, will be queen of the city's Rose Festival.

Immediately, the city editor knows he is in for a tedious trek through the copy. The reporter has failed to single out an interesting characteristic of the new queen to add to her age and year in school, common identifying factors.

Glancing through the copy, the editor notices deep in a rambling quote about Foster's home life that her mother was named Maid of Cotton some 25 years ago. At the end of the story, there is a fleeting mention that her father is a gardening enthusiast.

The editor runs his fingers through thinning hair. Masking his exasperation, he circles the two sections and suggests to the reporter that there just might be a lead in the mother-daughter relationship and that a logical question to have asked the new queen was whether her father grew roses. Without good reporting no story can shine, much less be complete.

Subject- Verb- Object

Next, to the fourth and fifth of our five guides to writing leads. The fourth question the reporter has to answer is: Is there a colorful word or dramatic phrase that I want to work into the lead? The ability of the reporter to answer the question often depends on the reservoir of language the reporter has accumulated through reading.

In 1979, Florida conducted the first execution in the United States since 1967 in which a person was put to death against his will. The issue of capital punishment had not only been considered by several federal courts, it had involved the nation in a debate about the morality of such an act. How best to put this culminating action into words? Here is the lead Wayne King wrote for *The New York Times:*

> STARKE, Fla., May 25—The state of Florida trussed Arthur Spenkelink immobile in the electric chair this morning, dropped a black leather mask over his face and electrocuted him.

The choice of the verb "trussed" is inspired. Not only does it mean to secure tightly. Its second definition is "to arrange for cooking by binding close the wings or legs of a fowl."

Caution: Sometimes during the thinking that precedes writing, a word or a phrase will pop into the reporter's head, and the decision is made instantly that it must go into the lead. Now and then, however, the choice points the reporter to dead ends. The word or phrase actually is inappropriate for the lead, but it clings tenaciously to the reporter's consciousness, and it is more hindrance than help.

The fifth guide takes us directly into the construction of the lead—the selection of the subject and verb for the lead.

The basic construction of the lead should be subject-verb-object, S-V-O. That is, the lead should begin with the subject, should be closely followed by an active verb and should conclude with the object of the verb.

The S-V-O structure has an internal imperative: It directs the reporter toward writing simple sentences, which are sentences with one main clause. This kind of construction keeps leads short, another major requirement for a readable beginning.

Here are some leads consisting of simple sentences. We will apply the S-V-O guideline to them:

> State Rep. Jack Campbell wants to run for governor.
> —*The Albuquerque Tribune*

S=Campbell; V=wants; O=to run for governor.

> SAN FRANCISCO—A federal judge has ordered the City of San Francisco to hire 60 women police patrol officers within the next 32 weeks.
> —*UPI*

S=judge; V=ordered; O=San Francisco.

> Businessmen generally like Ronald Reagan. They like his economic views, and they think he could beat President Carter.
> —*The Wall Street Journal*

S=Businessmen; V=like; O=Ronald Reagan.
(For the second sentence, a compound sentence: Clause No. 1: S=They; V=like; O=his economic views. Clause No. 2: S=they; V=think; O=he could beat President Carter.)

Not every lead lends itself to a simple sentence structure. But even leads made up of complex and compound sentences have at their heart the S-V-O news kernel.

The S-V-O construction is the staple of journalistic writing. Three-fourths or more of the sentences a reporter writes follow this pattern. Most direct news leads—whether for print or broadcast—have this construction. It parallels the usual pattern of discourse and conforms to the command: "Write as you talk." Also, the S-V-O construction is functional. It is consistent with the thinking pattern of the reporter as he or she structures the lead. It is the most direct way of answering the first two questions the reporter asks when trying to find the lead.

Although the S-V-O guideline may seem rigid, it does permit a variety of styles. Let us look at several leads written the night of a heavyweight championship fight:

Variety is Possible

```
    BULLETIN
  CHICAGO, Sept. 25 (UPI) SONNY LISTON KNOCKED
OUT FLOYD PATTERSON IN THE FIRST ROUND TONIGHT TO
WIN THE HEAVYWEIGHT CHAMPIONSHIP OF THE WORLD.
    M95Oct
```

CHICAGO, Sept. 25—Nobody got his money's worth at Comiskey Park tonight except Sonny Liston. He knocked out Floyd Patterson in two minutes six seconds of the first round of their heavyweight title fight and took the first big step toward becoming a millionaire.
—Robert L. Teague,
The New York Times

CHICAGO, Sept. 25—Sonny Liston needed all of two years to lure Floyd Patterson into the ring and only two minutes, six seconds to get him out of it in a sudden one-knockdown, one-round-knockout at Comiskey Park last night.
—Jesse Abramson
The Herald Tribune

CHICAGO, Sept. 25—Floyd Patterson opened and closed in one tonight. It took Sonny Liston only 2:06 to smash the imported china in the champ's jaw and, thereby, record the third swiftest kayo in a heavyweight title match—a sudden ending that had the stunned Comiskey Park fans wondering wha' hoppened. The knockout punch was there for everyone to see. It was a ponderous hook on Patterson's jaw. But the real mystery was what hurt the champ just before that; how come he suddenly looked in trouble when Liston stepped away from a clinch near the ropes?
—Leonard Lewin,
The Daily Mirror

CHICAGO, Sept. 25—It was short, sweet and all Sonny Liston here tonight. The hulking slugger with the vicious punch to match his personality teed off on Floyd Patterson, knocked the champion down and out at 2:06 of the first round and won the world heavyweight championship without raising a bead of sweat on his malevolent countenance.
—Gene Ward,
Daily News

All the reporters agreed on the news angle or theme—Liston's quick knockout of Patterson. The thinking of these reporters was along the S-V-O line:

S=Liston; V=knocked out; O=Patterson.

The first lead, written for the UPI, whose reporters are told to remember that there is a deadline every minute, has little more than the S-V-O structure in the lead. Written within seconds of the ten-count, the story was designed to meet the needs of newspapers and broadcast stations on deadline.

The other reporters, who worked for New York City newspapers when the city had four morning dailies, were under less pressure and were able to fashion more distinctive leads. Some put personal observations and their interpretations into the leads—a practice permitted byline reporters, particularly on the sports pages.

Four Essentials

Looking back at the direct news leads in this section, we can generalize about their essentials.

First, we notice that each lead has something *specific* and *precise* to tell the reader. The reporter moved directly to the heart of the event.

Next, the *time* element is almost always in the lead. Then, there is usually a *source* of the information or action, and the source is often identified. And finally, the *place* of the action is often included.

Keep It Short

When a reporter writes a lead, he or she must navigate between divergent currents. One pull is toward writing a longer-than-average sentence as the lead must be precise and must offer significant information. The other is toward a short sentence, since short sentences are more readable than long ones. The long sentence may be difficult to grasp; the short sentence may be misleading.

There is no outright prohibition against long leads, but good long leads are difficult to write. They must have rhythm, symmetry and balance. Only experienced writers can successfully handle long leads. Here is an example of a good long lead from an article about Rockefeller Center, "The City Where Nobody Lives," by Joe Alex Morris:

> The most magnificent city in America is an irregular block of limestone, steel, glass and masonry snugly set into a dozen acres of solid rock, with its foundations anchored sixty-eight feet below the surface and its towers rising 850 feet toward—and frequently into—the clouds. Nobody lives there.
> —*Saturday Evening Post*

Notice the short second sentence, which balances the longer first sentence. The content of the two sentences also offers the reader a contrast in ideas.

Leads should adhere to a 30–35 word limit whenever possible, for visibility as well as readability. Long leads occupy so much of the narrow newspaper column that they appear forbidding. There is beauty in economy, and there can be meaning, too, if the reporter tries hard enough.

There are several techniques reporters use to keep leads short. The most fundamental method is the relentless removal of all but essential material. The adage about placing the answers to the Five W's and an H in the lead is journalistic history, although it may be helpful to the beginner struggling to shape a story. The experienced reporter will pick the single most important or most compelling element.

A common but unnecessary space-and-time consumer is the precise time—11 a.m. today or the redundant 11 a.m. this morning or 12 midnight. Unless the exact time is essential to the story—tax returns must be postmarked before midnight—"today" is sufficient. Unnecessary attribution also wastes space.

Should attribution go at the beginning of the lead or at the end? If a title or descriptive phrase is long, how can the reporter keep the material from cluttering the lead? The answers are provided by an editor who spent many years breaking in young reporters at *The New Mexican,* a daily newspaper in Santa Fe, N.M.: "Remember that the basic sentence structure is subject, verb, object. So the subject, the source of the lead, should go first when it is necessary to carry attribution in the lead. Also, I want to know immediately who's talking. It makes a difference whether a corner druggist or the mayor says that the mill levy should be lowered. You would not write a lead this way:

Placing and Condensing Attribution

> City taxes are much too high and must be lowered as soon as possible, Albert Quigley, owner of the Owl Drug Store and former city councilman, said today in a Rotary Club luncheon address.

"You wouldn't do it this way because the reader has to go to the end of the lead before he realizes that it's old Al Quigley, that constant complainer, sounding off again," the city editor continues.

"Now to the second point. Suppose you're covering the Rotary luncheon and we have a speaker in town from Chicago, Dr. Robert Cohen, a physician who's done cancer research. He says it's necessary that middle-aged men and women have annual checkups. Dr. Cohen is unknown among our readers. But we must tell the reader who he is so that his statements are authoritative. We could write it this way:

> A cancer specialist said today . . .

"Or if the paper prefers more specific attribution and is not worried about a slightly longer lead, we could write:

> The head of the cancer clinic at the Roosevelt Hospital in Chicago said today . . .

"This is also the way people describe their experiences," the editor concludes.

Unlike this editor, some editors prefer attribution at the end of the sentence, unless the source is more important than what is said. This would reverse the S-V-O structure. For reporters, the argument is theoretical; they do what their editors demand.

Keep It Fresh The journalist may roam the world for ideas and stories, but his time dimension is a narrow confine—the few hours of his news day. The journalist moves through the world of today. Such is his anxiety about old news that his writing has been parodied in this lead for an obituary:

> John Smith was dead today. He died yesterday.

Leads of this sort do appear in newspapers, and they occasionally run on the wires of the press associations. Here is a lead that was sent over the wires of one of the press services:

> INDEPENDENCE, MO., Oct 10-William Sermon today was no longer mayor of Independence.
> In a short, prepared statement, Sermon told the city council last night he wanted to resign because of "ill health" . . .

This ran several years ago, and reporters nowadays are a bit more sophisticated about how they freshen up leads. But they still adhere to what they were taught on their first day at the typewriter—news must be up to date. Many journalists try to abide by an unwritten commandment: Thou shalt not use "yesterday" in thy lead.

There is some reason for this insistence on the most recent development. Readers and listeners are not paying for yesterday's news warmed over. Unfortunately, they have been conditioned to believe that their newspapers and broadcast stations are always able to deliver today's news today. Thus, even when yesterday's news is being printed or broadcast for the first time, reporters feel they must make it appear to be today's news, an extreme application of the unwritten commandment. Most newspapers, particularly morning newspapers, accept yesterday in the lead. The wire services strive for today leads.

Follow-Up Stories The task of updating or freshening stories is not difficult with important, continuing events. Usually, it is possible to find an authority to comment on a new development or to track down people affected by a new program or policy. Causes, consequences, reverberations are useful for leads on follow-up stories.

> Service and maintenance workers were returning to their jobs today following a vote to end a 10-day strike against three Baltimore-area hospitals.
> –*The* Baltimore *Sun*

Disasters are updated without difficulty. If the cause of the airplane crash is unknown, investigators can be asked about the progress of the inquiry. If there were serious injuries, the condition of the victims can be checked, and if there are additional fatalities, a new death toll can be used as the basis of the lead. New facts are not difficult to find for stories on unsolved crimes. The status of the investigation is the obvious "today" lead. If the crime was solved yesterday, the arresting officers can be interviewed, or the detective who solved the case may be willing to talk about how he cracked it. The limits to updating are the reporter's imagination and the availability of sources.

Delayed leads are often used to freshen day-old stories. The reporter finds a new angle that lends itself to narrative telling and the story gradually works back to the fact that the event occurred yesterday. These stories begin something like this one about a baseball game:

Second-Day Leads

> Preacher Stowe knew he was heading for a long, hard day's work when he had to borrow his roommate's pants.
> "The hotel mislaid my luggage, and in order to make the bus to the stadium I had to borrow a pair of pants," Stowe said. "I knew right then there would be trouble."
> There was.

The two-word sentence is the transition or tie-in paragraph to the news, which is contained in the next paragraph:

> Stowe lasted four innings last night. He was shelled from the mound after giving up four runs. The Red Sox defeated the Tigers 9–2.

Most fans knew the score before reading the newspaper, and they enjoyed the little tale, which we presume came from the experience of Preacher himself and not from the imagination of the club's public relations man.

Whenever possible, a new fact is put into a second-day lead. Or else a fact that was not mentioned prominently in the original story is put into the lead—when appropriate.

When a midwestern morning newspaper ran a piece about a police hunt in five counties for a suspected killer, the police reporter for an afternoon paper in one of those counties noted that the suspect was thought to have murdered a woman from his county. That became his lead:

> State police today widened their search for a 25-year-old farmhand suspected of three slayings, including the murder of a Mt. Pleasant woman.

Sometimes, it is impossible to find a new angle for a second-day story and a delayed lead has to be used.

Here is the second-day lead that the AP put on the wire about the conviction of Claus von Bulow:

> NEWPORT, R.I. (AP)—Claus von Bulow left behind the lunch-hour throng that chanted he was innocent, the lawyers who attacked and defended him and the jury that found he tried to kill his wife, and went home to his luxury apartment.
>
> The jury decided Tuesday that von Bulow had twice tried to kill Martha von Bulow by secretly injecting her with insulin so he could inherit $14 million of her fortune and marry his ex-actress lover. . . .

The second-day lead can be stretched to absurdity, particularly when the end becomes the means, when the purpose of the updating is word play. Some reporters become so adept at rewriting leads that they can fool experienced editors into believing old news is new. They will dig out a secondary fact of no great consequence and fluff it into importance with clever writing.

A less objectionable form of word play to freshen old stories is the simple switch to the present tense, present perfect tense or future tense. When there are no new developments, "yesterday" in the lead can be avoided by a tense change:

> `Two municipal pool lifeguards are under suspension for`
> `allegedly collecting city paychecks while attending`
> `school.`

> `Local officials have asked the governor to increase funds`
> `for community colleges throughout the state.`

Some reporters consider the present tense an easy way out and contend that the only imaginative second-day lead that tests writing talent is the lead that contains "today." The intention may be laudable, but the results are sometimes transparent fabrications:

> Billie Jean King today reigned as the queen of women tennis players.

In the next paragraph we learn that King won the women's final yesterday at the United States Open tennis tournament in Forest Hills. Equally unimaginative are the today leads that fall back on "after," "following," "still," "despite" and other subordinate conjunctions. Here are a couple of leads that fall into this category:

> Calm settled over Crown Heights today *after* a riot left two persons dead and 14 injured on neighborhood streets.

European political leaders were *still* awaiting China's response today to their plea for an end to Sino-Soviet tensions.

Sometimes an overnight lead—a lead on a story for early editions of afternoon newspapers that usually contains no new information—is overly imaginative. The overnight desk of the press associations usually has to fabricate a dozen overnight leads a shift, and sometimes the creative juices flow abundantly. Here is an overnight lead fashioned by a rewrite man in the Miami bureau of one of the press associations:

> MIAMI, FLA., Jan 8—Five thousand chickens are clucking around homeless today.
>
> Their home, the longest chicken coop in Dade County, burned down last night. Firemen say the chickens, smarter than horses, which sometimes stay in a burning barn, fled the coop immediately. None was fried.
>
> Damage was estimated at $25,000.

Whether this is the thirteenth lead turned out by a rewrite man suddenly wearied of inventing overnight leads for a dozen stories, or whether this is the height of the art is up to the reader to decide. In either case, it is a classic.

A reporter handed in this lead:

> The city planning office today recommended adding a section to the zoning code regulations on classification for residential use of property.

The editor puzzled over it and then instructed the reporter to simplify the lead and to say specifically what the proposed section would do. The reporter tried again.

> The city planning office today recommended that property zoned for two-acre, one-family dwellings be rezoned to allow the construction of cooperative apartment houses for middle- and low-income families.

The city editor looked this over and seemed pleased. "Let's take it a step further," he said. "What's the point of the recommendation? To change the code so people can move into that wooded area north of town near the Greenwich Estates section. Let's try to get people into the lead." The reporter returned in 10 minutes with these two paragraphs:

```
    Low- and middle-income families may be able to buy
apartments in suburban areas north of the city.
    This is the intention of a proposal made today by the city
planning office. The recommendation to the city council
would rezone property in the area from the present
restrictions that permit only single-family dwellings on
two-acre lots.
```

In this process of writing and rewriting, the reporter went from a jargon-loaded, impenetrable lead to one that stated quickly and clearly what the proposed regulation was intended to bring about. Accuracy was not sacrificed for simplicity and readability.

Readability stems from the ideas that make up the sentence, the order in which they are presented and the words and phrases chosen to give the ideas expression:

Ideas—When possible, the lead should contain one idea. "The sentence is a single cry," says Sir Herbert Read, the British critic and author, in his *English Prose Style*. Too many ideas in a sentence make for heavy going. Also, the idea selected should be easy to grasp; complexities should be simplified.

Sentence Order—The S-V-O construction is the most easily understood. "Reduced to its essence, a good English sentence is a statement that an agent (the subject of the sentence) performed an action (the verb) upon something (the object)," says John Ciardi, an American teacher and poet.

Word Choice—Since the lead moves on its subject and verb, the choice of nouns and verbs is essential for readability. Whenever possible, the subject should be a concrete noun that the reader can hear, see, taste, feel or smell. It should stand for a name or a thing. The verb should be a colorful action verb that accelerates the reader to the object, or makes him pause and think. It is not so much the presence or absence of the verb that matters, but the choice between a transitive and an intransitive verb, the American teacher and critic E. F. Fenollosa points out.

If we apply these guidelines to the three leads about the proposal of the city planning office we see immediately why the first two were rejected. They contained more than one idea, and the ideas were complex, disembodied. In addition to its structural simplicity, the third lead has a vivid subject. We can visualize and identify with a family more readily than we can see or feel a planning office.

Good leads are well written. But they do not spring solely from the fountain of inspiration. As we have seen, good reporting is the source of good leads. Intelligence—an ability to grasp the meaning and consequences of the event—helps the reporter. So does a feeling for the tragic and the comic and a sense of irony. These are as important as the ability to turn a phrase.

How to Write Readable Leads

1. Find the essential element(s) of the story.
2. Decide whether a direct or a delayed lead better suits the event.
3. If one element is outstanding, use a single-element lead. If more than one, choose between a summary and a multiple-element lead.
4. Use the S—V—O construction.
5. Use concrete nouns and colorful action verbs.
6. Keep the lead short, under 30 or 35 words.
7. Make the lead readable, but do not sacrifice truthful and accurate reporting for readability.

A student journalist who covered the University of Kansas campus for the *Kansas City Star* wrote this lead over a story about a discussion on agriculture in the Soviet Union:

> LAWRENCE, Kan.—As 35,000 football fans watched the University of Kansas play Texas Christian University yesterday, 50 persons sat in the Kansas Union building up the hill from the stadium and listened to a discussion of Soviet agriculture.

It is long, and it contains two ideas. But the irony carries the lead over these obstacles to readability.

Watch a reporter at the typewriter. Look at the city editor bent over a news story. More time is being spent on the lead than on any other single part of the story. When the lead sings, the reader hums along. Reporters have built reputations on their ability to fashion a memorable lead. Newspapers—the San Francisco *Chronicle* for one—have become famous for their leads. The Chicago brand of journalism has been stamped on generations of young reporters through the writing of Ben Hecht, Ed Lahey and Mike Royko, whose leads capture the reader's attention.

In 1966, the editor of *The Chicago Daily News* asked Lahey, then a Washington columnist, to return to Chicago to examine the administration of Mayor Richard J. Daley, the city's boss. Here is how Lahey's six-article series began:

> Chicago is a principality and Richard Joseph Daley presides over it—from the shores of Wolf Lake on the Indiana line to the saloons on Howard St. where the citizens of bone-dry Evanston can sneak down to dip their bills.

Leads to Running Stories

At 4:27 p.m. on a Saturday in March, 1976, 12 jurors filed into the jury box in a courtroom in the federal courthouse in San Francisco. The jury foreman handed an envelope to the court clerk who slit open the envelope, took out the verdict form and handed it to the judge.

Guilty.

After 12 hours of deliberation, Patricia Hearst—the 22-year-old daughter of the publisher of the San Francisco *Examiner* and a granddaughter of William Randolph Hearst, the founder of the vast Hearst publishing empire—was found guilty of armed bank robbery and the use of a gun to commit a felony.

The verdict ended the most intensively reported trial since the one for Bruno Hauptmann, who was accused of kidnapping the Lindbergh baby more than 40 years earlier. Reporters from over the world—400 of them—had converged on the courthouse, drawn by the Hearst name and the incredible story of an heiress who had been kidnapped by a revolutionary political group and who then allegedly had joined it in crime. The picture of her holding a submachine gun during a bank robbery was used all over the world.

But the story was not over for the reporters in the courtroom. Most of them had only minutes to catch the early editions of their Sunday newspapers. Radio, television and wire service reporters had to react immediately. The world was waiting for the news.

Despite the tremendous pressure on these reporters, they met their deadlines. Although some reporters only called in the single word "Guilty" over the telephone, full stories appeared. The reason: *B copy*.

Use of B Copy

"Lead Hearst," one shouted into a telephone, and dictated:

> SAN FRANCISCO-Patricia Hearst was convicted by a federal court jury this afternoon of armed bank robbery and the use of a gun to commit a felony.

Then the reporter hung up. He knew that the desk would put this on B copy, the background material that the reporter had written and dictated that morning while the jury was deliberating. His B copy had begun this way:

> The verdict ended a 39-day trial in which 66 witnesses had testified and 1,000 exhibits had been entered.
>
> Miss Hearst had testified that she had helped a revolutionary political group rob the Sunset branch of the Hibernia Bank in San Francisco on April 15, 1974. She said she had done so on the threat of death.
>
> Miss Hearst's testimony was considered by a jury of seven women and five men, who heard Federal Judge Oliver J. Carter tell them yesterday that they alone had to decide the key issue at the trial: Had Miss Hearst acted as a willing participant in the bank robbery?

After calling in the lead, the reporter returned to his typewriter to fill in details for the next edition. He then called in this material, an *insert* to go after the lead and before the second paragraph of the B copy. The insert ran for six paragraphs. Before he hung up, his city editor asked him to write another lead to try to put more drama into the story for the final edition.

The new lead that the reporter wrote was slugged just that, "New Lead." At a wire service desk, which had been running leads during the day for radio and television clients, the verdict was labelled "Fourth Lead" since three previous leads had been written. One of the services used the designation "Lead All" for the verdict.

Don't Write Writing

Immersed in words, the reporter is tempted to write writing, to make meaning secondary to language tricks. This is fine when a Dylan Thomas plays with words, but it is dangerous for a journalist, whose first allegiance is to straightforward meaning. Word play can lead to flippancies such as this lead from one of the press associations:

> JACKSONVILLE, Fla.—Like justice, the new judge of the Duval County Court is blind.

Good journalism is the accurate communication of an event to reader, viewer or listener. As Wendell Johnson, a professor of psychology and speech pathology at the University of Iowa, put it, "Communication is writing about something for someone . . . making highly reliable maps of the terrain of experience." Johnson would caution his students, "You cannot write writing."

The temptation to make writing an end instead of the means is enormous. Janet Cooke, a feature writer for *The Washington Post,* could not resist. She wrote a moving story about Jimmy, an 8-year-old heroin addict in the Washington ghetto. The Pulitzer Prize jury was impressed and gave her its feature writing award for 1981.

Background information about Cooke distributed by the Pulitzer office aroused the suspicions of a newspaper which checked her claims that she had graduated from an elite woman's school in the East—she had not—and that she spoke several foreign languages—she did not. It emerged that her story was also a fabrication. There was no 8-year-old heroin addict named Jimmy.

"I did not want to fail," she said in a television interview after she had been exposed. There is an undercurrent at the *Post* of "competitiveness and the need to be first, to be flashiest, be sensational."

She was stripped of her Pulitzer Prize and fired by the *Post,* but the damage had been done. Journalism had been tarnished in its efforts to maintain public trust.

The reporter who puts writing first on his priority list will achieve notoriety of a sort, if he or she is clever enough. Such fame is fleeting, though. Editors and the public eventually flush out the reporter whose competence is all scintillation.

This is not a red light to keep the reporter from trying to write well. In fact, the fashioning of well-written stories is our next objective. We have only skimmed the writer's art. Now for the plunge.

7

The Writer's Art

Well-written stories have these qualities:

- They **show** the reader through anecdotes, quotes, examples rather than directly **tell** the reader.
- They use quotations and human interest high in the story to sum up the event or the person the story is about.
- The language is precise, clear and convincing.
- Sentences are short. Transitions take the reader smoothly from one theme to another.
- The writing style is appropriate to the event.

Whether three-paragraph item or Sunday feature article, the news story is carefully constructed. We have discussed some of the rudiments of the well-crafted story:

The structure. The lead that states the essential elements of the event. The body that amplifies and expands the lead.
The content. Facts, derived from direct observation or reliable sources, that are accurately presented by telling the reader or listener what happened, who was involved, when and where it happened, and the causes of the event, its how and why.

Stories that contain these elements will satisfy readers because logical order and the precise and economical use of language are pleasing. But more is expected of the reporter. The news story should be well written.

The well-written story is clear, easy to follow, easy to understand. Good writing helps the reader to see the truths that the reporter is trying to tell. George Orwell said, "Good prose is like a window pane."

The window pane, unlike the stained glass window, does not call attention to itself. Good writing does not shout for attention. It calls attention to the people in the story, the event, the information.

There is a saying that great writers are born, not made. If so, it is unlikely that a course or a textbook can impart the gift that separates journalists like Red Smith or Ernie Pyle from the many capable reporters on newspapers, magazines and broadcast stations. Still, it is possible to learn to write well. It is also possible that during the learning process latent talents will emerge. The sudden discovery of the power and the beauty of words has transformed many young men and women into accomplished writers.

For years, journalistic writing had the reputation of being bad writing—a reputation probably well deserved. This kind of writing was best described by the city editor of a California newspaper who dismissed the writing of much of his local staff as "basic hack minimum." Nowadays, much more than the minimum is required. Genius, no. Craftsmanship, yes. Editors want reporters who can write the truth with a flair.

Gifted or journeyman journalist, experienced or beginner, the men and women who write for a living work at learning their trade. They have an "idea of craft," as the English scholar Frank Kermode put it, the drive toward "doing things right, making them accurate and shapely, like a pot or a chair." To sharpen their craft, journalists read writers who inspire them to move beyond themselves and who teach them the skills they always must be polishing. And they write. There is no way to learn to write without endless hours at the typewriter.

Ernest Hemingway read five hours a day, and he wrote and rewrote. He wrote, he said, 39 versions of the ending of *A Farewell to Arms,* a luxury no journalist is granted. But editors complain that reporters too often are satisfied with the first version out of their typewriters. While in his 70s, the poet Carl Sandburg remarked, "All my life I have been trying to learn to read, and to see and to hear. If God lets me live five years longer, I hope to be a writer."

Every writer is familiar with the agony of chasing elusive words. The writer knows that words can be brought to life only by strenuous and continued work. The aim is perfection of expression, the absolute match of words to the event. Walt Whitman described the writer's goal this way:

A perfect writer would make words sing, dance, kiss, do the male and female act, bear children, weep, bleed, rage, stab, steal, fire cannon, steer ships, sack cities. . . .

Following the masters is good practice. Creative workers and craftsmen know that the path to individuality begins with emulation. In teaching students at the Royal Academy about their study methods, Joshua Reynolds, an eighteenth century English painter, advised: "The more extensive your acquaintance is with the works of those who have excelled, the more extensive will be your power of invention, and the more original will be your conceptions."

Journalists read to master style and technique, to learn the tricks of the writer's trade that have served short story writers, poets, novelists, playwrights and other journalists. Poet or police reporter, the writer struggles to find words and phrases to match his observation of the event. When Hemingway covered the police court for the *Kansas City Star,* he would take his notes home and work over them hour after hour to simplify the testimony of witnesses until, in a few words, he had captured the essence of the evidence. He would always use the words he had heard in court.

This practice, as much as the influence of Ezra Pound and Gertrude Stein, may have been responsible for Hemingway's objective prose, what the critic Maxwell Geismar called "his famous flat style: the literal, factual description of the 'way things are.' "

This style, more brother than cousin to journalism, is evident in the ending to *A Farewell to Arms,* over which Hemingway labored. Frederic has just pushed the nurses out of the room where Catherine has died. He wants to be alone with her:

> But after I had got them out and shut the door and turned off the light it wasn't any good. It was like saying good-bye to a statue. After a while I went out and left the hospital and walked back to the hotel in the rain.

"The recognition of truth and the clear statement of it are the first duties of an able and honest writer," writes Hal Boyle, for many years one of the AP's top reporters. "The problem of good writing doesn't vary whether a man is writing a good novel or a good news story. He must look at the situation, find the kernel of truth he is seeking and record it in a durable book or a newspaper which, proverbially, will be used to wrap fish tomorrow."

The Reporter's Task

Although the poet W. H. Auden was describing the poem, his definition applies to the news story as well: "Firstly, it must be a well-made verbal object that does honor to the language in which it is written. Secondly, it must say something significant about a reality common to us all, but perceived from a unique perspective."

Unlike the novelist and the poet, the journalist cannot spend hours searching for the truth, much less the right word. No other writer is asked to commit words to paper with such speed, under such pressure. All the more reason, then, for the journalist to borrow from those whose struggles have cleared paths toward good writing. There are writing rules that apply to a three-paragraph item about a service station holdup and to a detailed investigative story on the state's deposits in non-interest-bearing bank accounts.

We might start with Tolstoy who, in describing the strength of his masterwork *War and Peace,* said, "I don't tell; I don't explain. I show; I let my characters talk for me."

Show, Don't Tell

In short, one of the reporter's first writing rules might be: Show, don't tell. Telling makes the reader or listener passive. Showing engages him. Good writers let the words and actions of the participants do the work. John Ciardi elaborates on Tolstoy's advice: "One of the skills of the good poet is to enact his experiences rather than to talk about having had them. 'Show it, don't tell it,' he says. 'Make it happen, don't talk about its happening.' "

When the reporter makes it happen, the reader moves into the story. The reporter disappears as middleman between the event and the reader.

Covering the funeral of a child killed by a sniper, a reporter wrote, "The grief-stricken parents wept during the service." Another reporter wrote, "The parents wept quietly. Mrs. Franklin leaned against her husband for support." The first reporter tells us the parents are "grief-stricken." The other reporter shows us with the picture of the mother leaning against her husband.

In a review of a movie, Stanley Kauffman of *The New Republic* writes: "We are told later that he (George C. Scott) is a cool man—which, presumably, is why his wife left him—but we are only *told* it; it's characterization by dossier, not by drama."

In a three-sentence paragraph, Sam Blackwell of the Eureka (Calif.) *Times-Standard* shows us a lot about teenage romance in the 1980s:

> They had met cruising the loop between Fourth and Fifth streets in Eureka. She fell in love with Wes' pickup truck, then fell in love with Wes. Wes gave her an engagement ring the day she graduated from high school.

Louis Lyons, a Boston newspaperman and later curator of the Nieman Foundation for journalists at Harvard, never forgot the lesson his night editor taught him early in his career. "When I was a cub reporter I had a story to do on the quarterly report of the old Boston Elevated system, whose history then as now was a nearly unbroken record of deficits," Lyons recalled. "This time they were in the black. I knew just enough to know how extraordinary that was.

"I wrote: 'The Boston Elevated had a remarkable record for January—it showed a profit. . . . '

"The old night editor brought my copy back to my typewriter. He knew I was green. In a kindly way, quite uncharacteristic of him, he spelled out the trouble.

"He pointed out that the word remarkable 'is not a reporting word. That is an editorial word.' " Then he advised Lyons to write the story so that the reader will say, "That's remarkable."

Good Quotes Up High

A corollary of the rule about showing, not telling is: Put good quotes up high. The reporter is alert to the salient remark, the incisive comment, the words of a source that sum up the event. Quotations help to dramatize the story as they permit the reader to visualize the person who is speaking. Quotes are also an aid in achieving verisimilitude, the feeling of truth. After all, if these are the words of a participant, the reader reasons, the story must be true. The higher in the story the quote appears, the better, although good quote leads are rare.

Notice the use of the poignant remark of the child in the second paragraph of this story:

> Mary Johnson, 9, lay alongside the bodies of her slain family for nearly two days. She believed she, too, would die of the bullet wounds inflicted by her mother.
>
> But Mary lived, and told ambulance attendants on her way to the hospital yesterday: "Don't blame mother for the shootings."

In an interview with an opponent of the U.S. government's policies in El Salvador, a reporter used this quote high in her story:

> "Why are we on the side of those who are killing the nuns?" he asked.

Human Interest Up High

A working rule for reporters: Try to place as close to the lead as possible the high quality incident or anecdote that spotlights the theme of the story. Often, this will be an anecdote or example about the persons involved in the situation that is being written about. Events become newsworthy because of their connection to human beings. When delayed leads are used, the incident begins the story. With direct leads—which often stress the formal aspect of the event—the human-impact illustration or example should be close to the lead. Readers and listeners want drama and excitement in their stories, and the reporter tries to oblige by finding and then using dramatic and personalized material.

We are all a little like Alice (of *Alice's Adventures in Wonderland*) when she says: " 'What is the use of a book,' thought Alice, 'without pictures or conversations?' " The newspaper reporter lets the illustrations and anecdotes serve as his pictures, and the quotations are his conversations.

Chicagoan, 15, wins $5,000 as champion of video game

Video Champion. An attention-grabbing lead. Showing, not telling the reader. A good quote high in the story. Human interest. This UPI story taken from *The Miami Herald* has all these ingredients of the well-written and interesting story.

WASHINGTON — (UPI) — Zap! Crunch! Swoosh!

With his eyes riveted on the TV screen and his hands dancing over a control stick, 15-year-old Andy Breyer of the Chicago area scored 142,910 points Saturday to win the world championship of the popular Asteroids video game.

Breyer, of Arlington Heights, Ill., beat out 17 other finalists from around the world to win the first-place prize of $5,000 from the competition's sponsor, Atari Inc.

"I don't like Asteroids that much," Breyer later told reporters, much to the chagrin of Atari officials standing nearby.

Well, what about that other popular Atari game, Space Invaders?

"That's kind of boring," Breyer replied.

The sponsors cringed.

A sophomore at Buffalo Grove High School, Breyer said he began playing video games about two years ago and bought a video game system with money he received for his bar mitzvah.

How much money have you spent playing these games at arcades?

"Oh, about 50 cents at the most. I don't like to waste my money on this stuff."

The sponsors faded into the crowd.

Breyer said he began playing Asteroids about three weeks ago, and practiced about five hours a day to get ready for the competition. He had only scored more than 100,000 points twice before. His all-time high is around 157,000.

"I don't think I could play any better than I did today," he said. "I would say at least 75 per cent of it is luck."

The youngster said he probably will use his prize for college tuition.

The second place winner was Gary Wong, 18, of San Francisco, with a total 128,780 points, and third place went to Dirk Mueller, 18, of Hamburg, West Germany, with 123,540 points. Wong got $3,500, Mueller $2,500.

The contestants played two games each.

The game consists of a player directing a space ship in the middle of an asteroid belt and using the ship's ray guns to blow up the asteroids before they hit and destroy the ship.

Breyer described his winning technique:

"I stay in the middle, then I go up left diagonally for just a fraction of a second and shoot all of the asteroids on the left side and then I shoot the right side. I don't like to use hyperspace."

After some prodding by the sponsors, Breyer said he did like their Football and Missile Command video games.

Do you feel like a champion?

"No, not really," the Asteroids champ replied. "I'm going to put the game away for a while and do something else."

The competition was staged in a room decorated to resemble a TV game show studio. One of the finalists, who had come all the way from Singapore, was unable to leave his hotel room because of an upset stomach.

Seventeen TVs, with computer games attached, were lined up in front of the dimly lit room. In the background was a mural of a Martian landscape, and music included themes from the movies *Superman* and *Star Wars*.

The master of ceremonies introduced each contestant game-show style and advised the audience "you're going to see some real guts ball play here."

Mark Twain's Principles

Before we invoke any more writing rules, let us listen to what a master craftsman, a former reporter, said about writing.

Mark Twain had volunteered to read the essays submitted by the young women at the Buffalo Female Academy for a writing contest. He was delighted by what he read, and in his report to the Academy he pointed out the virtues of the two prize essays.

He described them as "the least artificial, least labored, clearest, shapeliest and best carried out."

The first prize essay "relates a very simple little incident in unpretentious language," he said. It has "the very rare merit of *stopping when it is finished.*" (Twain's emphasis.)

"It shows a freedom from adjective and superlatives, which is attractive, not to say seductive—and let us remark, in passing, that one can seldom run his pen through an adjective without improving his manuscript.

"We can say further that there is a singular aptness of language noticeable in it—denoting a shrewd facility of selecting just the right word for the service needed, as a general thing.

"It is a high gift. It is the talent which gives accuracy, grace and vividness in descriptive writing."

In summing up the assets of the winning essays, Twain talked of "unpretentiousness, simplicity of language and subject, a marked aptness and accuracy of wording . . . excellence of treatment . . . naturalness."

Although many editors would contend that Twain's suggestion about stopping when finished is all a journalist needs to know about writing, his other principles are equally applicable to news writing. Good writing has four characteristics. It is:

- *Accurate:* The language matches the situation. This is Twain's "accuracy of wording," "using just the right word."
- *Clear:* Through proper use of form and content, the story is free from vagueness and ambiguity.
- *Convincing:* The story is believable.
- *Appropriate:* The style is natural and unstrained. In Twain's words, "unpretentiousness, simplicity of language . . . naturalness . . . selecting just the right word for the service needed."

The categories are not islands unto themselves. Causeways and bridges connect them. If we write that a congressman "refuted charges" that his proposal will cause unemployment, when he actually "denied" the charges, the language we use is inaccurate. As a consequence, the story is not clear. When we quote persons as they use the language—not in the homogenized dialogue that passes for the spoken word in too many news stories—our stories are more likely to convince readers they are true. The use of natural language is also part of the appropriateness of the well-crafted story.

Let us examine each of these characteristics. Before we begin, a reminder and a qualifier.

The reminder: A great deal of work is done before the reporter confronts the typewriter. The observing, note-taking and thinking that precede writing shape the story in major ways. The writing gives form and direction to ideas the reporter has in mind. Good journalistic writing is the result of good reporting. Clever writing cannot conceal a paucity of facts, stale observations or insensitive reactions to people. But bad writing can nullify superior reporting.

The qualifier: In the rest of this chapter—and in other chapters, too—rules, formulas and injunctions are presented. They are offered as guidelines, as ways to get going. They should not be considered inviolate rules. But it is best to accept them for the time being, until the beginner proves his or her competence. After this apprenticeship has been served, the experienced reporter can heed Anton Chekhov's comments about writing made in the play *The Seagull:* "I'm coming more and more to believe that it isn't old or new forms that matter. What matters is that one should write without thinking about forms at all. Whatever one has to say should come straight from the heart."

Accuracy

The city editor of a medium-size Iowa daily stared at the lead in disbelief. A reporter who had covered a city commission meeting the night before had written that the commission adopted a controversial resolution "with one descending vote." The proper word is "dissenting," the city editor lectured his errant reporter. "You've got to develop an accurate vocabulary or you can't function."

Without accuracy of language, the journalist cannot make the story match the event. The obvious way to check words for accuracy is by using the dictionary. But reporters who misuse the language often do so without knowing it. They could be saved from embarrassment by widening their reading. Watching the good writers put words to work might jar some journalists to the realization that their vocabulary is uniquely their own. Young reporters fall into the trap of using words and phrases of their age group that are meaningless to most readers.

Use Words With Referents

An accurate vocabulary also comes from the development of a feel for words, a feel for the way people use the language, which sometimes is not dictionary usage. "The true meaning of a term is to be found by observing what a man does with it, not by what he says about it," says P.W. Bridgman, a physicist. Journalists use words that have meanings that correspond to specific objects and identifiable feelings and ideas. When the journalist writes about the state treasurer's annual report, he is describing a specific person who has issued a document that can be examined. But when the reporter takes it upon himself to describe the report as "sketchy" or "optimistic," he is moving into an area in which there are no physical referents. He may use such words in an interpretative story, but only if he anchors them to specific facts and figures. Words such as progress, freedom, patriotism, big business, militant, radical and others like them cause trouble because they float freely, without referring to anything specific, concrete or identifiable. Reporters will quote sources who use these words and phrases, but they usually have the good sense to ask sources just what the words mean.

The reporter is obligated not to let language like this pass through his or her hands without making an attempt to ask the source to explain the non-specific words:

"This bill violates the spirit of *free enterprise.*"
"If we have any more *reactionary* proposals, the country is in real trouble."
"She certainly is an *exceptional* child."

Unwary reporters can become participants in brainwashing the public. When an oil company distributed a press release announcing the construction of an "oil farm" outside a Massachusetts town and the reporter dutifully wrote in her lead that the "oil farm will occupy a tract southeast of the city," the reporter was not only using language inaccurately, she was helping the oil firm obscure the truth. The so-called "farm" was to be used for oil storage tanks, which have a grimy image. A farm, with visions of white houses and green pastures, is what the oil company would like readers to imagine so that potential opposition can be diverted.

Euphemisms

When congressmen were discussing taxes, they sought to soften the impact of that dread word with a phrase—revenue enhancement. That sounds much better than the actuality. In Northern California, where marijuana is a major agricultural product, the polite term for its cultivation is "cash-intensive horticulture." Such attempts to blur truth are called euphemisms.

Some journalists may consider themselves compassionate for letting euphemisms slip by. After all, what is the harm in permitting people who work with convicts to describe them as the "consumers of criminal justice services?" What, for that matter, is wrong with "senior citizens" for older people or "sight deprived" for the blind? Surely, these euphemisms hurt no one.

Actually, they do damage us because they turn us away from reality. If the journalist's task can be reduced to a single idea, it is to point out reality to people. Words should describe reality, not blunt or distort it.

The absurdity of substituting an agreeable or acceptable expression for unpleasant but accurate language was demonstrated several years ago by a Chicago newspaperman. Returning from an assignment, he was reminded by his desk of the newspaper's prohibition of what the publisher considered earthy language. "Rape," he was told, was taboo. In his second paragraph, he wrote, "The woman ran down the street screaming, 'Help, I've been criminally assaulted! Help, I've been criminally assaulted!' "

During the Vietnam War, the violence and carnage were softened by euphemisms. Worse, words were used for propaganda purposes, and the press fell into line. "Destruction" became "pacification." "Destroy" became "save," as in the classic statement of an officer, "We had to destroy the town in order to save it."

These misuses of the language are dangerous shoals on which many reporters have gone aground. If we could mark the reefs that threaten writers, the most dangerous clearly would be where reporters have gone under while fishing for synonyms for the verb "to say." Let it be said at once, loud and clear, the word "said" cannot be overused for attribution. If tempted to replace it with affirmed, alleged, asserted, contended, declared, pointed out, shouted, stated or whispered, see the dictionary first. Better still, recall Ring Lardner's line: "Shut up he explained."

Don't Fear "Said"

If neither the dictionary nor Lardner work, try Donald Barthelme's short piece, "Snap Snap," in his collection *Guilty Pleasures,* (New York: Dell Publishing Co., 1976), pp. 31–37. Barthelme leafed through *Time* and *Newsweek* one summer and found a fascination for snap, cry, and warn:

"Ridiculous!" snapped Hollywood's Peter Lawford. . . . (*Newsweek,* June 21.)
"Adolescent," snapped Author Ralph Ellison. . . . (*Time,* June 25.)
Americans are "abominable," Russell snapped. . . . (*Time,* June 25.)

Sixteen snappers appeared in *Time* in June and July, fewer in *Newsweek.* The criers included an Egyptian, a Brazilian and Cuba's Castro (twice in *Time,* June 18 and June 25). "Strongman Castro nearly always cries in newsweeklies," writes Barthelme. "Sometimes roars. He has been heard to snort. But mostly cries."

During those two months, Barthelme found, a French novelist warned, economists warned, a philosopher warned, the Chancellor of the Exchequer warned.

Generally, it is wise to be wary of fishing for synonyms. Writing in which the same word appears and reappears may seem uninspired and dull to the writer. It is not to the reader. Consider the experience of the reporter who wrote a piece about the major export of a Central American country, the banana. As he looked over his copy, he noticed the word banana in the lead, then in the second sentence. In the fourth sentence, banana was replaced by fruit. But there in the fifth, it loomed up again. Hardly a paragraph was free of the word, which by now he had come to hate. But what to use in its stead?

Beware of
Synonyms

Suddenly, he hit upon it. "In Costa Rica, the elongated yellow fruit is harvested on both coasts."

The journalistic world has long forgotten what this creative journalist wrote, but the phrase "elongated yellow fruit" has come to represent a type of elegant and silly writing that journalists should shun.

This does not mean the news writer should steer clear of words and phrases that help to make writing picturesque or dramatic. In an interview, a reporter quoted an official in a peace organization as saying, "55,000 young Americans came home in rubber bags" from the Vietnam War. That image hits the reader more effectively than saying 55,000 were killed.

Facts First, Words Second

One of the impediments to accuracy stems from the reporter's unceasing desire for the well-written story that will perk up the reader. This desire is a healthy impulse, but it can lead to the selection of words—as well as facts—that are more colorful and exciting than the event merits. Reporters sometimes are so stimulated by the urge to be creative that they separate their language and their stories from the reality that inspired them. As writers, they feel an occasional liberty with facts and language may be granted them. In his novel, *The Deer Park,* Norman Mailer describes the lure of a well-crafted story for a movie director, Charles Eitel, and Mailer indicates the corruption of such temptation: "The professional in Eitel lusted for the new story . . . it was so beautifully false. Professional blood thrived on what was excellently dishonest."

Inaccurate writing often stems from finding the words and phrases first, then hanging on to them despite the facts. Every writer is carried away by the beauty and incisiveness of his or her writing. Watch the faces of students receiving their corrected essays from their instructors. Experienced writers find it equally difficult to cut or change their work once it has been put on paper.

But just as the broadcast journalist should never use the camera as an end in itself—despite the vast technical feats it permits—so the print reporter must not use words as an end. The objective is to communicate information accurately, not to display technical brilliance with the zoom lens or tape splicer, not to use words like a virtuoso. Technique has its place; its proper role is to aid in accurate communication. As Pauline Kael, the movie critic, put it: "Technique is hardly worth talking about unless it's used for something worth doing."

The handwritten manuscript of *The Great Gatsby* reveals that F. Scott Fitzgerald ruthlessly eliminated long sections of beautiful writing because they interfered with the narrative flow. He also worked unceasingly to find the accurate word, replacing "looked" with "glanced" in one place, changing "interrupted" to "suggested" in another. Fitzgerald knew Tolstoy's rule, "Show, don't tell." He eliminated sections that told the reader about his characters and instead let the action and dialogue do the work.

Hemingway's writing was simple, but it was not simplistic. He shaved language to the bone, but at no sacrifice to meaning. This accomplishment, of course, required hard work. He was asked why he had rewritten the ending to *A Farewell to Arms* so many times. "Was there some technical problem?" he was asked. No, Hemingway replied, the problem was not that complicated: It was "getting the words right."

Spelling

A few words about the bane of the copy editor, the misspelled word. A word incorrectly spelled is a gross inaccuracy. It is like a flaw in a crystal bowl. No matter how handsome the bowl, the eye and mind drift from the sweeping curves to the mistake. A spelling error screams for attention, almost as loudly as an obscenity in print. Intelligent reporters—good spellers or bad spellers—use the dictionary. Many editors associate intelligence with spelling ability because they consider the persistent poor speller to be stupid for not consulting the dictionary—whatever his or her native intelligence.

Argentina Says Its Ready for Peace or War

Clarity

The words and phrases the journalist selects must be put into a setting, into sentences and paragraphs that make sense to readers. "If you're going to be a newspaper writer you've got to put the hay down where the mules can reach it," said Ralph McGill of the Atlanta *Constitution*. Although he ranged over subjects as complex and touchy as race relations and foreign affairs, McGill wrote for ordinary people. His journalism was never vague, or incomprehensible to his readers. A reader of the King James version of the Bible, he learned early the strength, vigor and clarity of the precise word in the simple declarative sentence.

"A word fitly spoken is like apples of gold in pictures of silver," McGill said of the journalist's craft, quoting from Proverbs in the Old Testament. We know several ways to make these pictures—these sentences and paragraphs—clear to our readers.

First, there are the essentials of grammar and punctuation. Although there is greater leeway than ever in journalistic writing, the beginner should have complete control over these writing tools before experimenting.

Grammar

In grandfather's day, students stood at the blackboard and diagrammed sentences. They broke sentences down into nouns, verbs, pronouns, adjectives, adverbs, prepositions, conjunctions and interjections. From there, they went into phrases—verbal, prepositional, participial, gerund and infinitive. Then they examined clauses—main and subordinate. This is the way they learned how sentences are constructed. In most schools today, the only grammar students learn is through the study of a foreign language. For a journalist, this is inadequate training.

Five Fatal Flaws

After reading through dozens of freshman compositions, Loretta M. Shpunt, an English teacher at Trinity College in Washington D.C., said she seriously considered buying a red ink pad and a set of rubber stamps that read:

NOT A SENTENCE
"IT'S" EQUALS "IT IS"
"ITS" IS POSSESSIVE
DANGLING PARTICIPLE
"I" BEFORE "E" EXCEPT AFTER "C"

One way the beginning journalist can cope with this inadequacy is to invest in a handbook of grammar. It will not only solve grammatical problems quickly, but it will also expand the student's writing range. Some journalists stick with a limited style because it is all they can handle. No matter what the story, it is written with the same flat sentence structure the reporter used on the blues-singer interview yesterday and the bus-truck collision the day before that.

One of the most troublesome grammatical areas for the beginning journalist is the use of tenses. Improper and inconsistent tense changes are frequent. Since the newspaper story is almost always told in the past tense, this is the anchoring tense from which changes are made.

WRONG: He *looked* into the briefcase and *finds* a small parcel.
CORRECT: He *looked* into the briefcase and *found* a small parcel.

Not all changes from past to present are incorrect. The present tense can be used to describe universal truths and situations that are permanently true:

The Court *said* the Constitution *requires* due process.

When two actions are being described and one was completed before the other occurred, a tense change from the past to the past perfect is best for reader comprehension:

The patrolman *testified* that he *had placed* his revolver on the table.

In the course of the story, the tense should not make needless shifts from sentence to sentence. The reader is directed by the verb, and if the verb is incorrect, the reader is likely to be confused:

Moore said he *shot* the animal in the back. It *escaped* from the pen in which it was kept.

The reader wonders: Did the animal escape after it was shot, or did it escape and then it was shot? If the former, inserting the word "then" at the start of the second sentence or before the verb would help make it clear. If the animal escaped and then was shot, the second sentence should use the past perfect tense to indicate this:

It *had escaped* from the pen in which it was kept.

Dangling Modifier

Another trouble spot for young journalists, and for many of those who try to set their ideas to paper, is the dangling modifier—the word, phrase or clause that does not refer logically or clearly to some word in the sentence. We all know what these look like:

Walking through the woods, the trees loomed up.

The italicized phrase is a dangling participle, the most common of these errors. There also are dangling infinitive phrases:

To learn to shoot well, courses in marksmanship were offered.

The way to correct the dangling modifier is to add words that make the meaning clear or to rearrange the words in the sentence to make the modifier refer to the correct word. We can easily fix the two sentences:

Walking through the woods, *the runaway boy* felt the trees loom up at him.
To learn to shoot well, *the police* were offered courses in marksmanship.

Punctuation is the writer's substitute for the storyteller's pauses, stops and changes in voice level. The proper use of punctuation is essential to clarity. Misuse can change emphasis or meaning:

Punctuation

She could not convince him of her innocence, however she tried.
She could not convince him of her innocence; however, she tried.

Although the rules of punctuation are important, the sentence has been liberated from the strict restrictions of period, semicolon and comma. Dashes are used with greater frequency, and parentheses manage to make their way into news columns now and then.

The period is used to mark the end of the one point the sentence makes. The period is a full stop; the comma, semicolon and colon are slight pauses. To use them properly, a writer must develop a sense of rhythm.

Each paragraph should make a major point, and when the subject shifts, a new paragraph should be started. Sometimes, the development of a single idea will run six, seven, eight sentences. Set in type in a newspaper's narrow columns, a paragraph of this length would appear forbidding to readers, a block of black. So we must add a corollary to the rule. Start a new paragraph after the fourth or fifth sentence.

There is more to this corollary then typographical necessity. We know that readers pause at the ends of sentences and paragraphs. These short interruptions in the flow of the story help the reader absorb what he or she has read. Broadcast copy needs even shorter sentences and more frequent paragraphing. Short as these stops are, they are important to comprehension, particularly to the listener, who cannot reread something unclear to him. Even Gertrude Stein, the author of non-stop prose ("Rose is a rose is a rose is a rose."), came to recognize the value of the period. In *Lectures in America* (Boston: Beacon Press, 1957), p. 217, Stein said:

When I first began writing, I felt that writing should go on, I still do feel that it should go on but when I first began writing I was completely possessed by the necessity that writing should go on and if writing should go on what had colons and semi-colons to do with it, what had commas to do with it, what had periods to do with it. . . .

What had periods to do with it. Inevitably no matter how completely I had to have writing go on physically one had to again and again stop some time then periods had to exist. Besides I had always liked the look of periods and I liked what they did. Stopping sometimes did not really keep one from going on, it was nothing that interfered, it was only something that happened, and as it happened as a perfectly natural happening, I did believe in periods and I used them. I never really stopped using them.

Sentence Length

Spurred by an anxiety to cram facts into sentences, some inexperienced reporters write block-busters that send the reader down line after line in increasing confusion. When the reporter spots a sentence running three lines or more, he might recall the self-editing of Isaac Babel, a Russian writer whose short stories are highly-polished gems:

> I go over each sentence, time and again. I start by cutting all the words it can do without. You have to keep your eye on the job because words are very sly. The rubbishy ones go into hiding and you have to dig them out—repetitions, synonyms, things that simply don't mean anything.
>
> Before I take out the rubbish, I break up the text into shorter sentences. The more full stops the better. I'd like to have that passed as a law. Not more than one idea and one image to a sentence.
>
> A paragraph is a wonderful thing. It lets you quietly change the rhythm, and it can be like a flash of lightning that shows the landscape from a different perspective. There are writers, even good ones, who scatter paragraphs and punctuation marks all over the place.

The maxim that each sentence should, if possible, carry only one idea has been assumed to be an injunction limited to journalism. Not so, as we see from Babel's comment. The fact is, good journalistic writing is based upon the principles of good writing. Journalism is a part of the world of letters.

Babel was aware of the dangers of spending too much time on polishing. He warned that "the most important thing of all is not to kill the story by working on it." He described the writer's task of balancing spontaneity and precision as "walking a tightrope."

The Shorter, the Better

The press associations have concluded after a number of studies that one of the keys to readable stories is the short sentence. Here is a table distributed by the UPI:

Average Sentence Length	Readability
8 words or less	Very easy to read
11 words	Easy to read
14 words	Fairly easy to read
17 words	Standard
21 words	Fairly difficult to read
25 words	Difficult to read
29 words or more	Very difficult to read

Notice that a reader will have no trouble with an average sentence of 17 words.

Like any formula, the short-sentence rule can be overworked. One sentence after another under 17 words would create a staccato effect. Readers and listeners would feel as though they were being peppered with bird shot. The key to good writing is variety, rhythm, balance. Short and long sentences are balanced. Even a long sentence can be well written and as understandable as one of those eight-word wonders. Take this one-sentence story from *Time* magazine: "A mite miffed when wooly-mopped pianist Van Cliburn begged out from their ceremonial dinner (reason: a prior engagement), the U.S. Junior Chamber of Commerce brooded once more, decided that Prodigy Van was not really one of the nation's ten outstanding young men of 1958 after all, instead named fresh-faced crooner Pat Boone."

There are events whose nature dictates a relaxed style with long sentences. A public official retiring after 45 years of work with the state attorney general's office recalls in an interview the gradual evolution of civil rights. The story—told leisurely with rolling, conversational sentences—is written with a style far different from the short-sentence style employed to describe a bank holdup. This is a matter of appropriateness of style, and we shall go into it in more detail later. But it is important to point out here that although we want short sentences, the nature of the event determines how we tell the story. (See "A Pulitzer Prize Story.")

A Pulitzer Prize Story

Here are the first seven paragraphs in a story by Royce Brier of the San Francisco *Chronicle*. The sentence count runs as follows in these seven paragraphs: 14, 57, 16, 26, 36, 18, 9, 15, 5, 24, 24. Although the average sentence length is 22 words, which puts this section of the story in the "fairly difficult to read" category, according to the press association's study, the variety of sentence length and sentence structure make it eminently readable. Notice the quotation in the sixth paragraph, as high in the story as the reporter could place it. The story was awarded the Pulitzer Prize for reporting in 1934.

San Jose, November 26—Lynch law wrote the last grim chapter in the Brooke Hart kidnapping here tonight. Twelve hours after the mutilated body of the son of Alex J. Hart, wealthy San Jose merchant, was recovered from San Francisco Bay a mob of ten thousand infuriated men and women stormed the Santa Clara County Jail, dragged John M. Holmes and Thomas H. Thurmond from their cells, and hanged them in historic St. James Park.

Swift, and terrible to behold, was the retribution meted out to the confessed kidnappers and slayers. As the pair were drawn up, threshing in the throes of death, a mob of thousands of men and women and children screamed anathemas at them.

The siege of the County Jail, a three-hour whirling, howling drama of lynch law, was accomplished without serious injury either to the seizers or the thirty-five officers who vainly sought to defend the citadel.

The defense of the jail failed because Sheriff Emig and his forces ran out of tear-gas bombs. Bombs kept the determined mob off for several hours.

Help from San Francisco and Oakland officers arrived too late to save the Hart slayers.

"Don't string me up, boys. God, don't string me up," was the last cry of Holmes as the noose was put about his neck in the light of flash lamps.

Thurmond was virtually unconscious with terror as the mob hustled him from the jail, down the alley, and across the street to his doom. . . .

Use Short Words and Human Interest Words

Two other writing devices can help to make sentences clear: The number of syllables in the words used, and the use of human interest words.

Long words should be used infrequently. One study advises no more than 150 syllables for every hundred words. Obviously, no reporter can or should count syllables. The point is that short words are best. But we did not have to wait for the press association study to tell us, for in the *Fifth Reader,* Edward Everett Hale's fourth rule was: "A short word is better than a long one."

Participles add unnecessary syllables to sentences. Not only that, they turn sentences around, as in this lead:

> Expecting heavy traffic over the July 4th weekend, the state police today assigned all available manpower to duty over the three-day weekend.

It would take no great effort to make the lead conform to the S-V-O construction and to eliminate extra syllables. With a few pencil marks, clarity can be achieved:

> The state police today assigned all available men to duty for the three-day July 4th weekend to handle the heavy traffic that is expected.

The use of human interest words also helps to make writing clear and easy to follow. These words range from the simple "you," "your," "his," "her," "me," "mine," "my," to proper nouns and the names of familiar persons and subjects. It is better to write "the pansies" than "the plants," "the Stones" than "a rock group."

Clear Leads

A clear lead usually begets a clear story. For many years, the presumption was that only a short lead—under 35 words—could be clear to readers. For broadcast writing, the lead had to be even shorter.

The point is to make clarity the purpose, not brevity. Certainly, brevity does help. But as we have seen, a carefully written long lead can also be readable.

Theodore Bernstein, the driving force at *The New York Times* behind the campaign for the one-idea sentence, said, "The test is not the length but the clarity."

A member of the *Times*'s Washington bureau, Tom Wicker, described as a "useless exercise" discussions of how many words a lead should contain, how many ideas a sentence can carry before breaking down and how many sentences a paragraph must include.

"Nobody ever made a writer out of a hack by setting up rules," Wicker said. He said he followed Pulitzer's advice for good journalism: "Terseness—intelligent, not stupid, condensation."

These men would be fit company for Babel who, despite his concern for brevity, warned against following "a set of dead rules." But the beginner is no Wicker, much less a Babel, and there is reason for the young journalist to stay with a few rules until confidence develops and he or she can fly free from these restrictions.

Some reporters have trouble writing short sentences because they cannot handle transitions, the links between sentences and paragraphs. Because these reporters have no mastery of the device that enables a writer to move smoothly from sentence to sentence, their tendency is to think in large clots of words. The journalist with fingertip control of transitions thinks in smaller sentence clusters.

There are four major types of transitions:

1. *Pronouns*. Use pronouns to refer to nouns in previous sentences and paragraphs:

   Dr. Braun began teaching history in 1927. *He* took *his* Ph.D that year. *His* dissertation subject was the French Impressionists.

2. *Key words and ideas*. Repeat words and ideas in preceding sentences and paragraphs:

   He has been accused of being an *academic purist. Those words* make him shudder.

   "Academic purist is made to sound like an epithet," he said.

3. *Transitional expressions*. Use connecting words that link sentences. A large array of expressions function as connectors. Here are most of the major categories of conjunctions and some of the words in each category that can be used as transitions:

   Additives—Again, also, and, finally, furthermore, in addition, next, thus, so.
   Contrasts—But, however, nevertheless, instead, on the other hand, otherwise, yet.
   Comparisons—Likewise, similarly.
   Place—Adjacent to, beyond, here, near, opposite.
   Time—Afterward, in the meantime, later, meanwhile, soon.

   He tried twice to obtain permission to see the paintings in the private museum. *Finally,* he gave up.

   Dr. Braun's *next* project centered on the music of Berlioz. *But* his luck remained bad. An attempt to locate a missing manuscript proved a *similar* failure.

   In the meantime, he continued his study of Spanish so that he would be able to do research in Spain.

4. *Parallel structure*. Sentences and paragraphs are linked by repeating the sentence pattern:

   No one dared speak in his classes. *No one* ventured to address him in any but the most formal manner. *No one,* for that matter, had the courage to ask questions in class. His lectures were non-stop monologues.

Transitions emphasize the logical order of a news story. But they cannot create coherence where there is none. Transitions are used after the reporter has planned his piece by blocking out the major sections. Transitions link these blocks as well as the smaller units, the sentences. Transitions are the mortar that hold the story together so that the story runs smoothly from start to finish.

Logical Order A news story should move smoothly from fact to fact. When natural sequence is disrupted, the story loses clarity. Here are two paragraphs from a story in an Oklahoma daily newspaper:

> "There is nothing new in the allegations," Bartlett said. "We've heard them all before."
> "When we first heard them we thought there was nothing to it, but then we had a second look," Tillman said.

Although the first paragraph is closed by a quotation mark, which means that the speaker (Bartlett) is finished, most readers jump ahead to the next quote and presume that Bartlett is still talking. They are jolted when they find that Tillman is speaking. The solution is simple: When you introduce a new speaker, begin the sentence or paragraph with his or her name.

Jumps in time and place must be handled carefully to avoid confusion.

> NEW YORK (April 13)—A criminal court judge who last month ruled that a waiter had seduced but not raped a college student sent the man to jail for a year **yesterday** on a charge of escaping from the police after his arrest.
>
> **On March 19,** Justice Albert S. Hess acquitted Phillip Blau of raping a 20-year-old Pembroke College student. The judge said a man could use guile, scheme, and be deceitful, but so long as he did not use violence, rape did not occur.
>
> **At that time,** women's groups protested the decision.
>
> "Despite the protests of outraged feminists who demand your head, or other and possibly more appropriate parts of your anatomy," the judge told Blau **yesterday,** "I shall punish you only for crimes of which you have been found guilty."

The changes in time are clearly indicated at the start of the second and third paragraphs. From "yesterday" in the lead, the reader is taken to "March 19" in the second paragraph, and is kept there in the third paragraph by the transition "At that time" that begins the paragraph. When the quote begins the fourth paragraph, the reader is still back in March. Midway through the paragraph the reader realizes the judge spoke yesterday. Also, some readers might begin reading the fourth paragraph with the assumption that the quotation is by the women's groups referred to in the preceding paragraph. The jolts in time and place could have been avoided with a simple transition paragraph:

> In sentencing Blau yesterday, Justice Hess commented on the protests. He said: . . .

This may seem to be nitpicking. It is not. The journalist knows that every sentence, every word, even the punctuation marks he or she uses, must be carefully selected. For the reader does read from word to word, pushed, maneuvered, teased, sped and slowed through the story by the way it is written. When major disturbances to the reader's assumption of logic and order in the story do occur, the reader is confused, just as a quick jump cut on television destroys the continuity of the event for the viewer.

Logical order is based upon the organizing concept or principle that the reporter selects. The most frequently used organizing principle is chronology, a narrative device that is particularly useful on longer pieces with some drama—police stories, disasters, the passage of important legislation, profiles.

Some critics of journalistic writing scoff at what they consider the absurdity of a news story whose climax is presented in the headline, then again in the lead, and again in the body of the story that then builds to a climax, already twice-told. These critics are not disturbed by hearing *Carmen* for the third time; nor do they balk at rereading *Hamlet*. No news story can match the brilliance of a work by Bizet or Shakespeare. But people do read interesting stories even when they know the outcome, whether it be from having seen it themselves, from the headline and lead, or from seeing last night's 11 o'clock news account. The power of the written word to recreate an event in greater detail and with greater drama and clarity than it can be experienced will always attract readers.

Avoid Jargon

Beginning writers sometimes try to impress their editors with their grasp of their beats by using the specialized language of the field they are covering. The effort is wasted. No one knows what these words mean. They are usually used to avoid being specific or to cover up ignorance.

For those who would like to master jargon, here's a list that made the rounds of newspapers in Colorado:

Personal Jargon Generator

	1st digit	2nd Digit	3rd Digit
0	Long Range	Conceptual	Alternatives
1	Comprehensive	Facilitating	Objectives
2	Community	Regional	Interface
3	Ecological	Functional	Capacity
4	Schematic	Infrastructure	Analysis
5	Infill	Transportation	Matrix
6	Inter-Related	Open-space	Mitigation
7	Coordinated	Esthetic	Densities
8	Integraded	Planning	Relationships
9	Multi-Phase	Impact	Coefficient

Select any three-digit number. Apply it to the list above. Insert the phrase in copy when confused about the facts. If your editor is savvy, try it on friends. If they treat you with greater respect, drop them. They are too easily impressed.

The Longer the Story, the Greater the Organization

No matter how badly organized a short news story may be, readers will suffer through it if the information is essential. But no one will tarry on a disorganized longer piece. Coherence, focus and organization are essential to the feature, the analytical or interpretative article and certainly to the magazine article.

Here is the way the story, "On Chuck Hughes, Dying Young," by Barnard Collier, began in the February, 1972, *Esquire*. The transitions involving the characters have been marked. The underlinings (references to Hughes), circles (Butkus) and rectangles (doctors) in the first four paragraphs show how Collier has kept his central figure (Hughes) and the two minor figures (Butkus and the doctors) on stage. These provide human interest. They weave in and out of the paragraphs, moving the action forward in a continuous flow:

In the fourth quarter of the Sunday-afernoon pro-football game on TV, a twenty-eight-year-old Detroit Lion named Chuck Hughes dropped dead of a heart attack on the fifteen-yard line in front of the gathering of millions of Americans.

You did not know right away he was dead, but you knew something was very wrong. The cameras showed a close-up of Dick Butkus of the Chicago Bears standing over him and waving in a scared and frantic way for the referees and then for the doctors on the Lions bench. A player must wave for the referees before the doctors can come out on the field or it is a violation of the National Football League rules. A player might be lying there faking an injury to stop the clock. The Lions were behind by five points and they needed a touchdown before the clock ran out in order to win. But an incomplete pass had already stopped the clock, so Chuck Hughes had no reason to fake. He must have looked very bad off to Dick Butkus, because you knew that Butkus is mean and ornery when he is out there on the football field and doesn't normally come to the aid of an injured man who is not on his team.

The doctors ran out and started moving around too fast. You knew from looking at it on TV that this wasn't just a man with the wind knocked out of him. He was too still. Nothing of him moved. The doctors were working too hard. Instead of just loosening his pants like they do when a man is down with the wind knocked out, they went for his chest and mouth.

One doctor was pounding on Chuck's chest with his fist, and the other gave mouth-to-mouth breathing. This football player was not going to get bravely to his feet and walk off the field under his own steam, hanging from the shoulders of the trainers and dragging a leg. This man was not just injured. You knew

After describing the on-the-field scene, Collier begins the fifth paragraph, "Chuck's wife Sharon was in the stands." Then he describes her reaction to her husband's collapse. Collier's intention in this story is not to describe a football player's death but to tell us about Hughes's life as an athlete, beginning with his childhood in Texas. To move from Sharon in the stands to this background, Collier uses a transitional paragraph: "She kept thinking about their marriage and how much Chuck was in love with football." This is followed by a new paragraph that begins: "When Chuck was a little boy in Breckenridge, Tex., he carried a football around with him nearly all the time." We are now moved into a chronology of Hughes's life.

The story uses most of the writing devices we have explained, and in the four paragraphs reproduced above, Collier uses every one of our four transitional devices to move the reader through his story.

Conviction

To some people, the news they read, hear and see is as unconvincing as some of the advertising that accompanies it.

"What's the real story?" reporters are asked, as though they were prevented from revealing the truth by incompetent or venal editors, powerful advertisers or friends of the publisher or station manager. These pressures rarely influence reporters nowadays. More often, the pressures of time and the inaccessibility of documents and sources impede truth telling, and just as often, reportorial and writing failures get in the way of the real story. Let us examine the components of a news story that carries the conviction that it is accurate, true and complete:

Reporting:
1. Relevant factual material from personal observation and physical sources.
2. Authoritative and knowledgeable human sources for additional information.
3. Significant and complete background information.

Writing:
1. Simple language.
2. Illustrations, examples and quotes.
3. Human interest.
4. Appropriate style.

We will go into reporting in detail in the next chapter. Here, we might point to the reporting principles that are closely linked to writing.

Relevant Material

As we have seen, writing is dependent on the facts the reporter unearths. In his reporting, the journalist must have an eye for detail along with a nose for sniffing out the importance of the event. The journalist will use details just as any writer does—to build a picture, to show us the full extent of what is going on, and to convince us of the truth of his account. The journalist—whose eye catches the color of the trees felled in the disease eradication program and the tears of the child at the dog show whose puppy takes third place instead of first—convinces the reader he is an accurate observer and that his account can be trusted.

The journalist is always conscious of the backdrop, the scene. It may be that the press conference took place in the mayor's office, or that the rescue was made in a calm sea at dusk. Then he focuses on the important particulars: The mayor spoke seated at his desk, with seven microphones from radio and television stations in front of him and a dozen journalists in attendance; the Coast Guard boat was manned by six seamen and an officer.

A journalism teacher, a veteran of many years on small-town and big-city newspapers, still shudders at his recollection of the night he was sent out to the suburbs by a San Francisco newspaper to cover the death of a large family. Fumes from an unvented heater had poured into the house, killing the entire family. Only the dog had survived. The reporter gathered the relevant information—names and ages of the victims, occupation of the head of the household, approximate time of death, schools the children attended, how long they had lived in the house, whether the vent was legal, even the name of the dog (taken from its collar). Racing to a pay phone to make the final edition, he was dictating the story when he was stunned by the rewrite man's question: "What kind of house was it? Wood? Stucco? Brick?" The reporter had no idea, and there was no time to dash back to the house to find out.

To some editors, the construction of the house would be irrelevant detail. Details should be relevant to the story's theme or mood or they waste space and divert the reader. The political profile of a major presidential appointee in a national news magazine described him as: "neat, careful, conservative, reverent, industrious, polite without pretension, but incredibly smooth and self-controlled, always keeping his distance, maintaining the inner core of his being inviolate and locked. . . . He generates great sincerity in avoiding the direct answer, although he is by nature decisive and succinct."

Some of these details are the kind of comments a college admissions officer might make after interviewing a high school senior. Others indicate the reporter is possessed with extrasensory perception that allows him to penetrate his subject's "inner core." We want to know the official's record and his opinions on issues, not whether he is sincere. Who can tell whether he is sincere anyway? Reporters throughout their careers are always relearning that their judgments and inferences about human nature are as fallible as a teenager's opinions of his parents.

Authoritative Sources

Readers and listeners suspect declarations, opinions, judgments and explanations that are unaccompanied by material that supports them. They may even suspect facts offered only on the authority of the source. This suspicion and distrust, the result of the manipulation of facts by public officials and of commercial hard-sell, make life difficult for the reporter who prefers to let the name and title of his sources serve as authority. Readers want supporting material—data and documentation provided by the source and the reporter and a description of the context in which the statements and opinions were delivered.

As we have seen, some stories involve large areas of judgment and opinion that cannot be verified or supported with objective evidence. In such cases, if the reporter wants a convincing story, the source must be authoritative and knowledgeable. Here are the first four paragraphs of a story that appeared in a Kentucky newspaper:

This country must return to law and order if America's free institutions are to survive, Lexington businessmen were told Monday night.

And, it is the responsibility of businessmen on the local level to educate Americans, particularly the youth, in the importance of these free institutions and what they mean.

Speaking at a general membership meeting of the Greater Lexington Area Chamber of Commerce, Dr. Kenneth McFarland, author, educator and businessman, said that the current situation must be turned around.

"We can no more co-exist with this than we can co-exist with a cancer," he said, "We've got to take the handcuffs off the police and put them back on the criminal where they belong."

These statements are serious, and we wonder who is making them. We are told about the source's background in the third paragraph. And later in the story he is referred to as a "master's degree candidate from Columbia University." But the identifying material raises more questions than it answers: Author of what? Educator where? What kind of business? And does he own or manage the business? Why is a doctor studying for a master's degree? Or if he holds a Ph.D., why the need for a lesser degree?

Since the story is so vague about the qualifications of the source, readers will be reluctant to accept the speaker's analysis. He may have been qualified to speak out on the need for businessmen to educate the youth of the nation, but the story does not give his qualifications to do so.

The authoritative source is not necessarily the most knowledgeable. In fact, one of the reasons readers and listeners find some news unconvincing is that the sources that journalists use are officials or so-called experts who do not know what they are talking about because they have not lived through the situations they are describing. A story about unemployment that quotes only officials and data is inadequate. Unemployment is more than a set of figures released by a man sitting at a desk. It is men and women standing idly on street corners or sitting in anterooms waiting for job interviews day after day.

It is, of course, easier for a reporter to call an official for material than it is to seek out people affected by events. Taking the easy way out has led to stories with which readers and viewers cannot identify—educational stories written without interviewing students, health services delivery stories that lack comments from persons who use the clinics and emergency rooms of public hospitals. A glance at the evening newscast or afternoon newspaper will supply additional examples.

An event that is not placed in context lacks meaning. As the general news editor of the AP, Jack Cappon, put it:

> The dictionary defines context as "parts which precede or follow a passage and . . . its meaning."
> In news writing, nothing is more basic than making sure that any event, speech, situation or statistic is reported in sufficient context to fix the meaning accurately.
> Most of the time we do it right: A story about relaxed marijuana penalties puts it in the framework of current figures for offenses and convictions. A Moscow dispatch about Russian-American trade talks harks back to the collapse of an earlier trade agreement in December.
> When the proper context is given, you don't notice it—any more than you notice the oxygen you breathe. When it's missing, the effects are instantaneous and harmful.

One of the results of inadequate or improper context is an unconvinced reader. As Cappon pointed out in a story about the Army's pleasure over an unusually heavy crop of volunteers in 1975, the "story cited every factor except the main one: The economy was down, unemployment up, and enlistments always rise under those circumstances."

It is possible to isolate four writing components that add to the readers' and listeners' conviction that the story is accurate, true and complete.

One of the journalist's justifications for his unique privilege is that he fashions his stories for all people so that they can understand events and act immediately. Even the most complex idea must be taken to the people if it is an idea that affects them. This can be done. One of the biggest best sellers in this country's history was a political treatise, *Common Sense,* by Thomas Paine. Within three months of its publication in 1776, 120,000 copies were sold in the Colonies, whose population was about 2.5 million. Today, a book selling as well would reach almost 10 million readers in this country. Paine used the language of the people. He began his pamphlet: "In the following pages I offer nothing more than simple facts, plain arguments, and common sense."

Restraint in writing leads to simplicity in language. Young writers, and some older hands who have never overcome their youthful exuberance at making words dance and sing, sometimes will write with a sense of urgency where there is none, or exaggerate what should be understated. In reviewing one of Saul Bellow's novels, the critic Granville Hicks says of Bellow that "he is a master of style, without ever yielding, as John Updike sometimes does, to the temptation to show off."

The good reporter is content to let others engage in linguistic acrobatics while he or she remains firmly rooted in the language of the common people, which, because it is comprehensible, is convincing.

Illustrations, Examples and Quotes

The world is filled with wondrous events, exciting ideas and interesting persons. Fact has supplanted fiction. Wallace Stevens, the insurance company executive who wrote poetry that influenced a generation of poets, wrote with some incredulity about the situation: "In the presence of extraordinary actuality, consciousness takes the place of imagination."

Why, then, is so much journalism dull and unconvincing? One of the answers is that journalists sometimes do not use in their stories what they see and hear. They paraphrase good quotes. They reach for the complicated example and illustration, or they explain everything instead of letting the example show the reader.

Here are two paragraphs from a book by Studs Terkel, *Working: People Talk About What They Do All Day and What They Think of While They Do It* (New York: Pantheon Books, 1972), p. xliii. Terkel is a radio reporter based in Chicago. The speaker is a 14-year-old newsboy, Terry Pickens:

> I don't see where being a newsboy and learning that people are pretty mean or that people don't have enough money to buy things with is gonna make you a better person or anything. If anything, it's gonna make a worse person out of you, 'cause you're not gonna like people that don't pay you. And you're not gonna like people who act like they're doing you a big favor paying you. Yeah, it sort of molds your character, but I don't think for the better. If anybody told me being a newsboy builds character, I'd know he was a liar.
>
> I don't see where people get all this bull about the kid who's gonna be president and being a newsboy made a president out of him. It taught him how to handle his money and this bull. You know what it did? It taught him how to hate the people on his route. And the printers. And dogs. . . .

No paraphrase or summary would have the impact of Terry Pickens' own words as he talks of his disillusionment with the adult world. For that matter, few psychologists with their understanding of the problems of adolescence and growth can express so succinctly and convincingly—and with such simple emotion—the realities of the working world. Journalists can.

A single quote can throw a shaft of revealing light on a character. Lillian Ross, a writer for *The New Yorker* magazine, wrote a profile of Sidney Franklin, the only citizen of the United States who was ever recognized as a matador. Franklin was born in the Flatbush section of Brooklyn. In her profile, "El Único Matador," Ross wrote that Hemingway "maintained that to take to bullfighting a country must have an interest in the breeding of fighting bulls and an interest in death, both of which Hemingway felt were lacking in the United States."

Then she follows this with a quote from Franklin: "Death, shmeath, so long as I keep healthy."

When the Virginia State Bar Association voted to admit its first black member despite a determined effort by some senior members to block the move, a news story on the event quoted a Richmond lawyer as praising the applicant as a "commendable person with a high standing as a lawyer." Then the story quoted him as adding, "But he is a Negro and therefore I am opposed to accepting him as a member of this association. . . . I have a good many Negro friends, but I don't invite any of them to my home or club to socialize with me."

In three sentences, the reporter crystallized an aspect of race relations by letting one of the participants in the relationship speak.

A UPI story from Knoxville, Tenn., about a former light-heavyweight champion, Joey Maxim, describes his descent from a Madison Square Garden headline boxing attraction to a second-rate wrestler. The reporter quotes Maxim as saying about his former fight manager, "He probably doesn't want to see me any more—afraid I might want to borrow some money." That one quote tells us a great deal about Maxim, the manager and the boxing business. When a reporter hears a statement like that, he perks up. He senses that here, in a few words, is a summary of the story. The same excitement rushes through a reporter when he or she spots an incident that will illustrate the event.

Sally Grimes covered juvenile court for *The* Philadelphia *Bulletin*. Overworked and understaffed, the court was unable to cope with the cases before it. Also, the judges were generations away from the reality of street life, the reality of the world of youth. Here are some sections of a story Grimes wrote to make this point about the distance between the court and the youthful offender. A judge is speaking to two boys in court:

"You should stand still and be respectful when approached by a police officer. Then the officers will respect you. . . .

"I imagine they roughed you up a little bit, huh? I'd have given you a couple of good ones, too, before I took you in.

"In the old days, we used to have Irish policemen and we'd get it over the legs and then we'd get it again at home when the police took us to our fathers.

"We didn't call it police brutality then, and I'm concerned about the disrespect shown here for the policemen. . . .

"The next time you see a policeman, think positively. You can even say, 'Officer, what can I do for you?' The police are paid to protect us. When I see them I feel safe.

"You work, you pay taxes, the police are there to protect you."

Grimes ends her story by quoting the court-appointed lawyer of one of the boys:

> "The policeman is somebody who arrests you," the lawyer said, "If one boy is being beaten up by three others, he doesn't want the police because when the policeman comes he'll arrest all four. The one boy would rather just be beaten than be beaten and arrested."

Caution: Important as quotations are, it is improper to put into direct quotation what has been heard second or third hand. This device, used by imaginative reporters influenced by the New Journalism, is unethical. Reconstructed quotes are best left to the novelists.

Illustrations and examples can become symbols of ideas and events. When a reporter was covering a long and complicated discussion by the city council that led nowhere, she recalled that during the desultory debate, the mayor had built a pyramid with paper clips and matches. She wrote this into her story to illustrate his reaction to the discussion.

Human Interest

As we saw earlier, the two press associations consider the use of human interest words and incidents to be important elements in readability. Human interest also is essential to credibility. Readers who can identify with people in news stories are likely to believe the stories.

Frederick C. Othman, a veteran reporter for UPI, advised reporters to put as many personal references as possible into each sentence, "meaning he, she, King George, uncle, boy, girl or any such word describing a human being. The more such words, the more interesting the story." One way to begin is to replace definite articles—*the, a,* and *an*—with pronouns:

He picked up *the* gun and fired into the crowd.
He picked up *his* gun and fired into the crowd.

When a television reporter returned with a film story about a local store that was selling books, posters, pictures and other material based on the science-fiction show "Star Trek," his editor praised his enterprise in developing the feature. But after viewing it they both recognized immediately that it lacked human interest. The film concentrated on the material sold, but there was little mention of the customers, the "Star Trek" fans.

"We missed," the editor said. "We should have followed a customer around and used him as the center of the story."

Here is some other advice from Othman: "If a gent wears a dark-brown coat, say it's chocolate-colored. Not only is that descriptive, but it gets food into the story. Any word connoting food adds interest value.

"Tell about the taste of things and, especially, smells. Both good and bad. Take the man smoking a Turkish cigarette; it smells like burnt chicken feathers. Say so."

Othman worried about stories concerning ideas and things. He said, "Don't write about ideas, or even things, but about the people who have the ideas, or who build (or break) the things."

Othman gave this advice when much of journalism emphasized reporting actions and events rather than ideas, even though reporters knew that many of the events they covered stemmed from ideas. In 1945, when Othman's advice was distributed to United Press reporters, the world had undergone a catastrophic war whose origins lay in the racial and political theories of Adolf Hitler. The tens of millions who died in the gas chambers and on the battlefield were tangible proof that ideas can kill and thus must be the subject of journalism, even when they cannot be animated.

Actually, most ideas can be dramatized and personalized by putting them into human terms. The simplest way to do this is to show to people the consequences of these ideas, or to infuse the article with the personality of the person holding or advancing or opposing the ideas and theories.

Sometimes reporters fail to personalize events that easily lend themselves to human interest. When a puppy fell into the shaft of an abandoned well in Carlsbad, N.M., the rescue operation became a front page story in many newspapers. (There is truth in the adage that people like to read stories about dogs. It used to be monkeys and parrots as well.) One press service story that used the name of the puppy, Wimpy, was widely preferred to the competition's story that lacked the pup's name. The public could visualize Wimpy at the bottom of the well.

As we have seen so often, no amount of good writing can compensate for inadequate reporting. As William Burroughs, the novelist, said of the writer: "Generally speaking, if he can't see it, hear it, feel it and smell it, he can't write it."

Here is an example of a story that fails because it lacks human interest.

```
All doctors hope their patients never have occasion to
use the Poison Control Center recently established in the
emergency room of the Community General Hospital. However,
it should be reassuring to citizens, particularly parents,
to know the center exists for use in an emergency.
    Springfield is one of only eight cities in the state which
have official "recognized" centers to handle poisoning
cases. The other seven cities are. . . .
```

Here is how the same kind of story was handled by another reporter:

```
A frantic mother called her physician and cried that her
two-year-old had been at the oven cleaner. The child's lips
were smudged with the liquid.
    The label said poison. What should she do?
    Her call set in motion a series of checks and other calls.
In a short time her physician knew precisely what chemicals
were in the cleaner, which were poisonous, and what should
be done.
```

The child was treated and beyond a few small burns on the
lips and tongue the baby is doing well.

This happened the other day, and it was the first case for
the Freeport Poison Information Center in the Community
General Hospital.

Readers can visualize the inquisitive youngster and can identify with the mother's fears and her frantic phone call to the physician. The journalist who wrote the second piece did a better job of writing because his reporting was superior. Also, he contributed a greater public service. The picture he painted is etched in the minds of parents.

The second story is also more appropriate to the event. That is, the material is consistent with the nature of the event being reported. Clearly, the reporter sought material pertinent to the situation, and he wrote it in a style consistent with the event. The average sentence length of the first five sentences, which describe the poisoning incident, is between 11 and 12 words. The next three average 21 words because the reporter was seeking to give an air of calm after the frenzy of the incident. This brings us to the fourth and last of our guidelines for good journalistic writing.

Appropriate Style

Every event has its own tone, texture and pace that good reporters try to reflect in the way they write their stories. They do this through the careful selection of words and the patterning of sentences as well as through the choice of material to be included in their stories. The way a story is written is known as its style. An understanding of style might start with Cicero, the Roman statesman and orator: "Whatever his theme he will speak it as becomes it; neither meagerly where it is copious, nor meanly where it is ample, not in this way where it demands that; but keeping his speech level with the actual subject and adequate to it."

This congruity between theme and speech is what the journalist means by fitting the story to the event. Cardinal John Henry Newman in his book *The Idea of a University* said, "Matter and expression are parts of one; style is thinking out into language."

In a review of Lillian Ross's *Reporting* (New York: Simon and Schuster, 1961), the reviewer, James F. Fixx, says that Ross in her stories shows how reporting can be made into an art. She "somehow makes commonplace things interesting, but she never overdramatizes, never gains falsely heightened effects through dishonest juxtaposition or phony cuteness." He continues:

The result is an uncommon steadiness of tone that seldom lets her writing sink either into banality or that shrieking, supercharged prose that, in the hands of some journalists, makes the reader wonder whether life could ever have been all that exciting. Miss Ross's style is, in fact, a manner of reporting that all but eliminates the reporter.

In this story of a murder, the reporter uses a matter-of-fact style. The short sentences and simple language add to the starkness of the event:

Fight for Hat Cited as Motive in Boy's Slaying

Sixteen-year-old Kenneth Richardson was killed Thursday over a floppy brown hat, police said.

"It was just a plain old hat," Metro Homicide Detective Hugo Gomez said.

Richardson was wearing it. Someone tried to take it. Richardson refused.

Others entered the fray. The youth ran. They chased him.

"It was a running and shooting type thing. They were shooting directly at him," Gomez said.

Richardson still had the hat when taken to International Hospital, where he died in surgery, Dade's 554th homicide this year.

He was shot in the parking lot of the Miami Gardens Shopping Plaza at 12:15 a.m., soon after the nearby Gardens Shopping Skating Center closed for the night, police said.

No arrests have been made.

"They were all Carol City kids," Gomez said. "There was talk of several guns."

About 25 youths were in the area at the time, police say. "But there was nothing but the dust settling when we got there," Gomez said.

–*The Miami Herald*

Since journalists are obliged to tell their stories briefly because of limited space and time, they are aware that they must choose words that count, words that quickly and efficiently paint pictures. Every word, every sentence must work toward the end of telling the reader or viewer what happened. The story is most effective when the journalist selects words in which the denotative and connotative meanings, the explicit and implicit meanings, mesh.

During New York City's financial crisis in 1975, the city appealed for federal aid. President Ford brusquely said no, that the city's profligacy and incompetence had caused its fiscal misery and that it had to put its house in order itself. Pondering the story on the president's refusal, William Brink, the managing editor of the *Daily News,* cast about for the five or six words he could fit into the *News*'s page one headline for the story. He tried:

FORD REFUSES
AID TO CITY

The headline was dull, and the top line was half-a-unit too long. He tried again:

FORD SAYS NO
TO CITY AID

This fit, but it was as dull as the first. Brink recalls that in the back of his mind was the idea that "Ford hadn't just declined to help us. He had, in effect, consigned us to the scrap heap." He then wrote two words on a piece of copy paper. After a few moments, he put three other words above them. The headline:

FORD TO CITY:
DROP DEAD

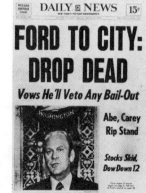

The headline was instantly famous. Television news stations displayed it that night, and *Time* and *Newsweek* ran it in their summaries of the city's plight.

Cicero would have been proud of Brink. The headline was appropriate to the subject.

The key to appropriateness and stylistic excellence is a wide vocabulary and a sensitivity to language that will guide word choice.

For instance, when the treasurer of a large utility is arrested for taking $25,000 in company funds, a reporter can write:

- The *employee* was x x x.
- The *official* was x x x.
- The *executive* was x x x.

Each noun has a different connotation. *Employee* would be appropriate for a lower-ranking worker. Although he is an *official* of the company, the word usually is used in connection with public officials. *Executive* seems most appropriate.

Let us look at some verbs:

- He *pilfered* $25,000 x x x.
- He *took* $25,000 x x x.
- He *appropriated* $25,000 for his own use.
- He *embezzled* $25,000 x x x.
- He *stole* $25,000 x x x.

Pilfered seems to trivialize the event. *Took* is prosaic: we *take* a rest, *take* cream in our coffee. *Appropriated* suggests an official action: Congress *appropriates* funds. *Embezzled* and *stole* are strong words and probably the best to use, properly attributed.

Some reporters play word games in their leisure moments. They make lists of synonyms: wound, laceration, gash; mistake, error, boner, blunder, blooper; car, automobile, limousine, jalopy, hot rod, vehicle; went, trotted, ran, scampered, scurried. Each suggests, implies, connotes a slightly different meaning.

Good reporters are not reluctant to borrow from their notes in English courses. The use of words whose sounds imply the object or action being described is a useful writing device.

- He *babbled* into his beard.
- The knife *slashed* through the fruit.
- The snake *slithered* through the grass.
- He *drooped* in the heat.

This stylistic device is onomatopoeia. Journalists will also borrow metaphor, simile, even hyperbole when it suits their purpose and when it is appropriate to the event.

Style is, Alfred North Whitehead wrote, the best way "to attain your end and nothing but your end." Whitehead said that style, a sense of the appropriateness of the work, is "an aesthetic sense based on admiration for the direct attainment of a foreseen end, simply and without waste. . . . Style is the fashioning of power, the restraining of power . . . with style the end is attained without side issues, without raising undesirable inflammations. . . ."

The stylist is prized in every newsroom, just as an individual style is valued in every field. Fortunately for journalists in the English-speaking countries, the English language has a great number of colorful nouns and verbs.

Yet journalistic writing continues to be dull and flat. Reporters are unimaginative in their selection of facts to use in their stories, and their writing is uninspired. A vapid writing style begets stereotyped observations and vice versa. Compare these two stories about Memorial Day. Determine which one is more appropriate to the event.

Topeka Reminded Of Debts to Dead

An Army general officer and a Navy lieutenant commander reminded Topekans of their debt and responsibility to America's war dead in two Memorial Day services Tuesday morning.

Brig. Gen. John A. Berry, commanding general of Fort Riley, spoke to representatives of 18 veterans organizations at ceremonies at Mount Hope Cemetery.

Earlier, Lt. Cmdr. John G. Tilghman, U.S. Navy Reserve, talked briefly at services on the Topeka Avenue Bridge.

"It is good for us to gather this morning to think of—and thank—those men and women who gave their lives in wars past that you and I may have the full benefits and privileges and responsibilities of our American heritage," said Cmdr. Tilghman.

"Many men in World War II and the Korean War did not always understand all the causes behind the war in which they fought, but they were sure they wanted those of us at home to continue to enjoy the birthright and heritage which is ours, and gave their lives that we might do so.

"You and I must realize our responsibilities in making sure our children and those to come in future generations will be sure of the same promise.

"Today, thousands are fleeing from those who would take away their birthright and their heritage. You and I may someday join their flight unless we get off the fence and take a stand for that which is right—morally right and right patriotically."

Tilghman told his audience protection of its heritage may not always be in combat dress and on a battlefield.

—The State Journal

Fresno Rites Honor Fallen War Heroes

Walk with me early this Memorial Day through the Liberty Cemetery before the ceremonies begin and a thousand feet scatter the dust over these quiet gravestones.

Here are the dead of many of our nation's wars.

A Flag flutters beside each grave and flowers grace them all. No one is forgotten.

Some died in uniform. Others, like Sergeant William J. Dallas of the 2nd Tennessee Infantry in the Spanish-American War, went to war and returned to live a long life—80 years long.

Many stones stand upright, their marble veined with the passage of time. What stories lie behind some of these stones? The passerby cannot tell. The inscriptions simply say:

Michael O'Connor, US Navy, Spanish-American War. Or, in the Civil War section: Isaac N. Ulsh, Company B, 13th Kansas infantry.

Other markers do tell their stories:

Jack T. Martin, Jr., 1922–1942, USS Langley, Lost At Sea.

James S. Waggoner, CEM, USN, USS Kete, 1917–1945, Lost At Sea.

Sergeant Keith A. Matthew, 877th Bomber Squadron, USAAF, 1918–1945, Lost At Sea.

Two Petersons

Side by side are these two:

T. Sergeant Maurice Peterson, 9th Air Corps, 330th Bomber Group, 1917–1944, Ploesti, Roumania.

Sergeant Sterling Peterson, Airborne Infantry, Company B, 1919–1944, Normandy, France . . .

The sun rises higher and friends and relatives of the dead come bearing flowers.

Families come and decorate graves with snapdragons, roses, stocks, hydrangea, marigolds and others. While the adults place the flowers, the children roll in the grass and shout to one another.

Then the ceremonies begin.

Veterans organizations march to the cemetery, and the Colors are massed at the War Veterans Memorial Shaft.

"Let us pray that we may always honor those who have given the last full measure of devotion to their country," Dean Emeritus James M. Malloch says.

"Let us pray that the United States may ever be the land of the free and the home of the brave and the advocate of peace in the councils of nations."

Pay Tribute

At the Belmont Memorial Park, military units stand at attention while tributes are paid to the dead.

Mayor C. Cal Evans reminds the quiet crowd Memorial Day has a new significance, paying "homage to the heroes of peace as well as to the heroes of war."

The main speaker, Legislative Commissioner Ted C. Wills, says:

"Although the bodies of our loved ones are consigned to the earth, their souls have winged their way to the Father in Whose house there are many mansions, where, for all eternity, theirs will be the fullness of joy."

The oratory is carried to the treetops and fades away and the soldiers march off.

–The Fresno Bee

The first story is much like dozens of Memorial Day stories. The oratory, while perhaps passionately uttered, has little emotional impact because it lacks reference to the people most directly involved in the event—the victims of war. The second story teeters on the edge of sentimentality in the lead, but soon settles into understated narrative that seeks to match the solemn nature of the event.

Ten Rules for Writing the News

1. Don't write until you understand the event.
2. Don't write until you know what you want to say.
3. Show, don't tell.
4. Put good quotes high in the story.
5. Put good illustrations or anecdotes up high in the story.
6. Use concrete nouns and colorful action verbs.
7. Avoid adjectival exuberance and resist propping up verbs with adverbs.
8. Avoid judgments and inferences. Let the facts talk.
9. Don't raise questions you cannot answer in your copy.
10. Write simply, succinctly, honestly and quickly.

Journalistic style is more free-wheeling than ever. Much of the writer's new freedom can be traced to the non-fiction novel of the 1950s and the New Journalism of the 1960s. Tom Wolfe, one of the founders of the New Journalism, has written about how he came upon the new style. In a *Wall Street Journal* review of an anthology of Wolfe's works, *The Purple Decades: A Reader* (Farrar Straus and Giroux: New York, 1982), Ellen Wilson describes Wolfe's inspiration:

> In the early Sixties, Tom Wolfe went to the New York Colosseum to cover a Hot Rod and Custom Car show, and came back with the New Journalism. As he tells it in the introduction to "The Kandy-Kolored Tangerine-Flake Streamline Baby," he felt frustrated by his inability to recreate the atmosphere of the show, with its "nutty-looking, crazy baroque custom cars, sitting in little nests of pink angora angels hair," in standard journalese. He needed a style flexible and uninhibited enough to capture everything a straight news story would miss: the carnival atmosphere and the thoughts and emotions of the participants.
>
> He came up with a style incorporating slang and contemporary speech patterns, stream of consciousness and abrupt switches in perspective. The first step was painstaking research and close attention to detail. After that, he was free to select from the novelist's whole bag of tricks.

One way to develop a distinctive style is by way of a suggestion made at the outset of this chapter: Read the masters. Whom shall the journalist read? Begin with the advice of British author and critic Sir Herbert Read in his *English Prose Style:*

Reading for Writers

> The great strength of the English language lies in its splendid array of transitive verbs drawn both from the Anglo Saxon and Latin. Their power lies in their recognition of nature as a vast storehouse of forces. . . . Shakespeare's English is immeasurably superior to all others. . . . It is his persistent, natural and magnificent use of hundreds of transitive verbs. Rarely will you find an *is* in his sentence. A study of Shakespeare's verbs should underline all exercises in style.

Abraham Lincoln, who had little formal schooling but wrote forceful, compelling prose, read Shakespeare and the Bible.

Few journalists realize how much they owe the Bible. Almost every virtue of the prose style the journalist uses can be traced back to the influence of the English Bible: direct simplicity, exactness and economy of language, rapid pace, even the S-V-O construction. The writings of John Bunyan, Emily Brontë and scores of others were influenced by the Bible. Peter Abràhàms, a South African black author, said he had a teacher who "whenever I used big words or made clumsy and almost meaningless sentences, sent me to the Bible. I read the Bible and I saw."

This is no place to make a plea for taking up the Bible. But look at these sentences and consider the possibility of some extra-curricular reading:

- For many are called, but few are chosen.
- Who is this that darkeneth counsel by words without knowledge?
- We all do fade as a leaf.
- Man shall not live by bread alone.
- A word spoken in good season, how good it is.
- The rich rules over the poor, and the borrower is the slave of the lender.
- How forcible are right words.
- Let thy words be few.

Gilbert Millstein, a network television newswriter after jobs with *Time* magazine, *The Saturday Evening Post* and *The New York Times,* recommends reading 19th and 20th century American fiction: Hawthorne, Melville and Nathanael West. Of West's novels he said:

For example, any television newswriter who reads *Miss Lonelyhearts* or *The Day of the Locust* by Nathanael West would find in them an economy and vividness of language achieved without adjectives that would surprise the life out of him. I would offer those two books as models for any person who wants to write factual news. The economy of *Miss Lonelyhearts* is unbelievable. There isn't a single word that could be dropped. The same is true for *The Day of the Locust.* But young people appear not to read these kinds of books anymore.

All reporters have favorite authors and books that influenced them. Fred L. Zimmerman, an editor with *The Wall Street Journal,* recommends Shakespeare, Ibsen, Dostoyevsky, Joyce, the plays of O'Neill and Arthur Miller, and the modern American authors, Updike, Capote, E. B. White, Salinger and Styron. He has read and reread Hemingway's *The Sun Also Rises,* Steinbeck's *The Grapes of Wrath,* John O'Hara's short stories and James Agee's *A Death in the Family.*

Among the magazines reporters read are the newsmagazines, *Time* and *Newsweek,* and the monthlies, *Atlantic* and *Harper's.*

An article in the *Public Opinion Quarterly* states: "There is no single leading intellectual journal and no monolithic intellectual establishment in the United States, but there is an oligarchy of influence. Eight journals—*New York Review of Books, New Republic, Commentary, New York Times Book Review, New Yorker, Saturday Review, Partisan Review,* and *Harper's*—account for 60 percent of the choices of our sample of intellectuals."

Much of what has been said in this chapter has presumed a rational, disciplined approach to news writing. Sometimes, diligent thinking and careful planning are of no avail. The right lead will not come; the exact words lurk just beyond our reach; sentences stumble over each other; and the whole business looks a mess. But the deadline is on us and we have to keep going.

Write, Write and Rewrite

Then—too often only minutes before the edition closes or the newscast is to go on—the story comes together. The theme of the piece is clear. There it was, hiding in the fourth graf. And there, that quote on the second take, the perfect second graf. We toss out four tortured pages; adrenalin flows and the words fly; everything fits; on deadline, too.

Every writer has gone through this scene. Sean O'Faolain, the Irish writer, points out that ideas sometimes become clear "by, and only by, the very act of writing."

Some reporters can function only under this kind of pressure. Given a day to do a story, they dilly-dally until the deadline is an hour off. Then they can write. True enough, they rarely miss their deadlines. But the wear and tear they undergo, and the frenzy their editors must face, is frightening to behold. Better to develop good writing habits now, gradually and without too much pressure, so that on-the-job writing most often is a calm, deliberate process. That means writing, seeing your mistakes and rewriting. The student might heed the advice of Samuel Butler: "It is by doing what you can that you gradually get to know what it is you want to do."

Once you know what you want to do, writing comes easier and is accomplished more quickly. On the job, the reporter must function efficiently. No matter what his or her gifts may be, if the reporter cannot put words on paper before the deadline, he or she will not hold the job.

The managing editor of a Scripps-Howard newspaper fired a beginning sports reporter because he could not finish his stories on time, although the editor felt the reporter was a skilled writer. "On his first writing assignment, Jim was still working on his 'rough' draft while the slotman was asking for the story," the managing editor said. "We do not operate on a schedule that gives reporters time for rough drafts."

Then he advised Jim's journalism teacher that students should be told about the realities of journalism. "Someone within the journalism school should warn students that their first job out of college may not challenge them in any anticipated way," he said. "This is to say there is a lot of tedium and routine involved in many newspaper jobs."

Jim's sad story has a happy epilogue. He went to work for a newspaper in Denver and covered sports and politics and wrote profiles. He did so well that a couple of years later the managing editor who had fired him offered him a job at a considerable increase in salary.

8 Features, Long Stories and Broadcast Writing

Preview

Features are written to entertain. The feature writer lets the actions and comments of the personalities carry the story. Most features follow this structure:

- Beginning—Usually a delayed lead, an incident, example or anecdote that illustrates the point of the feature.
- Body—Additional incidents, quotes, examples plus background.
- Ending—Clincher or climax that sums up the person or situation.

Some editors say there are three types of news stories. Although there are no precise lines that can be drawn to separate the three, they can be distinguished as follows:

Spot news story—Contains material of such significance that it must be reported immediately to the public.

News feature—Uses information that supplements the spot news, usually by providing the human element behind the breaking news event or by giving background through interpretation and explanation.

Feature—Aims to entertain through the use of material that is interesting but not necessarily important.

THE FEATURE

Coverage of spot news takes up most of the news budget of newspapers and broadcast stations. But an increasing amount of time and space is being given over to features.

The Suspect Feature

The feature has had a reputation much like Canadian mining stock, slightly suspect. Although it has worthy antecedents in the satire and parody of poets and essayists who used the pen to attack individuals in public and private life, the feature has been approached gingerly by many editors because of its abuse by the penny press and, later, by some publishers, notably William Randolph Hearst. Most editors have subscribed to the philosophy of Richard Draper, who wrote in his Boston *News-Letter* in the 18th century that he would use features only when "there happens to be a scarcity of news." But the allure of the feature always has been irresistible.

Conservative editors reacted with distaste to the features published by the penny press from the 1830s to the Civil War. Directed to the working class being enlarged by the country's industrial revolution, these inexpensive newspapers ran stories about domestic tragedy and illicit sex, stories that editors like Horace Greeley found unworthy of the mission of journalism. When he established the *Tribune* in New York in 1841, Greeley announced that his newspaper would avoid the "immoral and degrading Police Reports, Advertisements and other matters which have been allowed to disgrace the columns of our leading Penny Papers." But Greeley was soon running some of the material he had condemned in his competitors' newspapers.

The feature story was a weapon in the great circulation wars between Pulitzer and Hearst in New York at the turn of the century. Comics, crime stories, advice to the lovelorn, sports, society, science news—all of it embroidered with sensational details often as much invented as factual—were used to attract readers. This type of feature became synonymous with Yellow Journalism.

The Hearst newspapers were perhaps the most successful of the sensational and flamboyant papers of their day. W. A. Swanberg in his biography, *Citizen Hearst,* describes them:

> They were printed entertainment and excitement—the equivalent in newsprint of bombs exploding, bands blaring, firecrackers popping, victims screaming, flags waving, cannons roaring, houris dancing and smoke rising from the singed flesh of executed criminals.

In the days of Front Page journalism—see Ben Hecht's book *Gaily, Gaily,* which is about Chicago journalism around 1910, when the philosophy was never to let the facts get in the way of a good story—the feature writer's job was to wring tears from the bartender, smiles from the policeman, and gasps of wonderment from the tenement dwellers. The tales of the city as spun out by the feature writers of the day were long on drama, short on fact.

As the United States grew to world power and its citizens had to confront the consequences of World War I and then a pervasive depression, some of the press graduated to more serious pursuits. The feature came to be seen as too frivolous for the responsible newspaper. Newspapers that held on to the old formulas declined in popularity. The Hearst chain dwindled from 22 newspapers to eight.

In 1947, when Joseph G. Herzberg, city editor of *The New York Herald Tribune,* put together a series of essays by *Tribune* staffers for the book *Late City Edition,* not one of the 29 chapters was devoted to the feature story.

A comment by one of the writers may explain the reason: "The last fifteen years, including the late depression and the recent war, have brought an overall improvement, believe it or not, in public intelligence and good taste. A companion phenomenon has been the attraction to the newspaper business of a different kind of editorial employee, educated, serious, ambitious, and frequently competent."

The writer buried, with nary a tear, "the stalwarts of the roaring twenties," those "characters [who] dominated the business in the newspaper towns like Chicago and San Francisco, and were part of it everywhere else."

The problems that have plagued the world in the four decades since World War II have been as serious as those of the darkest days of the depression and the war. McCarthyism, the civil rights struggle, Vietnam, Watergate, and unemployment kindled national confrontations that led anguished citizens to seek an understanding of these problems. As in the earlier decades, the educational system continued to turn out intelligent and inquisitive men and women. This discerning audience demanded a serious journalism that might help it discover solutions. (The story of how such developments spurred CBS, *Time, The Washington Post* and the *Los Angeles Times* to the high levels of journalism they occupy is told by David Halberstam in *The Powers that Be,* New York: Alfred A. Knopf, 1979.)

Editors discovered that serious journalism does not have to be tedious. They rediscovered the fact known to the Greek playwrights 2,300 years ago, that almost all news events have a human dimension. Indeed, it is the human aspect of the event that makes it newsworthy. In his play *The Frogs,* Aristophanes has the playwright Euripedes say, "I made the drama democratic. I staged the life of every day, the way we live." Euripedes challenges Aeschylus, another playwright, "You ought to make people talk like people."

In addition to this humanizing of the news—usually through use of the news feature—editors found that an unvarying diet of seriousness will be rejected by the mass audience. To reach that audience, the newspaper or broadcast station must present a variety of news, the same kind of variety that marks the lives of most of us. There is a time to think about economic problems and a time to laugh at someone's humorous predicament. The news must include a story about how a family of five is faring in the fifth week of a strike that has made the head of the household jobless (news feature) along with a story that reveals how furniture wholesalers show off their new line to prospective buyers (straight feature).

The feature story has come to maturity. In 1978 the advisory board to the Pulitzer Prizes created a new category, feature writing. The guideline is: "For a distinguished example of feature writing giving prime consideration to high literary quality and originality, one thousand dollars ($1,000)."

Nowadays, editors see only a fine line between news and features. Lew Powell, a feature writer with *The Charlotte Observer,* points out, "The distinctions between news and features are increasingly blurred these days.

"Features are busting out of the back-of-the-book ghetto and changing the way stories are written throughout the paper. The old 'Mayor Harris said today . . .' kind of straight news story is just as likely to begin with an account of a testy exchange between the mayor and a councilman or with an analysis of how the mayor's statements fit in with his re-election campaign or with his previous statements."

The fact of the matter is that a well-trained journalist can handle any kind of story in the manner the event demands. That is, if the situation calls for a light touch, the reporter can churn out a feature. If the event is serious, demanding the careful recitation of facts, data, dates, dollars and cents, then the reporter knows how to adjust his or her style to the requirements of the straight news story.

On most newspapers and stations, reporters are expected to do double duty, handling spot news and features. But on some, particularly the larger papers and stations, a few reporters are regularly assigned to handle features.

Laughter and Tears "You have to let readers have a breather now and then," says a midwestern editor who has two full-time feature writers on his staff. "Even Shakespeare has comedy in his tragedies. Our paper serves up death, taxes and disaster day after day. So we use features whenever we can. We know there's more to life than struggle. People need to be able to relax, maybe smile.

"Of course, a feature can also entertain by moving a reader to sympathy or sorrow. Our feature writers are expected to be able to make readers laugh and sometimes shed a tear."

What makes the reader chuckle or cry? This is the feature writer's private misery. Young reporters usually say they prefer to write features rather than hard news because the feature is easier to handle, but this is the blather of the uninformed. The momentum of the news event carries most spot news stories. True, it is not easy to learn to organize a tight news story, and the skill to devise succinct leads that quickly take the reader to the news point is not easily mastered. But the feature writer must carry these burdens and more.

The feature, by being an exception to some of the rules of reporting and writing, imposes on the writer the task of pioneering in each piece, beginning anew to find form, a story tone, the appropriate words and the telling of scenes for this particular story. Readers demand more of feature writers than of straight news writers, and so do their editors. After all, said an editor, feature writers are given plenty of time to do a piece. It had better be good.

The Rules The few rules for feature writing cut to the heart of writing itself:

- Show persons doing things.
- Let them talk.
- Underwrite. Let the action and the dialogue carry the piece.
- Keep the piece moving. This requires a plan that gives the piece a beginning, a middle and an end.

Few reporters have ever gone wrong by making the individuals in their stories carry the action. But this requires a discerning eye and a discriminating ear. The telling action and the illuminating quote must be caught if the feature is to tell us something about ourselves or our friends.

When reporters were assigned to cover the opening of an off-track betting parlor in a prosperous suburb of New York City, most of them were content to report such obvious facts as the size of the crowd and the name and address of the first bettor on line. Leonard Levitt of *Newsday* resisted the routine and did some checking about the 62-year-old grandmother who was first in line. He did not want to settle for the obvious. As good feature writers know, no feature can be any better than the reporting. Snappy writing cannot sustain the under-reported feature.

Through interviews with the woman, her husband and children, Levitt learned that the woman was a chronic gambler who bet $50 and $100 a day. Her husband told Levitt, "It was hard when the kids were growing up. I used to hold three jobs." The woman told Levitt, "My husband doesn't approve of my betting. Neither do my kids. None of them bets. But they love me." In these few quotes, a family's tragedy is unfolded.

The feature writer also sees the absurd and hears the preposterous. In his piece about the Southern Furniture Market in High Point, N.C., where the new styles in furniture are previewed each year, Lew Powell tells us about Dr. Samuel Dunkell, "psychotherapist and author of the bestselling 'Sleep Positions.' " Just to make sure we know this event is hardly the stuff of which significant news is made, Powell sets the mood for Dunkell's findings in the first paragraph:

> Today in Washington reporters are awaiting Koreagate revelations. In Memphis, the latest on Elvis. In Minneapolis, the Billy Graham audit. In High Point we're crowded into a mattress showroom waiting for the inside poop on sleep positions.

From the serious to the silly. Powell does this in a few sentences. The words "inside poop" tell the reader that what follows in going to be fun. And that's what Powell provides:

> Enrico Caruso slept with 18 pillows. Neil Sedaka rubs his feet over each other. The late Hannah Arendt, author of "The Origins of Totalitarianism" and not someone you'd expect to be spilling this kind of stuff, favored the "water wings" position.
>
> And have we got a photo opportunity for you! As Dunkell discusses the "royal" position, the "flamingo," the "mummy," the "sphinx" and the "swastika," model Norma demonstrates. Her yellow sleep-shirt keeps riding up, ensuring undivided attention. When she's joined by a male model for the "hug" and "spoon" position, a sockfooted TV cameraman clambers onto an adjacent Maxipedic for a better angle.
>
> "Republicans sleep face down, Democrats on their backs," Dunkell says. Scribble, scribble. "Surprisingly few people fall out of bed—perhaps 20 percent in their lifetime." Scribble, scribble. . . .

The furniture piece, Powell says, was not totally lacking in redeeming value. The reader, Powell says, "may have painlessly learned something about the workings of one quirky corner of the world of commerce."

The feature writer must see universals as well as aberrations. What is there about this soccer player, that pianist, this dancer with dreams that strike chords common to all of us? The feature writer knows that great writers inspire us to see ourselves, as in Tolstoy's Natasha, Fitzgerald's Nick Carraway and Melville's Captain Vere. The feature writer must be open to human experience. As an art critic said of Rembrandt, he "rejected nothing human."

Most of us are curious. As youngsters, we took apart the kitchen clock. Later, we experimented with the forbidden; and as adults we wonder about each other's lives. What are we missing? What are the others doing? The feature writer understands this curiosity and envy and gives us some answers.

A Tale of Cheerleading

Frank Barrows, a sports writer for *The Charlotte Observer* had, like other fans, been watching cheerleaders for some time. He decided to do a piece about the acrobatic young men and women who lend color and excitement to the moments between plays and the intermissions between periods. Nothing earthshaking about that. But because of the probable interest in the feature his newspaper allowed Barrows enough space for 2,500 words. Barrows followed the cheerleaders at Clemson University as they prepared for an October game. Barrows knows that many people wonder what kind of youngsters these are who will spend hours doing calisthenics to prepare for their brief hour upon the stage. Are they really the empty-heads some presume them to be? The feature writer often offers another perspective of subjects people think they know something about. He interviews one of the cheerleaders:

> George Langstaff lounges at Sourdough's Sandwich Emporium, a subs-and-beer hangout near campus and talks cheerleading. . . .
>
> "You'd think," he drawls flatly, "cheerleaders would be real outgoing people, willing to do crazy stuff anytime, just to get attention. That's what you'd think, isn't it? Well a couple of us were kicking that around a day ago and we figure the people we've got for the most part are quiet. They're not true introverts—but they need something to help them climb out of themselves. It's easy to cut loose when 12 others are there. And they want to cut loose once in a while. So they're cheerleaders." He shrugs. "I think I'm like that."

Barrows' quotes sound authentic. He knows that the people in feature stories must be made realistic. We accept the cardboard cutouts that straight news stories make of our officials and others in public life. The characters in features must be individuals. After all, this is why they are being written about—it is their individuality that makes them interesting.

Feature stories must be written with care, for they are often held for days, sometimes weeks, until space opens. (At *The Wall Street Journal,* features are called "evergreens" in recognition of their perpetual freshness.)

This individual touch brings joy to an editor's heart. Confronted by the dull prose of the usual local or wire news story, the feature is like the single rainbow trout in a creel of brown trout.

Good and Bad

Asked to assess several features in his newspaper, an editor came up with the following evaluations, beginning with the personal touch that the feature should show:

"This story has the writer's signature on it, the kind of writing touches that make the story have a personal hallmark. There is also a relaxed feel to it. The reader glides through the piece.

"This next story has vivid writing that at times becomes eloquent. The writer has a good eye for character and scene, an ear for the language of the people interviewed. The youngsters speak differently from the school principal."

Turning to a couple of less successful features, he said:

"The construction is too loose. Just because it's a feature, there is no need to have a loosely constructed story. I think the reporter failed to arrange his thoughts carefully. As a result, they were not clearly in his mind throughout the writing.

"This other one is also on the wordy side; worse, it's glib, slick, too smooth. You get the feeling that the reporter really doesn't care about what he's writing about. Sometimes features come out that way, as writing exercises rather than as interesting ways to tell a story."

The novelist Philip Roth could be describing the well-crafted feature in this comment about one of his books: "*The Great American Novel* exists for the sake of no higher value than comedy itself: the redeeming value is not social or cultural reform, or moral instruction, but comic *inventiveness*."

To Barrows, careful planning of the feature is essential.

Planning

"Simply because a feature is not written to be cut from the bottom—as a news story might be—does not mean that the material can be randomly set down on paper," he says.

"For a feature to be something other than puffery, you must do the type of serious preparation and thinking that leads to organization. For instance, you might not want to put all the straight biographic data in one place."

Barrows knows that such material is usually tedious. Beginners tend to bunch up background. More experienced hands break up background like biographical material and place bits and pieces into the moving narrative.

For example, Barrows says, when a reporter comes to a place in the story where he or she is showing how the person's hometown influenced his life, that is the place to put something about the person's birthplace and a few other details of his upbringing. In other words, the ordinary background details are spotted into the ongoing story.

Another fault of beginners is the leisurely pace they set at the outset of the piece, as though they are feeling their way toward the theme of the story.

"Too often in features the writer does not tell his reader soon enough what he or she is writing about," Barrows continues. "A long and involved anecdotal lead is okay, but you must somehow slip in the first few sentences what the story is about, then proceed with the anecdote."

On his feature about cheerleaders, Barrows left no doubt about the subject of the piece. It began this way:

The subject is cheerleaders. And obviously, the matter is nothing to trifle with.

Look at how Eric Lawlor of the *Houston Chronicle* slides the reader right into his piece about a truck stop restaurant outside town. He sets a scene in the first paragraph, pulls us into the restaurant in the second paragraph, and in the third paragraph we meet a waitress who introduces us to a dialogue that, while not exactly out of *Hamlet,* gives us a good idea of what goes on at the truck stop:

The truck stop on the North Freeway is ringed with rigs. Trucks glide past one another with the grandeur of sailing ships: 16-wheel galleons bearing—not spices from the Indies or gold from the New World—but auto parts and refrigerators.

Truckers weave as they enter the restaurant; like sailors on shore leave, they are still finding their legs.

Tina Hernandez, an 18-year-old waitress here, serves an order of ham and eggs.

"Where are my grits?" asks the recipient.

"You don't get grits unless you ask for them," she tells him. "If you want grits, you gotta say, 'I want grits.' "

If this sounds unnecessarily acerbic, it's not, in fact: Tina and her customers are actually fond of one another. An affection that masquerades as good-natured abuse.

"Give me a bowl of split-pea soup,"

says a man whose face looks curiously flat. Perhaps someone sat on it. "Is there any meat in there?"

"There's meat in there all right," says Tina. "The problem is finding it."

"How are you and Billy (not his real name) doin'?" he wants to know.

"We don't talk anymore," says the waitress. "He got scared. Just checked out."

"Oh, I don't believe that. I'll bet you are goin' out and just don't want anyone to know about it."

"I'm tellin' ya: that man is scared of women."

"Maybe, he just doesn't like YOU," offers Myrtle, another waitress.

At a nearby table, a driver is telling a colleague about a recent fling.

"I had to leave her finally because she was so cold-blooded. You could get pneumonia sitting next to a woman like that."

With the arrival of new telephone directories, bells ring in the memories of many editors, and they respond by assigning a reporter to do a feature on the entries. Here's how Mary Voboril of *The Miami Herald* began her piece:

Lyons and Tigers and Bears and 293 Foxes are ensnared in the White Pages of the new edition of the Greater Miami Telephone Directory, the annual gift from that mythical matriarch known as Ma Bell.

A record 1,679 pages contains every listed human customer from Faye Aaker to Vladimir Zzzyd—plus corporate clients with such names as the Aaaaaall Together Escort Service, My Refugee Market and Your Island Dream.

The 700,000 customers in the area can Dial a Maid, a Meal, a Translator or a Jewish Story, but it still takes a long-distance call to New York City to Dial a Joke.

Have a message for Garcia? Good luck—there are 40 columns of them.

There are Blacks and Whites, and Thelma, Latin. Laurel and Hardy. Salt and Pepper. Sainte and Sinner. Manet and Monet. A Kitchen but no Sink. Lots of Gays and a few Straights. A Freud, a Jung—and, in the two-volume Yellow Pages, 10 columns of psychiatrists.

Southern Bell spokesman Don Mathis is unsure which is the most common surname in the directory these days. His betting still is with Smith, though Gonzalez may be closing in—if it hasn't already taken over.

Southern Bell's hired help began distributing the first of three million telephone books Friday and will be unloading 80,000 to 120,000 of them a day for the next two to three weeks . . .

In another feature story, this one about a school for bartenders, Eric Lawlor of the *Chronicle* gets right down to business, thrusting the reader into the classroom:

Using All the Techniques

> K. C. Stevens is explaining the difference between a godfather and a godmother.
>
> "To make a godfather," she tells her class at the Professional Bartenders School, "use amaretto and scotch. A godmother, on the other hand, combines amaretto and vodka."

Then Lawlor steps back for a few paragraphs to let the reader survey the scene, telling us something about the teacher and her students:

> K.C., a onetime barmaid, has been teaching people to mix drinks for four years now.
>
> "I didn't want to find myself at the age of 40 wearing orthopedic shoes behind some crummy bar," she says. "Being a bartender is a young person's game."
>
> Her class nods agreement. If that isn't to exaggerate this barely perceptible movement of heads. This is a pretty lethargic group. They slump at the school's mock bar as if drink had ravaged them. They wouldn't look out of place in Pompeii.
>
> It's hard to imagine these people doing anything as animated as tending bar. Indeed it's hard to imagine them doing anything as animated as standing up.
>
> K.C., a good soul, is inclined to agree.
>
> "A lot of them are spaced off somewhere," she says. "I was telling a couple of them just this morning, 'Look, you're gonna have to put more time into studying.' But once they get the picture, things usually work out. Many people come in here expecting to party. They don't realize there's a lot of work involved."

From the first sentence, the reader is as hooked on this story as an alcoholic on his gin and tonic. This is the object of the writer who seeks to entertain readers—grab them and keep them reading. Move the reader along with quotes and action.

Lawler goes on:

That's putting it mildly. To qualify for certification, these students must memorize 150 cocktail recipes and learn to mix as many as eight drinks in no more than 10 minutes. That's 75 seconds a drink. Try it sometime. It's not easy.

This is a class of six—three males, three females. Two of the guys are about 45; the others are in their early 20s.

One kid looks hardly old enough to drink. Another is barely visible when she goes behind the bar.

At what stage in this 40-hour program will these people begin to resemble bartenders?

"Early next week," says K.C. "This crowd is just starting out, but come Monday, you won't recognize them. And by the time they finish, well, you'd think they'd been bartenders all their lives.

"For the first couple of days, I just tell them to relax, to take it easy until they can find their way around."

For the moment, these incipient bartenders wander about like wraiths. They blink at the bottles ranked eight deep in front of them and handle their glasses as if they were live grenades. Movements are clumsy—so many bulls in so many china shops. Glasses are filled until they overflow; drink is sloshed onto counter tops; garnishes roll onto the floor.

K.C. is now taking them through Lesson 6: Hot Toddy, Hot Buttered Rum and Irish Coffee.

"Put these on your recipe cards," she says. "They're served where it's cold and snowy." It's 93 degrees outside. "They're not popular down here," she goes on, "but go up North, and they'll run you crazy."

The young blonde in the class yawns.

"But Irish coffee is popular most places. You'll get lots of sweet old ladies weighing 400 pounds ordering them instead of cheesecake. They don't know that cheesecake has only 400 calories; Irish coffee's got 750.

"Irish whiskey is fairly potent," she warns, "I want all of you to see how much I put in this cup." The cup passes from hand to hand, and student after student peers inside. It might have been the Holy Grail.

"And now we're going to talk about customer service." K.C. continues. "We're going to talk about money. And let's not forget what keeps us in this business: It's the money; the green stuff.

"If you can hook someone on your Irish coffee, he's going to come back for more. And he's going to tell his friends about you, and they'll tell their friends. And how do you do that? How do you personalize a drink?"

"With a garnish," someone says. K.C. looks gratified. It's the answer she'd been looking for. And more important, a sign of life.

This story has already run 750 words, almost a full column of type, and there is more to come. But few readers will quit now. The story will run another 500 words, and most readers will go on reading. Why?

If we can answer the question perhaps we will make a start toward understanding what makes a good feature.

First, the subject is interesting. Even if you can't tell a Hot Toddy from a Hot Buttered Rum—and care less—you wonder about these people who stand behind bars and are able to throw together scores of different concoctions from the amazing array of bottles behind the bar.

But even the most interesting subject in clumsy hands will be dulled. Lawlor is not awkward. He knows what he is doing. Let's analyze his craft.

The reader is put into the action.

The quotations are vivid.

The descriptions are colorful.

Back to the story:

These students are virtually assured of finding work.

"Frankly, we have more jobs than we have graduates," says Alex Tarasenko, the school's director and "resident maniac," as he puts it. "Houston is a boom town." And boom towns tend to drink a lot.

"A barman can make as much as $15 an hour. That's real good money."

Bartending attracts nomads, people with road hunger.

"A barman can go anywhere," says K.C. "He can go anywhere in the country and always find work."

What kind of people make the best bartenders?

"It helps to be crazy."

On the radio, Heart is shrieking its way through *Barracuda*. The din is merciless.

A recent graduate comes by to give K.C. a bottle of grand marnier. It's a present.

"Didn't I tell you I'd give you this?" he says.

"You sure did."

"I gave you my word. My word is my bond."

"Get me a glass," says K.C.

"Wow," he says, "she's gettin' fancy."

She pours him a little. And he likes it.

"Hey, this is nearly good enough to make me give up Irish whiskey."

"What brand do you drink?" she asks. "Murphy?"

"Hell, no." he says. "Murphy ain't worth nothin'. You can buy that stuff for $1.98 a gallon. I drink Bushmills." Now that's a man who knows his drink.

K.C. is back at the bar again.

"I'm going to show you how to make a Good 'n' Plenty," she says. And pauses.

"Didn't you love to eat Good 'n' Plentys at the movies when you were a kid?"

The question is intended to put the class at its ease. Inexplicably, it has the effect of making it acutely embarrassed. People shift in their seats, cross and uncross their legs, bob their knees, tap their feet.

K.C. looks crestfallen. Obviously, this ice is thicker than even she can have realized.

Desperate measures are called for. She looks in the direction of Alex who springs into action.

"Want to know how to lift three cordial glasses without using your hands?" he asks.

The trick is fairly elaborate and would require considerable skill to describe. When he finishes, Alex has one glass in his mouth; two others are stuck to his forehead.

It works a treat. Suddenly, people are talking to one another.

The blonde and one of the middle-aged men are getting on like a house on fire.

"Hey," K.C. tells him. "Your wife just called. She want you to pick up some Pampers on the way home."

It's not true, of course. K.C.'s joking.

Tone and Style

In any discussion with feature writers, the words tone and style come up often. This is the voice of the piece, and it is determined by the nature of the event or the person being interviewed. The tone of the piece on the bartending school is light, relaxed. A feature writer uses one tone for a piece about a classical guitarist, another for a guitarist with a rock group. Tone is established by selection of facts, quotes, illustrations, by word choice, length of sentences, even by the length of paragraphs. The rock musician may be quoted in short, one or two sentence paragraphs to match the rock beat, whereas the classical musician's quotes may run on longer to give the reader the sense of the sonority of classical music.

The profile of a businessman who crashes big parties will have a humorous cast to it, whereas the profile of a survivor of the Holocaust who recalls the concentration camps will be written in somber grays, the sentences running longer than those in the profile of the businessman. The choice of verbs will be different too. The piece about the businessman will have short, crisp action verbs. The rule about avoiding the intransitive verb "to be" may be broken in the other piece in a deliberate effort to underplay the reporter's writing and to allow the source's quotes to carry the piece.

The tone of this piece about a pool player is clear from the outset:

His complaint is stated with a mixture of annoyance and pride: Larry Lisciotti says nobody wants to play with him.

This sort of rejection might be hard for someone with a weak ego to live with. Fortunately, Lisciotti, master pool player, suffers from no such complex.

Lisciotti (pronounced Liscotty) was world pool champion in 1976, and by self-assessment, is among the top five in

the world at any given moment. "Any of us could beat each other," he says of those he deigns to admit are in his league.

Larry Lisciotti, 31, affects a demeanor of studied nonchalance. He can be clever and playful, but his basic nature, if rubbed away to its foundation, is that of a wily risk-taker.

This is no surprise. He has been living by his wits for years. He has never held a job, but instead has learned to make a neat living by exploiting his athletic and mental skills and the various suckers he has met along the way.

"There's no money in pool," says Lisciotti with irritation. "They have a lot of tournaments, but they're small. The first prize will be maybe $1,500 and second prize $1,000," he says. "If you have to travel and spend a week, if you come in second you break even." The tournaments he says, are just for prestige. . . .

The reporter, Barbara Shulgasser of the *Waterbury* (Conn.) *Republican,* is writing about a fellow who lives by his wits, and so Shulgasser is, in turn, witty. She realizes her source may be engaged in an occupation few mothers would choose for their sons, but she writes respectfully, though playfully, for Lisciotti is a master of his trade, and deserves as much respect as any doctor, lawyer or accountant.

The new field of neuroscience interested Jon Franklin, chief science writer for *The Evening Sun* in Baltimore. Franklin had been talking to Dr. Thomas Ducker, chief of neurosurgery at the University of Maryland Hospital, about brain surgery, and Dr. Ducker had agreed to call him the next time he planned an especially difficult surgical procedure. Late in 1978, Dr. Ducker called, and Franklin set out to follow the story of Edna Kelly, who was afflicted with what she calls her monster, a tangled knot of abnormal blood vessels in the back of her brain. She was born with the malformation but in recent years the vessels had ballooned inside her skull and were crowding out the healthy brain tissue.

Mrs. Kelly agreed to be interviewed, and she allowed Franklin to use her name. She also permitted Franklin to watch the surgery. Dr. Ducker agreed to cooperate, whatever the outcome of the delicate operation.

Here is how the first story in Franklin's two-part series begins:

A Pulitzer Prize Winner

In the cold hours of a winter morning, Dr. Thomas Barbee Ducker, University Hospital's senior brain surgeon, rises before dawn. His wife serves him waffles but no coffee. Coffee makes his hands shake.

Downtown, on the 12th floor of the hospital, Edna Kelly's husband tells her goodbye.

For 57 years Mrs. Kelly shared her skull with the monster. No more. Today she is frightened but determined.

It is 6:30 a.m.

"I'm not afraid to die," she said as this day approached. "I've lost part of my eyesight. I've gone through all the hemorrhages. A couple of years ago I lost my sense of smell, my taste, I started having seizures. I smell a strange odor and then I start strangling. It started affecting my legs, and I'm partially paralyzed.

"Three years ago a doctor told me all I had to look forward to was blindness, paralysis and a remote chance of death. Now I have aneurisms; this monster is causing that. I'm scared to death . . . but there isn't a day that goes by that I'm not in pain and I'm tired of it. I can't bear the pain. I wouldn't want to live like this much longer." As Dr. Ducker leaves for work, Mrs. Ducker hands him a paper bag containing a peanut butter sandwich, a banana and two fig newtons. Downtown, in Mrs. Kelly's brain, a sedative takes effect.

Franklin's intentions are made clear at the outset. This is to be a detailed account of the confrontation of a skilled surgeon and a woman in desperate need. Franklin takes the reader into the operating room:

Now, at 7:15 a.m. in Operating Room 11, a technician checks the brain surgery microscope and the circulating nurse lays out bandages and instruments. Mrs. Kelly lies still on a stainless steel table.

A small sensor has been threaded through her veins and now hangs in the antechamber of her heart. Dr. Jane Matjasko, the anesthesiologist, connects the sensor to a 7-foot-high bank of electronic instruments. Wave forms begin to move rhythmically across a cathode ray tube.

With each heartbeat a loudspeaker produces an audible popping sound. The steady pop, pop, pop, pop isn't loud, but it dominates the operating room.

Dr. Ducker enters the operating room and pauses before the X-ray films that hang on a lighted panel. He carried those brain images to Europe, Canada and Florida in search of advice, and he knows them by heart. Still he studies them again, eyes focused on the two fragile aneurisms that swell above major arteries. Either may burst on contact.

The one directly behind Mrs. Kelly's eyes is the most dangerous, but also the easiest to reach. That's first.

The first story ends at 11:05 a.m. Dr. Ducker has managed to find and clip off one of the two deadly aneurisms. The second article begins with Dr. Ducker peering into the neurosurgery microscope in search of the second. The going is slow, dangerous.

At 1:06 p.m. there is trouble and Dr. Ducker worries that his patient's heart has been slowed too many times. He decides not to continue. If she recovers, he says, he will try again.

If she survives. If. If.

"I'm not afraid to die," Mrs. Kelly had said. "I'm scared to death . . . but . . . I can't bear the pain. I wouldn't want to live like this much longer."

Her brain was too scarred. The operation, tolerable in a younger person, was too much. Already, where the monster's tentacles hang before the brainstem, the tissue swells, pinching off the source of oxygen.

Mrs. Kelly is dying.

The clock in the lounge, near where Dr. Ducker sits, says 1:40.

"It's hard even to tell what to do. We've been thinking about it for six weeks. But, you know, there are certain things . . . that's just as far as you can go. I just don't know. . . ."

He lays the sandwich, the banana and the fig newtons on the table before him neatly, the way the scrub nurse laid out instruments.

"It was triple jeopardy," he says, finally, staring at his peanut butter sandwich the same way he stared at the X-rays. "It was triple jeopardy."

It is 1:43, and it's over.

Dr. Ducker bites, grimly, into the sandwich.

The monster won.

Franklin was awarded the 1979 Pulitzer Prize for the feature story for his two-part series, the first time a Prize was given in this category. You might want to go back to our four rules for writing the feature and note in the margins of Franklin's piece where he follows these guidelines.

Franklin's story is a news feature, a story designed to throw some light on a subject by emphasizing the human element. Peter R. Kann, a *Wall Street Journal* reporter, found that the facts and figures used in a *Journal* news story about Bangladesh were inadequate to explain that country's misery and despair. He decided on some vignettes and a highly personal approach in a news feature that begins:

DACCA—Bangladesh may well be the world's poorest and most hopeless nation.

An article yesterday reported on some of Bangladesh's many economic and political problems. But facts and figures don't do justice to misery and despair, and so this article offers some voices and vignettes from the land that cruelly, but all too aptly, has been described as "an international basket case."

The Nun's Tale

An Irish nun is visiting Bangladesh, staying at a Christian hostel in Dacca. On her second evening in the city, she steps outside for a breath of air and finds an emaciated baby deserted on the doorstep. She takes the baby in, feeds it, doctors it, bathes it, and then goes out searching for the mother, who is nowhere to be found.

The next morning the nun finds a second starving baby lying in the street in front of the hostel. So she takes the second baby in. Then she goes off to the local police station to report the missing babies and to seek advice.

That advice is to put the babies back in the street or, the police officer says, you will find four more babies tomorrow.

"What on earth am I to do?" the nun says later in the day. "Am I to put them out to starve?"

The news feature usually has its origins in some news event that is worth covering. When Carl Hiassen of *The Miami Herald* dug deeper into the court case involving a doctor and his millionaire wife, he came up with a fascinating tale of greed preying on loneliness. His story begins:

To Dr. Edward Gordon, love meant never having to say he was out of money.

Six years ago, the solicitous Miami Beach physician married a patient who was worth more than $8 million. Her name was Elizabeth Buffum, and she was a lonely alcoholic.

With Gordon, she stayed lonely and she often stayed drunk. She just barely stayed wealthy.

Today, as lawyers doggedly try to retrieve her scattered fortune from all over the globe, the former Mrs. Gordon lies in a Fort Lauderdale nursing home, permanently brain-damaged. Relatives say her life was destroyed by four ruinous years as the doctor's wife. They say it wasn't a marriage, it was a matrimonial Brink's job.

"Unbelievable," says one son, Peter Beaumont. "It's sort of a classic: elderly lady with lots of bucks heads down to Retirement City and gets fleeced by local doctor."

It began as a September love affair. He was 62, silver-haired and single, with a new medical practice in Florida, She was 60, a bit overweight and twice divorced, given to irascibility and depression.

By the time it was over and the details tumbled out in court, the marriage of Betty Buffum to the man she called "my darling Eddie" emerged as a Machiavellian horror.

Buffum said her husband beat her, injected her with tranquilizing drugs against her will, forged her name to get her money, defrauded her of property, sent her to bed with bottles of booze and threatened to institutionalize her forever if she did not obey.

She said she became a stuporous prisoner in her own home. The doctor, she said, even rigged the telephones so she couldn't call out.

Gordon said he did only what his wife told him. He said she was eccentric and unpredictable with her money. He said he tried everything to cure her alcoholism.

A Dade Circuit Court judge decided the evidence pointed to a brazen scheme to strip Buffum of everything she had. The schemer, ruled Judge Harold Featherstone, was Gordon himself.

"The doctor came incredibly close to pulling the whole thing off, had he not been so greedy," says Buffum attorney Alan Greer.

Florida medical officials took action Feb. 17 against Gordon. He has been charged with lying about his criminal history when he applied for a Florida medical license nine years ago—a violation for which he could lose his right to practice.

The doctor has not been charged with any crimes in the Buffum case. Under Florida law, a husband cannot be prosecuted for stealing from his wife.

Gordon's lawyer, Andrew Boros, says his client currently is "traveling out of the country" aboard a ship to Australia. He says the doctor has done nothing wrong.

At this point, Hiassen stops and begins a chronological account, a device many writers use on long pieces:

How It Began

The story begins in autumn 1973, a few months after Dr. Gordon opened his general practice here.

Elizabeth Buffum, Vassar graduate and former Cleveland socialite, had been drinking again. A barman recommended a doctor who could drop by her Surf Club apartment and treat her. His name was Edward Gordon, and he soon became a regular visitor.

The doctor was charming and distinguished, Buffum would say later. She liked his company. During the summer of 1974, she invited him along on business trips to New Hampshire and Australia. They began living together.

Gordon learned this about Buffum: Her assets included an inherited stock portfolio valued at more than $7 million, a 2,400-acre ranch in Arizona, 70 acres of lakefront property in New Hampshire and at least $1 million in cash and jewelry.

He also learned of her fear that the United States economy was about to collapse and her obsessive desire to store much of her fortune abroad. . . .

Notice the devices Hiassen uses to make the reader stay with the story.

The lead is inviting. Nobody, every writer knows, ever tires of reading about love, money and violence. In this story, two of the three jump out at the reader. The third comes soon. Hiassen is using Stanley Walker's description of the three basic elements of news—women, wampum and wrongdoing.

The second and third paragraphs are like the coming attractions at a movie, or the come-on advertising on television. The reader is given a summary of the story's most dramatic facets.

The fourth paragraph drives home the theme: A woman ruined by her marriage. And in the fifth paragraph, a quote is used to sum up the theme.

No student will be able to do as polished a job as this for a while. But by analyzing good feature stories, it is possible to learn how to put them together.

Here is a news feature that appeared in *The Detroit News*. It could have been written as a straight news story. But the writer, Nancy Manser, took the more readable approach. She is writing about the problems that older women face in pregnancy:

She's over 40 and her doctor has told her she's pregnant.

That may be good news or bad news, depending on her reaction to having a child in middle-life.

But, one thing she'll have to face is the increased health hazards to both herself and the child—hazards which younger women usually don't encounter.

Doctors say the primary hazard for pregnant women over 40 is mongolism.

"There is an increase in all birth defects, but nothing as specific as mongolism," said Dr. Milton Goldrath, acting chairman of the department of obstetrics and gynecology at Detroit's Sinai Hospital.

Dr. Goldrath said the incidence of Down's syndrome, or mongolism, in those under 30 is one in 1,500; between 30 and 35, one in 750; 35 to 40, one in 300; 40 to 45, one in 100 and over 45, one in 40.

No one knows why being over 40 increases the susceptibility of birth defects, said Dr. Goldrath.

Through a test called amniocentesis, a technique used for about five years, a pregnant woman can learn if her child has birth defects.

"The amniotic test is used for congenital birth defects and primarily for mongolism," said Dr. Goldrath.

The test, usually done during the 14th and 18th week of pregnancy, involves inserting a five inch hollow needle into the amniotic membrane in the uterus. . . .

Feature Ideas

The feature writer makes journalism out of daily experience. Shopping in the supermarket, the reporter notices the stacks of snacks and gum and other small items near the checkout counter. A story idea pops up, and another. Listen to the reporter think:

How important is impulse buying? How do merchants determine what goes on the bottom shelves, what on the top shelves? Getting back to those snacks: How much do people spend on junk food? What is junk food anyway? Are things like potato chips, pretzels, soda, corn chips junk food? Do students really spend a disproportionate amount of money on such items? How much do Americans spend on potato chips, soda?

And there the reporter's train of thought bumped up against a specific story concept. Going to the files, the reporter finds that annual per capita consumption of soft drinks was 36 gallons in 1978. Wholesale sales amounted to $13 billion. Soft drinks overtook coffee in 1975 and milk in 1976, and at the rate people are drinking soft drinks the per capita consumption of water (now at 58 gallons) will eventually be surpassed.

The reporter then does some arithmetic, translating the gallons into quarts and into glasses. He finds annual consumption of soft drinks in 1978 was 576 glasses a year. Dividing by 365 the reporter gets a glass and a half a day for every man, woman and baby in the land. Next, he will bring the 1978 figures up-to-date for his lead.

Feature writers read widely, looking for story ideas. They also like to listen in on conversations—in laundromats, at lunch counters and in hotel lobbies. And they tend to use much more of what they see and hear than do writers of straight news pieces. Feature writers always keep in mind the first two rules of the feature: Show individuals doing and show individuals talking.

Like everyone else in Buffalo, Barbara Snyder of the *Evening News* was shaken by what became known as the Love Canal disaster. The area around the canal had been used as an industrial dumping ground in the 1940s. But since 1953, homes had been constructed over the area. In 1978, health authorities concluded that the area was a danger zone. An unusually large number of miscarriages had occurred and many babies had been born deformed. An investigation revealed that the area was highly toxic. Residents were told to leave at once, and 300 families were evacuated. Pregnant women in an even larger area were advised to go elsewhere.

"Our two reporters were doing an excellent job covering the news angle," Snyder recalls thinking.

"But one night as I was going home I thought, what would a reader like to know about the Love Canal? I felt nobody was asking the human beings involved how they felt."

Her news feature begins this way:

Fear follows Joann Hale to bed every night.

Fear wakes her up in the morning.

"It just doesn't go away," she says.

Mrs. Hale, 25, is seven months pregnant with her second child.

Two weeks ago her address was 643 99th St., Niagara Falls.

The Love Canal.

As long as she lives she will not forget the day she read in the paper, "Pregnant women must leave the area immediately."

The oozing chemical mess surrounding her house was a danger to her and her unborn child, the paper said.

She cried that day. There have been many tears since.

The Hales were one of the first families to be evacuated. It was the beginning of a nightmare.

"Would it really matter that I moved out of the house at seven months pregnant?" she remembers thinking. "Isn't the damage done already?"

A determined woman, she began inquiring about birth defects. What were the chances for her unborn child?

***

Nobody seemed to have an answer, but she kept asking . . . and asking . . . and asking. . . .

The powers-that-be called her a pest, but she got some answers. They weren't easy to hear:

Some children of the Love Canal area are mentally retarded. Two are deaf. Many suffer physical deformities.

"I think if they had told my husband and I we wouldn't have gone through the tears we did," she said. "When you don't know your mind goes wild.

"You know, up until a few weeks ago I thought this was a beautiful pregnancy," she says quietly. "I don't know if I got the chemicals through me. . . ."

A Short Feature: A Man Beset

A feature story need not be long. By making every word count, a reporter for *The Fresno Bee* captured the mood of a man beset by a problem:

Ben Karp is a patient man. Like most of us he can shrug off life's little onslaughts in hopes of a better day.

But Karp has been shrugging and dodging and hoping for six months now, and his patience finally snapped. He called the *Bee* and asked for a reporter to see him at his general merchandise business at 1837 Mariposa Street.

"Very important," he said. On the scene, Karp whipped off his hat, pointed a slightly trembling finger at a brownish spot the size of a half dollar on it and then wordlessly pointed skyward.

There, cooing happily and roosting comfortably in corners and on window sills, were pigeons. Dozens of pigeons.

"I've called the mayor, the public works commissioner, the health department," Karp said. "They promised me to do something. Nothing is done. It's ruining my business. People don't like to walk in here past that line there.

"I'd like to get a shotgun and scare them off. But you can't shoot a gun in the city. The health department says it can't do anything because it can't prove pigeons carry disease. The humane society says I can't trap or poison them. The mayor's office says he was going to have a meeting on it. Nothing happened.

"This is bad for the city, I tell you. Thousands of people go in and out of the bus depot and they see this and I hear them say to each other, 'Fresno can't be such a clean city. Look at this.'

"I don't blame people for not wanting to come into the store. What can I do about it?"

And Karp looked up at his feathered friends and shrugged.

Spotting the Feature

Some of the ideas that pop up are natural features. But how is a beginner to know a natural feature from an idea that will bomb? Here are some suggestions culled from the advice of *The Charlotte Observer* feature writers.

The story must have a good plot. This usually means the idea must be rich in human interest. The interviewees must be interesting enough for the reader to take notice.

The situation should be unusual, unique. If it is a commonplace, then the reporter should be able to find in it facets that most of us do not usually see. This shared discovery makes good copy.

The idea should be dynamic. It should have possibilities for conflict, drama, contrast, excitement.

The story should benefit the reader. If it's about people, for example, it should allow the reader to learn about how others conduct their lives.

Land Mines on the Way to a Good Feature

- Overwriting: Often the results of trying too hard for effect. Sometimes the result of inadequate reporting.
- Overreporting: One good anecdote or quote that proves or illustrates the point is enough.
- Concern for the subject: Be fair and give an accurate, complete and balanced account. Do not sacrifice facts for effect. But do not be overly concerned with at the subject will think of the piece.
- Bogging down in background: Look for the highlights of the career, the situation. A year-to-year, or day-to-day account fogs the point, bores the reader.
- Lack of guts: If everyone says your subject is a tightwad but still a charming guy, say so. Give the full profile, blemishes and beauty.

Avoiding the Pitfalls

The feature writer who botches a story suffers the agonies of those who make public spectacles of themselves. Since the feature aims to appeal to the widest readership possible, when it fails it collapses in full view. In the newsroom, colleagues excuse the spot news writer's failures more readily. After all, breaking news is written under pressure of deadline before all the facts are in. The feature writer has plenty of time to report and write and usually is given ample space.

To avoid the pratfalls to which feature writers are susceptible, here is some advice from several writers, beginning with Mark Twain, the country's greatest humorist.

"There are several kinds of stories, but only one difficult kind—the humorous," Twain wrote in an essay, "How to Tell a Story."

"The humorous story depends for its effect upon the manner of the telling. . . . The humorous story is told gravely; the teller does his best to conceal the fact that he even dimly suspects that there is anything funny about it."

The following suggestions are from a dozen feature writers around the country:

Single-source stories are rarely as good as multi-source stories. No one cares to read about the author who talks about his life, unless this personal perspective is supplemented by interviews with fellow writers, critics, his family, friends, maybe even some readers.

Do not have such a love affair with quotes that you fail to paraphrase dull material. Worse: Do not use quotes chronologically from the interview as a prop for failing to organize the piece. Good features can be written that are almost all quotes, but the quotes in many of these stories are drastically reorganized, a quote from the last part of the interview going into the lead, followed by what might have been the first words of the source in the interview.

Know what you are going to say, and the tone in which it is to be said before starting. Otherwise, the story will never get off the ground.

Develop an enthusiasm for the piece. Sometimes features are marred by an objectivity that keeps the reader at a distance. "The idea of a feature is to involve the reader," one reporter said. "But this is often taken to mean good craftsmanship through bright and colorful writing, the use of many anecdotes and quotes. Period. That's not enough. In many features, the writer needs to take a point of view, not simply to say, 'Look at this guy who was put into an institution for the retarded at the age of six, and when he was 18 some worker in the place saw that the kid wasn't retarded at all but had a learning disability.'

"The writer of this kind of piece has to be indignant at the tragedy. How can you be objective about this kind of inhumanity? A reader should be moved to indignation, not by the reporter's sounding off. We don't want that. But this kind of piece has to have the kind of facts and a story tone that gives a strong sense of human waste and bureaucratic inefficiency."

THE LONG STORY

Preview

■ Reporting: Develop the theme as quickly as possible so that material can be gathered relevant to it.

■ Structuring: Organize notes under the main theme (lead) and sub-themes that have been written on cards. Organize cards and notes in the order the story will take.

■ Writing: Find a tone or style appropriate to the theme. Use ample quotes and action to keep the reader interested.

Newspapers have responded to the clear advantage of broadcast journalism in covering the spot story by emphasizing reporting in depth. This has meant that newspaper reporters need to be able to handle series of stories and complex pieces that run more than 900 words. Broadcast journalists who do documentaries also must master the techniques essential to handling the long piece.

A simple recital of events is not enough for the long story. Readers, viewers and listeners will not waste time on a lengthy story or documentary unless the reporting has developed insights for them and the writing is a cut above the pedestrian prose often accepted in the short news story written under pressure. Thorough reporting and high-quality writing are two essentials of the long piece.

When John McPhee, whom many consider one of the best reporters in the country, was at *Time* he wrote many of the magazine's longer pieces. "Each had to have a beginning, a middle and an end, some kind of structure so that it would go somewhere and sit down when it got there," he said.

This is the third requirement exacted of reporters who take on long pieces: The story must be well-organized. Let us examine these essentials of the long piece: perceptive reporting, precise focus and good writing.

The Reporting   "The first point about reporting a depth story," says Jeffrey Tannenbaum of *The Wall Street Journal,* "is that it usually requires a lot of work. For a profile of Rockefeller University, I conducted at least 20 interviews in person, and the typical interview lasted 90 minutes. I also did several more interviews by phone and read a great deal of background material from the Rockefeller files and from news clips."

The long story, he says, "is an interplay between the specific and the general." By general he means the themes that the reporter has selected as the basis of the piece. A story about a breaking news event may have one or two themes. The long story may have half a dozen. Specific refers to the material that amplifies the themes.

"For every generalization or theme in the story," Tannenbaum continues, "there should be specific illustrations to buttress it. This means the reporter has to identify his or her themes and then must dig out the proof for them. The more specific and colorful the details that are used as proof or buttressing material, the more effectively the generalization or theme will be brought home to the reader."

Proof and buttressing material can consist of anecdotes, quotations, observations and pertinent background. But before the reporter can gather these, he or she must determine the heart of the story, its main point or major theme. Like all experienced journalists, Tannenbaum tries to sketch out his theme as soon as possible. This may come before any reporting is done, or soon after the reporting begins. It can come from a tip, an editor's assignment, the reporter's hunch. Or it may simply be the logical step following a series of developments on a beat.

After his first few interviews, Tannenbaum had a theme in mind for his Rockefeller piece: The institution's scientific freedom was being threatened by changes in its financial status. "From that point on, I pressed in interviews for material—the more colorful the better—to buttress my theme. I needed to show how wealthy Rockefeller University once was and how it was now comparatively less well off. I needed to show in detail the problems that had developed as a result. At the same time, I still had to convey a sense of what Rockefeller is like and what its accomplishments are.

"For each key point, I want two things: Good quotes stating the point and colorful illustrations, anecdotes, examples," he says. "I knew exactly what I was looking for from each subsequent interview subject."

In the reporting, additional themes will develop often, and these, too, must be buttressed with specific quotes, illustrations, data and anecdotes.

In a story Tannenbaum did for the *Journal* about violence in junior and senior high schools, his main point or major theme was that school violence is increasing:

> Acts of violence—shootings, beatings, rapes and strong-arm robberies—are cropping up with unnerving frequency.

This sentence occurred in Tannenbaum's third paragraph. Like many long pieces, Tannenbaum's had a delayed lead. He began the piece with the most telling of the illustrations his reporting turned up:

> In a second-floor washroom at Franklin D. Roosevelt Junior High School in Cleveland, four pupils recently cornered a 15-year-old classmate, Kenneth Wagner, and authorities say the foursome executed him by firing six rifle bullets into his head.

Tannenbaum used other incidents to illustrate the themes in his story. At Nottingham High School in Syracuse, N.Y., when black students and white students were fighting in the cafeteria, the principal tried to restore order. He was cracked over the head from behind with a chair.

Statistics are essential in a story of this sort. They provide conviction. Tannenbaum found government data that showed a seven-fold increase in pupil attacks on teachers and a two-and-a-half-fold increase in pupil attacks on other students.

The *Journal* wants reporters to include a "significance paragraph" high in their stories, a few sentences telling the reader why this story is important. Tannenbaum wrote that as a result of "growing violence, students in a number of cities face not only the increased possibility of being physically harmed but also near certainty that the quality of their education will suffer."

The idea that school violence affects learning needed buttressing, and so Tannenbaum sought out an authority to shore up the conclusion, and he wrote:

> An atmosphere of violence, says Richard T. Frost, director of urban studies at Syracuse University Research Corp., which has studied violence in the schools for the U.S. Office of Education, "mortally threatens the capacity of some schools to educate anybody."

Elsewhere, he quotes a seventh grade teacher at Franklin D. Roosevelt in Cleveland saying that violence "adds to the anxiety of the children—they're always anticipating something's going to happen, and then they begin to fear getting into arguments and spats."

If the story describes a problem, the reporter must find out what is being done to solve it. Tannenbaum learned that school security forces are being increased, city police in some cities are assigned to school grounds, and changes in the curriculum are being made with student participation.

Organizing the Story

The major difficulty writers have with the long story is controlling its several themes and ideas, the half dozen building blocks that must be arranged in logical and interesting order. It is not easy. McPhee says he goes "nuts trying to put it all in focus."

McPhee's first step is to structure the piece by typing up his notes and organizing them by subject or theme. He then types the themes on index cards and tacks them to a bulletin board. Some reporters spread their cards on a flat surface. The story is plotted by arranging the cards in the order that seems best for the story.

By attaching the typewritten notes to the appropriate cards with the thematic material, the reporter has the story laid out in a form easy to scrutinize and to rearrange if necessary. This physical arrangement tends to give the reporter a sense of control over the story, and control of themes and reporting detail is the key to mastering the long piece. The long article must move logically and coherently from beginning to end, from idea to idea.

Wayne Booth, of the University of Chicago, was distressed by the inability of writers—college students and experienced writers—to join thematic conclusion and factual material (the general and the specific) in their written works so that the articles had logical movement. He wrote:

> The simple painful task of putting ideas together logically, so that they "track" or "follow" each other, as we say, doesn't seem to appeal to many of us anymore. I once heard Professor George Williamson of our English Department explaining his standards for accepting articles for *Modern Philology.* "I can't really insist on anything that could be called a 'standard'," he lamented. "I'm happy if I can find essays which show some kind of connection between the conclusions and the evidence offered."
>
> You don't have to read much of what passes today for literary criticism, or political argument, or social analysis, to recognize that the author's attention has not been primarily, or even secondarily, on constructing arguments that would stand up in a court of law. Leslie Fiedler spoke at Chicago a couple of years ago and said that all the younger generation is really imitating Negro culture, and that the cultural warfare between what he calls palefaces and redskins accounts for our literature today. I protested to a student afterward that Fiedler had offered no evidence, no proof. "But that doesn't matter," the student replied, "because it was so interesting."

For Booth's "arguments" the journalist can substitute the words proof, buttressing material, illustrations, quotes. If the journalist is to convince the reader that the themes of the piece accurately portray the reality of the event, the piece has to be much more than merely "interesting." The article must have the convincing detail that comes from directed reporting. Then, it must "track," as Booth puts it.

The system of organizing copy suggested here may not work for every reporter. Some reporters do not need to write out their plan but can keep it clearly in mind as they write. Others need only to jot down a few words to remind them of the themes and the order in which they will be handled.

Whatever the method, organizing is essential. All stories begin with some kind of organization: "First the idea. Then the words." Strange as it may seem to the beginner anxious to set words to paper, structuring the story challenges a reporter's creative talents as much as the writing.

"What's most absorbing is putting these stories together," says McPhee. "I want to know where I'm going from the start of the piece. It's my nature to want to know."

The following system is useful in the organization of material for the long, magazine-length article:

1. Identify all themes. Summarize in a sentence or two.
2. Place each theme on a separate index card. Put the cards in the order that the themes will appear in the story.
3. Cut up notes by theme and place them next to cards. Arrange cards and notes in the order they will be used in the story.
4. Look through the cards for the major theme for the piece and write this on a card that will serve as the lead or the integrating idea for the article.

Writing Preparations

As the notes are lined up (Step 3), a reporter may discover that he or she does not have adequate documentation or illustrative material to buttress some of the themes. More reporting will be necessary.

Good reporters check their notes thoroughly at this stage for the high-quality quotes and illustrations that can be placed high up in the various sections of the story. One might be used to begin the article if the piece lends itself to a delayed lead. Some reporters use a colored pencil or pen to mark these quotes, anecdotes and incidents so that they are highly visible during the writing.

Caution: Resist the temptation to use a dramatic quote or telling incident simply because it is attention-getting. The material must illustrate the theme it accompanies. If the fit is loose, put the example with a more appropriate theme or toss it out, however much work went into digging it up, however exciting the material.

Remember: Keep clearly in mind or in view the major theme for the piece (Step 4). Toss out any material that clearly is irrelevant to this integrating idea.

Changing Directions

Once the organization of the story is completed, do not assume that the structure cannot be changed. If the piece does not seem to be flowing properly, shift some of the elements around.

Some of the other problems that come up are:

- A theme is too big and unwieldy. *Divide it into sub-themes that can be handled more easily. Consider dropping, or at least drastically subordinating, some themes.*
- A theme is too minor to be worth the space being given it. *Blend it into another theme or discard it.*
- The transition from one theme to another is awkward. To go from one theme to another smoothly, *reorder the themes so that the linkage is more natural.*
- A long block of background material does not move; it impedes the flow of the article. *Break up this background, history, explanatory material and blend it into the narrative.*

A discerning student might think the last piece of advice contradicts earlier instructions about organizing the story. It was said that the story should be broken into several building blocks. The background of the event or situation would certainly seem to be an important part of the article, one of the blocks. It is. But background can also be dull. A clump of dates and history can be boring.

Look at this paragraph in a long article about an evangelist:

> The search for miracles is virtually an American tradition. Throughout American history and literature, "the quest"—for hope, for answers, for reasons and fulfillment—has been a pervasive theme. In the 18th century. . . .

This could be the beginning of a long historical section. But the reporter, Mary Ann Wallis, is aware that every so often she must move the reader back to the present, to the faith healer, Bishop Bryant in Yonkers, about whom she is writing. After another paragraph of history, she writes:

> But the hope of fulfillment through religion and a longing for miracles has always been a consistent example of the American quest. Bishop Bryant's revival service, with its thick stifling air of expectation, was a symbolic microcosm of this American theme. . . .

Then another paragraph of background and history—enlivened with quotes and anecdotes to keep the reader's interest. Wallis then describes the current religious revival, the Jews for Jesus, Catholic Charismatics and the born-again Christians:

> The Born Again reject the unemotional nature and conservatism of staid Catholic and Protestant church services.
> Like the congregation in Yonkers, they celebrate their new-found faith with loud, boisterous services, filled with frenzy and emotion. These Christ-lovers say the reborn experience is a joyful one. They insist Christians must shout out their love for the Lord and put down the traditional ways of conventional religion.

Notice how Wallis slipped into the background paragraph the phrase, "Like the congregation in Yonkers." She is constantly aware of the necessity to blend the major theme of her story—the Yonkers evangelist—with the background to keep the reader's attention on the theme of her piece, the Bishop.

The poet Ezra Pound spoke disparagingly of those who "seem to think that a man can write a good long poem before he learns to write a good short one, or even before he learns to produce a single good line." The same could be said of the reporter who attempts a long article. The art and craft for doing the shorter piece must be under the reporter's control first. McPhee trained for his long-article writing by mastering his craft at *Time.*

"I must have written 200,000 words a year," he recalls. "Writing teaches writing."

Every writer hews to his or her craft every day. Students have fewer writing demands on them than the professional journalist and thus must impose writing quotas on themselves—500 to 1,000 words a day, even if the writing is for a personal journal. Such discipline is not easy. Tongue only half in cheek, McPhee says that sometimes he ties himself to his typing chair with a sash.

"If anyone has an alternative to writing for a living, he should take it," he says. "No writer likes writing. And it gets harder the older you get. I do get a kick out of writing—about two minutes a day."

These are the words of a master craftsman who knows the terrors of confronting the empty sheet of paper in his typewriter with a mind equally empty. But he also knows the ecstasy of filling that page, and those precious few minutes make the anguish worthwhile.

The task is made easier by unremitting work. As Norman Podhoretz, an editor and writer, says, "Articulateness on paper is a gift which does not differ in principle from the gift of physical coordination we call athletic skill; like muscle, it needs to be exercised not only in order for it to develop but because it exerts a pressure of its own on the possessor to use it, to keep working it out, and to no special purpose beyond the pleasure of feeling it function as it was meant to do."

One of the most difficult tasks in writing the long piece is finding a distinctive tone and style. This search precedes the writing. Podhoretz says: "The act of writing can be controlled by that magical key, a key in that it is musical. It is the tone of voice in which this particular piece of writing will permit itself to be written. To find that tone is to unlock the floodgates."

Writing in *The New York Review of Books,* the critic Nigel Dennis says, "Where good prose is concerned, there is the all-important ability to match the words to the chosen tone—to know the key that the subject requires."

The key or tone may be matter-of-fact, analytical, reserved. We would use this for a long piece about a technical subject. A lengthy profile of an old sea captain might call for a relaxed, anecdotal style. A piece about the author of mysteries might itself mimic the mystery style of writing.

Though it is good to have the style in mind before writing, often only the act of writing makes the writer receptive to the proper tone. "It's a matter of waiting for sentences to sound as I wish them to sound," says McPhee.

If there is a single difficulty the writers of long pieces have, it may well be the inability to keep from straying. Given all that space and having done all the reporting, it is no wonder that the long article tends to become diffuse, to lack focus. Reporters

The Writing

Story Tone

insist on tossing in everything they have turned up in their reporting so that the story sometimes has the appearance of a kitchen sink after a meal has been prepared: potato peels in a corner, onion skins under the tips of beans, a discarded ear of corn, the ends of carrots and some discarded fat from the roast.

The story should be like the meal set on the table, not the remnants in the sink. Everyone who sets words on paper for a living goes through the anxieties of cutting back, of discarding quotes, of tossing out details. Once the theme is set, cutting and discarding are essential. But this cannot be done until the theme is clearly identified. Let us watch the producer of a television documentary as he tries to focus on a theme for his complex subject, the decline of many of the country's older cities.

A Television Documentary

The deterioration of the inner city has had the attention of planners, politicians and journalists since the 1950s. If the city is civilization, then the troubles afflicting the city cores of Detroit, Cleveland, Philadelphia, Boston, Baltimore, St. Louis, New York and dozens of others threaten a way of life—cultural, commercial, educational, religious. For in the cities are the opera houses and philharmonic halls, the factories and the offices, the schools, and the churches and the cathedrals. The city gives a center to life.

To make journalism out of the decline of the older cities is no easy task, even for local reporters whose concern is a single community. The decline is the result of complex social, political and economic forces. The reporters with a national audience have even greater difficulty. They cannot write about all the cities in trouble. They must make one or two illustrate the plight of the many. They must draw from the tangled problems of many cities their common elements and then find a city that symbolizes most of these elements.

When Howard Weinberg, a producer of "Bill Moyers' Journal" on the Educational Broadcasting Corp. network decided to look at the near-collapse of the inner cities he cast about for some central themes and a city to symbolize them.

Before any reporter can begin writing, he or she must conceptualize the story, define the scope and the limits of the piece. With long articles, this planning is especially important. The reporter doing the long piece may also want to settle on a point of view. These decisions enable the reporter to develop the ideas that will direct the reporting toward a defined goal.

Weinberg's idea was to show the forces, especially racism, at work in causing neighborhood deterioration.

"I went to Chicago," Weinberg says. "My associate and I spent a week there, interviewing realtors, mortgage bankers, open housing leaders, community leaders, journalists, government officials and others on the south, west, north sides of Chicago."

When he returned to New York he felt frustrated. He had no idea how he would tell such a complicated story in half an hour. Tentatively, he decided to use the neighborhood of Austin on the west side where black and white community groups had organized to preserve and improve their neighborhood. Also, a woman organizer, Gale Cincotta, lived in Austin, and Weinberg wanted to have an individual as a focus for the program.

"In discussions with Bill Moyers, I was forced to rethink and refine my outline," he says. Weinberg had too many ideas to cover in 30 minutes. In looking back at his original outline, Weinberg found he had written, "It is beginning to be understood in communities of the inner cities that deterioration is not an accident, it is the inevitable result of a lack of faith. Expect deterioration—and you'll get it."

This idea of a self-fulfilling prophecy kept coming back to Weinberg, and he continued to do more reporting by telephone. Gradually, a theme and a strong point of view emerged.

"It became clearer that 'redlining' was the story I wanted to tell, not the FHA abuses, not the efforts to relocate blacks in the suburbs or to 'stabilize' a threatened neighborhood."

Redlining takes its name from the red circles banks and other lending agencies reportedly draw on maps around neighborhoods that the lenders decide will not be given mortgage money. The practice makes it difficult for residents to improve their homes or for buyers to come into the neighborhood. Neighborhood deterioration usually results.

Weinberg was struck by the material he turned up in his reporting.

"A savings and loan association was licensed to serve a neighborhood—and clearly, it was not doing that when it openly admitted that it received 80 percent of its deposits from its neighborhood and reinvested 20 percent in its neighborhood," Weinberg says.

Weinberg visualized the booming suburbs—which the savings of inner city residents was helping to build—and the deteriorating inner city. This would make dramatic film.

He decided to shift the main focus from Austin to Rogers Park, which was beginning to go the way of Austin. He used the woman organizer in Austin as a link to move the viewer from Austin to Rogers Park.

Here is how the script of "This Neighborhood is Obsolete" begins:

BILL MOYERS: The skyline of Chicago thrusts a handsome profile above the shores of Lake Michigan, suggesting the serene self-assurance of a city and its architecture, its wealth and its power and its tolerance for new ideas in urban living. But opulent skylines point up and away from the reality in their shadows. And in Chicago, as in every large American city, the grand vista is misleading.

Out beyond the soaring, secular temples of commerce, before you reach the shopping centers of suburbia, the future of Chicago is being decided every day in less spectacular surroundings: in neighborhoods where drugstores and delicatessens, taverns, laundromats, barbershops, and small churches on tree-lined corners express a life-style in danger of extinction.

For the way the economic game is played these days, these neighborhoods hardly have a chance. There's a profit in moving people out and hang the human cost.

In the next half hour, we'll look at two Chicago neighborhoods where the neighbors are fighting back.

I'm Bill Moyers.

This neighborhood is obsolete.

The people who live here don't think so, but some of the banks and savings and loan associations do. They stopped lending money because they believe the community's deteriorating and the risk is too great. But without money to improve people's homes or to give them a chance to buy another, the decay speeds up and the fear becomes a self-fulfilling prophecy.

In this and similar neighborhoods in Chicago, people accuse the savings and loan associations and the banks of redlining. Redlining means an entire geographic area can be declared unsuitable for conventional loans and mortgages. A redline is, in effect, drawn like a noose around a neighborhood until for want of good housing the working and middle classes are driven to the suburbs and the neighborhood is left to the very poor.

A side effect of redlining is something called disinvestment. You probably haven't heard of that term before. I hadn't until I came here. Disinvestment is a process of collecting deposits in one neighborhood and investing them somewhere else. The lending agents say it's necessary to spread the risk, but it leaves a neighborhood like this short of capital and hope. Gasping for its very life.

The people who could afford to, move on. And that's what the savings and loan associations would like to do. After they've helped to build up the suburbs and make them affluent and attractive, they want to move there, too, or at least to open a suburban branch. Only then does an old neighborhood like this discover where its money has gone, but by then it's too late.

MARY LOU WOLFF: This federal savings and loan is the largest savings institution in the state of Illinois. It's the leading savings and loan that sets the tone for the rest of savings and loans that will not give us money for our neighborhoods. Okay? The savings and loan industry has got to take us seriously. We are not kidding around. . . .

Like much good journalism, the documentary and the campaigns of local stations had results. The month after the Moyers' documentary, the Illinois Savings and Loan Commissioner issued a regulation against redlining. The regulation prohibits savings and loan associations from refusing to lend money in a neighborhood because of its age or changing character. The following year, Congress passed the Home Loan Mortgage Disclosure Act, which requires lenders to list the location of their mortgages for the public's scrutiny. Disclosure, it was felt, would help to end redlining by the banks.

Notice that Weinberg had to reduce his ideas to the dimension of his program. Strange as it may seem, reporters who are assigned long pieces find that they must do just what they do when they sit down to write a 300-word story or a 30-second news item for the 6 p.m. news—focus on a single theme and toss out all extraneous material. The journalist never escapes the chore of selecting from the vast array of material available the quotations and examples that help to animate the theme he or she has selected as the organizing concept for the piece.

That basic theme can always be expressed in a simple sentence or two. David Belasco, the American theatrical producer, once remarked, "If you can't write your idea on the back of my calling card you don't have a clear idea."

Some writers prefer to work on their own rather than put in an eight-hour day in a newsroom. These article writers are known as freelancers. Some do this full time, and others use freelance writing to supplement their income from other work. The freelance market is competitive: Freelancers compete with each other and with the staffs of the publications for which they hope to write. Here are some suggestions about developing markets for freelance articles. The advice is offered by Wilmer C. Ames, Jr., who has written articles on a freelance basis and is on the reporting staff of *Sports Illustrated:*

Freelancing Articles

1. Read the magazine for at least the previous six issues before submitting anything, even a query letter. This will allow you to familiarize yourself with its style, its contents, the types of articles published, and how many are written by staff writers as opposed to freelancers. This will also tell you how much space is allotted to a particular subject.

2. Study the masthead. Determine, through as much investigation as is required, which editors handle which sections and subjects in the magazine. Once you do get an assignment this will help you to know what the particular editor expects in a story. This will also provide you with some indication as to which editor has the most power on the staff (something that is important when a freelancer's story is competing against a staff writer's).

3. It is probably always best to send a query letter the first time around. This should be written as carefully as one would write the finished article. In fact, all of your basic research will probably have been completed by the time you sit down at your typewriter to compose the query letter.

4. The most difficult job to do when breaking into a magazine, is to find an article idea that either an editor or a staff writer has not already come up with. Your idea should be something that lends itself to the magazine's format, and is not so timely as to necessitate immediate publication. Make it newsworthy, but make sure it can sit in-house until the powers that be decide they have the space to run it.

5. From the very beginning, treat everyone nicely that you come in contact with. Most secretaries are important to an editor—they sometimes not only screen unsolicited manuscripts, but also unwanted phone calls. They can either help or hinder you. When your letter or copy comes in there are many things they can do with it. The better they feel about you, the more quickly and gently your copy will be handled.

6. Again, after you are given an assignment, it is important to have studied the style of the magazine in order to make sure that your piece will be done similarly. Don't worry, initially, about showing your specific style. The most important thing is that your piece be able to fit in the magazine's pages. After you've gained some recognition with the editor as a competent writer, then is the time to take liberties with your copy.

7. Part of your job is to be more thorough than a staffer. Do all of your homework before talking to an editor about a piece—*you* have to sell him on your knowledge and your abilities.

8. Be neat. An editor may say he doesn't mind typos in your copy, but you never know who will see it and pass judgment on it. Besides, the less someone can find fault with something the better he or she may feel about the article.

9. Call in periodically after the assignment has been completed. Volunteer to make any changes necessary, to help with the research, and to assist in any way you can. While you're writing, check in with the editor and let him know how things are developing. But don't make a pest of yourself.

10. Don't fight against making changes on your first few articles—at least until an editor respects your abilities and knowledge. Editors will only deem your objections an obstacle to their work, and you a pain.

11. It is not unheard of to rewrite copy, especially for a freelancer. Initially you may find it difficult fitting into a magazine's style.

12. Always be prompt. The only thing a freelancer has, initially, is his or her reputation, and the most important part of that reputation is dependability. If an editor says a piece needs to be in-house on a specific date, be sure to have it in or notify the editor well in advance that a problem has arisen and it might be a little late. Remember the managing editor is depending upon the senior editor and the senior editor is depending upon you. If the M.E. gets angry with the editor, the editor will get angry with you. A freelancer always has the most to lose.

13. Remember that most magazines are ethical organizations, and will at least give you the opportunity to write the article and then to rewrite it if necessary. They will not steal your idea or assign it to a staff writer. If you fail to deliver what they need, they may then buy you off and assign your idea to someone else to write.

14. Maintaining contact and establishing a casual relationship with "your" editor after a story is completed is very important. Remember there are many others out there who also want to appear in print, so it is important for an editor to always have you at the top of the list.

BROADCAST WRITING

Preview

Broadcast stories are written to be understood quickly and easily. Radio and television writers:

- Use everyday language.
- Write short sentences that follow the S-V-O sentence structure.
- Use the present tense for most sentences.

Broadcast news takes its form and its format from the fact that it is written to be read aloud by newscasters and to be heard or seen by listeners or viewers. This means that stories are written to rules considerably different from those for print journalism. Copy is prepared differently and stories are shorter and are written in a conversational style.

Tune in a radio station and time the items on a newscast. Watch the evening news, stopwatch in hand. Most of the "tell stories"—stories read by an announcer or reporter without film or tape—are short, one to five sentences running 10 to 40 seconds. Most hard-news radio and television stories are kept under two minutes. If all the news on a half-hour newscast were to be printed, it would not fill a single page of a standard-size newspaper.

To communicate the complexities of the day's events in such succinct pulses to an audience that cannot read or hear the material again, a special set of rules and a certain state of mind are required.

Like the jockey or the weight watcher who must think twice about every slice of bread, the broadcast journalist has to examine every idea and every word. Each

word and idea must be essential. Too many words and the story may run long and not fit precisely into the timed program. Too many ideas in a news item and the listener or viewer may be confused.

Broadcast newswriters set their writing rhythm to a series of near-inflexible rules. Keep it tight, editors warn their writers. Write simple sentences. Keep one idea to a sentence. Start with the attribution.

Rewriting the Wires

Much of the writing that broadcast newswriters do is actually rewriting. The tell stories and pieces read on camera usually are stories that have been pulled from the news wires and have been rewritten to broadcast style. The news wire stories are compressed, condensed and simplified. Let us watch Mervin Block rewrite a UPI piece into a 20-second tell story for the network news. Here is the wire copy Block had before him:

```
   ROUEN, France (UPI)--Police have arrested a
disgruntled employee who admitted he tried to
slowly irradiate his boss to death by planting
three radioactive discs under the driver's seat
of his car.
   Guy Busin, an executive at a nuclear rod
treatment plant, is the world's first known
intended murder victim by use of nuclear waste.
   Noel Lecomte, 27, who was arrested Wednesday,
told police Busin ''was always questioning me and
```

bothering me'' and confessed that he decided to
kill him by exposing him to nuclear radiation.

Busin was Lecomte's supervisor at the Nuclear
Treatment Center in La Hague near the Channel
Coast, the world's largest plant for the
treatment of nuclear fuel rods.   .

Busin has been under medical observation since
he found the intended radioactive murder weapon
in his car more than a month ago. Doctors say he
apparently suffered no ill effects from the
material except extreme fatigue.

Lecomte told police he was alone in the plant
one night in either May or June of 1978 when he
stole three nuclear discs used to move nuclear
fuel at the plant, and planted them under the
driver's seat of Busin's car.

Busin found the discs March 21, eight months
after they were planted.

He said he had not used the car for five months
because it had been damaged in an accident that
occurred when he was returning home from a
wrestling match.
        ---------=
    UPI 05-10 02:46 aed=

Here is Block's story:

French police say that a worker in a nuclear plant has
admitted trying to kill his boss by planting radioactive
discs under the driver's seat of his car. The worker
explained that he was angry because the boss irritated him.
So he decided to irradiate the boss. But the boss discovered
the deadly discs in his car. He seems to have suffered no
harm, except for extreme fatigue.

Here is how Block says he thought the story through:

I start off by establishing the location of the event with "French police." I
wouldn't use the name of the town because even if I did use it, what would it
mean to listeners? They wouldn't know where it is, and if I had to tell them I
would be taking up valuable time.

The second paragraph of the UPI story says the executive was the world's
first intended murder victim by use of nuclear waste. I avoid all absolutes and
superlatives: the first, the biggest, the highest, the most, the least. How would
anyone know? Who keeps track of that?

I wouldn't use the name of the executive, nor of the suspect or his age, or
the name of the plant or the site. Incidentally, site is a word to avoid in
broadcasting because it could be confused with sight.

Obviously, the story was of no great significance but was used because of its bizarre nature. This gave Block some liberty to featurize the piece. "If I were writing it today with more time," Block said, "I would restructure it. I think the script would have been improved if I had put the two sentences, 'The worker explained . . . irradiate his boss', at the end of the item."

"Newsbreak" runs on the CBS television network several times a day. In less than a minute, a few major stories are read. One day, Block compressed seven wire stories into 50 seconds. Here is his script (left) and his explanation of how he did it (right):

A former
employee
of the
Westchester
Stauffer's Inn,
~~outside~~
near New York
City, was
arrested today
and charged
with setting
the fire
that killed
26 corporate
executives last
December.

Rather than start a story with a place name, "In White Plains, New York," I always try to fix the place up high but unobtrusively. In the fifth line, I wrote "outside," then realized that "near" is closer and shorter. I didn't use his name because he was an unknown and his name wouldn't mean anything to anyone outside White Plains, which is largely unknown itself except as the site of a Revolutionary battle.

The
government's
index of
leading
economic
indicators
~~rosexslightly~~
~~lastx~~
last month rose
slightly, one-
point-four
percent. The
increase
reversed three
straight months
of declines.

To save words, I didn't say the U.S. Department of Commerce issued the statistics. It's sufficient to say "the government." In the fourth line, I originally wrote, "rose slightly last." Then I caught myself, remembering Strunk's rule to "place the emphatic words of a sentence at the end." (What do the statistics signify? Even if I knew for sure--and probably no one did--I wouldn't have had room to tell.)

235

Pennsylvania
Congressman
Raymond Lederer
said today
he's resigning
because of his
conviction in
the Abscam
scandal.
Just yesterday,
the House
Ethics committe
called for his
expulsion.

Again, a story that a newspaper might give hundreds of words. But newscasts don't have the luxury of roominess. I didn't have space for his party affiliation, his hometown or the particulars of his crime. I did try to put the news in perspective by writing a second sentence. (In my haste, I left an "e" off "committee." When not under pressure, I spell it with ease.)

A British truck
driver admitted
today he was
the "Yorkshire
Ripper,"
pleading guilty
to manslaughter
in the deaths
of 13 women.By
not pleading
guilty to
murder, Peter
Sutcliffe could
be sent to a
hospital for
the criminally
insane--and not
prison.

This is a simple, straight forward, no-frills account of a dramatic development in a sensational story. But there's no need here for any supercharged language to "sell" the story. (As architect Ludwig Mies van der Rohe used to say, "Less is more.") My second sentence gives the "why" for his plea. I underlined "murder" because I thought it was a word the anchor should stress. (Some anchors welcome this. In any case, in the pressure-cooker atmosphere of a network newsroom, the stress is usually on the writer.)

Israeli
warplanes
swept into
action over
Lebanon for
the fourth
straight day,
~~poundingRaies~~
bombing
Palestinian
guerrilla bases
just across the
Israeli border.

This one-sentence story does not
provide details, of course, but
there's no time for details.
Details are secondary. Most
listeners, I suspect, aren't
even interested in details.
Anyway, casualties and the
extent of damage are usually in
dispute. If I'd had word of many
casualties--and I didn't--I'd
have said so.

China announced
today its
population is
982-million.
Next year, it's
expected to
reach a
billion.

This strikes me as a "so what?"
story, especially because for as
long as I can remember there've
been forecasts of China's
population approaching a
billion. I doubt that our
listeners were interested in
hearing this non-news, and I
wasn't eager to tell them, but
we had nothing better to fill
the time.

The world's
Longest-
reigning
monarch,
Hirohito of
Japan, emperor
since 19-26,
today observed
his eightieth
birthday.
~~anniversaryx~~

Another non-story, but as
sailors at sea say, "Any port in
a storm." I used the word
"anniversary" because I was
taught that a person--even a
personage--has only one
birthday, that from then on that
date is an anniversary. My
editor deleted "anniversary."
Apparently, he came from another
school.
Before the last item in a
newscast, some editors and
anchors like to add "and" or
"finally." I don't.

Block was given the following wire story and told to write a lead-in and 20 seconds of voice-over videotape for the CBS Evening News. Here is the beginning of the wire service story:

```
     CRESTVIEW, Fla. (AP)--Tank cars carrying
acetone exploded and burned when a train loaded
with hazardous chemicals derailed here today.
Thousands were evacuated as the wind spread thick
yellow sulfur fumes over rural northwest Florida.
     Only one injury was reported. A fisherman
trekking through the woods near the wreck inhaled
some of the fumes and was hospitalized for
observation.
     Okaloosa County Civil Defense director Tom
Nichols estimated that 5,000 people had fled
homes or campsites in the 30-square-mile
evacuation area, which included several villages
and about half of Blackwater River State Forest.
     "It's a rural area and houses are scattered all
through it," said Ray Belcher, a supervisor for
the Florida Highway Patrol. "It's about half
woods, half farms."
     Civil Defense officials put the approximately
9,000 residents of nearby Crestview on alert for
possible evacuation as approaching thunderstorms
threatened a wind-shift that would push the fumes
in that direction. . . .
```

Block was writing "blind" to the tape. That is, he did not have access to the videotape his copy would refer to. We will see how he handled that problem. Block recalls his thinking:

First, I see the dateline, Crestview, Fla., and I know that in writing for broadcast I have to put the dateline up near the top in as unobstrusive a way as possible. It has to be done deftly.

When I started writing for broadcast, I was told by one of the editors that it's inadvisable to begin a story by saying, "In Crestview, Florida . . .." The editor told me that was a lazy man's way of starting a story. In London today . . . In Paris today. . . . He didn't say never. But in 90 or 95 percent of the cases, it's best not to begin that way.

We see in the first line of the AP story that one of the trains is carrying acetone. My reaction is that most people don't know what acetone is. That probably is a reflection of my lack of knowledge. If we were to use it on the air, it could sound like acid-own. In any case, there's no need to identify the chemical, or any of the chemicals, perhaps. The most important element is the explosion and the evacuation.

In the second paragraph of the story, it says that only one injury was reported. I didn't mention the injury. It seems slight. The third paragraph gives the name of the county. In writing news for broadcast you have to eliminate the details and focus on the big picture.

In my script, beginning with the second paragraph there is silent film and I had to write 20 seconds of voice-over. As so often happens, I had no chance to see the videotape in advance, so I had to write in a general way without getting specific. I made an assumption at this point, and although it's dangerous to assume, I have seen so many derailments on TV films or tape that I figured the opening shot would be of derailed cars. So I presumed my paragraph covering the tape of the accident would be appropriate.

I was looking for facts in the AP story that would be essential in my script. As you can see, my script consists of about a five second lead-in and 20 seconds of voice-over for the tape. Within the tight space I can use only the most important facts because a script cannot consist of a string of dense facts.

Here is the script as Block wrote it:

mb DEAN	A tank car explosion in the Florida Panhandle today led to the evacuation of about five-thousand people ⑦ from their homes.
SIL/VO :20	The explosion was one of several that ripped through 18 cars that derailed at Crestview, Florida.

Several were carrying toxic and explosive chemicals.
Because of the danger of various fumes and the chance of further explosions, officials ordered the evacuation of one-fourth the population of the county.
~0~

⑳

Block rewrote the piece for the next morning's "Today" Show on television:

```
    Several railroad tank cars blew up in northwestern
Florida today, causing the evacuation of about five-
thousand people. The cars were carrying hazardous
chemicals near Crestview, Florida, when they derailed,
exploded and burned. Thick yellow sulfur fumes spread over
the area, and one man was hospitalized. If the winds change,
thousands more might have to be evacuated.
```

He prefers the second version because "northwestern Florida" locates the accident more clearly than the "Florida panhandle."

From our window into the thinking of a broadcast newswriter, we can generalize about writing for the ear.

Sentence Structure and Language

Write short, simple sentences. Use everyday language. Make the structure of most sentences conform to the S-V-O rule: Begin the sentence with the subject and follow it closely with an action verb that leads directly to the object. Keep one idea to a sentence.

- Begin sentences with a source, with the attribution:
  WRONG: The city needs new traffic lights, the mayor said.
  RIGHT: The mayor says the city needs new traffic lights.
- Avoid introductory phrases and clauses:
  WRONG: Hoping to keep the lid on spiraling prices, the president called today for wage-price guidelines for labor and industry.
  RIGHT: The president is calling for wage-price guidelines to keep prices down.
- Use ordinary, one-syllable words whenever possible:
  WRONG: The unprecedented increase in profits led the Congress to urge the plan's discontinuance.
  RIGHT: The record profits led Congress to urge that the plan be stopped.
- Use vigorous verbs. Avoid adjectives and adverbs:
  WEAK: He made the task easy for his listeners.
  BETTER: He simplified the task for his listeners.
  WEAK: She walked slowly through the mud.
  BETTER: She trudged through the mud.
- Use the active, not the passive, voice:
  WEAK: He was shown the document by the lawyer.
  BETTER: The lawyer showed him the document.
- Write simply, directly. Omit useless words. When Block was the in-house editorial consultant at CBS, he issued an occasional bulletin of praise and criticism. Here is some errant writing he spotted. His comments are in parentheses:
  "Boats literally cannot move." (If boats can't move, they can't. "Literally" only adds bulk.)

"While they are in the process of sorting out the nation's economics, Lance and the other Carter appointees are also in the process of rearranging their own financial affairs." ("In the process of" adds nothing but length. Also, ditch "also.")

"Gas officials say the reason there's a gas shortage is because. . . ." ("the reason . . . because" is redundant. Recast this sentence to read: "Gas officials say there's a shortage because the price. . . .")

Simple, direct writing can be elegant. This is the language of Mark Twain, Dickens and Edward R. Murrow. Here is a lead by Charles Kuralt, a correspondent for CBS television who was doing a piece about exploitation of the environment:

Men look at hillsides and see board feet of lumber. Men look at valleys and see homesites.

Some beginning broadcast writers confuse simple, direct writing with simplistic writing. They fall into clichés and trite expressions with the ease of a tired commuter slipping into his or her loafers at the end of a long day. Broadcast writers usually are under pressure to produce large amounts of copy in short periods of time, and in their groping for everyday language they often come up with comfortable, familiar phrases, some of them too familiar. Hear Block on this subject:

"After six days of hearings and 33 witnesses, the Senate Judiciary Committee met late on Inauguration Eve to bite the bullet on Jimmy Carter's. . . ." ("Bite the bullet" is a cliché, heavily gnawed.)

"In the aftermath of a chain of tanker mishaps, the Coast Guard has apparently invested in an ounce of prevention. . . ." ("In the aftermath of" is a cliché; so is "in the wake of." They're wordy ways to say "after" or "following." As for "mishap," it's hardly more than bad luck with slight consequences, so "mishap" is inappropriate for an environmental disaster. Further, "an ounce of prevention" needs a gram of curare.)

"The Supreme Court said this morning that a community does not have to change its zoning laws in order to. . . ." (Skip "in order" unless you're paid by the word.)

Use a phrase to indicate someone is being quoted—as he said, in his words, as he put it.

WRONG: He said, "The industry needs protective tariffs."
RIGHT: As he put it, "The nation needs. . . ."
        As he told the Senate, "The nation needs. . . ."
        In his words, "The nation needs. . . ."

Also: Always keep in mind the fact that the copy is being read aloud. Place titles before names. Spell out all numbers. Do not use initials for agencies and organizations unless they are well known, such as FBI and CIA. Use contractions for informality. Paraphrase quotations unless the quote is essential or unusual. Keep sentences to fewer than 20 words.

Tenses   The anchoring tense for broadcast copy is usually the present or the present perfect tense. At times, it is impossible to avoid the newspaper-writing construction of the past tense with "today." With a little effort, however, it can be avoided.

Present
> The state highway department <u>announces</u> a six million dollar improvement program for farm-to-market roads.

Present Perfect
> The state highway department <u>has announced</u> a six million dollar improvement program for farm-to-market roads.

When the present tense is used in the lead, the story usually continues in that tense. When it is impossible to put the lead in the present tense because the event clearly is not new and no follow-up story is possible for a new lead, then the present perfect tense is used in the lead. The story can then shift to the past tense to indicate when the event occurred:

Present Perfect
> A federal judge <u>has issued</u> a temporary order stopping efforts to put a reservist on active army duty because he refused to shave off his beard.

Past
> District Judge Edward Day in Providence, Rhode Island, yesterday <u>gave</u> the army ten days to answer a suit filed Friday by the American Civil Liberties Union.

Following the past tense, the story can shift back to the present perfect or even to the present tense if the writer believes the situation is still true or in effect. The AP radio story continues:

Past
> The ACLU <u>filed</u> the suit on behalf of high school teacher Edward Leveille of Bristol, Rhode Island.

Present
> The suit <u>asks</u> the court to declare unconstitutional a regulation forbidding beards and <u>claims</u> Leveille was marked absent from several drill meetings which he, in fact, attended.

But shifts from the present directly to the past sound silly, as in this piece from the radio wire of one of the press associations:

Present
> The New Jersey Taxpayers Association <u>says</u> a recent government report shows the state's per capita property taxes are the highest in the nation.

```
The association reported yesterday that only Massachusetts        Past
had a higher property tax average than New Jersey.
```

The writer would have been better off had he used the present perfect in the lead and then shifted to the past:

```
The New Jersey Taxpayers Association has reported that a         Present Perfect
recent government. . . .
```

```
The association reported yesterday that only                    Past
Massachusetts. . . .
```

Avoid complex leads. Remember, the newspaper lead can be reread for understanding. The broadcast lead must be understood immediately or the piece will not make sense. But some events are too complex to plunge into immediately. Or there may be a confusing array of personalities or numbers. The listener then has to be set up for the theme of the piece.

The Lead

> NEWSPAPER LEAD: As President Carter neared the end of his seven-day working vacation aboard a Mississippi riverboat today, White House aides said that he was unconcerned about some editorial criticism that he had become an absentee president whose administration was adrift.

> BROADCAST LEAD: Some newspaper editorials have criticized President Carter as an absentee president. They have contended that his administration has gone adrift. Today, White House aides aboard a Mississippi riverboat with the president said that the criticisms don't bother Mr. Carter. The president is nearing the end of his seven-day working vacation on the boat.

The broadcast lead may read like an old enemy of the newswriter, the lead that backs into the story. But this is precisely what some broadcast stories require—a gradual buildup to the nub of the event.

Conversational Writing

"A script has to be conversational. It has to flow. There has to be a certain rhythm to it," says Block. One way to achieve this, says Joan Bieder, who teaches broadcast journalism at Columbia University, is to read the wire story, turn it over and relate it to a friend or classmate. "In telling the story first, rather than writing it out, the student will approximate the conversational tone required in broadcast writing," she says.

This technique also forces the student to get to the heart of the story so that the point can be made clearly and concisely. In their way, even old hands at broadcast journalism do this when they reconstruct a story. They will talk it out or think it out to themselves—but in a matter of seconds.

Checking the Wire Story

No broadcast writer should go directly from the wire to the typewriter. This is as egregious a fault as that committed by the rip-and-read news announcers. All stories need a calm, deliberate reading and appraisal before use, despite the pressure of time. Haste leads to the acceptance of weak or ambiguous phrasing, clichés or lengthy sentences from the wire version.

If the story has a hole or does not seem to make sense, independent reporting will have to be done. If the writer cannot clarify the story or verify the questionable material and a check of the wire service is not helpful, then the story should be passed up.

The longer pieces on radio and television usually are not rewrites from the wires but are the result of staff-originated reporting. But unlike the print journalist who has a fairly simple technology to cope with, the broadcast journalist contends with a complex technical apparatus. Some critics of broadcast journalism say that the broadcast technology sometimes becomes an end in itself, leading broadcast journalists to differentiate between stories for newspapers and stories for radio and television. True or not, the technical demands on the broadcast journalist are considerable and require careful study.

Reporting and Writing to Film and Videotape

The breaking news story—a fire, a press conference, a major arrest—must be handled quickly and under pressure. The event is stripped to its essentials, a summary of the news and film or tape that elaborates or describes that theme. The feature or "timeless" piece is the product of considerable planning and group effort. The story may include an interview, voice-over silent tape or film, or tape or film with sound of a situation and the reporter summarizing the situation. The two or three minutes that the story runs on the evening news may be the result of days of planning and hours of shooting, writing and editing.

A number of decisions are made in the planning stage of a film piece. Cover or background will be needed. The locations to shoot and who to interview will have to be planned.

For a story on a new reading program in the city schools, an interview with the superintendent of schools may set out the intent of the curriculum change. Additional interviews would allow viewers to hear the specific plans of teachers. School children would be interviewed. Locations might include classrooms, the teachers chatting over the program at lunch, the superintendent in his office. All this has to be planned within the reporting time limits set by the producer of the news program.

The producer is one of the several persons who would be involved with the piece. The camera crew, usually three persons, has to be directed to shoot wide shots to establish the event and the usual array of medium, closeup and cutaway shots that are necessary for the film editor to build a coherent picture story to go along with the reporter's narration and interviews.

The reporter usually deals with a producer who may edit the script. When it is finally put together, and if there is time, script and film are shown to the executive producer, who may choose to change either picture or script yet again before the story is aired.

Editing Decisions

Interviews in news pieces must be short and to the point and represent the essence of the source's thinking or emotions. The three or four minutes of raw film or tape may become not much more than a 15-second sound bite.

The cover footage of the president's boat trip down the Mississippi may contain some excellent natural sound, such as bands on shore welcoming the president as his riverboat pulls up to a river town. Should that natural sound be played full—sound up—and without narration, or should the three or four seconds be played sound under with the reporter using that time for a voice-over film? Which would make the more effective story?

The writer's task is to marry natural sound, visuals, interviews and the reporter's words. Sometimes the writer muffs the opportunity. In a piece about a cloistered order of nuns who vow perpetual silence, the reporter wrote a narration with no pauses. He wrote about silence but never stopped talking. In effect, the viewer could not "hear" the silence. The event would have been captured in its essence had he stopped talking in some places, a few seconds at a time, to allow viewers to hear the clatter of knives and forks at a silent dinner, the footsteps of nuns in darkened hallways.

Packaging Short News Features

In her television course at Columbia University, Bieder uses her own experiences to show how a television reporter, Cathy, puts together a news feature. The story is about a federally assisted program designed to prevent children from committing crimes when they grow up. Cathy has an interview on film of the psychologist who developed the idea behind the program. She has also filmed the children in the program as they talk to the psychologist and play. Cathy has film interviews of the children's reactions to the program.

Bieder describes Cathy's activities after four hours on the scene. As Cathy and her camera crew leave with about 40 minutes of tape, Cathy has to block out the story, which she starts doing on her way back to the station. Here is Bieder's description:

> Cathy knows that if all goes well she has a chance of having it ready for air that night. She will tell her editor to start with general pictures of the children in a circle for 20 seconds while in her script she will give some facts about the project.
>
> Then a 20- to 30-second sound bite from the psychologist explaining the "substitute family" technique. As he talks about the substitute parents, the editor will show pictures of the children and parents greeting each other affectionately.
>
> Then she will write a short transition into the interviews. She thinks that to get into this section she will pose the question, "But does the program work?" and have three or four short interviews with the answers.
>
> She'll close with a good quote from the psychologist for 20 seconds and then her own wrap-up to fill in any holes she feels have been left unanswered. By her calculations, the spot will run from 2:30 to 2:45, just what the producer wants.
>
> The crew pulls up in front of the office, hands Cathy the tapes, and drops her off.
>
> It's not finished yet; it's still a work in progress. But Cathy knows that when she and her editor turn the tapes into "packaged reality," she'll have an effective piece that sheds light on an important story.

Interviewing

Much of what Cathy did was the result of planning. For her interviews, she devised questions ahead of time that sought to get to the heart of the event quickly. Interviews have to be kept short, to the point. This requires gentle but firm direction by the reporter. Here are some rules in use in broadcast writing classes at Columbia University:

1. Don't ask questions that can be answered yes or no.
2. Don't ask long, involved questions—the subject might not understand what you want him or her to answer, and the goal is to let *him* or *her* explain, not to do all the explaining yourself.
3. Build on the subject's answers—don't ask questions just because you prepared them. Listen to his or her answers and ask questions about what he or she says. Otherwise you'll probably end up asking questions the subject has already answered.
4. You need to develop a sense of *TIMING*.
   You need to cut in if the subject starts to get repetitive or long-winded. Yet you must learn not to cut the subject off just when he or she is about to reveal something important.

5. Make the subject comfortable before the interview:
   a. Describe the general area your questions will cover, but don't tell the subject exactly what they will be. The first, spontaneous response to a question is often the truest.
   b. Explain the setting—which mike the subject should speak into and so on. But tell him or her to look at *you* or other questioners—not the camera—unless he or she is going to show the audience how to make a soufflé or do something else that requires more direct communication between speaker and audience.
   c. Chat easily to dispel any nervousness prior to the interview—show some interest in the subject's area so he or she will gain confidence.
   d. Don't act like you know it all—or you will end up looking foolish when the truth comes out. But *prepare,* so you *do* know enough that your subject feels you understand what he or she says. It's a good idea to learn as much as you can about the interviewee and the topic before the subject arrives.
   e. Know what you are looking for. Most short news items are carefully focused because of time limits.
6. Stay on one topic if possible.
7. Adjust the tone of the questions to the interviewee's experience. A politician may need to be prodded and pushed, asked tough and direct questions.
8. If the subject tends to be long-winded, tell him or her ahead of time that answers should be kept as short as possible.

No reporter can anticipate what a source will do, and no one can prepare fully to handle spontaneous events. When John A. Ferrugia, a reporter for KCMO-TV in Kansas City, Mo., was investigating the sale of flood-damaged cars by Allstate Insurance Co., he asked the firm for interviews with officials—without fully disclosing the nature of his story. Ferrugia said he wanted to find out how the company handled claims following the flood.

"Well into the interview, we asked the company official to explain the company role in auto claims. He outlined it, and at that point we laid out material that contradicted everything he said."

Ferrugia had found that open titles were passed on to used-car dealers and that this enabled the dealers to fill in company names and make it appear as though the cars had been sold directly to them. Thus, purchasers had no idea the automobiles were damaged. Many people over the country bought the cars at premium prices as they appeared to be in good shape.

"We wanted to let them know that the shining used car they bought might be mechanically unsafe and could cost them thousands of dollars in repairs," he said.

In his interview, Ferrugia laid out the material he had gathered as the cameras were shooting.

"Cut the cameras," the official suddenly said, and stood up and left.

As a result of the KCMO series, six companies were forced by a state investigation to reclaim flood-damaged cars from all over the nation.

Copy Preparation

Copy is written to give the newscaster as much help as possible. The rules for copy preparation differ from station to station. Some require the slug in the upper right-hand corner and the time the story takes to run above it. The date is lower left and the writer's name is lower right.

Copy for television is written in the right two-thirds of the paper. The left-hand column is kept open for instructions. Some stations also ask that radio copy be written this way.

Depending on the size of the typewriter characters, a line of 45–50 units will take two and one-half to three seconds to read. By keeping lines to the same length, it is easy to estimate the time it will take to read the story without the use of a stopwatch.

End each page with a full sentence. Better still: End on a paragraph. Do not leave the newscaster hanging in the middle of a sentence or an idea as he or she turns the page. Keep paragraphs short.

Each page should be slugged. Numbering should appear in the top left-hand corner:

    Page 11111 of 2.
    Page 22222 of 2.

Place the word more, circled, at the bottom of stories of more than one page, and use a clear, large end mark when finished.

Some stations require copy to be written in capital letters for easier reading, although studies have shown that all-capital text is more difficult to read than cap-and-lower-case. For television, visual directions should be written all caps.

Electronic News Delivery

In many cities, the all-news radio stations have a counterpart in all-news and information cable television channels. The news on these channels is displayed in written form on the screen, sometimes with still pictures. The stories are tightly written, many no more than 40 or 45 words. Known by a variety of titles, these services can be properly called cable news or cable text. Many of these news services often are cooperatives, ventures between newspapers and cable television companies. Most accept advertising, and some offer color. Often, background music is played as the news is flashed on the screen.

Newspapers and cable companies decided to finance home-delivered news and information text because of their belief that people remain interested in the news but are as willing to accept it from a screen as from a newspaper. In 1967, three of four people surveyed said they read a newspaper every day. Fifteen years later, one of those three had stopped daily newspaper reading; only two of four said they read the paper daily.

The newspaper's loss was the screen's gain, but many newspapers want to recapture that lost reader, and perhaps others. They have adjusted to changing times by supplying news, and sometimes personnel, for news on the screen. Large and small newspapers and newspaper chains have arranged with cable television companies to broadcast news. Some offer limited service. In Denton, Tex., the *Denton Record-Chronicle* presents 10 minutes of local news every hour on the "Cable Chronicle." The other 50 minutes are used for classified ads.

Most cable-newspaper arrangements offer international, national and local news on a 24-hour-a-day schedule. The newspaper is the source for the news, which is rewritten for quick visual impact. The news is described as an "extended headline service, a convenience service" by the director of TelePress, which serves viewers in Lexington, Ky.

News for TelePress is provided by the local staff of the *Lexington Herald-Leader*, which is owned by the Knight-Ridder newspaper chain. National and international news is taken from the newspaper's press services. The cable system is TeleCable Corp. Here is the news channel schedule for TelePress:

Time Past Hour	News Type
02	National News
06	World News
10	NYSE Stock list (10 second pages)*
14	Financial News
18	AMEX Stock list (10 second pages)**
22	People in the News
26	Local News
30	Newsbreak
34	National News (repeat)
38	World News (repeat)
42	NYSE Stock list (10 second pages)*
46	Financial News (repeat)
50	People in the News (repeat)
54	Local News (repeat)
58	Newsbreak (repeat/update)

*Weekends replaced with Potpourri
**Weekends replaced with movie reviews

Writing Cable News

The screen, or page, can hold eight to a dozen lines. Each line has 32 characters. Most stories run a page. For major stories, cable news may run two or three pages. A page remains, "dwells," on the screen for 17 seconds.

Let's look over the shoulder of Lisa Power as she prepares news for the morning news program on TelePress.

Power has arrived at 6:30 a.m. and is looking over local and AP copy she has called up on her VDT. Since the *Herald-Leader* deadline is 11:30 p.m., her VDT copy is from the previous evening and so she checks the AP wire in the TelePress newsroom for late national and international developments. Sports scores from late ball games last night are fed into another TelePress channel which broadcasts only sports news.

Cablenews Copy. Lisa Power of TelePress in Lexington, Ky., edits the news story she has written for the four-minute local news program. She cuts all unnecessary words, makes one word do the work of three. Most of the stories she writes contain no more than 45 words.

Power separates local, national and world stories. She knows that she has 12 pages for each of the four-minute segments allotted to each category. She decides which stories she will use and then begins to rewrite. She keeps in mind the TelePress guideline for its news writers: "Stories should be kept simple and written in simple sentences."

Power has to set the first two words of each story in capital letters. "We have to catch the viewers' attention in a few words," she says. "These words have to be real grabbers—like rioting, taxes, murder.

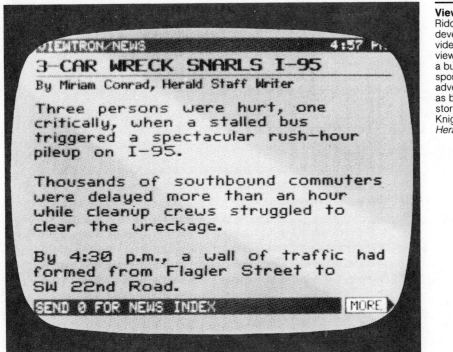

Viewtron News. The Knight-Ridder Newspapers are developing an interactive videotex system which allows viewers to select by touching a button: news, weather, sports, reference material, advertising and services such as banking. Here is a news story based on an article in a Knight newspaper, *The Miami Herald.*

"By writing this way, you end up using the passive voice often, which we are told never to use in journalistic writing."

She takes a wire service story from Washington that begins:

> The White House and Senate Republican leaders agreed Wednesday night on a federal budget compromise that would increase federal taxes over three years by $95 billion. . . .

Her version begins this way:

> TAX INCREASES of $95 billion over the next 3 years are called for in a compromise budget OK'd Wednesday night by the Senate Budget Committee. . . .

Notice that the numeral 3 is used and not spelled out, that she uses OK'd instead of approved or agreed to. Held to 45 words, 32 characters a line, Power saves space whenever possible. The wire story ran more than 500 words. Hers had 45 words.

A local story from the *Herald* began this way:

> PIKEVILLE—A recent decision to
> allow people who hunt with guns to shoot
> male deer near Jenny Wiley State Re-
> sort Park this November is meeting re-
> sistance here, largely from people who
> hunt with bows and arrows.

Power's story begins:

> BOW-HUNTERS are taking aim at a recent decision that
> allows gun-toters to shoot deer near Jenny Wiley Resort
> Park this November. . . .

"A lot of times you feel frustrated because you can't go into detail," Power says. "You have to give the reader enough information in eight lines to make sense. Then, you hope, the reader will go to the newspaper to get more information."

Power has problems with attribution, which takes space. "When you say that rioting broke out in Poland yesterday, do you have to add: 'the Polish News Agency said'? This takes up a lot of space."

TelePress—indeed all of cable news—is novel and has had to solve problems such as attribution. First to go was the AP Stylebook. Too many items are spelled out in the Stylebook. The formal news writing style was dropped because it made for long sentences, long stories.

Power sits in on the *Herald-Leader*'s news conference to learn what stories the newspaper plans to emphasize that day. This helps to put the day's news into perspective for her, although she is not obligated to run the same stories. Then, in the evening, she looks at the CBS Evening News to compare its news judgments with hers.

Power had worked for newspapers in Cincinnati before going to TelePress. She had to unlearn much of her newspaper craft.

"The hardest thing to get used to," she says, "is that you are breaking the rules you have been taught."

Reporting Principles

9 Gathering the Facts

Preview   The reporter's job is to dig out facts and to gather information that help people to understand events that affect them.

This takes the reporter through what we can describe as the three layers of reporting:

- Surface facts: press releases, handouts, speeches.
- Reportorial enterprise: verification, investigative reporting, coverage of spontaneous events.
- Interpretation and analysis: significance, causes, consequences of event.

The reporter is like the prospector digging and drilling his way to pay dirt. Neither is happy with the surface material, though sometimes impenetrable barriers or lack of time interfere with the search, and it may be necessary to stop digging and to make do with what has been turned up. When possible, the reporter keeps digging until he or she gets to the bottom of things, until the journalistic equivalent of the mother lode—the truth of the event—is unearthed.

The reporter, like the prospector, has a feel for the terrain. This sensitivity—the reporter's nose for news—is helpful. In addition, the reporter has access to some tangible guides.

First, the reporter knows that his observations generally are more reliable than those of many of his sources, who have not been trained to see and hear accurately. Nor do some of these sources have the reporter's motivation—the revelation of the truth.

When forced to rely on someone else's observations, the reporter uses various tests for determining the reliability of the source. When the reporter must use second-hand or third-hand accounts—or when he doubts his own observations—he knows where to look for verifying materials.

As the journalist goes about his work of digging up information, he is guided by an understanding of the nature of reporting:

> Reporting is the process of gathering facts—through observation, reasoning and verification—that when assembled in a news story give the reader, viewer or listener a good idea of what happened.

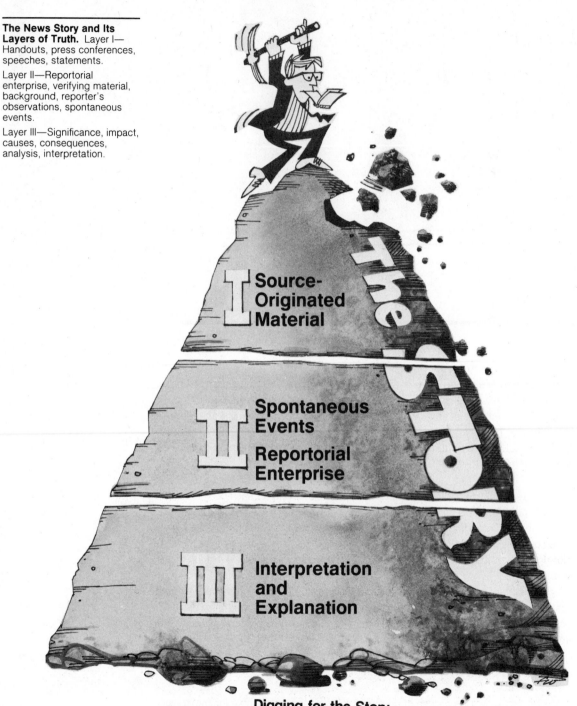

The News Story and Its Layers of Truth. Layer I—Handouts, press conferences, speeches, statements.

Layer II—Reportorial enterprise, verifying material, background, reporter's observations, spontaneous events.

Layer III—Significance, impact, causes, consequences, analysis, interpretation.

I Source-Originated Material

The STORY

II Spontaneous Events

Reportorial Enterprise

III Interpretation and Explanation

Digging for the Story

The reporter's job is to look beneath the surface for the underlying reality. Lincoln Steffens, the great journalist of the muckraking period, said the reporter's task is "the letting in of light and air." Many reporters base their work on the same conviction that guided Steffens: Their job is to seek out relevant truths for people who cannot witness or comprehend the events that affect them. As a member of the staff of *The Washington Post* defines reporting, it is the task of "uncovering the layers of truth that are around us, the layers of understanding that defy us."

Layer I Reporting

Layer I reporting is objective reporting, the careful and accurate transcription of the record, the speech, the news conference. Its strengths and its limitations are those of objective journalism.

Layer I is the source for facts used in most news stories. Information is mined from press conferences, handouts, statements, speeches, declarations, orders, decrees, decisions and opinions. This material originates with and is controlled by the source. Fact gathering at this level of journalism may involve going to the mayor's office to pick up a transcript of the speech he is to deliver this evening or it may involve calling the mortuary holding the body of the child who drowned last night. The stories based on these facts rely almost wholly on information the source has supplied.

Fact gathering at Layer I is the journalistic equivalent of open pit mining. The reporter sinks no shafts into the event, but is content to use the surface material, some of which is presented to him by public relations specialists and press agents. Much of the reporter's task is confined to sorting out and rearranging the delivered facts, verifying addresses and dates and checking the spelling of names. On some newspapers, the task of handling these releases is done by rewrite men and women, because the work is basically rewriting, not reporting. Most stories appearing in newspapers and on radio and television are based on source-originated material.

Manipulation by Source

News organizations, as well as sources, thrived under the arrangement implicit in Layer I journalism. Material for news stories could be obtained quickly and inexpensively by the newspaper or broadcast station. In a sense, the success of Layer I became its undoing. As the mass media, particularly television, became the dominant dispensers of experience in American life, sources sought to manipulate the media for their purposes. They realized that press releases and announcements unaccompanied by visual material of action events would not merit more than 20 seconds on most newscasts, if that. Only a genuinely newsworthy announcement could break into television's preoccupation with action. As a result, sources learned to stage events for the press that resembled spontaneous events (Layer II), but were, in fact, as much under the control of the source as the press release and the prepared speech. These staged events also are known as media events or pseudo-events.

Pseudo-Events   The press shares responsibility for the development of the fabricated event. The press could use the stories and pictures of the first female window washer in San Francisco, even if the event had been dreamed up to publicize the availability of rental space in a new office building. By providing the media with an endless stream of events, the managers of staged events enable the 11 p.m. news to be different from the 7 p.m. news and the afternoon newspaper to take the morning news a step further. The flow of contrived events feeds the insatiable news maw, for the public has been conditioned to demand action-packed, vivid, dramatic news with every newscast and edition. Television stations—creating and responding to the demand—devised news programs with titles such as Eyewitness News and Action News.

Following a presidential State of the Union speech, Russell Baker of *The New York Times* asked one of the president's advisers "if it was not mostly a media event, a nonhappening staged because reporters would pretend it was a happening."

"It's *all* media event," the adviser replied. "If the media weren't so ready to be used, it would be a very small splash."

Daniel J. Boorstin, the social historian, originated the phrase "pseudo-event" to describe these synthetic occurrences. He points out in his book, *The Image, A Guide to Pseudo-Events in America* (New York: Atheneum, 1961, p. 11) that a "larger and larger proportion of our experience, of what we read and see and hear, has come to consist of pseudo-events." In the process, he says, "Vivid image came to overshadow pale reality." His book opens with this short dialogue:

ADMIRING FRIEND: "My, that's a beautiful baby you have there!"
MOTHER: "Oh, that's nothing—you should see his photograph."

Boorstin says the pseudo-event has these characteristics: "It is not spontaneous, but comes about because someone has planned, planted or incited it. . . . It is planted primarily (but not always exclusively) for the immediate purpose of being reported or reproduced. Therefore, its occurrence is arranged for the convenience of the reporting or reproducing media. . . . Its relations to the underlying relativity of the situation is ambiguous. . . ."

Political Manipulation   The orchestration of events for public consumption reached the height of manipulation during the national political conventions in 1972. Aware that millions of potential voters were watching, the GOP party leaders structured their convention for maximum viewer excitement. The stage managing was just about total. Because President Nixon was certain of renomination, Republicans faced a publicity problem: How could reality—the routine renomination of the president—be made exciting? If there were no real drama, how then would the White House press managers keep the public tied to the television screen and how would they be able to provide the raw material from which reporters could fashion their stories?

The GOP's solution was to override reality with a staged event of enormous dimension. The White House wrote a 50-page scenario for the convention, a full script that called for "impromptu remarks" from delegates, "spontaneous" shouts of "Four more years," and allotted—to the minute—screams of enthusiasm. At the moment the president would be renominated, the chairman was instructed to attempt "unsuccessfully" to quell the "spontaneous" cheering.

The document fell into the hands of the press. *The Wall Street Journal,* among others, ran news stories on how the White House had organized the convention for television viewers. As the *Journal's* reporter put it in his story, the "convention was perhaps the most superorganized ever . . . the delegates' only function during the formal proceedings was to serve as a necessary backdrop for the TV show."

The reporter, Norman C. Miller, went offstage and tried to dig up the real story— Layer II. He interviewed delegates, watched a pep rally for Republican women and found no one had showed up at the "Poor People's Caucus."

Media managing has flourished at the state and local levels, too. An article by Richard Kotuk in the *Village Voice* describes how a state legislator used the media for publicity. Accompanied by a television crew and reporters from four newspapers the legislator's publicity man had alerted, the assemblyman drove to a farm on Long Island that was supposedly exploiting migrant workers. After unsuccessfully seeking comments from workers, the camera crew decided to film the assemblyman in action. Here is a concluding section of Kotuk's story of his day with the press and politician:

Then the CBS crew set up just outside the camp, but with the shanties, the kids, the wash on the line in the background. The interview—CBS: "Why are you here?" Stein: "This is a national disgrace! (Motioning to the rotting cabins behind) These people work hard. We're not asking for anything for them for free. They deserve a decent wage." CBS: "What do you hope to accomplish here?" Stein: "I want to get the Legislature to act on workmen's compensation for them, unemployment insurance. And I want a guarantee that the local authorities won't intimidate the United Farm Workers. We want to keep the pressure on. We want the people to know these horrible living conditions exist." The cameras clicked off. Stein mopped his brow.

Riding back to the city, Stein told me:

"This situation has existed for the last several decades. No local authorities, including Duryea, have made any attempt to deal with it."

I wrote dutifully, then put away my pen. Stein turned to his aide. They talked politics. Bobby, Teddy, Lindsay, Herman B., and all the fiery questions of the game.

"I want to keep plugging on this," Stein told me. "I want to keep the pressure up for the migrants."

But later, Orin said softly to Stein: "This is just a one-shot deal isn't it? I don't want to keep driving out to the island."

"Yes," Stein said, "we can't spend anymore time out there."

The city was close, traffic got heavy, Andrew Stein began to think of other things. . . .

News reporters handling stage-managed events rarely do what Miller and Kotuk did, even when the staging is the most significant or interesting part of the event. There has been an unwritten agreement that such events are treated as legitimate news. And to some extent they are, even though the photos are posed, important statements are repeated for the television crews that missed them the first time around,

Reporting the Manipulation

and the entire event is set up to sell something. When reporters heard that Joe Namath, a quarterback for the New York Jets, would have an important announcement at a press conference the next day, a group of them showed up. Namath had just turned down a lucrative offer to jump to another team in a rival league. Would he announce a new contract with the Jets? Fans across the country wanted to know about the plans of the most colorful quarterback in action. What they were told was that Namath was signing a multi-million dollar contract with an international cosmetics firm.

Though they knew they had been taken, most reporters mentioned the name of the firm. One of the few who did not was a sports columnist for *The Press* in Asbury Park, N.J., who advised his readers that if they wanted the name of the firm they could call Namath's agent, and he printed the agent's telephone number.

When Pelé, the Brazilian soccer star, agreed to play for the New York Cosmos, the team arranged a press conference for Pelé's contract signing. The event obviously was legitimate news: Pelé, the best-known soccer player in the world, had led the Brazilian national team to three world championships and then retired. He was to be paid $4.7 million, making him the highest-paid team athlete in history at the time. H.L. Stevenson, editor-in-chief of the UPI, describes the scene for his press association's house publication, the *UPI Reporter:*

In a dark-paneled room adorned with 18-inch beer steins and stuffed antelope heads, more than 300 persons showed up, twice the capacity of the place. There were scores of interlopers. A large contingent of foreign reporters, nearly a dozen television stations or networks and one man from *Advertising Age*. Pelé promotes Pepsi-Cola in his spare time.

The bedlam that resulted went something like this:

11:00 a.m.—There is no sign of Pelé at the announced hour. "You knew about Pelé before you knew that a soccer ball was black and white," says Ron Swoboda, the former New York Met now doing television sports.

11:05 a.m.—Two large trays of hors d'oeuvres placed in the middle of the room. Few pay attention to the Pepsis in silver ice buckets around the room.

11:10 a.m.—Hors d'oeuvres gone. Pepsis remain. Bar still busy.

11:20 a.m.—"The armored car bringing him had a flat tire," a sports writer quips.

11:35 a.m.—Clive Toye, general manager of the Cosmos, enters waving contracts in red folder.

11:37 a.m.—"Down, down, down, down," TV cameramen shout at the still photographers.

11:40 a.m.—"Ladies and gentlemen," booms Toye, "now the legend, the great one, the king." Pelé, in a black brocade suit, enters flashing a "V" sign. He smiles—sometimes shyly, sometimes broadly—all the time.

11:41 a.m.—Pelé starts signing the contracts amid continuing shouts from the mob of photographers. "Let's not get anyone killed," pleads a Cosmos official. "Please, gentlemen, be calm."

11:45 a.m.—Punches are thrown between American and South American television cameramen in the crush in front of the ceremonial table. Cameras turn from Pelé to record the fight, a draw.

11:50 a.m.—Still photographers are ordered to the rear of the room. They refuse. "O.K., gentlemen, unless you move back we'll have to leave this platform," threatens Cosmos official. The photographers grin, and agree to sit or kneel on the floor.

11:55 a.m.—Pelé signs more papers for the TV cameras. His attractive wife kisses him on right cheek. More shouts of "down, down, down" from the cameramen.

12:03 p.m.—"It is like a dream to be here," Pelé says in Portuguese, his first words. "You can spread the news all over the world that soccer has arrived in America." Someone in the rear drops a glass.

12:07 p.m.—"I had a dream that one day the United States will be known for soccer," he says in response to a question about his coming out of retirement. Pelé says he feels he can help and that Brazil would be proud of its contribution to the game. He is sincere. Is there another athlete who can say the same thing with a straight face?

12:12 p.m.—There had been speculation he would get up to $9 million for three seasons, with the Cosmos. True? "The money is no problem," Pelé says. "You made the confusion in the press."

12:13 p.m.— "Well, you solve the confusion for us," a reporter yells. Pelé ducks the question, saying his contract is a "package" that includes promotional fees and exhibition games. "I don't want to discuss money at this time," he adds. Another glass shatters somewhere in the packed room.

12:15 p.m.—Pelé, asked to say a few words in English, responds: "Listen, I don't speak well in English. But after three months, you come and I make an interview with you."

12:30 p.m.—Pelé leaves clutching a soccer ball and still smiling. Radio Free Europe man says his tape recorder has vanished.

Now, read the story the UPI sent out on its wires:

NEW YORK (UPI)--Pelé, the greatest ambassador the game of soccer has ever known, came out of retirement Tuesday to join the New York Cosmos, insisting he's not doing it so much for the $4.7 million he'll be paid, but because he had a dream he could help popularize the sport in the United States.

Edson Arantes do Nascimento, known the world over as Pelé, was more than a half hour late signing his Cosmos contract at a news conference which sometimes had overtones of pure bedlam.

When he finally was able to speak, Pelé said: "Everybody in life has something to do, a mission, a goal. The only country in the world where soccer is unknown is the United States. I had a dream that some day soccer would become known in the U.S., and that's why I came out of retirement."

Pelé spoke primarily in Portuguese through an interpreter, Julio Mazzei, during a wild session at the famed "21 Club" in midtown. At one point the conference was temporarily halted while

cameramen from rival television networks got
into a fist fight as they jockeyed for a better
shooting position.
        Pelé remained calm throughout the brief scuffle
in a room never meant to hold the more than 300
people who attended the conference. He was
flanked by his wife, Rosa, Cosmos general manager
and vice president, Clive Toye, coach Gordon
Bradley and Neal Walsh, representing mayor Abe
Beame, who presented Pelé with a soccer ball on
behalf of the city.
        "I promise to speak better English in three
months," Pelé said in broken English with a broad
smile. . . .

Although the story did capture some of the atmosphere, the in-house account of the staging as well as the signing is more interesting. It tells the reader not only about the signing, but reveals something of the social phenomenon known as a news conference.

Dangers of Layer I

When reporting is confined to Layer I, the distinction between journalism and public relations is hard to discern. The consequences for society can be serious. Joseph Bensman and Robert Lilienfield, the two sociologists who wrote *Craft and Consciousness* (New York: John Wiley and Sons, 1973), explain what the consequences can be in their section on journalism (p. 213):

> When "public relations" is conducted simultaneously for a vast number of institutions and organizations, the public life of a society becomes so congested with manufactured appearances that it is difficult to recognize any underlying realities.
> As a result, individuals begin to distrust all public facades and retreat into apathy, cynicism, disaffiliation, distrust of media and publication institutions . . . the journalist unwittingly often exposes the workings of the public relations man or information specialist, if he operates within a genuine journalistic attitude.

Tom Wicker of *The New York Times* says the press has been weak—because of its concentration on Layer I—at picking up new developments before they have become institutionalized, acquired spokesmen, and their sponsors have learned to stage media events to attract attention.

Correctives

The journalistic attitude these sociologists discuss requires that the reporter make his own observations whenever possible and verify the information supplied him when observation is not possible. Properly reported, an event then would reveal behind-the-scenes stagecraft. Far from being an unwitting exposé of the public relations person's work that the sociologists describe, the story would be like Miller's or Kotuk's, an intentionally written statement of the orchestration.

Some staged events produce news—Pelé's signing, the civil rights demonstrations across the South in the 1960s, picketing by the local teachers union. And certainly the dozens of news stories that are based on source-originated material—such as the text of the mayor's speech, and the details the mortuary supplies about the child's death—are legitimate news. But the reporter must always ask about Layer I information whether it reflects the truth of the event and whether reportorial enterprise is needed to supply the missing facts.

Occasionally, a staged or managed event moves beyond the control of those staging it and becomes spontaneous. Such was the case in Selma, Ala., in March, 1965, when state troopers with rifles, whips and tear gas charged whites and blacks on a Freedom March to Montgomery. The blacks were to petition the governor for the right to vote. Suddenly, what had been a pseudo-event staged for the media became a spontaneous event.

The transition from Layer I to Layer II is rarely that dramatic. Usually, it is like the transition at a press conference from the reading of a statement to the reporter's questions. The reading provides the source-originated material. The give-and-take of the question and answer period is spontaneous. When the source declines to answer questions, however, the reporter should clearly understand that he or she is back in Layer I, dealing with material totally controlled by the source.

When the event moves beyond the control of its managers—press relations experts, publicity men and women, sources—the reporter is taken into Layer II. However, good reporters do not wait for news to become spontaneous before they enter this second layer. Important events demand that the reporter dig into the information supplied by the source. The reporter must show some enterprise rather than act as a passive receptacle for facts. Simple events should be examined critically also. The unchecked story at any level may carry errors. Without reportorial enterprise, the story also may lack the kind of detail readers and listeners expect.

Layer II Reporting

The young reporter in chapter 1 who sought verification from a second source that the governor would appear at the Lions Club ceremony was moving into Layer II. So was the reporter who, after she was told by the police that the hotel was robbed at 5:46 a.m., checked the newspaper to determine the time of sunrise that day. The check enabled her to write: "The holdup man left the hotel in the early-morning darkness."

When they have time, all good reporters verify source-originated material which takes them from Layer I to II. At the other extreme of Layer II is the investigative reporter, whose work is based almost wholly on material gathered through enterprise, digging and checking. It is the investigative reporter who often reveals misleading official stories and who exposes what other reporters accept as reasonable and logical explanations and assertions. The reporter who writes that the state purchasing agent has awarded a contract for large highway equipment to a local dealer is engaged in Layer I journalism. The investigative reporter who digs into the records to learn that the contract was awarded without bids is working at the second level.

Going from I to II

Street Kids. Reporter Gail Roberts of *The Sun-Bulletin* in Binghamton, N.Y., had heard stories about a growing number of young people making their homes on streets, in basements and in parks. Rather than ask city officials about the situation, she sought out the street people themselves. They told her they managed to survive by selling sex, fencing stolen items and asking for handouts.

Not passive, not satisfied with the stenographic function, the reporter working in Layer II verifies material, seeks out additional facts, describes the staging of pseudo-events and employs his or her knowledge as a source of facts for the story.

When an official of a city struck by recession recommends a city-financed plan that he says will increase employment, the reporter will ask him for precise details. Who helped draft the plan? Why should the city act? What will be the reaction of private business? Those questions belong mostly in Layer I reporting. Then the reporter will check the data the official has supplied. He will also look into the program the official said has been working in another city in the South. This checking is the kind of work that moves the reporter into Layer II.

Finally, the reporter will seek comments from other city officials about the feasibility of the proposal and its prospects for adoption. Untold numbers of stories have been written about proposals that went nowhere because they were badly drafted or were introduced or recommended by people with no influence. Local newspapers usually play up a legislator's proposals or his intentions, but give no attention to the fact that he is a freshman with no influence, a member of the minority party, or that the committee chairman has vowed never to let such legislation move through his committee.

If we look back at the reporters at work in chapter 1 we can see how practicing journalists often move from Layer I to II:

- *The Chicago Daily News* reporter who went on the campus to see the demonstrations for himself rather than accept second-hand information.
- Carol Falk, a general assignment reporter in *The Wall Street Journal*'s Washington bureau, did not accept the president's version of the tapes but read the actual transcripts before reaching any firm conclusions.
- Much of the work Dick did on his story about the Black Parents Association after receiving the handout from the group was on his initiative. The group did not name the authors of the books it sought to remove from the schools. Dick inserted the names. He also gave the plots of the novels, and he interviewed the students for their reactions.
- Cammy Wilson's investigative stories in the *Minneapolis Tribune* were carried out entirely in Layer II.

Every one of the reporters we saw at work moved beyond merely relaying information originated and controlled by a source. Each checked the information, supplied missing facts, explained complex matters, clarified vague ideas. None of these efforts is the activity of a reporter content to stop gathering facts at Layer I. Statements, speeches, press conferences and handouts can be useful, but most of the time they should be the start of the reporting process.

The reporter who digs often finds his or her appetite whetted for the kind of information that such digging produces. Reporters who hear about strange doings in the athletic department of the local university do some checking. Their first checks lead to additional digging, and in time a major scandal is unearthed. Such checking and digging led to a Pulitzer Prize in local reporting for Clark Hallas and Robert B. Lowe of *The Arizona Daily Star* for their investigation of the University of Arizona athletic department.

Investigative Reporting

When Judy Johnson of *The Anniston Star* heard some people in the Alabama community she worked in were having trouble getting credit from banks and finance companies she decided to look into the situation. She spent months looking through records of mortgages and land transfers.

"I compiled them into lists year by year, looking for patterns, building a history," she said. She found private lenders were making loans at exorbitant interest rates.

She talked to people affected by these practices. Through the years of borrowing from a local businessman, one woman had accumulated a $50,000 loan. Among the loans he had made to the woman was $3,400 for a four-year-old car she and her husband had bought from his used car lot. When new, the car would have cost $3,036 to $4,599, depending on options.

Johnson showed how the poor, who cannot obtain credit from large lending institutions, are victimized by private lenders. Her series won national recognition.

Investigative reporters have looked into inadequate care in local hospitals, industries that pollute the environment, fraud and corruption in local government and police brutality.

Handling the Handout

"Don't be a handout reporter," Harry Romanoff, a night city editor on the *Chicago American* used to tell young reporters.

One of Romanoff's young charges was Mervin Block, who recalls an encounter with Romanoff:

"I remember his giving me a fistful of press releases trumpeting Movie Monarch Louis B. Mayer's expected arrival at the Dearborn Street Railroad Station. An hour later, Romy asked me what time Mayer's train would be pulling in. I told him, and when he challenged my answer, I cited the handouts: one from the Santa Fe, one from Mayer's studio (MGM), and one from his destination, the Ambassador East Hotel. All agreed on the time. But that wasn't good enough for Romy.

" 'Call the stationmaster and *find out*.' "

Reporters ignore Romanoff's admonition at their peril. When food chains in Chicago announced price cuts on thousands of items, the three Chicago newspapers bannered the stories on their front pages. One such headline:

Inflation Breakthrough— Food Prices to Drop Here

–Chicago Sun-Times

Despite the rash of stories about how the shopper "may save 15% in price battle," as *The Chicago Daily News* said in a headline over one of its stories, consumers were actually paying more on a unit, or per-ounce, basis.

The Chicago commissioner of consumer affairs demonstrated that the city's consumers were being misled by the announcements of the stores, and consequently by the newspaper stories that took the handouts at face value. The commissioner showed that many of the items that were reduced in price were also reduced in weight. Peanut clusters went from 72 cents a packet to 69 cents, an apparent saving of 3 cents. But the packet went from 6 ounces to 5¼ ounces. With a little arithmetic, a reporter could have figured out that this was actually an increase of six cents a packet. Some items were publicized because they stayed at the same price "despite inflation," according to the stores. A 30-cent can of beef stew was still 30 cents. True enough. But the new can contained half an ounce less than the old can. Consumers were actually paying more.

Reporters might have dug this out had they followed Romanoff's advice. If they had been enterprising, or had followed Tolstoy's advice, "Show, don't tell," they might have done some simple calculations to show the savings per ounce. Had they done so, they would have noticed that the so-called savings did not exist.

During the uprising in Nicaragua in 1979, the National Guard announced that a brigade of Venezuelan, Panamanian, Mexican and Costa Rican guerrillas had crossed the border from Costa Rica and been repulsed. The spokesman, an army colonel, said several of the invaders had been wounded. Then the AP reporter asked the colonel how he knew the troops had come from the various nations.

He responded, "Because I said it."

And that is just how the AP account quoted the colonel.

The wire service reporter was doing his job of refusing to accept at face value statements from a source that require verification. The assertion is carried for the record (Layer I), but so is the proof, or lack thereof (Layer II).

When 53 school children and their teachers were felled by creosote fumes in a Paterson, N.J., school, the school officials said the fumes were non-toxic. Rita Jensen, a reporter for the *News,* asked hospital authorities and the fire department about the chemicals. They said the fumes were toxic, and that is what she put in her lead. Other newspapers described the fumes as "noxious chemical vapors" and "non-toxic fumes." Jensen had a feeling the school authorities would try to minimize the situation, and so she checked with an independent source, the fire department.

Bob Greene, a prize-winning investigative reporter at *Newsday,* has a reputation for asking the necessary, if impolite, questions. He advises:

- Demand the file instead of having it read to you.
- Check comments and statements for factual content before printing them.
- Carefully collect all facts, then make sure to put them into context.
- Anticipate developments.

When a reporter moves from the first to the second level of reporting, he often discovers that his reporting has uncovered facts that contradict what he had been told by his original source. We saw in chapter 2 how E. W. Kenworthy of *The New York Times* used information from his files to clarify and correct assertions made by a presidential candidate. Here is another example of Kenworthy's work, a paragraph from a story about Edward Kennedy's campaign for the U.S. Senate in 1964:

> Edward Kennedy thereupon launched into a speech on medical care for the aged, declaring that while the Republicans in the Senate had opposed it, "every Democratic Senator voted for it," a statement not borne out by the Congressional Record.

Kenworthy did not wait for another source to deny Kennedy's assertion. He corrected it on his own, in the same story in which the misstatement was made.

A city planner from San Francisco commented in an interview in a journal that a portion of Sixth Avenue in New York City should have been dug up and an underground traffic-way constructed so that the area could have a plaza. The reporter who rewrote the interview for *The New York Times* interjected an observation of his

Asking Questions

Correcting the Source

own, that during the interview the planner "was not asked to explain how Sixth Avenue could go underground without driving the Sixth Avenue Subway further underground." Sweeping statements should have some grounding in reality. If they do not, the reporter is obligated to shoot them down.

Trusting the Reporter

For many years, the source's version—not the reporter's—was the basis of news. Attribution of almost every fact was necessary. The press associations placed this particularly rigid requirement on their reporters. Bob Frazier of the *Register-Guard* of Eugene, Ore., recalls covering an early-morning fire at an old and famous resort hotel on the Oregon coast. There was a steady rain and a stiff wind coming in from the north. After telephoning his newspaper to dictate the story, Frazier called the AP and gave the facts to a rewrite man. He mentioned the rain and wind.

"Who says so?" the rewrite man asked, needing the name of the authority for that fact.

"Hell's bells," Frazier said he recalls answering. "I said it. I'm standing here in a phone booth that's about to blow off its slab." Nevertheless, the AP insisted on knowing the name of the fire chief, which Frazier dutifully supplied. The story in the *Oregonian* the next day carried a line about the rain and the wind, and attributed the north wind to the fire chief. (As Frazier later remarked, "The chief would have been an ass to have said that. He might as well have notified the spectators that it was raining cats and dogs.")

The incident occurred in 1950. Absurd as it may seem, it was not unusual. Reporters were held to what their sources said and did. The hold sources had on reporters began to loosen when good editors realized that sources were not revealing what they knew and that their reporters were often as knowledgeable as some sources.

The Alternative Press

Some of the impetus in the movement away from reliance on sources to trust in the reporter came from the small newspapers and magazines that proliferated during this period. Known as the alternative press, these publications offered news that seemed to come closer to the truth than did many of the stories published by the commercial press. The reporters for these publications understood what Murray Kempton, a veteran political reporter and writer, meant when he said: "One of the big mistakes people who write for newspapers make is to assume the participants, speaking to them as reporters, are telling them the truth."

One of these new publications was the *Texas Observer,* which began publishing in 1954. An *Observer* reporter of the period, Larry Goodwyn, recalls that the weekly newspaper "thrust its reporters into the very maw of the on-going political world."

The *Observer,* says Goodwyn, "played an absolutely crucial role in fashioning the ground rules for a new kind of American journalism. It was one that went quite beyond the 'who-what-when-where-and-why' of the old school to provide the essential background information necessary to coherent interpretation."

The commercial press was quick to use the techniques initiated by the new journalism. Gradually, the press associations changed, too. Newspapers that had to rely for national and international news on the press associations were complaining that competing newspapers and broadcast stations with special correspondents and access to such syndicated news services as The *Los Angeles Times/Washington Post* and *The New York Times* News Services were doing a better job of reporting the news than they were.

A shift had to be made away from total reliance on Layer I reporting, and it was. Although press association reporters still do not have the freedom of special correspondents, they have more leeway than they did when Frazier was an AP stringer. Note the reporter's observation in the first sentence of the third paragraph of the following AP story:

WASHINGTON, April 1 (AP)— Secretary of Transportation John A. Volpe has responded to allegations that Federal funds have been wasted on a Federal transit show, saying that a success could have a "positive impact" on the United States economy and balance of payments.

Senator William Proxmire, Democrat of Wisconsin, had said that much of the $5-million that Congress paid out for the Transpo '72 exhibit has been wasted on luxury hotels, first-class plane fares, $15 dinners and $3,000-a-page memos.

In a letter to Mr. Proxmire on Monday, Mr. Volpe did not answer all of the allegations. However, the Secretary pointed to some specific cases and said Government regulations were followed. Mr. Volpe said the exhibit, to be held at Dulles International Airport near Washington, will show "potential customers the advantages of having us as their transportation hardware suppliers."

Politics and Public Affairs

The coverage of politics and public affairs often tests a reporter's ability to move into Layer II, for candidates and officials seek to set the agenda for public discussion. That is, they prefer to select the issues and to discuss these on their own terms. Left to their own preferences, they would avoid what they consider embarrassing or politically dangerous subjects. When that cannot be done, they would deflect or blunt the tough questions.

In politics and the area of public policy, the news media have replaced the traditional political institutions. The Social Science Research Council reports, "Elections are now waged through the mass media, which have supplanted the political parties as the major intermediary between the office seekers and the electorate." Officials turn to the media to activate and mold public opinion in order to win support for their policies. If the press permits itself to be used as a megaphone, the office seeker and the official are able to manipulate public opinion.

A case study rich in detail exists that reveals this manipulation. The tapes, documents, and Watergate hearings and trials turned up a vast amount of press-related information. Clearly, the administration sought to use the press—as any official does. But never has the record been so fully disclosed.

One of the vulnerabilities of the press that the Nixon administration sought to exploit is its penchant for color, drama and personalities, and its willingness to settle for appearance rather than significance. An incident involving the appointment of a party spokesman during the 1972 campaign underlines the necessity of Layer II journalism, the necessity to dig into the event to determine its full meaning rather than to settle for what social historian Boorstin describes as the "vivid image." The only significant difference between national press manipulation and the kind done at the local and county levels is that we know a great deal more about presidential and congressional shenanigans because they are played up in the national media.

To win "those outside middle America," particularly the youth vote, the deputy director of the president's re-election campaign, Jeb Magruder, proposed that a young Nixon assistant, Martin Anderson, be used as a party spokesman. A memo that Magruder sent to H. R. Haldeman, the White House chief of staff, makes it clear that Magruder understood the appeal Anderson would have to journalists, as well as to young voters.

"Who better than Marty Anderson can 'turn on' young people about draft reform?" Magruder wrote. "Young Metroamerica won't listen to Mel Laird, but they will to Marty Anderson, not because Marty's any more liberal (he probably is less liberal than Laird) but because he's got more *hair,* a Ph.D., a sexy wife, drives a Thunderbird, and lives in a high-rise apartment."

In the margin of the memo, Haldeman noted: "*Absolutely.* Really work on this."

This is, in its most unsophisticated form, the kind of political image-making Boorstin describes as "reducing great national issues to trivial dimensions."

The press has matured sufficiently to catch obvious attempts to exploit its weaknesses. But the tendency of the politician and public official to try to sell the image rather than the reality is always present. Reporters have to battle the willingness of their papers and broadcast stations to use a personality feature rather than to give time and space to the less scintillating story on a public issue.

The general failures of political reporters and the inadequate coverage of the 1968 and 1972 presidential campaigns were cited by Wes Gallagher, AP president and general manager, in a letter he sent to all AP staffers in preparation for the 1976 campaign.

"Political coverage produced for the 1968 and 1972 campaigns must be improved this year," he said. "We must make a greater effort than ever before to get to the specifics. We should not accept without challenge any political promise which is not detailed as to how it will be carried out.

"If the candidate cannot or refuses to answer questions, we should clearly state so in the story—a warning flag to the reader that the whole promise may just be hot air."

In short, Gallagher was telling AP reporters that unless they report at Layer II they will fail to inform their readers.

The inability of reporters to move beyond Layer I was probably responsible for the failure of the White House press corps to uncover the Watergate story. It was not a member of this massive group, but two young metropolitan reporters for *The Washington Post* who broke the story, even though the White House is the most intensively covered office in the world. Where were the reporters? The answer is instructive for all reporters.

Why the
White House Press
Failed

Most were covering the "large, regular flow of presidential news announcements," says Robert Donovan, former Washington bureau chief of The *Los Angeles Times*. Donovan is quoted in an article, "Why the White House Press Corps Didn't Get the Watergate Story," by Charles Peters in the July/August 1973 issue of *The Washington Monthly*. Peters says that reporters "are left exhausted and stupefied by the interminable string of staged events. . . . The correspondents are like a herd of seals waiting for the fish that are reliably tossed their way instead of looking elsewhere for sustenance."

Peters quotes Bill Moyers, President Johnson's press secretary, as saying, "The White House press corps is more stenographic than entrepreneurial in its approach to news gathering. Too many of them are sheep. Sheep with short attention spans. They move on to tomorrow's story without pausing to investigate yesterday's."

Many journalists and a significant number of historians are convinced that an aggressive press that demanded specific answers on U.S. strategy and intentions in Vietnam might have set the climate for an earlier end to the war. Some historians have described the policies of President Johnson and President Nixon as talking peace and waging war. The press bears some responsibility for allowing the presidents to have access to the public—which is necessary—but failing to represent the public by asking tough questions.

Covering Vietnam

A few journalists like David Halberstam and Charles Mohr moved to Layer II in their coverage of the early and middle parts of the war. We saw in chapter 2 how Schanberg refused to accept the official press handout and made his way to the bombed area in Cambodia late in the war when officials still sought to keep reporters in Layer I.

At the battlefront or in city hall, the reporter is flooded with Layer I-type information. He cannot discard all of it, for he knows that the official must have access to the public. That is, statements, handouts and press releases must be reported faithfully so that the public is informed of the actions and ideas of its officials. Once this Layer I reporting is completed, there may be little time for enterprise.

Barriers

Another impediment facing the reporter who wants to dig beneath the surface is the reluctance of some sources to cooperate. After the reporter has allowed a source access to the public, the public has a right to access to the official. But what does the reporter do when a source prefers to keep the reporting at Layer I?

Pushing the Source

Reporters have a few techniques to make sources responsive to the public's need to know. When a source will not come to grips with legitimate questions about public events and issues, the reporter can state that the source "refused to answer" a particular question or that he "did not explain his answers." Other sources can be asked to comment on the issue and on the source's silence, and these answers can be used. When there is demonstrable falsification, the reporter is free to indicate this.

Another device is the use of background material to supply needed information. This is an excellent technique because it can often be unearthed without recourse to the original source. The reporter makes independent checks and uses sources other than the reluctant one.

Layer III Reporting

People are not content with knowing only what happened. They also want to know why it happened, what it means and what may occur as a result—causes and consequences. Sometimes, this information is not immediately available to the journalist, and the only fact gathering that can be done is at Layers I and II. But when the story is important and the material can be dug up, reporters should not hesitate to mine Layer III, the area of interpretation and analysis.

Layer III reporting tells people how things work and why they work that way, or why they don't work. Such reporting moves beyond telling us what people did yesterday and what they say they will do tomorrow (Layer I). It is the journalist's way of helping people understand complex events. Layer III reporting is analytical. It may move beyond the recital of fact into the subjective area of judgment and inference. Obviously, this kind of journalism requires reporters who have command of subject matter along with their mastery of the craft skills.

In wire stories reporting Argentina's invasion of the British-controlled Falkland Islands, reporters gave the necessary added dimension to the spot news report with sentences like this one from an AP story:

> The invasion came at a time of increasing domestic trouble for the Argentine government, and the issue of the islands' sovereignty has always been a patriotic rallying point for the country.

The AP story said that Argentines celebrated the takeover whereas "only last weekend Argentines had demonstrated against the junta's economic policies."

When the New Jersey state legislature passed a bill banning state Medicaid payments for abortions, it ignored nine federal district court decisions in eight states that ruled similar bills were unconstitutional. The reason for the legislators' action was described in this Layer III sentence from *The New York Times:* "Approval of the measure reflects the influence of the Catholic Church, which opposes abortion, in New Jersey: About 55 percent of the state's registered voters are Catholic."

The battle over the need for interpretative reporting has long been over, although some newspaper and broadcast station editors are adamant about its dangers and rarely permit it. Dangers there are, but the risks are only slightly greater than those inherent in other areas of journalism. The benefits to the reader outweigh these risks.

Compare these two short pieces that were published when hostilities in the Middle East broke out in 1973. The first is Layer I journalism; the second paragraph of the second is Layer III journalism:

KARACHI, Pakistan, Oct. 7— Prime Minister Zulfikar Ali Bhutto, today condemned "Israeli aggression" and reaffirmed Pakistan's support for the Arab countries in messages to the presidents of Egypt and Syria.

According to an official spokesman in Islamabad, Mr. Bhutto also sent a message to Secretary General Waldheim of the United Nations, expressing Pakistan's concern over the outbreak of hostilities. He reminded Mr. Waldheim of the Security Council's responsibility for peace in the area.

Mr. Bhutto discussed the Middle East situation with Arab ambassadors in Islamabad. Later he held separate meetings with the Iranian and Turkish ambassadors.

NEW DELHI, Oct. 7—An Indian Government spokesman declared today that Israel's "intransigence" caused the outbreak of hostilities. India's sympathies are "entirely with the Arabs whose sufferings have long reached a point of explosion," he added.

Behind India's traditional pro-Arab position in any outbreak of fighting in the Middle East is believed to be her awareness of the importance of Arab votes in the United Nations on the question of Kashmir. For more than 25 years Kashmir has been the subject of a territorial dispute between India and Pakistan, a Moslem country.

The story above adds a dimension that the reader needs in order to understand India's motivation. This addition explains the "why" of the event. When explanation and interpretation are lacking, the reader is left with questions.

The political reporter is pulled by his or her sources toward Layer I reporting, while at the same time trying to ply his or her trade in Layers II and III. When Governor Jerry Brown of California announced that California would lend 10 billion cubic feet of natural gas to eastern states fighting a hard winter, reporters who had been following the situation pointed out in their copy that the utility companies made the decision, not Brown, not the state of California. But when Brown talked about $1 billion worth of sewage projects pumping life into the state's economy, the press quoted the governor—Layer I reporting. Later, reporters learned that the Supreme Court had released the funds impounded by Nixon. Brown had taken credit for something he had nothing to do with.

The fact that public figures can get away with media manipulation has led them to use advertising and public relations experts as their political advisers. When polls showed that President Carter did not have the confidence of a majority of the public, he installed Jerry Rafshoon, an Atlanta advertising man active in the Carter presidential campaign, in the White House.

In a memo to the president's staff before a State of the Union address, Rafshoon wrote: "It is important that the State of the Union speech be 'sold' properly." With the cadence of a coach calling on his team to give its all in the second half, Rafshoon says: "It is an important speech. . . . It is *Carter's* speech. . . . The theme is quintessential Carter. . . . It is positive. . . . It is moderate. . . ." Just what the president was saying is not made explicit in the memo.

The political hucksters presume they can sell style, and journalists who do their reporting at Layer I help to make politics into national entertainment.

But sometimes it is impossible to communicate the full flavor of an event or a personality even through interpretative reporting. When this happens, there is a recourse.

The Interpretative Column

In an issue of *UPI Reporter,* editor-in-chief H. L. Stevenson wrote, "Jerry Brown, just about everyone agrees, possesses charisma. He also is endowed with what can only be described as an abundance of arrogance." This was proper for the *Reporter* newsletter, but would hardly be appropriate for the UPI's news wires. What does a reporter do to give readers his or her insights and judgments? Increasingly, newspapers are granting beat reporters the privilege of the editorial page column. City hall reporters may take an overview of the week's activities in a weekend column. An education reporter may be permitted to give his or her opinion of a curriculum change in a Sunday column.

After Norman C. Miller of *The Wall Street Journal* had spent some time watching Brown, he wrote a column that began: "Gov. Jerry Brown's success in playing opportunistic politics is almost scary." He wrote of Brown's "record of flip-flops that would have broken the backs of most politicians." He said Brown engaged in "double talk," and he described the California governor as "a cold, seemingly humorless person." Miller concludes his column with a summary that could not appear in a news story but is permissible in the interpretative column:

> The picture that emerges is that Gov. Brown uses people to further his own ambition—an ambition that obviously extends to another presidential candidacy. He is a master at sensing mass opinion and manipulating it in his favor. It is a rare—and scary—kind of talent.

Sources for Interpretation

One device reporters use to add interpretation to their news pieces is simple enough. They ask a source to size up the situation. Sometimes, however, the explanation of a single source is not adequate to explain complex stories. The how and why of the event may be so elusive that no single explanation is sufficient. Then the reporter must move on to several sources to find a range of explanations and cross-explanations, analyses and cross-analyses. This kind of reporting will give the reader or listener several alternatives on which to base his or her conclusions.

Interpretation and analysis can be supplied by the reporter as well as by sources. How much the reporter is permitted to do depends upon the policy of his newspaper or station and the confidence his editor has in his ability. When an editor assigns a reporter to do an interpretative piece, or backgrounder, then the reporter will work primarily in the third layer.

When reporters depart from so-called objectivity, they enter uncharted territory. The immediate facts are firm and relatively certain. Motivation, meaning, consequence may be more revealing, but they do take reporters away from solid ground.

One of the classic examples of the problems inherent in interpretative reporting occurred in 1960 at a session of the United Nations. The Communist delegations, led by Premier Nikita Khrushchev of the Soviet Union, rejected a statement by the secretary-general. Khrushchev smiled and thumped his desk. What did this apparently contradictory behavior mean? Khrushchev was not immediately available to answer the reporters' questions, and so they fell back on reporting what had happened (Layer I) and interpreting it (Layer III). The interpretations ranged widely.

The AP stayed on solid ground. Its reporter wrote: "Communist contingents, possibly to show their disagreement, failed to join the applause, but smiled and thumped their fists upon their desks."

The UPI drew a conclusion, saying Khrushchev was "livid with anger" and had gone into "a desk-pounding rage that sounded like an anvil chorus." His behavior was "a display of anger that astonished the world of diplomacy," the UPI said. As for the smile, it was "a wide grin" of pleasure at the commotion his antics had caused.

The *Chicago Tribune* called Khrushchev's behavior "a Russian 'raspberry.'" The *Daily News* said the Russian had "bubbled with mock rage," and the *Detroit Free Press* said that while he was pounding his desk, Khrushchev's "face was beaming." *The New York Times* noted that desk-pounding is "a customary demonstration of disapproval in many parliaments." The *Chicago Sun-Times* said, "Khrushchev was displaying his personal friendliness" toward the UN secretary-general.

Asked later for an explanation of his behavior, Khrushchev said he meant to show his disapproval of the secretary-general's statement.

Another example of the risks of interpretative reporting:

In Warrentown, W.Va., 63 indigent mothers were sterilized with their permission. Reporters were sent to the city to do follow-up stories. Here are the headlines over two of these folos in New York City newspapers:

Town in Uproar
Over Sterilization

Virginians Calm
On Sterilization

Troublesome as these examples show interpretative reporting to be, reporters have little choice but to try to explain the events they cover. Walter Lippmann, one of the few original thinkers about American journalism, observed that during the 1930s with the advent of the New Deal "events started happening which were almost meaningless in themselves. It was the beginning of the era when Why became as important as What, when a Washington correspondent left his job half done if he only told what happened and failed to give the reasons and hint at the significance." Journalism has no rule that states that what Washington reporters can do is prohibited to local reporters.

While editor of *The Christian Science Monitor,* Erwin Canham weighed the pros and cons of interpretative journalism: "News interpretation, with all its hazards, often is safer and wiser than printing the bare news alone. Nothing can be more misleading than the unrelated fact, just because it is a fact and hence impressive. Background, motives, surrounding circumstances, related events and issues all need to be understood and appraised as well as the immediate event. . . .

"Interpretation requires integrity and knowledge and understanding and balance and detachment."

Putting I, II and III to Work

Let us watch a reporter mine these three layers for his story:

City Planner Arthur calls the local stations and the local newspaper to read to reporters a statement about a new zoning proposal. The release contains facts 1, 2 and 3. At the newspaper, reporter Bernard looks over the handout, tells his city editor that 1 and 2 are of no news value but that 3—elimination of two-acre zoning north of town—is important and worth exploring in an interview with Arthur. The editor agrees and assigns Bernard to the story.

Before leaving for the interview, Bernard checks the newspaper library for a story about a court decision he recalls that may be related to the proposed regulation. He telephones another city official and a real estate developer to obtain additional information. With this background and Arthur's statement, Bernard begins to develop ideas for questions. He jots down a few, 4, 5 and 6.

During the interview, City Planner Arthur repeats 1, 2 and 3. Reporter Bernard asks for more information about 3, the elimination of the minimum two-acre requirement for home building. Bernard also brings up his own subjects by asking questions 4, 5 and 6. New themes develop during the interview, 7, 8 and 9.

Back in the newsroom, Bernard looks over his notes. He sees that his hunch about 3 was correct—it was important. Arthur's answer to question 5 is newsworthy, he decides, and fact 7—a plan for low- and medium-cost housing in the area—that developed during the interview, may be the lead, especially since the broadcast stations will probably not have it. But 7 could have serious implications for real estate developers, and Bernard needs comments on its impact. A couple of calls and the possible consequences—10—emerge. Looking over his notes, he spots background from the morgue—11—that is now relevant and also will go into the story.

The story will contain facts 3, 5, 7, 10 and 11. Bernard decides he will fashion 7 into a lead, and he worries about how to blend 10 and 11 into the story at a fairly early stage without impeding the flow of Arthur's explanation. Background and consequences are important, but sometimes they are difficult to work smoothly into the story. He writes this lead:

```
A proposed change to eliminate the two-acre zoning
requirement for home building north of town could open the
area to people who can afford only low- and medium-cost
housing.
```

The Process of Reporting—
from Layer I to III.

Well, Bernard thinks, at least it's a start.

Referring back to the layers of the news story, we can see that Bernard's story will consist of the following:

Facts	Layer
3	I
5, 7, 11	II
10	III

Bernard has used almost all the techniques reporters have at their command to gather facts for stories. He was given information by a source. Then he used the newspaper library—a physical source—for background. He then interviewed his original source—a human source—and made independent checks by calling up additional sources.

Some Practical Advice About Reporting

Here are guidelines several working reporters suggested for fact gathering.

- There is a story behind almost any event. Remember it was a third-rate break-in in a Washington building that began the Watergate revelations and ended in the resignation of a president.
- Always check all names in the telephone book, the city directory and the morgue to make absolutely sure they are spelled correctly.
- Follow the buck. Find out where money comes from, where it is going, how it gets there and who's handling it. Whether it is taxes, campaign contributions, or donations, keep your eye on the dollar.
- Be counter-phobic. Do what you don't want to do or are afraid to do. Otherwise you'll never be able to dig into a story. And you might spend another year on a beat you dislike.
- Question all assumptions. The people who believed the emperor was clothed are legion and forgotten. We remember the child who pointed out his nudity.
- Question authority. Titles and degrees do not grant anyone infallibility.

10 Building and Using Background

Preview   Reporters are always at work building up their background knowledge. Background consists of two kinds:

- General—The over-all knowledge that the reporter takes to the job. It is based on wide reading and general experience. This type of background helps to put the news into context.

- Specific—The knowledge that helps the reporter cope with his or her beat. It includes, for example, the way the city judicial system is structured, or one judge's preference for jail sentences and another's penchant for probation.

The reporter is expected to know a lot. An error, a missing fact or a misinterpretation cannot be explained away by the reporter.

Demanding as this may seem, it is the lot of the professional that he or she be competent, unfailingly certain in performance. The doctor is expected to identify precisely the ailments that plague the patient. The attorney is a compendium of the law, a Clarence Darrow and Perry Mason in the courtroom. The teacher is a wise, unfaltering guide who takes students through the complexities of phonics, French and William Blake.

But we know they are all fallible. Doctors can misdiagnose, and sometimes they fail in their operations. Lawyers can lose cases through incompetence and ignorance. Teachers are human, too, like the grade school teacher who assigned her class the task of writing sentences containing words from a list she supplied. One youngster, whose father had taken him to a baseball game the day before, chose the word "cap," and he wrote: "Catfish Hunter wears a cap." The teacher returned the boy's paper with the sentence corrected: "A catfish hunter wears a cap."

Should the teacher have known Catfish Hunter was a baseball player? Well, perhaps we do make excuses for teachers, as well as for doctors and lawyers. But we do not excuse the journalist who errs through ignorance.

Should the journalist really be expected to know everything? "Yes," replies Murray Kempton, journalist and author. "When you're covering anything, and you're writing about it at length, you use everything you know. And in order to use everything you have to be interested in an extraordinary range of things."

Twain's and Mencken's Complaints

In Mark Twain's *Sketches,* he describes his experiences as a newspaperman in "How I Edited an Agricultural Paper." Twain is telling someone that little intelligence is needed to be a newspaperman:

I tell you I have been in the editorial business going on fourteen years, and it is the first time I ever heard of a man's having to know anything in order to edit a newspaper. You turnip! Who write the dramatic critiques for the second-rate papers? Why, a parcel of promoted shoemakers and apprentice apothecaries, who know just as much about good acting as I do about good farming and no more. Who review the books? People who never wrote one. Who do up the heavy leaders on finance? Parties who have had the largest opportunities for knowing nothing about it. Who criticise the Indian campaigns? Gentlemen who do not know a war whoop from a wigwam, and who never have had to run a foot race with a tomahawk, or pluck arrows out of the several members of their families to build the evening camp-fire with. Who write the temperance appeals, and clamor about the flowing bowl? Folks who will never draw another sober breath till they do it in the grave.

H. L. Mencken, a journalist whose prose skewered presidents, poets and bartenders with equal vigor, used some of his most choice execrations to denounce his fellow journalists. In an editorial in the *American Mercury,* October, 1924, he wrote:

The majority of them, in almost every American city, are ignoramuses, and not a few of them are also bounders. All the knowledge that they pack into their brains is, in every reasonable cultural sense, useless; it is the sort of knowledge that belongs, not to a professional man, but to a police captain, a railway mail-clerk or a board boy in a brokerage house. It is a mass of trivialities and puerilities; to recite it would be to make even a barber or a bartender beg for mercy. What is missing from it is everything worth knowing—everything that enters into the common knowledge of educated men. There are managing editors in the United States, and scores of them, who have never heard of Kant or Johannes Müller and never read the Constitution of the United States; there are city editors who do not know what a symphony is, or a streptococcus, or the Statute of Frauds; there are reporters by the thousand who could not pass the entrance examination for Harvard or Tuskegee, or even Yale. It is this vast ignorance that makes American journalism so pathetically feeble and vulgar, and so generally disreputable no less. A man with so little intellectual enterprise that, dealing with news daily, he goes through life without taking in any news that is worth knowing—such a man, you may be sure, is as lacking in true self-respect as he is in curiosity. Honor does not go with stupidity. If it belongs to professional men, it belongs to them because they constitute a true aristocracy—because they have definitely separated themselves from the great masses of men. The journalists, in seeking to acquire it, put the cart before the horse.

Well, that was 50 and more years ago. Journalists are now college-trained, often in schools of journalism (a hopeful sign, thought Mencken in the same editorial). Yet what are we to make of the current generation, one of whose representatives wrote in a college newspaper about a presentation of "The Merchant of Venus," instead of "The Merchant of Venice."

And what can we say to the journalism student who wrote of the sculptor Michel Angelo?

Should the journalist be expected to know the plays of Shakespeare, the world of art and the names of baseball players? Would it terrify would-be journalists to suggest that the answer has to be yes?

This storehouse of knowledge is the reporter's background. As Kempton, Twain and Mencken suggest, it should be kept full and constantly replenished—if such a feat is possible.

The term background has three meanings:

A reporter's store of information. This knowledge may be amassed over a long period or picked up quickly in order to handle a specific assignment. Without background knowledge, a reporter's fact-gathering can be non-directed.

Material placed in the story that explains the event, traces its development and adds facts that sources have not provided. Without background, a story may be one-dimensional.

Material a source does not want attributed to him or her. It may or may not be used, depending on the source's instructions.

Our interest at this point is in the first meaning—the reporter's store of information.

Reporters have a deep and wide-ranging fund of knowledge. Much of this stored information concerns processes and procedures: the workings of the political system; the structure of local government; arrest procedures; government finance. The good reporter is also aware of the past and its relation to the present. The *Dred Scott* and the *Brown* v *Board of Education* Supreme Court decisions are kept in mental drawers, ready for use. When a speaker refers to the New Deal, the reporter knows what he means.

The knowledge of how things work can turn a routine assignment into a significant story. When a reporter for a Long Island newspaper was sent to cover a fire in a plastic factory, she noticed that the plant was located in a residential zone. On her return to the office, she told her editor, "I've got the information on the fire, but I want to check out how that factory was built there in a residential zone. Was it zoned industrial when the factory was built, or did the company get a variance?" The reporter knew that variances—exceptions to general zoning patterns—are sometimes awarded to friends or for favors. Though the reporter was not a city hall reporter or a specialist in covering construction, she knew about zoning through her overall understanding of city government. Her curiosity and knowledge led to a significant story.

When Joe Munson, a photographer for *The Kentucky Post* in Covington, Ky., was covering the Indianapolis 500 the daring tactics of a driver caught his eye. Munson knew that there is an imaginary line that race car drivers must follow around bends in order to keep their cars under control.

The Contents of the Storehouse

Casualty at the Indy 500. Photographer Joe Munson had noticed that the driver of this car was cutting turns too closely. He kept his camera trained on driver Danny Ongais and was able to take several shots of this crash.

"I noticed driver Danny Ongais straying six inches from that imaginary line and I suspected he was destined for a crash," Munson recalled.

"So I kept my camera focused on him."

Munson was ready when Ongais lost control and his car cracked into the wall around the track. Munson was able to run off 20 shots of the fiery crash. One of them took first place in the sports category of the National Press Photographers Association regional competition in 1981.

"I use my experience with cars when I take pictures," he said. "I watch the drivers, particularly around the bends of the track, and I know when they're in trouble."

Munson was a race car driver on tracks in Ohio, Indiana and Kentucky. He says all journalists could do better "if they'd keep their heads about their business." Learning the business is essential. It pays off with better pictures and better stories.

Beat reporters have a ready and detailed knowledge of their specialties. The reporter assigned to cover the city planning agency knows about zoning regulations and variances, land use and city planning. When a developer calls to announce he will file a request to rezone an area north of town for a new housing development, the reporter need make no hurried calls for background. If he is on deadline, he can start writing as soon as he hangs up the telephone. His later calls to other sources and his examination of clips will fill in details and verify his recollections.

The courthouse reporter knows the diffference between an arraignment and a preliminary hearing. When prosecutor and defense attorney huddle at the judge's bench, the reporter assumes plea bargaining is occurring and he knows what questions to ask.

A frequent criticism of U.S. journalists is that although their mastery of the journalistic craft is unexcelled, their general knowledge is limited. American journalism lacks a strong tradition of scholarship, critics contend.

Such knowledge is important because it is the bedrock on which news stories are built. The American philosopher John Dewey said, "We cannot lay hold of the new, we cannot even keep it before our minds, much less understand it, save by the use of ideas and knowledge we already possess." Irving Kristol, a writer on social and political affairs, says, "When one is dealing with complicated and continuous events, it is impossible to report 'what happened' unless one is previously equipped with a context of meaning and significance."

Marcia Chambers, who covered the Criminal Courts Building for *The New York Times,* scored many exclusives because she had mastered the procedures of the criminal justice system. If a case was moving through the courts slowly, she could describe the history of the case by tracing the numerous continuations and delays. Her knowledge of the criminal justice records and processes enabled her to describe the system in New York City as revolving-door justice: Nine of ten defendants were allowed to bargain down their charges. Often, men and women accused of felonies were back on the streets right after pleading guilty or after a short term in jail.

Knowing the Records

Chambers used files, records and background for a piece she did on the arrest of a mass-murder suspect. Without the background material, the arrest story would have had some interest but little significance. Here is her description of how she went about digging up the information for her story:

"On the day Calvin Jackson was arrested, I covered the arraignment where the prosecutor announced that Jackson had been charged with the murder of one woman and had 'implicated himself' in ten others. At the time, we wanted to find out more about Jackson's prior criminal record, but given the hour—5:30 p.m.—we couldn't get the information. In a sidebar story that appeared the next day, Joe Treaster, the police reporter, said Jackson's previous arrest had occurred 10 months before. But the disposition of the case, the story said, was unknown.

"From my experience, I knew that nearly all cases were disposed of through plea bargaining, the process whereby a defendant agrees to plead guilty in exchange for a lesser charge. Several weeks before I had obtained from the Office of Court Administration data that showed that last year only 545 out of 31,098 felony arrests went to trial, including drug cases.

"I had not been assigned a story relating to the Jackson case, but I had a feeling that a check would turn up something interesting. On Monday, at 10 a.m., I went to the court clerk's office to test my premise. The premise was that Jackson's last arrest, like the thousands of others that pass through the criminal court system, had probably involved plea bargaining, a reduction of charges and a minimal sentence. If so, he might have avoided a lengthy prison sentence.

"From the docket book, I obtained the docket number of the mass-murder case, and since case records are public information, I asked the clerk for the case. I took it to the side of the room, and quickly copied the entire file that contained information about his previous arrests. (Reporters should carry at least two dollars in dimes at all times for the copying machine.)

"I did not write the story that day because I was assigned another story. More important, I didn't have all the information I needed. On Monday night, I read the file and the rap sheets. And I listed the dates of each murder.

"On Tuesday, having obtained the dates of Jackson's previous arrests from the rap sheets, I checked the docket book again, obtained the cases and copied them.

"I called several prosecutors and defense attorneys to find the reasons so few cases went to trial.

"At about 2 p.m., I called my desk to say I thought I had a good story. I had a general outline, but said I was uncertain whether it would be ready to go that night. I left the courthouse and went to the *Times*.

"First I went to the law library at the *Times* to check the Penal Code and Criminal Procedure Law. I knew from the complaint that Jackson had been charged with two felonies in his prior arrests, which had been delineated on the court papers by statute number. From the law books I learned the maximum sentence for each crime. In this case, the original charges were "C" felonies, punishable by up to 15 years in prison.

Suspect in Slayings Once Got
30 Days Instead of 15 Years

By Marcia Chambers

Calvin Jackson, who is said by the police to have "implicated himself" in the murder of at least nine women, was arrested in Manhattan 10 months ago on felonious robbery and burglary charges that could have sent him to prison for 15 years, an examination of court records disclosed yesterday.

Instead, the 26-year-old former convict was sent to jail for 30 days after the felony charges against him and two others were reduced to misdemeanors.

He had pleaded guilty in plea bargaining in Criminal Court to the lesser charges, which arose from the robbery last November of a young man, a resident of the Park Plaza Hotel, where Mr. Jackson lived and where six of his alleged victims were killed.

Mr. Jackson's experience is no different from that of thousands of others who yearly pass through the city's court system.

In 1973, the year of Mr. Jackson's last arrest, there were 31,098 felony arrests in Manhattan, according to the crime analysis unit of the Police Department. Of these, only 545 cases went to trial on the original felony charges, including possession or sale of narcotics.

Four out of every five of the 31,098 felony arrests were subject to plea-bargaining and were disposed of at the very outset of the court process—at arraignment before a Criminal Court judge or at a subsequent hearing. That is what happened in the Jackson robbery case. . . .

—The New York Times

"By 3:30 p.m., I was still missing information. I wanted to talk to the victim who had pressed the charges against Jackson and his two accomplices on his last arrest, but a check at the Park Plaza Hotel, where a half dozen of the murders had occurred and where he lived, turned up the fact that the complainant had moved out four months before and left no forwarding address or telephone number.

"I wanted to talk to the judges involved. Two were unreachable; one was on the bench.

"At 4:30 or 5 p.m., I told my editors the status of the story. We decided that while it was important to speak to the participants, the records clearly spoke for themselves. The decision was made to write the story at about 5:15 p.m., for a 7 p.m. deadline.

"After I finished writing, a young intern came over to my desk and asked to read the dupes (duplicate copies). When he finished he said, 'Boy, that was a good leak.'

"I was startled by his comment and told him how the story came about. His statement indicated to me one of the major failures of journalism today—an overreliance on leaks and insufficient attention paid to enterprise, most of which is based on relating seemingly unrelated events."

General and Specific Knowledge

Without a reservoir of general information, fact gathering is limited. Unless the reporter has the background knowledge against which to place new facts, they will appear to him to be of equal importance, or unimportance.

Also, a good grasp of subject matter allows the reporter to check source-originated material. When a reporter says something does not ring right, he or she means that when the information supplied by a source is placed against background knowledge, the reporter hears discordant sounds. These warning signals ring loudly and clearly to the knowledgeable journalist.

Furthermore, reporters with ample background knowledge do not embarrass themselves or their editors by blundering in print or on the air. Witness these bloopers:

In one of her columns, Harriet Van Horne referred to Canada as having a "tough and happily homogeneous population. . . ." (The columnist ignored the almost six million French-speaking Canadians, who have their own schools in an officially bilingual country. Not only is the country not homogeneous, the French and English-speaking Canadians are hardly happily ensconced together. Many of the French-speaking people contend they are second-class citizens, which has led to a separatist movement in the province of Quebec.)

When the basketball coach at Boston College accepted the head coaching job at Stanford, a CBS sports announcer said that the coach had "followed Horace Mann's advice to go west." (The advice was given by Horace Greeley, founder and editor of *The Tribune:* "Go west young man." Horace Mann was an educator.)

In a feature on food served during the Jewish holidays, a reporter for the *Press-Enterprise* in Riverside, Calif., described Yom Kippur as "marked by rich, indeed lavish meals." (Yom Kippur, known as the Day of Atonement, is the most solemn of all Jewish holy days and is observed by fasting.)

During a televised National Basketball Association game, a player let the man he was covering drive past him for a basket. The player looked disgusted with himself, and from the broadcast booth the announcers could see his lips moving. "What do you think he's saying, Bill?" an announcer asked his colleague, Bill Russell, one of the great defensive stars in basketball and the first black coach in the NBA.
Russell replied, "I know how Walt feels. I can hear him muttering a four-syllable word." Russell's co-announcer laughingly corrected him: "You mean four-letter word, Bill." Slowly, deliberately, Russell said, "No, I mean four-syllable word."
There was a long pause, a smothered gasp, and then a commercial. (Russell's long playing career had given him a vast store of knowledge about the game, from strategy to the little things like the specific obscenities players use in moments of futility.)

General knowledge can be accumulated by reading widely (see chapter 7). Mark Ethridge, an editor and executive for many years of the *The* Louisville *Courier-Journal,* advised student journalists to "take all the liberal arts they possibly can and get a broad educational base. . . .If you haven't a sound liberal arts education you haven't anything to write. Then you're in the position of knowing how to do something, but not having anything to say."

All knowledge does not come from books, and the academic community does not have exclusive access to knowledge. The young men and women who are determined to be journalists are alert to the world around them. They listen closely to people and observe them carefully. They welcome new ideas, and they form ideas of their own. They are interested in history, current affairs, and the things that make people and organizations tick. They speculate about what motivates people; they wonder about the role of money in society, and they are interested in how geography, history and the weather affect what people think and do. Although they are present-oriented, they know something of the past.

No reporter can be such a compendium of past and present knowledge that he or she is prepared for every assignment. Specific background usually has to be gathered before, during and after the event is covered.

When Barbara Walters was assigned to cover the wedding of Princess Anne, she spent days preparing in her London hotel room.

"I didn't go out," she says. "I didn't accept invitations." She and her assistant, Mary Hornickel, "sat in that hotel room day and night and studied," she recalls.

"We had papers all over the floor, and we had a notebook with everything cross-indexed so that, on the day of the wedding, no matter what came up, we could point to it.

"Nothing that could have happened would have thrown us."

The payoff was obvious to television viewers. Walters was able to recognize everyone the camera pointed to, and she was able to give specific, detailed information about all aspects of the wedding.

Walters did not use all the information she had gathered. No good reporter does. When reporting and gathering background material it is impossible to predict what will be useful for the story. It is better to have too much rather than too little background information.

When a reporter was assigned to handle the appointment of a local lawyer as an assistant attorney general, a wealth of background was available from the clippings, from the attorney general's office and from the appointee himself.

The reporter noticed in one clipping that the lawyer had been a star athlete in college and had held the mile record in the Big Eight at one time. In law school, he had been the editor of the law review. The lawyer's personal background revealed the following: He is married, has three children and belongs to the Elks. A clipping about a decision by the First Presbyterian Church to offer its facilities to the Head Start program states that as an elder of the church he initiated the church's action. He is a member of the firm of Davenport, Herbert, Evans and Smythe. He recently won a suit against the state welfare department for an elderly woman.

What goes into the story of the appointment? Whatever specific information the reporter picked up in his reporting and research that is relevant to the appointment. The editorship of the law review will be used; the mile record probably will not. The appointee's personal life will be abbreviated; his professional work will be emphasized.

Specific Information

Pairing Facts

Good reporters collect stray pieces of specific information that often have no particular use at the moment. Sooner or later, another bit of information will come along that when paired with the first will make a good story.

For example, a statehouse correspondent for an Albuquerque newspaper who made it his business to look in on the state penitentiary every few weeks was talking to a guard one day when an old man walked by. He was an inmate with a long record, a farmer with an inability to earn an honest living, the guard said. Swindler, thief and bad-check artist, he was always in trouble. A few weeks later, the reporter was chatting with the warden about a well-known prisoner from Albuquerque who was a troublemaker. Despite a long record of violent crime, the troublemaker was in for an eight-year term, which meant he would be out in a little more than half that time. The farmer was in for life.

The disparities interested the reporter, but he did little with the information. Disparities in sentences were not new to him. Well-to-do defendants were never convicted for drunk driving but instead were allowed to plead to reckless driving charges; the poor were usually convicted of drunk driving. He had done a story on that. The short prison terms imposed on white collar criminals was also an old story.

Every so often, the reporter would go through the penitentiary's records of the arrests, convictions and sentences of the inmates. One day, while leafing through the record book, he noticed that the farmer had been sentenced under something called the "habitual criminal law," which required stringent sentences for frequent offenders. Other convicts were also sentenced under the same law, some to less than life. The reporter's interest was piqued. The Albuquerque convict, with a long record of more serious crimes, was not sentenced under that law. Putting these facts together, he wrote a series of articles pointing out that judges and district attorneys over the state were ignoring and misapplying the habitual criminal law so that of the 72 frequent offenders in the state penitentiary who should have been sentenced under the law, only fourteen were doing time under it.

Many Prosecutors and Judges Ignore New Mexico Habitual Criminal Laws

(New Mexico has a stringent law concerning habitual criminals. But a Journal survey has shown that it is being consistently ignored by law enforcement officers. This is the first in a series of articles on this important law.)

SANTA FE, Jan. 4—New Mexico's habitual criminal laws, which were designed to increase punishment for the frequent offender, are ignored, inconsistently used, and misunderstood by many of the state's law enforcement officers and judges, a study of official records disclosed today.

Although the laws are clearly mandatory and require district attorneys to bring charges under the act when they can be applied, few district attorneys follow the statutes.

The habitual criminal laws apply to persons who have been found guilty of more than one felony.

Yet of the 72 men now behind bars at the state penitentiary who have committed three or more felonies, only 14 were sentenced under the habitual criminal act. The number of second offenders who could have been sentenced under the law but were not were too numerous to check.

In a few cases where men have been convicted under the law, district judges have handed down illegal sentences and have not applied the law consistently.

For some time the legal profession has been aware of these facts, but little has been done either to repeal the laws or to make them work fairly.

The habitual criminal act was passed in 1929 and establishes a table of increased prison sentences for law violators who have committed more than one felony. . . .

—*The Albuquerque Journal*

Always Use Background

Few stories are complete without some background information. Reporters who disregard this advice do so at the peril of inadequately informing their readers and listeners. Events do not spring from nowhere. The reporter's task is to discover their origins and to place them in a continuum, even in the shortest of pieces, as did the reporter who handled this two-paragraph item from the Burlington, Iowa, *Hawk Eye:*

Won't Allow Encroachment

City officials said Friday they will begin enforcing right-of-way encroachments in the remaining weeks before Burlington's city commission elections.

Campaign signs posted in rights-of-way, normally the parking areas between streets and sidewalks, will be removed if found to be encroaching, administrative intern Randy Peck said. A similar approach was followed in the city elections two years ago, and several signs were removed by street crews. Peck said the city would show favoritism to no candidates.

The third paragraph in the following short item from *The New York Times* gives meaning to the story. Without this background, readers would have been deprived of possible motivation:

Negro Business Aid Group Backs Carswell Nomination

WASHINGTON, April 4—An organization called N.E.G.R.O. has taken a full-page advertisement in tomorrow's edition of *The New York Times* to endorse the nomination of Judge G. Harrold Carswell to the Supreme Court.

N.E.G.R.O., an acronym for National Economic Growth and Reconstruction Organization, Inc., gives technical aid to black entrepreneurs to help them establish businesses.

The advertisement was signed by the group's president, Dr. Thomas W. Matthew, a New York neurosurgeon. Earlier this year, Dr. Matthew was pardoned by President Nixon after he had served two months of a one-year sentence for income tax evasion.

11 Finding, Cultivating and Using Sources

Preview   Reliable sources are essential. There are two basic types of sources:
- Physical sources, which consist of records, documents, newspaper clippings, direct observations.
- Human sources, which consist of authorities and people involved in events. They are often less reliable than physical sources because they may have interests to protect, are untrained observers and sometimes tell reporters what they think the reporter wants to hear. When using human sources, find the person most qualified to speak—an authority on the subject, an eye-witness, an official.

Journalists depend so much on their sources that it is a reporter's axiom that a reporter can be no better than his or her sources. These sources include officials, spokes persons, participants in events, documents, records, tape recordings, magazines, films and books. The quality of the reporter's story depends on the quality of the sources.

Reporters spend a lot of time looking for and cultivating good sources and contacts. A county courthouse reporter in California estimates that he spends a couple of hours a day chatting with people, testing the knowledge and reliability of some of them and just passing the time of day with the others who are his regular sources. He also chats with guards, secretaries, elevator operators. He describes these as contacts, people who can lead a reporter to a story with a tip. Once an elevator operator tipped him off about a well-known businessman who had been summoned by a grand jury and was escorted into the jury room via a back elevator.

During his first weeks covering Congress for *The Wall Street Journal,* Fred L. Zimmerman quickly learned that finding and cultivating dozens of sources and contacts was essential.

"If you can establish a friendly relationship with a committee chairman's secretary, she will tell you where he can be found in a hurry," Zimmerman says. "Or she will put you through on the phone sometimes when she wouldn't do it for a reporter she doesn't know.

"It's impossible to cover Congress well unless a reporter works hard at establishing good relations with dozens of these people whose names never get into the newspaper."

Zimmerman is describing the cultivation of one type of source, the human source. The two basic types are human and physical sources. The distinction between the two, and their relative reliability, was nicely put by Sir Kenneth Clark, the British writer and critic: "If I had to say who was telling the truth about society, a speech by the Minister of Housing or the actual buildings put up in his time, I would believe the buildings."

The difference is often on the reporter's mind, for no matter how much of his or her work depends upon interviews, the reporter seeks physical evidence whenever possible. This kind of material includes newspaper clippings, books, records and documents as well as the reporter's direct observation.

The coverage of an assassination attempt against President Ford illustrates the importance of the physical evidence provided by direct observation. During his visit to Sacramento, Calif., Ford was to walk from his hotel to the state capitol where a crowd was awaiting him. In the hotel, Richard Lerner, a UPI White House correspondent, looked out the window and debated with himself whether to join the president. He was exhausted after 20 hours of tracking Ford, and he knew that two other UPI reporters would be walking the few hundred yards with the president to the capitol. On the other hand, perhaps he should test the recent promise of the president's press secretary that the Secret Service would allow reporters to stay close to the president.

In one of those blindingly lucky decisions reporters make, Lerner says he figured, "What the hell, I'm going to tag along."

When a young woman, Lynette "Squeaky" Fromme, pulled a .45 caliber pistol from a leg holster, Lerner was only eight or ten feet away. He saw the woman, the gun and an agent grabbing the woman before she could shoot.

Later, the Secret Service told the press that the gun had never been higher than the level of the woman's mid-thigh. But Lerner had seen the gun come near her waist, and he also saw the president spot the gun before the Secret Service agents had.

"Ford moved on his own, I'm certain of that," Lerner says. "I was startled and froze on the spot. By then the Secret Service had seized the woman and there was a scuffle going on for the gun."

Lerner recovered quickly and sprinted about 200 yards back to the hotel. He called his Washington bureau and began dictating a bulletin and his eyewitness account. The AP had reporters close to Ford, too, but they had not seen the pistol in the woman's hand. Along with other reporters, the AP had to await official confirmation. The wait cost the AP much of the newspaper play because editors around the world had the UPI bulletin on their desks before the AP story began to move. The AP admitted that it was beaten because "it took precious minutes to obtain confirmation that the gun had been wrestled away from a would-be assassin."

Lerner had the facts from a physical source—his own observations. They were reliable, and they were immediate. Since the other reporters had not witnessed the event, they had to rely on human sources, and their accounts were not only later than the UPI's but did not have the conviction that direct observation carries.

Let us examine these two types of sources in detail.

Human Sources

A person with information the reporter needs for a story or for background is described as a source. Sources include the woman who saw an airplane fall short of the landing strip, and Deep Throat, the informant who cooperated with *Washington Post* reporters Woodward and Bernstein on the Watergate investigation. The stockbroker friend of a reporter on the business beat who explains complicated financial matters is a source, although his name may never appear in a story.

Here is how Arthur L. Gavshon, the diplomatic reporter for the AP, defines a source in an article on sources in the *AP World Magazine:*

> To me anyone on the inside of any given news situation is a potential source. But they only turn into real sources when they come up with a bit, or a lot, of relevant information. In writing thousands of stories over the years I have been helped in varying degree by prime ministers, even a president or two, members of cabinets, politicians, diplomats, doormen, police officers and pretty secretaries. Not to mention regular spokesmen who, at times, have to go on background terms.

Gavshon says he finds sources:

> Anywhere and everywhere. Particularly whenever the affairs of men and nations are discussed. For there you'll always find the politicians. And if you don't find them they, being politicians, soon enough will find you. And always remember politicians need newsmen quite as much as newsmen need politicians.

And he develops his sources:

> Just as you would get to know a friend and nurture a relationship in everyday life (always assuming you can live a normal life as a newsman!)—through the exercise of patience, understanding and a reasonable capacity to converse about shared interests.

Sometimes, if sources seem inaccessible, Gavshon uses two techniques to open their doors:

> There's nothing quite like trying the direct approach through normal channels as a start. Working for AP, of course, opens many doors although far more in the United States than abroad. My own private way of establishing a line to someone really worthwhile has been to suggest a meeting for the purpose of writing a profile-cum-interview with the person. Few public people find it in them to resist that sort of thing.

Contacts Pay Off. A summer barbecue came to a sudden end for reporter Diane Goldie when she was ordered by beeper phone to hasten to a Jersey City police station where an officer had shot another police officer. Unable to change clothes—her deadline was little more than an hour off—she raced to the station, only to be informed of a press blackout. Goldie telephoned a friend on the force who passed her the police report.

Sources need not be directors of companies, mayors or congressmen. As we have seen from Zimmerman's experience, excellent sources and contacts can be found in the so-called anonymous posts—secretaries, clerks, assistants. The city hall reporter knows that the town clerk who has served a succession of mayors has a comprehensive knowledge of the community and the inner workings of town government.

The courthouse reporter befriends law clerks, court stenographers and security guards. Business reporters cultivate switchboard operators, secretaries, the mailroom help. They know the names of company board members who do not hold executive positions and may discuss new developments.

Reporters have gone out of their way to do favors for their mid-level sources. At one newspaper in California, the reporters who handle obituaries send candy and flowers on birthdays to mortuary employees who call to report the deaths of important people. A death called in near deadline means the newspaper or station called first will have that much more time to write the obituary. A difference of two minutes can be the difference between making or missing the last edition or the 6 p.m. newscast.

Some reporters cultivate sources by reversing the news-gathering process. One Midwestern newsman says that instead of always asking sources for news, he puts his sources on the receiving end. "I see to it personally that they hear any gossip or important news. This pays off. When I want news, I get it," he says.

Most of the sources we have been talking about are essential to a beat. The source needed for information on a single story need not be cultivated with the care reporters lavish on essential sources. But courtesy and consideration are always important, regardless of the nature of the source. In speaking to a source for the first—and perhaps the only—time, the reporter will identify himself or herself immediately and move to the questions quickly. A different pace is necessary for the source essential to a beat. Gavshon cautions:

> Don't ever rush things. Don't make the ghastly mistake of thinking only in terms of tomorrow's headline. A serious political-diplomatic correspondent will see source relationships against the sweep of years ahead. One-night stands rarely satisfy anybody.

Keeping the Source

The source is the reporter's life blood. Without access to information through the source, the reporter cannot function. The reporter is just as necessary to most sources, for without the journalist the source has no access to the public. Most sources need public approval—through votes and support of policies—to function. Out of this mutual need a source-reporter relationship develops.

The source will provide the reporter with information and will brief him or her on developments. In return, the reporter will write a fair account of the material supplied.

As events become more complex, the reporter's dependence on sources increases. Briefings to explain complicated information are essential. A municipal budget officer can take days to brief a reporter about the budget to be submitted to the city council. When a reporter learns of a probable future event, he or she may ask a source for background so that a difficult story can be written without deadline pressure. The courthouse reporter who learns through the grapevine that the grand jury is about to return an indictment against the city clerk will ask the district attorney for a briefing, promising not to break the story before the indictment is returned. The district attorney usually is happy to comply, because he prefers a detailed, accurate story to a rush job.

Some reporters manage to score exclusives by rushing into print with tips and by disregarding embargoes. But sources eventually freeze out such reporters, unless the beat is so large that there is always someone available to talk. Still, it is risky to go ahead with a story before the facts are confirmed or verified. Writing a story on an indictment before it has been returned, for example, can lead to disaster for a reporter. It has become common practice among prosecutors to threaten to indict the subject of an investigation so that he or she will inform—"turn" is the prosecutor's word—on a bigger target. The Watergate inquiry was replete with examples of this tactic. Gullible reporters, or scoop artists, can be used by clever prosecutors. The harmonious reporter-source relationship avoids these exploitative activities.

Protecting Sources

Sometimes reporters have to protect the identity of a source. An investigative reporter learns from a police officer that a convict serving a life term for murder was convicted on perjured police testimony. In return for the tip about the frame-up, the reporter must promise to keep the source's identity secret.

In half the states, the reporter can make this promise because shield laws protect confidential sources. All states have some kind of protection, but recent state and federal court rulings indicate a trend away from full protection to a more limited type. In some states, a reporter who tries to protect a confidential source may face contempt charges and jail. State press associations usually distribute pamphlets about reporters' rights.

Protection of another kind can also be troublesome to reporters. Sometimes a reporter is too close to a source and is reluctant to hurt or embarrass him or her with a tough story. To avoid this dilemma, reporters have to learn to mark a line between their professional and personal lives. Walter Lippmann said there must be a "certain distance between the reporter and the source, not a wall or a fence, but an air space." Once a friend becomes an official, he said, "you can't call him by his first name anymore." Often the reluctance to criticize stems from the fear that a critical story may dry up the source.

After the newspaper *Newsday* ran a series of articles describing the financial affairs of a Florida financier who was close to President Nixon, the newspaper was excluded from the president's trip to China. Also, the presidential press secretary refused to speak to the newspaper's White House correspondent for three months. President Johnson forbade his press secretary to give any inside information to a reporter for the *St. Louis Post-Dispatch* because Johnson felt the reporter's questions at press briefings had been too aggressive. Good reporters are willing to sacrifice favors from this kind of source.

Still, reporters protect certain sources. The reason: Without some sources, the reporter cannot function. Jack Anderson, a Washington columnist who specializes in inside information, states his philosophy as follows: "We will give immunity to a very good source as long as the information he offers us is better than that which we've got on him."

The young reporter has still another problem that sometimes leads to the overprotection of sources. Mixing with the kinds of people the reporter had once only read about or seen on television—governors, congressmen, movie stars, generals—can be a heady affair. Without knowing it, the journalist may lose objectivity. Veteran reporters suffer from another form of this ailment. They become source-oriented. Forgetting that they are responsible to the general reader, they write copy for their source's approval. After all, the reporter may say to himself, the readers don't really know the score and their opinions aren't worth much.

Important as human sources are, they are not the most reliable. The beat reporter finds that his sources often have interests they wish to protect, programs and ideas they want to push, enemies they want to hurt.

Reliability

The Washington Post reported that outgoing President Jimmy Carter had planted a recording device in Blair House while incoming President Ronald Reagan and Nancy Reagan were staying there. When Carter protested, the *Post* apologized and said its source had been in error.

The source's motive was unclear. Some reporters concluded that the source was out to embarrass Carter.

The reporter who has to rely on transient sources for quick information on a breaking story knows that most people are notoriously inaccurate. A woman who says she saw an airplane crash in a ball of fire may not be relaying what she saw three hours ago but what she has seen on television shows and in movies over the years.

In 1968, eyewitnesses said that they had seen a UFO (unidentified flying object) in the sky on March third. They said that it was cigar-shaped with airliner-style windows and jet exhaust coming out the back.

Scientists had an opportunity to check on this sighting, for this was the date a Soviet Zond 4 satellite reentered the atmosphere. The satellite was not cigar-shaped, did not have airliner-style windows and was not shooting jet exhaust out the back.

Philip J. Klass, a flying saucer investigator, says that the public, "drawing on information it had acquired through the years from news-media accounts, supplied specific details that their eyes had never seen."

The conjurings of the mind took over the observations of the eye.

An eyewitness can seduce a reporter by the sheer drama of his or her story. Instead of being enthralled, the reporter should be cautious, for his knowledge of human nature should tell him that most people seek attention and tend to overdramatize events they have witnessed.

Erving Goffman, the sociologist, says everyone is a performer trying to put his or her stamp of individual identity on things. Individuals find it hard not to exaggerate their observations or feelings when they know that the more dramatic they are the more likely they or their remarks will be in the news. Having seen what is used on television newscasts, people tend to give the reporter what they think the reporter wants. This phenomenon is one reason for the stereotyped responses of most people interviewed at breaking news events.

People also forget aspects of what they have seen. They remember selectively, recalling mostly that which fits their preconceived notions or is pleasant to keep in mind.

If the average person who is sometimes called upon as a source can be so unreliable, how can the reporter test the source's reliability? Here are some measures of reliability:

Was the person an observer of the incident, or did he or she hear about it from someone else?

Is the person a competent observer? An airline employee would be a better source for information about an airplane crash than a student or a salesperson.

Can the source supply precise details that have the ring of truth and seem consistent with the facts?

For the sources essential to a reporter's beat, only the best-qualified persons should be called upon or cultivated. These sources should be selected because of their knowledge of the area, their contacts with others, and their reputations for intelligence and honesty.

False Credentials

Sometimes reporters use sources because of who or what they are, not because of what they know. Reporters can be blinded by the title, the organizational affiliation, the alma mater or the social position of a source.

Most people tend to believe those in authority. The greater the title or position, the more faith people have in the expert or authority. This is known as the "hierarchy of credibility"—the higher on the scale the authority is, the more believable he or she is thought to be. When the journalist surrenders to this tendency, he or she loses independence to those who hold power, allowing them to define events and situations.

Reporters also must be careful to use sources only within their area of expert knowledge. Asked questions within the narrow range of their expertise, sources are useful: A banker can talk about banking, a general about the strategy and tactics of war. But it is dangerous to rely on a banker for comments on the nation's economy or on a general as an authority on international affairs. The glitter of their jobs and titles attracts reporters to them as general-purpose sources, but they may be less useful than the lesser-known labor department area representative or the assistant professor of international affairs at a local college.

A reporter's best sources are those who have demonstrated their knowledge and competence as accurate observers, interpreters and forecasters of events. Reporters should drop sources who are proved wrong in their observations and assessments, whether they served in the president's cabinet, ran a multi-million dollar import business or graduated *summa cum laude* from Harvard.

Testing Steady Sources

Before the reporter decides to depend on an individual as a steady source of information, a simple test can be made of that person's reliability. The reporter can corroborate facts from other sources, physical as well as human. The individual's recollections can be checked against reference works or news clippings. If the potential source is found to be inaccurate, he or she is dropped. Sources should be re-evaluated periodically, particularly after a change in jobs. The city zoning administrator may lose effectiveness as an authority on certain topics after he becomes executive secretary of the local real estate board. Political reporters usually limit their use of the government official who goes to work as a lobbyist for industry.

Sometimes the information necessary for a story is so complex that no one person can know everything about the situation. And even the source with the best intentions can supply biased or misleading information because of his or her limited knowledge. In these situations, a second source is essential.

During *The Washington Post*'s Watergate investigation, when the reputation, if not the survival, of the newspaper hung on the reliability of sources, a corroborating source was always sought so that all the facts lacking supporting physical evidence were attested to by at least two individuals.

AP diplomatic reporter Gavshon uses a fairly simple device to test reliability, although he cautions that "in the end you, the reporter, are going to have to learn for yourself if you're being told something or sold something. . . . My own rough-and-ready rule is to test out the new-found source with questions to which I already know the answers."

Despite all these tests, the reporter has to keep in mind that he or she is relying on someone else, and that fact alone makes the story vulnerable. No reporter can ever feel certain that another person's observations are as accurate as his own.

Physical Sources

The range of physical information is enormous—from newspaper clippings, the telephone directory and the almanac to the reporter's direct observations. Physical sources are limited only by the reporter's imagination and the newspaper's or station's resources.

Many reference resources are free to the journalist: the law library of the district attorney or the nearby law school; the public and private libraries in town whose librarians delight in visits or calls from journalists; the files of local and state agencies in town, and the considerable resources of the nearby college or university. Many of the larger state educational institutions have on their campuses various state-supported and private programs for governmental studies that are well stocked with materials for stories as well as for background.

One reporter who leafed through the office copy of the *Congressional Record* each week often turned up interesting stories about area congressmen. A couple of thousand miles from their constituents, the congressmen apparently felt free to say what they might not tell local reporters. Once the reporter happened on a congressman's eulogy for Generalissimo Francisco Franco, the Spanish dictator. The piece drew considerable comment from the congressman's constituents.

All Sources Are Not Equal

As we have seen, reporters prefer the physical source to the human source. But not all physical sources are of equal reliability. The annual tables of vital statistics are more reliable than the city official's summary introducing the tables. The *World Almanac* is more reliable than a newspaper clipping of the same event, for the *Almanac* is usually the work of professional researchers, and the news story may have been written in a hurry before all the facts were in. Although reporters know they make mistakes, they sometimes use other reporters' work as the basis of their stories and the results can be embarrassing.

Veneration for Print

Journalists have a tendency to venerate the printed word, no matter what its source. Perhaps it is because the journalist spends his or her life in close harmony with words on paper.

Whatever the reason, the journalist's esteem for the somber black characters of print can be misplaced. In fact, print sometimes solidifies an original error. Once a story is written and filed in the newspaper morgue, it is difficult to correct an error, which may later be repeated, even magnified.

Here is the chronology of a printed error that was given added circulation because the journalist assumed that the published word was true. The journalist, Tom Wicker, wrote this explanation in his column:

> A Memorial Day column detailing the problems of Vietnam war veterans stated that 500,000 of them had attempted suicide. This statistic was derived from an article in *Penthouse* magazine. The author of that article obtained it from a pamphlet of Twice Born Men, a veterans' group in San Fran- cisco, now defunct. That organization's former director, Jack McCloskey, says he got the figure from the National Council of the Churches of the U.S.A. The council disavowed any knowledge of the statistic, which must therefore be considered unsupported. Its publication in this space is regretted.

The figure 500,000 should have seemed preposterous on its face. But reporters sometimes are influenced by their attitudes. Wicker may have been predisposed to believe the figure because of his opposition to the Vietnam War.

As for photographs, everyone knows by now that pictures can distort, if not lie. Camera angles, close-ups and the time appropriated to incidents in film can emphasize irrelevancies or capture an atypical moment.

Ultimately, the reliability of physical information comes down to the journalist's ability to spot inaccuracies and to double-check whenever possible. The inaccuracy of the physical source is no excuse for a reporter, who understands and accepts the rule of survival in journalism: Too many mistakes and you are out. Taught by experience and informed by a familiarity with his or her beat, the reporter makes surprisingly few errors, given the pressure under which he or she produces stories. One of the reasons is the journalist's reliance on and careful use of physical sources.

Using the Mails

The advantages of relying on physical evidence are demonstrated in the experience of a California reporter who needed some key information in his investigation of a faith healer. He wanted to determine whether the healings had been permanent.

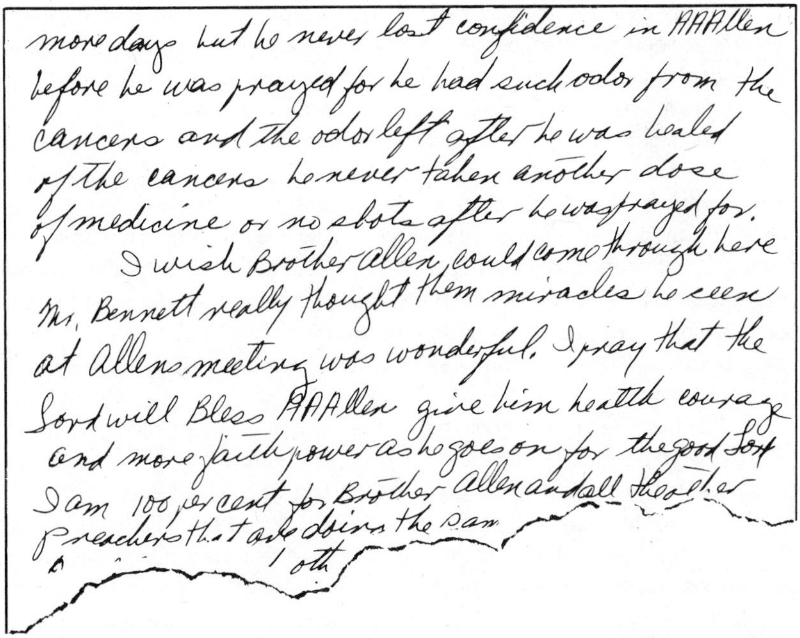

more days but he never lost confidence in AAAllen
before he was prayed for he had such odor from the
cancers and the odor left after he was healed
of the cancers he never taken another dose
of medicine or no shots after he was prayed for.
I wish Brother Allen could come through here
Mr. Bennett really thought them miracles he seen
at Allens meeting was wonderful. I pray that the
Lord will Bless AAAllen give him health courage
and more faith power as he goes on for the good Lord
I am 100 percent for Brother Allen and all the other
preachers that are doing the sam

Figure 11.1

Rather than make telephone calls, he wrote to those who had claimed healing. Their written replies, he felt, would carry more weight as documentation than their oral statements on long distance telephone calls.

One man had traveled more than a thousand miles from his home in Colorado in search of a cure for stomach cancer. A letter was sent to the man's physician. (During the healing sessions, a reporter had managed to learn the names of physicians who were treating some of those who sought healing.) The Colorado man's doctor wrote back that upon the patient's return from California he had been hospitalized and shortly thereafter died of stomach cancer.

The reporter then wrote the man's widow to ask if her faith remained strong in the evangelist. She replied in a lengthy, handwritten note that her faith was unwavering. Quotes from her letter revealed the strength of conviction of the evangelist's followers and described the kind of people who had made him a wealthy man of the cloth. (See figure 11.1.)

How Reporters Use Sources

Let us accompany four reporters as they work with various kinds of sources for their stories. The first story is the type that puts reporters on their mettle, the late-breaking event that must be handled quickly and accurately.

A Fatal

The story takes us to a New Jersey newsroom where a reporter is making late police checks, which consist of calling area police departments not personally covered by the police reporter. Here, the reporter must rely on human sources. There is little opportunity to examine police records.

Police reporters often turn up good stories because the police are the first to know of accidents, crimes, public disturbances and other deviations from the normal run of community life. They even know when parades will be held since the police usually are asked to barricade streets and may have to arrange for special escorts.

This night, the reporter turned up something more serious than a parade: A car had plowed into a motorcycle at a stop light and the two young people on the motorcycle were killed. The driver was arrested three miles down the highway and charged with drunken driving. The reporter knew this was a big story, but little time remained before the last edition closed. The rule in the newsroom, she remembered her editor telling her, is simple: "In baseball, if you get your glove on the ball and don't handle it cleanly, it's an error, no matter how hard it's hit to you. If you get a story before deadline and don't have it written for the next edition, you're not a reporter."

She had seen several baseball games in which fielders managed to touch a ball but were not given errors when they failed to throw the man out. But she had never wanted to call that to her editor's attention. She knew better.

She quickly learned the names of the victims and the driver and the location and circumstances of the accident. Knowing that the investigating officers were still writing their report, she asked if they were available at the station. She knew they would have details she needed, especially about the chase for the driver. She then called the mortuary to obtain background about the victims. Mortuaries will usually have the exact spelling of the victim's name, age, address and occupation. She glanced at the clock to see whether she had time to call the parents of the victims for more precise information. She decided she did not, particularly since the grief-stricken parents probably would have been incapable of talking. However, relatives often are on hand to help out, and they might be able to tell her something about the deceased youngsters. But she decided that first she would try the clippings to see if the victims' names were in the newspaper library.

During her interviews with the investigating officers, one of them mentioned that this was the third motorcycle accident in the last month, and she had noted that on her pad for a quick check in the library, too.

The check of the library, made by a reporter at a nearby desk who had some free time, disclosed this was actually the fourth motorcycle accident in the county, one of the others having been fatal to a young man. The clippings also turned up a story about the young woman who had been killed. She was the daughter of a prominent local family, and the story indicated she used a middle name, which was not in the reporter's notes.

The reporter then decided she should try to locate the parents of the young man who had died in the accident. She realized that she had decided not to make those calls because of her distaste for intruding on the family's tragedy. At some newspapers, reporters do not have to make such calls, she recalled a colleague telling her, but that was not the case at this one. She made the call and the younger sister of the boy answered the telephone and was able to supply some details about him.

In watching the reporter at work, we see how she used physical and human sources and that one of the keys to the story was her knowledge that the investigating police officers might be at the police station writing up the report of the accident. She knew that the best sources are those close to the scene. Although they had not seen the accident, they had arrived quickly and had conducted the investigation. The names of the officers would add authenticity to the story.

With her notes on one side of the typewriter and the library clippings on the other she began to type, some 20 minutes before the last edition would close. She knew she had time because she had organized the story during her reporting.

A Shooting

Although reporters sometimes use the telephone when they should be on the street talking to people or in meetings observing the give-and-take of open debate, on occasions direct observation is impossible. We have just seen a reporter handle a fatal accident by telephone. When the deadline is imminent and the source or the event is more than a short walk or trip away, the only recourse is the telephone.

Using the telephone can be an art. Properly used, it is a boon to reporting. But good reporters know its limitations. Let us watch a television news reporter cover a shooting 50 miles north of her station, WKTV in Utica, N.Y.

Early one fall evening, Donna Hanover was told by a cameraman that he had picked up a police report that two persons had been shot in separate incidents as they drove past an Indian encampment near the town of Big Moose. Hanover knew immediately this was a big story. Some Mohawk Indians had moved on to state-owned land in the Adirondack Mountains six months before and had refused to leave. Nothing had been done to the squatters. But the sudden burst of gunfire—apparently from Indians at the encampment—indicated something important might have happened.

Hanover's major problem was her impending deadline and the distance to Big Moose. Her newscast was at 11 p.m., which gave her no time for the trip up, reporting and the return trip with the film. She had to use the telephone.

By 10:15 p.m., her calls to the state police had turned up little information—a few details on the shooting and the names and ages of the injured. Apparently both were wounded by shots fired at the cars in which they were riding. Hanover then called a medical center near Big Moose to check the condition of the victims, a 22-year-old man and a 9-year-old girl. She also hoped to learn something more about the incident. She was told that the young man had been taken to a hospital in Utica and that the girl was on her way. When she called the hospital, the girl had just arrived.

She asked for information about the relatives of those who were injured. A hospital attendant gave her the name of the injured man's father. "I then called information for the home telephone number, hoping that some member of the family would have stayed at home in Big Moose," Hanover said.

She was lucky. The father was not there, but the person who answered the telephone was the victim's brother, and he had been riding in the car with his older brother at the time of the shooting.

DH

INDIANS

A 22 YEAR OLD MAN AND A 9 YEAR OLD GIRL WERE INJURED TODAY IN TWO
SEPARATE SHOOTING INCIDENTS ON BIG MOOSE ROAD NEAR EAGLE BAY.
STEPHEN DRAKE OF INLET, NEW YORK, IS IN THE INTENSIVE CARE WARD OF
ST. LUKE'S MEMORIAL HOSPITAL IN SATISFACTORY CONDITION.
HIS BROTHER, 20 YEAR OLD MICHAEL DRAKE, WAS WITH HIM WHEN HE WAS
SHOT, AND EXPLAINED WHAT HAPPENED. MICHAEL SAID THE TWO WERE DRIVING
                                    WITHOUT WARNING
DOWN BIG MOOSE ROAD WHEN THREE SHOTS WERE FIRED AT THEIR VEHICLE BY
             A GROUP OF THE INDIANS WHO   MOVED ON TO THE LAND
                                            DRAKES
ABOUT SIX MONTHS AGO. THEY KEPT DRIVING UNTIL THEY WERE OUT OF RANGE,
AND SPENT ABOUT 20 MINUTES AT BIG MOOSE LODGE. ON THE WAY BACK, AT
          AGAIN WITHOUT WARNING,
5:30, THEY CAME UNDER HEAVY FIRE AT THE SAME SPOT. STEPHEN, WHO WAS
DRIVING, WAS HIT IN THE LEFT SHOULDER. MICHAEL SAID THERE WERE ABOUT
15 MEN, AND THAT AT LEAST FIVE OF THEM WERE ARMED WITH RIFLES AND
SHOTGUNS. AFTER THE DRAKES WERE OUT OF RANGE AGAIN, MICHAEL TOOK
OVER THE WHEEL. STATE POLICE HAVE SET UP A ROADBLOCK ACROSS THE
BIG MOOSE ROAD TO PREVENT ANYONE FROM ENTERING THE AREA.
          MICHAEL'S PARENTS, ALLAN AND AUDREY DRAKE,
OPERATE DRAKES INN ON ROUTE 28 ABOUT 6 MILES FROM BIG MOOSE. THE
BUSINESS IS A FAMILY OPERATION IN WHICH THE FIVE CHILDREN PARTICIPATE,
AS DOESN STEPHEN'S WIFE, ELLEN. MICHAEL DRAKE SAID THAT THE INDIANS
                                        TWO
HAVE NEVER BOTHERED HIM BEFORE, BUT THAT   CUSTOMERS HAVE REPORTED
BEING FOLLOWED, PULLED OVER, AND WARNED TO STAY OFF INDIAN LAND.
                                            AT DRAKE'S INN
MICHAEL SAID THE INDIANS OCCASIONALLY STOP FOR GAS, BUT RARELY INDULGE
IN CONVERSATION.   STEPHEN DRAKE WAS TREATED
AT AN OLD FORGE MEDICAL GROUP BEFORE BEING TAKEN TO ST. LUKES. ALSO
TREATED AT OLD FORGE AND THEN ST. LUKES WAS A NINE WHO WAS RIDING
                                          YEAR OLD
                                          GIRL
                                          IDENTIFIED AS APRIL MADIGAN

2-

WITH HER FAMILY ON BIG MOOSE ROAD, AFTER DINING AT BIG MOOSE LODGE.
SHE WAS REPORTEDLY IN THE BACK SEAT WHEN THE CAR WAS FIRED ON.

A COMMAND POST HAS BEEN SET UP AT THE
EAGLE BAY FIRE HOUSE. STATE POLICE HAVE
BEEN BROUGHT IN FROM TUPPER
& SARANAC LAKE AS WELL AS FROM
THE SURROUNDING AREA.
MAJOR, ROB'T CHARLAND, COMMANDER
OF THROOP D, IS CURRENTLY AT THE
SCENE, HEADING THE INVESTIGATION.

10-28-74   dh

Figure 11.2 A Shooting. The script for the shooting incident was written under deadline pressure. Hanover was still bringing the story up-to-date at air time.

This piece of good fortune enabled Hanover to use an eyewitness, always a better source than someone with a secondhand account. He told Hanover that they had been fired at twice by the Indians. The first time they had missed. But on the return trip, the car had come under heavy fire and one of the brothers was hit in the shoulder.

The girl was in a car that passed by the Indian encampment a few hours after the boys were fired on. Apparently still angry, the Indians fired at the vehicle as it was disappearing down the road. One bullet entered the trunk, went through the rear seat and struck the girl in the back.

As a result of her calls, Hanover was able to make the 11 o'clock news with a report of the incident. She did not have all the information she needed, but she did have the interview, information from the state police, the condition of the 22-year-old and the name of the 9-year-old girl who was also injured. (See figure 11.2.)

The next day, with plenty of time, Hanover and two photographers drove to Big Moose to do an on-the-scene report. She interviewed the injured man's brother again, this time in front of a camera, photographed the damaged automobile and interviewed local residents and the state police.

The youth told Hanover that as he and his brother drove past the encampment they had shouted out some war whoops. He said that they had not shot at the Indians at any time.

Hanover checked his story with the police. They confirmed that the 20-year-old had been in the car with his brother when it was struck by bullets, and they said that no weapons had been found in the car.

"The interview with the brother was important," Hanover says, "because he was a primary source. The police report wasn't, and our job is to give our viewers the best and most accurate information about what has happened."

The interview also added an essential ingredient for television news—visual identification.

"I always try to make the viewers feel close to the scene, to make them feel they were there as it happened," says Hanover, who later went to television stations in Columbus, Ohio, Pittsburgh, Miami and New York.

One patrolman was photographed indicating where the bullets had entered the vehicle. The Indians were not available for interviews. Later, they told her they had been shot at and were returning the fire.

Her script began:

```
New York state police are manning roadblocks near Eagle
Bay and are escorting cars on Big Moose Road where two
people in passing cars were shot Monday. Nine-year-old
April Madigan of Geneva, New York, is in critical condition
at St. Luke's Memorial Hospital Center. . . .
```

After describing the Madigan shooting, she turned to the incident involving the brothers. She let the 20-year-old brother describe for one minute and 37 seconds how he and his older brother drove by, let out some war whoops and suddenly were fired on. His segment ended with, "I didn't bother them."

We turn from these spot news stories to a story that began with a chat between college classmates.

An Enterpriser

Jeffrey A. Tannenbaum, a reporter with *The Wall Street Journal,* was in the newsroom when a call came in from a friend, Ralph Sanders, one of Tannenbaum's classmates at Columbia University. Sanders, who is blind, told Tannenbaum he was active in an organization called the National Federation of the Blind and that the group was planning a demonstration to publicize the plight of blind people. Sanders said that the blind were tired of being denied rights granted to sighted people.

He invited Tannenbaum to the demonstration and suggested that it would make a good story. Sensing a broader story than the coverage of an event that was being staged for the media, Tannenbaum arranged to have lunch with Sanders.

"I was fascinated with the possibility of writing a story about the blind comparable to early stories on the civil rights movement," Tannenbaum says. "In the course of a long interview, Sanders provided the theme for the story. I used it in the sixth paragraph of the finished story.

"What I needed to do after the interview was to document the central thesis. I needed to find examples of ways in which blind people are discriminated against. And I needed to find cases of discrimination in which blind people were militant."

Sanders provided some sources and examples of militancy. Tannenbaum found other examples by calling organizations of the blind. He learned about the alleged discrimination by checking with social agencies and human rights commissions. He was able to find more than a dozen examples of discrimination.

"As a rule of thumb," Tannenbaum says, "I like to have half-a-dozen highly-readable, colorful, to-the-point examples in a story. Each one should illustrate a different aspect of the general problem, buttressing the main theme but not precisely duplicating one another."

He checked with people who might have another point of view on what the blind had charged was discrimination.

Tannenbaum says, "More than fairness is involved here; a good reporter knows that the best stories are multi-dimensional. Conflict and controversy do make a better story, but they also accurately reflect reality."

Tannenbaum now had sources with specific complaints and incidents they recalled. He had a feeling an incident at a Washington, D.C., airport described by Keith and Elizabeth Howard would be well up in his story, perhaps the lead. But he needed some general information.

He interviewed the head of Sanders' organization, and eventually came upon a blind professor of American history at Seton Hall College in New Jersey, who provided an excellent quote that gave an overview of the problems of the blind. He consulted some references for data about the blind. He had now interviewed 40 people and was ready to write.

The writing was relatively painless, he recalls. "A well-reported story—one reported logically with a central theme in mind—tends to write itself." He began with an example—a delayed lead—and presented the theme in his own words in the fifth paragraph, then in Sanders' words in the sixth paragraph.

The next two paragraphs were perspective, background. Originally, he had the blind professor's quote lower in the story, but he remembered the guideline that good quotes should be put up high in a story and he raised the quote as high as he could.

"A reporter can usually improve a story by rewriting it a second, a third, even a fourth time, if he has time," Tannenbaum says.

"While writing, I realized I needed to do more reporting to bring home an example. For instance, in writing about the blind seeking jobs I decided to add a paragraph putting credibility into the claims of the blind that they can handle jobs, which is hard for most sighted people to believe. So I called back a source and got some more information."

Tannenbaum spotted some holes in his story, questions he thought readers might ask, and so he did additional reporting.

THE WALL STR

© 1975 Dow Jones & Company

VOL. CLXXXVI NO. 7 ★★ EASTERN EDITION THURSDAY, JU

New Crusaders

Angry Blind Militants, Seeking 'Equal Rights,' Try Tougher Tactics

Sightless Stage Walkouts, Sue Landlords, Bosses, Reject 'Excessive' Pity

The Fight With Sky Glider

By JEFFREY A. TANNENBAUM
Staff Reporter of THE WALL STREET JOURNAL

Keith and Elizabeth Howard were all set to board an Allegheny Airlines flight from Washington, D.C., to Philadelphia. The airplane wasn't fully booked. Yet an airline official suddenly insisted they must take separate flights.

The reason: The Howards are both blind.

The couple say they were told the pilot didn't want more than one blind passenger on the flight because he assumed that blind people might cause a safety problem or require extra service. While his wife went on ahead, the 43-year-old Mr. Howard waited for the next flight.

Far from being helpless nuisances, the Howards both successfully manage their own lunch counters in Washington. They angrily protested to Allegheny, which confirms their story. Allegheny apologized, and says that Ransome Airlines, which operated the flight under contract, has changed its policies to prevent a repeat of the incident. But the Howards figure their problems are far from over. They say the airline incident was typical of the "common discrimination—a normal thing" that society practices almost routinely against the blind.

But nowadays, blind people like the Howards are moving with increasing fervor to protest such discrimination. They are voicing complaints, turning to the courts and even staging strikes and demonstrations. As a result, employers, landlords and businesses generally are finding they must either change their policies or face protests and lawsuits.

"A Dash of Leprosy"

"Society will give charity to the blind, but it won't allow us to be first-class citizens," charges Ralph W. Sanders, president of the Arkansas unit of the National Federation of the Blind. "Like the blacks, we've come to the point where we're not going to stand for it anymore," he adds.

Ironically, this militancy occurs at a time when conditions for the blind are improving significantly, particularly in the realm of jobs. Several states in recent ~~have gr~~ ~~approv~~ ~~broad~~

What's News—

* * *

* * *

Business and Finance

OIL'S EXPORT PRICE was cut by Ecuador in what may be the first major crack in the oil cartel's pricing structure. Ecuador's cut was through a reduction in the income-tax rate charged oil companies.
(Story on Page 3)

* * *

A tax on most crude oil and refined petroleum products of up to three cents a barrel was proposed, as expected, by President Ford to help pay for damages caused by oil spills.
(Story on Page 3)

* * *

A Honduran commission urged steps to nationalize the concessions and property of units of United Brands and Castle & Cooke to increase that country's participation in the banana-export business.
(Story on Page 2)

* * *

Developing nations' efforts to negotiate new international agreements fixing commodities prices will be resisted by the U.S., a top Treasury official said.
(Story on Page 2)

* * *

General Motors is being countersued by a former dealer for $33 million in connection with a tangled series of criminal and civil cases involving alleged warranty fraud. Separately, GM said its supplemental benefit fund for laid-off employes could soon resume payouts for a brief period.
(Stories on Page 4)

* * *

Ford Motor confirmed that it quietly paid for repairing about 69,000 rust-damaged 1969-73 models even though normal warranties had expired.
(Story on Page 4)

* * *

Great Atlantic & Pacific Tea reported a $6.5 million loss, less than predicted, for its May 24 first quarter; a year earlier it earned $10.3 million.
(Story on Page 4)

* * *

International Paper's second quarter earnings slid 37% to $47.2

World-Wide

A MIDEAST AGREEMENT isn't "anywhere near," Kissinger said.

The Secretary of State, beginning a European trip during which he will meet with Israeli Prime Minister Rabin, said reports that an Egyptian-Israeli accord had been all but wrapped up are "totally wrong." Hearst Newspapers quoted Egyptian President Sadat as indicating that basic terms of a new interim Sinai agreement had been worked out. But Prime Minister Rabin said some key issues remain to be settled.

Sources suggested that an agreement would involve an electronic surveillance system, operated by the U.S., to warn of any attack through the Gidi and Mitla mountain passes in the Sinai.

Rabin conferred with West German Chancellor Schmidt in Bonn, who urged the Israeli premier to take advantage of the current chance to win a settlement with Egypt. Kissinger arrived in Paris and will meet with Soviet Foreign Minister Gromyko in Geneva before seeing Rabin Saturday in Bonn.

The Palestine Liberation Organization said in Beirut that it had failed to win the release of an American Army colonel kidnapped last week. It said the colonel was being held by two radical Palestinian groups that don't belong to the PLO. The deadline the abductors set for the U.S. to meet their ransom demands passed.

* * *

A TURKISH-ARMS COMPROMISE was offered to the House by Ford.

After meeting with 140 House members, the President proposed legislation partially lifting the ban on military aid that was imposed after Turkey used U.S. weapons in invading Cyprus. Under the plan, undelivered arms already paid for by Turkey would be shipped and more weapons could be bought for cash, but Turkey wouldn't be eligible for grants. Ford would report to Congress every two months on arms sales and on the chances for a Cyprus settlement.

The three leading House opponents of arms for Turkey weren't invited to the meeting with Ford. One of them, Rep. John Brademas (D., Ind.), denounced the proposal as a fraud.

Speaker Carl Albert predicted the House would approve Ford's plan. The Senate last month voted 41-40 to end the arms embargo. Turkey has demanded that negotiations on the status of U.S. bases begin next Thursday if the embargo hasn't been lifted by then. It wasn't known whether Turkey would accept Ford's compromise.

* * *

PORTUGAL'S ARMED FORCES will form local units bypassing political parties.

Then the story moved to the copy desk. "An editor sharpened some of my transitions and, as editors often do, axed several paragraphs to make the story shorter. He also asked me some questions, eliciting answers that enabled him to improve the background paragraphs. A good editor is helpful since a reporter can become so close to a story that he doesn't see ways to simplify it."

The story appeared much as Tannenbaum had written it.

Tannenbaum's story is known as an enterpriser—it originated with the reporter. From the outset, he had an idea of the theme clearly in mind. This planning enabled him to line up his sources, persons who would illustrate through their experiences the two parts of his theme—militancy and discrimination. Authoritative sources were used to give some over-all perspective to the theme—the college professor, a state insurance commissioner, lawyers.

Because Tannenbaum's story did not have the immediacy of breaking news, he was able to spend some time on it. Such stories can be run at any time and are known as time copy, or, in the language of the *Journal,* as timeless or evergreens. Our fourth story is also time copy.

Does Johnny Read?

The reporter, Mullins, is told by his city editor to find out whether people are reading as much as they used to—a vague assignment, but Mullins thinks he knows what his editor has in mind. The editor has talked so often of the impact of television in the home and the "deficiencies of the young" that Mullins gathers he wants to know if youngsters can read as well as they used to. The reading scores in local schools have been steadily declining in recent years, and the editor has played up those stories.

"If you find out anyone is still reading, tell us what they're reading," was the editor's parting comment as Mullins left for the library downtown.

After visiting that library and talking to clerks in bookstores, Mullins concludes that books are selling as well as ever and that library use has remained steady.

As Mullins is looking over his notes in a library, he notices some youngsters chatting at a table near the window. Unobtrusively, he moves over to listen.

"What did you find out about the clipper ships?" one of the boys asks another. A few minutes later, a girl asks the boy next to her if he knows when the first transcontinental railroad was completed. Apparently they are doing research for an assignment on transportation. Mullins asks one of the boys, and he is told the work is for an honors history class in one of the local high schools. That is worth noting, Mullins decides.

As he passes three boys, he glances at the books they are reading—Jack Kerouac's *On the Road,* Hermann Hesse's *Demian,* and a book that appears to be about race car driving, judging by its title. That, too, goes into Mullins's notes. Suddenly, it strikes him that this is just what he needs to be doing, that he has been relying too heavily on human sources and not enough on his own observations. He knows that sources often will tell reporters what will make them or their organizations look good, and yet he has been relying on interested sources—librarians and book store owners and their clerks—instead of physical sources.

He decides to make his observations the basis of the story.

Mullins strolls around the library, hoping to see what adults are reading. As he passes one shelf, he observes that most of the books, which bear numbers ranging from 200 to 300 on their spines, are hardly used but that a few are well worn. The well-read books are on eastern religions. He jots down their titles, and he makes a note to himself to look into that by talking to the librarian. She might have some of the titles of books that have been borrowed frequently.

The physical evidence seems to show that youngsters on school assignments are major library users as are older people with time on their hands. The older readers congregated around the newspaper rack, and much of their borrowing and reading was among the historical romances, adventure novels and mysteries. Considerable activity by all age groups focused on the ''how-to'' books that offered instruction on investments, gardening, home repair and sex.

As a result of these observations, Mullins is able to supplement what he has been told by the people he had interviewed. His story is a blend of physical and human sources, the one supplementing the other. By adding his observations of the people in the library, he is able to inject human interest into his story. He *shows* his readers the students and adults using books, newspapers and magazines.

To summarize the work of the reporters we have been watching, we can make these generalizations:

- Use direct observation whenever it is possible. Make yourself the source.
- When it is necessary to rely on second-hand accounts, use high-quality published sources, records and documents and the most knowledgeable and authoritative human sources available.
- Stay with the central character(s) or source(s) in the event you are covering—the speaker, the performer, the witness, the official.
- Line up ahead of time, or have in mind, human sources who can provide official or authoritative versions: police, fire chief or marshal, press secretary, spokesmen, authorities in the field. Stay close to them. But remember: The official version is not always the correct one.
- Use insiders whose information will serve as a check on official accounts.
- Know the limitations of human and physical sources.

12 Making Sound Observations

Preview   To make the kind of reliable and relevant observations essential to the news story, the reporter must:

- Know what readers and listeners are interested in and what they need to know.
- Find a theme for the story as early in the reporting as possible.
- Look for the dramatic, the unusual, the unique aspect of the event that sets it apart from other events like it.

In addition to the standard methods of reporting, journalists use unobtrusive observation (the identity of the reporter is unknown to those being observed) and participant observation (the reporter becomes part of the event being reported).

The Congo was torn by civil war in the early 1960s. Because the war had serious international implications, the United Nations dispatched a peace-keeping force and then sent Secretary-General Dag Hammarskjold to the African republic to try to arrange a cease-fire.

At dusk, reporters at the Ndola airport in Northern Rhodesia awaiting Hammarskjold's arrival saw a plane land and a fair-haired man emerge. The reporters, who had been held behind police lines a hundred yards away, ran to file bulletins on the secretary-general's arrival. Anticipating Hammarskjold's next move, the press association rewrite men soon had stories on the wires describing Hammarskjold's conferring with President Moise Tshombe about a cease-fire. Many of these stories ran in early editions of the next day's newspapers.

But the man the reporters saw disembark was not Hammarskjold. He was a British foreign affairs official on a fact-gathering tour. At the time the reporters were filing their stories, Hammarskjold was aboard another plane that was to crash in a forest 10 miles north of Ndola, killing the secretary-general and the others on board.

Hammarskjold was dead when stories about his arrival and his conferring with Tshombe were being broadcast and were in print. It took eight hours for UPI to correct its erroneous story and four more hours for the AP.

How did it happen? The UPI reporter told his boss later, "I saw a man I thought looked like Hammarskjold. Other reporters claimed they were sure it was. After comparing notes, all agreed to file stories."

The incident reveals some of the basic problems reporters face in covering spot news stories. One is obvious: To make sound observations, the reporter has to see and hear the event clearly. In this case, the reporters did some things reporters do when their observations are uncertain and they are under pressure. They made an inference, and they formed a consensus.

Because the man was light-haired and his build approximated that of the secretary-general, the reporters jumped to the conclusion that he was Hammarskjold. This violated the reporter's maxim, "Beware of inferences. Do not jump from the known to the unknown."

To guard against individual error, they checked with each other. The result, as we have seen, was an egregious blunder, a classic of journalistic incompetence.

The difficulty in identifying what is news often causes journalists to consult each other for reassurance, and this leads to what is known as herd or pack journalism. In his book *Reporters and Officials,* (Lexington, Mass.: D. C. Heath, 1973), Leon V. Sigal says that since news cannot be defined clearly the reporter is always uncertain as to what news is. He calls this the "uncertainty factor" in the news gathering process.

Reporters tend to chat with each other about the lead, the credibility of the source, the reliability of the documentation they have been offered. They seek agreement in resolving the uncertainties. Should anything go wrong, the reporter can always point to his colleagues' reporting.

The life of the loner is difficult, even when his or her copy is accurate and revealing. The editor may query the reporter, asking why his copy is so different from that of others on the story. Editors, too, confront the uncertainty factor in news, and they also find security in unanimity. Although the loner may be doing the job well, he or she may grow weary of the call-backs and decide to join the pack. There is group pressure against the reporter who does not go along. Because no reporter can be everywhere, everyone is expected to lend a hand at filling in his or her colleagues. Also, no reporter wants to be beaten by an enterprising competitor. The line between herd journalism and legitimate cooperation is difficult to draw, but most reporters usually will share routine stories and keep enterprisers and exclusives to themselves.

Alone or in a group, the reporter's search for accurate, usable and relevant facts is not easy. Making sound observations begins with the reporter's ability to distinguish useful from irrelevant information.

Relevant Observations
Generally, the reporter on assignment is confronted by a flood of facts. A meeting can last two hours, cover seven different topics and include four decisions. A speaker may deliver an address containing 4,500 words. To handle these stories, the reporter may have at most a column for each story, about 750 words.

There are three major guidelines to selecting relevant facts:

1. *Know the community:* Develop a feeling and understanding of what readers need and want to know.

2. *Find the theme:* Carefully identify the theme of the story so that facts that support, buttress and amplify the theme can be gathered.
3. *Look for the drama:* Develop a sensitivity to the unique, the unusual, the break from the normal and routine.

Let us examine these guidelines in some detail.

Know the Community

We saw in chapter 2 that facts that are relevant to readers in one section of the country may be insignificant to readers in another area and that the story that fascinates some readers may bore others. It is essential that the reporter know what interests his newspaper readers or broadcast viewers. This news sense is part intuition, part common sense and part knowledge acquired from living and working in the community. A grizzled city editor once remarked that metropolitan newspapers started to go downhill when reporters and editors moved to the suburbs.

Reporters who move from one area to another often have trouble adjusting to their new readers and listeners. The story is told about the veteran reporter for *The Chicago Daily News* who decided to forsake the big city for the more relaxed life style of Texas. He accepted a job as the city editor of a west Texas daily newspaper. One day a fire broke out in town and the reporter's blood stirred in the city editor. He decided to go out on the story himself.

On his return, he batted out a story in *News* style, dramatic and well-written. The managing editor was pleased with his city editor's handiwork, but for one hole in the story.

"How much water did they use to put out the fire?" he asked. In parched west Texas, that fact was as important to readers as the number of fire units answering the call would have been to Chicago readers.

Find the Theme

Our second guideline is based upon the form of the news story, which places certain demands on the reporter that he must satisfy in his fact gathering.

We know that the story consists of the statement of a central theme or idea (the lead) and the elaboration of that theme or idea (the body). According to the second guideline, the reporter should begin concentrating on those facts that support, buttress and amplify the theme as soon as he or she senses the direction the story is taking.

When the Salvation Army dispatched 4,000 of its soldiers to New York City to do battle against "sin and evil," a reporter for *The New York Times* accompanied some of the troops through the streets. Impressed by the work of the Army men and women, the reporter decided to emphasize their dedication and singled out this detail in her account to illustrate her theme:

"The Army believes in total abstinence," a young soldier was saying to a disheveled-looking man, whose breath reeked of alcohol. "You are the temple of the Lord and if you destroy yourself, you're destroying Him."

"Am I?" the older man asked, as they stood in front of the entranceway of the Commodore. "No, I'm not."

"Sure you are," the soldier replied, resting his hand on the man's shoulder. The man reached out his hand, too, and began to cry. So did the Salvation Army soldier.

This approach—confining observations to the theme—is not unique to journalism. All writing that is intended to communicate an idea or an event should be written with the theme clearly in mind. Irrelevant details are gravestones marking dead prose, despite the apparent liveliness given by the flood of detail.

A reporter may spend some time gathering facts before the theme emerges. Or the theme may be clear from the outset, as it usually is with spot news stories like the shooting and the motorcycle accident, or with enterprisers like the militancy of the blind. As soon as the theme seems to be set, the reporter must focus on observations relevant to that theme. This does not mean that facts contrary to the theme should be discarded. If the reporter discovers facts that contradict the basic idea, then the idea is discarded and a new theme is adopted. In this way, the reporter is like the scientist whose conclusion can be no stronger than his or her evidence.

Of course, some events will have secondary themes. The same rule about gathering only material that buttresses the theme applies to the secondary ideas.

Look for the Drama

Our third guide to making relevant observations—a sensitivity to the unusual—stems from our definition of news. News, we discovered, is often the novel, the different, the unexpected.

Learning to distinguish the break from everyday routine seems simple. But to the reporter covering his tenth fire, his thirty-third ball game and his third board of education meeting this month, events seem to settle into a familiar pattern. Spotting the differences between this fire, this game, this meeting and the others is difficult. After all, most people cannot differentiate the Delicious from the Jonathan, the Jersey from the Holstein. To them, all apples are alike and all cows are alike.

The reporter has to learn to look at the world through the eyes of the infant, who views everything as new and different. At the same time he applies to the world the discerning eye of the wise elder, who can differentiate the significant from the meaningless.

Red Smith, a sports writer who covered so many baseball games he lost count, explained the basis of his artistry: "Every ball game is different from every other ball game—if the reporter has the knowledge and wit to discern the difference."

When Gustave Flaubert, the French novelist, was teaching Guy de Maupassant to write he told the young man to pick out one of the cab drivers in front of a railway station in Paris and to describe him in a way that would differentiate him from all the other drivers. To do so, de Maupassant had to find the significant details that would single out that one man.

Reporting Gone Wrong

The reporter who ignores these guidelines may waste time pursuing facts to dead ends. Worse, the stories will leave readers and listeners dissatisfied because they lack essential information. Let us look at a few examples of what happens when a reporter loses his or her way while gathering facts.

This story appeared in a Chicago newspaper:

> Miss Rosemary McGrath, 28, was struck on the head early today by a burglar in the rectory of St. Veronica Roman Catholic Church, 3300 N. Whipple St., where she is a housekeeper.
>
> Miss McGrath was treated at Belmont hospital for two cuts on her scalp. Police found that the burglar entered by prying the rear door.

Our first guideline would apply here. If the reporter had anticipated the reader's questions, the obvious question he or she would have asked is, "How much and what was taken by the burglar?"

In another example, a Maine newspaper reported the arraignment of a Brunswick youth on charges of possession of a narcotic and resisting arrest. The story described the youth's plan: He called a drug store, claimed to be a physician and instructed the druggist to fill a prescription for a man who would pick it up. When the 19-year-old appeared to pick up the prescription, police picked him up. Nowhere did the story give the type of narcotic the youth sought. To a generation of readers conscious of drugs, this is an inexcusable omission. Though the material is not essential to the story, our guideline does instruct the reporter to anticipate what the reader *wants* to know as well as what he *needs* to know.

The students in the story that follows were never named:

Pulliam Fellowship Winners Announced

Eight graduating college seniors have been named winners of Pulliam Journalism Fellowships for 1975.

The winners were announced by Harvey C. Jacobs, editor of *The Indianapolis Star* and director of the fellowship program.

In addition to receiving a cash award of $1,000, each fellow will take part in an 8-week seminar of work and study in Indianapolis through August 1. The seminar began June 9. Work will include assignments on the staff of either the *News* or *The Indianapolis Star*.

The fellowships were established in 1974 by publisher Eugene C. Pulliam to encourage the pursuit of newspaper careers and provide outstanding journalism students an opportunity.

—Editor & Publisher

Sometimes the reporter, try as he or she will, has trouble obtaining the information the public needs and wants to know. When sources do not divulge the needed information the reporter must pose questions that will unearth the needed material. Here is an example of a story that to some readers lacked essential information. During the Goldwater-Johnson presidential campaign in 1964, a New York City daily newspaper printed a long profile of Gerald L.K. Smith that described Smith's political activism. Smith was characterized as the "epitome of the really extremist forces—the several dozen year-around anti-Negro and anti-Semitic organizations of the country—that, to the discomfort of many Republicans, are rejoicing in Senator Barry Goldwater's candidacy for the president." Smith was quoted as an enthusiastic Goldwater supporter. He was also quoted as saying that the United States "was established as a white, Christian country. . . . I'm against permitting Jews to dilute our Christian tradition. I don't think our country should be mongrelized by the weaker elements."

Nowhere is there an indication that the reporter asked Smith to reconcile his statements about Jews with his support of Goldwater, an Episcopalian whose father was a Jew—a fact well known to New York City newspaper readers.

Individuality

Although no two reporters will see an event the same way, experienced reporters usually do agree on the major facts, the theme and the direction the story will take. Beyond that, each reporter puts his or her individual stamp on the story. Some of that individuality comes from writing style. Much is based on the observations the reporter makes. What is relevant to one reporter may be irrelevant to another.

When Homer Bigart, the winner of two Pulitzer Prizes and one of the country's great reporters, was sent to cover the trial of Lt. William Calley, who had been accused of murdering civilians in the My Lai massacre during the Vietnam War, Bigart observed how Calley was brought into court. He placed this observation against his observations at another army officer's trial and he wrote:

> Although he had just been found guilty of twenty-two
> murders, Calley was treated far more gently than was Army
> doctor Captain Howard B. Levy four years ago after
> receiving a sentence for refusing to give medical training
> to Green Berets on the grounds that the training would be
> used unlawfully in Vietnam.
> Unlike Levy, Calley was not handcuffed and left the court
> unfettered. An officer explained: "His conduct has been
> exemplary throughout and he'll continue to be treated as an
> officer."

Bigart's editors at *The New York Times,* apparently considered his references to the Levy trial to be irrelevant, for the section read simply:

> Lieutenant Calley was not hand-
> cuffed when driven to the stockade.

Whose judgment was better, Bigart's or his editors'? Bigart's reference to the Levy trial provides the reader with some idea of the intense feeling of the military against the peace movement—of which Levy was a symbol—and its consideration for the accused murderer of civilians, who was a career army man.

There are so many impediments to accurate observation that reporters are sometimes astonished at how often they are on target. The Hammarskjold incident illustrates one of the most common difficulties—the absence of a vantage point from which to view the event. Obviously, a good view is essential. But it is not such a simple matter as it may seem. Just as the reporters at the airport in Northern Rhodesia erred because they were too far away, it is sometimes disadvantageous to be too close to the scene. Proximity may cause the reporter to lose the scope of the event.

The reporter sent to a nearby city to cover the debut of a local singer is seated in the orchestra among the staid patrons of the opera. He hears only polite applause after the singer's first major aria as Florestan. If he had been seated high in the opera house he would have heard the vigorous applause of the younger opera goers and the knowledgeable standees. What, then, is the audience reaction?

The lesson: When in doubt, move about. Find a variety of perspectives, if possible and if it makes sense for the story. The opera-going reporter could have shifted seats quietly in time to relocate himself for the singer's second aria. Obviously, he should have seen to it ahead of time that he had a seat on the aisle and that he knew just when the singer would be in the spotlight. On breaking news stories, vantage point is often out of the reporter's control. In organized events, like the opera, the reporter can control his location.

In moving about, reporters have to be firm, for sometimes they must shoulder their way to the front of the crowd. A reporter for a college newspaper was unable to find a seat near the front of the Poetry Hour lecture she was assigned to cover and took a place in the back of the room. The lecture was on political satire, and the speaker seemed to be direct in his language. When she returned to the newsroom, she wrote this lead:

"Political satire of today stinks," Dennis Quinn, assistant professor of English, said at yesterday's Poetry Hour.

A few days later, the newspaper received a letter from Prof. Quinn. With some restraint, he wrote that he had actually said, "Political satire is practically extinct." The *University Daily Kansan* printed his letter, and despite the reporter's embarrassment she stayed in journalism and went on to do distinguished work as an AP correspondent in Vietnam.

The incident also illustrates the necessity of checking—when possible—strong quotations with the source and others if the reporter is unsure of what has been said. No source should be permitted to back down from a strong statement, but sometimes reporters cannot hear well and need to verify what they think they have heard.

Even when accurately seen or heard, some events can be misleading or uninformative if stated flatly. They need to be placed in a setting the reporter provides from his own knowledge and that of competent persons acquainted with the event. When a fact is so unusual that it makes reporters—who are noted for a skepticism Diogenes would envy—take special notice, then that wonderment should be acted on. Every attempt should be made to examine possible causes.

Editors attending a luncheon during the annual convention of the American Society of Newspaper Editors in 1959 were astonished when they saw Fidel Castro, the guest of honor, reach across the table and swap plates with the president of the Society. Some of the editors concluded this was boorish behavior.

Had one of them acted on that astonishment at the banquet and done what reporters are supposed to do—ask why—the editor might have been informed that Castro feared assassination. And had the editor not laughed that off but checked into Castro's assertion, that editor might have changed history. For in 1975, the Central Intelligence Agency admitted that during the administrations of presidents Eisenhower, Kennedy and Johnson the United States government had indeed tried to murder Castro.

The Castro incident points up an unseen dimension of reporting. Although the reporter is guided by logic, he must be open to the most implausible facts and observations. Time after time reporters find aberrant facts and extraordinary observations and put them aside as too unusual for further examination. After the revelations of the 1960s and 1970s about politics, international affairs, and the business world, no observation should be dismissed—no matter how outlandish it seems—without at least a quick check.

Limitations of the Story

Although we may agree that the reporter's task is to continue the search for relevant facts until the pattern of a story emerges, we also must admit that the search can never be completed, that there are facts beyond the reporter's reach. Just as a map can never be the complete guide to a territory, so a news story is rarely the definitive statement of reality.

Here are some of the obstacles reporters face:

- The source the reporter could not locate.
- The record, document or newspaper clipping that was missing.
- The incident the reporter could not see or hear properly.
- The facts the source would not divulge.
- The material the copy editor cut out of the story.
- The reporter's own limitations.
- The book or magazine the reporter failed to read. Yesterday's newspaper left unread beyond page one.

The Tyranny of Time

Add to this formidable list the reporter's slavery to the tyrant of time. It is the clock that is the journalist's major obstacle to truth-telling. Unlike the historian or the sociologist, who face few daily or weekly deadlines in their work, the journalist submits to the requirements of publication and air time while still seeking to present a complete account.

Although the journalist tends to give the public a sense of completion and truth in the accounts, limited observations permitted by the allotted time result in only an approximation of the event. This is one reason reporters are always looking back at stories they have written. They want to see whether they should give the story another go, to tidy up loose ends and to present facts they did not have when the story was written.

Complex events require an ability to find relationships that link seemingly disparate events. The reporter may find the hidden patterns difficult to nail down or he or she may find that the newspaper or station is not interested in this kind of investigative reporting. Tiring of the endeavor to find these patterns, the reporter sometimes settles for a rudimentary form of truth, the recital of what sources declare (Layer I journalism), which is truth of a sort.

Style as a Barrier

The journalistic style also may obstruct truth. The journalist is required to tell a story in simple, dramatic, personalized prose. Some important events are complex, prosaic and abstract. The reporter who seeks to make these events—usually ideas, trends, concepts—come alive may distort them by using too many exciting details that are colorful but irrelevant. For several years, the news magazines specialized in this kind of exciting detail. Their reporters sent in the name of the wine the diplomat drank, how many cigarettes he smoked during a tense hearing and his mannerisms. The significance of the event often was lost in the human-interest trivia.

The Reporter as Intruder

The act of reporting can itself be an impediment to accurate observations. Walter Lippmann characterized the journalist as a "fly on the wall," a detached observer whose presence does not affect the event being observed. But if reporting requires close-at-hand observation, scrupulous note-taking, photographs, film or tape, how unobtrusive can the reporter be? The fly descends and buzzes around the event. The participants can no longer ignore its presence.

We know what happens when a television crew arrives at an event. Drones become animated. Restrained people suddenly begin to gesticulate. Reality is altered.

At a political rally in Central America, a reporter noted the calm, almost serene atmosphere. Even when a speaker released a dove from the center of the plaza, the crowd was hushed. Then the television and still photographers arrived, and the event suddenly took another shape. Fists were shaken. A Cuban flag was unfurled for the photographers, and revolutionary slogans were shouted into the recording equipment. When the photographers departed, the rally returned to its placid pace. In the next day's newspaper, accompanying the reporter's story of a peaceful protest meeting against the United States, was the photograph that the picture service had distributed—a shot of a fist-shaking mob.

Even the reporter's pencil and paper can change the situation and distort the event. Every reporter experiences the trying moment when, after chatting with a source to put him or her at ease, it is time to reach for a pencil and notepad. In an instant, the mood changes. The simple tools of the reporter's trade have spooked the source.

Unobtrusive Observation

This type of reaction can be avoided by non-reactive or unobtrusive observation, methods that have the merit of allowing the reporter to be a fly on the wall. Let us follow a reporter as he uses this reporting technique.

Among the dozens of reporters gathered in central California to attend a Republican state conference was a reporter who was determined to prove to his editor that he could handle political coverage. The newspaper's political reporter was assigned to the main political story. The reporter we are following was to do sidebars and pieces on secondary issues.

Unlike the other reporters at the convention, our man was unknown to the delegates. He was able to mix freely, smiling and shaking hands with delegates. He knew he was being mistaken for a young delegate, and when one of the central committee secretaries told him there was an important meeting, he went along with her. They walked into the meeting together, and he sat near her, apparently doodling absent-mindedly on a pad in front of him.

All day long he moved in and out of caucuses, meetings and powwows. He heard Orange County delegates denounce the president, a Republican, as a liberal, a spendthrift, an enemy of the party's conservative principles. He listened as deals were made to try to attract the labor and minority votes.

His story, played prominently on page one, was exclusive and other newspapers were forced to quote from it. Republican leaders were chagrined. Our young reporter was jubilant.

Although the meetings, caucuses and small sessions were private—indeed all sessions were conducted behind closed doors—the reporter had no qualms about his unobtrusive observation. His tactics were no different, he felt, than those he had used the week before when another political group—a national organization of right-wing activists—held a convention. The reporter had plumped down in a soft chair in the lobby of the hotel and listened. He had heard delegates talk about bringing back the gold standard, the threat of communism from minorities, the radicalism of the labor movement and the dangers of sex education in the public schools.

Today, that reporter has second thoughts about his coverage of the Republican meeting. He is not so concerned about his hotel-lobby listening, for that was done in a public place, and if people want to talk in public, they suffer the consequences. But his intrusion at a private meeting was another matter. He was eavesdropping in a place from which he would have been barred had his identity been known.

Many reporters justify eavesdropping if the public interest is served by disclosure, particularly if the event involves public bodies and officials. A city council meeting surreptitiously held in a downtown hotel may be covered by a reporter hovering in a hall, ear to the door or eye to the keyhole. Public officials have no right to do public business in private, and the reporter is willing to risk appearing undignified if that is what he must do to dig out the news.

Reporters have hidden in closets, rented hotel rooms next to politicians, even used hidden tape recorders in order to dig out the news.

Some journalists condemn this kind of observation. Their criticism stems from their concern about widespread intrusions into privacy by insurance firms, credit investigators and the federal government. Federal agencies have poked into the lives of persons through wiretaps and mail openings. What right, then, should the journalist have to do what it is his business to expose as a violation of privacy?

The journalist who uses unobtrusive observation, and more devious means of fact gathering, defends his prying into private as well as public affairs on the ground that the story—the search for truth—justifies the means if the story reveals wrongdoing or aids the public in decision making. As for a check on the prying journalist, he would have none but his conscience. "Let me use my judgment," he would say. "I will not use material irresponsibly."

Opponents of the ends-justify-the-means argument contend that the reporter cannot adopt methods he condemns in others, that he cannot set himself apart from the rules that apply to others.

The concerned journalist seeking to do his or her job but confused by the conflicting opinions might find some guidance from a debate that occurred in the pages of *Society* magazine following the publication of an article, "Tearoom Trade: Impersonal Sex in Public Places," about homosexual activity in public men's rest rooms.

The author, Laud Humphreys, a sociologist, posed as a voyeur interested in homosexual activity. The homosexuals accepted him and stationed him outside the rest room as a "watchqueen," a lookout to warn of the police or other intruders.

"I played that part faithfully," he writes in the January, 1970, issue. By peeking in the window, he continues, he was able to observe the activities of the men. When they left, he took down the numbers of their automobile license plates and learned their identities. A year later, he interviewed 50 of the 100 men of whom he had a record.

Humphreys' techniques have increasingly become the methods of the reporter, who began in the 1960s to utilize the ethnographic methods of social scientists.

Humphreys anticipated criticism of his method of observation, for in a short article accompanying his research, he defended the work on what he described as three ethical assumptions:

1. The social scientist should not avoid an area of research because it is difficult or socially sensitive.
2. He should "approach any aspect of human behavior with those means that least distort the observed phenomena."
3. He "must protect the respondents from harm."

Humphreys' second item is a restatement of Lippmann's fly-on-the-wall concept and a defense of unobtrusive observation. But the articles and their author's defense were shrugged aside by one of his critics, Nicholas von Hoffman, a columnist, who attacked the methods of observation as an invasion of privacy. As for the argument that the information served a good purpose, von Hoffman wrote, "Everybody who goes snooping around and spying can be said to have good motives. . . . No information is valuable enough to obtain by nipping away at personal liberty."

In reply, two editors of the magazine, Irving Louis Horowitz and Lee Rainwater, defended Humphreys on these grounds:

1. People have a right to "learn the truth" about themselves and each other.
2. The article served a "socially constructive purpose" in helping readers to understand deviant behavior and the activities of the police in this victimless crime.
3. Such research is consistent with the social scientist's "demystification of human life and culture."
4. The "tearooms" were public rest rooms on public land.

Balancing the right of privacy with the right to know, the editors cited information gathered by the Census Bureau, health and welfare departments and other agencies that collect information for the common good but intrude on privacy.

The link between the journalist's unobtrusive observation and Humphreys' methods is close. Journalists who use this technique may therefore want to ponder the objections to and the defense of the method. A guideline: For private activities, think twice; for official activities held in private, act in the public interest.

The reporter's ethics are discussed further in chapter 16.

Participant Observation

Another research method—participant observation—also links social science and journalism strategies. A West Coast reporter who managed to fold his six-foot frame into a third grader's seat at school was a participant observer. The reporter who worked as a telephone operator and then wrote a series of articles based on her observations was basing her stories on personal experience. At the simplest level, a reporter can spend a day with a meter reader, a public health nurse, or another person of interest. Mary Voboril of *The Miami Herald* took an exercise class with actress Jane Fonda.

In participant observation—the opposite of unobtrusive observation—the reporter discards his or her role as the uninvolved, detached observer and joins the activity of the person or group he or she is covering. Unlike the unobtrusive observer, the participant observer's identity is known to those he or she is observing.

The newspaperman who became a third-grader for a story participated in the children's school work, ate lunch with them and played ball at recess. The school children took him for a friend, a bit older and awkward about some things, but a companion nevertheless. They talked to him as an equal. His relationship with the students enabled him to gather material that the usual interview and observation techniques would not have revealed.

Workout with Fonda.
Reporter Mary Voboril of *The Miami Herald* asks actress Jane Fonda a wide range of questions while taking part in Fonda's exercise class.

William Foote Whyte, in his classic study of an Italian-American slum, *Street Corner Society,* (Chicago: The University of Chicago Press, 1943), talks about the difference between the traditional perception of what is news and the reality of the way people live, which participant observation allows the reporter to view:

> If the politician is indicted for accepting graft, that is news. If he goes about doing the usual personal favors for his constituents, that is not news. The newspaper concentrates on the crisis—the spectacular event. In a crisis the 'big shot' becomes public property. He is removed from the society in which he functions and he is judged by standards different from his own group. This may be the most effective way to prosecute the lawbreaker. It is not a good way to understand him. For that purpose, the individual must be put back into his social setting and observed in his daily activities. In order to understand the spectacular event, it is necessary to see it in relation to the everyday pattern of life. . . .

Whyte learned how to be accepted by the street corner people. ''If you ask direct questions, people will just clam up on you,'' he writes. ''If people accept you, you can just hang around, and you'll learn the answers in the long run without even having to ask the questions.''

When Whyte used some obscenities to try to gain acceptance, one of his new friends advised him, "Bill, you're not supposed to talk like that. That doesn't sound like you."

Whyte had to be careful about influencing the group he was observing. "I tried to be helpful in the way a friend is expected to be helpful."

The results of his observations allowed the reader to have a moving picture of the street corner society, not the still photograph that the brief glimpse allows.

The Live-In

Journalism students at Columbia University have been doing participant observation in an assignment known as the Live-In, which sends students into private homes and working places. To move closer to their sources, students have tutored addicts in drug rehabilitation centers and children in ghetto schools. They have slept on the floors of mission houses in the Bowery, in sleeping bags at a residence of the Catholic Workers and on cots in communes.

Students have walked the beat with police officers, gone on home visits with social workers and accompanied ambulance drivers on their calls. These experiences were not one-shot affairs. They met the policeman's family, talked to the welfare mother's children and went into wards to talk to patients.

Charles Young, a white, middle-class student from Wisconsin, did his Live-In in a junior high school in West Harlem in New York City. Young is waiting for the assistant principal in his office. The room is filled with students. Young describes the scene at the beginning of his Live-In:

Gus Marinos, known simply as "Marinos" to everybody, a Greek immigrant in his twenties with dazed but kindly eyes beneath his Coke-bottle glasses, returns to his office on the fourth floor. The room erupts with a deafening chorus of his name.

"MAH-*REE*-NOS! HER FINGERNAILS BE POISON!" a girl screams, holding up her scratched right hand.

"So die," says Marinos, examining some smudged papers on his desk.

"WHY 'ON'T CHEW DIE!"

"You wanna go home?"

"YEAH, BUT CHEW CAN'T TELL ME HER NAILS AIN'T POISON!"

"So go home."

"HER NAILS GOT DIRT AN' SHIT IN 'M!" The girl leaves with a pass home.

"MAH-*REE*-NOS!" another girl demands. "GIMME A PENCIL!" He hands her a pencil from his desk. "I 'ON'T WANT NO PENCIL LIKE THAT! I WANNA BLACK PENCIL!"

"This *is* a black pencil."

"I MEAN A YELLOW PENCIL THAT WRITES BLACK!"

"We don't sell those here."

"I 'ON'T WANT TO BUY NO PENCIL! I WANT CHEW TO GIMME IT!" She grabs the pencil from his hand and in the process drops a text book. "NOW SEE YOU MADE ME DONE DIRTY MY BOOK!"

"I made you done what?"

"DIRTY MY BOOK!" She leaves for class.

These girls read an average of two years below the national norm for their grade level (slightly ahead of the boys), but the ghetto has already taught them how to get what they want from life: yell until somebody gives it to you. The lesson is apt, because when they are graduated in three years or so, they won't be equipped to do anything anyway.

That these girls (all sent to the office for disciplinary reasons) want something is obvious. What they want is less obvious and increasingly important as the market for unskilled labor dries up.

The first step in finding out what they want is learning a new vocabulary, some of which would be useful to define here. To "come out your mouth" is to communicate. "On time" is an adjective or adverb of approbation meaning you have done something according to socially accepted procedure. "On cap" is synonymous with "in your head," referring to intelligence. . . .

Young interviewed the assistant principal in charge of discipline, who, he writes, "carries a cane in one hand and a leather whip in the other when she wades into a group of warring Dominican and Puerto Rican youths."

His description continues:

She resembles an army tank—solid, low-to-the-ground, unstoppable, paradoxically maternal.

She is in fact known as the mother of the school. Teachers speak with awe of the dedication that brings her to the otherwise deserted building on weekends and vacations. Students speak with equal awe of her omniscience. Because they trust her, she knows exactly who is pushing what drugs and who is fighting with whom.

Standing at the main entrance to the building at 3 o'clock one Friday afternoon in anticipation of a gang fight, Williams catalogues a gathering of a dozen or so Puerto Rican school alumni.

"That one is on parole now. . . . That one is pushing. Look at his station wagon. . . . That one has a sawed-off .38 in his pocket. We'd tell the police about it, but it will pass fifty hands by the time they can react. . . ."

On Thursday, one of their little brothers dropped a piece of chalk from the fourth floor that hit a Dominican on the head. In the ensuing melee, another Puerto Rican was badly cut on the arm with a broken bottle. The Puerto Ricans seek vengeance.

Having no stake in the matter, the blacks are blasé and leave the area immediately. They've seen it all before and even the prospect of serious violence is a bore. The Hispanics gather in groups along the sidewalk and buzz with rumors, with more energy than they have shown all day in class.

Williams crosses the street and puts her arm around one of her former students who has an Afro bigger than the rest of his body. She makes small talk for a couple of minutes, then kisses him on his pock-marked cheek as the gang scatters off down the street. A group of Dominicans, observing the enemy from a block away, disappears to its lair on 133rd Street.

The aborted fight is typical of junior highs anywhere in that the participants seem willing to do battle over nothing. What is frightening is that the involved alumni range in age from 16 to the mid-twenties. They never grew up, just became better armed. They are the fruit of the American system of education.

"Even five years ago they at least expressed an interest in college," says Williams back in the dormitory-room-sized office which she shares with three other school officials and usually seven or eight students who have been thrown out of class. . . .

Young befriended a bright young black student in the school. After Young graduated and went to work for *Rolling Stone,* he decided to look up the youngster for a story for the magazine about his dream of becoming a basketball star. He found the youth in high school, playing basketball, struggling with his classes, and still filled with hope. Young's piece in the Oct. 6, 1977, issue of *Rolling Stone,* "Above 125th Street: Curtis Haynes' New York," begins:

I'M GROWIN' PLANTS ALL THE TIME," says Curtis Haynes, pouring half a glass of water over a geranium. The floor and window ledge of his bedroom are covered with leafy pots. "Plants are everything. They give us oxygen and food. They also a home for insects." He brushes an aphid off a leaf. "Insects gonna inherit the earth."

He continues the tour of his room—recently painted electric blue by his mother—by pulling a picture off a shelf full of basketball trophies. Judging by his fleeting eyes and reticent tone of voice, he doesn't know what to make of me—a pale, white, 26-year-old, bearded magazine editor with thick glasses from a myopic childhood of too much TV watching and book reading in Madison, Wisconsin. Nor do I know what to make of him—a handsome, ebony-skinned, 16-year-old, short-haired high-school student with sharp vision from a childhood spent on the basketball courts of Harlem. "This my brother, Footie," he says, holding a blurred photograph of a teenager bearing a strong resemblance to Curtis. "Remember, remember, remember. . ." is inscribed around the margins. "We named him that because he had such big feet," he says. Curtis' Pro Ked basketball shoes equal my own 11½ Adidas—and I am 6′ 2″ while he is just 5′ 10″. "He died in a fight two years ago. Puerto Rican friend got in an argument at a party and the other dude pulled a gun. My brother jumped between them. I never go to parties no more."

The concept of the Live-In is based on the work of anthropologists such as Margaret Mead and Oscar Lewis and the psychiatrist and author Robert Coles. They spent considerable time with the people they were observing. In describing the field work that went into her book *Coming of Age in Samoa,* Mead wrote:

I concentrated on the girls of the community. I spent the greater part of my time with them. I studied most closely the households in which adolescent girls lived. I spent more time in the games of children than in the councils of their elders. Speaking their language, eating their food, sitting barefoot and cross-legged upon the pebbly floor, I did my best to minimize the differences between us and to learn to know and understand all the girls of three little villages on the coast of the little island of Tau, in the Manua Archipelago.

Some reporters arrived at the Live-In technique on their own. Concerned by the direction of journalism toward centers of authority, reporters realized that they were observing only one facet of reality. As some journalists realized, a concentration on the formalities of life—its ceremonies, meetings, announcements—was not helping them relate the reality of human experience. They became anxious to develop techniques that enabled them to report this reality. Sally Grimes, a reporter in Philadelphia, said after she had been covering the juvenile court for a year, "I wonder why so many reporters insist on quoting people in positions of power rather than observing people who are affected by power."

She listened closely to the young defendants in court, and she sought to understand the effect of the system on youngsters by talking to them. One day she learned that an 11-year-old boy—who was brought into court in handcuffs—had been held in a detention center for nine months although he had not committed a crime. He was a runaway. Grimes asked to talk to the youngster, who had been sent to foster homes after his parents were judged neglectful. He had not liked the foster homes and had run away. Here is part of the story she wrote:

"Jones, Jones," the guard's voice could be heard as he walked up and down the cell-block. Amid a few undistinguishable low grumblings behind the rows of bars came a small, high voice. "Yes, that's me."

Johnny was brought out to an anteroom. No longer crying, he sat with downcast eyes in dungarees and a gray sweatshirt. Quietly and slowly he answered questions.

He wished he had somebody to bring him soap because the institutional soap gives him a rash. He would like to leave YSC (Youth Study Center) and would go "any place they send me."

How does it feel to be handcuffed? In a barely audible voice, he answered: "It makes me feel like a criminal."

It is a natural step from this kind of reporting to participant observation, for the only way the reporter can understand some situations is to experience them. Without this intense personal experience, some reporters contend, the people they write about become cardboard figures.

These reporters would agree with Chekhov's observation in his short story, "Gooseberries," that journalism has not dug deeply enough into the lives of people:

We see the people who go to market, eat by day, sleep by night, who babble nonsense, marry, grow old, good-naturedly drag their dead to the cemetery, but we do not see or hear those who suffer, and what is terrible in life goes on somewhere behind the scenes. Everything is peaceful and quiet and only mute statistics protest: so many people gone out of their minds, so many gallons of vodka drunk, so many children dead from malnutrition. And such a state of things is evidently necessary; obviously the happy man is at ease only because the unhappy ones bear their burdens in silence, and if there were not this silence, happiness would be impossible. It is a general hypnosis. Behind the door of every contented, happy man there ought to be someone standing with a little hammer and continually reminding him with a knock that there are unhappy people, that however happy he may be, life will sooner or later show him its claws, and trouble will come to him—illness, poverty, losses, and then no one will see or hear him, just as now he neither sees nor hears others. But there is no man with a hammer. The happy man lives at his ease, faintly fluttered by small daily cares, like an aspen in the wind—and all is well.

Without being dramatic about it, some reporters see themselves as the man with the hammer.

Problems of Involvement

But participant observation also entails some problems. In addition to the possibility that the reporter's presence may affect the event, the participant observer can become too deeply involved with his or her sources, risking the possibility that compassion and friendship may precede responsibility to the facts. Identifying with persons and their causes has led some journalists to romanticize ghetto life and poverty and to make heroes of street criminals.

Participant observation has also been criticized as exploitation of the source. After all, the journalist is using the lives of people as the basis of a story, which, if it is good, will lead to the reporter's acclaim, help him win a pay raise and possibly a promotion. But the alcoholic, the addict, the welfare mother, the assembly-line worker and the policeman are not reimbursed for their contributions. They are used to enhance the career of the reporter, and usually little or nothing is done about the problems that overwhelm some of these people.

The journalist James Agee agonized over prying into the lives of Southern sharecroppers and their families. He and the photographer Walker Evans were assigned by a magazine to do an article on cotton tenantry, the system by which farmers worked the fields of landowners in return for a share of the crop less what is advanced to them for seed, living quarters and tools. The sharecroppers were poorer than dirt poor, for not even the earth they tilled was theirs. The magazine article was not published, but in 1940 the work became a book (*Let Us Now Praise Famous Men*, Boston: Houghton Mifflin Co., 1980). Agee knew the justifications for his intimate observations, but they did not console him. Early in the book, he describes his reservations:

It seems to me curious, not to say obscene and thoroughly terrifying, that it could occur to an association of human beings drawn together through need and chance and for profit into a company, an organ of journalism, to pry intimately into the lives of an undefended and appallingly damaged group of human beings, an ignorant and helpless rural family, for the purpose of parading the nakedness, disadvantage and humiliation of these lives before another group of human beings, in the name of science, of "honest journalism" (whatever that paradox may mean), of humanity, of social fearlessness, for money, and for a reputation for crusading and for unbias which, when skillfully enough qualified, is exchangeable at any bank for money (and in politics, for votes, for job patronage, abelincolnism, etc.). . . .

Nevertheless, Agee went ahead, and the work he produced, *Let Us Now Praise Famous Men,* belongs on every reporter's shelf next to a copy of Lincoln Steffens' *Autobiography.*

In rebuttal to criticisms of participant observation, reporters who use the technique say that public awareness is increased by stories about the lives of people. They say this awareness can lead to reform by involving the public emotionally in the situations described by the reporter.

Also, participant observation can help correct the objective detachment that can lead to callousness. A Columbia University student who said he considered drug addicts weak and worthless conducted a Live-In project with a young female addict. The woman's daughter was being put up for adoption because her mother had been judged unfit to raise her. The woman's agony at the prospect of losing her daughter—which the student felt intensely—led him to do a series of revealing articles about the city's adoption laws.

The experience of participant observation allows the young reporter to know a stranger who is unlike family and friends and to see this person as an individual. It helps the reporter to step outside routines and familiar environments to achieve new insights.

This and other methods that lead to better stories also help the reporter to avoid yet another trap—the tendency to stereotype. Stereotyping is a natural human process, all the more understandable in a reporter working under pressure. Stereotyping permits the journalist to simplify complex events, situations and people and to communicate them to his or her audience in easily understood terms. Forgetting that life is endless variety and change, some reporters look at the world through a kaleidoscope that is never turned. As a consequence, their observations reflect only the narrowest vision.

Next, we shall examine these stereotypes and the feelings and ways of thinking that determine how reporters look at events.

13 Hunches, Feelings and Thinking Patterns

<u>Preview</u>   Reporters rely on hunches, intuition and feelings as well as rational, disciplined thinking for their reporting.

■ Hunches and intuition spring from the application of the reporter's intelligence to the vast range of material the reporter has accumulated from reading and general observations.

■ Feelings and emotions can distort reporting. But they can also motivate a reporter to expose wrongs in society.

■ Disciplined thinking leads reporters to see relationships among apparently unrelated facts and events. The patterns the reporter discovers help readers move closer to the truth.

Reporters go about their work in a rational, almost scientific way. They assess events with detachment, breaking them down into facts that the reporters weigh against each other and against their knowledge of the background of the event. They draw conclusions on the basis of their observations, not in accordance with their hopes and beliefs. Then they reconstruct these events into coherent, orderly stories.

Analysis and synthesis, the application of reason to experience—these are the processes underlying the reporter's work.

Yet, this summary is misleading. It ignores hunches and intuitions and emotional reactions that include feelings such as bias, prejudice, hatred and love.

Hunches and Intuition

Every reporter has had the experience on assignment of intuitively sensing its meaning, of suddenly seeing through the thickets of facts to the one idea that shapes the event. In fact, the process by which the news media determine what they will cover, and the thinking of the reporter as he or she selects the facts for use in a story may well be based on hunches.

Some reporters seem to possess extrasensory perception that enables them to detect stories. "I can smell something a mile away. It's just a fact of life," says Seymour Hersh, whose stories on the My Lai massacre and other investigative reports won numerous prizes.

Hunches, guesswork and intuition come into play as soon as a reporter is given an assignment. Before leaving the newsroom, before gathering a single fact, the reporter usually has ideas and feelings about the story, and these reactions influence his or her coverage.

There is nothing wrong with this. The psychiatrist C. J. Jung said, "Feelings are not only reasonable but are also as discriminating, as logical, and as consistent as thinking." Even scientists admit the nonrational in their universe. Einstein wrote of the "underlying uncertainties of all knowledge and the function of intuition." Aleksandr Solzhenitsyn, the Russian novelist, describes the strength of emotional reactions in this conversation between two inmates of a Russian prison camp for scientists. It is from his novel *The First Circle* (New York: Harper & Row, 1968), p. 325:

"I am not objective?" Rubin demanded. "Me? Then who is objective?"
"No one, of course," the artist exulted. "No one! No one ever was and no one ever will be. Every act of perception has an emotional coloring. The truth is supposed to be the final result of investigation, but don't we perceive a sort of truth before any investigation has begun?"

Hunches Lead to Stories

On a slow news day, a reporter decided to look into a proposal that had been made for a regional education plan for several Southwestern states. He wanted the comments of the governor of his state and he made a call to the governor's office. The governor's secretary said the governor was on a brief vacation. Instantly, the reporter had a hunch something was amiss. Something did not ring true. He called another state official he knew was close to the governor, and when he was told that the official was "out of town" he was not surprised. Another hunch and the reporter called the state party chairman. His whereabouts were "unknown" to his secretary. A pattern was emerging, but what idea would put the pieces together? Another hunch: The party was to be the host for a large gathering of western Republicans who were to discuss the various candidates for the party's presidential nomination. Assuming that the state party leaders were discussing arrangements for the conference, he was about to dismiss the affair as routine when his intuition—or reason—told him that the plans for secrecy were too elaborate for such a routine meeting.

The reporter knew that one of the issues the party faced—one that would probably surface at the conference—was what role Senator Joseph R. McCarthy should play in the presidential campaign. As host to the conference, the state's party leaders might be adopting a neutral position, or possibly one critical of McCarthy, whose charges of subversion and treason against the Democratic administration had caused turmoil within the country. The reporter knew that the state chairman and the governor were disturbed by the charges and had little use for McCarthy's tactics.

The reporter's hunches paid off. After many calls and some sleuthing, he managed to track down the state party officials. He learned that they were meeting to consider an anti-McCarthy statement. The story was given play around the country.

When President Kennedy was assassinated in Dallas, the AP distributed an unconfirmed report that Vice President Johnson had been wounded. Tom Wicker, covering for *The New York Times*, was instructed by his desk to check the report.

Wicker said later that he dismissed the report immediately because he felt it was based on Johnson's holding his arm as he entered the hospital, and Wicker knew that the peculiar posture was a Johnson mannerism. It was an accurate hunch, fortunately for Wicker.

During the confusion that followed the shooting, Wicker and the other reporters were told many things they had no time to check. They had to make quick decisions. Wicker said rumors, statements and reports flew through the city. Wicker said he had to go on what he knew of the people he talked to, what he knew of human reaction, what two isolated facts added up to in sum—above all on what he felt in his bones.

Summing up the reporter's use of his feel for a story, Wicker writes, "In a crisis, if a reporter can't trust his instinct for truth, he can't trust anything."

Experience as the Basis

We have seen a reporter who smells out stories (Hersh), and another reporter who trusts his instincts (Wicker) to guide him in his coverage. Clearly, neither of these reporters depends completely on intuition, hunches and feelings. Like the reporter for the southwestern newspaper who broke the story of the anti-McCarthy meeting, their fact-gathering is underlined by discerning observation directed by disciplined intelligence.

What seems to be the play of intuition and hunches is the crystallization of experience. Reporters who have mastered their beats have stored thousands of facts about people, events, policies, concepts and the various other elements that go into their daily experience. This vast storehouse is organized, almost subconsciously, so that when a new situation develops, it is seen in terms of the pertinent stored material.

Hunches and instinct usually work for the good reporters, rarely for the talentless. Ability plus experience equals excellence in all fields.

During the 1982 hockey season, a talented young center for the Edmonton Oilers set records no one thought possible. Wayne Gretzky had fans comparing his feats with those in other sports. His goals and his assists for the season would be the equivalent of a .425 batting average in baseball, 55 points a game over a basketball season, 3,000 yards gained in a season of professional football.

Pure instinct, say those who watch him. Not so, says Gretzky.

"Nine out of ten people think my talent is instinct," he said. "It isn't. It's all practice. I got it all from my dad."

When he was a three-year-old in Brantford, Ontario, Gretzky's father iced down the backyard and had the youngster practicing. At the age of 10 he was skating five hours a day.

Good reporters make use of this same combination of talent and experience.

The reporter who discovered the purpose of the meeting of the state's party leaders had more than intuition going for him. As he looked back on the event, he realized he knew from the tone of the voice of the governor's secretary that something was unusual about the governor's "vacation." Dozens of conversations with the secretary had prepared him for that.

The reporter's mind is like an advanced computer in its capacity to store information. Unlike the machine, the mind is able to make creative link-ups, as the reporter did when he put together the governor's "vacation," the scheduled party conference and the animosity of the two party leaders to McCarthyism. This fusion of stored and new material is the reporter's highest achievement. It is accomplished through the application of logical thinking, inspiration and intuition to observations and background information.

Awed by a technological society in which computers and data processing machinery seem to minimize the human mind, reporters should retain their faith in the mind. "The largest computer now in existence lacks the richness and flexibility in the brain of a single honeybee," writes Peter Sterling, a brain researcher at the University of Pennsylvania Medical School.

Robert S. Lynd, the famous sociologist, says that "knowledge cannot advance without both insight and data." Both must be put to work on subject matter, "the one constantly checking the other in an endless game of leapfrog between hypotheses and evidence. . . ."

Feelings

The reporter usually welcomes his or her hunches and intuitive guesses, but is less cordial toward feelings—that uncontrollable emotion that can hold the reporter captive without warning, lift him or her to ecstasy at a glance or a touch, and plunge its victims to bleakest despair with a word or a gesture.

This wilderness of feeling frightens most people, and it terrifies those who depend on their rationality, as reporters do. But reporters are human and must function within the limitations of the rationality of human behavior.

Feelings, in fact, can be an asset. "How can you write if you can't cry?" asked Ring Lardner. Feelings help develop value systems and keep them nourished. A sense of moral indignation can direct a reporter to crowning achievements. The muckrakers, whose journalism may well have been the supreme journalistic achievement in this century, were propelled by a monumental moral indignation. Anyone who reads their work can sense the intensity of feeling behind it.

This same intensity drives most investigative reporters, who talk of their inability to tolerate wrongdoing. It is this strong emotional reaction to the abuses of power by public officials and the titans of commerce and industry that propels investigative reporters to their discoveries. The Teapot Dome scandal was exposed by a reporter for the *St. Louis Post-Dispatch* who spent years investigating and proving that powerful oil interests had bribed the Secretary of the Interior in the Harding administration. The reporter, Paul Y. Anderson, was driven throughout his journalistic career by the need to expose wrongdoers, the same intensity of feeling that motivates reporters who expose corruption and systemic abuses now.

Auditing Feelings

Nevertheless, the reporter is right to check his or her emotions, for they can distort observations and impede the process of analysis and synthesis that is the foundation of reporting and writing.

A city hall reporter who finds the personal lifestyle and ideas of a councilwoman abhorrent may discover he is looking only for negative facts about her, or that his writing bears an unmistakable undertone of hostility. A political reporter whose personal allegiance is to the Democratic Party may find she is not paying sufficient attention to the other parties or that she is overly critical of the Republican Party and its leaders. The idea of welfare payments to the able-bodied poor—or subsidies to farmers—might so violate a reporter's economic beliefs that his or her coverage of these activities is distorted.

The feelings that feed these opinions and the reporter's values come into play constantly on the job, and reporters should examine them regularly. Here are some questions a reporter might also ask himself or herself every so often:

Does my need for ego-gratification—which runs high among journalists— lead me to see an event a certain way? (The blandishments of governors and presidents can lead to a journalism of cronyism and self-censorship. Clever sources know how to play to a reporter's need for praise.)

Have I so committed myself to a person, an organization or an idea that new facts that contradict the commitment are ignored?

Does my need for immediate and frequent reward—a byline, a front page story—make me push a story so that I think it is ready to be written before all necessary facts are gathered? (The journalist often must write before every fact is in. Journalism is legitimately described as history in a hurry. But sometimes reporters make stories from skimpy material, particularly when they have not had a good story in a week or two.)

Is my competitive drive so great that I will ignore, underplay, or try to knock down another reporter's legitimate story on my beat?

No reporter can be neutral about life. Nor should a journalist be neutral. But all reactions that swing to one extreme or the other should be examined for their causes. The reporter should watch out for uncritical enthusiasm or unreasonable hostility.

Some reactions may be based on what the semanticists call "short-circuited responses," feelings that burst forth without thinking. A reporter may be positive about doctors or judges and negative about salesmen or plumbers without distinguishing among the individuals in these groups. This kind of knee-jerk thinking is known as stereotyping. It is a dangerous way to think, particularly for a reporter.

Stereotypes

Attitudes, fears, assumptions, biases and stereotypes are part of the baggage we carry with us from an early age. We see the world the way our parents, friends, schools and religious community have defined it for us. We are also creatures of the culture that surrounds us—our jobs, the reading we do, the television programs we watch, and the kind of government and economic system we live under.

All these elements influence the way we think and how we see and hear.

Victim of Images

Despite the journalist's pride in the ability to question assumptions, he or she too, is a child of his own or her own culture.

The power of parents in shaping the child is described by Christopher Lasch, a historian, in a review, "The Family and History," in the Nov. 13, 1975, issue of the *New York Review of Books:*

> As the chief agent of "socialization," the family reproduces cultural patterns in the individual. It not only imparts ethical norms, providing the child with his first instruction in the prevailing social rules, it profoundly shapes his character, in ways of which he is not even aware. The family instills modes of thought and action that become habitual. Because of its enormous emotional influence it colors all of a child's subsequent experience.

The journalist sees much of the world through lenses tinted by others. The maker of images and stereotypes, the journalist is also their victim.

Difficult as it may be to shed these images, the journalist must always question these ways of looking at the world. The young man who has grown up in a politically liberal home in a Northern state may find on close examination that some of his attitudes are based on the stereotype of Southerners as diehard conservatives. The daughter of a doctor may discover she presumes that people who work with their hands—electricians, plumbers, auto mechanics—are not as intelligent as those who work with their minds—lawyers, teachers, engineers. Purging one's self of these ways of thinking and seeing is not easy.

From Plato's time to the present, great thinkers have speculated about how and what people see. In the "Simile of the Cave" in Plato's *Republic,* he describes a cave in which people are shackled so that they can only look straight ahead at one of the walls in the cave. They cannot see themselves or each other. Outside, a fire burns, and between the fire and the cave dwellers there runs a road in front of which a curtain has been built. Along the road are men carrying figures of men and animals made of wood, stone and other materials. The shadows that these figures cast up on the wall are all the cave dwellers can see.

"And so in every way they would believe that the shadows of the objects we mentioned were the whole truth," Plato has Socrates say of what the prisoners can see.

The parable is striking, almost eerie in its perception of image making. It takes little imagination to replace the cave with the movie theater or to visualize the shadows on the wall as the images on a television screen.

Plato goes still further with his insight into how images pass for reality. He examines what happens when the prisoners are "released from their bonds and cured of their delusions." Told that what they have seen was nonsense, they would not believe those who free them. They would regard "nothing else as true but the shadows," Socrates tells us. The realities would be too dazzling, too confusing.

Now let us jump some 2,250 years to the speculations of Walter Lippmann, whose classic description of how persons see is contained in his book, *Public Opinion* (New York: Macmillan, 1922), p. 81. Here is that description:

> For the most part we do not first see, and then define, we define first and then see. In the great blooming, buzzing confusion of the outer world we pick out what our culture has already defined for us, and we tend to perceive that which we have picked out in the form stereotyped for us by our culture.

The Seduction of the Stereotype

To Lippmann, as to Plato, reality can be too complex and confusing. Lippmann says that the "attempt to see all things freshly and in detail rather than as types and generalities is exhausting. . . ." Stereotypes allow us to fit individuals into categories defined for us, categories that are comfortable because they save time in a busy life and defend our position in society, Lippmann says. They also "preserve us from all the bewildering effects of trying to see the world steadily and see it whole," he writes.

But see it whole the reporter must. When a student movie reviewer at Barnard College saw a film made by Luis Buñuel, she wrote, in amazement, "How Buñuel at age 70 can still direct such marvelous, memorable, intelligent and worthwhile films is beyond me." Her comment illustrates one of the stereotypes common to youth, the belief that with age comes not wisdom but decrepitude.

Stereotypes are held by every age group for its comfort and protection. And by religious groups, nationalities and the sexes. Sexual stereotypes are common: Women are passive, men aggressive; women are good at spelling, men make better scientists.

Class and racial stereotypes seem to lie deep in the psyches of many persons. One of the veteran reporters on a large metropolitan daily newspaper was sent to do a major story on the unusual circumstances involved in the rape and murder of three children within a two-year period. The reporter pointed out that the children lived in rundown areas of the inner city, a euphemism for saying they were from poor families. He tried to determine how the slayings might affect the community. But he based his assessment on interviews with suburban parents. He ignored the inner city parents who might be more directly affected.

He wrote:

> It is hard to measure the effect of the murders on residents of this sprawling metropolitan area, many of whom seldom, if ever, enter the inner city, since their places of employment, homes and shopping centers are situated on the periphery. Their lives seldom intersect with those of the poor who have been left behind.

The reporter presumably knew that there were parents in the poor sections of the city, but he did not consider them worth interviewing. Implicit in the way the reporter handled the story is his class bias.

Sexism Sexual stereotypes are extraordinarily powerful. The word sexism was coined to indicate how close discrimination based on gender is to racism. The stereotypes begin in infancy, carry through school and are retained in the workplace and home. Women are seen as weak, men as strong. Women are destined for jobs as secretaries, nurses, teachers, and when a woman becomes an engineer or a plumber, that is news. Obviously, journalists not only are victims of sexual stereotyping, but they also are its promoters when they write such phrases as the following taken from news stories:

> . . . his bride-to-be, attractive, blonde Claudette Fournier, 35 . . .
> . . . the cleaning lady said she . . .
> He had the girl check his coat and . . .

How to Tell a Businessman from a Businesswoman

An anonymous but acute and mischievous observer of the office scene compiled this telling commentary:

A businessman is aggressive; a businesswoman is pushy.

He is careful about details; she's picky.

He loses his temper because he's so involved in his job; she's bitchy.

He's depressed (or hung over), so everyone tiptoes past his office; she's moody, so it must be her time of the month.

He follows through; she doesn't know when to quit.

He's firm; she's stubborn.

He makes wise judgments; she reveals her prejudices.

He is a man of the world; she's been around.

He isn't afraid to say what he thinks; she's opinionated.

He exercises authority; she's tyrannical.

He's discreet; she's secretive.

He's a stern taskmaster; she's difficult to work for.

To avoid sexism in copy, or any other kind of stereotyping, it helps to think of people as individuals. Each has his or her own identity. Sexist writing identifies women through their relationship with men. Language itself often reflects male-centered thinking. The column on the left contains what is considered to be sexist language. The column on the right is preferable:

Sexist	**Preferred**
policeman	police officer
fireman	fire fighter
salesman	sales person
mankind	people, human beings
manpower	human resources, workers

There are also inconsistencies in referring to men and women:

Wrong	**Right**
man and wife	husband and wife
men and ladies	men and women
Jack Parsons and Ms. (Miss, Mrs.) Sloan	Jack Parsons and Joan Sloan
Parsons and Joan	Jack and Joan
	Parsons and Sloan

Substitutes for Observation

A news story grows out of the interaction between the reporter and the event. If the reporter sees the event in pre-fixed forms, he or she will pre-judge the event, making it conform to the stereotyped pictures carried in his or her head. Robert L. Heilbroner describes an experiment performed with college students that shows how powerful these pictures can be. The students were shown "30 photographs of pretty but un-identified girls, and asked to rate each in terms of 'general liking, intelligence, beauty' and so on," Heilbroner writes in an article, "Don't Let Stereotypes Warp Your Judg-ment," in the June, 1961, issue of the magazine *Think.*

"Two months later," he continues, "the same group were shown the same photographs, this time with fictitious Irish, Italian, Jewish and 'American' names attached to the pictures. Right away the ratings changed. Faces which were now seen as representing a national group went down in looks and still farther down in likability, while the 'American' girls suddenly looked decidedly prettier and nicer."

Stereotypes are, as the semanticist S. I. Hayakawa points out, "substitutes for observation," and reporters tend to fall back on them unless they are careful. Persons and events are stereotyped in story after story. A computer fed the different names, addresses, and locations could write these stories.

Pandering to Stereotypes

Reporters may sometimes be unknowing victims of their own stereotypes. This is excusable. But when the reporter believes the reader, listener or viewer cannot grasp anything but stereotypes, the reporter becomes a knowing violator of the journalistic ethic that requires him to tell truths.

A television reporter preparing a documentary on a country-style singer learned that the entertainer's wife was hardly the rustic lass she pretended to be for the public. She was, in reality, a serious drama student who conceived the role she was playing. The reporter had to make a decision: Should the documentary present the stereotyped version, which would fit public expectations, or should it dig deeper into her personality and character? The truth introduced a complicating factor, as it inevitably does. The decision was to go ahead with the stereotyped version, and the woman emerged as just plain folk, just the way people expected her to be.

David Halberstam, journalist and author, says that when a television special on President Kennedy was being edited, the producers noticed that when CBS correspondent George Herman asked tough questions the president appeared to give vague answers. The producers eliminated the questions and answers. "They weren't sharp, they did not make a good show," says Halberstam.

The television producer—and all journalists who believe in meeting the lowest common denominator—might heed the warning of F. Scott Fitzgerald: "Begin with an individual and before you know it you have created a type; begin with a type and you have created—nothing."

Patterns and Relationships

John Dewey said that "the striving to make stability of meaning prevail over the instability of events is the main task of intelligent human effort." In finding these meanings, the journalist seeks to find the patterns that establish relationships between facts and events. The great journalist of the muckraking period, Lincoln Steffens, said that his thinking about reporting was transformed by a prosecuting attorney during his investigation into municipal corruption in St. Louis.

"He was sweeping all his cases of bribery together to form a truth out of his facts," Steffens wrote later. "He was generalizing . . . he was thinking about them all together and seeing what they meant all together." Steffens said that this thinking led the prosecutor to conclude that the corruption was "systematic."

People whose business it is to strip events and activities down to their meaning try to find new and different patterns and relationships that underline the situation. Mystery writer John Le Carré describes how George Smiley suddenly finds the key to a strange suicide in the mystery novel *Call for the Dead*. Smiley is stumped but suddenly sees

there was another quite different solution to the case of Samuel Fennan, a solution which matched every detail of circumstances, reconciled the nagging inconsistencies apparent in Fennan's character. The realization began as an academic exercise without reference to personalities; Smiley maneuvered his characters like pieces in a puzzle, twisting them this way and that to fit the complex framework of the established facts—and then, in a moment, the pattern had suddenly reformed with such assurance that it was a game no more.

No additional facts were necessary for Smiley to reach his breakthrough—only the ability to see them in a new way. This ability to put things together, as a journalist does when writing a news story, is called synthesizing.

Writing about a pioneer scientist, Randolph Kirkpatrick, a Harvard history of science instructor, says, "He had a passion for synthesis and an imagination that compelled him to gather truly disparate things together. He consistently sought similarities of geometric form among objects conventionally classified in different categories. . . ."

One of the most common relationships journalists form is the causal relationship. Here is an example of such a relationship. These are the first few sentences from a news story:

> Dozens of teen-agers threw bottles and rocks at a youth employment office today after the governor announced he was closing it and five others in the state to save money.
>
> Police said they dispersed the youths and made no arrests at Eighth Avenue and Essex Street.
>
> The incident followed an announcement yesterday by the State Director of. . . .

The sentences seem straightforward, clear, the kind of Layer I reporting in which the reporter quotes authorities about the incident. The story implies cause and effect: Because the governor closed the office, the youths demonstrated. The reporter did not visit the scene. He put two events into a pattern and established a causal relationship.

Causal relationships are the result of thinking that goes this way: Because A preceded B, A caused B. The tip-off to such thinking often comes from the use of the words "after" or "following" in copy.

There are legitimate causal relationships. But when reporters do their job and move into Layer II to check out their assumptions about these relationships they often find the situation is more complex than it appears at first glance. In the rock-throwing incident, if the reporter had questioned the youngsters it might have turned out that most of them were hot and bored that day and were angered when the supervisor bawled out a couple of youths who were lounging at the front door. The truth could well be that none of them knew of the governor's action.

Causal relationships are less certain in human affairs than they are in the world of mechanics and dynamics where physical forces have visible consequences. However, when a reporter has enough facts to indicate a relationship exists, he or she should be willing to make an inference on his or her own. The reporter will be cautious about it, for he or she knows that ultimate truths are rarely available to a reporter. Nevertheless, risks can be taken. In 1974, reporters for the *Minneapolis Tribune* looked into the records and came up with proof that the milk producers' lobby had channeled hundreds of thousands of dollars into the Republican Party treasury through dummy committees. Following these contributions, the reporters wrote, the White House decided to increase milk support prices.

There was no absolute proof that the contributions had caused the policy decision. But the reporters decided that the suggestion of a causal relationship was legitimate.

In the obituaries of Joe Pyne, a television and radio talk show host, and Hal March, a master of ceremonies on television quiz shows, *The New York Times* reported the men died of cancer. Then the stories noted that Pyne had been a "heavy smoker" and that "Mr. March had smoked two packs of cigarettes a day for many years." No absolute causal relationship had been demonstrated between cigarette smoking and cancer at the time the obituaries ran, but the data collected by the surgeon general's office had indicated a high probability of such a relationship, and the newspaper was willing to suggest the cause-and-effect for its readers.

Making causal relationships in print or on the air represents a certain risk to the reporter, but good reporters take risks. In fact, risk-taking may be one of the marks of a successful journalist. The British mathematician, G. B. Hardy, remarked that high intelligence is not important to the success of most persons. He granted that judgment is important, but not as essential as application to the task at hand, a capacity to take risks and luck. No one, he said, can make the most of his or her talents without constant application or without taking frequent risks.

Storing Information

Sometimes the journalist is unable to see the story because he or she cannot visualize relationships and possibilities. Thinking can become trapped in grooves that are difficult to escape. We have seen how the reporter stores information. Sometimes this material affects thinking. Research seems to indicate that people in the communications field not only organize new information to suit their audiences but that they will remember it in that particularly limited way.

In one study, journalism students were divided into two groups to listen to the same speech. One group was told it would write a story for readers favoring the viewpoints of the speaker; the other group was to write for a publication whose readers opposed the speaker's views. The two groups turned out dissimilar stories. Reporters in each group remembered material that seemed to suit the readership of the publication they were told to write for.

Another example: A police reporter may keep in mind the accomplishments of the men he covers, not their failures, for the beat reporter too often is concerned only with those within the narrow confines of the beat, not the general reader.

Polar Alternatives

Another potentially dangerous line of thinking that is common among harried reporters is the polar alternative. For instance, the reporter may think: Either the Black Parents Association is right, or it is wrong in its stand on school books. The candidate was open about the bond issue, or he was secretive. This either-or thinking can save the reporter time and energy, but it can lead to superficial journalism.

Causes and actions are complex, a combination of many factors. The reporter who looks only for the white and black of situations, the yes or no, will be limiting his or her observations to the most obvious facets of the event. The world is hardly bilateral and the reporter must attempt to see several of its infinite faces.

Confronting this multitude of facets, faces and facts is only half the task. The most difficult job the reporter faces is to put them into some meaningful pattern, the story. But that is what journalism is about—linking facts to make stories.

Look back at the work of the reporter we watched as he tried to figure out the reason state GOP party leaders were meeting secretly. He was trying to link facts. But he had to provide the concepts to link his facts.

This kind of reporting takes us into the mainstream of contemporary journalism. It would have been what we have called Layer I journalism to have written that the governor had taken a vacation. Because of the reporter's hunch that there was more to the official's absence than a desire to try the Royal Coachman on a trout stream, the reader was taken closer to the truth of the situation. In other words, by digging for the significant relationship between the absence and the current political situation, the reporter moved into Layer II journalism.

We could say that the discovery came in an intuitive flash, a sudden insight. Reporters have the ability to make these sudden discoveries of the concept or idea that puts observations into order in a meaningful pattern. As we have seen, these leaps to significant relationships are actually launched from solid ground. These insights are based on experience and the logical thinking of the kind described by the philosopher Isaiah Berlin: "To comprehend and contrast and classify and arrange, to see in patterns of lesser or greater complexity is not a peculiar kind of thinking, it is thinking itself."

The ability to pattern observations is the mark of the thinking person, whether we look at a reporter covering a story, a youth who identifies the make and model of a car at a glance, or a second grader on a children's television program who sees a unique relationship.

Four youngsters on a children's program were shown pictures of a dog, a rooster, a cow and a monkey. The children were asked to find something that at least two of the animals had in common, which is a good exercise to develop the kind of thinking we have been describing. One youngster pointed out that the monkey and the rooster walked on two legs and that the dog and cow used four legs. Another pointed to the long tails of the dog, cow and monkey. The hand of another youngster suddenly shot up and her eyes shone with excitement.

"The rooster and the cow," she announced triumphantly. The host was perplexed and asked her to explain.

"Those pink, soft things," the child said. The quiz master looked even more puzzled. Slowly, enlightenment spread over his face, and he, too, joined in the youngster's glee. Wordlessly, he pointed to the rooster's comb and the cow's udder.

That child could become a fine reporter, for she had begun to develop what the philosopher Alfred North Whitehead describes as an "eye for the whole chessboard, for the bearing of one set of ideas on another."

Reporters are always looking for facts that relate to each other. The obituary writer wants to know the cause of death, especially if the death is sudden, unexpected. A reporter covering such a death was given the explanation—accidental gunshot wound. But the reporter wonders: The death seems staged. Could it have been a suicide? That's playing games, he says to himself. Still, the death looks like that of one of the characters in a novel.

Thinking of this sort led this reporter to learn that Ernest Hemingway had killed himself, contrary to the explanation put out by the authorities, who had agreed to cover up the truth to save the family embarrassment.

A reporter assigned to write a year-end summary of traffic fatalities begins with the data the police department has supplied. As she scans the figures of deaths on city roads and streets, she notices that pedestrian deaths are up 16 percent, whereas the over-all increase in fatalities over the previous year is 8 percent. She decides to concentrate on pedestrian deaths for her story.

Further examination of the data indicates that most of those killed were 14 years old and under. The reporter recalls that some months ago a parents organization petitioned the city council to provide more play streets for the warm-weather months in downtown areas where there is a heavy concentration of low-income families and few open spaces. She wonders whether the number of children who were killed in traffic accidents was high in the summer. She also checks the location of the accidents. A pattern is beginning to take shape in her mind. Now she must determine whether the facts support her ideas.

As she moves through the data, she also notices the traffic department lists the times at which deaths and injuries occurred. She is surprised at the number of children who were killed or hurt in the evening. Well, she reasons, perhaps that is logical. Where else can kids play on hot summer evenings, especially youngsters from homes without air conditioning? Television viewing in searing-hot summer tenements is no fun. She looks at her newspaper's clip file to check her recollections of the city council meeting. All this takes less than an hour. Next, she makes several telephone calls to gather additional information.

A reporter's approach to the story is as important as her fact gathering. She could have settled for Layer I reporting. Had she done so, her story might have begun this way:

> **Pedestrian deaths in the city last year were 16 percent higher than the previous year, a year-end summary of traffic deaths disclosed today.**

Instead, after her first hour of thinking and checking the clips, and another 45 minutes of calls, she is ready to write a story that she begins this way:

> **For 17 of the city's children the streets they played on last summer became a death trap.**

She then gives the total figures for all deaths and injuries to children under 14 and the total traffic deaths for the city. Then she works into her story the petition the parents had presented to the city council. Her finding that the evening hours were particularly dangerous for youngsters had not been discovered by the parents, who had asked for daytime restrictions on traffic. Before writing, the reporter calls the head of the parents group and tells her about the evening accident rate. The reporter is told that the group probably will renew its petitioning, this time with the request that in the summer some streets be permanently blocked off to traffic. This new material—the concept of 24-hour play streets—goes into the story, also.

The reporter not only turns out a meaningful story by linking up certain facts but performs a public service for her community as well.

Patterning is done all the time. Here is a simple example from a San Francisco newspaper:

TEN LIVES IN TEN HOURS— Such was the appalling toll yesterday of two head-on crashes that chalked up the grimmest period in Bay Area traffic history.

Not one person in the four cars involved survived. An entire family of five was snuffed out. That family, and a sixth individual, were innocent victims.

Speed was the killer. And liquor a confederate.

Three died in an explosive, flaming smashup on the Bay Bridge at 11:40 p.m. yesterday. The killer car was going 90 miles an hour.

Just ten hours earlier, at 1:40 p.m., seven met death in a jarring smackup on the divided Altamont Pass near Livermore. The speedometer needle of that killer car was stuck at 80 miles an hour.

The identified dead in the bridge crash. . . .

The relationships, the patterns, are obvious: First, the reporter took two fatal accidents and put them into a single story based on their having occurred in the San Francisco area. Next, he noticed that in both accidents, alcohol was involved and the cars that struck other vehicles were speeding. This leads to the nicely phrased third paragraph. We can excuse the clichés in the lead—"appalling toll" and "chalked up"—if that is the price we have to pay for the imaginative and terse third paragraph.

Roundups such as this story from San Francisco depend upon organizing ideas to keep them from being a laundry list of separate items. These ideas not only can link facts that are already on hand, they also can lead the reporter to do more fact-gathering, as did the reporter who handled the city's year-end traffic fatality report.

Risks and Responsibilities

5

14 Reporters and the Law

Preview   The laws of libel and privacy limit what reporters may write. Stories that damage a person's reputation can be libelous, unless the material is privileged or can be proved to be true.

- Libel—Most libelous stories are the result of careless reporting. All material that might injure someone should be double-checked. The courts protect journalists who libel public figures or public officials; but recent court decisions have limited these exceptions.

- Privacy—The right to privacy is protected by law. The personal activities of an individual can be reported if the written material is about a newsworthy person and is not highly offensive.

One of the most dangerous areas for the journalist is libel. To the beginner, the region is a land of mystery in which all the guideposts read *Don't*. To the experienced reporter, who has lost his fear of legal language, it is a cautionary presence in the newsroom.

Broadly speaking, libel is published defamation of character. That is, it is writing or a picture that exposes a person to hatred, contempt or ridicule, or that injures his reputation or causes him to be shunned or avoided, or that has a tendency to injure him in his occupation.

Of course, many articles and pictures do libel individuals. In most cases, the defamatory material may be safe for publication if it is privileged. By this we mean that the article is a fair and true report of a judicial, legislative, or other public official proceeding, or of anything said in the course of such sessions, trials or proceedings. Those who made our laws recognized that open debate of serious issues would be impeded unless the public had full access to official actions.

Another defense against libel is truth. No matter how serious the defamation may be, if the statement can be proved to be true and to be made without malice, the defamed individual cannot successfully bring legal action.

A third defense, fair comment and criticism, most often involves the writing of editorial writers and reviewers. So long as the comment or criticism is directed at the work and is not an attack of the individual, the writing is safe.

In summary, the libel laws generally have held that a reporter is not in danger if the material is from a privileged proceeding (public *and* official) or if the material is substantially true or constitutes fair comment.

For broadcast journalists, defamatory statements made from a prepared script fall under libel, whereas extemporaneous defamatory remarks are treated as slander, which can be defined as oral or uttered defamation.

Grounds for Libel Suits

Matter that might be held libelous by a court would have to:

1. Imply commission of a crime.
2. Tend to injure a person in his or her profession or job.
3. Imply a person has a disease, usually a loathsome disease that might lead to the individual's ostracism.
4. Damage a person's credit.
5. Imply a lack of chastity.
6. Indicate a lack of mental capacity.
7. Incite public ridicule or contempt.

For years, libel was a great weight on the shoulders of the press, particularly for newspapers that handled controversy and emphasized investigative reporting. The press associations had special concerns, for libel law was state law and was beyond the protection of the Constitution. What was legal in one state might be libelous in another. The wire services thus tended to take few risks.

So, for that matter, did the press as a whole. Although prior restraint clearly is unconstitutional, what happens to the press when lawmakers decide that the publication of certain material is illegal—as legislators have decided in the case of supposedly seditious, obscene and immoral material? As Zechariah Chafee Jr., an authority on freedom of expression, put it in commenting on press freedom in England in the eighteenth century: "A death penalty for writing about socialism would be as effective suppression as censorship."

In effect, libel laws restrained the press, as the Supreme Court recognized in an epochal decision in 1964 that was to lighten the burden on the press. The court ruled that defamatory statements could have First Amendment protection. Our seven danger points are still to be watched, but the press now has much stronger defenses, thanks to the Supreme Court. To understand that decision—and to understand the organic nature of the law—we must travel back in time to Montgomery, Ala.

An Incident on a Bus

When Mrs. Rosa Parks boarded the Cleveland Avenue bus in Montgomery in December 1955, she spotted an empty seat toward the rear, just behind the section reserved for whites. Tired from a day's work in a downtown department store, she eased into the space, only to be ordered to move. Seats were needed for white passengers.

Mrs. Parks, a quiet, reserved woman, refused to give up her seat. She was taken off the bus and arrested.

The following weekend, plans were made by the black community to boycott the buses.

Martin Luther King, Jr., a black minister involved in the boycott plans, later recalled how he awoke early Monday morning to look out a window of his home at a nearby bus stop to see whether Montgomery's black residents would heed the word that it was better to walk in dignity than to ride in shame. The bus line that passed by the King home carried more blacks than any other line in the city. The first bus went by at 6 a.m. It was empty. Another, 15 minutes later, was empty, too.

That was the beginning of the boycott. Some 42,000 Montgomery blacks said they would walk to and from work or use volunteer vehicles and black-owned taxis until the bus system altered its seating arrangements and hired black drivers for buses along the predominantly black routes.

For 381 days they stayed off the buses rather than be told to move to the back. Many persons went to jail for violating the state's anti-boycott laws, including Mrs. Parks and Dr. King. Finally, the Supreme Court ruled bus segregation illegal.

Tension Mounts

To some blacks, the action of Mrs. Parks and others in Montgomery was more significant than the decision of the Supreme Court the year before that prohibited the segregation of public schools, for in Montgomery blacks had banded together and had brought about change by themselves. This effort helped accelerate the mass movement of non-violent resistance to discrimination among blacks. It was to develop slowly in the 1950s and to spread in the early 1960s in marches, lunchroom sit-ins, Freedom Rides and picketing throughout the South, in which a number of communities openly defied the 1954 school desegregation ruling and were unwilling to follow other court orders.

Tensions mounted, and blood was spilled. In 1963, Medgar Evers, a black civil rights worker, was murdered in the doorway of his home in Jackson, Miss. The following year, three young civil rights workers were murdered in Philadelphia, Miss.

Newspapers and television stations sent waves of reporters to the South to report the conflict. Viewers saw fire hoses, police dogs and cattle prods used on blacks in Birmingham, and they saw the clubs of state troopers in Selma. The press reported that blacks themselves were now voicing the cry for an end to humiliation, economic exploitation, segregation in schools and discrimination at the polls.

It was also obvious the South was hardly budging. The border areas, yes. Portions of Tennessee and Kentucky, and metropolitan communities like Atlanta and Richmond were being pushed by non-violent action toward accommodation. But not the towns and parishes of the Black Belt—Selma, Plaquemines, Yazoo City. Here, non-violence met intractable resistance. Blacks might wait patiently outside the courthouse in Selma to register to vote. But the doors would stay closed to them, unless they were battered in by the blacks, or broken down by the federal government along with the National Guard, the powers of the attorney general and the courts.

Press Coverage Increases

Because of the intensive coverage in the press, a consensus was developing outside the Black Belt. Most of the nation saw the anguish of the blacks who were hurling themselves against the wall of segregation, and some believed the nation was heading toward a cataclysm. Some foresaw a race war in the making.

In 1963, President Kennedy, aware of the developing conflict, declared that the struggle of blacks for civil rights was a "moral issue." Then four young girls attending Sunday school in the black Sixteenth Street Baptist Church in Birmingham died in a bomb blast at the church.

The press stepped up its coverage. In some northern newspapers and on network television, the South was presented as a forbidding region of racism, its law officers openly defiant of the law, its white citizens unwilling to adjust to the changing times. Southerners were dismayed by the coverage, and some whites assaulted reporters covering civil rights demonstrations. The retaliation also took the form of suits against the press and television.

A Legal Club

Millions of dollars in damages were being claimed by officials, who asserted they had been defamed by press and television. By 1964, libel suits seeking $300 million in damages were pending against news organizations covering the racial story. One of the largest suits was brought against *The New York Times* by five officials in Alabama who contended that they had been inferentially damaged in an advertisement in the *Times* in 1960 that sought to raise funds for the civil rights movement. The advertisement, headlined "Heed Their Rising Voices," attacked the treatment of blacks in the South. The five officials brought suit for a total of $3 million.

The first case to be tried involved L. B. Sullivan, one of three elected Montgomery city commissioners, who was responsible for the police department. At the trial, it was evident that the advertisement contained errors and exaggerations. An Alabama state court jury awarded Sullivan the $500,000 he had sought from the *Times*, although the advertisement had not named him but had made erroneous statements about the Birmingham police. The press and television reporters wondered what would happen next.

In a headline over the story about the suits against the *Times*, a Montgomery newspaper seemed to reveal the motives behind the libel suits. The headline read: "State Finds Formidable Legal Club to Swing at Out-of-State Press."

The Court Acts

It was in this atmosphere that the Supreme Court considered the appeal of the *Times* from the state court decision. The case of *The New York Times v Sullivan* (376 US 254) in 1964 was to mark a major change in the libel laws. But more important, by granting the press wider latitude in covering and commenting on the actions of public officials the decision gave the press greater freedom to present issues of public concern, like the racial conflict that was tearing the country apart.

The Supreme Court realized the unique nature of the appeal. The Court commented: "We are required for the first time in this case to determine the extent to which the Constitutional protections for speech and press limit a state's power to award damages in a libel action brought by a public official against the critics of his official conduct."

In its decision, the Supreme Court took from the states their power to award damages for libel "in actions brought by public officials against critics of their official conduct." The Constitutional protections for free speech and free press would be seriously limited by state actions of the kind the Alabama court took, the Court said.

Justice William J. Brennan wrote: "The Constitutional guarantees require, we think, a federal rule that prohibits a public official from recovering damages for a defamatory falsehood relating to his official conduct unless he proves that the statement was made with 'actual malice'—that is, with knowledge that it was false or with reckless disregard to whether it was false or not."

The court was moved to this change in the libel laws because it saw the laws being used to stifle free discussion of public issues. The Court apparently agreed with the argument of Herbert F. Wechsler, who wrote in a brief for the *Times:* "This is not a time—there never was a time—when it would serve the values enshrined in the Constitution to force the press to curtail its attention to the tensest issues that confront the country or to forgo the dissemination of its publications in the areas where tension is extreme."

Justice Brennan noted in his opinion that the Supreme Court had seen in the use of such legal concepts as "insurrection," "contempt," "breach of the peace," "obscenity," and "solicitation of legal business," attempts to suppress the open discussion of public issues. Now it was libel.

In the Sullivan libel case, the Court extended the First Amendment in order to accomplish a social-political purpose: The protection of dissident voices in a repressive atmosphere.

The Brennan decision, establishing what became known as the "Times Doctrine," noted that the "Constitutional safeguard was fashioned to assure unfettered interchange of ideas for the bringing about of political and social changes desired by the people." In order to accomplish this, there must be "maintenance of the opportunity for free political discussion to the end that government may be responsive to the will of the people and that changes may be obtained by lawful means, an opportunity essential to the security of the Republic. . . ."

Running through the decision are such reminders as the above, that free discussion will lead to a peaceful settlement of issues. The Court seemed to be addressing itself to the millions of Americans in trauma because of the racial conflict.

Justice Brennan wrote, ". . . it is hazardous to discourage thought . . . the path of safety lies in the opportunity to discuss freely supposed grievances and proposed remedies . . . right conclusions are more likely to be gathered out of a multitude of tongues, than through any kind of authoritative selection. . . ."

In summary, the decision in the case makes it clear that under the Constitution no public official can recover damages for defamation in a newspaper article or "editorial advertisement" concerning his official conduct unless he can prove the article false and also show that:

1. The publication was made with the knowledge that it was false; or
2. The statement was made with reckless disregard of whether it was false or not.

Items 1 and 2 constitute the Court's concept of "actual malice."

The decision is the law in every state and takes precedence over federal and state laws, state constitutions and all previous court decisions, whether they are state or federal.

Extension and Contraction of "Times Doctrine"

In the decade following the enunciation of the "Times Doctrine," the Court went beyond applying it to public officials and included public figures, then private individuals involved in matters of public concern. In a significant case, a businessman lost a libel suit that involved a clear case of error by a radio station.

A distributor of nudist magazines was arrested while delivering the magazine to a newsstand. The Philadelphia police reported the incident to a local radio station, which broadcast an item about the distributor's arrest on a charge of selling obscene materials. Further, the station stated that the magazines were obscene. In a subsequent trial, the distributor was acquitted. The distributor said he had been defamed by the radio station and sued. The case went to the jury, which awarded him general and punitive damages.

The radio newsman had obviously violated one of the first rules a beginner learns: Never state as fact what is only charged and therefore subject to determination in the courts.

However, the reporter and his station were fortunate. The Court of Appeals reversed the lower court verdict, and in 1971 the Supreme Court upheld the reversal on the distributor's appeal (*Rosenbloom v Metromedia, Inc.* (403 US 29). The Court ruled:

> We thus hold that a libel action, as here by a private individual against a licensed radio station for a defamatory falsehood in a newscast relating to his involvement in an event of public or general concern may be sustained only upon clear and convincing proof that the defamatory falsehood was published with knowledge that it was false or with reckless disregard of whether it was false or not.
> Calculated falsehood, of course, falls outside the "fruitful exercise of the right of free speech."

Rosenbloom was neither public official nor public figure. But he was involved in an event of "public or general concern," and ordinary citizens so involved can successfully bring a libel action only by a showing of actual malice, the Court stated.

Rosenbloom might have been luckier had his troubles occurred later, for the Supreme Court in 1974 reversed directions and did so again in 1976 and 1979. The rulings significantly narrowed the category of "public figure." By doing this, the Court made it possible for many more libel plaintiffs to collect damages for defamatory falsehoods since for private citizens the proof of defamation may be negligence or carelessness, not the actual malice necessary for public figures to prove.

In commenting on two Court rulings made in 1979, Bruce W. Sanford, a partner in a firm that handles communications law for UPI, Scripps-Howard and other news organizations, said, "They deal a series of staggering, unexpected blows that will cost the industry millions of dollars and that will have an immeasurable but definite effect on aggressive news coverage."

Sanford said the 1979 opinions "gloss over the vast importance of having a person classified as a public figure." In libel cases, public officials and public figures rarely reach the costly trial stage because they usually do not survive a pre-trial defense motion for summary judgment when a judge can dismiss a suit because the plaintiff cannot show actual malice.

Floyd Abrams, a lawyer for *The New York Times,* said of the 1979 decisions—*Hutchinson* and *Wolston*—"We have been deeply wounded." Let us examine these two and the 1976 and 1974 opinions that have contracted the Times Doctrine.

In the 1974 case of *Gertz v Robert Welch, Inc.,* (418 US 323) the Supreme Court suddenly ceased the steady expansion of First Amendment protection to publications in libel actions. Elmer Gertz, a civil rights lawyer in Chicago, had been defamed by *American Opinion,* a monthly magazine published by the conservative John Birch Society. The magazine described Gertz as a "Communist-fronter" and said he had designed a national campaign to discredit the police. Although the trial judge had found no evidence the magazine had published recklessly, a jury awarded Gertz $50,000. The decision was appealed by the magazine.

A Change in Directions

The Supreme Court ruled that as a private citizen Gertz could recover actual damages more easily than a public official or a public figure. Gertz, the Court said, did not have to show "actual malice" but was entitled to damages if he could prove the material was false and defamatory and that it had been the result of negligence or carelessness by the publication.

In 1976, the Court altered slightly the definition of a "public figure" in a case involving *Time* magazine, which had appealed a Florida court decision awarding $100,000 in damages in a libel suit brought by Mary Alice Firestone. She alleged *Time* had incorrectly reported the grounds on which Mrs. Firestone's husband had been granted a divorce. The court agreed that *Time* had been inaccurate. *Time* contended Mrs. Firestone was a public figure, which would have required her to submit proof of "actual malice" by *Time.* Mrs. Firestone had not submitted such proof. But the Court ruled that although Mrs. Firestone was a well-known socialite she "didn't assume any role of especial prominence in the affairs of society. . . ." (409 US 875).

In 1979, the Court further constricted the definition of a public figure. The cases, decided 8 to 1, were *Hutchinson v Proxmire,* (443 US 111), and *Wolston v Reader's Digest Assn., Inc.,* (443 US 157). The Court said there are two kinds of public figures: "A small group of individuals" who occupy positions of "persuasive power and influence" and people who have "thrust themselves to the forefront of particular public controversies in order to influence the resolution of the issues involved" and have, therefore, become public figures for the limited purpose of comment on their connection with these controversies.

Sanford says that unless the two-part test is applied expansively, both categories "become limited to a few prominent people or limelight-seekers who, as a practical matter, will rarely risk rankling the news media with a libel suit in any event." But in *Hutchinson* and *Wolston* the Court gave narrow application to the test.

In *Hutchinson,* the Court ruled against Sen. William Proxmire, who, in bestowing one of his Golden Fleece awards, had belittled a project by Ronald R. Hutchinson, a scientist who had used monkeys in an effort to find an objective measure of aggression. Several of the federal agencies that had granted Hutchinson $500,000 were cited by Proxmire as wasting public money. Hutchinson brought a libel action against Proxmire, seeking $8 million. He said the senator had caused him mental anguish and loss of income. A lower federal court ruled against Hutchinson in two areas. First, it said that by soliciting and receiving federal grants Hutchinson had become a public figure. Also, it ruled that Proxmire had legislative immunity.

The Supreme Court rejected the defense contention that Hutchinson was a public figure. The Court said that the scientist "did not have the regular and continuing access to the media that is one of the accoutrements of having become a public figure." As for Proxmire's immunity, the Court said that the Golden Fleece award was made known by the senator's newsletter and press releases, and these do not enjoy the same protection as words said on the Senate floor as part of the legislative process. The court rejected the assertions of House and Senate leaders on behalf of Proxmire that his public relations activities were part of the "informing function" of Congress. The case was returned to the lower court for trial. Proxmire settled out of court with a payment of $10,000 to Hutchinson.

In the other 1979 case, Ilya Wolston contended he was libeled by *Reader's Digest* when it falsely listed him in a book as being a Soviet agent. The book used an erroneous FBI document as its source. In 1958, Wolston had failed to appear before a grand jury investigating a spy ring. He later pleaded guilty to contempt and was given a suspended sentence. Wolston's case attracted considerable attention at the time.

But the Court ruled that Wolston did not "voluntarily thrust" or inject himself into the controversy over the inquiry. "It would be more accurate to say that Wolston was dragged unwillingly into the controversy," Justice William Rehnquist wrote.

"A private individual is not automatically transformed into a public figure just by becoming involved in or associated with a matter that attracts attention," the justice wrote. A person who engages in criminal conduct does not automatically become a public figure. "To hold otherwise would create an 'open season' for all who sought to defame persons convicted of a crime," Rehnquist said.

Suspects and Defendants— Not Public Figures

Sanford, usually a temperate observer of the Court, described Rehnquist's remarks as "unbelievable language. Reporters and editors don't go hunting for people (least of all criminals) to defame." The Court, he said, had made a "startling" ruling by rejecting—here Sanford quotes the Court—the "contention that any person who engages in criminal conduct automatically becomes a public figure for purposes of comment on a limited range of issues relating to his conviction." This is a significant shift in the Court's views since *Rosenbloom*. Sanford states that the "impact of this one sentence will be stunning" since the person most often involved in potentially libelous copy—the criminal suspect or defendant—"now will probably not be classifiable as a public figure."

But there is even worse in the opinions. Richard Schmidt, general counsel of the American Society of Newspaper Editors, finds in a footnote in *Hutchinson* a remark by Chief Justice Warren E. Burger that would "throw out the window" summary judgments in libel cases and force them to go to trial before "juries which will stick it to the press if they can."

In another footnote, Chief Justice Burger notes that the category of public official "cannot be thought to include all public employees, however." Sanford says that this footnote on public officials "undercuts the public official test and with it the whole rationale underlying the Court's own finding in *The New York Times*—that the press should be allowed to encourage robust debate about public affairs."

These four decisions since *Rosenbloom* impose greater burdens on reporters. Since most journalism is concerned with the activities of officials and public figures, the Court's new definitions of such persons require reporters to be careful in their reporting so that mistakes are avoided and to be cautious in their assumptions about the law. Different courts interpret the laws differently.

Courts Differ

The Washington Post escaped a libel judgment when a federal court ruled a police informant was a public figure and had to prove actual malice. The *Post* had incorrectly stated the informant was a drug user. But three months later a federal judge in Maryland ruled that a police informant was a private individual and thus need only prove that the Baltimore *News-American* was careless in mistakenly stating he had broken into a lawyer's office to steal documents for the police.

In state courts, a Kansas judge ruled that a lawyer appointed to defend a penniless criminal defendant was a public official. Two months later, a Michigan judge said that an attorney appointed to represent a poor defendant was neither public figure nor public official.

Caution: Events that are the subject of gossip or public curiosity and have no significant relation to public affairs usually do not confer on the persons involved in them the status of public figures. This means that no matter how public a person's marriage rift may be, or however notorious the person's sexual escapades are, that person is not therefore a public figure. Nor does the usual kind of crime or violence confer on the person involved the status of public figure.

Public Officials and Public Figures

Public officials—Government employees who have responsibility for governmental activities. This would cover elected officials, candidates for political office, appointed officials such as judges, police officers and some others engaged in the criminal justice system. The Supreme Court has said that not all public employees are public officials.

Public figures—People who have considerable power and influence and those who "voluntarily thrust" or inject themselves into public controversy are defined as public figures. Newspaper columnists, television personalities, and some celebrities who seek to influence the public are included. But not all prominent people are covered.

If the reporter can prove that the events in question relate to public affairs or an important social issue, then the persons involved may be classified as public figures. For example: If a physician or a lawyer injects himself or herself in a controversy over a local bond issue, then the person has made himself or herself a public figure for news about the bonds, but not about his or her personal life.

Repeating a Libel

In a story about neighborhood politics, a student newspaper reporter wrote and the newspaper printed this paragraph:

> A member of Board 9, who asked not to be identified, charged that Lawrence and Fine were involved in a kickback scheme in which the district manager, who is the board's paid administrator, pushed along projects beneficial to Chevra in return for an unspecified kickback.

Asked if he knew that the allegation about kickbacks is clearly libelous since accepting a kickback is a crime, the student replied, "But I attributed it." His instructor could only shrug in exasperation.

A reporter can be held liable if he or she repeats a libelous statement or quotes someone making such a statement unless the original material was privileged. Thus, a district attorney's assertion that a man had been convicted of a crime is defamatory if untrue. And the reporter who quoted the prosecutor might lose a libel suit if the man sued and could prove he was a private individual and the reporter had failed to check the material.

However, if the district attorney made the assertion in court during a trial, the statement—even if untrue—would be privileged and the privilege would be a defense against claims for damages.

The privilege to those participating in court cases and legislative sessions is an "absolute privilege," meaning the participants—the judge, lawyers, witnesses—cannot be held legally accountable even for malicious and deliberately false statements that are made within the scope of their participation in the proceedings. A newspaper or station, however, cannot use absolute privilege as a defense in libel suits. Their protection is known as "conditional" or "qualified privilege." The newspaper must present full, fair and accurate reports that are free of actual malice to be granted privilege.

A candidate for re-election to Congress who says of his opponent, "That man is a swindler" on the floor of the House of Representatives can make the statement with impunity, and a reporter can publish the accusation. (Obviously, the reporter would also carry the accused's reply.) But should the Congressman make the charge in a political rally and the reporter's newspaper print the allegation, both are in trouble, unless the reporter can prove the man is indeed a swindler, and this would require proof of the man's conviction on that charge.

Warning: These protections do not cover proceedings, meetings, or activities that are private in nature. The news story must deal with a judicial, legislative or other official proceeding.

"Swindler" is just one of many words that alert the careful reporter to the possibilities of libel. Any word that is associated with the seven danger areas listed at the outset of this chapter is carefully examined to see that it is (1) privileged or (2) provably true, by which we mean that a document (not someone's assertion) supports the charge. Here are some dangerous words and their danger areas from the list, "Grounds for Libel Suits" at the beginning of this chapter.

1. Thief, loan shark, shoplifter, gangster—implies commission of a crime.
2. Incompetent, failure, quack, shyster, slick operator—injures a person in his or her profession.
3. Wino, leper—implies a loathsome disease.
4. Unreliable, bankrupt, gambler, failure—damages a person's credit.
5. Loose, seducer, B-girl, immoral, mistress, hooker, streetwalker—implies a lack of chastity.
6. Screwy, nutty, incompetent, strange, out-of-it—indicates a lack of mental capacity.
7. Phony, coward, hypocrite—incites public ridicule or contempt.

The danger is not avoided by preceding these words, or others like them, with the words "alleged" or "reported."

Some federal courts have adopted the concept of "neutral reporting" which allows a newspaper to report a defamatory charge—in effect to repeat it—if the charge is made by a responsible organization and is accurately reported. The concept emerged in *Edwards v National Audubon Society* [556 f. 2d 113 (1977)] in which *The New York Times* was sued by three scientists that a Society spokesman accused of misusing bird counts to suggest that DDT did not harm birds. The Second Circuit Court of Appeals ruled unanimously that the "First Amendment protects the accurate and disinterested reporting" of charges "regardless of the reporter's private views of their validity." The Supreme Court refused to review the case.

Time Copy Not Exempt

The Supreme Court has been generous to reporters who make mistakes under pressure of deadline. But reporters who have time to check material may not fare so well under the Court's distinction between "hot news" and "time copy." The differences were spelled out in two companion cases decided in 1967, *Curtis Publishing Co. v Butts* and *Associated Press v Walker* (both 388 US 130).

Edwin Walker was a former Army general who had become involved in the civil rights disputes in the South and had taken a position against desegregation. He was on the campus of the University of Mississippi in September, 1962, when it erupted over the enrollment of James Meredith, a black student.

The AP moved a story on its teletype wires that Walker had taken command of a violent crowd and had personally led a charge against federal marshals on the campus. The AP said Walker had encouraged rioters to use violence and had instructed white students how to combat the effects of tear gas. He sued for a total of $800,000 in damages. In his trial, he testified that he had counseled restraint and peaceful protest and had not engaged in any charge against the marshals. The jury believed his account and awarded him the sum he sought. The trial judge cut out the $300,000 in punitive damages because he found no actual malice in the AP account.

Wally Butts was the athletic director of the University of Georgia in 1962. He was employed by the Georgia Athletic Association, a private corporation, and so, like Walker, he was a private citizen when he supposedly committed the action that led to his libel suit.

The Saturday Evening Post accused Butts of conspiring to fix a football game between Georgia and Alabama in 1962. An article in the magazine said an Atlanta insurance salesman had overheard conversation between Butts and Bear Bryant, coach of the Alabama football team, in which Butts outlined Georgia's offensive strategy in the coming game and advised Bryant about defending against the plays.

Butts sued for $5 million in compensatory damages and $5 million in punitive damages. The jury awarded him $60,000 on the first charge and $3 million on the second, which was subsequently reduced to $460,000. The Curtis Publishing Co., publishers of *The Saturday Evening Post,* and the AP appealed to the Supreme Court.

Butts won his appeal, but Walker lost. The Court ruled that the evidence showed that the Butts story was not "hot news," but that the Walker story was. The *Post*'s editors, the Court stated, "recognized the need for a thorough investigation of the serious charges" but failed to make the investigation.

In the Walker case, the Court noted: "In contrast to the Butts article, the dispatch which concerns us in *Walker* was news which required immediate dissemination. . . . Considering the necessity for rapid dissemination, nothing in this series of events gives the slightest hint of a severe departure from publishing standards. We therefore conclude that Walker should not be entitled to damages from the Associated Press."

In its opinion in the Butts case, the Court said that stories involving investigation and research require greater care and attention than spot news. In a ruling that bears on the work of the investigative reporter, the Court found *The Saturday Evening Post* had sought to expose Butts, which required considerable care. The Court stated:

> Elementary precautions were, nevertheless, ignored. *The Saturday Evening Post* . . . proceeded to publish the story without substantial independent support (of the source's assertions). . . .
> The *Post* writer assigned to the story was not a football expert and no attempt was made to check the story with someone knowledgeable in the sport. . . . *The Saturday Evening Post* was anxious to change its image by instituting a policy of "sophisticated muckraking" and the pressure to produce a successful exposé might have induced a stretching of standards. In short, the evidence is ample to support a finding of highly unreasonable conduct constituting an extreme departure from the standards of investigation and reporting ordinarily adhered to by responsible publishers.
> Where a publication's departure from standards of press performance is severe enough to strip from him the Constitutional protection our decision acknowledges, we think it entirely proper for the state to act not only for the protection of the individual injured but to safeguard all those similarly situated against a like offense.

The Court points out that the magazine had failed to check further after Butts had told a reporter the article was untrue. In other words, the *Post* had proceeded with "wanton and reckless indifference," and this plus Butts's showing that the information was false constituted the "actual malice" that the Times Doctrine said had to be proved before the individual could win a libel suit. Butts won his case; the *Post* lost its appeal.

The Court's recognition of the difference between a spot or breaking news story and investigative or interpretative news articles is important to contemporary journalism since publications are increasingly emphasizing in-depth articles.

A study by the Libel Defense Resource Center conducted from 1978–1982 found that out of a sample of 54 defamation and invasion of privacy suits brought against the media, the defendants were ordered to pay damages in 47.

Assessing the Times Doctrine

In these 47 cases, juries made damage awards of more than $100,000 in 30 cases, more than $250,000 in 12 cases and more than $1 million in 9 cases. In addition to these awards for damage, punitive damages were assessed in 30 cases, 17 of them for more than $250,000 and 7 for more than $1 million.

Some of these awards are being appealed. But the media have spent large sums defending themselves; in one case, legal fees cost one defendant $7 million.

Looking over this data, Irving R. Kaufman, a judge in the prestigious U.S. Court of Appeals for the Second District, said that "the constitutional standards developed in the Sullivan case and thereafter no longer provide any meaningful protection to the media in a defamation action." He described the court's establishment of the Times Doctrine as a "stunning, if well-intentioned, failure."

The reason, he said, is that juries do not understand the complexities of the Doctrine. They are, he said, "lost upon even the most conscientious jury."

The consequence of these large awards, said Kaufman, is "a substantial chilling effect on the media's performance of its vital role."

Privacy

While truth is the strongest defense against libel, it is the basis of invasion of privacy suits. Invasion of privacy is said to occur when an individual is exposed to public view and suffers mental distress as a consequence of the publicity. Unlike defamation, which has deep roots in the common law, the right to privacy is a fairly new legal development, and one in which there is even less certainty for the reporter than in the area of libel.

As in libel, the balance must be struck by the courts between the public's right to know—a right commonly accepted though not in the Constitution—and the individual's right to privacy.

Three categories of privacy concern the reporter:

1. Publicity that places a person in a false light in the public eye. The Times Doctrine applies, provided the matter is of public interest.
2. Public disclosure of embarrassing private facts about an individual. If the facts are in an official document, they can be published, but not if they are private acts of no legitimate concern to the public.
3. Intrusion by the journalist into a private area for a story or a picture without permission. The use of electronic devices to invade a home or office is illegal. Newsworthiness is not a defense.

Except for intrusion, the newsworthiness of the event is a defense against invasion of privacy suits. A public event cannot have privacy grafted on it at the behest of the participants. However, the reporter cannot invade a person's home or office to seek out news and make public what is private. Nor can he or she misrepresent the purpose of reporting to gain access to home or office. There is, however, no prohibition against following and watching a person in a public place, but the reporter cannot harass an individual.

Although the law of libel and the right of privacy are closely related, they involve distinctive legal principles and are fundamentally different. Libel law is designed to protect a person's character and reputation. The right of privacy protects a person's peace of mind, his or her feelings, spirits and sensibilities. Generally, privacy guarantees an individual freedom from the unwarranted and unauthorized public exposure of the person or his affairs in which the public has no legitimate interest.

The right of privacy is the right of the person to be let alone unless he or she waives or relinquishes that right, the UPI tells its reporters. Certain persons, defined by the federal courts as "newsworthy," lose their right to privacy, but the material published about that person cannot be "highly offensive."

In making rulings on the claim of invasion of privacy, the Supreme Court has applied the Times Doctrine. That is, even when the claimant can prove that the report was false, if it was a matter of public interest the person bringing the action would have to show the error was made "with knowledge of its falsity or in reckless disregard of the truth."

In one case, decided in 1974 by the Supreme Court, such disregard of the truth was proved by a claimant. The Court in *Cantrell v Forest City Publishing Co.* (419 US 245) upheld a $60,000 award against *The* Cleveland *Plain Dealer* on the ground that a reporter's story about a visit to the home of the claimant "contained significant misrepresentations." Although the woman was not at home when the reporter visited, the article said she "will talk neither about what happened nor about how they were doing. . . ." He wrote that the widow "wears the same mask of nonexpression she wore at the funeral." A lower court jury awarded her $60,000 to compensate for the mental distress and shame the article caused. An appeals court reversed the verdict, and the woman appealed to the Supreme Court, which found the reporter's statements implying that the woman had been interviewed were "calculated falsehoods."

The decision was 8–1. Some months later in March, 1975, in another 8–1 decision, the Supreme Court ruled on the second category involving privacy—the rights of private persons to keep their personal affairs from public disclosure. In this case, the Court nullified a Georgia law that made it a misdemeanor to print or broadcast the name of a rape victim. The case involved the father of a young woman who had been raped and killed in 1971 by a gang of teenage boys. An Atlanta television station had used the victim's name, and the state court found for the father under the state law.

In setting aside the Georgia law, the Supreme Court stated that "once true information is disclosed in public court documents open to public inspection, the press cannot be sanctioned for publishing it." The Court stated (in *Cox Broadcasting Corp. v Martin Cohn,* 420 US 469):

> The commission of crimes, prosecutions resulting therefrom, and judicial proceedings arising from the prosecutions are events of legitimate concern to the public and consequently fall within the press' responsibility to report the operations of government.

In both cases, the Supreme Court cautioned against broad interpretations of its rulings. Nevertheless, the first case clearly indicates that the press must take care in publishing material about individuals that is false, and the second indicates the Court may not extend the right of privacy to private persons involved in actions described in official documents.

A quick guideline in matters of privacy is provided by a case involving a surfer who gave an interview to a *Sports Illustrated* reporter and then sued because the published report contained unflattering material about his personal life as well as information about his surfing activities. A Federal appeals court ruled that the public had a legitimate interest in him and that the facts reported were not so offensive as "to lose newsworthiness protection." The guideline:

> A reporter or publication that gives publicity to the private life of a person is not subject to liability for unreasonable invasion of privacy if the material is 1) about a newsworthy person—who need not be an elected official or a celebrity—and 2) is not "highly offensive to a reasonable person, one of ordinary sensibilities."

Newsgathering Not Protected

The use of hidden electronic mechanisms for newsgathering may result in trouble if stories are based on the material gathered by hidden cameras and microphones. A federal court in California ruled in 1972 that a man who was healing people with herbs, clay and minerals could sue for invasion of privacy because of the tactics used by employees of *Life* magazine in gathering information. A woman employed by *Life* had a radio transmitter in her pocketbook. The transmitter relayed to other reporters the healer's conversation as he examined her. Also, a picture was taken with a hidden camera; the picture was later published in the magazine.

Secret use of telephone wiretapping devices and tape recorders, considered unethical by some newspapers and broadcast stations, is illegal in 13 states. These states' laws require both parties to consent to the taping. Federal law, however, permits a third party to tape a conversation if one party to the conversation approves, which means that if the reporter approves, another reporter can record the conversation without violating federal law.

The ground rules of journalism require reporters to tell sources when they are being photographed, taped or quoted. The broadcast journalist, for example, should inform his or her source when the camera is on, unless it is made clear beforehand that anything and everything may be filmed and recorded. But such full disclosure usually is impossible in investigative reporting, said the attorneys for *Life* in their defense. However, the appeals court stated:

> We agree that newsgathering is an integral part of news dissemination. We strongly disagree, however, that the hidden mechanical contrivances are "indispensable tools" of newsgathering. Investigative reporting is an ancient art; its successful practice long antecedes the invention of miniature cameras and electronic devices. The First Amendment has never been construed to accord newsmen immunity from torts or crimes committed during the course of newsgathering. The First Amendment is not a license to trespass, to steal, or to intrude by electronic means into the precincts of another's home or office. . . .

Avoiding the Dangers

The guide in libel and invasion of privacy suits seems fairly clear. Caution is necessary when the following are *not* involved—public officials, public figures, public events. When a private individual is drawn into the news, the news report must be full, fair and accurate. Of course, no journalist relies upon the law for loopholes. He or she is always fair and accurate in coverage.

The reporter who follows the guidelines in chapter 2 on the basic components of the news story need not worry about being hauled into court.

Libel suits usually have been the result of the following:

- Carelessness.
- Exaggerated or enthusiastic writing.
- Opinions not based on facts.
- Statements of officials or informants made outside a privileged situation.
- Inadequate verification.
- Failure to check with the subject of the defamation.

Although libel judgments may well be difficult to sustain before the Supreme Court, defending against them is a costly business for a newspaper and few editors are sympathetic to the reporter whose mistake may be technically within the area of exemption set by the Court but will cost tens of thousands of dollars to appeal. Rather than fight some suits, newspapers have, in fact, settled out of court.

When a libel has been committed, a retraction should be published. Although a retraction is not a defense, it serves to lessen damages and may deprive the plaintiff of punitive damages.

The Reporter's Rights

The press carries a heavy burden. It has taken on the task of gathering and publishing the news, interpreting and commenting on the news, and acting as watchdog in the public interest over wide areas of public concern. The burden of the press has been lightened by the foresight of the Founding Fathers through the guarantee in the First Amendment of the Bill of Rights that Congress shall make no law abridging freedom of speech or of the press. This has meant that the press has the right to publish what it finds without prior restraint.

To journalists, it also came to mean that they had the freedom to gather and prepare news and that the processes involved in these activities were shielded from a prying government and others. Also, journalists understood that their sources, their notes, their thoughts and their discussions with sources and their editors were protected.

They had good reason to believe all this. State legislatures and the courts had interpreted the concept of press freedom to cover these wide areas of news gathering and publication. In 1896, for example, the state of Maryland passed a law allowing reporters to conceal their sources from the courts and from other officials. The concern of the public traditionally has been that the press be free and strong enough to counterpose a powerful executive. This sensitivity to central government began with the revolution against the British Crown. It was reinforced by the generations of immigrants who fled czars, kings, dictators and tyrants. Old as the story of the abuse of power may be, and as frequent as the exposures of its ruinous consequences have been by the press, the dangers implicit in centralized government are always present, as the Watergate revelations taught U.S. citizens.

This tendency of government to excessive use of its power was foreseen by the American revolutionaries who sought to make in the press a Fourth Estate outside government control and free to check on government by publishing reports of the government's activities.

There is, however, no clear-cut consitutional statement giving the press the privileges it had come to consider immutable. Absolute freedom of the press has never been endorsed by a majority of the Supreme Court, but the federal courts usually have been sympathetic to the rights of the press. However, in the 1970s following Watergate, as the press started to dig and check with growing tenacity, a former ally in its battles with governmental power—the judiciary—began to render decisions the press found to be increasingly restricting. Many of these decisions—particularly those of the Supreme Court—convinced the press that its assumptions about its privileges were false. The press, the courts ruled, has no greater rights than any citizen of the land.

To the press, the rulings appeared almost vindictive. To the judiciary, they were necessary to balance constitutional rights. In its decisions, said Justice William J. Brennan, the Supreme Court must weigh the First Amendment's protection of the "structure of the communicative process against a variety of social interests." The press's ability to gather and publish the news may be outweighed "by society's interest in the enforcement of criminal law," Brennan said in explaining two decisions—*Branzburg* and *Zurcher*—that the press has found hobbling its freedom to protect sources.

In its balancing of the public right to know against individual rights to privacy and the accused's rights to a fair trial, the courts denied the confidentiality of sources, the protection of unpublished material and the privacy of the editorial process. The courts gradually limited the press's access to information, and some newsgathering was specifically prohibited.

These restrictive rulings continued into the 1980s, and they seemed to be welcomed by the public. Opinion polls showed that the public was becoming disenchanted by the press because of what it saw as inaccuracies and unfairness. Also, the public was worried about the power of the press to pry into private affairs—never mind the fact that many people delighted in the publications that play up these revelations.

The love affair between the press and the public inspired by Watergate was dim history. The public wanted the press harnessed, it appeared.

The Right to Gather News

There are, of course, still wide areas of newsgathering open to the press. Generally, the actions of official bodies are accessible to journalists. Judicial, legislative and executive activities can be freely covered—with exceptions. A reporter has the right to cover a city council meeting, except for executive sessions. But the reporter has no legal right to sit in on a meeting of the board of the American Telephone & Telegraph Co., a private company. In a Florida court case involving a newspaper that sought to examine the records of a disciplinary proceeding that had been held by a bar association for a lawyer who later became a public official, the ruling went against the newspaper because the lawyer had been in private practice at the time of the proceeding and the alleged infraction was not a criminal matter. Criminal matters following arrest, charge or indictment are public record. Had the infraction involved the lawyer in his official activities, that would have opened the matter to the press.

Journalists have rights—along with all citizens—to vast areas of official activities. The Supreme Court has ruled *(Branzburg v Hayes)* that the press has protection in some of its newsgathering activities. The Court stated that "without some protection for seeking out the news, freedom of the press would be eviscerated."

But the Court has refused to grant protection in some areas of newsgathering. A reporter cannot protect information a grand jury seeks, and grand jury proceedings are closed to the press. When *The Fresno Bee* published material from a grand jury inquiry and its staff members refused to tell the court how they had obtained the information, they were sent to jail for contempt of court.

Executive sessions of public bodies are closed to the press, but the reason for holding closed-door sessions must not be trivial. Usually, state laws define what may constitute an executive session. Reporters are free to dig up material discussed at executive sessions.

Material of a confidential and personal nature held by such agencies as health and welfare departments is not available to the press. A reporter has no legal right to learn if a certain high school student was treated for gonorrhea by a public health clinic. But the reporter is entitled to data on how many were treated last month or last year, at what cost, how many persons the clinic has on its staff and so on. Nor are there prohibitions against a reporter interviewing a clinic user who is willing to talk about his or her treatment, just as a person who appears before a grand jury may tell reporters about his testimony to the jury.

Most of these limits have been in existence for some time, and reporters generally have recognized them. But in the 1970s the limitations were considerably extended.

In 1978, the Supreme Court ruled that the press has no "special privileges" of access. A sheriff had kept reporters and photographers from entering a California county jail to follow through on an investigation reporters had made of the sheriff's activities. The Court said the sheriff could keep the gates closed to the press.

The most serious constrictions of access to information have occurred in the coverage of the courts.

Free Press-Fair Trial

"The press is having an increasingly difficult time going about its task of covering the courts," wrote Paul J. Levine, a Miami attorney, in his annual review of press freedom for *Editor & Publisher*. In his survey of rulings in 1978, he wrote that "whenever pre-trial publicity is substantial, trial judges will not hesitate to hold closed hearings." Levine's remarks were prophetic, for the following year, 1979, the Supreme Court handed the press a major blow. It ruled that closing pretrial hearings to the press does not violate the Constitution.

The restrictive 1979 Supreme Court decision came in *Gannett v DePasquale* (443 US 368). Judge Daniel A. DePasquale had ordered reporters to leave his Seneca County, N.Y., courtroom during a hearing on a pretrial motion to suppress evidence in a murder trial.

Furthermore, in 1982, the Court upheld a ruling that excluded the press from pretrial hearings in non-criminal cases.

These rulings were based on the contention of many judges that some news can prejudice jurors and thus compromise a defendant's Sixth Amendment "right to an impartial jury," making a fair trial impossible. An increasing number of criminal convictions in lower courts had been set aside because of such publicity.

Pretrial hearings do involve material that is potentially prejudicial. At these hearings, decisions are made as to whether a confession is voluntary, whether a wiretap violates constitutional safeguards, whether the defendant is competent to stand trial, whether a search leading to physical evidence was conducted with constitutional protections.

A judge may toss out a confession. He or she may rule that certain evidence cannot be admitted at trial—the issue before Judge DePasquale. News reports of the matters before the court at the pretrial hearing might be heard or read by jurors who would not be allowed to hear such information at the trial.

The Sheppard Case

Obviously, there is considerable material about a person charged with a crime that emerges before any pretrial hearing, and this, too, may be prejudicial, so much so that courts have overturned convictions made in this atmosphere. Probably the most famous, or infamous, example of such coverage occurred in the 1950s. On July 4, 1954, Marilyn Sheppard, the pregnant wife of a Cleveland osteopath, was found bludgeoned to death at the couple's lakeside home. For some time, the police had made no arrests, and Louis B. Seltzer, editor of the *Cleveland Press,* was restless. Why had not the police taken in Dr. Sam Sheppard? That's what his newspaper asked one day in an eight-column banner across page one:

Why Isn't Sam Sheppard in Jail?

Coverage of the trial was no less sensational. A columnist reported the judge's remark that the defendant was "guilty as hell." A radio station reported that Sheppard had conceded his guilt by hiring a prominent criminal attorney. News stories carried discussions between Sheppard and his lawyer and between the lawyer and the judge.

Sheppard was convicted and given a life sentence. He appealed, alleging "trial by newspaper," and in 1966 the Supreme Court threw out the conviction because "virulent publicity" had denied him a fair trial. The Court placed most of the blame for the "carnival atmosphere" at the trial on the trial judge.

The press, however, was chastened. A free press-fair trial committee of the American Society of Newspaper Editors urged the press to report criminal matters "with restraint, good taste and scrupulous regard for the rights of defendants." It also insisted on the right to print the details of crimes and arrests as the press sees fit. The ASNE report stated:

> In a community, for example, where crimes against a given race or group are traditionally tolerated, publication of the facts about the crime may be an instrument that forces rather than obstructs justice. Much the same is true when the malefactor has friends in high places or is closely aligned with the political structure of a community. And when similar forces are bent on railroading an innocent man, his protection as well as the proper ends of justice are served by the publication.

Since 80 to 90 percent of all criminal cases are disposed of prior to trial through dismissal and plea bargaining, closure orders put most cases beyond the scrutiny of the press and the knowledge of the public. Thus, little can be known of police conduct, of the prosecution's activities or of judicial conduct. Sometimes, publicity from pretrial hearings brings forth key witnesses unknown to prosecutor or defense attorney. Coverage also helps to explain plea bargaining, which many citizens find suspect.

Judges have ways to protect the defendant from damaging publicity that would compromise the defendant's right to a fair trial. In *Nebraska Press Association v Stuart* (427 US 539), the Supreme Court discussed changing the location of the trial, adjourning the trial until pretrial publicity that may be prejudicial has dissipated, careful questioning of jurors during the voir dire (jury empaneling), sequestering the jury and other methods.

There seems to be little question that pretrial publicity does influence jurors. Studies of actual and simulated jury trials have indicated that when jurors have been given pretrial publicity about prior criminal records and information about confessions the jurors are prone to find guilt. Jurors not exposed to such pretrial material are less likely to find the defendant guilty. Nevertheless, the traditional position of the judiciary had been, in the words of an opinion of the Third Circuit Court of Appeals, that "secret hearings—though they be scrupulously fair in reality—are suspect by nature. Public confidence cannot long be maintained where important legal decisions are made behind closed doors and then announced in conclusive terms to the public, with the record supporting the court's decision sealed from view."

Gannett v DePasquale

When Judge DePasquale ordered reporters to leave his courtroom, one of them, Carol Ritter, who was covering the proceeding for the Gannett Rochester newspapers, the *Times-Union* and the *Democrat and Chronicle,* called her editors. They dictated a statement to the judge asking that the hearing on suppression of the evidence be postponed until the newspapers' attorney could argue for an open hearing. It was too late. The judge did not get the message until the closed pretrial hearing was over.

Gannett appealed, won in one state court but lost in the New York State Court of Appeals. The newspaper organization then took the case to the Supreme Court.

In their brief, the Gannett lawyers said that closing pretrial proceedings "may mask collusion among the participants harmful to the defendant and of which he is personally unaware. Alternatively, a closed proceeding may unduly benefit a criminal defendant to the detriment of the public interest.

"An order excluding the public and press from a suppression hearing at the request of a criminal defendant thus has profound constitutional significance since it at once deprives the public and press of their right to a public trial, infringes upon the right to gather news, and restrains the press from observing and commenting on public institutions."

The attorney for Judge DePasquale argued that while the public has the right to know, "without an impartial jury, any other right granted to the accused is meaningless." He pointed out that the judge did not enjoin the media from publishing information about the case. That is, he said, there was no gag order, no prior restraint. There was only a denial of access, which he contended was legal.

Gag orders against the press clearly violate the Constitution. The *Nebraska Press* case classified a gag order as prior restraint. Reporters could publish whatever they could find out about matters before the court. But closures—denials of access—had been upheld, and it was this area of the law that the Supreme Court was being asked to rule on in the *Gannett* case. Could a pre-trial proceeding be closed to the press despite the phrase in the Sixth Amendment about a "public trial"?

When the ruling was issued in July 1979 it stunned everyone. Although the Court had indicated in other rulings that it had no special sympathy for the claimed privileges of the press, the opinions of the majority seemed to go well beyond the issue before the Court and appeared to show an antipathy to the press.

The Court ruled that judges can close pre-trial hearings on motion of the defendant, which was the issue before it. But it went further. One of the justices, William H. Rehnquist, concurring with the majority in the 5–4 decision, said the majority reasoning was broad enough to authorize court-clearing orders in most cases without giving "any reason whatsoever" to outsiders.

Judges immediately interpreted the ruling to mean that criminal trials, even sentencing, could be carried out in secrecy. In several courtrooms, reporters, but not other spectators, were thrown out of courtrooms. The situation was such that Chief Justice Burger took the unusual step a month after the ruling was handed down to comment that the ruling referred only to pretrial hearings, not to trials or sentencing. But the opinions of the majority justices seemed to state clearly that all criminal court proceedings could be closed on agreement of judge, defendant and prosecutor.

Less than a year after *Gannett* there were 239 motions to bar the public and the press from criminal justice proceedings, the Reporters Committee for Freedom of the Press reported early in 1980. At least 37 of these were motions to close actual trials or sentencing proceedings. More than half the attempts at closure were successful.

The Supreme Court clearly was troubled by the response to its ruling. After Chief Justice Burger had sought to clarify the opinion, Justice Harry A. Blackmun publicly differed with the interpretation of the chief justice. Two other justices then spoke out.

One of the justices, Justice Brennan, said *Gannett* "holds the judges, as officers of the government, may in certain circumstances remove themselves from public view and, perhaps, also holds that they can make this decision without even considering the interests of the people. I believe that the framers [of the Constitution] did not conceive such a government."

Aware of the confusion of its ruling in *Gannett,* the Court in 1980 took up the issue **The Court Acts**
of whether criminal trials must be open to the public.

In *Richmond Newspapers, Inc. v Virginia* (448 US 555), the Court decided 7–1
that "openness" is essential to the criminal trial and that media representatives should
enjoy the same right of access to the trial as does the public.

In his opinion, Chief Justice Burger stressed the importance of access to the
workings of society's institutions. He wrote:

> People in an open society do not demand infallibility from their institutions,
> but it is difficult for them to accept what they are prohibited from
> observing. . . .
> Plainly it would be difficult to single out any aspect of government of higher
> concern and importance to the people than the manner in which criminal trials
> are conducted. . . .
> What this means in the context of trials is that the First Amendment
> guarantees of speech and press, standing alone, prohibit government from
> summarily closing courtroom doors which had long been open to the public at
> the time that amendment was adopted. . . .
> Absent an overriding interest articulated in findings, the trial of a criminal
> case must be open to the public.

But what of pretrial hearings? Although the press at first welcomed *Richmond*
as opening these hearings, a close examination of the decision led to despair. The
Court clearly did not reverse its ruling in *Gannett v DePasquale.* Pretrial hearings in
criminal cases could, it appeared, still be closed to the press. Since only about 10
to 20 percent of all criminal cases go to trial, a huge area of coverage remained
closed to the press and thus to the public.

The limitations of *Richmond* were made evident in a 1982 Court action when
three California newspapers appealed a state supreme court ruling barring the press
from covering jury selection in a murder trial in which the death penalty was a possible punishment.

The newspapers argued that the decision in *Richmond* should take precedence over the California court's ruling. However, the U.S. Supreme Court rejected
the newspapers' plea—probably because *Richmond* refers only to the coverage of
criminal trials, not to pretrial activities.

Two other rulings in 1982 disheartened free-press advocates. The Court threw out **More Bad News**
a Massachusetts law that made mandatory the exclusion of the public and press
during the testimony of a minor who is a rape victim. In doing so, however, the justices said that the right of access to criminal trials is not absolute. This leaves states
free to authorize judges to decide on a case-to-case basis whether to close their
courtrooms to the press. Some in the press were encouraged by the Court's statement that the public and the press have a general constitutional right to attend the
proceedings. Further, Justice Brennan asserted that exclusions of public and press
would have to be based on "weighty" justification.

The other discouraging ruling in 1982 came in the Court's refusal to review a federal appeals court ruling that barred press and spectators from a trial. A federal district judge had cleared the courtroom of all but court personnel while he discussed with prosecution and defense lawyers the admission of evidence in a drug-trafficking case. *The Sacramento Bee* took the case to the circuit court of appeals, but that court said that the newspaper had no need to publish the material at the moment it was discussed in court.

"An easy solution," the court ruled, "would have been to acknowledge that immediate publication was unnecessary and that the *Bee* would await later developments in the trial until the material withheld from the jury might be printed without inconveniencing the jury."

By not reviewing the case, the Supreme Court seemed to agree with the expulsion of press and spectators during a criminal trial.

Obviously, *Gannett, Richmond* and subsequent cases have left muddy waters in their wake. In an attempt to clear up some of the confusion, federal court administrators proposed a rule to allow the court to bar the press when there is "reasonable likelihood" that information could prejudice the defendant's right to a fair trial if the material were to be used. The proposed rule provides for a hearing of any motion or action to close the court to the public and press.

The proposed rule provides for a hearing of any motion or action to close the court to the public and press.

Rap Sheets

Reporters often encounter information that would be prejudicial to a defendant on trial. This includes reports of confessions and information about the prior record of the defendant. Federal law enforcement officials recommend that limits be placed on the access to criminal records or "rap sheets." Some states expunge all details about arrests that did not result in convictions. Others prohibit access to criminal records, and some states limit what police in the state may release. A few prohibit use if information is obtained, making such use a misdemeanor.

Generally, reporters are able to track down criminal records since they are kept by a variety of sources—police, the courts, the prosecutor's office, probation officers and others. Reporters should first learn their newspaper's policy and the laws of their state and then decide in each case whether usage is justified.

In the matter of confessions, many reporters usually will state: The arrested person (or the defendant) made statements to the police about the crime. Few details will be given.

Protecting the News Process

The way in which events become news stories involves dozens of decisions by editors and reporters. Journalists contend that these decisions are made rationally, against a set of criteria that are as objective as possible. But they also concede that there is a good deal of imprecision, guesswork and intuition. The delicate nature of this decision-making process was opened to public exposure by the Supreme Court in 1979 in a ruling that journalists say makes the decision-making process even more difficult. The Court ruled that the First Amendment does not grant journalists immunity from answering questions about the process. These are questions put by litigants who claim to have been injured by the news. The Court's logic was that since an official or a public figure in a libel suit must prove "actual malice" he or she should be able to determine this by inquiring into the editorial process (*Herbert v Lando*) (441 US 153). Malice, the logic goes, is obviously a state of mind, and it can only be proved by evidence from the alleged defamer's thoughts.

Barry Lando, a producer for CBS, had produced a program about Col. Anthony Herbert, who had accused the Army of covering up reports of civilian deaths in Vietnam. The program questioned Herbert's role in Vietnam and was disparaging. Lando also wrote an article about the program, which was called "The Selling of Colonel Herbert," for *The Atlantic Monthly*. Herbert sued Lando, *The Atlantic Monthly* and television reporter-interviewer Mike Wallace for $44 million. He said he had been libeled.

Herbert's lawyers wanted to question Lando about his feelings toward Herbert and about other matters. The lawyers reasoned that if the plaintiff in a libel suit must show actual malice, as *Sullivan* stated, then inquiries about the reporter's state of mind are pertinent. How else could malice be shown but by asking what Lando was thinking?

The Second Circuit Court of Appeals turned down Herbert's argument. To allow questions about how a journalist "formulated his judgments on what to print and what not to print" would condone judicial review of the editorial thinking process. Such an inquiry, "which would be virtually boundless," the Court ruled, "endangers a constitutionally protected realm, and unquestionably puts a freeze on the free interchange of ideas within the newsroom."

The Supreme Court was less concerned about the free interchange of ideas than it was by the right of the libel plaintiff, Herbert, to be allowed to obtain "direct evidence through inquiry into the thoughts, opinions and conclusions" of journalists, in the words of Justice Byron White, who wrote the majority opinion in the 6–3 ruling in April 1979.

"Inevitably, unless liability is to be completely foreclosed, the thoughts and editorial processes of the alleged defamer would be open to examination," he wrote, accepting Herbert's argument.

The knowledge that they will have to testify in libel cases about the actions they took and the decisions they made will, journalists say, inhibit the open discussions between editor and reporter. Faced with the prospect that the courts can now make judgments about their editorial decisions, journalists may make only safe decisions. Since confidential, unedited and unused material may be exposed in libel cases, a process that is complicated enough has been made even more difficult. The threat of government looking over journalists' shoulders is, to news workers, ominous.

The counter-argument is that the press cannot escape responsibilities for what it publishes and broadcasts. If it makes errors, it must be held to account, just as the rest of us are. Those who are injured must have recourse to the courts.

But the press is by nature a risk-taker, and it will err. Indeed, a centuries-old tradition tells us that the best path to truth is through the dissemination of a variety of doctrines, ideas, explanations, theories. A press that was concerned that it could be held accountable in court for its thoughts might not have published the Pentagon Papers, exposed the disasters the United States experienced in Vietnam, or dug into Watergate.

Newsroom Searches

In 1978, a year before the *Herbert* decision, the Supreme Court clearly limited the rights the press claimed for itself to resist the intrusion of government. The *Stanford Daily* had run stories and pictures of a campus demonstration and the police obtained a search warrant for them. The student newspaper went to court, and two federal courts ruled that a search warrant could not be issued against a newspaper if the employees were not suspected of criminal activity. The material would have to be obtained through a subpoena, the federal courts ruled.

These rulings helped the newspaper, and the press in general, because a subpoena can be contested in court by a motion to quash the subpoena. Search warrants are requested by law enforcement officials in *ex parte* proceedings—hearings at which only one side is represented. Unlike the subpoena, which requires notice to the party to turn over the requested material, the purpose of a search warrant is surprise.

The lower court rulings were appealed to the Supreme Court and in *Zurcher v Stanford Daily* (436 US 547) the court ruled 5–3 that people not involved in a crime—"seemingly blameless" third parties—have no greater rights to resist a search for evidence of a crime than those directly implicated. The press is no different from any other third person involved in such a search, said the Court. As Justice Brennan later was to summarize the case, the Court held that "whatever First Amendment rights were implicated were outweighed by society's interest in law enforcement."

The only question, then, is the method by which law enforcement agencies may obtain evidence. To require a subpoena, the Court said, "could easily result in the disappearance of the evidence, whatever the good faith of the third party."

The *Columbia Journalism Review* found the majority opinion of Justice Byron R. White to be "redolent of indifference or malice toward the press." The *Review* characterized as an "offhand judgment" Justice White's assurance that searches authorized by warrant will not deter "normal editorial and publication decisions."

Congress then stepped in. Overwhelmingly, it voted that federal, state and local law enforcement officers could not, except under limited circumstances, use a search warrant for notes, films, tapes or other materials used by those involved in broadcasting and publishing. The authorities would have to obtain a subpoena, which would give news organizations the chance to oppose the request in court.

Confidentiality Requires Protection

Just as the press argues that freedom to publish without prior restraint is meaningless without freedom to gather the news, newspapers and broadcast stations contend that confidentiality is essential to freedom of the press. The press points out that the power of the government to punish people involved in unpopular causes led the courts to safeguard anonymity in many areas. Also, the courts have come to recognize the doctor-patient and lawyer-client relationship as generally beyond legal inquiry. Journalists have sought the same protection for their sources.

If the press is to be the watchdog of government, as the press believes the Founding Fathers intended, then the press must be free to discover the actual activities of officials, not merely to print what officials say they are doing. In order to ferret out these activities, insiders and informants are necessary. These informants usually must be promised anonymity.

Clearly, the exposures of Watergate were fueled by inside information provided by sources within government who were told their identities would not be made public. To this day, most have not.

Reporters contend that their notes—which may include the names of confidential sources as well as the reporters' own investigatory work—should be treated as confidential. Many state shield laws grant the reporter this protection unless in a criminal case the defense can prove that the notes are material and relevant and that alternative sources of information have been exhausted.

But some state shield laws have been struck down, and some courts have indicated that reporters may not hold back the identity of their sources should a trial judge require such identification. The most publicized case of this type involved Myron Farber, a reporter for *The New York Times*. In 1978, the *Times* was fined $285,000 and Farber was jailed for 40 days on contempt charges for refusing to give a New Jersey court his notes about a doctor on trial for murder. Farber's investigative work for his newspaper had led to charges against the doctor. The defense sought to have the judge in chambers review Farber's raw investigative materials on the ground that the Sixth Amendment grants compulsory process to obtain evidence. This evidence, the defense contended, might contradict testimony by witnesses.

In his defense, Farber argued that the judge's request to have the material delivered to him for his personal scrutiny was illegal on two different grounds. First, the *Times* argued that the New Jersey shield law provides that in any legal proceeding a journalist "has the privilege to refuse to disclose" any "source" or "news or information obtained in the course of pursuing his professional activity." The second argument contended that whatever the legality of the state's shield law, the judge's order violated the First Amendment rights of the journalist to "freedom of the press." Under these two umbrellas, the defense argued, Farber's notes and the identity of his sources was privileged.

In turning down the arguments of the *Times,* the New Jersey Supreme Court in effect said shield laws must give way to the constitutional right under the Sixth Amendment to a fair trial. As for the First Amendment argument, that appears to have been lost in the 1972 *Branzburg v Hayes* (408 US 665) decision when the Court denied that the First Amendment automatically grants reporters the privilege to withhold sources and other information in legal proceedings. News reporters, *Branzburg* stated, have no greater rights than other citizens.

As a result, the press decided to raise in the courts, state by state, the question of privilege and to seek a qualified privilege under the First Amendment. James C. Goodale, general counsel to *The New York Times,* says that under the privilege, "no reporter could be required by a court to produce testimony or documentation unless there is a showing of (1) a high degree of relevance, (2) materiality and (3) exhaustion of alternate ways to obtain the same information."

The press strategy paid off, and a growing number of state courts and most federal circuit courts have granted the qualified privilege. In 1983, for example, the court of appeals in the state of Washington held that newspapers have a qualified privilege under common law to protect their sources, but that judges may make a "balancing test" with the defendant's right to a fair trial. If the information the defendant seeks is found to be crucial to the case, then the information may not be withheld.

In New Jersey, the state supreme court did agree that reporters should not be required to produce their notes in criminal cases unless a show of relevancy and exhaustion of alternate sources was made. But the court said the ruling did not apply retroactively to Farber, and it stated that the trial court knew the information was relevant—although no hearing was granted Farber on the matter. In the future, such hearings would be necessary, the state supreme court held.

By not protecting fact-gathering as reflected in the notes of reporters, the courts in those states that had not granted qualified privilege had succeeded in doing what no belabored public official had managed to bring about. A few journalists were not so alarmed. Some felt the press was seeking to claim immunities and privileges no other institution is granted.

Generally, the criticism of the courts came from journalists who have been in the forefront of aggressive, investigative journalism. The courts' defenders have been journalists who take a more restrictive view of the role of the press, less adversarial, more inclined to accept than to question authority.

Causes and Consequences

The turnabout in the Supreme Court reflects, many observers agreed, the growing public antagonism toward the press. In the 1970s, the press became more dogged in its pursuit of wrongdoing. No newspaper wanted to live through the guilt the press underwent immediately after Watergate when the public was given to understand that despite the presence of several hundred experienced Washington correspondents, the president was undone by two young reporters who were not part of the White House or Congressional press corps.

In their pursuit of the malefactors in public life, the press was seen as a critic not only of sacred cows but of sacred institutions. "Nothing to be left untouched" may have been an excellent guide for the reporter, but it disturbed many people. Most people want and need ideals and heroes, men and women to look up to, to be loyal to. Few individuals or institutions can stand up under the scrutiny to which the press subjects them.

This conflict can be resolved by the ancient technique of destroying the messenger, and in a way this is what the public seemed to be seeking in its assertions that the press had become too powerful, too elitist.

Tyrone Brown, a law clerk to Chief Justice Earl Warren in the 1960s, and then general counsel for Post-Newsweek Broadcasting and later a member of the Federal Communications Commission, said the Court's rulings reflect public antagonism toward the press.

"All those so-called absolute principles like the First Amendment are functions of the time when they're decided," Brown says. "The Justices' role is a process role—making accommodations between various power groups in the country at various times. The Warren Court balanced competing interests more in favor of the First Amendment. The Burger Court appears to be doing otherwise."

To some observers, the decisions have a simpler source: The personal antagonisms of conservative lawyers toward an inquisitive, independent press.

Whatever the cause, most observers agree that the turnabout began with the *Branzburg* decision in 1972.

The key finding of *Branzburg* was that the First Amendment has to move aside before "the general obligation of a citizen to appear before a grand jury or at a trial . . . and give what information he possesses."

Joel M. Gora, author of the book, *The Rights of Reporters* (New York: Avon Books, 1974), saw *Branzburg* as a "severe setback in the campaign to secure constitutional protection for the newsgathering process in general and, in particular, for the right of reporters to safeguard their sources of information.

"For the first time, the Supreme Court explored the nature of the newsgathering process and the reporters' need for a Constitutional right to protect confidential sources. The reporters lost."

Chilling Effect

"You just don't know what subconscious impact the decisions have on your judgment to go or not to go with certain stories," says Frank McColloch, managing editor of *The Sacramento Bee*. Other editors talk of telling their reporters not to take notes during interviews because of the lack of protection reporters now have.

Certainly, few small newspapers or stations will be willing to go to court to protect their reporters and sources. It is just too expensive. So, fewer chances are taken.

Reporters usually like to hang on to their notes. Not everything makes the story they are working on, and the leftovers are sometimes useful for later pieces. Also, the notes serve as a handy reference when someone calls to protest. But nowadays reporters are tossing their notes away after a week or so. They fear a subpoena for their notes. The same concern affects photographers.

By their nature, journalists over-react. Certainly, many of the judicial decisions over the past 15 years have been inimical to an inquiring and free press. But many judges on state and federal benches maintained a firm belief in and a commitment to the First Amendment. In 1978, a federal district court in Chicago quashed subpoenas for a reporter's notes. Unlike some of his colleagues, Judge George N. Leighton ruled that "even if the information sought is relevant . . . the publisher and its reporters are constitutionally protected. . . ." (*Gullivers Periodicals Ltd. v Chas. Levy Circulation Co., Inc.*).

In one of the few federal rulings that has recognized a newsman's privilege under a state shield law, U.S. District Court Judge Maurice B. Cohill ruled that WTAE-TV in Pittsburgh need not turn over unused outtakes of interviews. The station's consumer affairs reporter had investigated a steak sale, and the program raised questions about the quality of the firm's frozen packaged steaks and the fairness of its advertising and sales methods. The firm alleged it was libeled and asked the court to order the outtakes be submitted on the ground that they were essential to show malice. The station said the Pennsylvania shield law provided that no person connected with a television station "shall be required to disclose the source of any information . . . in any legal proceeding." Compelled disclosure, the court ruled, would interfere with the station's exercise of editorial control and judgment in violation of the First Amendment (*Steaks Unlimited v Deaner*).

These decisions preceded the *Herbert* ruling, and so it is not certain whether such lower court rulings as these will recur. And to add to the press's pessimism, while Pittsburgh station WTAE-TV escaped having to reveal to a court its outtakes, CBS's "60 Minutes" was ordered to do just that by a California state court of appeals.

"60 Minutes" had filmed the sale of PCP, also known as Angel Dust, at the Santa Clara County Fairgrounds. Two of those filmed making sales to undercover agents were later arrested and charged with illegal sale of narcotics. The program did not include the films or recordings of the two suspects, but their attorneys sought all videotapes, sound tapes and photographs of the sale from CBS. The network contested the subpoena on the ground that it violated the state's shield law, which specifically protects all unpublished information, including outtakes. CBS also said the First Amendment gave it the right to protect confidential material.

A Santa Clara Superior Court rejected CBS's arguments. The judge said that the shield law and the network's First Amendment rights had to yield to the defendants' Sixth Amendment rights to a fair trial.

An appeal by CBS was lost, although the appeals court modified the lower court's order to require the trial court judge to examine the material and said that only voice tapes and not film tapes could be examined (*CBS v Superior Court of California*).

Reconciliation Sought

The alarm of the press was clearly communicated to the courts, and attempts were made to bridge what seemed to be a widening gap between the two. Justice Brennan noted "in the present controversy a new and disturbing note of acrimony, almost bitterness," and urged a recognition of the "fundamental and necessary interdependence of the court and the press." He continued:

> The press needs the court, if only for the simple reason the court is the ultimate guardian of the constitutional rights that support the press. And the court has a concomitant need for the press, because through the press the court receives the tacit and accumulated experience of the nation and— because the judgments of the court ought also to instruct and inspire—the court needs the medium of the press to fulfill this task. This partnership of the court and the press is not unique; it is merely exemplary of the function that the press serves in our society.

In his book on the rights of reporters, Gora tells reporters to know their rights and to assert them. He notes:

- The police cannot arbitrarily deny a press pass to a reporter.
- Except for reasonable restrictions on access to events behind police lines, the police cannot interfere with a reporter engaged in newsgathering activities in public places.
- Reporters cannot be denied access to open meetings of legislative or executive bodies.
- The reporter can try to use state law to open certain hearings of public bodies that have been closed as "executive sessions." But there is no constitutional right to attend. Several states have adopted "sunshine laws" that require public agencies to have open meetings and open records.
- Reporters do not have a constitutional right to documents and reports not available to the general public. (The Supreme Court has equated the press's right to access with the right of access of the public.) There are, however, state and federal laws granting access to official information.

The Reporters Committee for Freedom of the Press runs a Legal Assistance Hotline from Washington, D.C. The telephone service assists those who run into government censorship, receive subpoenas for confidential sources, are threatened with libel and privacy suits or prior restraints on publication. The number is 202 466–6313.

Never before have reporters been under greater pressure to be absolutely accurate in their work. The leeway the courts had granted for honest mistakes has been narrowed in libel cases. Fewer individuals can be considered public figures, and the courts are narrowing the definition of a public official.

Reporters:

Summing Up

- Have no special right of access to news.
- Have no right to attend pretrial hearings.
- Should be careful about what they print about the records of criminal defendants.
- May be asked to divulge their thoughts before they wrote a story.
- Can have their files examined by police.
- Cannot guarantee sources confidentiality.
- May be required to give testimony or documents to a grand jury.
- Should be careful about telling sources the press and the source are protected by a state shield law.

15 Taste—Defining the Appropriate

Preview   Material that is obscene, vulgar or profane offends readers and listeners. But it can be informative, and sometimes the reporter risks offending to move closer to the truth of the situation.

Decisions on usage depend on:

- Context—If the event is significant and the material essential to describing the event, offensive material may be used.

- Nature of the audience—A publication for adults will contain material that a mass medium may not.

- Prominence of those involved—Public officials and public figures lead public lives. What would be prying into the life of a private individual may be useful reporting of a public personality.

Two Cornell University astronomers had an idea for the Pioneer 10 spacecraft flight. For its journey beyond our solar system it would carry a drawing of a man and a woman as well as information about the planet Earth. Should the spacecraft then nuzzle down on some distant civilization the inhabitants could visualize what earth man and woman looked like.

The National Aeronautics and Space Administration accepted the suggestion, and when Pioneer 10 was launched in February, 1972, a gold-plated aluminum plaque engraved with a sketch of the earth and its solar system and a drawing of a naked man and woman standing next to each other was aboard. NASA released the drawing to newspapers, thereupon confronting many editors with a dilemma. The picture was newsworthy, but would its publication be in bad taste? (See fig. 15.1.)

The *Chicago Sun-Times* published the drawing in an early edition after an artist had removed the man's testicles. In a later edition, the rest of the genitals obviously were erased. *The Philadelphia Inquirer* did even more brush work: The male had no genitals and the nipples had been removed from the woman's breasts. The *Los Angeles Times* ran the drawing untouched. "Filth," a reader wrote.

Now, more than a decade later, the assertions of bad taste and the editors' anxieties seem as obsolete as the embarrassment pregnant women once were made to feel in the male-oriented society. (The word "confinement" to describe the term

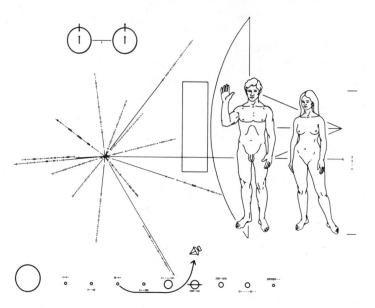

Figure 15.1 Filth! When this drawing, carried on the first man-made object to escape from the solar system into interstellar space, was reproduced in the *Los Angeles Times*, a reader wrote protesting it was "filth." Many newspapers removed various parts of the man's and woman's bodies before running it.

of pregnancy goes back to this period because pregnant women were kept at home to hide their supposed shame.) But no matter how liberated we may think ourselves in an age in which we have been counseled to let it all hang out for our own good, matters of taste still concern the reporter.

No one wants to write a story that offends readers or viewers. Nor—in the case of broadcast journalists—is there much sense in offending the Federal Communications Commission, which has rules about obscenity, indecency and profanity on the air. But how do we draw the lines that separate obscenity and profanity from revelation? What guidelines can we use to determine what is indecent and what is informative? How does a reporter or an editor decide what words and which subject matter are offensive or essential? Just what is the "good taste" that journalists are supposed to exercise?

Taste Is Relative

Taste is usually defined as a set of value judgments in behavior, manners, or the arts that is held in common by a group or class of people. Generally, these values help to keep society stable, to insulate it from sudden and possibly destructive change. Those who advocate strict controls on obscenity, for example, argue that such material will stimulate anti-social behavior or damage the young while their character is being formed.

Time

The values that determine decisions about taste are not absolute. They change with time, place and context. The word rape was taboo in many newspapers until the 50s. Wedding announcements were, and in some newspapers still are, platitudes.

In the 70s *The New York Times,* hardly the prime mover in changes in taste, ran these sentences in a wedding story:

One guest . . . who describes herself as the bride's "semi-mother," had second thoughts when [the bride] decided to wear nothing underneath her blue and white voile wedding gown.

"I didn't think it was right at first," [but she] relented, but stood by her decree that there would be "no pot smoking" at the ceremony.

In another wedding story, the *Times* reported that it "was not a happy day for the bride's mother. From the moment the engagement was announced, Mrs. Havemeyer has said she disapproved of the marriage."

When the wedding of Prince Charles, heir to the British throne, and Lady Diana Spencer was announced, the press covered the story in intimate detail, as in this section of a story from the Knight-Ridder News Service:

She has been forced to submit to a discreet but thorough gynecological examination to be proclaimed fertile enough to deliver royal heirs to the House of Windsor. No such results have been announced for the prince.

Questioned by reporters in the weeks after the engagement announcement, her uncle, Lord Fermoy, assured the public that the bride is indeed a virgin. It has been generally understood, in true double standards, that Prince Charles, 12 years older than Diana, is not.

The Washington Post tells its reporters that "society's concepts of taste and decency are constantly changing. A word offensive to the last generation can be part of the next generation's common vocabulary."

In 1939, the public was scandalized when in the movie *Gone With the Wind,* Rhett Butler turned to Scarlett and said, "Frankly, my dear, I don't give a damn."

In 1982, the AP castigated its copy editors because they sanitized the statement of a woman who had accosted Henry Kissinger at an airport and shouted at him. The woman, said the AP's first report, "asked Kissinger about his sexual preferences."

What she said was, "Do you sleep with young boys at the Carlyle Hotel in New York City?"

Louis D. Boccardi, executive editor of the AP, said the exact quote should have been used as it put "the incident in context."

During the 1960s, college newspapers sought to delve into subjects and to use language that had traditionally been forbidden. Despite the gradual lessening of taboos, student journalists had a hard time of it. At Villanova in 1964, the newspaper's adviser, called the brother-moderator at that Catholic institution, was horrified by a photograph to go on page one of the *Villanovan.* It showed a scene from the rehearsal of a campus theater production. A female student is seated on a chair, her skirt a couple of inches above her knees. Magic Marker in hand, the good friar sketched in a new hemline and all was well.

Forty Seniors At...

Vol. 40—No. 7 VILLANOV...

John McPeak slaps Bonnie Lucas during rehearsal of Belle Masque production of "Mask of Angels" (see below for details).

(Photo by Joe Harrison)

the **Vanguard**

Friday, May 19, 1967 Portland State College, Portland, Oregon Volume 22, Number 34

Ginsberg Vows 'Propriety'

By LARRY SMITH
Entertainment Editor

Allen Ginsberg will appear in Old Main auditorium 3 p.m. Monday.

Eligibility, Disapproval Narrow List . . .

Faculty Rate Mosser Money Con...

By BOB MEYER
Acting News Editor

eals Vanguard Pink 100

Senate Examines Club Sp...

By HUNTLY GOODHUE
Managing Editor:

Touching Bottom

"ARCHIE AND Mehitabel," with Gay Mathis, will open at the Ides Theater Thursday at 8 p.m.

House

College Papers Cause Problems. During the 1960s, many college newspapers deliberately sought to expand the boundaries of the acceptable, and they ran into trouble. Even when they did not seek confrontations they had problems with suspicious advisers: At Villanova University, the adviser added a hemline to a picture. But at Portland State College, the student journalists deliberately sought a confrontation over their right to print what they wished. The half-nude photo of poet Allen Ginsberg infuriated the college president; the following week the newspaper ran a picture of a scantily clad student actress. The newspaper was shut down.

In 1967, the president of Portland State College was in a running battle with the editors of the *Vanguard* because of what he considered their vulgarity and bad taste. He objected to a letter to the editor as an example of "lavatory humor." A picture of poet Allen Ginsberg, who was to speak on the campus, nude from pubic hair upward infuriated the president. The editors, unwilling to allow choleric rage to subside, then ran a shot of a black-stockinged young woman in tights—from the rear, bending over. That was it. The president suspended publication of the *Vanguard*.

In the mid-60s, the Wisconsin legislature threatened budgetary punishment of the state university unless the school's administration exercised more control over what legislators called the "moral climate" of the university. The legislative reaction was seen as a response to a movie review and a review of *Human Sexual Response* by Masters and Johnson that was published in the student newspaper, *The Daily Cardinal*. The book was based on a study of human sexuality, and the movie review contained a four-letter word that was used several times.

Commented one state assemblyman, Paul Alfonsi, "We don't feel the kind of tripe they printed was the kind of tripe students should read."

Today, the antics of the newspaper adviser, the college president and the state legislature seem absurd. With the passage of time, the criteria for good and bad taste have changed drastically.

Taste changes with place. Behavior appropriate in a football stadium would be considered boorish in an opera house. Language inoffensive to most residents of San Francisco would be tasteless, if not worse, to residents of Salt Lake City.

Taste also is a function of the context in which the material is used. A story in *Rolling Stone* would contain language and references abhorrent to a reader of *The Christian Science Monitor*. Here is a sidebar to an article in *The Columbia Journalism Review*:

Meeting Mr. Scaife

Richard Scaife rarely speaks to the press. After several unsuccessful efforts to obtain an interview, this reporter decided to make one last attempt in Boston, where Scaife was scheduled to attend the annual meeting of the First Boston Corporation.

Scaife, a company director, did not show up while the meeting was in progress. Reached eventually by telephone as he dined with the other directors at the exclusive Union Club, he hung up the moment he heard the caller's name. A few minutes later he appeared at the top of the Club steps. At the bottom of the stairs, the following exchange occurred:

''Mr. Scaife, could you explain why you give so much money to the New Right?''

''You fucking Communist cunt, get out of here.''

Well. The rest of the five-minute interview was conducted at a rapid trot down Park Street, during which Scaife tried to hail a taxi. Scaife volunteered two statements of opinion regarding his questioner's personal appearance — he said she was ugly and that her teeth were ''terrible'' — and also the comment that she was engaged in ''hatchet journalism.'' His questioner thanked Scaife for his time.

''Don't look behind you,'' Scaife offered by way of a goodbye.

Not quite sure what this remark meant, the reporter suggested that if someone were approaching it was probably her mother, whom she had arranged to meet nearby. ''She's ugly, too,'' Scaife said, and strode off.   *K.R.*

The *Review's* editors wanted to show its readers the full dimension of Scaife's personality. Since most of the readers are journalists, the editors knew this brief excursion on the streets of Boston with Scaife and Karen Rothmyer, the reporter, would enlighten rather than offend them.

A vulgarity uttered by the president may be essential to the story, whereas an offhand obscene remark by an athlete may be unnecessary to the piece. During his negotiations with steel companies about price increases, President Kennedy said, "My father always told me businessmen were sons-of-bitches." *The New York Times* printed the president's remarks as made. But almost 20 years later the *Times* in-house bulletin, *Winners & Sinners,* was unhappy about a sports story that quoted Reggie Jackson, then with the New York Yankees, saying, "I can say this because George can do nothing to me. He can do nothing because I can hit the baseball over the wall. But when I can't hit, they'll screw me too. I know they'll screw me the same way they screwed Rosen." *Winners & Sinners* commented:

> Depending upon one's broad-mindedness, *screw* is either obscene or vulgar. Our stylebook, citing the 1974 precedent of the Watergate transcripts, says we use such language "only when the printing of the objectionable word or words will give the reader an insight into matters of great moment—an insight that cannot be otherwise conveyed." It adds that "most such instances would almost certainly involve a person of high standing—a president, perhaps."

And yet what are we to make of the coyness of *The New York Times* in a story describing the confrontation of Iranian diplomats with a State Department official? Frustrated and angered by its inability to free 50 American hostages held in Iran, the United States broke relations with Iran in 1980. Summoned to the State Department for the formal notification, two Iranian diplomats protested, whereupon, said the *Times,* the official told them "off with a blunt barnyard expletive." To Americans, the official "may have become something of a hero," said the *Times.* Surely, in the terms of the *Winners & Sinners,* this was something "of great moment." Nevertheless, what the official said was never made explicit.

A Guideline

These incidents supply us with our most important guide to the use of unusual subject matter and explicit language: The event must be significant and the questionable material essential to the situation to justify its use. *The Washington Post* advises reporters to "avoid profanities and obscenities unless their use is so essential to a story of significance that its meaning is lost without them."

But we must immediately qualify this guideline in two ways. First, there are legitimate differences of opinion as to what constitutes significance or importance. Second, place must be considered in the application of the guideline. When Charles Alexander, the editor of *The Journal Herald* in Dayton, Ohio, decided his readers should have the fullest possible account of a fatal quarrel between two agents with the Treasury Department, he approved the following quotation:

> "Gibson God damn it, you are fuck-
> ing with my family. You are fucking with
> my future. I am not going to let you do
> it. I'll kill you first."

The paper was quoting agent Casper Carroll Gibson's account of the quarrel. Gibson said the other agent then started to pull a gun out of his pocket. Gibson grabbed the gun; it went off and his colleague fell dead.

Alexander's bosses found the use of the words indefensible for Dayton readers. When Alexander would not back down and apologize, he was fired.

"It's a matter of truth," Alexander said. "To me, the telling of that message from an incident in real life, including in one instance the raw vulgarity used by a man blind with rage, is a lesson that every man, woman and child should perceive in all its dimensions. It is shocking—it surely should be. . . ."

Alexander lost his job in 1975. Four years before, *The Record* in Bergen County, N.J., across the Hudson River from New York City, carried a story about a Democratic party official's reaction to being told she could not attend a party meeting at the home of the state chairman. She went anyway. When she arrived, the chairman told her she would have been welcome but for the language the men used in their discussions. To which she replied, "I don't give a shit what kind of language you use."

The Record quoted her as saying just that. (The men then told her she could attend.)

On the same day the political story appeared on page one of *The Record,* another article was carried on the front page that also included an obscenity. After a convocation on the Newark campus of Rutgers University, the university's new president, Edward J. Bloustein, was confronted by a group of women waiting to see him about women's rights on the campus. He stopped to speak to the women.

The Record reported: "Listen, sweetie," he said to one undergraduate, who replied: "F--- you."

When the president protested the obscenity, a woman faculty member said the word "sweetie" was degrading to women, *The Record* explained.

Apparently, the editors of *The Record* felt their readers were ready in 1971 to see explicit language in print, whereas the management of the *Journal Herald* in Dayton four years later presumed their readers would be offended by explicit language. Editors and publishers set the standards for their publications in response to what they presume are community standards.

The Uses of Humor

Taken from letters received by the state welfare department in Oregon, the following examples of unclear writing have found their way into some newspapers. Is poking fun at the helpless in good taste?

> I am forwarding my marriage certificate and six children. I had seven but one died which was baptized on a half sheet of paper.

> I cannot get sick pay. I have six children. Can you tell me why?

> I am glad to report that my husband who is missing is dead.

> Unless I get my husband's money pretty soon I will be forced to lead an immortal life.

Changing Standards

Clearly, the standards for printed and broadcast material have been changing drastically over the past three decades.

Standards in taste traditionally have been set by the upper class and the respected elders of the community. Although these groups still carry some weight in these and other matters, their power has significantly diminished since World War II. As a consequence, taste-by-edict has all but disappeared, replaced by a more realistic and pragmatic set of guidelines. In two major areas, sex and death—the ageless taboos—the time-honored boundaries for the press are disappearing. Graphic language that had been presumed to be vulgar, obscene or profane, however it was used, is now appearing in newspapers and is heard on television and radio. The transformation has been startling, but these changes bother those who regard the loosening of standards for language and subject matter as a threat to the social fabric.

Journalists realized that the country had moved through a series of divisive and traumatizing events since 1945 and that old presumptions were properly subject to re-examination. The profanities and the obscene acts that accompanied the country's crises were symbols of the collapse of the old order. The increasing activity and power of the young (18-year-olds were given the right to vote in 1971) were obviously newsworthy, and although some of the more conservative members of the community considered the young to be the modern counterparts of the barbarians at the gates, the young unquestionably were causing significant changes in society. But to report the full dimensions of the changes the press would risk censure by the upholders of order in the community, the very people upon whom the newspaper depends for its survival. As for the broadcast industry, radio and television station managers were clear about their responsibility. The FCC, they said, required them to conform to contemporary community standards.

In 1968, the turmoil that was afflicting the country over Vietnam seemed to focus on Chicago where the Democratic presidential convention was being held. President Johnson had withdrawn as a candidate for re-election because of his feeling that his conduct of the war had divided the nation. Anti-war demonstrators were congregating in Chicago to try to convince the party to pledge an early end to the war by picking an anti-war candidate. There, in the summer's heat, they were met by Chicago police who, under Mayor Richard Daley's orders, sought to keep the demonstrators from disrupting the convention. The clash between police and demonstrators was bloody, violent and vicious. Profanities and blows were exchanged.

An inquiry by the National Committee on the Causes and Prevention of Violence concluded that the confrontation "can only be called a police riot." The report, written under the direction of Dan Walker, was graphic in its descriptions and quotations—so much so that the Government Printing Office refused to publish it unless Walker permitted deletions. He refused, saying that the obscenities by the police and the demonstrators were essential and that deletions would "destroy the important tone" of the report.

A number of private publishers rushed into the vacuum created by the GPO, and one newspaper organization, *The* Louisville *Courier-Journal* and *Times,* did carry some of the graphic language of the report.

On looking back at what his newspaper had done, the executive editor of the papers, Norman Isaacs, had misgivings. Although the younger members of the staff were pleased with the newspaper's frankness, the community was not.

"In my considered judgment we have made a grievous error in misjudging our own community," Isaacs said. "A newspaper under conditions of monopoly that exist in 95 percent of the American cities is no longer a free agent.

"It must have a community ethic. We can understand standards only in terms of community conscience," he said. "A family newspaper should not use language that some people find objectionable," he continued. Isaacs apologized to churchmen who were angered by the publication.

The incident raises several questions journalists have to consider in making decisions about matters of taste. Does a monopoly newspaper or broadcast station have responsibilities that differ from publications and stations with competition? To some degree, yes. The responsibility is to tend to carry controversial material, not to screen it out, for unless the single paper or station in town uses the material the public will be uninformed.

Next, what is the community conscience or ethic, and who defines it? The answers, never simple, were becoming more difficult in the 70s as vast social changes were occurring. Youth, women and blacks had rarely been consulted as part of the community. Isaacs' churchmen, who were offended by the Chicago riot report, had become less influential in the community, and their voices were by no means unanimous in matters of taste.

The community was in flux. Years of racial strife and urban crises, the consequences of the women's movement, the disenchantment with political and business leaders as a result of Vietnam, Watergate and business scandals had taken their toll of those who traditionally set standards. The standard-setters themselves had become suspect, for had not the best and the brightest of them led us into the Vietnam quagmire, and had not some of them urged us to vote for Nixon and stability?

The awareness that journalists themselves could define taste was slow in coming. But it was inevitable. Events had made it imperative that the press describe the changes, and to describe them accurately a new sense of the appropriate in language and subject matter was necessary. The way the press responded to these changes can provide us with guidelines by which to make judgments about questionable language and subject matter.

The Turning Point

In 1960, during a school integration demonstration in New Orleans, the AP quoted some of the women who were shouting at the leader of the school sit-ins, ''Jew bastard, nigger lover.'' In answer to many protests that the use of such words was in bad taste, the AP said it ''judged them essential to establishing the temper and the mood of the demonstrators.''

Gradually, pertinence was becoming the established guideline in determining whether an obscenity or profanity should be included in news accounts. The turning point may have been reached during the Watergate days when the tapes of the White House conversations revealed a profusion of vulgarities and profanities. As a West Coast journalism review, *feed/back,* put it, the ''Nixon administration made inoperative the detente that existed in the daily press against words once excised by editors.''

The words shit and fuck, used in the White House, appeared in such papers as *The Washington Post,* the *St. Paul Dispatch* and *Pioneer Press,* the Atlanta *Journal,* the *Kansas City Star* and *The Seattle Times.*

It would have been impossible, many editors felt, to have changed the emphatic language of a statement by President Nixon from the key tape of March 22, 1973:

> I don't give a shit what happens. I want you all to stonewall it, let them plead the Fifth Amendment, cover up or anything else if it'll save the plan. That's the whole point.

The AP made a survey of newspapers using the Watergate material and found nearly 30 percent of them printed all or nearly all of the words in their stories, without alteration. Slightly more than half sanitized the word shit or other words, and 15 percent of the papers completely edited out the vulgarities and profanities by paraphrase or deletion.

One of the newspapers that did not use Nixon's language was the Huntington (W.Va.) *Herald-Dispatch* and *Advertiser,* whose executive editor said, ''In this very Fundamentalist market, we came to the conclusion that there was no reason to offend unnecessarily.''

Turning away from some kinds of reality while daily parading man's most obscene acts—murder, torture, terrorism—seems an act of hypocrisy to some editors. Another kind of hypocrisy is revealed by an incident involving television station WGBH in Boston. The station decided to do a program a few days after the 1968 student demonstrations on the Harvard campus. It invited people from the community to have their say. One of the persons who showed up took the microphone at the beginning of the program and shouted, "What I have to say is fuck Harvard and fuck Pusey [Harvard's president] and fuck everybody." David Ives, the president of the public TV station recalled, "I was upstairs, and you have never seen so many telephone calls. The most interesting thing about them was the quality of what they said.

"One woman said, 'I just want you to know that no language like that has ever been permitted in this house.' And in the background you could hear a man saying, 'You know God damn well it has.' The prize came from a man who called and said, 'I'm just not going to have any of that kind of shit in my living room.'"

Subject Matter

As language that had been deemed unfit to print was gradually working its way into newspapers and magazines, subject matter once considered far beyond acceptance for the mass media became acceptable.

Here is the beginning of a story that was published in *The Sacramento Bee*, circulation 225,000:

Necrophiliac Takes Stand

By Jaime Diaz
Bee Staff Writer

Confessed necrophiliac Karen Greenlee, looking drawn and tense, took the stand before a jury in Sacramento Superior Court Friday and quietly admitted climbing into coffins to have sexual contact with corpses.

Under questioning by attorney Leo O'Connor, Greenlee, 23, said she had sexual contact in an embalming room and in other locations at the Sacramento Memorial Lawn mortuary, where she was an apprentice embalmer in late 1979.

She also admitted she drank heavily in her apartment at the mortuary during her employment there.

Greenlee and the mortuary are defendants in a suit by Marian Gonzales, who contends she suffered severe emotional distress when Greenlee stole the body of her son, John Mercure, 33, in a mortuary hearse Dec. 17, 1979.

The hearse containing Greenlee and the corpse were recovered the next day near Alleghany in Sierra County. After surrendering herself, Greenlee attempted suicide by swallowing pain relievers.

Greenlee pleaded guilty to interfering with a burial and illegally driving a hearse, and spent 11 days in jail and was fined $255 and placed on two years probation, with medical treatment recommended. She is now living . . .

Mort Saltzman, weekend editor of the *Bee,* says he made the decision to use the story because the arguments for its use outweighed those against it. His list:

Pro:
1. It's interesting.
2. It deals with a human being and with another facet of our complicated lives.
3. Freedom of the press.
4. It touches on the subject of necrophilia, a subject about which little is known and, more importantly, little is published or examined. Informative.
5. It's happening in our community.

Con:
1. Bad taste.
2. Who needs to know?
3. Lacks regard for the woman involved, shows a lack of compassion and sensitivity and ignores journalistic ethics.
4. Panders to the public's lust.
5. Not newsworthy or significant.

"What it really boils down to is that this story is extremely interesting, is being talked about by most folks in town and is being handled in what I consider good taste," Saltzman said.

"What is good taste to one person is pandering to another. What plays in Sacramento may not play in Sioux Falls, S.D., and then again may be considered very tame in San Francisco."

The ombudsman for the *Bee*—its internal critic—said he had received no more than five complaints about the story and said he thought that coverage had been handled with "good taste."

The wire service bureaus in Sacramento, however, moved little copy on the trial. AP and UPI reported scant newspaper interest.

Prominence a Determinant

In 1976, on a flight from the Republican presidential convention, a *Rolling Stone* reporter overheard and described in the magazine a conversation among John Dean, the singer Pat Boone and a member of President Ford's cabinet. Boone is quoted as saying:

"John and I were just discussing the appeal of the Republican party. It seems to me that the party of Abraham Lincoln could and should attract more black people. Why can't that be done?"
"I'll tell you why you can't attract coloreds," the secretary proclaimed as his mischievous smile returned. "Because coloreds only want three things. . . .
"I'll tell you what coloreds want. It's three things: first, a tight pussy; second, loose shoes; and third, a warm place to shit. That's all."

Rolling Stone ran the quotes in full but without attribution. The wire services and newspapers picked up the story. UPI handled the offensive comments with the paraphrasing "good sex, easy shoes and a warm place to go to the bathroom." *The*

Washington Post made it: ". . . Coloreds only want three things . . . first, a tight (woman's sexual organ); second, loose shoes; and third, a warm place to (defecate)." The quote was attributed to Earl Butz, secretary of agriculture.

AP paraphrased the statement in its story and used it in full in a note for editors. Later, it used language much like the *Post*'s.

A UPI survey showed that one newspaper, *The Capital Times* of Madison, Wis., had used the full quote. The fury of the public led to Butz's resignation, and then *The* Toledo *Blade* used the original comments. The *Blade* received eight calls, six protesting, two approving. The Erie, Pa., *Morning News* told readers in a front page editor's note that Butz's comments were in poor taste but that adult readers could see them in the newspaper office. More than 100 persons did just that. In Lubbock, Tex., the *Avalanche Journal* made a similar offer, and 350 persons showed up, including a farmer and his wife who drove 70 miles into town, copied the material to show their neighbors, and drove back.

The managing editor of *The Capital Times,* Robert Meloon commented on his use of the material: "We think readers have the right to know exactly what Mr. Butz said and to judge for themselves whether the remarks were obscene and racist in character; the paraphrasing we've seen doesn't carry off the same meaning as the actual words."

Clearly, direct quotes give the reader a sense of the person making them. In praising the *Minneapolis Tribune* for "defying community conventions by printing verbatim the crudities and obscenities of a truck driver assigned to the Human Relations Commission," the *Columbia Journalism Review* said the *Tribune* had portrayed "his racism, pugnacity, and know-nothingism as no 'doctored' quotations could have done."

When the UPI quoted Billy Carter, the president's brother, saying of Jews who had protested his ties with the leaders of Libya, "They can kiss my ass," there were some protests. The UPI replied that its decision was "based on the reality that members of the president's family are public figures and we have to chronicle their excesses, verbal or otherwise."

Thus, the prominence of the persons involved in news events as well as the importance of the event and the relevance of the explicit language to the event bear on the use of obscenity or profanity.

Limits on Broadcasting

Being regulated, the broadcast industry is more sensitive to complaints about language and subject matter than newspapers and magazines. The FCC is empowered to enforce federal statutes and the decisions of the courts in the area of obscenity, indecency and profanity. The FCC can fine a station or revoke its license if it finds that it violated section 1464 of the federal Criminal Code, which provides for penalties for uttering "any obscene, indecent or profane language by means of radio communication." ("Radio" includes television.)

But even broadcasters and the FCC have changed with the times. In 1960, NBC censored the use of the initials "W.C." on the Jack Parr show, the nightly televised network talk program that was a predecessor to the Johnny Carson show. W.C.

stands for water closet, which in Britain means toilet. A dozen years later, the Public Broadcasting Service showed an "education entertainment" called the "V.D. Blues." There were no protests about the initials, and there were surprisingly few objections to some of the language in such songs as "Don't Give a Dose to the One You Love Most" and "Even Dr. Pepper Won't Help You," which was about the futility of douching as a contraceptive practice.

Although some stations made cuts, and stations in Arkansas and Mississippi did not carry the program, the majority of public broadcast stations decided that the program was a public service. When "V.D. Blues" was followed by a 2½ hour hotline on the New York City station, 15,000 persons called with questions about venereal disease. One of the city's V.D. clinics reported the next day that the number of persons seeking blood tests went up by a third.

The program obviously was aimed at teenagers, whose venereal disease rate has approached epidemic proportions. But stations must be careful about approaching the younger audience.

The "Filthy Words" Case

In 1973, in a broadcast in the early afternoon over station WBAI (FM) in New York City, George Carlin gave a comedy monologue entitled, "The Seven Words You Can't Say on Radio and Television." Carlin said his intent was to show that the language of ordinary people is not threatening or obscene. The station later said in its defense that the broadcast was in the tradition of satire. In the broadcasts Carlin had said:

> I was thinking one night about the words you couldn't say on the public airwaves . . . and it came down to seven but the list is open to amendment and in fact has been changed. . . . The original seven words were shit, piss, fuck, cunt, cocksucker, motherfucker and tits. . . .

He repeated the tabooed words several times in what he said later was a purposeful "verbal shock treatment."

There was one complaint, and the FCC investigated. In 1975, it issued a declaratory order finding that the words were "patently offensive by contemporary community standards for the broadcast medium and are accordingly 'indecent' when broadcast by radio or television. These words were broadcast at a time when children were undoubtedly in the audience."

The station was not prosecuted under the federal statute. Nor was a fine imposed. The finding was, however, to be part of the station's file. It was, in effect, probation for the station.

The station appealed to the federal courts, and many stations and civil rights advocates joined the appeal against what was seen as a threat to freedom of expression. The case reached the United States Supreme Court, and in 1978 the court ruled 5-4 that radio and television stations do not have the constitutional right to broadcast indecent words. It said that the government has the right to forbid such words because of the broadcast medium's "uniquely pervasive presence in the lives of all

Americans." The Court stated that "of all forms of communication, it is broadcasting that has received the most limited First Amendment protection."

The Supreme Court emphasized the limits of its ruling:

> It is appropriate, in conclusion, to emphasize the narrowness of our ruling. . . . The Commission's (FCC) decision rested entirely on a nuisance rationale under which context is all important. . . . The time of day was emphasized by the Commission. . . .

Nevertheless, the Court's ruling was seen as a setback in the attempt by broadcasters to gain the same kind of freedom granted the print media.

On the specific matters of obscenity, indecency and profanity, the FCC is guided by court rulings, in particular *Miller v California* in which the standard for determining whether a printed work is obscene is whether:

a) The average person, applying contemporary community standards, would find that the work, taken as a whole, appeals to the prurient interest.
b) The work depicts or describes in a patently offensive way, sexual conduct specifically defined by the applicable state law.
c) The work, taken as a whole, lacks serious literary, artistic, political or scientific value.

For the work to be ruled obscene by the FCC all three elements must be present.

In the Carlin-WBAI case, the FCC defined indecent language as "language that describes, in terms patently offensive as measured by community standards for the broadcast medium, sexual or excretory activities and organs." The Commission also stated that when children are likely to be in the audience indecent language "cannot be redeemed by a claim that it has literary, artistic, political or scientific value."

As for profanity, the FCC said that the legal test is whether the words indicated "an imprecation of divine vengeance or implying divine condemnation, so used as to constitute a public nuisance." In other words, the FCC will not act when profanities clearly are not intended to be taken literally.

"Scared Straight"

Several of Carlin's Seven Filthy Words were used with dramatic impact in a film documentary, "Scared Straight," broadcast on television six years later. The documentary was aimed at young viewers. It described a prison program designed to show youngsters the consequences of crime. The cameras followed a group of youths as they toured the Rahway State Prison in New Jersey.

"You think you're tough or something? You think this is a fucking joke," says one of the lifers to a smirking youngster.

To another youth who wondered about life in prison, a murderer says: "We have sexual desires. Who do you think we get, and don't tell me each other. We get young, dumb motherfuckers just like you."

The program was given an Oscar at the 1979 Academy Awards for the best feature-length documentary of the year.

Sexual Matters   The taboos against the explicit reference to the sex act have been eased at a much slower pace than have the prohibitions against frank language. Still, there have been changes, hardly surprising in view of the vast alterations in society over the past three decades. If journalism is the mirror held to life, then a journalism that is prohibited from chronicling changes in how we live is worse than useless; it is misleading and irresponsible.

The press has followed the arts, which have always strained to journey wherever imagination soared. Fiction, the movies, magazines had flung off the fig leaf and discarded the asterisk and dash years ago. The press lagged, and this failure to keep up, some press critics say, led to a public uninformed on such issues as sex education, venereal disease and the role of sex in behavior.

When the University of Kansas Medical Center sponsored a symposium in 1969 on sex education, the institution was attacked as being part of the "communist conspiracy." Outraged, the medical students issued a statement that pointed out:

> It is our offices that will be filled by people with sexual problems arising from misinformation or lack of information concerning sexual matters. . . .
> Isn't it time that we admitted that man is a sexual being. Isn't it time that we stopped trying to keep our children from discovering that fact. Isn't it time that we spent more of our efforts informing our children of the reality of man's sexual nature and its concomitant moral responsibilities.
> We think so. . . .

The general press did not think so. Most editors thought of their newspapers as "family reading," and they steadfastly refused to admit to mankind's sexual nature. They contended the material about sexuality was available elsewhere to those who searched.

Once more, critics of the press were able to point out that the press usually follows the path of least resistance, that it reinforces the status quo, and that it seeks to entertain and to reassure readers and listeners rather than to inform them or to lead them.

But some publications gradually became aware of the necessity to report these matters and their consequences. They began to report fully such issues as family planning, abortion, birth control, homosexuality, sex education, teenage sex, family relationships, venereal diseases and laws affecting sexual behavior.

The pioneering work into human sexual behavior, Alfred C. Kinsey's *Sexual Behavior in the Human Male,* had been treated gingerly by the mass media when it was published in 1948. In 1966, another important work on sexual activity was published, *Human Sexual Response,* by Dr. William H. Masters and Virginia E. Johnson. The result of a detailed 11-year study of sexual physiology, the work was too important to be ignored. The question was not whether to run a news story—times had changed—but how the story was to be written.

The study was based on the direct observation of sexual intercourse and masturbation. The book was published to give those treating problems of sexual inadequacy information based on scientific observations. How this was made into journalism by *The New York Times* constituted a breakthrough of sorts.

The story that appeared in the April 18, 1966, issue of the *Times* used the words vagina, vaginal lubrication, intravaginal diaphragms, orgasm, and other sexually explicit words. As the story was being edited, a problem came up on the desk.

As the event is recounted by a *Times* copy editor, the desk noticed the frequent and explicit references to the female sex organ (six times before the continuation) and only euphemistic references (two) to the male organ—"genital organ" and "the organ." The question was referred to an assistant managing editor who served as the arbiter of language and taste at the *Times*. He decreed "vagina" for the woman and "organ" for the man as proper.

Two years later, the *Times* was more forthcoming in its use of explicit language. Reporting the changes *The Washington Post* and *Chicago Tribune* had made in a review appearing in their Sunday book review supplement, "Book World," the *Times* reported that the newspapers had called back a press run of the supplement to delete a section that "consisted of a paragraph containing reference to the penis in a discussion of the sexual behavior of primates."

The paragraph that so offended the sensibilities of decision makers at the *Post* and *Tribune* that they called back a million copies of the press run at a cost of $100,000 began:

> Many a cocktail party this winter will be kept in motion by this provocative chit chat: man is the sexiest primate alive; the human male and not the gorilla possesses the largest penis of all primates. . . .

The *Post* and *Tribune* were clinging to the concept of the newspaper as family reading, though *Life* and *Newsweek* had used the word in their stories about the book, *The Naked Ape* by Desmond Morris, and though it was commonplace among millions of nursery school children, who had been told to call a penis a penis. Child psychologists had been telling the mothers of America that calling it anything else—flower, yo-yo, carrot, seed-carrier—only necessitates further explanations and eventual hang-ups, neuroses and feelings of guilt.

In the 70s, birth control devices were distributed on college campuses. Women talked openly about their sexual needs. Abortion, once a hush word, was frequently in the news because of the suits brought by groups urging repeal of abortion laws, and the counter-drive waged by various groups to retain the measures. Venereal disease was reported as a serious health hazard.

In 1975, the *Argus Leader* in Sioux Falls, S.D., carried a streamer across the top of page one:

At Least 14 Sexually-Transmitted Diseases Spreading In Epidemic Proportions

Right above the headline and under the newspaper flag was the newspaper's motto, "A Newspaper for the Home." The decision to play the story this way may have been influenced by one of the quotes in the AP's account:

"The public would panic if any other disease were advancing at the rate gonorrhea is," declares Dr. Bruce Webster of New York Hospital-Cornell University Medical College.

In December, 1967, the *Times* had run a story about college coeds and their "first experience with sexual intercourse." It was published on page one under the headline;

MORE COEDS FIND
LESS GUILT IN SEX

Joy in First Experience Is
Likelier Now, Study Says

This was in the *Times* tradition of reporting significant events. Five years later, in May 1972, a reporter for the *Times* family section decided to find out "what happens when the 'liberated' young return for the weekend, with a friend of the opposite sex, and expect to share the same bedroom."

Whereas in 1967, the report on college sexuality was based on a study, the 1972 story was the result of enterprise by the *Times* itself. The newspaper understood the dimensions of the sexual revolution and did not wait for a study to be issued or for an authoritative source to make a statement on the subject.

This journalistic enterprise in areas that usually were approached with trepidation has extended to the coverage of the personal lives of public figures.

Personal Lives   For years, reporters had ignored the alcoholism of public officials. With the exception of Drew Pearson, a Washington columnist, reporters ignored senators and representatives who were drunk in Congress or committee. They confined their reporting to official activities, despite the obvious inability of some officials to function on their jobs.

In 1975, the escapades of Rep. Wilbur Mills, one of the most powerful men in Congress, with a burlesque dancer catapulted him and the issue of alcoholism to the front pages. Mills confessed he was an alcoholic. This admission, wrote Jack Anderson, Pearson's successor, caused reporters to ask "one another whether they should write more about the drinking habits of Washington dignitaries."

The answer by some journalists is that they should if the drinking affects the official life of the public figure. Clearly, conduct in office is an appropriate subject for journalism, particularly if the conduct incapacitates the official.

There is less agreement about coverage of the public but unofficial activities of officials and prominent persons. A movie star's nightlife may be subject to coverage as that is the world of the public personality, the star's allure. But is the nightlife of a mayor or governor a fit topic for coverage? Most reporters would say it is only if the hangovers make the official regularly miss work.

But then, suppose most people in town know that the mayor has an eye for the ladies and an insatiable thirst. Does not that public knowledge justify reporting? Most would say no.

And almost all would agree that what a public figure does in the privacy of his or her home—or apartment, or motel—is that person's own business. But not all. The sexual dalliances of another powerful congressman, Rep. Wayne Hays, were exposed by *The Washington Post* in 1976. The newspaper ran the revelations of Elizabeth Ray, a $14,000 a year employee of Hays. Her real job, the 27-year-old clerical worker said, was to serve as the congressman's mistress. Hays, chairman of the House Administration Committee, denied the allegations at first, then admitted them.

Three years later, another test of the propriety of publicizing the personal life of public figures emerged, this one more dramatic than the Hays story.

Nelson Rockefeller, for many years governor of New York, an aspirant to the presidency and vice president to Gerald Ford, died in the company of a young woman while ostensibly working on an art book he was preparing. A family spokesman released to the press the information about Rockefeller's fatal heart attack. But where Rockefeller died, when he died and the circumstances of his death were, it quickly turned out, garbled by the spokesman.

The truth, as it was pieced together by the press over the next several days, made increasingly vivid reading. There seemed little doubt that the 25-year-old woman who was with him in his townhouse at the time he was stricken (not in his office as the spokesman had announced) was more than simply Rockefeller's assistant. Although their relationship was never made explicit, there was no need. The usually staid *New York Times* took the lead in uncovering the details, among which was the fact that the young woman—whose salary was $60,000 a year—was clad in what appeared to be a black evening dress of some kind.

Although the other two New York City newspapers covered the story once the *Times* began, some journalists had misgivings. After all, Rockefeller was no longer a public official. Clearly, he was a public figure, but his notoriety was not that of a rock star or a movie idol whose reputation as a stud may be carefully cultivated.

A New York City television journalist, Gabe Pressman, found press accounts of the death to be an "effort to pander to the people of New York." He called the play the story received "salacious" in its use of "innuendoes and smears."

In their defense, editors pointed out that the first account of Rockefeller's death given by a family spokesman was almost completely erroneous. The press, always concerned about coverups, dug into the story when the spokesman's account began to crumble, and once the ferreting began it was unlikely to be halted by a sudden surge of second thoughts about propriety.

A case can be made for intrusion into the personal lives of public officials, even after they have left office. It is made effectively by Sanford Levinson, a lawyer who teaches in the department of politics at Princeton University. In an article in the May/June 1979 issue of the *Columbia Journalism Review,* Levinson justifies the Rockefeller coverage because of the spokesman's attempt to "make Rockefeller's death exemplary . . . to elevate it to the status of a public spectacle, and, so to speak, to invite the press to witness it after the fact." The spokesman sought to have Rockefeller die to rave notices, much like any public relations agent tries to orchestrate an event. Rockefeller had throughout his public career enjoyed excellent press coverage. He was rarely held to account by the New York press, Levinson points out. And so the spokesman "can be excused for expecting one last act of cooperation from the press."

But some of the press refused to go along with the expectation of the Rockefeller spokesman for the "one last act of cooperation." Their stories amounted to, in Levinson's words, "a rejection of the power that wealth has to transform reality in this society."

The official, sanitized version of the Rockefeller death certainly was accepted by some journalists. Two days after Rockefeller died, James Reston led off his column in the Sunday *New York Times* with this observation:

> It should particularly be remembered that Nelson Rockefeller died at his desk late on a Friday night after almost everybody else had gone home for the weekend. He was a worker, a yearner, and a builder to the end.

In an article, "Letter to Jimmy Carter," that appeared in the July/August 1979 issue of *The Washington Monthly,* the author, Charles Peters, writes: "Unlike Edward Kennedy, you do not get drunk, nor do you have to worry about explaining from whose bed you may be called at the moment of nuclear decision." In response to many protests, Peters said that the personal life of Sen. Kennedy was appropriate for discussion because the senator was considered a candidate for the presidency. Peters had made more explicit what other journalists had been alluding to in their profiles of the senator for several years.

The personal life of the public official or the private individual involved in public policy matters was considered relevant by *The Minneapolis Star.* Late in 1979, after an extensive inquiry, it published articles quoting prostitutes who said that many of the men who made and enforced laws against prostitution were their customers. The men were named and included a state district judge, a state senator, the United States Attorney for Minneapolis and St. Paul and the chief lobbyist for the Minnesota

Catholic Conference, who argued for legislation against prostitution. The response in Minneapolis was sharp and divided.

Levinson's comments seem appropriate here, too:

> Leaders play multiple roles in a society; their importance goes far beyond simply providing decisions about public problems. They become sources for the collective understandings and psychological bonds that define communities. And leaders are also made responsible for teaching their fellows about the right way to confront the full range of human dilemmas.

The politician who seeks our trust, and votes, because he proclaims himself virtuous must in truth be what he declares himself. It may be that the fury with which some reporters responded to the White House lies and coverups during Watergate was a declaration of anger and anguish that they had been had, that they had been party to a gigantic pseudo-event, the beautification of shallow, ruthless men.

After all, it was Richard Nixon in one of his famous debates with John Kennedy in 1960 who said of Harry Truman's cussing:

> . . . whoever is president is going to be a man that all children look up to or look down on, and I can only say that I am very proud that President Eisenhower restored dignity and decency and, frankly, good language to the conduct of the presidency of the United States.
>
> And I can only hope, should I win this election, that I could approach President Eisenhower in maintaining the dignity of the office and see to it that whenever any mother or father talks to his child, he can look at the man in the White House and, whatever he may think of his policies, he will say, 'Well, there is a man who maintains the kind of standards personally that I would want my child to follow.'

Journalists, hardly paragons of virtue themselves, do not expect saints to occupy public office. But they want the right to report the language and deeds of those who pass themselves off as white knights.

Photographs and Film

On May 25, the AP transmitted to its clients a partially nude photograph of Elizabeth Ray from *Playboy* magazine. Ray was shown lying on what seemed to be a couch, bare-breasted, her arms upraised, her fingers running through her hair.

The photo committee of the APME was interested in how many editors thought the AP should have transmitted the photo. Of 138 who replied, 98 said yes, the AP did the right thing. But only 24 said they used the picture, 20 of them cropping the photo to avoid showing Ray's bare breasts. Clearly, editors are not ready—or believe their readers are not—for nudity.

Pueblo Prisoners. When AP Wirephoto distributed this picture of men from the captured intelligence ship Pueblo in 1968, it ran an editor's advisory: "Your attention is called to the possible obscene nature of the fingers in this picture." *The New York Times* ran the picture and in the caption stated, "The defiant finger gesture by three of the men seems to have eluded the North Korean photographer."

But readers and television viewers are apparently ready for some pictures that once were considered offensive. Bodies of accident and murder victims are regularly shown on television. The breakthrough came during the Vietnam War. It made no sense for war coverage to hide war's consequences. Some writers believe that the frank coverage by television of death and disaster may have caused the eventual public disillusionment with the war that led to U.S. withdrawal.

In 1972, AP distributed gruesome pictures of torture and executions of Pakistanis by East Pakistanis following the war between India and Pakistan. Editors were asked whether the pictures were too strong for them or their readers. Here are some of the comments:

I do believe that these pictures help to bring home the point.
—Paul R. LaRocque, Battle Creek *Enquirer and News.*

Perhaps Americans are not interested in violence except as it affects them directly.
—Bob Tench, *News* and *Dispatch,* Tarentum, Pa.

Used one of the less brutal shots on Page 4 because we felt the others were too much to stomach at the breakfast table.
—Kuyk Logan, *The Houston Post*.

Received more than 20 phone calls, all against running the pictures. News editor said, 'I would do it again if we got those pictures again.'
—James Dooley, *Arizona Republic*.

We felt an obligation to let our readers see the brutality.
—John Stallings, *Corpus Christi Caller-Times*.

My feeling is that newspapers have done no favors in suppressing or playing down photos such as the Dacca offerings. In the absence of some of the stark truths about warfare, the public is left with John Wayne and Audie Murphy images.
—Ralph Langer, *The* Dayton *Journal Herald*.

The pictures were awarded the 1972 Pulitzer Prize for photography.

Not long after the Elizabeth Ray photo was distributed by AP Photo, another photograph containing offensive material was moved by AP Photo. This one pictured Nelson Rockefeller, then vice president, chortling as he "gave the finger" to hecklers at a political rally. Taken by Don Black of the Binghamton *Press* and *Sun-Bulletin,* it ran on page two of Black's newspaper but was given page-one display over three, four and five columns, in newspapers from *Newsday* on Long Island to the *Chronicle* in San Francisco, from the *Herald* in Portsmouth, N.H. to the *Democrat* in Tallahassee.

Black said he disagreed with the decision of his editors to put the picture on page 2, but he understood "the reluctance of the editor to give front page display to an obscene gesture, no matter who had made it." He speculated further about the picture:

"If Rockefeller hadn't confirmed his intent to make such a gesture, I would have had some doubt about whether it was intentional. If the photo had been one of those capturing a moment out of context which gave it a false meaning, then it shouldn't have been used."

The picture was prominently displayed on page one of the *Knickerbocker News* in Albany, where Rockefeller was governor for 15 years. Executive editor Bob Fichenberg said of his use of the photo, "Either we put ourselves in the position of protecting the vice president from his own actions or we report it pictorially, as well as in text, and let the public know. We decided to let them know."

Black's photo won the general news or documentary prize in the 34th annual Pictures of the Year Contest sponsored by the University of Missouri School of Journalism and the National Press Photographers Association.

Death

One of the most dramatic series of pictures taken by a newspaper photographer since the Vietnam War was criticized as tasteless and cheap, irresponsible journalism. The subject was death. Sent out to cover what he thought would be a routine rescue attempt of a woman and a child trapped on a fire escape in a tenement fire, Stanley Forman of the *Boston Herald American* was photographing a fireman on the fire escape as he reached for the ladder being inched toward the three. The firefighter had one arm around the young woman, who was holding the child.

Suddenly, the fire escape collapsed. The fireman managed to grab the ladder. The woman lost her grip on him and the child, and as Forman stood watching and automatically shooting, the two fell. His series of pictures ran across front pages over the country.

But many readers were disturbed. What purpose did they serve? In Boston, the photographs did call attention to lax safety enforcement standards, and one of the consequences was a stepped-up inspection program. Unquestionably, the pictures were dramatic. They have been described as one of the great achievements of news photography. In a sense, they were photographic high art. But does that justify their use?

The furor over the pictures was undoubtedly a response to their theme, death. Had they portrayed another subject as dramatically, the quality of the photography would have warranted their use. But calling attention to death is deemed tasteless.

Despite the heavy toll traffic accidents take, newspapers have been reluctant to use photos of traffic fatalities. They will show the photograph of a plane crash in another state but are reluctant to use the picture of a sheet-draped body of a local motorist killed on a highway.

A photograph of a family grieving at the funeral of a soldier killed in Vietnam, taken by an intern at *The* Louisville *Courier-Journal* and *Times* was not published because, said the photographer, Stewart Bowman, "They felt it was too powerful

from the standpoint that it involved personal feelings too deeply, and they were afraid
it may cause an adverse effect on the family should they see it in the next day's
paper.''

The AP did pick up the photograph and it was used in many newspapers around
the country. It was awarded the Mark of Excellence in the Sigma Delta Chi photographic competition in 1978.

In discussing the photograph of the grief-stricken mother of a young girl who
had been raped and killed, students at Central Michigan University were evenly divided over its use. Professor James Stanford Bradshaw said he sided with those
who opposed its use on the ground that this intensely personal picture was better
suited to a large-city daily newspaper than to a small-town newspaper where people
are more personally known.

Questionable. *The* Louisville Courier-Journal *did not use this series of pictures of an elderly woman committing suicide. But its sister newspaper, the* Times, *used one.*

A series of photographs taken by Bowman of a distraught woman jumping off a building in Louisville was not used by *The Courier-Journal* on the ground that the woman was not a public figure and that the incident had only minimal news value. *The Courier-Journal's* sister newspaper, the *Times,* used one of the pictures.

Claude Cookman, then photo editor of the *Times,* argued for its use. "In the first place, these were extremely powerful pictures, and they made me think about my own death.

"I think that we should show the entire range of human experience. We always run pictures of people singing and dancing. That's part of life, but death is, too. If we don't show suffering, then we aren't giving a complete view of life."

Three years later, Cookman was working on the photo desk of *The Miami Herald* when another decision had to be made involving pictures of death. This time the pictures were of Haitians who had drowned attempting to reach the United States and whose bodies had been washed up on Florida's shores. The newspaper used the photos.

Cookman says that in deciding about photo use, these questions must be resolved:

1. What do the pictures really show?
2. What are the readers likely to add or read into their interpretation of the photos' content?
3. What are the circumstances under which the photographs were obtained?
4. How compelling is the news situation out of which the photos arose?
5. How compelling or significant are the photos in terms of what they teach us about the human experience?
6. Do the positive reasons for publishing the photos outweigh the almost certain negative reaction they will elicit from a sizable portion of the readership?

End of a Dream. The body of a Haitian who drowned while trying to reach the United States lies on the sand in an exclusive Florida beach-front community. Use of the pictures of these refugees offended some readers of *The Miami Herald.*

Compare the two incidents—the Louisville suicide and the drowned Haitian—in terms of Cookman's guidelines and others you may devise.

In the Haitian drowning, the attempt of these people to reach the United States was a running news story. This was not an isolated death. Many others had drowned in the incident. The news situation (No. 4) was strong.

The news value of the woman's suicide was negligible. She was not prominent. This was not the one case that set a record for the city or county's number of suicides. Clearly, the pictures were dramatic. But that is not reason enough.

Cookman made the point that there is something that transcends news values—the human value, you might call it. If so, question No. 5 could be applied to the suicide as follows: The pictures of a 71-year-old woman leaping to her death show us that old age, ill health and loneliness take their toll in many ways that this youth-oriented culture prefers to turn its back on.

Nora Ephron, a media critic, says of pictures of death:

"I recognize that printing pictures of corpses raises all sorts of problems about taste and titillation and sensationalism; the fact is, however, that people die. Death happens to be one of life's main events. And it is irrresponsible—and more than that, inaccurate—for newspapers to fail to show it."

A sensitivity to personal feelings is essential to the journalist, not because invasions of privacy are illegal but because compassion is a compelling moral demand on the journalist. The photograph can be as callously intrusive as the television crew at the scene of a disaster poking camera and microphone in the faces of the bereaved. Yet, death is part of reality, and it is possible to be overly sensitive to the subject.

The subject of death has provided the press with almost as many problems as has sexual material. Most of us cringe from confrontation with our mortality. Morticians try to make death resemble life. Wakes are no longer fashionable. Black for the bereaved is a past practice. Children are kept from funerals by solicitous relatives.

Death is said to be the last taboo. A youth-oriented culture finds aging and death threatening.

Young reporters sometimes go to the other extreme. Carried away by the drama of violence, they may chronicle the details of death—the conditions of bodies strewn alongside the airliner, the mutilated homicide victim, the precise plans of the youngster who committed suicide in the garage.

This enthusiasm is as tasteless as prurient sexual interest, for it uses the tabooed subject as the means to shock readers, to call attention to the reporting rather than to the subject. Death can be terrible and horrifying. But its terror and horror are best made known through understatement. In sensitive areas, the whisper says more than the shout.

Reporters are often told that on matters of taste the decision as to what will be used will be made by an editor or the copy desk. However, reporters should set criteria for themselves for several reasons. Obviously, what the reporter sees and how he or she sees it is influenced by his or her attitudes and values. A censurious reporter may block out relevant material. A prurient reporter may over indulge his or her fantasies. An open attitude toward the matters we have discussed is a corrective to the natural propensity to be guided, and consequently victimized, by the impulses and sentiments that influence most people.

By their nature, editors are conservative. Like libel lawyers, when they are in doubt they tend to throw out questionable material. A reporter learns early in his or her career to fight for stories. The reporter who has a set of standards from which to argue his or her story past the desk will be better able to do a good job of presenting to readers and listeners the world of reality.

Clearly, the self-appointed guardians of good taste no longer have the power to issue dicta. Now, it's the journalist who decides what is essential and what is offensive and unnecessary. Guidelines are essential for responsible use of this power. Here are some:

1. Is the questionable material essential to a story of significance? If so, there is compelling reason to use it.
2. Use is subject to the kind of readers and listeners who use the medium. But care should be taken to see to it that all are considered, not just those who are most vociferous about taste.
3. The tone of the publication or station is a consideration.
4. The private as well as the public actions of public officials and public figures are the subject of journalism if they bear on matters of public concern.

16 The Morality of Journalism

<u>Preview</u>   Newspapers, broadcast stations and press organizations have adopted codes of ethics and guidelines that:

- Prohibit journalists from accepting anything of value from sources.
- Limit activities that may pose conflicts-of-interest.
- Stress the journalist's responsibility to society.

The reporter should also adopt a personal code. Such a code would stress the reporter's:

- Compassion for the poor, the handicapped, the different.
- Moral indignation when the powerless are victimized.
- Willingness to place responsibility for the failures of policies and decisions on those who make them.
- Commitment to the improvement of his or her skills.

"I don't mean to seem unfriendly," the fragile old man said, "but I just don't want people to see any stories about me." He looked down for a moment and then back to his visitor, Kevin Krajick, a reporter for *Corrections* magazine. Krajick was on assignment to interview elderly prisoners, and during his stop at the Fishkill, N.Y., state penitentiary he had been told about one of the oldest, Paul Geidel, 84 years old and in his 68th year behind bars for murder.

Geidel offered to make toast and tea for Krajick, and the reporter accepted. Geidel had turned away many reporters before, but a guard had suggested Krajick try anyway, and he had led the young reporter to Geidel's 10 × 10 room in the prison infirmary.

With the gentleness of his age, Geidel said he understood that Krajick's job was "to get a story." He respected that calling, he said, but he was afraid he didn't want to talk about himself.

"I began slipping in questions about his past, his feelings about his life," Krajick recalled. "He answered several of them, but he said several times he did not want 'any story.'

"He had tried to live in solitude and repentance, he said, and any notoriety upset him. He wanted to die in obscurity." A reporter had visited him a few years before and had promised that no story would come out of their conversation, Geidel told Krajick.

"I thought they would leave me alone, but then one day I pick up the paper, and oh, there's my name and my picture splattered all over the front page."

Geidel, the son of an alcoholic saloon keeper, was put in an orphange at seven. At 14, he quit school and worked at menial jobs. When he was 17 he broke into a hotel room in New York, stuffed a chloroformed gag in a guest's mouth, grabbed a few dollars and fled in a panic. The victim suffocated. Geidel was arrested, convicted and sentenced to life in prison for second-degree murder.

It was all in the newspaper, again, 60 years later.

"It was terrible, just terrible," Geidel said.

"I had decided at that point that I would not put him through the pain of printing a story about him," Krajick said. "I told him that I would not. I figured there were plenty of interesting elderly prisoners who wouldn't mind being written about."

The two chatted about an hour and parted good friends.

"Then I learned that Mr. Geidel had served the longest prison term in U.S. history. I started to waver. I checked the files and found that several magazines and television stations had run stories on him when he refused parole at the age of 81. I then called the state corrections and parole authorities to find out how Geidel had been held for such an incredible term—a point that had not been made clear in the previous articles.

"It turned out that he had been classified as criminally insane on what turned out to be a pretty flimsy basis and then totally forgotten about. He had not stood up for himself during all those years and had no one on the outside to do it for him.

"This obviously was a story of more significance than I had first thought. It was the most dramatic demonstration possible of the abuse of power under the boundless mental commitment statutes that most states have. What could be more moving than the story of the man who had spent the longest term ever, whom everyone acknowledged as meek and repentant and who, under other circumstances, would have been released before he reached the age of 40?

"The public clearly had reason to know about this man's life. It would be difficult to justify leaving him out since I was writing what was supposed to be a definitive article on elderly prisoners for the definitive publication on prisons."

Krajick faced a moral dilemma. Were the reasons for publishing his story sufficiently compelling to outweigh his promise to Geidel and the pain that the article would certainly inflict on the old man?

"I was anxious not to hurt a man who had, as prison records and he himself said, spent his life in mental anguish. I was sympathetic with his wish to remain obscure."

In his work, Krajick had faced situations in which people had been imprudently frank with him and had asked to be spared publicity. Those decisions had not been hard to make. He had reasoned that those who are hurt or embarrassed by the truth usually deserve to be. But Geidel deserved neither society's curiosity nor its condemnation. If anyone had paid his debt to society, certainly Geidel had.

In the balance Krajick was striking were two other factors: Articles had already been written about Geidel, and the fact that he had become a statistic in the *Guinness Book of World Records* would soon draw other reporters whose articles, Krajick felt, would be more flamboyant and less accurate than his.

"On this basis, I decided to print the article, though not without misgivings," Krajick said. "I realized that if Mr. Geidel were to see the article he would be distressed, and he would feel betrayed by the young man who was nice to him but ended up lying. I only hope those around him have the sense not to show him the article. That would be the only escape for my conscience."

The piece appeared in the March 1979 issue of the magazine under the title, "The Longest Term Ever Served: 'Forget Me.' " The concluding paragraph of the article reads:

> As his visitor left, he offered to write to Geidel. "Oh, no, please," he said. "Please. I don't mean to seem unfriendly. But please don't write. Forget me. Forget all about me." A distressed look crossed his face and he turned and hobbled down the hall to clean the teapot.

Solicitude for the feelings of persons like Geidel is fairly new to journalism. If there had been a practical guide for reporters during the past hundred years, it could well have been, "The story's the thing." For many years, outsiders had urged on the press a sense of responsibility, a caution that the First Amendment was not a license for money-making and sensation-mongering without corresponding responsibilities. In the 1970s, the press began to heed these criticisms, and this self-scrutiny included an examination of a variety of ethical problems.

We will go into the causes of this self-examination and then look at some codes and standards that emerged. These codes, we shall see, proscribe certain activities, such as the acceptance of gifts from sources. But the codes do not take the young reporter too far along the road toward establishing an individual moral code. By examining a variety of ethical problems journalists have encountered we shall try to provide suitable guidelines for the journalist caught on the horns of moral dilemmas such as the one Krajick faced, and we shall attempt to construct a series of signposts to help the journalist to set a general direction for his or her journalism.

Causes for Concern

James C. Thomson, Jr., the curator of the Nieman Foundation, noted in an article in the Winter/Spring 1978 issue of the *Nieman Reports* that during the previous five years there had been a "sharply increasing preoccupation both inside and outside the media, with journalistic ethics: the values and behavior of news organizations and individuals."

He found several causes for this new concern:

> VISIBLE NATIONAL POWER. A national press had emerged, consisting of the three television networks (ABC, CBS, NBC); the two weekly newsmagazines *(Time and Newsweek)* and at least two dailies *(The New York Times and The Washington Post).* These national media, with others, "helped end the Indochina War by turning many Americans against that conflict and forcing the virtual abdication of President Johnson," Thomson said. One, *The Washington Post,* forced the resignation of President Nixon.

NEWS CREATORS. The electronic media in particular "have been perceived as creators of, or at least as participants in, the news." This has affected the coverage of politics, which has become a media spectacle.

COUNTER-ATTACK. As a consequence of the growing prominence and power of the media, a "major and effective counter-attack was made on these national media." The attacks "produced within the press not merely temporary fear but also increased self-examination and widened access" through the creation of ombudsmen, opposite-editorial pages, journalism reviews.

RADICAL REPORTERS. Journalistic practices were criticized by a "new generation of younger and more radical reporters who assailed their elders for alleged collusion with the Establishment." Some young reporters went into alternative journalism and were later hired by the more orthodox media, which they influenced.

PUBLIC ACCOUNTABILITY. With the disclosures journalists made about the behavior of politicians, the accountability of all professions became a matter of concern to many Americans. "Inevitably, journalists themselves" became "increasingly preoccupied with the issue of journalistic ethics."

Some journalistic practices were embarrassing. *The Detroit News* made a study of the gifts staff members had received in 1972. The watches, offers of free travel, Christmas hams and poinsettia plants added up to $56,000, a tidy sum. *The Detroit News* decided that gift-givers should be put on notice that gifts would either be returned or given to charitable organizations.

Free travel was also an embarrassment. The American Society of Newspaper Editors examined free travel practices in 1972 and found that three-fourths of their members would accept offers of free travel for staff members. The situation changed considerably after the ASNE called attention to the practice and adopted its code in 1975. The code stated, "Journalists must avoid impropriety and the appearance of impropriety as well as any conflict of interest or the appearance of conflict. They should neither accept anything nor pursue any activity that might compromise their integrity."

Here are some of the comparisons the ASNE made on free travel:

	'72	'74	'77	'79
		(percentages)		
Would accept free travel from tax-supported agencies for reporters and photographers.	78	32	25	11
Sports writers accept free transportation to travel with team.	—	38	25	8
Editors accept free travel on airlines' inaugural flights.	—	37	19	15

As the self-examinations continued, similar declines were reported in the acceptance of gifts and the holding of part-time jobs that created conflicts of interest with the journalists' full-time jobs.

Two major organizations adopted codes and a third revised its code during the 1970s. Numerous newspapers and broadcast stations drafted codes of their own. Generally, the codes call on journalists to be impartial, independent, accurate and responsible. They prohibit certain practices, such as the acceptance of gifts, free travel and special privileges, and they condemn conflicts of interest. (The codes of the American Society of Newspaper Editors, the Associated Press Managing Editors and the Society of Professional Journalists, Sigma Delta Chi, are included at the end of this chapter.)

The codes established ethical norms for a craft with aspirations to professional status. The problems these codes address have tinged journalism with a grubbiness inconsistent with the standards of professional conduct. But they do not address many of the problems that grew out of the concerns Thomson cited in his article. To do so, Thomson writes, is not easy. Journalists have to "tangle with a number of ambiguities about journalism, news and the U.S. Constitution," he says.

"What codes, standards, or models could—or should—encompass the extraordinarily wide varieties of practitioners in, and avenues of approach to, journalism?" he asked. Then there is the definition of news. It is "undefinable," says Thomson. The news organization is "both a private, profit-making business and, simultaneously, a constitutionally-protected semi-public service. Such outfits are therefore operating both To Make Money (at the least, not to lose it) *and* To Do Good (or expose iniquity, and thereby to improve society). Therefore, a first and unresolvable tension is between greed and idealism."

Finally, the "difficult fact, for journalists, is that the Constitution, its amendments, and its judicial interpreters have recognized and guaranteed several other citizens' rights" in addition to the free-press portion of the First Amendment.

Thomson describes these ambiguities as "too endemic and ineradicable," journalism's "domain too wide and infinitely varied" for a code to cover.

"What code can be written for such a special craft other than those of the philosophers and saints who have tried to teach men how to coexist?" he asks.

Even if journalists were to find specific guidelines to codify, there seems scant chance that such a disputatious group as journalists could agree to any but the most general admonitions, injunctions and exhortations. In 1974, the National Conference of Editorial Writers, concerned that some syndicated columnists had undisclosed conflicts of interest, entertained a motion that the columnists "should be censured." After considerable debate, the group changed the wording to "subject to criticism."

The codes define dubious behavior and then tell the journalist it is improper to behave in that way. But most of the dilemmas journalists must resolve require choices between what journalists consider to be conflicting moral actions.

Krajick had to choose between what he saw as two positive ends. To print the story would reveal some truths about a system that crushed one prisoner and may still be affecting others. It would be morally right to use Geidel to illustrate the inadequacy of the mental competency process, he believed. Not writing the piece would also be a moral action because then Geidel would be spared the further agony of public exposure. Surely, a man who has spent 68 years behind bars deserves our compassion. Moreover, there was Krajick's promise not to use the material. Can a public need justify the reporter's compromising his integrity?

Looking to codes for guidance, we find in one of them, that of the Society of Professional Journalists, that the journalist should "serve the general welfare." Krajick would serve the general welfare with publication. The same code stresses "respect for the dignity, privacy, rights and well-being of people encountered in the course of gathering and presenting the news." Clearly, respect for Geidel would mean heeding his plea not to write about him. The codes, we see, are only a starting point. We shall have to go beyond them for guidelines to the practice of a moral journalism.

Sins of Omission

Most of the criticism of the press is addressed to what is printed or broadcast—the vast number of pseudo-events orchestrated by people in power and the disconnected tidbits of news that are only of momentary interest.

But the major sins of the press may well be those of omission—ignoring the significant actions of the powerful and the travails and the longings of vast numbers of invisible people in society. Since the end of World War II, the press has been criticized for not recognizing or for ignoring the enormous social changes in society. The press has responded to some of these criticisms by opening columns and air time to such news. But the independent men and women who operate newspapers, magazines and broadcast stations would never accept a code that tells them what to print and broadcast.

They argue, irrefutably, that they have the right to be as responsible or as irresponsible as they choose. No code, they would say, can make a journalist a person of good conscience. Only individual choice in particular situations or a personal commitment to a journalistic morality can determine that.

What code could be adopted that would have led *The Charlotte Observer,* for example, to address the fact that North Carolina's leading income producer, its tobacco crop, is the source of the single greatest cause of lung cancer? It was the conscience of the *Observer's* management and editors that caused the newspaper to examine the issue in detail in a special section.

Nevertheless, the codes and various principles adopted by the press have been effective in correcting abuses that diminished the press as the voice of conscience in a community. The codes of the 1970s trace their lineage back to the report of the Commission on Freedom of the Press, which sought to establish standards of responsibility for the press. The report was commissioned by Henry R. Luce of *Time* and released in 1947. The study team was headed by Robert M. Hutchins, then chancellor of the University of Chicago. Hutchins summed up the report in its preface:

"This report deals with the responsibilities of the owners and managers of the press to their consciences and the common good for the formation of public opinion."

The study was the culmination of extensive criticism of the U.S. press as insular, often sensational and sometimes irresponsible. It was carried out in a period of change. The United States had emerged from World War II as the leading world power. Vast social changes had been unleashed inside the country. The members of the Commission—most of them prestigious faculty members at leading universities—concluded that the press had not been "adequate to the needs of society."

In its report, the Commission included five requirements for the media that have been described as a "theory of responsibility" for the press:

1. The press must give a truthful, comprehensive and intelligent account of the day's events in a context that gives them some meaning.
2. The press must provide a forum for the exchange of comment and criticism.
3. The press must project a representative picture of the constituent groups in the society.
4. The press must present and clarify the goals and values of the society.
5. The press must provide full access to the day's intelligence.

Many newspapers ignored the recommendations when they did not assail the Commission, possibly because the Commission consisted of outsiders, and the press does not take kindly to being told what to do by any but the brethren, if by them.

Still, the Commission recommendations were a persistent reminder to the press of its shortcomings. During the 1950s and 1960s, one criticism was particularly rankling—that the press had failed to give "a representative picture of the constituent groups in the society." Vast segments of society had been ignored by the press, particularly the young and the aged, racial minorities, the poor and women. Generally, the press became responsive to external criticism. Journalists themselves became outspoken, and their criticisms began to appear in the various press reviews that sprang up around the country.

Journalists realized the need for a personal journalistic ethic. No journalist can escape confronting ethical questions in his or her work. Every reporter and editor must construct some kind of moral framework on which to build his or her journalism. Without such an approach, journalism eventually is reduced to an endless, repetitive chase after disconnected stories, and this becomes for the reporter a life empty of meaning and dignity.

Morality Underlies Journalism

Morality is basic to the theory and practice of journalism. The free press justifies its existence in terms of moral imperatives; it rationalizes much of its behavior with moral declarations.

If public consent freely given is essential to the proper functioning of a democracy, then for the consent to be meaningful the public must be adequately informed by a press free of government or any other control. Thomas Jefferson expressed this simply: "Where the press is free and every man able to read, all is safe." The First Amendment makes this consensual system possible. Although neither the Constitution nor any laws require that the press carry out its essential part in the system, the press does take on itself responsibilities and obligations. The decision to offer thorough coverage of those who have power—even at some risk—is a moral decision. Some publishers and station owners obviously choose otherwise, to maximize profits by offering vast quantities of entertainment and crowding the remaining news with advertising.

The highest praise in journalism goes to the reporter, the newspaper or the station that engages in public service journalism. Journalists are expected to be socially conscious, to have "at their heart a touch of anger," as Richard L. Strout, veteran Washington correspondent of *The Christian Science Monitor,* puts it. At what is their anger directed? Here is a list of awards made by the Associated Press Managing Editors organization recently:

> The Providence *Journal-Bulletin:* Bringing to light unsafe and unhealthy conditions in the state's jewelry industry.
> The Atlanta *Constitution:* Examining practices used to deny voting rights to blacks.
> The Jackson, Miss. *Clarion-Ledger:* Detailing the plight of poor farmhands in the Mississippi Delta.
> The Long Beach *Press-Telegram:* Exposing police brutality.
> The *Los Angeles Herald Examiner:* Revealing sweatshop conditions in the local garment industry, especially by firms employing Spanish-speaking aliens.
> The *Seattle Times:* Reporting that freed a man wrongfully convicted of rape.
> The Worcester, Mass. *Evening Gazette:* Describing the plight of elderly people forgotten by their friends, family and society.
> The *Albuquerque Tribune:* Uncovering the extensive dumping of dangerous wastes in New Mexico.
> The *Columbia* (Mo.)*Daily Tribune:* Investigating conditions at Missouri's hospital for the criminally insane.
> The *Greeley* (Colo.) *Daily Tribune:* Revealing conditions in some nursing homes.
> The *Longmont* (Colo.) *Daily Times-Call:* Covering the fatal shooting of two Hispanics by local police in what began as a routine traffic stop.

In 1982, the Pulitzer Prize for public service reporting went to *Detroit News* reporters Sydney P. Freedberg and David Ashenfelter for exposing the U.S. Navy's cover-up of circumstances surrounding the deaths of seamen aboard ship. The stories led to significant reforms in naval procedures. The special local reporting prize in 1982 was awarded to Paul Henderson of *The Seattle Times* for reporting that proved the innocence of a man convicted of rape.

The 1983 public service reporting award went to the Jackson (Miss.) *Clarion-Ledger* for its campaign to reform the state's public school system, and the special local reporting prize was awarded to Loretta Tofani, a reporter for *The Washington Post,* for her investigation of rape and sexual assault in the Prince George's, Md., detention center.

No codes, no mastery of the craft can lead newspapers and stations to cover stories like these. These stories grew out of the understanding by reporters and their editors that journalism is a moral enterprise.

In his book, *Deciding What's News* (Pantheon Books: New York, 1979), the sociologist Herbert J. Gans describes a set of "enduring values" that he says "can be found in many different types of news stories over a long period of time. . . ." These values, he says, "affect what events become news, for some are part and parcel of the definition of news." Some he says are "unfairly belittled as 'motherhood values.' " Among these are the desirability of economic prosperity; the undesirability of war (which does not extend to certain wars, Gans points out); the virtues of family, love and friendship, and the ugliness of hate and prejudice.

Gans also lists eight "clusters" of values that influence news decisions: ethnocentrism, individualism, altruistic democracy, responsible capitalism, moderatism, social order, small-town pastoralism and national leadership. Journalists see news in terms of deviations from these values. The belief in altruistic democracy, for example, is revealed, says Gans, in the "stories about corruption, conflict, protest and bureaucratic malfunctioning." The news stories about these deviations imply "that politics should follow a course based on the public interest and public service."

In their reporting and editing, journalists are always making choices: What to report, whom to interview, what to leave in the story, what to remove. Selection, the heart of journalistic practice, is guided by news values, and these values usually reflect the prevailing concerns of the society and are rarely disputed.

There is, however, considerable disagreement over ways to handle certain events. The disputes often come down to the choice between alternative actions, each of which has some claim to principle. This is no different from the decision-making most of us face in our daily lives. "The world that we encounter in ordinary experience," says the philosopher Isaiah Berlin, "is one in which we are faced with choices between ends equally ultimate and claims equally absolute, the realization of some of which must inevitably involve the sacrifice of others. . . . If, as I believe, the ends of men are many, and not all of them are in principle compatible with each other, then the possibility of conflict—and of tragedy—can never be wholly eliminated from human life, either personal or social. The necessity of choosing between absolute claims is then an inescapable characteristic of the human condition."

Life as Referent

Can the journalist refer to some universal values as guides to choice, or is decision subject to particular circumstances and individual decisions—what the philosophers call a situational ethic? Traditionally—perhaps instinctively—mankind has sought absolutes as guides. And as often as the priest or the guru has supplied them they have been found to be so general as to be impractical. Or they have been discovered to be a way of keeping a political, economic or social system from attack or criticism.

Even so, we may find in these searches for an ethic to live by some suggestions for a useful journalistic morality. The concern for the good life, the properly led life, is almost as powerful as the need for sustenance. We may find some guides from religion and philosophy, from the Prophets and Plato and from the guru who traces his ethic to the Bhagavad-Gita.

A Religious Perspective

- Peter Brown, professor of classics and history at the University of California at Berkeley—"The deep religious anger of the Prophet Muhammad at what he saw around him, wealth squandered, the weak oppressed, the insensitive pride of the well-fed. The Prophet's clear and chilling message: The possible perfection of a human being, living at ease with his fellows."
- Abraham Heschel, an Old Testament historian—The prophets were "intent on intensifying responsibility." They were "impatient of excuse, contemptuous of pretense and self pity." They "felt fiercely" and were "attuned to a cry imperceptible to others."
- Will Campbell, an activist minister with the Committee of Southern Churchmen—"Jesus judges us by what we do to the children, the prisoners, the whores, the addicts, the scared and the bewildered—to the 'least of them.'"
- Genesis, Chapter 18—The Lord tells Abraham that he will destroy Sodom and Gomorrah for their sins. "Wilt thou also destroy the righteous with the wicked?" asks Abraham. No, the Lord replies, "I will not destroy it for ten's sake." But ten righteous men could not be found. (The point is the same one that philosophers have made through the generations: The individual has an inescapable moral obligation to society. On him or her may depend its salvation and survival.)

"Life is the referent of value," says Allen Wheelis, a psychiatrist and a writer about moral issues. "What enlarges and enriches life is good; what diminishes and endangers life is evil." If we define life as physical survival and apply Wheelis's referent to one of the immediate problems of industrial societies, we can conclude that factories and automobiles that poison the air are bad. To preserve an atmosphere we can breathe is good. Industries that endanger the lives of their workers or nearby residents are bad. Safety procedures—or plant closures if this cannot be accomplished—are good.

Journalists have revealed many of these unsafe and life-threatening conditions. Water supplies contaminated by industrial waste and land that is permeated with toxic materials have been the subject of diligent journalism.

But the factory and plant owners and the automobile manufacturers have opposed strict environmental protection standards. To clean up a plant, to make a car that does not emit pollutants, to make a process safe in the factory would be costly, so costly the price of the car would have to be increased or so expensive the plant might have to shut down, owners have told the press. This means unemployment, a loss of taxes to the local community, a decline in business where the plant or factory is located. No wonder that workers, whose health is at stake, often are adamantly opposed to proposals for safety, clean air and clean water.

Is it the responsibility of the journalist to continue to point out that the factory is polluting or poisoning the air? Or does the reporter turn elsewhere to relieve the pressure on public officials to force industry to abide by clean air laws or to enact such laws? If attention is turned elsewhere, jobs may be saved, the profits of the company assured and taxes kept low.

The dilemma for the professional is not new. The playwright Henrik Ibsen describes it in *An Enemy of the People.* Dr. Thomas Stockman, medical officer of the municipal baths, a considerable tourist attraction, discovers that the baths—the source of the town's economic resurgence—are being poisoned by the nearby tanneries. He wants to close them as a menace to public health.

But the community leaders and the local newspaper editor point out that any revelation about the pollution will lead people to shun the baths, and this will cause serious economic problems, among them unemployment and higher tax rates for property owners. Dr. Stockman is reviled as an enemy of the people.

The practical concerns of a money-based society have occupied many writers. Dickens' novels cry out against the "cash-nexus" as the "only bond between man and man," as one literary critic put it.

"Breathe the polluted air," Dickens says in *Dombey and Son.* "And then, calling up some ghastly child, with stunted form and wicked face, hold forth on its unnatural sinfulness, and lament its being, so early, far away from Heaven—but think a little of its being conceived, and born, and bred, in Hell!"

If "life is the referent of value," what other choice has the professional whose reason for being is service to the public than to see and to speak out so that others may see and understand. In the calculus of values, life means more than the bottom line on a ledger sheet. Joseph Conrad said: "My task which I am trying to achieve is, by the power of the written word, to make you hear, make you feel—it is, before all, to make you *see.* That—and no more, and it is everything."

Harold Fruchtbaum, a Columbia University social scientist, describes as "one of the intellectual's primary functions" the task of placing "responsibility for the failures of our society on the people and the institutions that control the society." Translated into a moral concern for the journalist, this is the task of holding power accountable, whether the power be held by a president or a school superintendent.

Given these broad guidelines, the journalist can have some idea of how to direct his or her coverage.

Are there additional guidelines that we can find, some of more obviously direct use to the journalist? Through an examination of a few of the practical problems reporters face we may find some.

To Print or Not to Print

• In the six weeks of a libel trial against the San Francisco *Examiner* for $30 million, there was minimal coverage by the Bay Area news organizations. There was one brief spot on KPIX-TV, another on a local public television news show and a feature in the San Francisco *Chronicle,* which ran four weeks after the trial began. Why was there so little coverage?

"It wasn't a terribly good television story," the news director of one television station said. It could not be squeezed into the station's 90-seconds-per-story format, she said. The *Chronicle's* city editor said the story was of greater interest to reporters than to the general public.

One of the defendants gave another reason. "The story was sensitive and complex—and it didn't include the raciness of the stories they like." It was also embarrassing to the *Examiner*. The suit involved a story alleging illegal actions by law enforcement officers in a murder case.

• Mike Royko, the *Chicago Sun-Times* syndicated columnist, was arrested on charges of speeding and driving while intoxicated. The story was carried by the competing *Chicago Tribune*, local television stations and the UPI's national wire. The *Sun-Times* did not carry the story because of "simple news judgment," according to the newspaper's editor.

• The news shocked the people of Missoula. The 21-year-old daughter of a respected couple in the Montana community of 60,000 had been stabbed to death outside her downtown Washington, D.C., apartment house. The only daughter of one of the city's best-known families, she had been a high school honor student and an accomplished musician and had won a scholarship to Radcliffe. Her father was a music teacher at two local high schools and a director of the Missoula Youth Symphony.

Less than a week later, the managing editor of *The Missoulian,* a 32,500 circulation daily in the city, had an even more shocking story on his desk: The young woman had been a streetwalker in Washington, "a $50-a-trick prostitute" who "used to talk freely about her work and bragged about being 'a pro,' " according to a story *The Washington Post* planned to run the next day under the headline, "A Life of Promise that Took a Strange and Fatal Turn." The *Post* had learned she had returned to Missoula after dropping out of Radcliffe and one night in a bar she had been approached by a man who asked her to return with him to the East. He was a pimp who recruited young women around the country.

Rod Deckert, the managing editor of *The Missoulian,* was confronted with a difficult decision. If he ran the story, the family would suffer new anguish. If he did not, he would be suppressing news that was bound to get back to town anyway since the *Post* was moving the story on its news service wire and papers distributed in Missoula and nearby might carry the dramatic story of a small-town girl come to a sordid end in the East. It was, Deckert said, "the most painful day in my 11 years of life in the newsroom." Jack Hart and Janis Johnson recount the story in "Fire Storm in Missoula" in the May 1979 *Quill.*

Deckert reasoned that the description of the young woman's experience could be a warning to other young women in the university community. Again, however, he had to weigh the value of the story against the pain it would cause the family and friends.

Deckert decided to run an edited version of *The Washington Post* story with some locally-gathered inserts. Deckert played the story down. It ran on page 12 with no art under an eight-column headline. The last paragraph reads:

"She was a pretty nice girl," said Officer Geary Scott, who arrested (her) under the name Mika Jenson, and charged her with soliciting for prostitution November 9, 1977. She was convicted the following December.

The Silent College Daily

• In the early 1970s, college health services made a right angle turn. Long accustomed to being charged with a lack of concern for the needs of students—aspirin was a favorite prescription, according to students—the health services began to become important treatment centers for sexual and psychiatric problems. Sex counseling, contraception, abortion referral, venereal disease treatment and help with various emotional problems were provided. Some colleges set up separate gynecological clinics.

There was little opposition from parents and trustees and regents in many places, but at the University of Michigan, the student journalists at *The Michigan Daily* were concerned that the Board of Regents might object if publicity were given to the introduction of contraception information and birth control devices in the health service. The *Daily* decided not to run a story on the contraception clinic.

• Sylvia Porter, a financial columnist with an estimated 31 million readers in 350 newspapers, admitted in one column that she had information about internal problems in the financial community that could have had damaging consequences to it and that she had held back on printing the information for fear she might start "a panic."

To criticism that her job as a journalist required that she go into the matter, she replied, "If you're going to be an analyst and a columnist on economic life, don't you think you have a responsibility not to bring the whole structure down?"

• A local businessman died, and in preparing his obituary, the reporter noticed that the man had once been a county official and 30 years before had been convicted after a fund shortage was discovered in his office. He was given six months probation. Since that time, he had married, raised a family and had become a respected businessman. His life for 30 years apparently had been exemplary. Should the conviction be included in the obituary? *The* Louisville *Courier-Journal* decided to put it in. Several days later, the editor decided he had made a mistake and apologized to the family.

• In the mid-1950s, movie houses in downtown Tampa removed all racial barriers and blacks were no longer restricted to the balconies. The Tampa newspapers did not print anything about the change. The managing editor of one of the papers explained to Professor Arthur M. Sanderson of the University of South Florida in Tampa, "If we had announced this policy in our newspapers, we would have encouraged every redneck in four counties to roar into town that night in his pickup truck, armed with a baseball bat or a shotgun, and we could have had a riot on our hands."

A number of southern editors made the same decision when public schools were desegregated in the 50s.

Racial Identification

• The UPI moved a story about an unemployed Detroit automobile worker in the 1970s who said in an interview he had been reduced to eating popcorn for breakfast and had only a bottle of water in his refrigerator. He was drawing $165 a week in unemployment benefits. He was identified as a black. His apartment, the story continued, had two TV sets, a new, uncrated encyclopedia set and little furniture. He said he was ready to turn to crime if his needs were not met. When the *St. Petersburg Times* ran the story, readers protested, saying the story should not have been printed. Some said it belittled blacks. In his reply, editor Eugene C. Patterson said:

> The rationale for printing this story was to introduce to our readers an American who thought $165 a week was poverty. I found it a highly instructive story. The picture it gave is one reality of American life. To keep reality from our readers, because it might upset them, would be to serve them very poorly indeed. We print the news not because we necessarily agree with it, but because we judge it is significant that our readers know about it. Readers would get furious if a newspaper blinded them to news.

• In the mid-1970s, a Boston physician was convicted of manslaughter after he performed an abortion in the second trimester of a woman's pregnancy. Coming during a period of intense debate between pro- and anti-abortion groups, the story aroused national interest. Race and religion figured in the legal situation, as well as the volatile issue of abortion. Here are the comments of H. L. Stevenson, editor-in-chief of the UPI in answer to a criticism of a UPI story:

> Several letters have taken us to task for failing to make clear that Dr. Kenneth C. Edelin, involved in the Boston abortion case, is black. The jury which convicted him was all-white and predominantly Roman Catholic, another fact subordinated in our stories on the verdict.
> "If any previous stories from UPI referred to his race, we all missed it," writes John McCormally, editor and publisher of *The Hawk Eye* in Burlington, Iowa. "Was the downplay of race and religion deliberate by UPI?"
> There was no deliberate attempt to suppress these facts.
> Our feeling—and those involved in the coverage have been advised—is that the racial and religious identification was pertinent to this sensitive story. These facts should have been reported more prominently.

National Security

• In 1961, *The New York Times* withheld on security grounds publication of information it possessed about an impending U.S.-sponsored invasion of Cuba. In another international issue Jack Anderson came into possession of letters and memoranda said to be from the internal files of the International Telephone & Telegraph Company that showed the firm's effort to enlist the U.S. government's support to prevent Salvador Allende, a Marxist, from taking office as president of Chile. The publication would have embarrassed the United States in Latin America. Anderson printed the information.

• During my stint as correspondent in Central America, I sent stories to *The Christian Science Monitor* from Nicaragua detailing U.S. cooperation with the Somoza dictatorship. The foreign editor was concerned that the articles would feed growing anti-U.S. sentiment in the area and considered not publishing the material. Finally, the editor agreed that the stories merited publication, despite their implications. The editor's worries proved accurate. The stories were picked up by some Latin American newspapers to prove that the United States was an opponent of political, social and economic reform in Latin America.

• *The Progressive* magazine, which has described the concept of national security as the government's way of stifling open debate about important matters such as the arms race, in 1978 approved an idea for an article by a 36-year-old former Air Force captain about the hydrogen bomb. The free-lance writer, Howard Morland, said he wanted to show that the so-called "secret" of the construction of the bomb was no secret. Morland had been an economics major at Emory University, then a Vietnam War transport pilot (he flew aluminum coffins across the Pacific) and then an anti-nuclear activist. Morland visited plants where the components of the bomb are put together, and he read vast amounts of literature on the subject.

The Progressive scheduled Morland's article for the April 1979 issue under the title "The H-Bomb Secret: How We Got It, Why We're Telling It."

His point, Morland said, "is that the myth of secrecy is used to create an atmosphere in which public debate is stifled and public criticism of the weapons production system is suppressed. I hope to dramatically illustrate that thesis by showing that what many people considered to be probably the ultimate secret is not really a secret at all. The information is easily available to anyone who wants to acquire it."

The editor of *The Progressive,* Erwin Knoll, knew that the penalty for publishing restricted information is severe—prison and a fine. On the advice of his attorney, he sent the piece to the Department of Energy, which found that it contained restricted data and said all the drawings and 20 percent of the article would have to be removed.

As is often the case in moral dilemmas, the choice was between two courses of action that seem legitimate: To publish and expose the vast "nuclear warhead assembly line," as Morland put it, or to accede to the government and not risk the further proliferation of nuclear weapons by divulging possibly secret information.

Knoll decided on publication. The government asked for a restraining order (which was granted), the first injunction to suppress publication of an article in American history and the first case of prior restraint since the Pentagon Papers case eight years before, in 1971. (Knoll later said he regretted not having gone ahead with publication and risking prison instead of first seeking clearance from the Department of Energy.)

The press was divided on Knoll's attempt to publish the article. Many newspapers felt that the case was not important enough to risk further restrictive action by the Supreme Court. (The editorial positions themselves are a case study in morality.) In September 1979, the government dropped its prosecution of the magazine. The piece was published.

A Few Conclusions

Should these articles have been printed? Some generalizations are in order. Clearly the journalist speaks to all, for all. That is, the journalist's concern is the public, not the special interest. On matters that require the balancing of the press's self-interest (the San Francisco *Examiner* libel case) or the interest of a special group (Sylvia Porter's financial community) against the general interest, the latter should prevail. Defining the public or general interest is not easy, for, as some maintain, there is no public interest but a melange of special interests. But there are concerns shared by most people, and access to information is one of the basic needs of a democratic society.

The omission of news because of a station's format or a newspaper's involvement would seem to be immoral. True enough, there are special-interest publications that omit vast areas of news. But for newspapers and broadcast stations that serve the general public, the public interest takes priority. To whom was Porter responsible? In a conflict of choices, does she choose the public or the financial community?

The journalist with an overly acute sense of responsibility is sometimes as dangerous as the recklessly irresponsible reporter. A scrupulous regard for every interest can work to the disregard of the general interest. Too great solicitude can come close to cronyism in its consequences.

When *The* Louisville *Courier-Journal* printed the conviction of the deceased former county official, however, it did disregard a personal interest (the family's) for the general interest. Yet what was the general interest that was served? Disclosure of a crime of small magnitude committed 30 years before by a person who is dead seems to serve no end at all but the purpose—often sound enough—of full disclosure. If our goal is truth, and truth is served by presenting all the facts, then certainly we are on sound moral ground if we include this unsavory but factual detail in the obituary. But the journalist knows that he or she can never hope to learn everything about an event, that the most diligent reporting can never do more than approximate the truth. Moreover, the journalist is forced to select for use from this limited stockpile of information the few facts that can be fitted into the restricted time and space allocations. In this selection process, the journalist applies to the material the tests of utility, relevance and significance within a value system.

Many agencies and groups do take on themselves the task of providing full disclosure. The *Congressional Record*, minutes of council meetings, court transcripts and the like are available. But the journalist must summarize, condense, choose. Applying a value system to the county official's crime, we see that it adds little of significance to the story, for the crime was minor—the six months probation indicates that—and the man appeared to redeem himself. Although redemption is handled by another calling, journalists should consider compassion in their work.

Had the crime been well known at the time of the man's death, the journalist would have served no purpose in ignoring it. What the public knows the press cannot skip over. This could also apply to the Missoula case. There was no way the community would remain ignorant of the death of the young woman. Had the newspaper failed to run some story, accusations could have been made that the newspaper showed partiality to a middle-class family while day after day it chronicles the troubles of others less affluent and influential. The newspaper might have handled the story with an editor's note admitting its dilemma. Then the violent reaction—the newspaper's editorial writer condemned the story and scores of people protested by calls and cancellations—might have been avoided or alleviated. (Krajick's dilemma might have been less intense had he considered such an editor's note. Although readers need not be told the reporter's problems too often, situations such as these can be less troublesome with full disclosure.)

Suppose the Missoula newspaper alone had learned that the young woman died a prostitute. Should it have included the fact in its story? If her work had been an inextricable part of the crime, there would have been no way to avoid it. But she had been found dead near her apartment house, the victim of an unknown assailant. No newspaper dredges up every aspect of an individual's life for a story about a person's death, whether for an obituary or a straight news story.

In the first draft of this section, I used the woman's name, the instinctive reaction of a journalist to supply basic information. Surely, in a book that seeks to examine a subject in detail, the name would seem to be relevant. But is it? What does it add to the information necessary to understand the situation? Nothing, it would seem. It would appear to be information for the sake of information, which has some merit. But balance this against the damage revelation could cause. This textbook is used at the University of Montana and it could be the inadvertent cause of grief to the family. Still, there is a principle no journalist can turn from: What the public knows or will learn, the journalist cannot ignore. Surely, after the newspaper ran the story, most people in town knew the identity of the young woman. But the story is now a few years old.

The internal argument can continue indefinitely. Unlike the philosopher, who may spin out syllogisms for a lifetime, the journalist must act quickly. My decision in this case was against disclosure.

The principle that what the public will learn itself the journalist must tell if the event is significant could apply to the Tampa theaters, school desegregation in the South and the University of Michigan newspaper's decision to ignore the health clinic story. An event of considerable magnitude in the community soon becomes common knowledge, and the newspaper ignores the event at its peril. This is a pragmatic argument, but it has theoretical validity in that the journalist tends toward disclosure on the ground that publication usually serves a community better than does self-censorship, which permits rumor mongering.

It strains credulity to believe that the university regents and trustees would not have known of the clinics and that the so-called redneck would not soon hear of the changes in racial practices. True, publication can call attention to subjects people know about but prefer to ignore until they are forced to recognize the subjects. The stories might have been played down. But they cannot be ignored. These are significant events, and the journalist's task is also that of recorder of important events.

There will always be people who react and over-react to the word. The reporter who writes straight-forward accounts of events may indeed feed the fires of bigotry and violence. Not to print important news on occasion may seem responsible at first glance. But such decisions do corrode the journalist's moral injunction to be the carrier of information, bad and good. In the area of racial news, much has changed since newspapers gingerly approached racial and ethnic groups.

A dozen years ago, in a roundup on the ways the press was handling racial news, *The Wall Street Journal* summarized the journalist's dilemma:

> If the press hews to its ideals and holds a mirror up to society, reflecting all its evils, cankers and tensions as well as its virtues, it runs the risk of stirring dangerous passions. But if it deliberately distorts the image or blots out the parts that might inflame, it casts itself in the dubious role of censor and judge.

Some newspapers and stations, the *Journal* reported, had taken on self-censorship. Some agreed to arrangements whereby news of racial disturbances would be delayed. Most said they strove to be careful in handling sensitive racial news but would not limit coverage. "It is the public, not the press, that must in the end find a way out of racial crisis, they argue—and the public can't be expected to do that unless the press gives it an accurate picture of society, warts and all," the *Journal* stated.

The maxim that if a story about race is not positive it should not be carried has been discarded. The black poet Langston Hughes used to remark that he would know television—and society—had matured when TV shows could portray a black as a liar, a cheat or a criminal.

Progress is being made. In Salt Lake City, the National Association for the Advancement of Colored People (NAACP) condemned a state health department film on teen-age pregnancy—not because it portrayed minority teen-agers having illegitimate children, but because it did not.

"All the actors are white. Minority teens get pregnant too," the president of the local NAACP chapter said.

Stories involving national security pose complicated questions. But the experience of the press during periods of crisis—the Korean and Vietnam Wars, the Cuban invasion, the cold war following World War II—destroyed "the unspoken alliance between journalists and the government," as Thomson put it. Reporters learned that the government had systematically misled or lied to them on crucial issues. The government, reporters found, not only misled them about the facts but covered up by pulling the cloak of national security over matters of legitimate public concern.

A Journalist's Moral Framework

- Loyalty to the facts. "You inevitably develop an intense sense of revulsion or a mild attachment for one candidate or the other," said Joseph Alsop, Jr., a political writer. "But you have to be loyal to the facts or lose your reputation." John Dewey put it this way: "Devotion to fact, to truth, is a necessary moral demand."
- An involvement in the affairs of men and women that requires experiencing or witnessing directly the lives of human beings. Involvement generates compassion, which Thomson in his article on ethics in the *Nieman Reports* lists along with accuracy and fairness as guidelines for ethical journalistic conduct.
- The ability to distance one's self from experience to generate understanding. Antonio Gramsci, an Italian writer imprisoned by Mussolini for his commitment to freedom, said he had to learn the necessity of being "above the surroundings within which one lives, but without despising them or believing one's self superior to them."
- A reverence for rules, codes, laws and arrangements that give a sense of community. Such concern causes the journalist to keep careful watch for any action that can divide people into hostile groups, classes or races.
- Faith in experience when intelligently used as a means of disclosing some truths.
- An avoidance of a value-less objectivity. This kind of objectivity can lead to what philosopher Stuart Hampshire describes as an "ice age of not caring." He writes that this approach can lead to the end of civilization "not in a flurry of egotism and appetite leading to conflict . . . but in passivity and non-attachment, in a general spreading coldness. . . ."
- A willingness "to hold belief in suspense, the ability to doubt until evidence is obtained, the willingness to go where the evidence points instead of putting first a personally preferred conclusion; ability to hold ideas in solution and use them as hypotheses instead of dogmas to be asserted; and (possibly the most distinctive of all) enjoyment of new fields for inquiry and of new problems."—John Dewey.
- Belief in the methods of journalism—the gathering of relevant material and evaluation of those facts through analysis and the synthesizing of them in the story. Conviction that this method will lead to some kind of truth worth sharing.
- A moral vision of the future. "If you don't have that vision," says the Indian writer Ved Mehta, "sooner or later the system will collapse." Without a moral vision, the journalist's compulsion may be power, profit and place in society.

When the public cannot help guide national and foreign policy by choosing from alternatives openly presented, tyranny follows. In so-called national security matters, only one voice is heard—that of the state.

Clearly, the government cannot disclose all it knows. But who is to decide what protects the state and what protects the policy maker, what secrets are crucial to survival of the nation and what undisclosed truths protect an administration in office? The state says it shall decide. The press says history indicates that as irresponsible as the press may well have proved itself at times, press disclosure is the least dangerous alternative in a democracy. Support of South Korea or a Somoza, the nuclear arms buildup and arms pacts are debatable policy. But without disclosure of all information there can be no informed debate. The logic and the morality of democracy call for publication.

Knowledge as a Value

The journalist cannot in conscience be passive about a threat to public awareness. "If you are among brigands and you are silent, you are a brigand yourself," an Hungarian poem tells us. The brigands come in all shapes and sizes. Some are treated leniently by the press because they appear not to know what they do, censoring books and movies for what they truly believe is the public welfare. Others play on that part of us that fears knowing too much.

But the journalist must recognize these as threats to an immanent value, the necessity of knowing, of having information that will liberate us from ignorance, prejudice and the limitations of time and place.

This does not mean that journalists use everything they can find. All facts are not equal, and other values come into play in the selection of what is to be published and broadcast. But when the source is closed—as has been the tendency in vast areas of criminal matters from indictment through trial and imprisonment—the possibility of knowing is denied.

Every commentator about values in a democracy has agreed that the open society is a perilous one. When all the winds of doctrine are set loose, the turbulence can be overwhelming. The world since 1945 has seen democratic nations that were born in optimism succumb to the tyrant who promises order. The journalist hardly contributes to order, for the journalist's task is to broadcast widely competing ideas and doctrines. It is also the journalist's task, some journalists believe, to maintain an adversary relationship to the centers of power.

Adversary Journalism

Journalists are undecided on the adversary position. The choice is an important one, for how one approaches power determines much of the reporter's coverage. James Reston, a long-time Washington correspondent and columnist for *The New York Times,* said in a series of lectures before the Council of Foreign Affairs that "the rising power of the United States in world affairs, and particularly of the American president, requires not a more compliant press, but a relentless barrage of facts and criticism, as noisy but also as accurate as artillery fire. . . .

"Our job in this age, as I see it, is not to serve as cheerleaders for our side in the present world struggle, but to help the largest possible number of people to see the realities of the changing and convulsive world in which American policy must operate. . . ."

Yet when President Johnson in 1965 appealed to the nation's patriotism as he committed ground troops to Vietnam—an appeal for national unity so that "the enemy" would not be encouraged by the spectacle of a divided nation—Reston went along. Walter Lippmann did not.

Lippmann said:

If the president's version of history is correct, it follows that when there is an issue of war and peace, the only safe and patriotic course is to suspend debate and rally round the president. . . . It amounts to saying that debate on the vital issues of war and peace gives aid and comfort to the enemy. . . . This is an impossible course for a free people. . . . How else but by debate are the great questions of war and peace—of isolation and intervention and of military expansion onto the Asian continent—to be decided?

Increasingly, governments seek the cooperation, even the compliance, of the press. The reaction of the American Society of Newspaper Editors at its 1980 convention indicated the distance editors seek to put between their newspapers and the government. When the head of the Central Intelligence Agency, the U.S.'s spy service, told editors he reserves the right to enlist journalists in secret missions, the editors vigorously protested. Not only would it endanger reporters' lives, they said, it would make questionable the integrity of their reports. The editors stated that their reporters need to be what they represent themselves as, independent seekers after information for the public. In response to the charge that such a position is unpatriotic, which some editors said the agency head had implied, *The New York Times* stated in an editorial:

There is no higher service for a free press than to operate openly and independently to inform all Americans, including the intelligence agencies. That, too, is serving the nation. As Justice Hugo Black once observed, the press is "one of the very agencies the Framers of our Constitution thoughtfully and deliberately selected to improve our society and keep it free. That worthy ideal cannot be pursued if the line between the American press and the American government is so dangerously blurred."

The comment of the Italian journalist Oriana Fallaci may seem to trivialize the choice between adversary journalism and compliance with power, but it actually gets to the heart of the matter. She said, "Almost every time I have tried to absolve even partially some famous son-of-a-bitch, I have been bitterly sorry." After *The New York Times* had gone along with "national security" interests to keep secret President Kennedy's plans to invade the Bay of Pigs in Cuba in 1961, it confessed its decision had been wrong.

Journalists make these decisions with care and concern. Sometimes, their concern overcomes their journalism, as is the case early in the terms of most presidents. During Ronald Reagan's first year in office, *New York Times* columnist Anthony Lewis pointed to the massive Reagan budget deficit, the recession, the lack of a consistent foreign policy and an insensitivity to problems of race and poverty—all common knowledge in Washington. But "the press still holds back from giving an unvarnished picture of this president," Lewis wrote.

Lewis said the Washington press corps had refused to examine Reagan's competence. Why? Lewis's answer reveals journalists to be all-too-human:

"They care about their country, and they find it too upsetting to acknowledge—to the pubic or to themselves—that the enormous power of its leadership is in such hands."

The Democratic Commitment

The journalist who is committed to the open society, to democratic values, has a moral structure from which to work. It seems clear that the journalist must be alert to institutions and their activities that threaten the right of everyone to take part justly, equally and freely in some kind of meaningful community life. Any word or deed that denies this way of life to people because of their sex, age, race, origin, religion or position in society must be revealed by the journalist, who is committed to the democratic institutions in the society. We are here expanding our concept of "life as the referent of value" from simple physical survival to a way of life.

When *Times* columnist Lewis learned that the Nixon administration had made a deal with Vice President Spiro Agnew for his resignation in return for the promise of a non-prison sentence on his plea of "no contest" to a felony, he wrote that this was the correct action. It was right, Lewis said, on "political grounds: the need to investigate the president's wrongdoing without having as his potential successor someone who was himself under indictment."

But Lewis then had second thoughts. They followed the sentencing to prison of two businessmen whose confession of corrupt payments had led to Agnew's resignation from the vice presidency. "So they go to prison," Lewis wrote, "while the sleazy felon who soiled our politics earns $100,000 in his new career as 'business broker.'" Instead of trusting the democratic institutions of law and politics to work, Lewis wrote, the attorney general had made personal policy.

"That unhappy precedent was carried further in the pardon of Richard Nixon," he wrote. "Of course, Watergate is not alone in examples of law applied unequally. It is commonplace, and terribly damaging to our system of criminal justice, for the powerful to go free while the little wrongdoers go to prison."

In writing about the American philosopher John Dewey, Sidney Hook said that Dewey believed

> . . . the logic of democracy requires the elimination of economic, ethnic, religious and educational injustices if the freedom of choice presupposed by the ethos of democracy is to be realized.
>
> One man, one vote is not enough—if one man can arbitrarily determine the livelihood of many others, determine where and under what conditions they can live, determine what they can read on the press or hear on the air.

Dewey also believed that the community has the responsibility for eliminating hunger and poverty, that political power must be harnessed to solve the problems of group and individual welfare. Economic conditions must be such, he wrote, that the equal right of all to free choice and free action is achieved.

"Democracy means the belief that humanistic culture *should* prevail; we should be frank and open in our recognition that the proposition is a moral one—like any idea that concerns what *should* be," Dewey wrote.

Along with the general value systems we have discussed, the journalist must have some specific guidelines for application in particular situations. An examination of several incidents may help us to develop these guidelines.

The Pose and the Disguise

Reporters have disguised themselves as priests and policemen, as doctors and distraught relatives to get stories. Some of the great coups in journalism have come through lying and deception. Many of these stories made banner headlines, though they were of little significance. Although many of the questionable methods are now used for laudable ends—usually the exposure of corruption—questions have been raised about some of the methods. Should a reporter impersonate a policeman to pass through a police line? Did Raymond R. Coffey of *The Chicago Daily News* act responsibly in disguising himself as a student to gain access to the University of Mississippi campus to cover a student race riot?

If a reporter defends his or her act on the grounds that the events were of public interest, this means that the journalist, not the authority, is the judge of public interest. Is this proper? Clearly, vested interests have always sought to keep their activities secret and the press has served the public by breaking through barriers. Is there a dividing line we can locate between permissible deception and irresponsible impersonation? Is the line located at the point where an adversary press checks power to serve the legitimate public interest? If so, how is "legitimate public interest" defined?

Deception has had a long and, until recently, an honorable journalistic history. In 1886, a young and ambitious reporter who called herself Nellie Bly feigned insanity to enter a mental hospital and exposed inhuman conditions in the hospital. Ninety years later, a reporter from *The Washington Post* gained admission to St. Elizabeth's, a federal hospital in Washington D.C., with the same ruse. One of the most revealing and dramatic books about life for blacks in the South, *Black Like Me,* was written by a white man, John Howard Griffin, who darkened his skin to pass as a black.

The Mirage Watering Hole and Pub

In 1978, *Chicago Sun-Times* reporters won several prizes for their exposé of abortion mills that were endangering women's lives. The reporters posed as women in need of abortions. A complex subterfuge was worked by the same newspaper when it purchased a bar, staffed it with reporters and photographers and set out to gather proofs of payoffs and corruption. The newspaper obtained considerable information that led to reforms of the city inspection system, and the series was recognized with a number of journalism awards. But when the articles were recommended for a Pulitzer Prize in 1979 by the Pulitzer Prize jury, some members of the advisory board considered the operation of the Mirage Bar a deception.

Benjamin Bradlee, the executive editor of *The Washington Post* and a Pulitzer Board member, asked, "How can newspapers fight for honesty and integrity when they themselves are less than honest in getting a story?" Eugene C. Patterson, another board member, also objected, saying that the *Sun-Times* reporters should have interviewed bar owners. "That would have been the hard way to get the story," he said, implying that deception was the easy way out. (The Pulitzer board did not award a prize to the *Sun-Times* for the Mirage stories, although it stated it did not reject them on the ethics issue because it did not want to set a precedent for future entries.)

Interviewing bar owners—if they would have talked, which seems unlikely—does not provide the physical evidence investigative reporters always seek to support their stories. The accounts of human sources—here, the bar owners—are never as convincing as the physical evidence. But the requirements of journalism, as we have seen in the case of the San Francisco television station that could not fit the libel trial into its 90-second format, do not weigh heavily in balancing moral choices.

Is Bradlee's point—that the consequences of deception are damaging to the press—valid? One of the basic tests of an action is its consequences. If the action would have damaging consequences to individuals, it should probably not be taken. But in this case, the damage is to the press, and journalists are supposed to take risks to publish truths. But Bradlee's argument does have validity in that no person or group can claim exemption from the rules that the individual or group would set for others, unless that exception were so essential no other choice is possible. We do not condemn the physician for deceiving the terminally ill patient when he keeps the truth from the patient. In the case of the poses to expose Chicago bar inspectors or abortion mills, these arguments could be made:

1. If we adopt a disguise, we can help to reform the city inspection system or close down substandard abortion mills that endanger the lives of women. It may not be a moral tactic, posing, but the ends justify the means. We are acting morally because we are trying to right a wrong in our exposé.
2. To pose is wrong. It misleads persons who may take us into their confidence to tell us things they would not if they knew we were reporters. It treats persons as means. A corollary to the principle of life as a referent of value is that we may not treat a person as a thing to be used for the purpose of another. Here, for our purposes, for a story, we would be treating persons as things.

   But not to pose would mean we might not dig up the story, and if our function is to expose wrong then we are immoral in not acting.

If we use life as the referent for testing the moral validity of actions, then posing to gain access to health clinics may be reasonable and responsible since lives are involved. But the adoption of poses for routine stories would appear unjustified. The reporter who disguises himself as a health seeker to gain access to the tent of a faith healer may have greater claim to moral justification than the reporter who poses as a customer to expose a massage parlor as a front for prostitution.

We can apply some of these guidelines, and others you may design, to the following incidents:

Neva Flaherty of the Rochester *Times-Union* wore a wig and sunglasses to a town court to observe a judge without being recognized. "This was a public court session, so I didn't feel I was violating any rules or principles." She sought to capture the judge as he was, not as he would have been had he recognized the reporter in the courtroom.

On another story, Flaherty was forced, she said, to adopt a pose to work her way into a pyramid sales operation. She had gone to the session thinking there would be a large crowd and she could just listen. Instead, there were five spectators and five salesmen present.

"So I found myself making up a fake identity on the spot in a one-to-one conversation with a salesman. I didn't feel guilty about lying."

But she said she would not pose as an official, a lawyer or violate "laws and rules" in her posing. "When pressed to defend these tactics, editors and journalists usually say that the public's right to know justifies the breach of law," she said. "But the end-justifies-the-means argument was the same one Nixon's aides used throughout the Watergate cover-up and to justify illegal break-ins to get information on dissenters."

Flaherty's point about justifying apparently unethical techniques on the ground that the end justifies the means takes us back to the Mirage Bar story. There, we concluded that the reporter could not justify acts that he or she would condemn in others—unless the exemption were crucial.

One of the time-tested guides to behavior is Immanuel Kant's categorical imperative: "Act as if the maxim from which you act were to become through your will a universal law of nature."

Kant had another imperative: "So act as to treat humanity, whether in your own person or that of another, in every case as an end in itself, never as a means." Kant (1724–1804) was one of the great figures in the history of philosophy, and although his prescriptions for ethical behavior may appear old fashioned at first glance, their application can help to resolve some of the sticky moral questions journalists face.

In a sense, people are always means to the journalist's end, which is the news story. Even when deception is not used, the reporter maneuvers and manipulates sources to his or her end. The reporter justifies this on the ground that such actions serve useful purposes, even for the source since the individual is a member of the society that is being served by the reporter.

Here are additional examples of journalistic deception:

The Washington Bureau chief of *The Detroit News,* decided to witness the signing of the Egyptian-Israeli peace treaty at the White House in 1979. The ceremony was closed to the press. The reporter posed as a member of Congress and boarded a bus set aside to carry Congressmen to the event. "All it took was one call, one question, a little observation and one lie to get a police-escorted ride," he said in an article for the *News.*

The Standing Committee of Correspondents, a panel of five reporters that oversees the accreditation of congressional reporters, reprimanded the reporter, calling his pose "a serious breach of journalistic ethics." The censure seems appropriate. The reporter's deception served no other purpose than to give him a close-up view of a pseudo-event.

Mike Albertson, investigative editor of the *Pensacola* (Fla.) *Journal,* describes a story his newspaper covered:

> In Pensacola, during the Christmas holidays, a nightclub operator was putting customers in contact with a supplier of "cheap" quality perfume; a two-ounce bottle of Chanel No. 5 could be bought for $8. The perfume proved bogus. Tipped off, a reporter went to the nightclub and arranged a "buy." He told the nightclub owner his real name but faked his occupation. After buying the perfume and confirming through chemical analysis it was a fake, the reporter confronted the nightclub owner.
> "That's not fair!" argued the nightclub owner. "You didn't tell me you worked for a newspaper!" True, and it probably wasn't "ethical," but it saved scores of unsuspecting citizens from buying fake perfume at that nightclub and, as it turned out, other places as well.

Albertson says that if reporters were not allowed to hide their identities, it would "eliminate at least half the major investigative stories that have ever been written." This may be so. But the question the reporter must always ask is whether the story is of such importance that it justifies the exception to the moral injunction against deception. Few stories pass this test.

For their article on the campus health service, three student reporters at Northern Illinois University feigned illnesses and one gave the name of another student. They pretended to suffer from nervousness, anxiety and menstrual cramps. They reported that the doctors spent no more than 15 minutes with each of them and did not examine them or seek medical histories before prescribing tranquilizers, a sleeping medication and a barbiturate. The reporters for *The Northern Star* were criticized by the university for giving false information to officials but no formal action was taken. The university later announced that a panel of medical experts would examine the service to review "the quality of care exercised in prescribing medication" at the health service.

The Heifitz of the Telephone

One line of thinking that has allowed reporters an escape hatch from the moral dilemma presented by disguise, posing and deception is this: A reporter need not identify himself or herself as a reporter, and if a source presumes the person talking to him is not a reporter, so be it. An intentional disguise or pose would be deceptive and therefore unethical, but a telephone call asking for information need not be preceded by the reporter's identifying himself as a reporter. However, the techniques of Harry Romanoff of the defunct *Chicago American* would be prohibited by most editors.

Romanoff was known as "the Heifitz of the telephone" for his flawless performances. His greatest act of virtuosity was his coverage of the mass murder of eight student nurses in Chicago. Romanoff, who never left his desk to cover a story, extracted the details of the crime from a policeman by pretending to be the Cook County Coroner. He was also able to write a long story about the suspect, Richard Speck, by convincing Speck's mother that he was her son's lawyer.

Romanoff and others who have used deception to gather information usually do not disclose their tactics in their stories. Now it is considered responsible journalism to make full disclosure in the copy. Then the journalist can be held responsible for his or her tactics by an informed reader. A useful guideline: If the technique is such that it cannot be described in the story, then it is unworthy of use in the reporting.

There are some practical guidelines for the use of deception. Gary Seacrest, a lawyer for the Gannett newspapers, says "Reporters have to be very careful about how they obtain a story or a photograph. The use of deception is very risky. Journalists should identify themselves for what they are—reporters on assignment. This is crucial when a journalist invades a private place, but less important when operating in the public arena. Judges are often harsh on the imposter's technique."

Imposters come in different guises. The reporter who poses as a priest or a detective to reach a grieving widow is one form. The reporter who claims the work of another as his or her own is another.

During the 1970s and 1980s there was a surge in the incidents of plagiarism. Some reporters went so far as to fabricate incidents. A reporter for *The Washington Post* invented an eight-year-old heroin addict and wrote a harrowing tale that won the author a Pulitzer Prize in 1981. When the fraud was exposed, the reporter, Janet Cooke, said that the competitive pressure in the newsroom, the need to stand out, had led to her action.

Dishonesty

In their defense, some of these reporters contend their work should be judged like any creative writing—imaginative in detail but true in ultimate meaning. They say they have poetic license. Unfortunately for them, journalism issues no such licenses.

Others say they have been swept up in the head-long drive of journalism for ever-more fanciful writing. This does not exempt them from responsibility for their unethical actions, but there may be some legitimacy to this defense.

Some editors want clever writing above all else. They pressure their reporters to gloss over the facts that do not quite fit, to burnish the dull quotation so that it glistens. All of this is dishonest, and, says Roy Peter Clark of the Modern Media Institute, "Dishonest writing is bad writing, no matter how beautiful the style.

"We cannot tolerate self-indulgent over-writing, the creation of stereotypes, composite characters, improved quotations, rearranged facts, invented authorial presence or the omniscient looking into minds.

"If information is important it often needs attribution because we have a responsibility to let our readers know not only our knowledge, but the limits of our knowledge."

Clark added: "Good writing is not just a veneer to coat the facts. It is not style without substance. It is clarity, relevance, humanity and hard work."

The Anonymous Source

Reporters rely on their sources, but sometimes the price for information may be too high. When a reporter guarantees sources anonymity by quoting them without attribution, the reporter can be made an accessory to the management of the news. When he was secretary of state, Henry Kissinger used the press corps to aid his foreign policy. "He played the press like a cello," one reporter recalls. Not everything he said, or planted, turned out to be truthful. Indeed, some of his statements during the Vietnam War were calculated lies.

There is no problem with a reporter accepting information on a confidential basis if the material can be checked out and its accuracy independently determined. Then the reporter can attribute it in a story to other sources. However, the information offered on a not-for-attribution basis usually is non-verifiable. The reporter then bears some responsibility for the information he or she uses.

In the case of leaks, which often are planted to expose or injure, reporters often are asked to honor the source's anonymity. Again, if the material can be verified, a source can be found and named. If it is non-verifiable, the leak that makes accusations should not be used.

Individuals can do little to change the system of accepting material on a non-attribution or off-the-record basis. A single reporter who refuses to go along with a cabinet member or governor soon finds the desk shooting queries at him or her about missed stories. There are indications, however, that the not-for-attribution epidemic has gone too far and that some of the large press organizations are chafing at the arrangement and finding ways to eliminate it. *The Washington Post* ran an important story on U.S. foreign policy and quoted "an official speaking aboard Secretary of State Cyrus Vance's plane." Above the story was a two-column picture of a man with the cutline: "A senior U.S. official." To readers in this television age it was not difficult to know who was pictured—Cyrus Vance—and to identify him as the anonymous "official."

The Quid Pro Quo

Carl Bernstein says that while digging into the Watergate story he needed cooperation from the chief investigator for the Dade County (Fla.) state's attorney. To obtain it, Bernstein promised to dig up the military records of a man running against the state's attorney. A source in the Pentagon agreed to help Bernstein find out any material about mental illness, arrests or homosexuality. Bernstein says he did not have to transmit the information because the state's attorney decided he did not need it.

Jack Anderson describes how he turned over information to a good source, Senator Joseph McCarthy. In his book, *Confessions of a Muckraker* (New York: Random House, 1979), Anderson says that shortly after the senator made his famous speech in Wheeling, W. Va., in which he asserted he had the names of 205 Communists who were "shaping policy in the State Department," McCarthy asked Anderson's help. McCarthy had been challenged to produce the names. He did not have them, and he called on Anderson to gather some names.

"As I recall, the decision to help McCarthy was almost automatic," Anderson says. "I went to our files and pulled out what was the most promising." He said he told McCarthy the material was unsubstantiated. McCarthy found the material "terrific."

Anderson did not tell his boss, Drew Pearson, what he was doing but when Pearson decided to attack McCarthy as a witch hunter, Anderson tried to talk him out of it.

"He's our best source on the Hill," Anderson said.

"He may be a good source, Jack," Pearson said. "But he's a bad man."

Anderson stopped leaking to McCarthy, and soon began investigating the senator, and two years later wrote a book attacking McCarthy.

Jimmy Breslin is the most popular columnist in New York City. His columns in the New York *Daily News* are read by two million people a day. Breslin is courted by officials and politicians. In a column, he recalled the evening the governor of New York called on him for a favor.

They got together in a bar called Higgins. The governor, Hugh Carey, wanted Breslin's support for a congressman, Mario Biaggi, whose deals had given him the aroma of one of the flounders in the city's Fulton fish market.

"Biaggi's very important," Breslin said Carey told him. "We need his endorsement. One of the things he wants is a column rehabilitating him in the 'Daily News.' You could do that and it would be very important. We all have to have a little whore in us sometimes."

At the time, Breslin was known to favor a candidate in the city's mayoral primary, and the governor indicated he would find money for the candidate if the column appeared.

"Of course," wrote Breslin, "the conversation meant that I could not write anything with Biaggi's name on it for at least a couple of years. It is hard enough to put something together when it is your own idea. The dust hanging in the air begins to resemble words, and as you watch the light strike the dust, you think you can see the words falling into a lovely pattern, one that people would like to read, and then you reach out for these words and the dust is gone and you have a blank paper in front of you and now more dust dancing out of the air to taunt you. Therefore, the act of sitting and trying to write something that you don't want to is too painful."

This is a lyrical way for Breslin to make a simple point: No one in journalism makes a deal to cleanse anyone, whatever the enticement.

Many reporters swap information with their sources. But the Bernstein, Anderson and Breslin incidents put the reporter into a provocative role as the supplier of confidential information or publicity the source could not otherwise obtain. This is a dangerous role for a journalist to play, and an unethical one as well.

When Patrick Buchanan, now a columnist, worked for President Nixon, he twice leaked information to columnists Rowland Evans and Robert Novak about Senator Edmund S. Muskie that had been stolen from the Muskie presidential campaign and photographed. Clearly, Buchanan had an interest in eliminating Muskie as a potential candidate against Nixon. Did the columnists have an obligation to track down the full story and then to print the fact that the material had been filched from Muskie headquarters? Should a reporter accept stolen documents?

Other questions: Is it ethical to read material when a source leaves it unguarded; is there a difference between this and photographing the material? Should the press pay for information, engage in what some have called "checkbook journalism"?

Some working reporters might contend that anything that helps to develop a good story should not be rejected too hastily. Granted, so long as moral anarchy is not one of the alternatives in making a choice. In choosing between irreconcilably opposed moral claims, the choice can be defended with honor and dignity. The sociologist Max Weber said that when a man "is aware of a responsibility for the consequences of his conduct and really feels such responsibility with heart and soul he then acts by following an ethic of responsibility and somewhere he reaches the point where he says, 'Here I stand; I can do no other.' " The reporter who would use stolen material has the burden of proving his or her action morally defensible.

Responsibility to the Journalist

A young reporter who was asked to describe what journalistic ethics meant to her said the organization for which she worked had "only one type of morality—making money." The staff was too small to cover the community, she said. Most of the reporters were, like her, young, inexperienced and underpaid.

"The newspaper had no library to speak of and a small staff," she said. She was distressed by the coziness of some editors with the community power structure.

"Most reporters covered their stories through press releases and over the phone. They were rarely out on the street.

"No one cared."

The horror story is not typical, but it is not rare. When management fails to fulfill its moral obligations to the staff, little can be done by the most devoted reporters and editors.

For 15 years, the *Carnegie Quarterly* was edited by Helen Rowan. The publication contained articles about the work of the Carnegie Corporation of New York, which funded projects in a variety of fields—education, law, Mexican-Americans, discrimination, the labor market, the education of women. In a letter to the president of the corporation, Rowan summarized what every journalist seeks in the workplace:

> . . . great freedom and steady moral and intellectual support. I couldn't get along without any of them. Add to that the fact that I have never been asked to write a cheap or dishonest or trivial thing. And that I do get to write about important things and can hope that by reaching people I can do a little bit of good.

The newspaper or station that does not carry out its obligations to its staff—a decent salary, adequate staffing of reportorial and editing positions, full support for penetrating journalism, intelligent and independent leadership—cannot demand the loyalty of the staff. When he was dean of the School of Journalism at Columbia University, Edward W. Barrett advised students to have a "go-to-hell fund," a few dollars squirreled away that would enable the discouraged journalist to take off should he or she find the newspaper or station irresponsible.

A Personal Credo

"Not to decide is to decide," says the religious scholar Harvey Cox. To put off making the choice between difficult decisions is irresponsible. But for every story a reporter turns from because it poses too many complexities or too many difficult choices, there are two the reporter never sees because he or she has not developed a moral sensitivity.

Young journalists might consider the adoption of a personal set of values as guidelines in their work. From a variety of sources—from the Greek philosophers to police reporters—the following emerge as suggestions for consideration:

- A belief in and a commitment to a political culture in which the cornerstone is restraint in the use of power.
- Moderation in life and behavior.
- A secular, scientific attitude to the work at hand. Knowledge is allowed to speak for itself. The professional does not believe on the basis of hope but of evidence.
- An openmindedness that seeks out and tries to comprehend various points of view, including those in conflict with those the reporter holds.
- Responsibility to one's abilities and talent. To leave them fallow, to fail to labor to develop them through indolence or want of seriousness of purpose demeans the self and punishes the society whose betterment depends on new ideas vigorously pursued. In Homer, the king who failed to govern was immoral, for the good was the fulfillment of function. For Aristotle, the good was living up to one's potential, and for Kant the development of one's talents was a duty, and adherence to "duties" constitutes the moral life. The reporter who fails to report and write to his or her potential is immoral.
- An understanding of and a tolerance for the ambiguities involved in most important issues, and the ability to act despite these uncertainties and doubts. The willingness to take responsibility for these actions.
- The willingness to admit errors.
- A capacity to endure solitude and criticism, the price of independence.
- A reluctance to portray heroes and villains to the rhythm of the deadline.
- A knowledge of the pathfinders in fields of knowledge, including journalism.
- A commitment to work.
- A sense of the past. "Let us remember that though great artists of the past could not change the course of history, it is only through their work that we are able to break bread with the dead, and without communion with the dead, a fully human life is impossible."—W. H. Auden.

- Resistance to praise. Humility. "You have to fight against the praise of people who like you," says I. F. Stone, the crusading journalist. "Because you know darn well it wasn't good enough." He tells the story of the great conductor Arturo Toscanini who was engulfed by admirers after a concert. "Maestro, you were wonderful," one said. Toscanini knew the oboe had not come in at the right point and that the violins were off. And Toscanini burst into tears because he knew it had not been good enough.
- Duty. "If a man is burdened with an idea, he not only desires to express it; he ought to express it. He owes it to his conscience and the common good. The indispensible function of expressing ideas is one of obligation—to the community and also to something beyond the community, let us say to truth."—John Dewey.
- Avoidance of the desire to please. Self-censorship is a greater enemy than outside censorship. Pleasing an editor, the publisher or the source is commonplace. Setting one's values to the "pragmatic level of the newsroom group," as Warren Breed puts it, can lead to timid, status-quo journalism.
- Andre Maurois, the French writer and political activist, warns the writer to beware making words an end in themselves:

Power, Glory and Money are only secondary objects for the writer. No man can be a great writer without having a great philosophy, though it may often be unexpressed. A great writer has respect for *values*. His essential function is to raise life to the dignity of thought, and he does this by giving it a shape. If he refuses to perform this function he can be a clever juggler and play tricks with words such as his fellow writers may admire, but his books will be of little interest to anybody else. If, on the contrary, he fulfills it, he will be happy in his writing. Borne aloft by the world as reflected in himself, and producing a sound echo in his times, he helps to shape it by showing to men an image of themselves which is at once true and disciplined.

Some Guidelines to an Ethic of Journalism

Reporters should seek to give voice to all groups in society, not to report solely those who hold power.

The public's need to know is an immanent value.

The reporter has a moral obligation to express ideas.

In determining what shall be reported and what shall be included in a news story, the reporter should consider the relevance of the material to the real needs of the audience.

If the reporter cannot disclose in the story the tactics and techniques used to gather information for the story, such tactics should not be used.

The reporter should:

- Be wary of treating persons as a means.
- Believe on the basis of facts, not hope.
- Be committed to a value system but be free from ideologies and commitments that limit thought.
- Be wary of promising to help or give information to a source in return for material.

In balancing equally moral alternatives, the choice can be made on the basis of:

- The importance of the possible actions to life. (Life is the referent of value.)
- The public interest as against the private interest.
- The extent of knowledge of the event. If it is public knowledge or is likely to become so and the material is significant and relevant, the information should be used.
- Serving the needs of society. If the material assists people in participating justly, equally and freely in a meaningful community life, then it should be used.

(Adopted by the Society of Professional Journalists, Sigma Delta Chi, 1973)

Code of Ethics: Society of Professional Journalists

The Society of Professional Journalists, Sigma Delta Chi, believes the duty of journalists is to serve the truth.

We believe the agencies of mass communication are carriers of public discussion and information, acting on their Constitutional mandate and freedom to learn and report the facts.

We believe in public enlightenment as the forerunner of justice, and in our Constitutional role to seek the truth as part of the public's right to know the truth.

We believe those responsibilities carry obligations that require journalists to perform with intelligence, objectivity, accuracy, and fairness.

To these ends, we declare acceptance of the standards of practice here set forth:

RESPONSIBILITY: The public's right to know of events of public importance and interest is the overriding mission of the mass media. The purpose of distributing news and enlightened opinion is to serve the general welfare. Journalists who use their professional status as representatives of the public for selfish or other unworthy motives violate a high trust.

FREEDOM OF THE PRESS: Freedom of the press is to be guarded as an inalienable right of people in a free society. It carries with it the freedom and the responsibility to discuss, question, and challenge actions and utterances of our government and of our public and private institutions. Journalists uphold the right to speak unpopular opinions and the privilege to agree with the majority.

ETHICS: Journalists must be free of obligation to any interest other than the public's right to know the truth.

1. Gifts, favors, free travel, special treatment or privileges can compromise the integrity of journalists and their employers. Nothing of value should be accepted.
2. Secondary employment, political involvement, holding public office, and service in community organizations should be avoided if it compromises the integrity of journalists and their employers. Journalists and their employers should conduct their personal lives in a manner which protects them from conflict of interest, real or apparent. Their responsibilities to the public are paramount. That is the nature of their profession.

3. So-called news communications from private sources should not be published or broadcast without substantiation of their claims to news value.
4. Journalists will seek news that serves the public interest, despite the obstacles. They will make constant efforts to assure that the public's business is conducted in public and that public records are open to public inspection.
5. Journalists acknowledge the newsman's ethic of protecting confidential sources of information.

ACCURACY AND OBJECTIVITY: Good faith with the public is the foundation of all worthy journalism.

1. Truth is our ultimate goal.
2. Objectivity in reporting the news is another goal, which serves as the mark of an experienced professional. It is a standard of performance toward which we strive. We honor those who achieve it.
3. There is no excuse for inaccuracies or lack of thoroughness.
4. Newspaper headlines should be fully warranted by the contents of the articles they accompany. Photographs and telecasts should give an accurate picture of an event and not highlight a minor incident out of context.
5. Sound practice makes clear distinction between news reports and expressions of opinion. News reports should be free of opinion or bias and represent all sides of an issue.
6. Partisanship in editorial comment which knowingly departs from the truth violates the spirit of American journalism.
7. Journalists recognize their responsibility for offering informed analysis, comment, and editorial opinion on public events and issues. They accept the obligation to present such material by individuals whose competence, experience, and judgment qualify them for it.
8. Special articles or presentations devoted to advocacy or the writer's own conclusions and interpretations should be labeled as such.

FAIR PLAY: Journalists at all times will show respect for the dignity, privacy, rights, and well-being of people encountered in the course of gathering and presenting the news.

1. The news media should not communicate unofficial charges affecting reputation or moral character without giving the accused a chance to reply.
2. The news media must guard against invading a person's right to privacy.
3. The media should not pander to morbid curiosity about details of vice and crime.
4. It is the duty of news media to make prompt and complete correction of their errors.
5. Journalists should be accountable to the public for their reports and the public should be encouraged to voice its grievances against the media. Open dialogue with our readers, viewers, and listeners should be fostered.

PLEDGE: Journalists should actively censure and try to prevent violations of these standards, and they should encourage their observance by all newspeople. Adherence to this code of ethics is intended to preserve the bond of mutual trust and respect between American journalists and the American people.

(Adopted by the Associated Press Managing Editors, 1975)
This code is a model against which newspaper men and women can measure their performance. It is meant to apply to news and editorial staff members and others who are involved in, or who influence, news coverage and editorial policy. It has been formulated in the belief that newspapers and the people who produce them should adhere to the highest standards of ethical and professional conduct.

Code of Ethics: APME

A good newspaper is fair, accurate, honest, responsible, independent and decent. Truth is its guiding principle.

Responsibility

It avoids practices that would conflict with the ability to report and present news in a fair and unbiased manner.

The newspaper should serve as a constructive critic of all segments of society. It should vigorously expose wrongdoing or misuse of power, public or private. Editorially, it should advocate needed reform or innovations in the public interest.

News sources should be disclosed unless there is clear reason not to do so. When it is necessary to protect the confidentiality of a source, the reason should be explained.

The newspaper should background, with the facts, public statements that it knows to be inaccurate or misleading. It should uphold the right of free speech and freedom of the press and should respect the individual's right of privacy.

The public's right to know about matters of importance is paramount, and the newspaper should fight vigorously for public access to news of government through open meetings and open records.

The newspaper should guard against inaccuracies, carelessness, bias or distortion through either emphasis or omission.

Accuracy

It should admit all substantive errors and correct them promptly and prominently.

The newspaper should strive for impartial treatment of issues and dispassionate handling of controversial subjects. It should provide a forum for the exchange of comment and criticism, especially when such comment is opposed to its editorial positions. Editorials and other expressions of opinion by reporters and editors should be clearly labeled.

Integrity

The newspaper should report the news without regard for its own interest. It should not give favored news treatment to advertisers or special-interest groups. It should report matters regarding itself or its personnel with the same vigor and candor as it would other institutions or individuals.

Concern for community, business or personal interests should not cause a newspaper to distort or misrepresent the facts.

The newspaper and its staff should be free of obligations to news sources and special interests. Even the appearance of obligation or conflict of interest should be avoided.

Newspapers should accept nothing of value from news sources or others outside the profession. Gifts and free or reduced-rate travel, entertainment, products and lodging should not be accepted. Expenses in connection with news reporting should be paid by the newspaper. Special favors and special treatment for members of the press should be avoided.

Involvement in such things as politics, community affairs, demonstrations and social causes that could cause a conflict of interest, or the appearance of such conflict, should be avoided.

Outside employment by news sources is an obvious conflict of interest, and employment by potential news sources also should be avoided.

Financial investments by staff members or other outside business interests that could conflict with the newspaper's ability to report the news or that would create the impression of such conflict should be avoided.

Stories should not be written or edited primarily for the purpose of winning awards and prizes. Blatantly commercial journalism contests, or others that reflect unfavorably on the newspaper or the profession, should be avoided.

No code of ethics can prejudge every situation. Common sense and good judgment are required in applying ethical principles to newspaper realities. Individual newspapers are encouraged to augment these APME guidelines with locally produced codes that apply more specifically to their own situations.

A Statement of Principles: ASNE

(Adopted by the American Society of Newspaper Editors, 1975)

PREAMBLE: The First Amendment, protecting freedom of expression from abridgment by any law, guarantees to the people through their press a constitutional right, and thereby places on newspaper people a particular responsibility.

Thus journalism demands of its practitioners not only industry and knowledge but also the pursuit of a standard of integrity proportionate to the journalist's singular obligation.

To this end the American Society of Newspaper Editors sets forth this Statement of Principles as a standard encouraging the highest ethical and professional performance.

ARTICLE I—RESPONSIBILITY: The primary purpose of gathering and distributing news and opinion is to serve the general welfare by informing the people and enabling them to make judgments on the issues of the time. Newspapermen and women who abuse the power of their professional role for selfish motives or unworthy purposes are faithless to that public trust.

The American press was made free not just to inform or just to serve as a forum for debate but also to bring an independent scrutiny to bear on the forces of power in the society, including the conduct of official power at all levels of government.

ARTICLE II—FREEDOM OF THE PRESS: Freedom of the press belongs to the people. It must be defended against encroachment or assault from any quarter, public or private.

Journalists must be constantly alert to see that the public's business is conducted in public. They must be vigilant against all who would exploit the press for selfish purposes.

ARTICLE III—INDEPENDENCE: Journalists must avoid impropriety and the appearance of impropriety as well as any conflict of interest or the appearance of conflict. They should neither accept anything nor pursue any activity that might compromise or seem to compromise their integrity.

ARTICLE IV—TRUTH AND ACCURACY: Good faith with the reader is the foundation of good journalism. Every effort must be made to assure that the news content is accurate, free from bias and in context, and that all sides are presented fairly. Editorials, analytical articles and commentary should be held to the same standards of accuracy with respect to facts as news reports.

Significant errors of fact, as well as errors of omission, should be corrected promptly and prominently.

ARTICLE V—IMPARTIALITY: To be impartial does not require the press to be unquestioning or to refrain from editorial expression. Sound practice, however, demands a clear distinction for the reader between news reports and opinion. Articles that contain opinion or personal interpretation should be clearly identified.

ARTICLE VI—FAIR PLAY: Journalists should respect the rights of people involved in the news, observe the common standards of decency and stand accountable to the public for the fairness and accuracy of their news reports.

Persons publicly accused should be given the earliest opportunity to respond.

Pledges of confidentiality to news sources must be honored at all costs, and therefore should not be given lightly. Unless there is clear and pressing need to maintain confidences, sources of information should be identified.

These principles are intended to preserve, protect and strengthen the bond of trust and respect between American journalists and the American people, a bond that is essential to sustain the grant of freedom entrusted to both by the nation's founders.

Reporting the Spoken Word

6

Interviewing Principles

There are two kinds of interviews:

- News interview—The purpose is to gather information that will explain an idea, event or situation.
- Profile—The focus is on an individual.

For effective interviews of both types, reporters prepare carefully, and they ask questions that induce the source to talk freely. Questions are directed at obtaining information on a theme that the reporter has in mind before begining the interview.

If a more important theme emerges, the reporter develops it with questions related to the new theme.

In the stadium locker room, the half-dressed athlete was putting his warm-up suit and track shoes into a battered black bag. Seated on a bench nearby, a young man removed a pencil and a notepad from a jacket pocket.

"I'm from the paper in town," the young man said. "You looked sharp out there. Mind if I ask you some questions?"

The athlete nodded and continued his packing.

"First time you've been to this part of the West or this city?" the reporter asked. Another nod. This was not going to be easy, the reporter worried. The sports editor had told him to make sure he brought back a good story for tomorrow's paper, the day the National Association of Intercollegiate Athletics would begin its annual out-door track meet. The tall, lithe young man standing in front of the bench was a world record holder in the hurdles, the editor had said, and worth a long profile for the sports page to accompany the schedule of events.

The reporter tried again. "What do you think of our town?" The athlete seemed to see the reporter for the first time.

"I don't know anything about this town," he replied. "I'm here to run. I go to the East coast, the West coast, here. They give me a ticket at school and I get on a bus or a plane and go. My business is to run." He fell silent.

Rebuffed, the reporter struggled to start the athlete talking again. In the 20-minute interview, the hurdler never really opened up.

Back in the newsroom, the reporter told the sports editor about his difficulties. They seemed to begin with his first question about whether the athlete had been to the town before, he told his editor. His boss was not sympathetic.

"First, you should have checked the clips and called the college in town for information about your man," the editor said. "That way you could have learned something about him, his record or his school. That might have been used to break the ice. Or you could have asked him about the condition of the track, something he knows about."

Then the editor softened. He knew that interviewing is not easy for young reporters, that it can be perfected only through practice.

"I think you have a good quote there about the business of running," he told the reporter. "Did you get anything else about the places he's been? That could make an interesting focus for the piece."

Yes, the reporter said, he had managed to draw the hurdler out about where he had been in the last few months. With the editor's guidance, the reporter managed to turn out an acceptable piece.

This incident illustrates the four principles of interviewing. They are:

- Prepare carefully whenever possible.
- Ask questions that induce the source to talk.
- Establish a relationship with the source conducive to obtaining information.
- Listen and watch attentively.

Since much of the daily work of the journalist requires asking people for information, mastery of interviewing techniques is essential. The four principles underlie the various techniques the reporter uses. Clearly, the sports writer's troubles began when he failed to learn enough about the athlete he was to interview. Lacking background, the reporter was unable to ask questions that would draw out the source. Furthermore, he had failed to establish a rapport with the hurdler, so that the session was more like dentistry than journalism, with the reporter painfully extracting bits and pieces of information from an unwilling subject.

Fortunately, the reporter had listened carefully so that he managed to salvage something from the interview. Later in this chapter, we shall examine in detail the various techniques reporters use in applying the four principles. First, let us look at today's newspaper or listen to the evening newscast to see how often interviews are used.

We see that news stories are based on information from three kinds of sources: physical sources, such as records, files and references; the direct observations of the reporter, and interviews with human sources. Most stories are combinations of two or three of these sources.

If we had been able to watch a reporter sent to cover the governor's address at a party fund-raising dinner, we would have seen the reporter cover the speech (direct observation) and then question the speaker and some of the guests (interviews). Before and after the event, the reporter consulted clippings from the newspaper library (references) for additional material. Thus, the speech story contains material from the three kinds of sources.

An examination of the reporting that goes into most stories will reveal that the reporter interviewed one or more persons. This is true even when the story does not appear to include an interview. Let us look at a few stories to see how often interviews are used. In the process, we will also discover the two types of interviews.

The major story on page one of a September issue of *The Hawk Eye* in Burlington, Iowa, is about a three-alarm fire that destroyed a two-story building that housed an automobile sales agency and a body repair shop. The reporter interviewed several people for information to supplement his observations. Here are the people he interviewed and a summary of their comments:

Types of Interviews

- The owner—15 cars destroyed; exact loss as yet unknown.
- A fire department lieutenant—The building could not have been saved when his men arrived. They concentrated on saving the adjoining buildings.
- An eyewitness—"I didn't know what it was," the story quotes her as saying of the fire. "It just went all at once. I seen it a-burning and I was scared to death."
- The fire chief—The state fire marshal will investigate the cause of the fire.

Although the reporter was not present when firemen battled the fire during the early morning hours, the interviews with the lieutenant and the neighbor give his story an on-the-scene flavor. Since these interviews help to explain the news event, we might describe them as news interviews.

Another locally written front page story also relies on a news interview. A head-on automobile crash on Iowa Route 2 near Farmington took the life of a Van Buren County woman and caused injuries to four others. Although no source is quoted, the story is based on information from a call to the Iowa Highway Patrol. The story is a news interview also.

Next, let us look at another type of interview story, the profile or personality interview. Shortly after her graduation from journalism school, Mary Ann Giordano was assigned by *The Bergen Record* in New Jersey to interview a high school English teacher who had been involved in a dispute with his school administration over articles he allowed to run in the student newspaper of which he was the adviser. The *Record* had run news stories on the conflict. Giordano was to profile the teacher. (See story on next page.)

We now have described the two types of interviews:

1. The news interview whose purpose is to develop information about an idea or an event that is the focus of the story.
2. The profile or personality interview in which an individual is the center of the story.

The strong and quiet voice

A teacher's story

By Mary Ann Giordano
Staff Writer

He is the most unlikely looking rebel. Graying and middle-aged, scholarly and low-key, James Williams Downs resembles a college librarian or a junior-college humanities professor whose motto might be, "Happiness is never making waves."

Profile

Actually, Downs has been in the middle of turmoil and controversy for two years at Pascack Valley High School in Hillsdale, where he teaches junior and senior English.

Last year, he became embroiled in a censorship dispute with the administration after he allowed the school newspapers to publish articles on teen-age pregnancies and growing marijuana.

It was a matter of principle to Downs, but it cost him his job as the paper's adviser, his two journalism classes, and his health. This year, he was one of 10 teachers cut down by the budgetary ax, but managed to save his spot, thanks to a tenure technicality.

Students and friends say Downs never really looks for the trouble, that he is simply a man of principle. "I don't believe in blind obedience," Downs agreed in his quiet but emphatic way. "There's things I like to express my mind about."

Not the type

His readiness to express himself was developed over the years as a Harvard undergraduate, a drill-press operator, a private-school headmaster. The experiences have led Downs to believe in not giving up, even if the stand leads to a lot of trouble.

But if there is a classic type of "troublemaker" or "controversial figure," the 52-year-old Downs seems not to fit.

As one former student described him, "he lacks dynamics. He's not vocal enough." A soft, Midwestern twang can still be detected in his even, steady voice, revealing his Indiana upbringing. But when he wants, his words are sharp and emphatic. He chops the air with his right hand to punctuate his meaning. And the honesty and ease of his expression sometimes border on the daring.

"Throughout life, it seems there. . . .

The news interview is more often used. Rarely does a reporter cover an assignment without asking someone for information. A city clerk may be asked to verify an election result for a story about the next mayoral election, or a lawyer will be asked to clarify a suit he has filed in the county courthouse. In the course of the day, a reporter may interview a dozen or more people for the stories on which he is working. Usually, these are quick question-and-answer sessions conducted over the telephone.

When a reporter talks about doing an interview, usually he is referring to a more extended session with one or more sources that will form the basis of a story. These long sessions can be news or personality interviews, depending upon the purpose of the piece.

The extended news interview can provide readers and listeners with interpretation, background and explanation of events whose description in the basic news story may have been too sketchy for adequate understanding.

The News Interview

When Douglas Watson, a *Washington Post* reporter, was covering the extortion and tax evasion trial of a Baltimore County official, he heard the testimony of a stock manipulator who was a confessed white collar criminal and political fixer. Watson was told that the witness was being held by United States marshals in a special facility while testifying for the government. Watson learned there were several of these facilities—known as "safe houses"—and he decided to do a story on them. After the trial, he went to the office of the Marshal's Service and spent several hours talking to officials.

"In the interviews, I learned about other interesting and unreported aspects of the organization besides 'safe houses,' " Watson said. "One of the Service's activities is giving new identities to people who had been government witnesses. This enables them to start new lives in another part of the country."

Watson's interviews continued for two days, and the story he wrote was given good play in the *Post* and in many newspapers that subscribe to the *Post*'s syndicated news service.

Here is how Watson's story begins:

"Restricted Area — U.S. Govt. Training Center," says the sign on the barbed wire-topped fence surrounding a barracks at Ft. Holabird on the edge of Baltimore.

The sign doesn't say it, but the barracks is one of several "safe houses" that the U.S. Marshal's Service operates for the special care and feeding of very important prisoner-witnesses such as Watergate conspirator E. Howard Hunt, political saboteur Donald Segretti and stock manipulator Joel Kline.

Three to five "safe houses" have been in existence around the country for about a year, usually holding about 50, mostly white collar, "principals," as they like to call themselves. They are federal prisoners who usually were involved in organized crime and who are considered too valuable as government witnesses or too endangered by threats to be incarcerated in the usual prison. . . .

The Profile   The profile should be seen as a mini-drama, blending description, action and dialogue. Through the words and actions of the source, with some help from the reporter's insertion of background and explanatory matter, the character is illuminated. Profiles should include plenty of quotations. The reporter must resist his urge to paraphrase.

The major ingredients of the profile are:

- The person's background (birth, upbringing, education, occupation).
- Anecdotes and incidents.
- Comments by the source relevant to his or her newsworthiness.
- The reporter's observations.
- Ample quotations.
- Comments of those who know the interviewee.

News events can stimulate profiles. During the Vietnam War, hundreds of servicemen were listed as missing in action. After the war's end, many names remained on the missing list. To examine the human dimension of this tragedy, the UPI sent a reporter to the home of the wife of a Marine captain who had been missing for almost nine years. Here is the beginning of the story the reporter, Bernard Caughey, wrote:

CENTERVILLE, Mass.—Mrs. Barbara Mullen knows her husband is dead. So do her two sons.

But no one has verified it as fact. So they live with uncertainty. And with an ever-dimming hope that he might just be alive.

The Mullens are among that handful of Americans for whom the war in southeast Asia is not ended.

It was 8½ years ago, on April 29, 1966, that Marine Capt. William F. Mullen was shot down in Laos while on a bombing mission over the Ho Chi Minh Trail. During rescue attempts, searchers heard his radio three separate times, all within a mile of where the plane went down. But the 150-foot ground cover kept him from sight and prevented the rescuers from landing.

To this date, the Mullen family has heard not one word from or about him.

"We know he must be dead. There would be no reason for him to be held as a prisoner or a pawn," Mrs. Mullen said in an interview.

"But we'd like to know how he died, where he died and where he is buried," Mrs. Mullen said. "And, if he really is dead, we'd like to hold a memorial service—a mass—for him."

The tall, willowy Mrs. Mullen, in an attempt to start a new life, packed up her belongings a few months ago and moved with her two sons, Terrance, 11, and Sean, 13, to this Cape Cod seatown. . . .

Often, interviewing only the source will lead to a thin, possibly misleading story. When a young *New York Times* reporter turned in a piece about an alcoholic nun who counsels other similarly afflicted nuns, the story did not move past Charlotte Evans, an editor.

"As it stands," Evans told the reporter, "all you have is a moderately interesting interview with Sister Doody. You sat in a chair, and she sat in a chair and you had a chat. That's not very good, considering the story material.

"Did you talk to any nuns in treatment or just out of it?

"Where is the anguish, the embarrassment, the guilt?

"It doesn't sound as if you had done any real reporting, digging, pushing. Where are the people, the quotes, the color?"

For her profile of Les Brown, a black preacher and radio personality, Itabari Njeri of *The Miami Herald* talked to other ministers, a community activist and the heads of the local chapters of the Urban League and the National Association for the Advancement of Colored People, as well as to Brown. The views of Brown diverged widely:

"I will not allow anyone to manipulate or prostitute the black community, and that is what Les Brown is doing to the nth degree," Njeri quoted the Urban League official as saying.

"He is different . . . he's got guts. He is a challenge to the traditional black leaders here," the activist told Njeri.

The reporting and writing of a personality piece or profile can take several days. The profile should not be a hastily written account of an interview with the subject. When Giordano was assigned to profile the English teacher in a New Jersey high school who had been attacked because of his devotion to his students' freedom of expression, she decided on several "reporting areas," she said.

"I watched Downs in action with his students. I immediately sensed his warmth and communication, the easy-going and relaxed feelings between them. Instincts are not always correct, but unless I immediately learn otherwise, I try to follow my feelings as a hypothesis for the story."

Reporting and Writing the Profile

She interviewed other teachers and found that Downs was well liked and re-spected. "Like the students, they felt Downs was a good man, a courageous man and an inspiration to them."

She also interviewed his former students, administration officials, and Downs himself. She was surprised by Downs, "that a man so close to being fired would still remain unafraid to speak out.

"I watched Downs very closely during the interview. His features—his gray-ness, his tiredness, his restrained, gentlemanly nature—told me a lot about him. I noticed his clothing, the way he spoke. When he spoke, he chopped at the air with his hands to emphasize a point. I jotted all this down and included much of it in the story.

"I had to keep reminding myself as I wrote that the story was a personality profile, not a biography. Writing, rewriting and cutting, I finally put the story together the way I wanted."

Her advice for doing profiles: Take your time with the story. Keep your eyes open for revealing details. Talk to as many people as possible. Do not ignore negative instincts, but wait to draw conclusions.

Lew Powell, who has written many profiles for *The Charlotte Observer*, begins his work by gathering background about the subject. Since the profile usually has a chronological framework supporting it, Powell first goes through the newspaper's clippings.

"I make notes on things I'd like to know more about," he says. "I keep an eye out for quirks and holes in the public image that I can follow up."

He also is alert to a news peg on which he can hang the story. "It helps to have a peg for a profile," Powell says, "so that readers won't wonder, 'Why is he writing about this person?' This peg business may be more journalistic mythology than necessity, but it makes me feel better."

Sometimes, Powell says, a reporter finds himself at the mercy of the source's recollections. On items about which he is unsure, Powell tries to determine the sub-ject's credibility through careful questioning and by making a determination of the individual's frankness. In an interview in which the subject told some wildly improb-able tales of derring-do in World War II, Powell had his doubts. "They did fit in with the rest of his life, but I was careful to attribute them and disclaim responsibility for them.

"I can't overstate the importance of asking a lot of questions.

"In the interview, I ask a ton of questions. For one long piece about a man and wife who own a Charlotte radio station, I had three interviews with them, and I had telephone interviews with probably 20 people who have known them at one time or another. The interviews with other people can provide anecdotes and illustrations as well as facts the source may have forgotten or doesn't care to remember.

"You strike out a lot this way, but every now and then you hit a real gem.

"I look for little glimpses of the subject, incidents that will make people who know the subject say, 'Ah, that's Stan, all right.' "

As reporters increasingly sought to personalize news stories, the line between the news interview and the profile began to blur. The emphasis was on the human condition, and the talk was of "people-related stories." When the UPI questioned the editors of more than 100 daily newspapers about how to improve the UPI's wire stories, many of them said that news stories should have a human angle, even when they originate in Washington, the state capitals or overseas.

Blending the Two Types

What the editors were trying to tell the UPI was that their readers wanted the same kind of human element in stories about political, economic and international affairs as the UPI had been putting into many of its other stories. For example, when flood waters had surged through several Southern states, the UPI had assessed its effects by describing one family's suffering. The UPI's night lead began:

HATTIESBURG, Miss., Feb. 25 (UPI)—"We ain't never had too much, but we've never been this bad off."

J. W. Creel Jr., 47, a mechanic who has been struggling since before Christmas to stretch his $30 weekly unemployment compensation checks over the needs of himself, his pregnant wife and nine children, sadly surveyed his chattering brood at the Red Cross shelter in the Hattiesburg Community Center.

The Creels, and thousands like them, are the victims of disastrous floods ("Worse than 1900," one old gentleman commented) that are sweeping broad areas of southern Georgia, Alabama, and Mississippi.

The Creels lost everything but the clothes they wore.

Creel said he left his rented home briefly Wednesday to see the flood waters and returned to hear "the kids hollering at me, 'Daddy, water's coming in the house.'

"It was up to my knees," he said. "They were trying to sweep it out but I told them it wasn't no use to sweep and to grab the young 'uns and get out of there."

After a few more paragraphs about the Creel family, the story concentrated on the straight news:

The flood waters which boiled into Hattiesburg, spoiling and contaminating everything they touched, began a slow retreat today—an inch in an hour— as the flood moved swirling and broadening toward the gulf.

More than 6,000 persons were homeless in Mississippi, 5,500 of them from Hattiesburg. More than 1,000 left their homes in Alabama. Several hundred more were left homeless in Georgia, and North Carolinians braced for threatening floods. . . .

If the UPI could describe the human consequences of a flood, then it should not be much more difficult to have stories about the effects on people of a proposed increase in the federal excess profits tax, said the editors. No one disagreed with the suggestion.

This kind of journalism—the smooth blending of news and personality interviews in a single story—requires reporting skill. The reporter must gather information for the factual description and explanation of the event or idea and combine it with a lively or moving account of the people involved or affected by the situation. *The Wall Street Journal* has mastered this technique. The key to success with this type of story lies in fusing the thoughts or experiences of the individual with the news event. Here is the beginning of a *Journal* story about stormy economic times for Newfoundland fishermen:

BAY BULLS, Newfoundland—Cyril Mulcahy has seen some lean years in his 51 years of fishing, but he laments that "this is one of the worst."

It's late afternoon and Mr. Mulcahy is baiting fish hooks with pieces of squid in preparation for a full day of cod fishing tomorrow. At dawn, he will be several miles offshore in a 26-foot open boat setting his lines with the hope of catching enough cod so that he and his only crew member will each bring in $50 for a 12-hour working day. And that "would be a good day," he says. "I've been out days when I couldn't make $5."

Mr. Mulcahy, like most of the other older men in this tiny coastal village, has been fishing since he was a young boy, following a way of life that has been traditional in Newfoundland for 350 years. But Mr. Mulcahy, now 61 years old, sees himself as an endangered species. "The way things are, there's no youngster taking it up anymore. The youngest man fishing here (in Bay Bulls) now is 40."

These opening paragraphs do the job of giving the reader a taste of the fisherman's life, Mulcahy's own background and an indication of the problems he and other Newfoundland fishermen face. If we look back at the ingredients for the profile we can see that in the space of three paragraphs the reporter has covered all of them.

The next two paragraphs mark the shift to the situation—the news peg—that prompted the story. These contain information based on news interviews with Canadian employment officials:

Canadian employment statistics would certainly back him up. There are about 15,000 fishermen in Newfoundland today. That's several hundred less than a year ago and about 4,400 less than in 1968. Most of these are known as "inshore" fishermen who ply the Atlantic waters with nets or lines in small boats within a few miles offshore. Almost all of them have watched the size of their catches decline steadily over the past several years.

The main reason for their plight: overfishing, or more precisely, overfishing by fleets of foreign trawlers. The trawlers travel thousands of miles to fish in these waters, especially in the 80,000-square-mile Newfoundland Grand Bank. They seek mainly groundfish, such as cod, haddock and flounder, that are found close to the ocean floor. . . .

When Mark Patinkin and Christopher Scanlan were assigned to profile the black community in Rhode Island for *The* Providence *Journal-Bulletin,* they focused on individuals—the people who symbolize the facts and figures they were gathering.

For one of their stories, about the high rate of unemployment among blacks, they talked to a black man who was looking for work:

Voices: Stephen Gordon on Unemployment

"I felt like everything I was trying to build was worthless," said Stephen Gordon. "I was back at the bottom. Quite a few times, I'd just break down and cry. I couldn't even get a job on a garbage truck. I felt less than a man."

Stephen Gordon, 27, sits in the darkness of his kitchen in a Newport housing project, speaking of being black and jobless.

Back from Vietnam in 1971, he had gone through three years of the hardest of times. He had no high school diploma. He had no job. He had two children. His family survived on welfare.

Then came a federal job program that reached out and gave him hope, gave him training as a welder. He was a tradesman. For nine months, he strove to build the good life.

He was fired. He appealed the firing to the State Human Rights Commission, which found the company guilty of racial discrimination. That was two years ago, but the case remains on appeal. Meanwhile, Gordon went on unemploy-

ment, then welfare. He remembers the feeling.

"My inspiration was destroyed again," he said. "It was the same old rut."

Recently, he climbed out of the rut by finding a job as a cook in a Newport inn. For other black adults in the state, joblessness remains chronic.

Unemployment among Rhode Island blacks is higher than for any other group. There were 8,880 blacks in the labor force in 1976, and, state figures show, 11 percent were unemployed, compared to an overall state rate of 8 percent.

There are the thousands more the statistics don't mention.

Richard Torchia, head of CETA for Providence, estimated that actual black unemployment in the city is at least 17 percent. Black hunger for jobs, he added, runs even higher. Of the thousands now on Providence's federally supported CETA payroll, 47 percent are black.

"We take the most disadvantaged first," explained Torchia.

There is hope in the black community, and with the careful use of quotes and the selection of incidents, the reporters showed success:

Voices: Ed Blue on moving up

"I wanted the good life," said Ed Blue. "I wasn't going to settle. I figured, I'm a citizen, I'm a taxpayer. I have as much a right as anybody else. Just give me a chance."

Twenty-eight years ago, Ed Blue came to Rhode Island with a suitcase and $300, another poor black immigrant from a small town in the South. Today he is the state's chief bank examiner and lives with his family in the state's wealthiest suburb, Barrington. Barbara, his wife, is running for Town Council.

For most blacks, Rhode Island has not been a place of opportunity. It wasn't for Ed Blue either. It was a place of slammed doors.

They slammed as soon as he got out of college. One large retailer put an "X" on his application for a clerk's job. He demanded to know why. The interviewer admitted it was to mark black applicants. Next he went to a bank. The bank told him he'd never be anything more than a guard.

Ed Blue saw other blacks told the same thing and saw them accept it. Don't bother, they told him, you won't make it, they won't let you make it. Blue would not accept that. "I was new here," he recalled, "I figured hell, I'll give it a shot. I'm going to break that down."

He put his shoulder against the door and he pushed hard. And when it finally gave, and a higher door slammed, he broke that one, too. He did it, he said, by proving he was so qualified they had no choice but to hire him. Ed Blue made it because he believed in Ed Blue.

"This is one of the things I've instilled in my children," he said, "Don't say you can't. I don't want to hear 'You can't.'"

For their report on crime in the Providence ghetto, they interviewed a prostitute:

Voices: Debbie Spell on hustling

"Being a hooker is all I know," said Debbie Spell. "It's how my mother supported me. That's all I seen when I was a kid, broads jumping into cars. Put me in a factory and I just couldn't hack it."

In poor neighborhoods, where unemployment and welfare rates are high, many blacks turn to hustling to survive. Debbie Spell turned to prostitution. Although she is 20, she looks 15. She is already the mother of three children. She normally works on Pine Street in Providence, where most of her customers are white.

"If it wasn't for them, then I wouldn't have food for my kids," she said, "or Pampers for my baby." Nor would she have her color television and living-room furniture.

"I'm not proud of it," she added, "but it's the way I make a living. Why should I work in a factory for $100 a week when I can make that much on a Thursday night?"

Although blacks make up only 3.4 percent of the population in Rhode Island, they make up 24 percent of the population at the Adult Correctional Institutions and 7.5 percent of admissions to state drug abuse programs.

In Providence, blacks account for about 10 percent of the population, but a much higher percentage ends up in the city's arrest books. Last year, of the 243 juveniles Providence police arrested for major crimes, 37 percent, or 90, were black. As blacks get older, their arrest percentage grows. In 1977, of the 470 adults Providence police arrested for major crimes, 48.7 percent, or 229, were black.

Short as these pieces are, they say a great deal. The quotes reveal frustration, anger, futility, possibilities.

The story about Debbie Spell has a tragic epilogue. A year after she was interviewed for the series, she was arrested on charges of assault and loitering for prostitution. Two days after her arrest, she hanged herself in the shower room of the prison.

Scanlan returned to the streets Debbie walked to find out more about this woman who became a hooker at 12, was a drug addict, had three illegitimate boys, and was dead at 22.

Scanlan admits he was worried when he went out to interview Debbie's friends. He was concerned about how a prying reporter would be treated.

"What I found were two grief-stricken women who told me an illuminating story about life on the streets," he said. His interview with Debbie's prostitute friends begins:

PROVIDENCE—It's a little after 5 on a Friday afternoon. Pine Street, between Pearl and Portland Streets, is a desolate stretch littered with broken glass, where young women wait on the sidewalks for the men who drive slowly by to stop and pick them up for a few minutes of sex.

This part of South Providence was where Debbie Spell used to wait, too—until last Wednesday when the police arrested her. On Friday, she hanged herself at the Women's Prison in Cranston.

Maurine sits in the doorway of a vacant building, a tired-looking woman in her early twenties, wearing shorts and a halter top.

"Sometimes it's not even worth the money to me," she said. "I got stabbed three times. I got busted in the face with a bottle. Just crazy guys. I told the police, but they didn't do nothing. I even got his plate. They still didn't do nothing. They said, 'If that's the type of life

you want to lead, you got to take the bitter with the sweet.' "

Last summer, Debbie Spell told a reporter that she was a prostitute because the money was good. But times have changed, Maurine said.

"Hmph," she snorted when a reporter told her what Debbie had said. "Ain't no money here. Too many girls now. Some girls bring their little sisters down here, underage girls, 11 or 12 years-old, some of them."

A young man approached and slowed his car.

"Wanna go?" Maurine asked half-heartedly. He looked at her, shook his head and drove on.

Another young woman came up. A few minutes before, Tammy had been dropped off by a trick, and now she was back on the corner. She said she was Debbie's best friend. On her way to Pine Street, she learned that Debbie was dead. She spoke bitterly, her voice husky with grief, sharp with anger. Tears shone in her eyes. Like Maurine, she did not want her real name used.

"This was Debbie's life, right here on Pine Street," Tammy said. "This is all of our lives, right here."

She too was bothered by all the younger girls on the streets, but for a different reason.

"They don't know what they're getting into," she said, "This is no game. It's just step up and make money. But they don't know that yet." A man stopped his car at the corner. She talked to him for awhile, leaning on his car door, but he, too, drove away. . . .

Lifestyle Interviews

Although the reporter seeks to make journalism out of the events that affect people, certain issues, ideas and events were approached with great care, even reticence, by the press. Social taboos and respect for privacy stood in the way. Sometimes the public preferred the ostrich position in the belief that it is possible to know too much, and journalists went along.

Beginning in the mid-1960s and continuing into the 1970s, this reticence melted away under the friction generated by the turmoil and movement in American society. Incomprehensible to most people, the churning and conflict had serious consequences. The social, political, sexual, religious and economic fabric as it had been stitched together through two centuries began to unravel, and many people wanted to know what was happening and why. There was an explosion of curiosity. The age of candor was born.

The New Journalism

Journalists, who had been influenced by Truman Capote's book about a mass murder in Kansas, *In Cold Blood*—published in 1965 and described as a non-fiction novel—sought to use Capote's techniques in their journalism. Two of them, Gay Talese and Tom Wolfe, eventually found daily journalism too confining and turned to writing books. Like Capote, they sought to dig into the inner lives of their characters, to reveal motivation, emotion and other feelings and thoughts daily journalists were prohibited from speculating about. Their work became known as the New Journalism.

Wolfe said that the new journalists derived their techniques from the realistic novelists whose powers could be traced to four devices:

1. Scene-by-scene reconstruction; moving from place to place to witness events as they occurred.
2. Full dialogue. " . . . realistic dialogue involves the reader more completely than any other single device. It also establishes and defines character more quickly and effectively than any other single device."
3. The third-person point of view. This required interviews with people involved in events, asking about "thoughts and emotions, along with everything else." The first-person story based on the reporter's point of view was "irrelevant to the story and irritating to the reader."
4. Recording everyday "gestures, habits, manners, customs, styles of furniture, clothing, decoration, styles of traveling, eating, keeping house, modes of behaving toward children, servants, superiors, inferiors, peers, plus the various looks, glances, poses, styles of walking and other symbolic details that might exist within a scene."

Much of the work of the new journalists appeared in magazines, but the techniques had a lasting effect on newspaper reporting and writing.

In newspapers, the interview became an even more important reporting tool. The profile was expanded to include the personal lives of public figures, and reporters looked into the lives of so-called ordinary individuals who seemed to typify a class or a group of people. In their work, journalists were granted greater freedom. Not only were the barriers lifted on subject matter, but reporters were encouraged to write their stories imaginatively.

Newspapers and television stations began to concentrate on the human condition—the plight of the family around the block, the girl next door. The reporters took their themes from the questions people were asking.

Stories on the Human Plight

Parents wanted to know why their children were turning away from them and towards friends. Instead of developing values from the family, children were taking on the outlook of their peers. What happened to marriage, parents wondered. And what about acceptance of homosexuality as a lifestyle?

Parents worried about what their children were learning in grade school. They wondered whether social mobility was leading to a new value system in which they had little faith.

Into the arena stepped the reporter, ready to ask questions on behalf of a concerned public. Across the country, editors wanted interviews with sociologists and psychologists, homosexuals, unmarried couples, women running group sessions, psychiatrists, college dropouts. The working man and woman were rediscovered and made the subject of interviews.

Berkley Hudson, a young reporter for *The Bulletin* in Bend, Ore., (circ. 12,000) wrote several stories that revealed aspects of community life of which most residents were unaware. Hudson knew that the metropolitan press and network television had been carrying news and features about homosexuality as a lifestyle, but he realized that little had been written about the lives of homosexuals in small- and medium-sized cities.

"Homosexuals have made the cover of *Time*," he said, "but the small-town homosexual still leads a life of secrecy and is still ignored by journalists." Hudson set out to tell the story of Bend's homosexuals.

To meet homosexuals, Hudson ran a classified advertisement in *The Bulletin* inviting them to discuss "the joys and woes of being gay in Central Oregon" and promising confidentiality.

The word was soon around town about what Hudson was up to. Bend was not sure it liked the idea. Several residents protested in letters to the editor, and two Jehovah's Witnesses visited Hudson in the newsroom to try to dissuade him. Hudson turned the visit to good use; the visitors inspired him to do a story on the sect.

Hudson received about 10 replies to his advertisement, and he selected two single men and two couples—one male couple, one female couple—for his interviews. Each interview lasted two to four hours. Some of the interviewees were open about their sexual preferences. One was terrified and would meet Hudson only in out-of-the-way places. Only one let Hudson use his real name. Most feared loss of jobs and community ostracism.

Sensitive Topic. Reporter Berkley Hudson caused controversey in the community with these stories about homosexuals in Bend, Ore.

THE BULLETIN **Lifestyle**

Central Oregon homosexuals dream of freedom

If you are a homosexual in Central Oregon, you probably lead a secretive existence.

Traditionally, and especially in America, theological, medical, and legal theorists have considered homosexuals to be deviants who should be shunned and kept in society's skeleton closet with the other minorities and aberrant types.

However, this view is changing. In recent years, homosexuals, along with other groups, actively have sought and partially have gained "liberation."

Yet, in Central Oregon, homosexuals still dream of freedom, as blacks have dreamed of equal job and housing opportunities.

"There is no such thing as a Christian homosexual. They could change and become a Christian," Rev. Rex E. Blott, presiding minister of the Bend Jehovah's Witnesses, said without hesitation.

The minister quoted from the Bible, Romans 1:26-27, which reads:

"God therefore handed them over to disgraceful passions. Their women exchanged the normal practices of sexual intercourse for something which is abnormal and unnatural. Similarly the men, turning from natural intercourse with women, were swept into lustful passion for one another.

"Men with men performed these shameful horrors, receiving, of course, in their own personalities the consequences of sexual perversity."

Rev. Leopold O'Riordan of St. Francis of Assissi Catholic Church, Bend, said homosexuals can be Christians, but like other problems, such as kleptomania, homosexuality needs to be overcome.

In the field of psychology, the debate continues, with the views of Sigmund Freud gradually being shaken. Freud said homosexuality is an incurable mental illness and perversion.

His theory of an Oedipus complex stated a child may develop homosexual tendencies after becoming strongly attached to the parent of the opposite sex and rejecting the other parent. Also, an overprotective parent combined with an absent or brutal parent may contribute to a child becoming homosexual, he said.

The Freudian view prevailed for more than 50 years. Only this April, the American Psychiatric Association (APA) decided to uphold its board's decision to drop homosexuality from the group's listing of mental diseases.

The organization now considers it a mental illness only when homosexuals "are bothered by or in conflict with or wish to change their sexual orientation."

This year a study, which has become a book — "Male Homosexuals: Their Problems and Adaptations," by psychiatrists Martin Wienberg and Colin Williams — found male homosexuals not under psychiatric care to be as psychologically adjusted as other males.

This survey, taken of 2,437 men in Denmark, the Netherlands and the United States, recommended an end to legal and social harassment of homosexuals. It said the United States was the most anti-homosexual of modern Western nations.

The professors are continuing the work of Dr. Albert Kinsey, of Indiana University, who in 1948 said 40 to 50 per cent of the male population had experienced a homosexual situation and psychiatry should reassess its idea that persons should conform to a particular sexual standard.

The 1974 survey, which included 1,057 American men, said 67.8 per cent of homosexuals still attempt to hide their sexuality from heterosexuals.

But more than half disagreed with the statement, "I wish I were not a homosexual."

Twenty-eight per cent said they would like to give up homosexuality and 27 per cent said they weren't sure. Seventy-six per cent said they were happy or pretty happy and about the same number said they weren't depressed, anxious or ashamed of being homosexual.

In Deschutes County, Charles Whitchurch, a psychiatric social worker, says the few homosexuals who seek help from him have problems not with their homosexuality but with living in a small town and having to be discreet and not as free as if they were in a large city.

"Married homosexuals have the problem of leading a double life, being bisexual. They have a similar problem as someone who is cheating on his wife," he said.

"Homosexuality in a small community is still a scary thing. Our country works on the national average mentality. If you don't have 2.5 kids, aren't mortgaged on house and car, aren't white, Protestant, Catholic or Jew, then you don't fit," said Jim Henson, director of the Deschutes County Family Counseling Center.

In Oregon, no law prohibits consenting persons over 18 years old from engaging in homosexuality, according to Warren West, Deschutes County assistant district attorney. However, he said there are laws against solicitation in public places or homosexuality involving adults and those who are under 18 or mentally incompetent.

A bill which would have made it illegal to discriminate against homosexuals in the areas of jobs and housing died last year in an Oregon Legislature committee. That bill proposed a law similar to ones existing in Seattle, Wash. and San Francisco, Calif.

———

It's 10:30 p.m. in a Bend tavern one night last week. At the bar, all six stools are occupied. The male customers laugh and drink and joke with each other and the barmaid.

One man throws a verbal barb to another at the end of the bar. The target of the barb, who is a homosexual, replies, "You better watch out, I've got my broomstick parked outside."

(Later, he says, "Everybody knows fairies ride brooms.")

"Oh, I thought you were going to hit me with your purse," the joker counters, and everyone laughs.

Less than 10 months ago, that homosexual, Ricky (not his real name), had written in his diary on Nov. 30, 1973: "At one time Central Oregon wasn't big enough for both of us (Ricky and his father). I have returned not in vengeance or contempt, but to live my life in my own way."

"Not just as a gay, but as a proud gay. And not afraid to admit the fact. Why live a lie and be something you're not or what somebody else wants you to be?...be yourself open and freely."

Ricky, one of the estimated 11 million homosexuals in American, says it has taken him many months to be accepted by his friends with whom he now jokes about his homosexuality. His story and brief profiles of several other area homosexuals accompany this article.

Ricky:

'. . . I realized chicks weren't the thing for me'

Ricky was born and has lived in Central Oregon for most of his 25 years, except for a brief period in the Navy and short stints working in Portland and Seattle.

"When I was 15 or 16, I realized chicks weren't the thing for me. I had a lover (male) down the street, but when we were 16, a girl broke us up. I went with her for two or three years. That was very frustrating," Ricky recalled.

In his diary, on Nov. 5, 1972, Ricky — who now works for a restaurant in the area — wrote: "Remember you at that age? What a crazy mixed up kid you were. Kept trying to change from gay life to hetero. Each time you changed, the more dissatisfied you became. And not just with women. You became that much more disgusted with yourself.

"Even became suicidal. Then you tried, almost succeeded, if...your ex-wife's son, 16 years old and damn good looking, hadn't of pulled your body from the surf. The tide was going out and nobody would've missed you."

After being dismissed from the Navy for a nervous condition related to problems with his homosexuality, Ricky went to Portland and became very successful in his job there.

He "came out" (a gay term for publicly asserting one's homosexuality) and joined the scene there with lavish parties and old, rich "sugar daddies" cruising in their sleek, fancy cars, looking for young homosexual partners.

In Portland, Ricky was married to an older woman for six months. The marriage was a "social " marriage for tax purposes and to maintain appearances of being "straight" or heterosexual.

Returning to Central Oregon, he worked in various restaurants and "quit" at one after the boss accused him of making sexual advances toward another male employe.

Ricky said, "I don't mess around on the job. That's a no-no."

Although Ricky spent several years learning to cope with his sexuality, he feels comfortable now as a homosexual. He enjoys his job and sees a positive future in it.

Ricky's boss knows he's gay.

His relations with his family, who still live here, have varied. Now, he considers the situation good. He again is thinking of marrying to maintain the apppearance of being heterosexual.

"To a certain extent, I'm a recluse. But I have a very pleasant life," Ricky said.

He likes the slow, unhurried pace of Central Oregon and puts most of his energies into his job.

After quoting verbatim, Romans 1:26-27, Ricky — who grew up as a member of the Christian Church — said the Bible's hostile view toward homosexuality is outdated.

Another portion of his diary, on Nov. 30, 1973, reads as follows, "Even though I feel I have no family, the fond memories linger...Thank you, God, for giving patience and understanding, not to mention that great gift only you can give — love."

Barbara:

'It's like we belong in another country . . .'

When Sue and Barbara moved eight months ago from the Willamette Valley to Central Oregon, someone scrawled on the door of their home: "Fairies wear boots."

This greeting was a harbinger of many experiences they would have in Bend.

On several occasions in bars, they have been ridiculed for being "queers" and mocked with obscene jokes about their homosexuality.

Twice, Sue (not her real name) has been denied a change of job location by her employer.

She describes herself as a professional and says, "I don't want to force the issue by being identified."

She said her homosexuality is the unofficial reason given for the transfer denials.

"Right now I would like people not to think of me as gay or straight, man or woman, but that I do a job well," she said.

We would just as soon see a people world," instead of one segmented sexually, racially and religiously, said Sue, who is 27 and grew up in the Pacific Northwest.

"I don't want to be snickered at or hear dirty jokes said behind my back at work and loud enough so I can hear them. I'm tired of explaining myself to people. I just want to go some place and to live. And if people don't accept me, to hell with them," Sue said.

Barbara, who lived in various places as her father traveled around the world in the Army, said she is not unhappy in Bend, but she couldn't live here for any prolonged periods.

She said, "Compared to our other friends, we haven't had much trouble, though."

Barbara (not her real name either) is 25 and works for a motel in the area. She and Sue have lived together for more than three years. They consider their relationship unusual among lesbians. Both regard themselves as monogamists.

"I don't feel I need to have children to make my life complete," Barbara said.

It we could just find some friends here," she says.

They know one married couple besides the people they know at work. They say the unfriendliness they feel in Bend stems from their being outsiders and homosexuals.

"It's like we belong in another country. And people think that we don't vote and we just are perverted with our whips and chains" Barbara said.

Sue, who deals with the public in her job, said once when working she approached someone who said, "Here comes that dirty queer again."

Sue said, "If you don't have hair down to your waist and big boobs, you're not a woman."

Barbara said, "I believe in God. I'm not a Christian Scientist but I lean towards that. God is love and that's all he knows. He can't condemn love when it doesn't hurt anybody. I don't feel we're perverted. I can't say because I'm a queer, I'm going to hell."

David:

'I think being homosexual is a positive thing'

Although David Buscemi knows Bend doesn't encourage homosexuality, he isn't reluctant to reveal his name. He came here in July with the man he's been living with for six years.

They left a tiny New Hampshire town after pressure was applied because they were activist homosexuals. Their trouble began when they handed out pro-homosexuality leaflets which said, in part: "Gay is not tragic. Gay is OK."

David's partner, Gene, which is his actual first name, was born in Bend and has lived here most of his life. He's 31 and was married but has been separated for six years. He has several children who live with his wife.

"I can see why gays would want to be discreet in Bend," David, 25, said. "The feeling here is of masculinity, with loggers and cowboys. I really feel self-conscious about being gay in Bend."

David, a native of Groton, Mass., attended Syracuse University for two years and later the University of Washington, where he met Gene.

Although David bitterly recalls being harassed as a youngster, he said, "I think being a homosexual is a positive thing. I think as far as our relationship goes, we're pretty free and easy. It's sensitive."

David said Gene is more radical than he because Gene grew up repressed in the Bend environment and he has reacted to that.

"I hope some of my children are homosexuals," Gene said. "Homosexuals should recruit more homosexuals because we're not going to make anymore."

"We're into gay liberation," said Gene, who graduated from Bend High School and now is a carpenter.

"My favorite thing is to go up to people on the street and ask them if they want to go to bed with me. The only reason people shun it, is they're afraid they might like it."

"There is a myth of homosexuals being milktoasts. That's why radical action, even shooting pigs who are down on homosexuals, would be good. Homosexuals are going to come out soon," Gene said.

Henry:

'There is quite a bit of cruising going on . . .'

Henry, a homosexual, came temporarily to Oregon. He is college educated and works with a film company recently in the area.

Henry says the "gay scene" in Central Oregon is far removed from the glittering, gay discotheques such as Le Jardin in New York, or San Francisco's sauna baths or Hollywood's bizarre, bisexual parties.

Henry isn't his real name.

"Knowing the way people feel here in Bend, there is a certain degree of paranoia about revealing my name," he said.

People fear homosexuality because, he says, "if everyone were homosexual, there would be no human race."

"The only woe of being gay in Bend is it's hard to meet people. There are more closet cases here than any other place I've been," Henry said.

Despite that, he said, "There is quite a bit of cruising going on around here."

Cruising is a subtle tango of the eyes which occurs among gays in several after hours bars in the area. Cruising is a necessary part of the game, Henry said, because only 15 per cent of homosexuals are identifiable by outward appearances.

Henry, however, has been reluctant to indicate his gayness in bars here.

"There is baiting in small towns. Also, if a gay here were afraid I would expose him, it might come to the point where he might kill me," he said.

During a recent two-week period, Henry said he met more than a half dozen gays who were cruising.

He said people in small towns should be more tolerant of homosexuals, for there is no reason to fear them sexually.

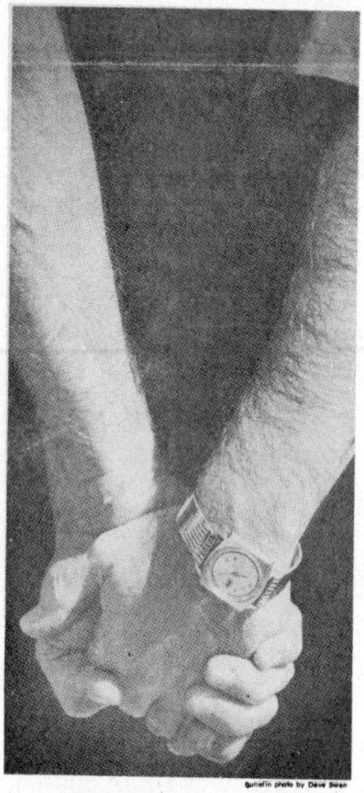

Bulletin photo by Dave Swan

Stories by Berkley Hudson

Lifestyle Interview. Hudson interviews a couple at home in preparation for one of his series of lifestyle interviews.

"Since I'm not gay, that caused a slight problem," he recalled. His sources were unsure of his motives and his understanding of their problems. But he was open with the six persons he interviewed, and his obvious sincerity established a rapport that led to a reciprocal openness.

"Before and during the writing of the story, I did a great deal of reading about the subject," Hudson says. "This impressed the people I interviewed and they were frank and honest."

The Bulletin devoted an entire page to Hudson's stories. There were more letters, including a few that contained the page from *The Bulletin* with the word "GARBAGE" scrawled across it, about 20 telephone calls and a few personal visits. More than a year after the article appeared, some people in town still shunned him. However, the response was not all negative. Some callers and letter writers praised Hudson's reporting.

Undaunted, Hudson continued to seek out stories about people with divergent lifestyles. Through interviews and research, he informed *The Bulletin*'s readers of the lives of people heretofore invisible to most Bend residents. Some of these stories struck home, particularly Hudson's piece based on interviews with unmarried couples.

If we could have followed Hudson from the time he developed his ideas for these stories through his interviewing, we would have noticed his careful preparations and the warm relationship between him and his sources. His questions were designed to elicit relevant information, and he listened more than he talked. In short, Hudson was putting to work the four interviewing principles we derived at the beginning of this chapter.

Putting the Principles to Work

Preparing for the interview, the reporter devotes as much time as possible to learning about the subject matter and the person to be interviewed. Questions will be carefully drafted, whether written or stored in the reporter's mind. During the interview, the reporter will establish a relationship that may be friendly, reassuring, threatening, naive or knowledgeable. Finally the reporter will listen carefully to what is said and will watch attentively to see how it is said and whether the scene is worth noting.

The Interviewer's Ground Rules

Both parties in an interview have certain assumptions and expectations. There are ground rules that both usually agree to follow in order to create an atmosphere of mutual trust. Generally, the reporter expects the interviewee to tell the truth and to stand behind what he or she has told the interviewer.

The interviewee presumes the reporter will write the story fairly and accurately. Both agree, without saying so, that the questions and answers mean what they appear to mean—that is, that there are no hidden meanings.

Having said this, we must now admit to the exceptions. As we have pointed out, sources may conceal, evade, distort and lie when they believe it is to their advantage to do so. The reporter must be alert to the signs that indicate a departure from the truth.

As for the reporter, the rules that govern his behavior in the interview can be detailed with greater certainty. Reporters, too, conceal, mislead and, at times, lie. A few reporters justify these practices, but most would agree the reporter should:

1. Identify himself or herself at the outset of the interview.
2. State the purpose of the interview.
3. Make clear to those unaccustomed to being interviewed that the material will be used.
4. Give the source an idea of how much time the interview will take.
5. Keep the interview as short as possible.
6. Ask short, specific questions the source is competent to answer.
7. Give the source ample time to reply.
8. Ask the source to repeat or to clarify complex or vague answers.
9. Read back answers if requested or when in doubt about the phrasing of crucial material.

10. Insist on answers if the public has a right to know them.
11. Avoid lecturing the source, arguing or debating.
12. Abide by requests for non-attribution, background-only or off-the-record should the source make this a condition of the interview or of a statement.

Reporters who habitually violate these rules risk losing their sources. Few sources are anxious to talk to an incompetent or an exploitative reporter. When the source realizes that he or she is being used to enhance the reporter's career or to further the reporter's personal ideas or philosophy, the source will close up.

For their part, sources also risk trouble when they exploit the press. Reporters are mature enough to understand that their sources will float occasional trial balloons and give incomplete, even misleading, information. But constant and flagrant misuse of the press leads to retaliation by journalists.

We are now ready to examine in detail the way reporters go about preparing for and conducting interviews.

In his first year on the job, a reporter sent this note to one of his former journalism instructors:

The Preparations

> I'm finding out that the greatest trouble I have is with interviews. Here you are in a man-on-man situation, you and the expert. You simply have to know everything that you can know about the man and his specialty. These people are busy. They do not have time to waste on you if you don't know what you are talking about. You have to go in with a specific idea of what you want, which you can get from the clips and from your general information. They will trust you to report something important if they realize you understand what they are talking about.
>
> Recently, I attended a press conference on a new method of revitalizing oil wells. There was a reporter from one of the local papers who obviously was sent down to get a feature story. She had no idea what was happening, and every time she asked a question, we all cringed. The fellow we were interviewing was a decent guy. He spent 10 minutes patiently explaining the essentials and she dashed off happy as a lark. I read her story later. It was absolutely unintelligible.

In the years following this first brush with the challenges of interviewing, *Wall Street Journal* reporter Fred L. Zimmerman had plenty of opportunities to sharpen his skill. He interviewed politicians, merchants and college students in the 1960s when blacks protested segregation by refusing to leave lunch counters and restaurants that would not serve them. Covering business activities, he interviewed corporation presidents and directors. In Washington, Zimmerman interviewed the directors of federal regulatory agencies on their programs and the meaning of their directives. Later, as his newspaper's White House correspondent, he had to cover the wide range from politics to international affairs in his interviews.

For each of these assignments, Zimmerman made intensive preparations. In addition to keeping abreast of developments on his beat, he would try to learn as much as possible about the subject of the interview. Based on his experiences, here are his suggestions to beginning reporters about how to prepare for an interview:

1. Do research on the interview topic and the person to be interviewed, not only so you can ask the right questions and understand the answers, but also so you can demonstrate, clearly but unobtrusively, to the interviewee that you cannot be easily fooled.
2. Devise a tentative theme for your story. A major purpose of the interview will be to obtain quotes, anecdotes and other evidence to support that theme.
3. List question topics in advance—as many as you can think of, even though you may not ask all of them and almost certainly will ask others that you do not list.
4. In preparing for interviews on sensitive subjects, theorize about what the person's attitude is *likely* to be toward you and the subject you are asking about. What is his or her role in the event? Whose side is he on? What kind of answers can you logically expect to your key questions? Based on this theorizing, develop a plan of attack that you think might mesh with his *probable* attitude and get through his *probable* defenses.

Obviously, there are many assignments the reporter takes on with scant time for these preparations. Whatever the time limit, however, the reporter can at least check the morgue, which is an automatic response on any assignment. Because a reporter may have to move quickly, greater dependence is made of the reporter's storehouse of knowledge, the background the reporter has picked up in reading, covering related stories, discussions with colleagues and sources. Under the pressure of deadline, these resources become the reporter's basis for designing questions in the interview.

Research

A. J. Liebling, a master reporter who moved from the newspaper newsroom to *The New Yorker* magazine, is quoted in *The Most of A. J. Liebling,* edited by William Cole (New York: Simon and Schuster, 1963): "The preparation is the same whether you are going to interview a diplomat, a jockey, or an ichthyologist. From the man's past you learn what questions are likely to stimulate a response."

Research begins with the library's clippings about the subject matter of the interview. If the topic has more than local importance or if the interviewee is well-known, *The New York Times Index* and *Facts on File* may have a reference that can be useful. *The Reader's Guide to Periodical Literature* also may list a magazine article about the topic or the person who is to be interviewed. For personality interviews, *Who's Who in America* and other biographical dictionaries can be consulted. Persons who know the interviewee can be asked for information, also.

Oriana Fallaci, an Italian journalist whose interviews appear in newspapers around the world, says, "I read as much as I can to prepare for an interview. For my interview with Marshal Tito—if you could see the amount I read: books, articles, other interviews. So much, it scares me. I took notes from it all." Her extensive reading gives her a framework from which to develop her questions, she says.

These resources provide material for three purposes: They give the reporter leads to specific questions; they provide the reporter with a feel for the subject, and they may provide useful background for the story.

Asking Questions

In the best of all possible worlds for the reporter, all sources love to talk, and they speak openly and to the point. Strange as it may seem, reporters sometimes realize these dreams. Television cameras seem to induce this mood, as does the prospect of seeing one's name in print. Sometimes the urge to talk wells up from a need that lies deeper than the desire to be seen on television. Persons occasionally have a compelling desire to share an experience or to call attention to a topic that requires public discussion. Most of us have this feeling after reading a good book, hearing an exciting concert, or seeing a close game.

Arthur L. Gavshon, the AP's diplomatic reporter, says that one of his first good stories after he had been assigned to the diplomatic beat came when Britain was administering Palestine. Jews who were fleeing Europe were entering Palestine in violation of the British limitation on Jewish immigration. The Arabs were pressuring Britain to stop the flow from Europe, and the Jews were anxious to flee the Continent where so many of their relatives and friends had been killed by the Nazis.

"Daily, I checked unhappy government men for their solution to a situation of deep sadness. Then, by chance, I saw a three-line newspaper report that said that the Royal Navy battleship *Vanguard* had sailed from Malta to Haifa," he says.

Gavshon knew that warships do not venture into dangerous areas without orders. He made several checks with his sources and was able to write that Britain was about to mount an air-sea blockade to halt the stream of Jews into Palestine.

Gavshon says he was able to score this exclusive because "some officials were ready to reveal a plan they did not much like."

Lucky is the reporter who finds a source in a similarly talkative mood. Luckier still is the reporter who finds a source in this mood who talks accurately and truthfully about matters in which the reporter is interested. Most often persons are too busy with their own affairs to talk. They must be prodded. Usually, sources are moved to talk by a series of questions that take shape from the reporter's preparations and from the reporter's use of situations and facts that develop during the interview.

The Basic Questions

For most interviews, some questions can be prepared ahead of time. Often, but not always, they are asked early in the interview. Fallaci carefully prepares her first questions. Most of her subsequent questions are based on answers she receives to her prepared questions.

In a personality interview, the reporter will want to know the vital data about the source—age, address, education, jobs held, family, and so on. Some of these may not seem necessary since the clippings and references may contain such material. But people move and change jobs, and clippings can be wrong.

Harold Ross, the brilliant and eccentric former newspaperman who founded and edited *The New Yorker*, slashed in exasperation at the pages of profiles and interviews that lacked vital data. "Who he?," Ross would scrawl across such manuscripts.

The reporter must also identify the source sufficiently to provide the reader or viewer with reason to give credence to the source's comments.

As obvious as these questions about identification may be, the beginning reporter may want to jot them down before setting out on an interview. Otherwise, the reporter may be embarrassed by having to call the source later for basic information. In her first week at *The Daily Register*, Shrewsbury, N.J., a journalism school graduate was sent to interview an Austrian organ maker who was installing a new organ in the United Methodist Church in nearby Red Bank. All went well until the reporter and the photographer were on their way out of the church. At the door, the photographer whispered to her. She looked crestfallen and ran back into the church.

"I had forgotten to ask the builder how old he was," she says, "and the photographer had to remind me. So I had to go back and ask."

These basic questions are usually neutral and therefore easy to answer, so asking them early makes the source feel at ease with the reporter. Sometimes a reporter will ask a question that is of little news value in order to break the ice with an interviewee he has never seen before. These lead-in questions must be carefully chosen for the public figure. The politician, athlete or diplomat usually expects to be queried about relevant matters and has little time for chit-chat.

Once the reporter moves into the serious business, he or she must ask questions that are aimed at revelation, disclosure and insight for the reader or listener. These questions, sometimes called leading questions, are designed to turn up material that will enable the public to learn something that has been unknown or that will clarify material that had been unclear.

Leading Questions

Most interviews are based on questions that the reporter believes will lead to newsworthy information. The questions follow what the reporter perceives to be the nature or the theme of the assignment. A reporter calls the state highway patrol and hears about a fatal accident nearby. Automatically, the reporter knows that he or she must find out who died and how and where the death occurred. The same process is at work on the more complicated interview.

A reporter is told to interview an actor who had been out of work for two years and is now in a hit musical. The reporter decides that the theme of the story will be the changes the actor has made in his life. He asks the actor if he has moved from his tenement walkup, has made any large personal purchases and how his family has reacted to his suddenly being away most nights. These three questions lead the actor to talk at length.

On another assignment, the reporter is to interview a well-known singer-composer. The reporter decides to ask about the singer's experiences that led him to write songs that call attention to war, poverty, sexism and racism. "Bread," says the singer in answer to the first question the reporter asks. "Money," he explains. There is a good market in such songs. The reporter then quickly shifts themes and asks questions about the economics of popular music and the singer's personal beliefs.

472   **Chapter 17**

The interview with the singer-composer illustrates the reporter's ability to shift from the tentative theme. Early questions will follow the prepared theme, but should the replies turn in a more rewarding direction, the reporter devises another theme and uses this as the basis for a new line of leading questions.

When the sports writer asked the hurdler, "What do you think of our town?" he was using what is known as an open-end question that could have been answered at length. The sports editor's suggestion that the reporter ask the athlete about the condition of the track would have elicited a specific response—fast, slow, or slick—as it was a closed-end question.

The open-end question does not require a specific answer. The closed-end question calls for a brief, pointed reply. Applied properly, both have their merits. Two months before the budget is submitted, a city hall reporter may ask the city manager what he thinks of the city's general financial situation—an open-end question. The reply may cover the failure of anticipated revenues to meet expectations, unusually high increases in construction costs, higher interest rates and other factors that have caused trouble for the city. Then the reporter may ask a closed-end question, "Will we have a tax increase?"

As we have seen, reporters often begin their interviews with open-end questions, which allow the source to relax. Then the closed-end questions are asked, which can seem threatening to a source if asked at the outset of the interview.

Television and radio interview programs usually end with a closed-end question because the interviewer knows there is time only for a brief reply.

The reporter who asks only open-end questions should be aware of their implications to the source. To some sources, the open-end question is the mark of an inadequately-prepared reporter who is fishing for a story.

Television reporters seem to have a tendency to ask open-end questions, even when a specific one is more appropriate. When a van containing radioactive materials was stolen in New Jersey, a youngster who had been in contact with the van was rushed to the hospital for checks. A TV reporter asked the boy's mother, "Weren't you a little nervous?"

A Chicago TV reporter in an interview with orphans asked a youngster, "Do you wish you had a mother and father?"

The most-famous of all these open-end questions that poorly prepared TV reporters ask is, "How do you feel about. . . ?"

Marvin Kitman, a television critic, comments: "Whether it's a press conference on funding or the neutron bomb, TV guys will ask the dumb, open-ended questions about the report. The print guys at the press conference often know the implications and meanings already. They have read the report, not just the press releases. They go deeper. The TV guys who are asking the inane, 'What does it mean?' don't want to go into the facts, which only complicate the story, and life.

"Asking inane questions is as much a part of a TV journalist's job as using hair spray."

Of course, there are many competent TV reporters who are well-prepared and ask specific questions.

Interviewing the Klan.
Reporter Peter Francis of *The Stockton Record* questions two leaders of the Ku Klux Klan about their plan to organize California chapters. Bill Wilkinson (with cigar), KKK national leader, and George Pepper, head of the California Klan, said their program of promoting racial segregation was attracting new members "every day." Although Wilkinson refused to shake his hand when they were introduced and both men were wary, Francis was able to draw them out about their plans for California.

Asking the Right Questions

Reporters are often criticized for belaboring the obvious, for the constant reworking of the same themes so that stories that may seem to contain new material are merely differently phrased reworkings of the same old story. The charge is valid. But by asking the right questions, reporters can write stories that put people closer to the truth than they have been.

A reporter's preparations must be wide ranging, well beyond reading the local newspaper and chatting with authorities. Reporters who hold themselves to these narrow confines usually are able only to operate in a linear fashion. That is, today's coverage is built on yesterday's newspaper stories and the council meeting of the day before. Good stories—by which we mean informative journalism—often are spurred by the question that breaks the chain of events. Remember Copernicus. All he asked was what would happen if the sun and not the earth were the center of the universe, and what had been centuries of linear thinking shot off into a new plane.

Asking the Tough Questions

Sometimes a young reporter finds that posing the right question is difficult because the question might embarrass or compromise the interviewee. There is no recourse but to ask. Some reporters will lead up to the tough questions with open-end questions so that the source starts talking freely. Then they will ask the difficult questions. Some reporters say that the abruptly asked question may be more likely to produce a reply because delay may only intensify the source's resolution to evade or to give the reporter a barrage of verbiage behind which the source can hide.

Whatever the technique, the tough question must be asked. This may be especially difficult for a young reporter interviewing a person in authority.

Fallaci says that her success may be the result of her asking the world leaders she interviews questions that other reporters do not ask.

"Some reporters are courageous only when they write, when they are alone with their typewriters, not when they face the person in power. They never put a question like this, 'Sir, since you are a dictator, we all know you are corrupt. In what measure are you corrupt?' ''

Remarkably, heads of state, kings and guerrilla leaders open up to her. One reason for this is her obvious courage. She lets her sources know that the public is entitled to answers to her questions. She will not be treated impolitely or with indifference. When Muhammad Ali belched in answer to one of her questions, she threw the microphone of her tape recorder at his face.

Another reason for her effectiveness is "her talent for intimacy," as one journalist put it. "She easily establishes an atmosphere of confidence and closeness and creates the impression that she would tell you anything. Consequently, you feel safe, or almost safe, to do the same with her," writes Diana Loercher in *The Christian Science Monitor*.

In her interview with Henry Kissinger, the U.S. secretary of state at the time, Fallaci had him admit that his position of power made him feel like the "lone cowboy who leads the wagon train alone on his horse." His image of himself as the Lone Ranger caused Kissinger later to say that granting Fallaci the interview was the "stupidest" act in his life.

In *All the President's Men*, Bob Woodward describes his telephone call to Kissinger to ask whether the secretary of state had placed wiretaps on his aides. Woodward explains to Kissinger that he had been told by sources in the FBI that Kissinger had done so.

> Kissinger paused. "It could be Mr. Haldeman who authorized the taps," he said.
> How about Kissinger? Woodward asked.
> "I don't believe it was true," he stated.
> Is that a denial?
> A pause. "I frankly don't remember."
> Woodward reminds Kissinger that his sources said that Kissinger had personally authorized the taps.
> A brief pause. "Almost never," he said.
> Woodward suggested that "almost never" meant "sometimes." Was Kissinger then confirming the story?

Kissinger gets excited and tells Woodward that the questioning is like a "police interrogation."

> "If it is possible and if it happened, then I have to take responsibility for it . . . I'm responsible for this office."
> Did you do it? Woodward asked.

There is no hesitation here. Woodward gets right to the point.

Kissinger did not like the questioning and called Woodward's boss, Benjamin Bradlee. He told Bradlee that it was "almost inconceivable" that he authorized the wiretapping. Woodward pointed out that this was not a denial.

Once the Watergate stories began running, Woodward and Bernstein became known as tough questioners. Some reporters gain this reputation and need not beat around the bush. When Jack Anderson, the Washington columnist whose specialty is political exposés, calls a congressman, the politician knows that he is unlikely to be asked for the text of a speech he is to give in Dubuque. Anderson is after meatier game.

Still, there are questions that few reporters like to ask. Most of these concern the private lives of sources—a city councilman's recent divorce, the mental retardation of a young couple's missing son, the fatal illness of a baseball player's wife. Some of these questions are necessary, some not. The guidelines for relevance and good taste are constantly shifting, and reporters may find they are increasingly being told to ask questions that they consider intrusive.

Often, this uneasiness stems from the anticipation that the source may be hurt or embarrassed by the questions. Yet, reporters who dislike asking these questions because they would prefer to spare sources anguish are sometimes surprised by the frank replies to their questions. A reporter for *Newsday* was assigned to follow up an automobile accident in which a drunk youth without a driver's license ran a borrowed car into a tree. One of the passengers, a 15-year-old girl, was killed. In doing his follow-up story, the reporter discovered that most of the parents were willing to talk. Some were anxious to be interviewed because, as one parent said, the lessons learned from the accident might save the lives of other youngsters.

Making Sources Talk

The early stage of the interview is often a feeling-out period for the source and the reporter. The interviewee balances the hazards and gains for him or his organization in divulging the information the reporter seeks, and the reporter tries to show the source the rewards the source will receive through the disclosure of the information—publicity, respect, and the feeling that goes with doing a good turn.

When the source concludes that the risks outweigh the possible gains and decides to provide little or no significant information or is misleading, the reporter has several alternatives. At one extreme, the reporter can try to cajole the source into a complete account through flattery—or by appearing hurt and surprised. At the other extreme, the reporter can demand information. If the source is a public official, such demands have some legitimacy because officials are responsible to the public. The reporter can tell the source that the story—and there will be some kind of story—will point out that the official refused to answer questions. Usually, the source will fall into line, for he eventually realizes he needs the press more than the press needs the source. This statement is true of all public figures, whether they are officials or not.

If the source is an authority, he cannot escape a question with the plea that he does not know the answer. A city controller, whose job it is to audit the financial records of city agencies and departments, told a reporter he had no idea whether a bureau had put excess funds in non-interest bearing bank accounts. Told by the reporter it was his business to know that and that the story would state so, the controller supplied the information.

Stephen P. Morin and Dan Stets of *The* Providence *Journal-Bulletin* revealed that committees of the Rhode Island state legislature hire 20 lawyers and that many ot them do little for their $4,000 to $6,000 a year. The jobs are usually awarded through patronage.

Accompanying their story revealing the expenditures was a sidebar that shows Morin trying to make one of the lawyers talk:

How Did You Get Your Job, Mr. Marzilli?

Frederic A. Marzilli has been legal counsel to the Senate's Health, Education and Welfare Committee since January, 1981. He served as counsel to the Judiciary Committee the year before that.

Reporter Stephen P. Morin asked him how he got his job:

A. Ah, I'm trying to think if I got a letter indicating that I wasn't going to be rehired for Judiciary. Ah, I don't know. I don't even have a file. I had one when I was in Judiciary, but I don't keep a file no more.

Q. I'm incredulous.
A. What does that mean?

Q. It's hard for me to believe that you don't know how you got selected for a job that pays $6,000.
A. Well, again, I don't think it's a job.

Q. What is it then?
A. A contract. It's no different than a garbage company. I'm not an employee. I'm a contractor. Look, I'm not trying to give you a tap dance.

Q. Work is a job, isn't it? Whatever you do is a job, right?
A. Right.

Q. How did you hear about this job?
A. I know how the General Assembly works. I was an intern for two years. I was a member of the Model Legislature. I go down there a lot. It wasn't something I was unfamiliar with.

Q. Do you know legislators?
A. Ah, yes.

Q. Are you related to anybody?
A. No. Definitely not. Nepotism is a bad word.

Q. How about cronyism
A. Ah, I don't call it cronyism.

Q. Well, how were you selected? Do you know Rocco Quattrocchi?
A. I know him. We've been involved in politics before.

Q. Is he your godfather? Do you have a godfather?
A. No.

Q. No one recommended you for the job?
A. I'll be candid with you. I don't want to be singled out. I don't know whether to . . .

Q. Why don't you just speak honestly? That would relieve your problems. How did you get the job?
A. I think, because of my previous experience down there. I think that point is valid.

Q. Previous experience doing what? Being a lawyer?
A. No, no. Knowing how the General Assembly works.

Q. You're saying you did not make any phone calls asking for this position?
A. Oh, I inquired. I inquired as to what the proper steps were for getting a job. I sent a resume and sent out an application, and I think I gave it to Jerry Mosca (Angelo Mosca Jr., head of Legislative Council). I wanted to work at Leg. Council.

Q. Legal counsel (to the committee) is second best?
A. I guess. They didn't say to me, 'If you don't want this, you want this job?' I went down and tried to talk to him (Mosca), but he's a real tough guy to get in touch with, and I'm trying to remember if I got a call from Rocco's secretary or not. I know it wasn't by mail. I know it was Christmastime, 1980.

Q. She gave you a Christmas present?
A. Christmas present? Boy, are you tough. I like reporters.

Q. Essentially Rocco selected you?
A. Yeah, I would say that was a fair estimate.

Q. Thanks.
A. Listen. Take it easy on me, will you?

Sometimes a source will seem to talk freely but will cover the important material with a layer of unimportant information. When the interviewer confronts this situation, it is often worthwhile to encourage the source to talk on. The reporter adopts a naive, innocent demeanor and listens, occasionally asking a simple question. Emboldened by the rapt attention of the reporter, who is studiously taking notes, the source may begin to exaggerate or fabricate. These assertions duly noted, the reporter may suddenly appear puzzled by statements that, he informs the source, contradict what the source had said earlier or what is known as fact. Given the opportunity to pull back gracefully, the source may do so by giving the reporter the desired information. If the source does not, the reporter says that he has no alternative but to print the source's fabrications and accompany them with the evidence that contradicts or corrects the statements. Confronted by the implicit threat to make the source look silly, evasive or duplicitous, the source often agrees to supply the necessary material.

Some reporters teach their sources that they cannot be misled or lied to by using the misleading or false information and to provoke other sources to issue denials, corrections or amplifications. This technique of setting sources into play against one another is well known to experienced reporters. As James Fallows writes in *The Washington Monthly*, "If there is one thing reporters in Washington understand, it is the necessity of playing ins versus outs, privates versus captains, agency A against agency B."

These techniques may appear unethical to the uninitiated. Properly applied to public officials, they are justified by the public's right to know and the requirement that journalists hold officials accountable to the public.

Wendell Rawls Jr., who has worked for *The Tennessean* in Nashville, *The Philadelphia Inquirer* and *The New York Times*, says of interviewing: "Most important of all, you just got to listen—just sit there and listen."

His advice was given to reporters at a conference of the Investigative Reporters & Editors organization and adapted for publication in the November/December 1982 *Columbia Journalism Review* under the title, "Interviewing: the crafty art." Rawls adds:

Another thing I would suggest is, don't tell people what you know. Ask questions. Then back off. Use diversion. I love to do that—talk with people about things you're not there to talk to them about. You ask a question that may be very meaningful. Then you move away from it. I do it sometimes even if the person doesn't get particularly fidgety, because I don't want him to think that I think what he has told me is necessarily important to me. I'll move to another question and say, "What is that on the wall? That's an interesting sort of. . . ." Whatever. Anything that will divert him, and he will start talking about that. And then maybe ask two or three questions about junk, and then come back and ask another very pointed question.

Rare is the reporter whose persuasiveness is so overwhelming or whose charm is so overpowering that he or she is never told, "No comment." Most reporters run up against stone walls, some frequently because of the nature of their assignments. Reporters must then resort to techniques and devices that will nudge information from unwilling sources.

Handling "No Comment"

One *Wall Street Journal* reporter says if he fails to convince the source that revelation will benefit him, he remarks that he already knows the other side of the issue and that "no comment" will mean that only the other side will be reported.

Another technique is to tell the source that although the available information is incomplete the station or newspaper will have to run it anyway. The source is told that with his help the story will be more accurate.

"One of my sources will never tell me anything if we start from scratch on a story," a business reporter said. "But he will talk if I have something. Sometimes I bluff that I know more than I really do," he said.

Investigative reporters are masters of the bluff. During the Eisenhower administration, Drew Pearson—a muckraking Washington columnist—sought to expose White House interference with the supposedly independent regulatory agencies such as the Federal Trade Commission and the Federal Communications Commission. Pearson's assistant, Jack Anderson, was given the job of gathering the information. Anderson heard that private attorneys who had lost cases before various commissions suspected political fixes. (A reporter's maxim: When investigating suspicious decisions in government, always talk to the losers.)

Anderson learned that Commissioner Richard Mack of the FCC had promised his decisive vote to an applicant before the commission proceedings began. The applicant, considered the least qualified of the four applicants by the FCC examiner, had hired an attorney to lobby his case. The attorney, Thurman Whiteside, was a friend of Mack and a notorious fixer in Washington.

Anderson found out that Whiteside controlled a trust fund. "I was half satisfied he was using this as a funnel for payments to Mack, but I had no proof," Anderson recalls in his book *Confessions of a Muckraker* (New York: Random House, 1979). He called Mack

. . . and tried to con the truth out of him before he could get his defenses straight.

After giving him the nerve-jangling news that I was Jack Anderson of Drew Pearson's office, I bluffed, 'I have an accountant who is prepared to testify that Whiteside has paid you money from the Grant Foster trust. I'd like to hear your side of it.'

There was a moment of dead air as Mack fell for the bait and groped for a way to reconcile the irreconcilable. 'Those were only loans,' he ventured, not seeming to realize that even in sweetening up the transactions he was admitting to the impermissible offense—taking money under any guise from an attorney in the Miami television case.

Mack dug himself into a deeper and deeper pit as he tried to parry Anderson's educated guesses. By the time the interview was over, Anderson had confirmed his suspicions: Mack was on the take.

Some sources try to avoid problems by avoiding comments. The reporter can open up silent sources by telling them that they will be quoted as saying "no comment," which might lead people to believe they are hiding something. Some reporters tell "no comment" sources that they will keep trying to dig up the information, and when they do they will make it a point to include the silent source's "no comment." Few sources want to be embarrassed this way.

Most reporters know that there is more than one source for a story, and that if they cannot budge the first source, they may find the information elsewhere. A reporter assigned to find out how the recession affected local automobile sales made no headway with the local dealers. Obviously hit hard by flagging sales, they did not want to admit that all was not well. The reporter was at sea and told his editor the story could not be broken. The editor suggested he check the motor vehicles department and the tax office. In many cities, new car sales are recorded for fee and tax purposes. Once the reporter had the basic data, the local automobile dealers opened up.

Anonymous Sources

Sometimes a source will allow material to be used on the proviso it is not attributed to him. Usually, the information can be used. But when the information constitutes an attack on an individual, it should be handled carefully. The victim, confronted by an anonymous attacker or detractor, has no idea where the information originated and may be hamstrung in making an adequate reply. Persons who criticize others should be asked by the reporter to stand by their words rather than to hide behind the reporter, who must assume responsibility for the story with no source.

Guidelines for Questioning

Zimmerman suggests some guidelines to asking questions that have worked for him:

1. Almost never should you plunge in with tough questions at the beginning. Instead, break the ice, explain who you are, what you are doing, why you went to him or her. A touch of flattery usually helps if it is not overdone. Try to establish rapport.
2. Often the opening question should be an open-ended inquiry that sets the man or woman off on his or her favorite subject. News rarely comes out of this kind of question. Its value is to get the person talking, to set up a conversational atmosphere, and to provide you with important clues about his or her attitude toward you, the subject and the idea of being interviewed.
3. Watch and listen closely as he talks. How is he reacting? Does he seem open or secretive? Maybe interrupt him in the middle of an anecdote to ask a minor question about something he is leaving out, just to test his reflexes. Use the information you are obtaining in this early stage to ascertain whether your preinterview hunches about him were right or wrong. Use it also to determine what style you should adopt to match his mood. If he insists upon being formal, you may have to become more businesslike yourself. If he is relaxed and expansive, you should be too, but beware of the possibility the interview can then degenerate into a formless conversation over which you have no control.
4. Start through your questions, usually in an arranged order, to lead him along a trail you have picked. One question should logically follow another.

Lead up to a tough question with two or three preliminaries. Sometimes it helps to create the impression that the tough question has just occurred to you because of something he is saying.

5. Listen for hints that suggest questions you had not thought of beforehand. And stay alert for the possibility that the theme you picked in advance is the wrong one, or is only a subsidiary one. Remain flexible. Through an accidental remark of his you may uncover a story that is better than the one you came for. If so, go after it right there.

6. Throughout the interview, keep reminding yourself that when you leave, you are going back to a typewriter to do a story. As he talks, ask yourself: What is my lead going to be? Do I understand enough to state a theme clearly at the typewriter and buttress it with quotes and documentation? Do I know his or her full name, his title? Do I have enough information to write a coherent account of the anecdote he just told me?

7. Do not forget to ask the key question—the one your editors sent you to ask, or the one that will elicit supporting material for your theme.

8. Do not be reluctant to ask an embarrassing question. Even if you go through all the preliminaries you can think of, the time finally arrives to ask the tough question. The thing to do then is just ask it.

9. Do not be afraid to ask naive questions, either. The subject understands that you do not know everything. Even if you have done your homework there are bound to be items you are unfamiliar with. The source usually will be glad to fill in the gaps in your knowledge of the subject. So do not try to seem omniscient.

10. Get in the habit of asking treading-water questions, such as "What do you mean?" or "Why's that?" This is an easy way to keep the person talking.

11. Sometimes it helps to change the conversational pace, by backing off a sensitive line of inquiry, putting your notebook away, and suddenly displaying a deep interest in an irrelevancy. But be sure to return to those sensitive questions later. A sudden pause is sometimes useful. When the subject finishes a statement just stare at him, maybe with a slightly ambiguous smile, for a few seconds. He often will become uneasy and blurt out something crucial.

12. Do not give up on a question merely because the subject says "no comment." That is only the beginning of the fight. Act as if you misunderstood him and simply restate the question a little differently. If he still clams up, act as if he misunderstood you and rephrase the question again. On the third try, feign disbelief at his refusal to talk. Suggest an embarrassing conclusion from his refusal and ask if it is valid. Later, ask for "guidance" in tracking down the story elsewhere, or suggest non-attribution, or get tough—whatever you think might work.

13. Occasionally your best quote or fact comes after the subject thinks the interview is over. As you are putting away your notebook and are saying goodbye he often relaxes and makes a crucial but offhand remark. So stay alert until you are out the door.

Zimmerman acknowledges that his list is long. His advice to the novice: "Pick the techniques you think you can use and then practice them. Eventually, they'll become so natural you won't have to think about them."

18 Interviewing Practices

Preview   A successful interview depends on:

■ Questions that put the source at ease and show the source the reporter knows the subject.

■ Role playing by the reporter. The reporter may adopt a personality with which the source feels at ease. Usually, the reporter is himself or herself—efficient, direct, unemotional.

■ Patience and accurate observations. The reporter lets the source talk without interruption while observing the physical surroundings and any revealing interactions between the subject and third parties.

When Liebling interviewed the jockey Eddie Arcaro, the first question he asked was, "How many holes longer do you keep your left stirrup than your right?"

"That started him talking easily, and after an hour, during which I had put in about twelve words, he said, 'I can see you've been around riders a lot.'

"I had," Liebling said later, "but only during the week before I was to meet him." In his preparations, Liebling had learned that most jockeys on counter-clockwise American tracks help balance their weight and hug the rail by riding with the left stirrup longer than the right. A rail-hugging journey is the shortest distance from start to finish.

Starting Off Right

Careful preparations such as Liebling's enable the reporter to establish an open, friendly relationship with the source, who usually is complimented that the reporter took time to learn something about him or his field. But no matter how carefully a reporter may prepare, it is impossible to guarantee a free-flowing interview. No reporter can predict precisely the mood of the source or the feelings a particular question will generate.

Liebling recalls going to a Washington, D.C., hotel early in World War II to interview General John J. Pershing for a profile. Pershing had been commander of the American Expeditionary Forces in World War I, and Liebling thought he might have worthwhile comments on the outbreak of fighting in Europe.

"I did everything I could to get the old man to loosen up, including some pretty obvious flattery," Liebling writes in "Interviewers" in *The Most of A. J. Liebling*.

" 'When they started to cut down the Army after the Armistice in 1918, General,' I said, 'you were against it, weren't you, because you foresaw this new European crisis?'

"The old boy looked at me in an angry, disgusted manner and said, 'Who the hell could have foreseen this?' "

Usually, it is not necessary to spend much time on the preliminaries with experienced sources the reporter knows. But people who are infrequently interviewed—the atomic physicist in town for a lecture at the university, the engineer sent out by his company to survey the area north of town for industrial development—must be put at ease and made to feel that the interview is a simple, natural activity. The reporter should take an interest in the person being interviewed. Such attention is reciprocated.

Reporters use all sorts of techniques to start the interview off right. One reporter who does many interviews usually glances around the source's home or room as soon as he enters. He tries to find something about which he can compliment the source. Before one interview, he noticed an ivy growing up one wall of the source's office.

"How do you keep the leaves against the wall?" he asked. "Magnets and small clasps," the source replied, and then she talked about training ivy for several minutes.

Although the tactic may appear contrived, the reporter usually asks about matters that interest him. In this case, the reporter was an avid home gardener.

Who's in Control?

One cause of trouble can be the reporter's misreading the source's willingness to be led. Some sources take over the interview situation, and if they supply the needed information, the reporter should be willing to assume the passive role. Most sources, unaccustomed to being interviewed, need guidance in the form of suggestions, leading questions, encouraging gestures and facial movements. Sometimes the reporter takes control of a domineering personality and the interview is unsuccessful.

A source may dominate the interview and intentionally or inadvertently avoid the issue in which the reporter is interested. The source may be at ease, even talkative, in such a situation. But the reporter must wrest control, subtly if possible. Control need not be overt. Indeed, a reporter bent on demonstrating that he or she is in charge will fail to achieve the balance among listening, watching and guidance that is necessary for the successful interview.

A source may allow the reporter to direct the interview on the strength of the reporter's reputation or his experience with the reporter. Some first-time sources consider reporters to be authority figures and become submissive. Generally, cooperation and a willingness to be guided depend on the source's immediate reactions on being confronted by the reporter. Some of the questions that the source may ask himself or herself are:

- Why is the reporter talking to me?
- What is her purpose? Is she here to hurt, embarrass or help me?
- What sort of story does she intend to write?
- Is she competent, or will she misunderstand and misquote me?
- Is she mature, trustworthy?
- Is she bright enough to grasp some of the complexities, or should I simplify everything?
- Will I have to begin at the beginning, or does she seem to have done her homework?

Sources answer these questions from the cues they pick up from the reporter's clothing, looks and behavior as well as from his or her reputation, conversation and questions.

One afternoon a journalism student cornered an instructor.

Appearance and Behavior

"Professor X (and here he named the journalism school's senior professor) told me I had better get my hair cut," the student said. "He said I would offend people I'm sent to interview."

The student's hair was long. "Have it cut and stop worrying," the instructor replied. "Most of the people you will be interviewing will be very proper people."

The student plunged deeper into gloom. "But it will ruin my love life," he said.

The instructor and the student thought over the problem, the student in deep despair.

"Why not have it trimmed, and see what happens?" the instructor suggested.

The student took an inch or so off his locks and had no further trouble with Professor X. Nor, presumably, did his love life suffer, for there were no further anguished visits from the young man, who, after graduation, became a long-haired and successful rock music critic for *The Village Voice*.

A few years later, when the hirsute look had become common on assembly lines and in offices and faculty clubs, the issue became women in pants. And so it goes: Youth expresses its independence through dress and grooming. And traditionalists—who are usually the majority and always in authority—take offense and condemn the new ways, until sometimes they join in and the fad becomes a trend and later a tradition. Until then, reporters in the vanguard risk offending sources, most of whom are traditionalists in politics, social activities, business and education.

A carefree, casual attitude and dress can tell a source that you, the reporter, do not take him or her seriously. Tone of voice, posture, gestures and facial expressions convey messages to a source along with hair and dress. Anthropologists say that what people do is more important than what they say, and the first impressions the reporter conveys with his or her dress, appearance, posture, hand and facial movements may be more important than anything the reporter may say.

A reporter can choose his or her garb, practice speaking in a steady, modulated voice and learn to control the hands. But age, race, sex and basic physical characteristics are usually beyond the reporter's control, and some sources are affected by these.

Age, sex and race

The attitude toward women has changed considerably over the past 20 years, but some men in authority still find it difficult to address a woman as an intellectual equal. The worlds of government and finance are male-dominated. Many of these men have formed their attitudes toward women from their relationships with their secretaries, switchboard operators, wives and daughters. As a consequence, women reporters sometimes have greater difficulty than men in establishing a suitable atmosphere in the interview situation. They find the sources are either cold and distant—possibly because they are uncomfortable being questioned by a woman. Or the source may be excessively friendly or protective—possibly because of a sense of *machismo* or paternal interest.

These reactions of sources are amply documented in sociological research. Where there is identification with the reporter, the source is much more likely to speak freely than he or she is with an interviewer of another sex, race, religion or age. People feel comfortable with those who are like them. They believe that only someone who has experienced their problems can relate to them. But no editor has an unlimited supply of reporters.

Most small- and moderate-size news staffs are dominated by young reporters, and it may well be that the prejudice among sources against youth is the most pervasive. Youth must prove itself. And until a source is sure that a young reporter can be trusted, the source may be uncooperative.

Reporters, too, can contribute to polluting the interview atmosphere. Reporters have prejudices and biases that can impede their work. One of the most common prejudices among the young is intolerance of the elderly.

Because of these limitations, some social scientists—and a few reporters—distrust the material they gather in interviews. In the book, *Unobtrusive Measures, Nonreactive Research in the Social Sciences* (Chicago: Rand McNally & Co., 1966, p. 1), the authors, Eugene J. Webb, et al., maintain:

> Interviews and questionnaires intrude as a foreign element into the social setting they would describe; they create as well as measure attitudes; they elicit atypical roles and responses; they are limited to those who are accessible and will cooperate; and the responses obtained are produced in part by dimensions of individual differences irrelevant to the topic at hand.

The interview is neither a natural nor a spontaneous event since the reporter is always an obtrusive "foreign element."

Striking a Balance. When interviewing authorities the reporter shows respect but is not submissive. The reporter gently guides but does not overwhelm the source. Dress is appropriate to the occasion. Here, Elizabeth Bumiller of *The Washington Post* interviews Ronald Reagan at the White House.

Although no reporter would surrender the interview as a useful fact-finding tool, some reporters prefer to use physical sources—records, documents and their own unobtrusive observations—as primary sources. They will use the interview to supplement what they have already learned from physical sources.

Role Playing

Sent to interview a pioneer developer of the polygraph, a reporter sensed that the man was easy-going and relaxed. In an attempt to be humorous, the reporter's opening remark was, "You're described as the country's leading polygraph expert. That's a lie detector, right?"

The interviewee suddenly stiffened. "If that's all you know, I'm going to call your city editor and have him send someone else over," he said. The reporter apologized, adopted a business-like approach, and the interview was conducted satisfactorily for both of them.

Another reporter sent to interview a retired state department official decided that the official was so forbidding that by acting naive and a little helpless she might break the ice.

"I see you have just returned from Rio de Janeiro," the reporter said. "That's in Brazil, on the coast, I believe."

The distinguished former ambassador peered at the reporter from under thick, white eyebrows. There was a long silence. The reporter decided to drop that gambit. She became more self-assured.

Both reporters were intelligent and had carefully prepared for the interviews, but they had decided to appear naive to open up the source. They were role playing, and although their interviews skirted disaster, role playing is generally successful—if the reporter acts out a role appropriate to the source. Experienced sources expect a neutral, business-like attitude from their interviewers. Some sources—particularly those who are unaccustomed to being interviewed—respond best to the stereotypical journalist they see on television or in the movies, the knowledgeable expert. Others talk more freely to the opposite type, the reporter who confesses he or she needs help from the source.

Obviously, the best role for the journalist is the one he or she fits most comfortably, which for most journalists is the impersonal, unemotional and uninvolved professional. Sometimes, the reporter finds he or she must be more personal, emotional and involved or the story will slip away. When one reporter was assigned to cover the rush week activities at a local college, she was struck by the depression of the young women who were rejected by sororities. In her interviews, she felt she was unable to break through the reserve of the young women until she remarked to one of them, "I know how you feel. I went through the same thing in school."

From Friend to Authority Figure

Reporters can adopt the role of friend, confidant and companion when sources appear to need boosting-up before they will talk. When a source indicates he will cooperate only if he is sure that certain benefits will accrue to him, his organization or his cause, the reporter may have to appear to be an authority figure, someone sufficiently powerful and prestigious to bring about such benefits.

Reporters have been encouraged by their editors to push their sources harder than ever before. Some stories require pressing sources to the point of discomfort, or implying a threat should they fail to respond. As someone once said, journalism is the business of making people say things they would prefer to keep to themselves. Many of these things are properly the public's business, and the reporter who shifts roles from friend to authority figure or threatening power figure may justify his role as being in the public interest.

Limits to Role Playing

No one doubts that reporters adopt different techniques with different types of sources. The issue is how far a reporter can go before such acting becomes unethical. Is there a line between the prohibition against a reporter posing as a coroner to speak with the widow of a murder victim and feigning ignorance in an interview? If there are no outright prohibitions against the latter behavior, then what does it do to the morale of the reporter? Does it generate a contempt for sources, for the reporter and his or her work?

One well-known Washington reporter said she did not mind letting a senator pat her on the fanny if it meant he would be more inclined to give her a story—an attitude many of her female colleagues find abhorrent. But is that much different from some role playing considered to be proper?

There are other questions. How well, after all, can a reporter assess a source so that role playing is useful? We saw how two reporters failed. Even psychiatrists admit to no special ability to make lightning diagnoses.

Reporters usually are best off when they are themselves—once they determine who they are—and then modify that behavior as the situation seems to demand. No reporter can make wide swings in his or her personality anyhow. When John McCormally, editor of *The Hawk Eye,* went to Cuba with a group of journalists, he studied television reporter Barbara Walters for a story he planned to write. In his story, he wrote:

> Does she use the fact that she is a woman? people ask. Of course she does. Just as I'm using my "old country editor" routine to try to outwit the big city boys; and Marty McReynolds of UPI uses the fact that he's an old Latin hand, and Joe Klein that *Rolling Stone* is a former underground sheet these revolutionaries ought to appreciate. You use what you've got in this rat race. But if that's all you've got, you're nothing.

Looking and Listening

Every story that makes a reader or viewer take notice contains sights and sounds the reporter has captured with such precision that the event and the persons in the story come alive. Behind the carefully chosen words of the story are the reporter's accurate and precise observations. In the interview story, these observations center on the person and his or her words and radiate outward to include the source's immediate surroundings and the general situation.

Watching carefully and listening attentively, the reporter is able to reconstruct on paper the scene that unfolded before him. Here is *New York Times* reporter John Corry's description of George Balanchine, the choreographer:

> He is, nonetheless, a slender, attractive man with high cheek bones, a chiseled face and a slight scimitar of a nose. Most often he looks as if he were about to be surprised, and if a caricature were to be done of him it could very well look like a bemused chipmunk.

Listening to Balanchine instruct the company in a rehearsal, Corry caught him in full swing:

> "No, you don't do 1, 2, 3; you do 1, 2, 3, 4 . . . Just once through because I don't even know what it is, I forgot . . . Slow, slow, slow . . . It's easy, chata-chata-cha . . . You know, like shish kebab when you put it on a spit, you want to see every side. . . .
>
> "Now you walk this way, da-da-da . . . The man needs the woman, or else how does he know what to do? . . . And now I have to go left . . . AH, THAT'S GOOD, GOOOOOD."

The reporter captured Balanchine's temperament by watching and listening to him interact with a dancer:

> Precisely then, Kay Mazzo, another principal dancer, walked in, unaccountably carrying a very small kitten. Balanchine was at her instantly.
>
> "Where you get the pussy?" he said. "Kitty, kittteeee. Animals are good. People are lonely. But you should give it to a kennel. You like it now. It's so soft. It feels good. Then it grows up. It scratches. It does things in your apartment. You should give it to a kennel now. . . ."

You are entering the office of the chairman of the English department, who is expecting you. You had telephoned him to ask if you could interview him about the department's plans to cope with the increasing numbers of high school graduates who arrive on campus poorly trained in reading and writing skills. He had told you to drop in about 3 p.m.

As you enter, you notice that his office is sparsely furnished. There are two pictures on the wall and some books on his desk. He also has books in a floor-to-ceiling bookcase against one wall. These fleeting impressions do not particularly concern you because this will be a news interview focused on the situation, not the individual. Nevertheless, the setting could provide an occasional break in the recital of facts.

The chairman is worried, he says, about the growing numbers of students unable to read and understand college-level material. The chairman pauses often in his answers and occasionally goes to a bookcase to take down a book that he reads to amplify a point.

"A friend of mine calls this the cretinization of American youth, and I used to laugh at him," says the chairman. He reads from a copy of *McGuffey's Readers*. "This kind of material is now at the high school level," he says. "I wonder if anyone cares." He then reads from a Wordsworth poem that he says used to be memorized in grade school. No more, he says.

As the interview proceeds, you notice that the chairman is toying with what appears to be a battered cigarette lighter. You wonder whether to ask about it.

Suddenly, you decide that the interview should include more than the plans of the department to offer remedial writing, grammar, punctuation and spelling. The story will include the chairman's personality as well as his plans and ideas. That will help to personalize it, to make it more readable.

Quickly, you re-examine the office to make note of the artists of the prints, the titles of the books on the desk, and you ask about the ancient cigarette lighter. (You learn that the lighter is a World War II memento the chairman uses to relieve tension; he is trying to stop smoking.)

As the chairman talks, you note his mannerisms, his slow speech, his frequent stares out the window. A student enters the office and asks for permission to drop a course, and you watch as the chairman gradually convinces the freshman to give the course another week.

Noticing the family pictures on the chairman's desk, you ask for their identities. Smiling, the chairman complies, then says, "You must be a believer in Whitehead's remark that genius consists of the minute inspection of subjects that are taken for granted just because they are under our noses."

You make a note of that, too, more for yourself than for the story.

Back in the newsroom, the editor agrees that the story is worth two columns, and he sends a photographer to take a picture of the chairman.

The Careful Observer

The Careful Observer.

Details, Details The reporter was acting in the best reportorial manner by noting specific details of the setting and the interviewee's mannerisms as well as watching for any interaction with third parties. In looking for details, the reporter was seeking the material that gives verisimilitude to an interview. Here is a report a *Time* correspondent wrote about Jacqueline Kennedy in Hyannisport during the Kennedy presidential campaign:

> Jackie settled back into a huge flowered arm chair, draped a striped beach towel over her knees, and spread out a vast clutter of paint tubes, palette brushes, a glass of water, a glass of rosé wine (left from dinner), a cup of coffee, a jar full of L&M cigarettes, and pulled an immense easel with a half-started painting to a spot between her and the TV screen. . . .

There are at least 10 concrete details in this short passage, and these specifics help to project the reader into the Kennedy vacation home.

Just how exact a reporter should be in his observations is reflected in the admonition of an editor at *The* Baltimore *Sun* when a reporter turns in a story that lacks precise details: "Which hand held the gun?"

It was not enough to say that the chairman toyed with a cigarette lighter. The reporter wrote of the "World War II-vintage lighter that he fingered to remind him of his no-smoking pledge." The reporter did not write that the chairman had read from an elementary school reader used in U.S. schools generations ago. He gave the book's title. The reporter did not merely quote the chairman when he spoke about the low scores of entering freshmen on the English Placement test. The reporter noted the dejected slope of the chairman's shoulders.

Listening and Hearing There is an adage that says that most people listen but few hear. For most people, the condition is harmless and understandable. Words assail us on all sides: Newspapers on the porch morning and afternoon, magazines in the mail, books to be read for courses, the omnipresent radio and television sets, and the questions, advice, and endless prattle of friends, neighbors, parents and teachers. It is a wonder that anyone hears anyone amidst the clatter. But the reporter must hear. His or her livelihood depends on it.

So many people are talking and so few listening with attention and courtesy that the reporter who trains himself or herself to hear will find people eager to talk to someone who cares about what they are saying.

To become a listener:

- Cut down your ego. You are in an interview to hear what others say, not to spout your opinions.
- Open your mind to new or different ideas, even those you despise.
- Grant the interviewee time to develop his or her thoughts.
- Rarely interrupt.
- Concentrate on what the person is saying and make secondary the person's personality, demeanor or appearance.
- Keep questions to the theme or to relevant ideas that turn up in the interview.
- Don't ask long questions.

Good listeners will have in their notes the quotations that give the reader or listener an immediate sense of the person being interviewed. Oscar Lewis, the anthropologist who wrote about Mexican families and other Spanish-speaking peoples, began his article, "In New York You Get Swallowed by a Horse," (*Anthropological Essays,* New York: Random House, 1964, and *Commentary,* November, 1964) about Hector, a Puerto Rican, this way:

> We had been talking of this and that when I asked him, "Have you ever been in New York, Hector?"
> "Yes, yes, I've been to New York."
> "And what did you think of life there?"
> "New York! I want no part of it! Man, do you know what it's like? You get up in a rush, have breakfast in a rush, go to work in a rush, go home in a rush, even shit in a rush. That's life in New York! Not for me! Never again! Not unless I was crazy.
> "Look I'll explain. The way things are in New York, you'll get nothing there. But nothing! It's different in Puerto Rico. Here, if you're hungry, you come to me and say, 'Man I'm broke, I've had nothing to eat,' And I'd say, 'Ay, Benedito! Poor thing!' And I'd give you some food. No matter what, you wouldn't have to go to bed hungry. Here in Puerto Rico you can make out. But in New York, if you don't have a nickel, or twenty cents, you're worthless, and that's for sure. You don't count. You get swallowed by a horse!"

Hidden Meanings

The careful listener encourages the source to talk as openly as possible, regardless of the subject. But some people will skirt a topic, and the reporter has to hear what is meant as well as what is said.

The concealed meanings in every interview can be found by the interviewer who notes gestures, facial expressions, slips of the tongue, half-uttered remarks and the peculiar uses of words. Good listeners pick up the source's inconsistencies. And they are alert to the undercurrents that may be more important than the torrent of information the source seems only too willing to provide.

The reporter may seem slightly passive in the interview, but he or she is working hard. The reporter is checking the incoming information against his or her preconceptions of the story. Is the source confirming or contradicting the reporter's ideas? Or is he avoiding them for some reason? Or is the source providing better thematic material for the interview? Just what does the source mean? What is he trying to say? Does he have any self-interest that affects the interview?

Taking Notes

The reporter who puts all his or her energy into taking notes often has a pad full of quotes but lacks the idea or theme that will give the story meaning and coherence. Most interviews provide much more material than can be used. It is necessary to note only the salient facts and the high-quality anecdote, quote or incident that will illustrate them.

This is why it is so necessary to have a firm idea of the theme or themes that the story will contain while interviewing. With the themes in mind, the reporter is able to concentrate his or her note-taking on relevant material. There is no way a reporter can keep up with the source's flow of information and still retain some control of the interview unless the reporter is constantly filtering the information.

As we saw in the discussion of how to write the longer story, the news story is an interplay between the general (the themes) and the specific (the buttressing material—quotes, incidents, anecdotes, illustrative detail). Any information not pertinent to theme or buttressing material is unnecessary.

A source, seeing the reporter stop his or her note-taking, may be discouraged from continuing. To avoid this, the reporter may want to seem to keep up note-taking while the source is supplying non-essential material. Actually, the reporter will be writing about the setting or the ideas he or she has from statements made earlier in the interview. With sources who inadvertently say more than they want to reveal, the reporter slows down note-taking or seems slightly disinterested so that the source does not take notice of the reporter's intensified interest.

Before leaving, or during the interview, the reporter may ask the source to repeat something in order to make certain the quotation is precise. But when the reporter feels the source may want to retract a statement or will argue that he meant something else, the reporter will risk relying solely on his or her notes. Under the careful guidance and rapt attention of an expert interviewer, sources sometimes say things that on second hearing they wish they had not said.

First Impressions

The adage that first impressions are the best usually works for the reporter. Lillian Ross, the brilliant *New Yorker* writer whose profiles are studied by serious reporters for their understated yet incisive perceptions, says that "first impressions and first instincts about a person are usually the sound reliable ones that guide you to the rest of what the person has to offer." These early impressions can give the reporter a sense of the entire scene, the whole person, whereas the later impressions tend to be narrower, to focus on details and particulars.

The fresh observation is unimpeded by preconceptions. The reporter new on the scene will sometimes out-report the old timer who has formed notions and drawn conclusions after repeatedly seeing the same events and persons. But veteran reporters can look at the scene and make discoveries, too. Sally Grimes says she would not have been able to write about the handcuffed boy in the juvenile court (chapter 12) had she stopped to think about what she wanted to see and say.

"If I had stopped to think about what I had observed, I would have lost my own experience for the reader," she says. "All I want to do in my articles is say, 'Look.' I think it is important for journalists to look carefully and be constantly aware, which involves forgetting yourself and your own hang-ups which only blind you to what is going on at the moment."

Sometimes a person being interviewed will suddenly stop and realize he has said something he does not want to see in print or hear on television or the radio.

"Please don't use that," he will say. "It's off the record."

Should the reporter honor that request? It depends. If the source is a good contact for the reporter and the material is not crucial to the story, the reporter probably will go along with the source's request, particularly if the source is not a public figure or official. If the source has said something important, or the information is of concern to the public, then the reporter will usually reply that since the source knew he was talking to a reporter, he cannot suddenly go off the record retroactively. When the reporter is doing investigative reporting, the possibility that he will go along with such a request is inconceivable.

When Jessica Mitford was interviewing Bennett Cerf, one of the owners of the Famous Writers School, he let his guard down and chatted freely with the amiable but sharp-penned writer. In the middle of his discourse, Cerf realized he sounded contemptuous of the people who took the school's correspondence course.

Here is how Mitford describes what happened, in her July, 1970, *Atlantic Monthly* article "Let Us Now Appraise Famous Writers":

> While Mr. Cerf is by no means uncritical of some aspects of mail-order selling, he philosophically accepts them as inevitable in the cold-blooded world of big business—so different, one gathers, from his own cultured world of letters. "I think mail-order selling has several built-in deficiencies," he said. "The crux of it is a very hard sales pitch, an appeal to the gullible. Of course, once somebody has signed a contract with the Famous Writers School he can't get out of it, but that's true with every business in the country." Noticing that I was writing this down, he said in alarm, "For God's sake, don't quote me on that 'gullible' business—you'll have all the mail-order houses in the country down on my neck!" "Then would you like to paraphrase it?" I asked, suddenly getting very firm. "Well—you could say in general I don't like the hard sell, yet it's the basis of all American business." "Sorry, I don't call that a paraphrase, I shall have to use both of them," I said in a positively governessy tone of voice. "Anyway, why do you lend your name to this hard-sell proposition?" Bennett Cerf (with his melting grin): "Frankly, if you must know, I'm an awful ham—I love to see my name in the papers!"

Here, Cerf spoke first, then requested that the material be excised from the reporter's notes. Reporters are reluctant to agree to such requests. But when the source states beforehand that something is off the record and the reporter agrees to hear it on that condition, the material may not be used. Never? Well, hardly ever. Witness how Clifford D. May handled his source in his article, "Whatever Happened to Sam Spade?" in the August, 1975, *Atlantic Monthly*. A private detective, Jeremiah P. McAward, has been describing his difficulties in shadowing people:

> "It's harder than you'd think," McAward continues. "Don't print this, but I once lost a pregnant Indian who was wearing a red blanket and had a feather in her hair, in Macy's." I reply that he cannot tell me something like that and expect that I won't use it. "Really?" he asks. I nod. "All right, then." There is a pause and then he adds, "But she just evaporated. A two-hundred-pound Indian."

Literal Quotes   Many reporters cleanse the language of free-speaking sources before putting their quotes into stories. They also correct grammatical errors and ignore absurd and meaningless statements that are not central to the story.

The authors of a book about Clifford Irving, who hoaxed a major publisher into believing he had written an authorized biography of multimillionaire Howard Hughes, reported overhearing this conversation between a *Times* reporter and a lawyer for Mr. Hughes named Davis.

"Mr. Davis, I wanted to ask you if you have any comment on the things Mr. Maheu has been saying about you and your behavior in Las Vegas."

"It's just bullshit."

"But Mr. Davis, we can't put 'bullshit' in *The New York Times*."

"Why not? You do it every day."

"No, I don't mean it in that sense. I mean it's a term we can't print."

"Oh, would you like it better if I said his remarks were utter nonsense?"

The next day, the authors say, the *Times*'s story on the interview quoted Davis as saying Maheu's remarks were "utter nonsense."

To some sources, reporters sometimes apply the whip of literal quotations. They know the validity of the statement by Arnold Gingrich, editor-in-chief of *Esquire* magazine, "The cruelest thing you can do to anybody is to quote him literally."

Racial and religious epithets are treated with care, but during the 1960s use of these terms increased to demonstrate the intensity of the feelings involved. "Nigger" became acceptable in some newspapers. In the early 1960s, *The Wall Street Journal* began a roundup on race relations in the South this way:

> How are white Southerners reacting to the intensified Negro drive for equal rights?
>
> Some are nonplussed by the very idea of demands for change. In the small East Texas town of Crosby, O. O. Hare, president of the Crosby State Bank, says incredulously: "The niggers are getting bolder and bolder. Some smart alecks come in here and think they can sign a note."

In an interview with the chief of police of Providence, R. I., for the *Journal*, Christopher Scanlan quoted the chief as saying:

> "Everyone knows you can stop crime if they gave the police the authority that they had. Nobody is going to tell me that you're going to stop crime by being nice to people. You have to push people around.
>
> "I believe that if you have to take a guy around the corner and give him a couple of shots, maybe that's what we should do.
>
> "If a guy commits a murder and we know he committed a murder, why don't they string him up the following day? That's my theory.
>
> "Everybody is trying to rehabilitate. They want to rehabilitate these people.

How can you rehabilitate an animal? You take a lion in the zoo they can't do anything with; what do they do with him after a while? They shoot him. That's realistic.

"In Providence we have the Puerto Ricans, we have the blacks, we have a lot of minority groups, and they're the toughest to control."

After Scanlan's story appeared, a state-wide black ministerial alliance asked the mayor to fire the chief. An arrangement was worked out whereby instructors from the Urban League and the National Association for the Advancement of Colored People would be on the teaching staff of the police academy.

Here is a section from a piece in the *New Yorker*'s "Talk of the Town." It is about a press conference attended by entrants in the Miss Universe beauty contest. Miss U.S.A. has just been introduced to reporters and is telling them that the Miss Universe contest has helped her express her feelings and widen her knowledge.

"For instance, Miss India has a red spot on her forehead. And do you know what? She says it's an Indian custom. . . .

"One of the experiences I've had was just this morning," Miss U.S.A. says. "I'm rooming with Miss South Africa, and I just saw their money. You see people, but you never realize their money was different."

The reporters try to think of another question. Finally, one of them says, "What do you think of the feminist movement?"

"Oh, I think femininity is the best thing on this earth," she says.

"What about masculinity?"

"That's just as wonderful."

At this, says the magazine's reporter, the journalists decided to leave. "As the zoom lens pulls back from the Roma di Notte Restaurant, from Manhattan, from the Eastern Seaboard, the reporters retire to the nearby Clancy's Bar and attempt to drink themselves into insensibility."

Let us watch a television reporter as he puts into practice some of the principles and techniques we have been discussing in the last two chapters on interviewing.

A Television Interview

It is 6:30 a.m. and we are in an automobile with J. J. Gonzalez, a reporter for WCBS-TV, a New York City television station. Gonzalez and the crew are driving to Kennedy International Airport. Louis Treitler, the electrician, is at the wheel. Gonzalez is next to him. William Sinnott, the soundman, and Joe Landi, the cameraman, are in the back seat.

"You see the assignment?" Gonzalez asks Treitler, who nods that he has read it. Gonzalez unfolds the typewritten note from the assignment editor and reads it again: "Go to Overseas National Headquarters at 175th St. off Farmers Blvd. (Right near the airport.) We will be able to get interviews with the passengers. Afterwards we were told that we would be able to get on the runway to film the boarding which has been delayed until 8:30 or 9. Crew should arrive 7:30 a.m."

Burning Jetliner. Clouds of black smoke rise from the broken fuselage of a jetliner after the flight of the DC-10 was suddenly halted when a flock of seagulls was sucked into an engine. Gonzalez used some of the film of the burning wreckage for his follow-up on the second attempt of the airline personnel to make their flight to Saudi Arabia.

The passengers the assignment refers to are airline personnel who had been on a DC-10 the previous week en route to the Middle East. The plane ran into a flock of seagulls on the runway, an engine ingested several of the birds, and before the plane could take off, one engine stopped turning over and dropped to the ground. The pilot managed to stop the plane and quickly ordered everyone out. Within seconds, the 10 crew members and 139 passengers were spilling out of the exits and down the escape chutes. The plane caught fire and in five minutes was a charred hulk.

No one was injured. But if those aboard had been the usual run of passengers, Gonzalez says, there might have been a catastrophe. He plans to ask some of the airline personnel whether they agree. The metropolitan editor had instructed Gonzalez to find out how the passengers felt about taking off a second time.

The Planning It is a 45-minute drive to the airport, and Gonzalez and the crew have plenty of time to chat about the assignment. They will be going to three locations—first, to the airlines building where the passengers will be assembling, then to the airplane the passengers will board, and finally to a runway to watch the plane take off. Film of the plane heading off into the rising sun will make a good closing shot, they agree. But they are not sure that they will be allowed on a runway, and they discuss going to the airport control tower. Sinnott doubts that the tower will be available either, and they talk about using the public observation platform.

Gonzalez knows there is newsfilm at the station that was shot the previous week of the burning plane. He will want to insert some of that dramatic film into what he anticipates will be unexciting film from today's assignment.

"This is really a bunch of talking heads," Gonzalez says. He means that the film shot today will show individuals talking into the microphone and camera.

If he uses film from the three locations he intends to visit this morning and the newsfilm of the airplane burning from last week, he will need a number of transitions, or bridges, to move the viewer from one place to the next smoothly. Gonzalez begins to think of possible bridges—long shots of the airport, the passengers milling about.

Gonzalez makes mental note of the questions he will ask the passengers. If he is lucky, he will be able to interview the pilot of the plane that burned. He knows the pilot will not be on this morning's flight, but if he should happen to be around the airline office, an interview with him could liven up the story. It would also be useful as a transition to the newsfilm of the burning plane and might even carry through as a voice over the film (VO) of the firemen battling the flames.

Fortunately for Gonzalez, the pilot is there, and after chatting with him to obtain some background about the first flight, Gonzalez asks the pilot one of the standard leading questions in the television reporter's repertory of simple, direct questions, "What went through your mind at this time?"

On the Scene

The pilot answers, "Basically, I thought we should be doing it some other way."

His reply makes everyone in the office laugh and it seems to break the tension.

"It's the understatement of the week," mutters one of the young women who was aboard the first flight. But when Gonzalez and the crew look toward her she has put on a sparkling smile, and in answer to Gonzalez's question about the mood of her fellow passengers she says that as professional airline people they are not too nervous.

Gonzalez is excited about his interview with the pilot. "This is the only real news here," he says. "No one else has had an interview with the pilot."

In his interviews, Gonzalez did not ask many questions. He knew that viewers are more interested in the interviewee than the interviewer. To keep from intruding when a source began to slow down in the interview, he would encourage the source with a smile or a headshake.

"I also use facial questions a lot," he remarked later. "When someone tells me something that is unclear or hard to believe, I will look incredulous or give the person a blank stare. This encourages them to go on and talk.

"Sometimes, the best question you can ask is one word, a simple, 'Why?' "

On the drive to the airport, Gonzalez had estimated the story to be worth "a pound and a quarter," a minute and 15 seconds. But it is Saturday, usually a dull news day, and there may not be many other local stories to compete with this story, so Gonzalez interviews several of the waiting passengers.

"How do you feel about taking the flight now? Uneasy?" he asks a young woman.

"No, I feel good," she answers as the cameraman shoots her reply. "I just want to get going."

In the Newsroom   Back in the newsroom, Gonzalez engages in another set of preparations. Before he writes his script, he jots down what he has on film and the voices that will accompany it. In one column, he lists the order in which he thinks the film will be put together and in another column, he indicates the lead-in for the anchorman, his own voice and those of the interviewees.

Later, Gonzalez learns his hunch about the length of the story was correct. There are few breaking news stories, and CRASH, as he slugged it, is given more than two pounds on the 7 o'clock news.

Summing Up   The interview is the basis of most news stories. Reporters should learn how to ask questions that induce sources to talk. They can do this by preparing carefully, when there is time, and by establishing an effective relationship with the source. During the interview, the reporter should concentrate not only on what is being said but on the source's gestures and mannerisms and on the surroundings, which may give some clues about the person being interviewed.

Whenever possible, the reporter should go into the interview with some idea of a theme for the piece. This will direct the course of the interview and provide the reporter with the control necessary to draw out relevant replies to questions. But the reporter should always be ready to switch themes if the original one is invalid or a more newsworthy theme comes up in the interview.

19 Speeches, Meetings and News Conferences

Preview

■ Speech stories must include the name and identification of the speaker, the theme of the talk, the setting and ample quotations. When a prepared text is used for the story, it should be checked against the actual delivery.

■ Meeting stories usually begin with the major action taken. They should also include the purpose of the meeting, background to the major action and quotes from those who spoke.

■ A news conference story should begin with the major point made at the conference unless a better lead turns up in the question-and-answer period. The story also should include background and topics discussed in the question-and-answer period.

"Ours is not to wonder why but to cover the speech or die," the reporter said as he put on his overcoat and prepared to step into the cold for a three-block walk to a downtown hotel where a testimonial dinner for the mayor was about to start. "I'll bet it's creamed chicken again," he muttered on his way out.

The reporter's exasperation was caused as much by the prospect of an ordinary dinner as by the fare he felt the speaker would offer.

Speeches, hardly the most exciting story a reporter covers, are a steady part of the journalist's day-to-day work. Often, a prepared text is delivered to the newspaper and broadcast station ahead of time so that the story can be written in the office. The reporter inserts the phrase, "In a speech prepared for delivery tonight . . ." or something similar.

Generally, it is a good idea to cover speeches personally. Even the dullest speech sometimes contains some spontaneous verbal gems if the reporter listens carefully. Speeches by prominent persons are always covered, regardless of the subject matter. Nothing could have been more mundane than the testimonial dinner set for Betty Ford, wife of President Ford, at the New York Hilton one warm June evening. She was to be honored at the dinner launching a $6 million fund drive for an American Bicentennial Park in Israel. Her remarks were expected to be routine. Indeed, as the evening wore on, reporters became restless. A few of them left, after asking those who remained to cover for them should anything unusual occur.

Naturally, the unusual did occur, and it was front page news in newspapers around the country.

As Mrs. Ford was being introduced, the president of the Jewish National Fund of America, who had just finished speaking, slumped down in his chair at the head table.

In the confusion, Mrs. Ford went to the microphone and spoke to the stunned guests: "Can we bow our heads for a moment and say a prayer for Rabbi Sage," she said. The New York *Daily News* began its story this way:

> First lady Betty Ford led a stunned benefit dinner audience in prayer at the New York Hilton last night for a Zionist leader who collapsed at the affair honoring Mrs. Ford, and died of an apparent heart attack at a hospital a short time later.

Basics for the Speech Story

Every speech story must include:

- Who spoke—name and identification.
- What he or she said—speaker's main point.
- The setting or circumstances of the speech.

Any of these can provide the lead and theme of the story, although the great majority of speech stories emphasize what was said.

The speech story takes its form from these three essentials. All three must be included in the first few paragraphs, as in the story on the opposite page by Itabari Njeri in *The Greenville* (S.C.) *News.*

Njeri began her story with a delayed lead and moved to the speaker's main point in the second paragraph. The third paragraph has the setting. In three paragraphs, she handled the essentials of the speech story: name and identification of speaker, main theme of talk and the circumstances of the speech.

In covering a speech, the most important task the reporter faces is grasping the speaker's theme. A tip-off to the theme may be in the title of the speech. Often, speakers will use forensic devices to drive home their major points—pounding the podium, raising the voice, a sudden slow-down in delivery, the summary at the end.

When the reporter cannot find the theme, it makes sense to interview the speaker when he has finished. When combining material from a speech and interview, the journalist should tell the reader or listener which information came from each. Otherwise, those who attended the speech or heard it on radio or television will find the report puzzling.

Occasionally, a reporter will find a lead in what the speaker considers a secondary theme. Then, the reporter should lead with what he considers the most important element, but high in the story he should summarize what the speaker considers as the major theme.

Fewer rules a goal, OSHA director says

By ITABARI NJERI
News staff writer

The three greatest lies, according to Dr. Eula Bingham, assistant secretary of labor: "The check is in the mail; Darling, I haven't looked at another woman in 27 years; and, I'm from the government and I'm here to help you."

The punchline got the desired laugh. But Dr. Bingham, who also directs the Labor Department's Occupational Safety and Health Administration, said she really is trying to help business and labor by eliminating or streamlining unnecessary government health and safety regulations.

Addressing the annual spring meeting of the South Carolina Occupational Safety Council, the former college professor and zoologist said: "We are attempting to revamp regulations that are burdensome and not meaningful. Our mandate is to protect the health, life and limb of working men and women. We are not interested in harassing or catching anybody."

Dr. Bingham said that when she was appointed to her position by President Carter in 1977 she came in with the bias of streamlining OSHA and giving businesses the flexibility to comply with health and safety regulations in a cost-effective manner. She said this is in keeping with the president's goal of a leaner, less inflationary government.

"We've taken 928 standards off the federal books and I have urged state programs to follow suit," she said. "Nine of those non-essential regulations accounted for 21,000 citations for OSHA violations being issued."

Dr. Bingham said that OSHA is currently rewriting its fire protection code which was 400 pages and will be 25 to 30 pages when it is completed in a few weeks.

"I hope to have that reduced to one paragraph of plain English," she said.

Dr. Bingham said that her agency must "speak to the needs of small businesses. It's not just General Motors that has safety difficulties."

She said OSHA provides on-site consultants to assist small businesses with safety problems.

"In an Alabama bakery employees were suffering from severe headaches. We sent a consultant there and discovered that the exhaust system was turned off after the bread was baked and carbon monoxide had built up in the bakery.

"In Tennessee, a paint shop was having problems with vapors from mixed solvents. Our consultant helped the company ventilate the shop at a very low cost," said the OSHA director. . . .

For example: The president of a large investment firm is speaking to a local civic club about "The Role of the Small Investor." The morning papers have a story from New York about a sudden selling wave on the stock exchange late yesterday that sent prices tumbling to a year's low. The speaker sticks to his subject that noon, but in a digression predicts that the bottom of the market has not been reached. Obviously, the lead is his prediction of a continued decline. The story will also include material from his talk. The reporter will probably want to nail the speaker after his talk for his comments on the market decline to give still more information to readers about the newsworthy prediction.

The Fuzzy, the Dull and the Funny Speech

Now and then a reporter sits through an incoherent speech in which illogic and vagueness prevail. What should he or she do? Confuse the reader with an accurate account? The reader will only blame the reporter. The reporter should seek out the speaker and attempt to clarify the confused points, ask others who know about the situation the speaker sought to discuss, and then play down the entire piece.

John R. Hunt, who turned from prospecting in the wilds of northwestern Quebec to newspapering, has been covering the North country of Ontario for the *North Bay Nugget* for almost 30 years. "As a small-town newspaperman, I have covered hundreds of speeches," Hunt says.

"It is an interesting fact that a dull and boring speech can often become an interesting story. But I don't know of anything more difficult to write about than a funny speech."

Hunt says a "high degree of craftsmanship is required to take the spoken word, translate it into type and somehow retain both the essence and the flavor of the talk."

A speech consists of spoken words. So must the story. Unless there is an incident during the talk which would make the circumstances and the setting the most newsworthy item, the story should emphasize what was said with ample quotations at the top of the story. But resist the quote lead unless there is a highly unusual statement.

Off the Record

Speakers occasionally insist that reporters agree to hold back on some of their statements. This request puts the reporter in a difficult situation, for at most speeches, the reporter is an invited guest. A reporter has the right to be present at an official and public meeting and to use all statements and actions there, but he has no legal right to attend a Rotary Club speech.

A reporter may have to leave if he or she refuses to go along with a request for off-the-record status of all or parts of a talk. But the reporter is under no compulsion to heed the request for silence, present or absent. A talk heard by dozens of persons cannot be kept confidential, and the reporter usually points this out to those making the request. He or she also points out that since those attending the session will talk to the reporter about the speech, the speaker may find the material somewhat garbled in the telling and should welcome an accurate report. This argument usually wins the reporter's battle.

The Washington Post distributed this memo about requests for off-the-record status at meetings:

> In a large gathering—say 20 persons or more—but sponsored by a private organization, club, committee, where the reporter is present in his role as a reporter but also as an invited guest, he must protest vigorously any attempt by the speaker to go off the record. He should point out that the meeting was scheduled as open to the press and should declare that he will not be bound by the limitation.

Remember, the reporter is not bound by requests for off-the-record status of any item if the request is made after the information has been disclosed.

Meetings

Meetings provide newspapers and broadcast stations with enormous amounts of news. Public bodies—school boards, city councils, legislatures, planning and zoning commissions—conduct much of their business at open meetings. Then there are the meetings of private groups—baseball club owners, the directors of corporations, protesting citizens. The list could be extended for pages.

The essentials of meeting stories are:

- Purpose, time and location of meeting.
- Items on the agenda.
- Major business transacted: Votes, decisions, adoption of policies.
- Discussion and debate. Length of session.
- Quotes from witnesses and experts.
- Comments and statements from onlookers, authoritative persons and those affected by the decision that the reporter gathers after the meeting.
- Background.
- Unusual departures from the agenda.
- Agenda for next session.

Not all meeting stories will contain every one of these items. Notice the items stressed in the first several paragraphs of this meeting story from The Brattleboro Reformer of Brattleboro, Vt. The reporter used a delayed lead to emphasize the scope and the nature of the protests rather than a direct lead saying the board made less than half of the requested cut. The first paragraph sets the scene for the major business transacted by the town school board, which is described in the second paragraph:

Public Protests Budget Cuts in Elementary Programs

By Gretchen Becker

Nearly 300 people came to an emotional Brattleboro Town School Board meeting at Green Street School Tuesday night to protest proposed cuts in the elementary school art, music, and physical education programs.

Purpose
Time
Location

Caught between the strong public opinion at the meeting not to make these cuts and a strong Town Meeting mandate to cut 5 percent from their budget, the school directors reluctantly approved almost $35,000 in budget reductions.

Major business transacted

Approved were elimination of the elementary art instructor's position, the second physical education position, a part-time vocal instructor's position, the fifth and sixth grade basketball program, and rental of space at Centre Church.

The board took no action on the administration's proposals to eliminate the instrumental music position and the part-time principal's position at Canal Street School. Approval of these cuts would have brought the total cuts to $46,000.

Salary Controversy

At Town Meeting March 22, the representatives voted to cut 5 percent, or $74,200, from the elementary budget. Those urging the cuts requested that teachers' salaries be frozen. However, WSESU Superintendent James Cusick has noted several times that the proposed budget included only $25,000 for increases in salaries. . . .

Background

Most often, the lead will focus on the major action taken at the meeting, as in this lead:

City Councilwoman Elizabeth T. Boskin persuaded council members to approve additional funds for the city police department last night.	Major action taken
The council had been cutting requested funds for the 1984–5 budget because of anticipated declines in tax revenues.	Purpose of meeting
But Boskin said violent crimes had increased 18 percent last year.	Amplification of major theme
"The only way to handle this is with more police officers," she said.	that includes direct quote on theme
The department had asked for a 15 percent increase in funds over the current year's allocation for hiring an additional dozen officers.	Background
The council has been making cuts in the requests of city departments and agencies ranging from 10 to 20 percent.	
But Boskin's plea was persuasive, and they voted unanimously to approve the request for an additional $87,000, an increase of 14 percent.	Amplification of theme
Then the council returned to wielding the hatchet. . . .	Transition to other actions

Sometimes a meeting continues past the reporter's deadline, and the reporter has to make do with what he or she has. It is possible, however, to catch the sense or drift of a meeting, as Robert T. Garrett did in this story in *The* Louisville *Courier-Journal*:

LEXINGTON, Ky.—The Fayette County school board appeared likely last night to reject the teaching of "scientific creationism" alongside the theory of evolution in local science classes.	Probable major action
The five-member board, which had been deadlocked 2-2 on the issue, heard opposing views from residents for several hours last night before a packed house at school headquarters.	Setting
The board had taken no vote as of 11:15 p.m.	
But the fifth and previously undecided member of the school board, Harold Steele, hinted that he would vote against the proposed "two-model" science curriculum.	Buttressing of lead with quotes and paraphrases

Steele said he had concern that "very definite parameters will endure" that ensure the separation of church and state.

As the school board prepares to face the question of tuition tax credits in coming weeks, it must remember that public education "is not permitted to teach sectarian courses," Steele said.

Before last night's debate, school board Chairman Barth Pemberton and board member Carol Jarboe were on record opposing introduction of creationism in the schools.

Board members Mary Ann Burdette and David Chittenden had said they support the teaching of creationist views. Mrs. Burdette moved that the creationist proposal be adopted, and Chittenden seconded it.

Scientific creationism is a theory closely aligned to the biblical account of creation.

It holds that man and the Earth were created by an outside force, such as God, in a short span of time less than 10,000 years ago and have changed little since. . . .

Probable position of others on major action

Background

The school board did vote 3–2 to reject creationism in classrooms, as Garrett indicated it would.

News Conferences

The UPI Day Book, a listing of daily events used by New York City newspapers and broadcast stations as an aid in making local assignments, carried this item one Wednesday evening:

Manhattan District Attorney Robert Morgenthau holds news conference to produce evidence that confirms existence of ancient civilization in Israel between 2000–1500 B. C., 155 Leonard Street 10:30 a.m.

To local editors, it sounded like a good yarn. Moreover, many New Yorkers feel a kinship with Israel. Thus, when the district attorney began his conference, half a dozen reporters and two television crews were on hand.

The reporters were told that a Manhattan school teacher on a honeymoon in Israel had unearthed a clay tablet with writing on it and had managed to take it out of the country. On trying to learn its value, the teacher had spoken to someone who discovered the tablet was an antiquity. Under Israeli law, no historical objects may leave the country and the teacher was therefore in possession of stolen property, which is an indictable offense.

But the district attorney had decided not to prosecute. He had worked out an arrangement between the teacher and the Israeli government. Although all of this could have been announced in a press release, a news conference was called so that the district attorney could play midwife in the delivery of the tablet to an Israeli representative. The district attorney, an elected official whose office is financed through legislative appropriations, would appear to the public as a man of compassion and wisdom. The reporters would profit, too, for the story seemed to be a good one.

The incident illustrates the mutuality of interests that the news conference serves. It permits an individual, group or organization to reach many reporters at one time with an announcement that will receive more attention than a press release, and it is an efficient and economical way for the press to obtain newsworthy material.

Although most people associate news conferences with the president, the device is a daily occurrence in most cities. News conferences are called by basketball teams and cosmetics manufacturers as well as by city councilmen and governors.

Usually, the news conference has a prescribed form. A prepared statement is usually distributed to the reporters beforehand. (See fig. 19.1.) Then reporters ask questions.

At the district attorney's news conference, reporters wanted to know the size of the tablet, when it was discovered, how it was recovered and other facts. The news stories that appeared differed substantially from the press release.

Here is how Marcia Chambers began her account that appeared in *The New York Times.* Compare it with the press release. Note that some material in the lead is not contained in the handout and was obtained through questioning. Also, the story stresses the action and places the district attorney in the third paragraph, whereas the press release begins with the district attorney's name:

A fragment of a clay tablet 3,500 to 4,000 years old that confirms the existence of the biblical city of Hazor in Israel was returned yesterday to the Israeli Government after a teacher who smuggled it out of Israel agreed to surrender it to avoid prosecution.

The odyssey of the 2-by-2-inch fragment, with a cuneiform inscription, began in 1963 when the young teacher was on his honeymoon. The teacher, an amateur archeologist, found the tablet at the site of an archeological excavation some 10 miles north of the Sea of Galilee.

It ended yesterday, at a news conference, when Robert M. Morgenthau, the Manhattan District Attorney, turned over the priceless piece to Amos Ganor, Israel's acting consul general here. . . .

**Figure 19.1 A District
Attorney's Press Release.**

DISTRICT ATTORNEY–NEW YORK COUNTY

For Release: November 20, 1975

Contact: Gerda Handler
        732-7300
        Ext. 603/4

   Robert M. Morgenthau, District Attorney, New York
County, announced today the recovery of a priceless
antiquity from ancient biblical times. The object is a
sherd–a fragment of a clay tablet–bearing a cuneiform
inscription of unique archaeological significance.
   Mr. Morgenthau today returned this antiquity, dating
from between 1500 and 2000 B.C., to Amos Ganor, Acting
Consul General of the State of Israel.
   The sherd was originally found at the site of the
archaeological excavation of the ancient city of
Hazor, located about ten miles north of the Sea of
Galilee in Israel.
   It was removed from Israel in violation of that
country's Antiquities Ordinance, which requires the
finder of any antiquity to notify the Government of
the discovery and afford it an opportunity to acquire
the object. A complaint was filed with the District
Attorney by the Government of Israel through Dr.
Avraham Biran, former Director of the Department of
Antiquities in Israel. An investigation was undertaken
by the District Attorney which resulted in the
recovery of the sherd.
   The sherd records a case of litigation, conducted in
the presence of the king, concerning real estate in
Hazor. It is of great historical value because it
confirms that the excavation, begun in 1955 near the
Sea of Galilee, is the ancient city of Hazor.
According to Professor Yigal Yadin, who headed a four
year archaeological expedition at Hazor, the sherd is
a major link in the identification of the excavation
as the ancient city of Hazor, that was mentioned in
the Egyptian Execration Texts of the 19th Century
B.C., the Annals of the Pharaohs Thut-mose III, Amen-
hotep II and Seti I and in several chapters of the
Bible.

News conference stories must include the purpose of the conference or the reason it was called. The atmosphere is less important than for a speech or a meeting story, unless something unusual occurs.

Some reporters who are dissatisfied with what they have learned at a news conference will gather around the speaker at its conclusion and ask further questions.

Reporters are sometimes sent to cover a symposium, colloquium or panel discussion. The presence of several speakers can pose a problem, but experienced reporters usually make their way through the tide of talk by emphasizing a thematic approach. They will seek out a basic theme and write a summary based on that theme, such as:

Panel Discussions

> Four members of the local bar agreed last night that probation is no longer a useful means of coping with criminal offenders.
> Although the speakers disagreed on most matters at the symposium on "How to Handle Increasing Crime," they did agree. . . .

Even when there is little agreement, a summary lead is possible, for disagreement is a theme, too. Here is such a lead:

> There was no accord at the College Auditorium last night as four faculty members discussed "Discord in the Middle East."
> The political scientists and historians disagreed on the causes of unrest in that troubled area, and they disagreed on solutions.
> All they agreed upon was that the situation is thorny.
> "We really don't know whether peace will break out tomorrow, or war is in the offing," said Prof. Walter. . . .

After the theme is developed for a few paragraphs, each speaker is given his or her say. Obviously, the more newsworthy statements come first. When one of the speakers says something clearly more interesting than what the others are discussing, then the thematic lead is dropped and the newsworthy statement becomes the lead. Later, the subject matter is examined. Here is how such a story runs:

A California research team may have found a potent opponent of the virus that causes the common cold sore.

The information was disclosed today at a discussion of bioscientists and physicians at the School of Public Health on the campus.

Dr. Douglas Deag, a naval biochemist, said that the enemy of the herpes simplex virus (types 1 and 2) may well be the popular seafood delicacy, seaweed. The red variety—known as Rho-dophyta—contains a species that has an active agent that prevents the herpes virus from multiplying.

Herpes is responsible for keratitis—a severe eye infection—and a genital disease as well as the cold sore. But the research is in the early stages, Dr. Deag said.

He was one of five speakers who discussed "Frontiers of Medicine," which was concerned primarily with careers in the medical sciences. . . .

Stories involving several speakers will sometimes require multiple-element leads. However, it is generally best to avoid them since the number of speakers and multiplicity of themes can be confusing. Obviously, when necessary to the accurate retelling of the event, a multiple lead will be used.

Space exploration can be man's salvation, a physicist said today, but an astronomer worried that man might over-reach himself and pollute the universe as well as his own planet.

The disagreement was voiced at a symposium last night, on "Space Travel," sponsored by the Science Club and held in the Civic Auditorium. More than 250 persons turned out, obviously drawn by the promise of hearing one of the speakers discuss Unidentified Flying Objects.

But if they came expecting to hear a defense of UFO's they were disappointed, for Dr. Marcel Pannel said flatly, "They do not exist." . . .

A Reporter's Checklist

7

Introduction   The preceding chapters have described the processes that underlie reporting and writing. The beginning reporter should approach assignments in the disciplined and logical ways that have been outlined. Now we are ready to move to specific stories. To help the new reporter handle these, we can devise a checklist of the necessary elements of any type of story.

For example: An obituary requires the name and identification of the deceased; the causes, time, place and location of death; the survivors; funeral and burial plans, and some background about the deceased. We can make similar lists of necessities for other basic story types.

In order to select the story types that most beginners encounter, many young reporters and veterans were canvassed for suggestions and for sample stories. The following chapters are the result.

Using the Checklist   When a reporter goes out on an assignment, the aim should be to gather information on the checklist, the essentials of the story. The checklist is only a starting point, however, a take-off for the application of imagination and enterprise.

Mastering these essentials is not an end in itself. No rote learning of what to look for and how to structure a particular kind of story can substitute for creative journalism, just as no memorization of writing techniques can transmute slaglike prose into apples of gold.

The elements on the checklist are not in exact order, although many stories will follow the checklist. Any one of the elements could be made into a lead, depending upon the circumstances. Reporters must use their judgment to determine what constitutes the news angle or theme of the event. Not all of the elements will appear in every story, but most will be used.

Students should not look at the checklist as a cook approaches a recipe, first buttering the pan, then adding salt, stirring for six minutes, adding half a cup of flour. . . .This volume is a textbook, not a cookbook. Creative cooks always depart from the recipes, anyway. The reporter's task is to put his or her personal stamp on copy. The checklist will help point the reporter in the right direction if it is used carefully along with the reporting, writing and thinking processes that have been described in previous chapters.

20 Accidents and Disasters

Preview   Stories about accidents and disasters must include:
- Names and addresses of dead and injured.
- Time, location and cause of accident.
- Comments from eyewitnesses and authorities when possible.

Motor vehicles kill, injure and maim an enormous number of persons each year. News of collisions, of trucks and cars careening into trees and smashing into each other on fog-bound freeways is given good play in newspapers and on local radio and television news programs. Only the routine "fender benders," as newsmen describe minor accidents, are ignored or summarized. Rare is the reporter who has never written "a fatal," a story about an accident in which at least one person died. Most newsrooms make periodic checks with authorities so that they have the latest accident reports right up to deadline.

Motor Vehicle Accidents

Four Dead, Three Hurt in Car Crash

Four men died and three others were critically injured when their speeding car smashed into a retaining wall in a residential section of Vallejo, police said yesterday.

Officers said six of the victims in the crash late Tuesday night were stationed at Mare Island Naval Base in Vallejo.

The dead civilian was identified as 23-year-old Patrick D. Hagen of Vallejo. The others, all in their early 20s and from the Mare Island Base were identified as Jonathon S. Cohen, Michael G. Williams and Manuel Guiterez.

The three injured men, who doctors at David Grant Hospital at Travis Air Force Base said are not expected to survive, were identified as Lucky V. Ramirez, Steve Criss and Conrad Anderson, also in their early 20s and stationed at the Mare Island Base.

Officers said the car carrying the men hit the retaining wall about a half-mile from the base at a speed of at least 70 miles per hour. Police described the road as narrow and twisted, with a posted speed of 25 miles per hour.

–San Francisco *Chronicle*

Sometimes the remarks of the coroner or an official provide material for the lead, as in this story from the *Herald-Dispatch* in Huntington, W. Va.,:

ELK CREEK, W. Va.— Two teen-agers died early yesterday when their car went off W.Va. 65, struck a tree and "practically disintegrated," a county official said.

The deaths were the second and third traffic fatalities in Mingo County in two days, said interim County Coroner Larry Wood.

He identified the victims as Jimmy Nichols, 16, of Varney, and Clyde R. Nichols, 18, of Columbus.

He said their car left the highway about 12:15 a.m., wrapped around a tree and "practically disintegrated."

Although wreckage was scattered over a wide area, evidence at the scene indicated that Jimmy Nichols was driving, the coroner said.

"From the appearance of the car and where it left the road, excessive speed probably caused the accident," said Deputy Bill Webb of the Mingo County Sheriff's Department.

There were no witnesses to the crash, he said. . . .

The story's importance is determined by the number of persons killed and injured and their prominence, the proximity of the accident to local readers or listeners and the circumstances of the accident.

**Checklist:
Motor Vehicle
Accidents**

_____ Victims: Names, identification of dead and injured.
_____ Type of vehicles involved.
_____ Location.
_____ Time.
_____ Cause (from official source).
_____ Names and identification of other drivers and passengers.
_____ Cause of death, injuries.

_____ Where dead taken.

_____ Where injured taken and how.

_____ Extent of injuries.

_____ Heroism, rescues.

_____ Latest condition of critically injured.

_____ Funeral arrangements if available.

_____ Damage to vehicles.

_____ Arrests or citations by police.

_____ Unusual weather or highway conditions.

_____ Accounts by eyewitnesses and investigating officers.

_____ Speed, origin and destination of vehicles.

State highway patrol; local, suburban police; sheriff's office; hospital; ambulance service; mortuary; coroner.

Sources

Art Carey of the *Philadelphia Inquirer,* says that one of the first warnings he received while covering an accident was to be careful of inadvertently attributing blame for the accident when writing about the cause. Unless one of the drivers has been cited or arrested, it is best to avoid a detailed description of the cause. The reporter must be especially careful about saying which vehicle struck the other since such statements often imply responsibility.

Cautions

News of airplane accidents makes headlines. A motor vehicle collision in which two are killed will not receive the attention given the crash of an airplane with the same number of fatalities. The romance of the airplane and the infrequency of such accidents probably cause this contrast in news play.

Airline crashes are big news because of the numbers involved. Local newspapers and stations will scan the casualty list carried on the wires for the names of local residents.

Airplane Accidents

_____ Number of dead and injured.

_____ Time, location and cause of crash.

_____ Origin and destination of plane.

_____ Airline and flight number.

_____ Type of plane: Manufacturer, number of engines.

_____ Victims: Names and identification (including home town).

_____ Survivors by name.

_____ Condition of injured.

_____ Where dead and injured taken.

_____ Cause of death: Impact, fire, exposure.

_____ Altitude at time of trouble.

_____ Weather and flying conditions.

_____ Last words of pilot.

**Checklist:
Airplane
Accidents**

_____ Police, fire, rescue units at scene.

_____ Unusual incidents; heroism.

_____ Eyewitness accounts of survivors.

_____ Eyewitness accounts of people on ground.

_____ Comments by air controllers, officials, airline.

_____ Cost of aircraft.

_____ Prominent people aboard.

_____ Fire and other destruction as result of crash.

_____ Direction aircraft heading before crash.

_____ Flight recorder recovered?

_____ If aircraft was missing, who found wreckage and how.

_____ Funeral arrangements.

_____ Survivors of deceased.

_____ Official inquiry.

_____ Previous crashes in area.

Material for this section was provided by Thomas H. Jones of the *Chicago Sun-Times* and Paul Peterzell of the *Independent-Journal* of San Rafael, Calif.

Sources
Airline; police, fire, and other rescue units; Federal Aviation Administration (which in many large cities has a special telephone number for accident information); air traffic controllers; airport officials; National Transportation Safety Board; hospital; mortuary; coroner; morgue.

Cautions
Eyewitnesses on the ground are notoriously inaccurate about aircraft crashes. Early reports of casualties tend to be exaggerated. Passenger flight lists can be erroneous; verify if possible.

Disasters

The line between accidents and disasters is difficult to draw. If the demarcation point is the number of lives lost, the amount of property destroyed or damaged, then who would set down the numbers that distinguish the two? The fatal plunge of a school bus into a river that takes the lives of six children is a tragic accident in a metropolis, but to the residents of a town of 25,000 it is a disaster and much of the news staff will be mobilized to cover the accident, the consequences to the families, school-mates' versions, means taken to prevent further such occurrences and so on.

When a bomb went off at a crowded New York City air terminal, the *Daily News* assigned a dozen reporters to the story. Perhaps one definition of a disaster is that it is a situation that draws maximum coverage. Some define a disaster as massive, widespread death and destruction of the kind usually associated with the vagaries of nature—floods, earthquakes, hurricanes, storms and drought. But in actual usage, the word disaster covers large loss of life:

> An American Airlines jetliner lost an engine and crashed shortly after takeoff from O'Hare International Airport this afternoon, killing all 272 persons aboard. It was the worst disaster in United States aviation history.

Notice the straightforward account of the tragedy. A sidebar gives the details, some of them horrifying:

> . . . red and yellow stakes marked
> the few charred bodies the firemen could
> reach.
> One of the first physicians to arrive
> at the scene was Dr. Robert Loguersio.
> "There were bodies all over," he said.
> "There were a lot of corpses on the
> scene. . . ."

The sources and checklist for disaster coverage are similar to those listed for accidents. Since disasters may cause widespread havoc, the National Guard is sometimes mobilized, and the Red Cross may dispatch units to help. Civil defense agencies may be present. State and federal agencies are often called upon to arrange access to the scene or to engage in rescue operations.

As in the accident story, the human toll is more important than the loss of property.

Checklist: Disasters

____ Dead.
____ Injured.
____ Total affected or in danger.
____ Cause of death.
____ Estimated death and injury toll.
____ Eyewitness accounts.
____ Property loss:
    Homes.
    Land.
    Public utilities.
    Permanent damage.
____ Rescue and relief operations:
    Evacuations.
    Heroism.
    Unusual equipment used or unique rescue techniques.
    Number of official personnel and volunteers.
____ Warnings:
    Health department, public utility commission, police and highway
    department statements.
____ Looting.
____ Number of spectators.
____ Insurance.
____ Suits.
____ Arrests.
____ Investigations.

There is no dearth of sources for disaster stories. Statements may be issued by presidents and kings; generals and prime ministers; local police and priests. The enormity of the destruction is so vast no one source can accurately assess the toll in human lives until the disaster begins to abate and energy can be devoted to gauging the human and property losses.

Eyewitnesses Essential

Edward A. Mahar, a reporter and editor in New York City for many years, recalled his first big story as a cub reporter on the *Albany Argus*. It was the wreck of a New York Central train near Scotia, N. Y.

"On that big story I was fortunate enough to get one of the finest lessons a reporter can learn," Mahar recalled. "That is, to get your story, if you can, from someone who saw it happen.

"When I arrived at the scene about 1 o'clock on that cool, spring morning I saw bodies laid in a row alongside the wreckage. I thought I'd get sick, then and there. I got to the sheriff who admitted he knew little about the wreck. He pointed to a fellow sitting on the ground nearby.

" 'He saw it—talk with him,' he said, gruffly, over the din of the wreck crews.

"Though wide-eyed with shock, the fellow, a young farmer, told me how he had seen a freight pull out of a siding onto the main tracks right in front of a speeding passenger train. I took notes as fast as he talked.

"Finished with him, I counted the bodies and streaked off to a telephone, a half mile away. I had been sent to the scene merely to preempt a telephone and hold the line open for the star reporters coming later.

"I called the office and gave the city editor the farmer's eyewitness story and the count of the dead. Without knowing it, I had given the paper a good story for an 'extra.'

"Since then I have always stressed the importance of getting the story from someone who saw it happen—not secondhand from a policeman or an ambulance driver."

Writing Disaster Stories

With stories of the dimension of a disaster the reporter is tempted to pull out every writing device he or she knows. Resist. If resistance is difficult, pause and reflect on the story—part fact, part fiction—told of the reporter from a Philadelphia newspaper sent to cover a mine disaster in Donora, Pa., where hundreds of miners were entombed dead or facing imminent death from mine gas. The mine was surrounded by weeping relatives, and when it was opened 200 bodies were taken out.

The Philadelphia newspaper reporter looked at this massive scene of death and grief and wired his newspaper the lead: God sits tonight on a little hill overlooking the scene of disaster. . . .

As these words came over the telegraph machine in the newsroom in Philadelphia, an editor shouted out, "Stop," and he handed the telegraph editor a message to send back to the reporter in Donora: Never mind disaster interview God.

Obituaries

Preview   Obituaries are among the most frequently read sections of the newspaper. The obituary should seek to sum up the background and outstanding qualities of the individual. The obituary must include:
- Name, age, occupation and address of the deceased.
- Time, place and cause of death.
- Survivors.
- Funeral and burial plans.

The obituary is a routine story that no reporter enjoys writing.

On the obituary page may be found the summing up of the glories, the achievements, the mediocrities, and the failures of a life which the rest of the paper chronicled day by day.

The first description is taken from a journalism textbook, the second from a veteran journalist's article about writing obituaries. Strangely, both summaries are accurate. Most obituaries in most newspapers are indeed routine, written by reporters who rigorously follow a formula so that only names, addresses, ages and the other vital statistics differentiate one obituary from another. However, the newspapers that ask their reporters to use their reportorial and writing skills on as many obituaries as possible find ready reader response. Obituaries are among the best-read staples in the newspaper.

Unless otherwise instructed, no reporter should ever approach any story with the intention of writing a routine account. Of course, some stories are difficult to make interesting, but the obituary hardly falls into this category, for the reporter has a wide panorama from which to select material—a person's entire life. No one's life lacks drama, if the reporter has the intelligence and the time and the desire to look for it.

Even when the life is brief, the obituary can be interesting or moving. Here is an obituary of a 12-year-old boy written by a young reporter, James Eggensperger, for the *Sanders County Ledger* in Thompson Falls, Mont.

Goodbye, Ron

Ronald Laws, a rising star in Thompson Falls athletic competition, died Friday night doing one of the things he liked best, playing baseball. He was 12 years old.

Ron, as his friends and teachers and coaches called him, was batting in a Little League baseball game when he was hit in the chest by a pitched ball.

Then, according to one witness, he started running. After about 20 feet, he turned to the call of his coach, fell to the ground and never rose.

Spectators at the game rushed Ron to the Clark Fork Valley Hospital at Plains where the game was being played, but efforts there to start his heart failed.

His funeral was Monday in Thompson Falls. The Rev. Bruce Kline performed the service with special feeling because he had known Ron through Sunday school and liked him greatly.

The Rev. Kline also performed graveside services at the Whitepine cemetery.

In fact, everyone who knew Ronnie liked him, teachers, classmates and teammates. He was a good sportsman and student and took pleasure in anything he undertook.

He left behind his parents, Mr. and Mrs. Larry Laws and two brothers, Larry Lee and Timothy, and a sister, Lori.

Fittingly, the Thompson Falls and Plains All Star baseball teams are planning a two-game fund raising baseball marathon for the 8th and 9th of July. Proceeds from the games will go to a memorial fund in Ron's name, a fund which will be used to support sports activities in both towns.

Other memorials for the fund may be sent to his parents.

Eggensperger recalls the day he took the call about the accident:

I remember feeling sick that such a thing should happen to such a good kid. But even more, that he had not had a chance to bloom into his potential and to enjoy all the things in life there are to enjoy. I put myself in his shoes and thought of all the memories, good and bad times, people and places I would have missed if I had not lived past 12, and the impact was overwhelming.

And in the back of my head was something I had been taught, which ran something like this: "An obit may be the only time a guy gets into the paper, and it's his last chance."

So I talked to some people and wrote what I felt.

The Druggist and the Laborer

Deborah Howell, managing editor of the *St. Paul Pioneer Press*, says that "too many big-city dailies report just the deaths of important people—captains of industry and political leaders. That's a mistake. These newspapers ignore the woman who always feeds the ducks in the late afternoon at the city lake, the tireless youth worker at the neighborhood park, the druggist dispensing sage advice along with medicine for 50 years."

Howell recalls obituaries about ordinary people that made interesting reading. A woman who died of cancer and who had asked for a party after her funeral was memorialized in an obituary that began this way in the *Pioneer Press:*

The ladies sat in a circle of lawn chairs in the neatly clipped backyard, between the pea patch on the right and the tomatoes and cucumbers on the left, sipping their gentle scotches and bourbons and beers, while the mosquitoes buzzed around their ears, and the evening slowly faded without pain into the night.

When Tom Flaherty died in St Paul, the paper was informed of his death by a friend of the family. "To most folks, Tom might have seemed quite ordinary," Howell said. "He worked his whole life as a laborer on the Great Northern Railroad, as did many of the Irish immigrants in St. Paul. At first, I worried how I was going to make an obit on Tom interesting. Then I decided that his life represented so much that is so Irish, so Catholic, so railroad, so St. Paul. When any Irish railroadman died, Tom was at the wake. At the St. Patrick's Day parade, Tom led the Flaherty section.

"I explained the kind of obit I wanted to one of our better writers. His obit began:

Tom Flaherty was an Irishman's Irishman, a John Henry of a man who for 50 years matched his mighty muscle against the hardest work the railroad had to offer.

"The trick is to make the dead person come alive again in an obituary, to remind family and friends and co-workers why someone was important.

"Too often reporters come away with just the basic facts about birth, education, marriage, vocation and perhaps a few war medals. Obituaries can be examples of the paper's best writing, meaning reporters must search for the kind of detail—the unusual facts—that makes any news story interesting to read."

Richard G. West, who was a city editor of *The New York Herald Tribune* and whose comments on the obituary appear in italics at the start of this chapter, says of the obituary: "Preparing an obituary is a delicate and exacting task, demanding the utmost diligence, insight and imagination. His obituary should be, as far as human judgment and ability may create it in the limits of a newspaper's space, a man's monument."

Monuments take time to carve, and the newspapers that attempt to carry an obituary for all or most of those who die within their circulation area cannot possibly devote much time or space to each. Still, some should be carefully prepared, and the others condensed.

Beginning reporters usually are broken in by a stint of obituary writing. Most reporters consider it a dull assignment of little consequence.

"What nonsense. What an opportunity," says Joseph L. Galloway, a foreign correspondent for the UPI. Galloway wrote his share of obituaries when he broke into newspaper work on a small Texas daily.

"The obits are probably read by more people with greater attention to detail than any other section of a newspaper," he says. "Nowhere else is error or omission more likely to be noticed.

"A good reporter gives each obit careful and accurate handling. He or she searches in the stack for the one or two that can be brought to life.

"Veteran of World War II, the funeral home sheet says. Did he make the D-Day landing on the beaches of Normandy? Taught junior high school English for 43 years? Find some former pupils who can still quote entire pages of Longfellow because somehow she made it live and sing for them."

Checklist: Obituaries

The following items are required in all obituaries:

_____ Name, age, occupation and address of the deceased.
_____ Time, place and cause of death.
_____ Birthdate, birth place.
_____ Survivors. (Only immediate family.)
_____ Funeral and burial arrangements.

Many obituaries will also include:

_____ Outstanding accomplishments and achievements.
_____ Memberships in fraternal, religious or civic organizations.
_____ Service in the armed forces.
_____ Anecdotes and recollections of friends and relatives.

Here is an obituary from *The Hawk Eye,* Burlington, Iowa, that includes most of these items:

Ray D. Miller

Ray D. Miller, 60-year-old owner of Burlington Beauty and Barber Supply Co., died in Burlington Memorial hospital Thursday, Sept. 18, at 1:30 p.m., after a long illness.

The son of Benjamin and Rilda Huntey Miller, he was born July 17, 1915, in Gorin, Mo. He married Margaret Marlin Feb. 22, 1941, in Burlington.

Mr. Miller served in the Army in World War II. He was a member of St. Paul church and the Knights of Columbus, Beauty and Barber Supply Institute, American Legion, and Elks Lodge.

Surviving: The wife; two sons, Mike and Jim D., and one daughter, Mary Rae Schnedler, all of Burlington; four brothers, Tom, LaGrange, Mo., Harry and Archie, both of Memphis, Mo., and Fred B., Burlington; four sisters, Hazel Kettle, Queen City, Mo., and Jewel Schelen, Alta Corso, and Eula Ridge, all of Burlington.

Funeral: 1:30 p.m. Saturday, St. Paul Church, Fr. James Quinlan; Sacred Heart Cemetery. Rosary this evening at 7:30 at Prugh's. A memorial has been established at St. Paul Church.

Note the last two paragraphs of the Miller obituary. This is *The Hawk Eye*'s style for these two standard components of the obituary. The other paragraphs are written in the usual manner.

B. A. PRUGH & SON
FUNERAL SERVICE
BURLINGTON, IOWA
52601

Name of deceased .... MRS. HAZEL F. COOKSEY ....

Residence ...... 1102 N. 8th St. Burlington, Iowa ....

Place of death .... Mercy Unit, Burlington Medical Center, Burlington, Iowa ....

Date of death .... April 22, 1976 .... Time 1:50 AM ....

Length of stay in hospital .... in city ....

Sex .... Female .... Color .... White .... Single, married, widowed, divorced

Name of husband or wife .... Peck N. Cooksey ....

Birth date of deceased .... February 18, 1894 .... Age ... 82 ....

Birthplace .... Canton, Missouri ....

Usual occupation .... Retired ....

Name of father .... William F. Lee .... Mother .... Maude Elaine Lewis ....

Military service .... None .... Soc. Sec. No. .... 480-01-6112 ....

Informant's name .... Mrs. Norma V. Cook ... (daughter) ....
                                              Address ... Same .... (2-3705)

Attending physician .... Dr. Todd ....

Cause of death ....

OBITUARY NOTES:

Duration of illness .... Brief .... Church affiliations ... Baptist Faith

Organizations .... None

Date and place of marriage .... September 7, 1912 at Canton, Missouri

Survivors:

One daughter, Mrs. Chester (Norma) V. Cook of Burlington and one son
Mr. Kenneth Cooksey also of Burlington, Iowa. Two brothers, Mr. James F. Lee of
Muscatine, Iowa and Mr. Merle Lee of Florida.

Preceded in death by her husband, parents and three sons, and two sisters.

SERVICE ARRANGEMENTS:

Day of funeral .... Saturday April 24, 1976 .... Time 1:30 PM ... Place .... Prugh's Chapel ....

Cemetery .... Aspen Grove Cemetery ....

Minister .... Rev. Mr. Charles Stevens ....

Other arrangements .... FAMILY WILL RECEIVE FRIENDS AT PRUGH'S FRIDAY EVENING FROM
7:30 UNTIL 9:00 O'CLOCK.

HAWKEYE THUR

Death notices

Mrs. Hazel F. Cooksey

Mrs. Hazel F. Cooksey, 82, of 1107 N. Eighth, died in Burlington Medical Center at 1:50 a.m. Thursday, April 22.

The daughter of William F. and Maude Elaine Lewis Lee, she was born Feb. 18, 1894, at Canton, Mo. She married Peck N. Cooksey Sept. 7, 1912, at Canton; he died earlier.

She was a member of the Baptist church.

Surviving: Son, Kenneth, and daughter, Norma Cook, both of Burlington; and two brothers, James F. Lee, Muscatine, and Merle Lee of Florida.

Funeral: 1:30 Saturday, Prugh's Chapel, Rev. Charles Stevens; Aspen Grove cemetery.

First news of deaths can come from several sources. Many newspapers rely on the death notices mortuaries send newspapers to be placed in the classified advertising section. The news department is given a carbon. Some mortuaries will call in the death of a prominent person, and on some newspapers reporters regularly make the rounds of mortuaries by telephone. The police and the coroner's office will have news of accidental deaths. Wire service stories are scanned for the names of local people who may have been involved in disasters or accidents out of town.

Sources

Material for the obituary can be gathered from many sources. Always begin with the newspaper library. Friends and relatives can provide information, some of it human interest material that makes an obituary interesting to read, and they can verify questionable or vague information. Here are the various sources:

- Mortuary.
- Relatives, friends.
- Newspaper clippings.
- References such as *Who's Who.*
- Police, coroner and other officials.
- Hospital.
- Attending physician.

Writing the Obit

Obituaries fall into two general categories, depending on the circumstances of the person's death. When the death is accidental—as in a traffic accident, disaster or airplane crash—the lead emphasizes the cause of death. When death is antici-pated—as it is for the elderly and persons who are seriously ill—the obituary con-centrates on the person's background and achievements. In both cases, of course, the obituary will list the vital facts from the checklist.

Here are leads from the two types:

Roberto Clemente, star outfielder for the Pittsburgh Pirates baseball team, died last night in the crash of a cargo plane carrying relief supplies to the vic-tims of an earthquake in Managua, Nic-aragua.

Walter Lippmann, the retired col-umnist and author and the elder states-man of American journalism, died today in New York City at the age of 85.

Find the Theme

As with any story, the obituary should concentrate on a major point or theme. Ob-viously, the overriding theme of all obituaries is the person's death. But that is not enough. The reporter must find the aspect of the person's life that is most notewor-thy.

When William H. Jones, managing editor of the *Chicago Tribune,* died at the age of 43 of leukemia, his professional accomplishments as an investigative reporter and an eminent editor were emphasized. The obituary noted his "tireless work, cre-ative thinking and total integrity."

The obituary writer found in the newspaper files a story about a talk Jones gave to a graduating class at the Medill School of Journalism at Northwestern University. The reporter quoted from that talk in order to show Jones's philosophy of journalism. Jones had spoken about journalism as a career:

> It's a commitment to use your skills to improve your community, to speak loudly for the victims of injustice and to speak out against those who perpetuate it. Some of the best reporting begins with a single, voiceless citizen who seeks help from a newspaper that is willing to listen, and to dig out the facts.

Then the obituary quoted an investigator with the city's Better Government Association who worked with Jones on a series of stories that exposed widespread corruption in Chicago's private ambulance companies, which won Jones the 1971 Pulitzer Prize when he was 31. The investigator said, "Bill hated to see people abused, especially the helpless."

When Emma Bugbee, a pioneer woman reporter in New York, died, her obituary stressed the unique niche Bugbee filled in the days when women were a rarity on newspaper reporting staffs.

> A founder of the Newspaper Women's Club of New York, Miss Bugbee was one of a handful of prominent female reporters who sought to expand the role of the women in what was the largely all-male world of journalism when she entered it in 1911.

Bugbee worked for *The New York Herald Tribune* for 56 years. For many of those years she was one of only two women reporters at the newspaper. They were not allowed to sit in the city room, the obituary recalled, "but had to work down the hall."

Not every obituary need lead with the news of the individual's death. Notice how Cary Stiff of the *Clear Creek Courant* of Georgetown, Colo., begins his story of the death of a prominent local citizen:

Delayed Leads

GEORGETOWN—When Tony Ricci was Georgetown's postmaster, he used to keep the Post Office open from 7 a.m. to 6:30 p.m.—seven days a week.

"Back in those days, the mail used to come in twice a day," his daughter, Irene Ricci Nelson, recalled Wednesday. "And he wanted to give the people good service."

Tony Ricci was proud of his appointment as the postmaster of Georgetown, perhaps because it proved that an Italian immigrant, a naturalized citizen, could amount to something in this big country of America.

The appointment was signed by the President of the United States himself—Franklin Delano Roosevelt, one of Ricci's heroes—and by the Postmaster General, James A. Farley.

And when Ricci died Monday in Denver just two months short of his 95th birthday, the document was still among his papers.

For his story of the funeral of a slain civil rights leader, Charles Bailey of the *Minneapolis Tribune* began this way:

> ARLINGTON, Va.—The humid haze of early summer lay hot and heavy on Washington, D.C., but here across the river, under the oak trees, the air was fresh and cool.
>
> The little girl sat on a folding chair, her mother on one side and her older brother on the other. The child's face was blank and bemused, almost dazed. Around her stood a thousand others. Closer in, a score of men with cameras crept and scuttled and snapped their shutters at her.

The little girl, the story goes on to say, is the daughter of the dead man. The story continues, and still the man's name is not given. Here are the final two paragraphs:

> Then the little girl and her brother and her mother were taken away, leaving their father and husband under the oak trees with the others who like him earned their right to lie there.
>
> In a few weeks, he too will have a little headstone, with an inscription like all the thousands of others on the hills and in the hollows under the trees. His will say:
>
> MEDGAR EVARS
> MISSISSIPPI

Use Human Details

Most obituaries read like the label on a bottle. The major ingredients are listed, but the reader has no idea of the actual flavor. The reporter's task is to help the reader to go beyond the basic data, to allow the reader to move close to the life of the person being written about. The kind of reporting Stiff did usually will turn up fascinating human interest details.

Because of time and other pressures, not every obituary can be made dramatic. But few lives lack drama, if the reporter digs deeply enough to find it. This point was eloquently made by a reader of the *Lubbock* (Tex.) *Avalanche-Journal* in a letter to the editor:

> To the Editor,
> A recent heading in the *Avalanche-Journal* read: "Relative of Ralls Negro found dead in an open chicken shack." Thin clothes, dirt floor, one quilt. Doctor gives probable cause of death as heart failure.
> At ten degrees below zero, these conditions could stop a powerful heart in a

young robust body. Still we wonder—what really caused death, a heart attack—or heartbreak? . . . Reckon how many bales of cotton Sam Jones picked in his lifetime? How many bales did Sam help grow? How many acres did he chop? How much profit did Sam's labor make for somebody the past sixty years? . . . Just before he died, he left a note asking to be buried near some cemetery. Sam was too modest to ask to be buried in a cemetery. . . .

In an obituary of Mrs. Helen Childs Boyden, who taught science and mathematics at Deerfield Academy, the reporter used several incidents from her life. When Mrs. Boyden had applied for work, the obituary reported, the principal was "not at all enthusiastic about the young applicant. But the school was too poor to insist on someone more experienced. He hired her on a temporary basis." She taught there for 63 years. The obituary continues:

. . . In a highly personal style she cajoled thousands of students through the intricacies of mathematics and chemistry.

Even in a large class she taught the individual, not the group. Her tongue was quick but never cutting. One boy, later a college president, recalls her telling him:

"Victor! When will you stop trying to remember and start trying to think?"

Some alert students at Syracuse University point out that the writer of the Boyden obituary has a "boy" doing the recalling in the second paragraph when obviously it is a man recalling something Boyden told him when he was a boy.

Here are some colorful paragraphs taken from obituaries:

Bill Stern, a radio and television sports announcer—While some radio and television critics and sportswriters contended that Mr. Stern's stories were sometimes taller than the highest infield fly, millions of listeners looked forward to his Sports Newsreel commentaries and anecdotes.

A wealthy retired business executive who lived on an estate—He knew the butcher, the baker, the news dealer and it was significant that he died in a moving-picture theater surrounded by a fireman, a policeman and the head usherette.

Duke Ellington, composer and musician— "Duke, he went all over the world after that, but nobody ever loved him better than we did," said an old-time tap dancer who goes by the name of Kid Chocolate.

Milton Bracker, a reporter for *The New York Times*—A restless, high-strung, energetic man whose unceasing productivity carried his work into just about every editorial corner of the *Times,* Mr. Bracker had a compulsion to write and his typewriter raced to appease his appetite for words.

The widow of a politician—She avoided the spotlight that focused on her husband through his long political career, but among teachers in local schools she was well-known as a tireless and cheerful volunteer who could be counted on to dry the tears of a newcomer to the first grade or to hand out graham crackers and milk at recess.

Sexist Obits   Most small- and medium-sized newspapers run at least a short news story on every-one who dies in town. Metropolitan newspapers may run as few as one out of a hundred deaths. In almost all cases, the preponderance of those selected are men. This is the consequence of the emphasis our society places on occupation and achievement. Traditionally, women have been housewives, clerks, typists and sec-retaries, not considered newsworthy occupations. But the perceptive reporter knows how important such tasks can be. There is as much drama—perhaps more—in the life of a woman who has reared three children as there is in a man whose obituary is justified by the fact that he headed a local concern for 25 years.

Here is the beginning of an obituary in a Maine newspaper:

> Mrs. Verena C. Hornberger, 92, died Tuesday at a Waldoboro nursing home. She was the widow of Hiester Hornber-ger.
> She was born at Bremen, daughter of Franklin and Emma (Hilton) Cha-ney. . . .

Not only is the obituary routinely written, it finds Mrs. Hornberger's prominence to be in her relationship to Hiester Hornberger, which might be newsworthy if her husband is shown to be prominent. He is not. But the obituary does contain some clues that, if followed up, might have made a fascinating story about Verena C. Horn-berger. Look at the possibilities:

> . . . She graduated in 1910 from Colby College where she was a member of Chi Omega sorority.
> She was a teacher, first working in local schools. She also taught in Essex, Conn., and Verona, N. J., following graduate work in Germany at the Uni-versity of Jena and Columbia's Teach-ers College.

Was she the last surviving member of the Class of 1910? Does the college have any information about her? She taught in local schools. Are there some stories from the principals or superintendents about her? Was it unusual in those days for a woman to do graduate work abroad? Is there someone who recalls her as a teacher? And so on.

Be Current   Current activities should be emphasized in writing the obituary. A man who was cap-tain of the local high school cross country team and then worked for the local power company as a lineman for 32 years will be remembered for his work and his activities with the local church rather than for his running.

Here are answers to some questions about writing obituaries.

Q. Does it make sense to prepare advance obituaries?
A. Yes, whenever possible, even before a prominent person is taken ill. Death is always sudden and often unexpected, despite the obituaries that report, as though unusual, that death came unexpectedly or suddenly. The AP keeps some 700 "biographical sketches" on hand, ready to be used and frequently brought up to date. A newspaper, depending on its size, may have a score or a handful. When a well-known person is near death, the background, or B Matter, as it is sometimes called, is ready so that all the reporter need write is a lead and the funeral arrangements.

Q. Must all second-day leads begin with the funeral or burial arrangements? Second-Day Leads
A. Not necessarily. An enterprising reporter can turn up interesting and significant material although a competing newspaper or station may have had the first story on the death. Although many newspapers do require the standard second-day lead, nothing is as likely to discourage a reader from a story as the lead that begins: Services for **(name)** of **(address)** will be held at **(time)** tomorrow at the **(church or funeral home)**. **(She/he)** died at **(her/his)** home **(date)**.

Q. Do I verify obituaries? Always Verify a Death
A. Always. Do so by telephoning relatives, the funeral home or mortuary, the police or hospital. Strange as it may seem, there are persons who call in reports of deaths, for revenge or because of some neurotic compulsion. Many reporters can recall experiences similar to that of a reporter on the *Evening News* in Newark who wrote an obituary only to find it was a hoax. This item had to be printed the next day:

> The Newark *News* yesterday printed an erroneous report of the death of James Barton of Westfield. The report, obviously a hoax, was received by the *News* in good faith from a source who purported to be an official of the company of which Mr. Barton is an executive. . . .
> The *News* regrets the error.

Q. Should I omit material from a person's life that might offend some readers Offensive Material
or embarrass survivors or friends?
A. Follow the policy of the newspaper or station. Generally, newspapers have become more frank since the 1930s when a new reporter for *The New York Herald Tribune* would be told by City Editor Stanley Walker that there were two rules for writing obits: "First, make sure he's dead. Second, if he's a rich drunk, call him a clubman and philanthropist."

We follow Walker's first rule by verifying deaths. The second rule may be applied to a local businessman everyone in town knows was a heavy and habitual drinker in the last years of his life and lost most of his business because of his drinking. But when the novelist Jack Kerouac died in 1970, *The New York Times* said he had "increasingly eased his loneliness in drink." And a former member of the Federal Communications Commission who died in a rooming house in Miami was described by physicians in an obituary as a "chronic alcoholic." We are also frank about the subject's legal entanglements, personal beliefs and even sexual preference.

Criminal activities from the person's past may be used. In the obituary of the FCC member, the lead described him as having been charged with plotting to fix the award of a television license. One obituary of Joseph P. Kennedy, the father of President Kennedy, reported that during the elder Kennedy's life there had been "whispers that Mr. Kennedy was anti-Semitic." Some of the obituaries of the writer W. Somerset Maugham referred to his homosexuality.

The taboos that once restricted such material are disappearing, and in time may completely vanish like the taboo against mentioning in an obituary that a person's death was a suicide. On smaller newspapers the tendency is to look at the brighter side. However, incidents well-known to the public cannot be disregarded. On the other hand, when a man or woman had led a useful life after making a mistake years past, no harm to truth is done by passing over the incident. The obituary of the former city treasurer who was sentenced to the penitentiary for graft 30 years before his death will be handled differently by different newspapers. Some will include his crime; others will not, on the ground that he paid for his mistakes and thereafter led a blameless life.

Some anecdotes and illustrations that friends may provide are hardly the stuff of which monuments to a man's memory are made. But those whose lives were marked by exceptions to the norm are best remembered for their unusual behavior. A. Kent MacDougall, in a piece on the obituary in *The Wall Street Journal*, writes that when an advertising man was dying of leukemia he told a friend to have his coffin ordered by Jessica Mitford, the author of *The American Way of Death,* a critical account of the funeral business.

"She's the only one who knows how to shop 'em," the friend recalled, and the anecdote went into the obituary, which was written by a friend of the dead man who knew that it would not offend his friends and relatives.

Please Omit Flowers

Q. When people request no flowers, what do I write?

A. Ask the caller if the family prefers that donations be made to an organization, scholarship or charity and name it. For example: The family requests that remembrances be sent to the Douglas County Heart Association.

Cause of Death

Q. Do I always use the cause of death?

A. The cause is given, unless policy is otherwise. For years, cancer—the country's second leading cause of death—was replaced in many obituaries by the euphemisms "long illness" or "lingering illness." For some reason, many people regarded cancer as a disease too horrible to name. Under the educational program of the American Cancer Society, newspapers have been encouraged to mention the disease. Cancer, cardiovascular diseases and the other leading causes of death should be mentioned whenever possible so that the public becomes aware of the major causes of death.

Sometimes, it is impossible to learn the cause. Relatives will not say, and physicians are not available or will give the answer, "heart failure." There are diseases that would embarrass relatives, such as cirrhosis of the liver, which often is the result of heavy drinking. If the person is prominent, the cause of death will sooner or later be revealed.

Ignoring the cause of death may be responsible for the public's failure to react to the major killers, such as alcoholism, which in some communities is the third or fourth leading cause of death. No one would know this from reading the obituaries, in which euphemisms for causes of death abound.

In an article in the *Nieman Reports,* "The Obituary as a Work of Art," June, 1971, Michael Gartner recalls reading a New Hampshire weekly newspaper in which the "townsfolk had an unusual characteristic; they died of but two causes: a long illness or a short illness." He asked the editor why. The editor answered that most obituaries are submitted by funeral directors who presumably used the stock phrases to spare survivors distress. He went on, according to Gartner:

> They do present difficulties at times, as for instance recently when a man who resides here was found dead in a New York hotel room having fastened a noose and hanged himself from a peg on his bedroom door. We reported him as dead of asphyxiation under circumstances being investigated, which was the literal truth, but something less than the truth.
>
> As a matter of fact this belies your allegation that we have only two types of *causa mortis.* The real fun comes when a respected citizen meets his Maker not by way of long or short illness, but because of a very short illness in the form of suicide or homicide. In such cases, small town journalistic practice demands that the cause itself be passed over in one hasty sentence. We then proceed to describe the profusion of flowers at the funeral, the high esteem in which said citizen was held by his townsmen, etc.

These practices are disappearing, along with all the other taboos and restraints that do not withstand the scrutiny and curiosity of a pragmatic and questioning generation. Cause of death should always be listed—unless policy is otherwise—certainly when the deceased is relatively young, say under 60. Readers want to know.

Q. How do I handle suicides?

Suicide

A. Follow the newspaper's policy. Most are frank. But be careful to attribute suicide as a cause of death to an authority, the medical examiner or the coroner.

Localizing Obituaries

Q. Should I try to localize obituaries whenever possible?

A. Yes, if the person is a resident of your community and died elsewhere or was a former well-known resident. For example:

> John A. Nylic, 68, a retired maintenance worker at General Electric Co., died Friday night after suffering an apparent heart attack while visiting in Lebanon Springs, N. Y.
> Mr. Nylic, who lived at 78 West Housatonic St. . . .
> —*The Berkshire Eagle*
> (Pittsfield, Mass.)

But the practice of localizing the deaths of well-known persons by putting into the lead the person's connection with the community, no matter how tenuous, is disappearing. Some newspapers localize deaths they find on their wires whenever possible. Here is such a lead:

> Former President Harry S. Truman, who stopped here on his "Give 'em Hell Harry" campaign trip in 1948, died today in Kansas City, Mo., at the age of 88.

Leads of this sort tend to trivialize the person's death.

Nowadays, such material might be put into the body of the story rather than the lead. There are, of course, legitimate local follow stories: The reaction of local residents to the death of a prominent person, memorial services, a drive to rename a local street or park after the deceased.

Humorous Obituaries

Q. Must the obituary always be solemn?

A. Most are and should be. Now and then the subject lends himself or herself to lighter treatment. When the screenwriter Al Boasberg died, his obituary reflected the man. Boasberg had written many of the gags that were used in the Marx Brothers movies. Some of his most famous sequences involved death, such as the one of Groucho Marx posing as a doctor taking a patient's pulse and intoning: "Either this man is dead or my watch has stopped."

For the lead on Boasberg's obituary, Douglas Gilbert wrote:

> The joke's on Al Boasberg. He's dead.

Some readers were shocked. Others thought it was appropriate for the subject.

On most newspapers, obituaries are handled by beginners and feature and general assignment reporters who happen to be in the office. A few newspapers have writers whose specialty is obituaries. Often, the specialist is given wide latitude.

Alden Whitman, for years the master obituary writer for *The New York Times*, was allowed to comment on the personal habits and the accomplishments of his subjects. When he wrote the obituary of Mies van der Rohe, the prophet of an austere modern architectural style, Whitman noted that the architect chose to live on the third floor of an old-fashioned apartment house on Chicago's north side.

In his obituary of André Malraux, the French writer, Whitman wrote that he was "a chain smoker of cheap cigarettes." In his lengthy obituary of the famous socialist, Norman Thomas, Whitman said Thomas's socialism "was to Marxism what Musak is to Mozart."

22 The Police Beat

Preview   Police reporters cover a vast array of news. Their beat calls upon them to handle:

- Breaking stories—Accidents, crimes, fires, arrests.
- Features—Profiles of police personnel, suspects, criminals; stories about police investigations.
- Interpretative articles—Stories explaining law enforcement policies, meaning of changes in departmental personnel and procedures.
- Investigative reporting—Examination of police activity such as false arrests, police-crime tie-ins, lax enforcement.

Few beats produce as much news as the police beat, and few reporters are called upon to do as much as quickly as the police reporter. Each day, a dozen or more potential stories develop on the beat. Here is the range of the police reporter's coverage:

Crime—Reports of crime, investigation, arrest, booking, arraignment.
Accidents—Traffic, airplane, drowning, suicide, rescue.
Fires—Reports and occasional on-the-scene coverage.
Departmental Activity—Coverage of the police department personnel, policies, efficiency and accountability.
Departmental Integrity—Standards, policies and procedures for dealing with internal and external allegations, assumptions and attitudes about corruption, systematic or sporadic.
Other Law Enforcement Agencies—Sheriff's office, state highway patrol, suburban police departments.

The complexity of the police beat is no concern to editors who assign beginning reporters to the police station in the belief there is no faster way to test a reporter's ability and to teach him or her about the city.

The new police reporter immediately becomes acquainted with the organization of the police department—from headquarters to precinct level—and sets about making contacts with key officers, particularly with commanders of the special units such as the detective bureau, patrol division, homicide squad, youth squad and internal affairs division. Survival depends on establishing a routine and developing good sources. Otherwise the police beat can become an impenetrable maze, and the reporter may be given only the information that the department deigns to hand out.

Police Department Organization

The police department is organized around the three police functions—enforcement of laws, prevention of crime, and finding and arresting criminals.

The department is headed by a chief or commissioner who is responsible to the mayor, director of public safety, or city manager. The chief or commissioner is appointed and although he makes departmental policy, broad policy decisions affecting law enforcement come from his superior and are often made in a political context.

The chief's second-in-command may be an assistant chief or inspector. Commissioners have deputy commissioners under them.

The rest of the organizational chart depends upon the size of the city. In large cities, deputy inspectors are put in charge of various divisions or bureaus—homicide, detective, robbery, juvenile, rape, arson, traffic. The larger the city, the more bureaus. As the patterns of criminal activity change, organizational changes are made. These new policies make good stories.

The next in command in large cities are captains, who are assigned to run precincts and are assisted by lieutenants. Sergeants are placed in charge of shifts or squads at the precinct house. The private in the organization is the patrolman or woman, usually called a police officer.

The beat reporter's day-to-day contacts are for the most part with sergeants and lieutenants. Police officers are traditionally suspicious of the press. An off-hand comment by a police officer that is quoted in the afternoon newspaper or evening newscast can cause trouble with superiors and make advancement difficult. Even the higher-ups can be hard to get along with, viewing the press as an impediment to their work, particularly when the reporter is working on an unsolved crime.

Reporters, trained to be suspicious of authority, are sometimes irritated by the para-military structure, secretiveness and implicit authoritarianism of the police department. Class antagonisms may also exist. Reporters are usually college trained and middle class, whereas police officers are often from working class families. This relationship has been changing as police work has become more attractive to college graduates and the police have come to realize their need for a friendly press.

Making the Rounds

In large cities, the police reporter is based at the police station. Here is how Larry Carroll, the police reporter for *The Fresno Bee,* a newspaper with a circulation of 110,000, describes his beat:

"My beat begins at 5:30 a.m. to ensure adequate time to make the first edition deadline if a story warrants all-edition coverage. I begin by checking with the city police department watch commander for a hint of what might have happened overnight. He usually has only the barest of details and a swing by the detective bureau is often essential.

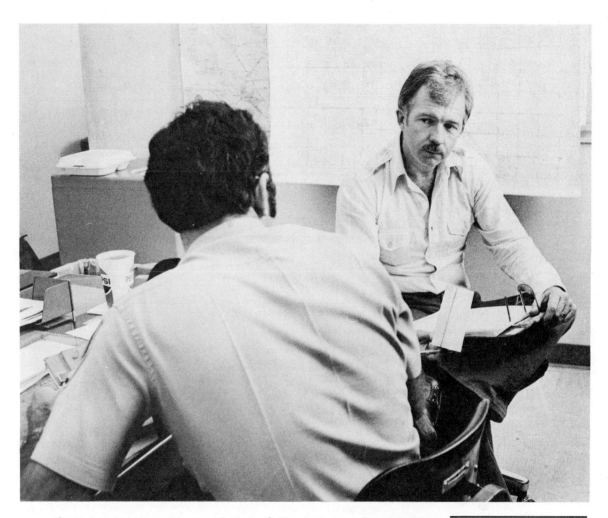

On the Job. *Fresno Bee* police reporter Larry Carroll interviews a deputy sheriff about a complaint called in by a county resident.

"Sandwiched between this are calls to the California Highway Patrol; Mid-Valley, North Central and Fresno fire departments; Clovis Police Department and any other agency necessary—for example, hospitals for condition reports on accident or crime victims.

"My next stop is the sheriff's office where once again the watch commander will give me a briefing of what transpired on the preceding shift.

"My beat becomes a series of scribbled notes consisting of quotes from the watch commander, detectives and sometimes the victims themselves."

Crime Reports

"Considerable time is spent leafing through crime reports, which sometimes number over 100 compiled through the night. However, from these reports often comes the necessary information for a good feature or human interest story."

(*Note:* In many cities, these reports are inaccessible to the press. Called "dailies" in New York and a few other cities, they are read to reporters by police officers.)

Left Form

CRIME REPORT

FRESNO COUNTY SHERIFF'S DEPARTMENT 1000

1 CASE NO. 76-0001

2 CODE SECTION	3 CRIME	4 CLASSIFICATION	5 REPORT AREA
PC 211	Armed Robbery	Convenience Market-Handgun	Beat 2

6 DATE AND TIME OCCURRED - DAY	7 DATE AND TIME REPORTED	8 LOCATION OF OCCURRENCE	
March 23 0400hrs.	March 23 0410	5555 S. Blank Ave.	

9 VICTIM'S NAME - LAST, FIRST, MIDDLE (FIRM IF BUSINESS)	10 RESIDENCE ADDRESS	11 RES. PHONE
DOE, John James	2222 S. Elm Ave.	222-2223

12 OCCUPATION	13 RACE - SEX	14 AGE	15 DOB	16 BUSINESS ADDRESS (SCHOOL IF JUVENILE)	17 BUS. PHONE
Clerk	WMA	30	3-31-46	2224 S. Elm Ave.	485-2020

CODE'S FOR BOXES 20 AND 30   V - VICTIM   W - WITNESS   P - PARENT   RP - REPORTING PARTY   DC - DISCOVERED CRIME

18. CHECK IF MORE NAMES IN CONTINUATION

19 NAME - LAST, FIRST, MIDDLE	20 CODE	21 RESIDENCE ADDRESS	22 RESIDENCE PHONE
	V		

23 OCCUPATION	24 RACE - SEX	25 AGE	26 DOB	27 BUSINESS ADDRESS (SCHOOL IF JUVENILE)	28 BUSINESS PHONE

29 NAME - LAST, FIRST, MIDDLE	30 CODE	31 RESIDENCE ADDRESS	32 RESIDENCE PHONE

33 OCCUPATION	34 RACE - SEX	35 AGE	36 DOB	37 BUSINESS ADDRESS (SCHOOL IF JUVENILE)	38 BUSINESS PHONE

MODUS OPERANDI: (SEE INSTRUCTIONS)

39 DESCRIBE CHARACTERISTICS OF PREMISES AND AREA WHERE OFFENSE OCCURRED
Convenience market in low income, high crime residential area.

40 DESCRIBE BRIEFLY HOW OFFENSE WAS COMMITTED
Suspect enters store, brandishes handgun and orders clerk to hand over money. Ties victim with rope and locks victim in storage area

41 DESCRIBE WEAPON, INSTRUMENT, EQUIPMENT, TRICK, DEVICE OR FORCE USED
Possibly .38-caliber revolver

42 MOTIVE - TYPE OF PROPERTY TAKEN OR OTHER REASON FOR OFFENSE
Robbery--currency,checks

43 ESTIMATED LOSS VALUE AND/OR EXTENT OF INJURIES - MINOR, MAJOR
$400

44 WHAT DID SUSPECT/S SAY - NOTE PECULIARITIES
''This is a holdup, don't try anything or I will shoot you.''

45 VICTIM'S ACTIVITY JUST PRIOR TO AND/OR DURING OFFENSE
Stocking shelves

46 TRADEMARK - OTHER DISTINCTIVE ACTION OF SUSPECT/S
Suspect stuttered and seemed to walk with a limp.

47 VEHICLE USED - LICENSE NO. - ID NO. - YEAR - MAKE - MODEL - COLORS (OTHER IDENTIFYING CHARACTERISTICS)

48 SUSPECT NO.1 (LAST, FIRST, MIDDLE)	49 RACE - SEX	50 AGE	51 HT.	52 WT	53 HAIR	54 EYES	55 ID NO. OR DOB	56 ARRESTED
unknown	WMA	30	5-9	155	Brn	Blu		YES☐ NO☒

57 ADDRESS, CLOTHING AND OTHER IDENTIFYING MARKS OR CHARACTERISTICS

58 SUSPECT NO.2 (LAST, FIRST, MIDDLE)	59 RACE - SEX	60 AGE	61 HT.	62 WT	63 HAIR	64 EYES	65 ID NO. OR DOB	66 ARRESTED
								YES☐ NO☐

67 ADDRESS, CLOTHING AND OTHER IDENTIFYING MARKS OR CHARACTERISTICS

68. CHECK IF MORE NAMES IN CONTINUATION

REPORTING OFFICERS	RECORDING OFFICER	TYPED BY	DATE AND TIME	ROUTED BY
Holmes				

FURTHER ACTION ☐ YES ☐ NO   COPIES TO: DETECTIVE☐ JUVENILE☐ DIST. ATTNY☐ SO/PO☐   CII☐ PATROL☐ OTHER☐

REVIEWED BY _____ DATE _____

CAL. JUS. CR #1 (REV 2-26-69) SO-6

Right Form

FRESNO COUNTY SHERIFF'S DEPARTMENT
Fresno, California

69 CASE NO.

70 CODE SECTION	71 CRIME	72 CLASSIFICATION
PC 211	Armed Robbery	Conveniece Market-Handgun

73 VICTIM'S NAME - LAST, FIRST, MIDDLE (FIRM IF BUS.)	74 ADDRESS ☐ RESIDENCE ☐ BUSINESS	75 PHONE
DOE, John James		

RO responded to 5555 S. Blank Ave. where victim, Doe, advised he had been robbed by a man who tied him up and then locked him in a storage area. Victim said he managed to crawl to door where he continued to make noises until a customer entered the store and discovered him. Victim said the suspect did not touch anything during commisssion of crime and only said the words described on face sheet. Victim feels he could identify suspect if seen again. Advised victim detectives would be contacting him for follow-up.

REPORTING OFFICERS	RECORDING OFFICER	TYPED BY	DATE AND TIME	ROUTED BY
Holmes				

FURTHER ACTION ☐ YES ☐ NO   COPIES TO: DETECTIVE☐ JUVENILE☐ DIST. ATTNY☐ SO/PO☐   CII☐ PATROL☐ OTHER☐

REVIEWED BY _____ DATE _____

CAL. JUS. CR #2   SO-7

Crime Report. This report, filled out by the responding officer, describes an armed robbery of a grocery. There were no arrests at this time.

''The police reporter looks through the crime report with emphasis on the penal code, the victim, and the suspect, if one has been arrested. The penal code is a number that refers to the specific crime that has been committed. In California, a PC 211 is armed robbery; PC 187, homicide; PC 261, rape. The body of most crime reports is usually poorly written and obtaining background from authorities may be necessary.

''All arrests are available from the crime reports. If a person is arrested several weeks after a crime, the information can be found on a follow-up crime report filed along with the daily reports. The follow-up would list the case number, victim and possibly some details on the original crime. A good crime reporter usually has a mental file of serious crimes and a case will leap up out of the thick pile of petty incidents.

''A reporter familiar with the city and its well-known residents can usually spot prominent persons by looking at the victim's name on the crime report. Another tip-off to prominence, if the name is not familiar, is the box which lists the victim's occupation or place of business. Finally, if a name tugs at the back of my mind, I usually refer to the city directory.''

"Care should be exercised in naming a suspect. Make sure the suspect has been booked on the charge and whether he is still in jail, has made bail or has been released. Many times a person is detained as a suspect and let go after perfunctory questioning.

"A person may be arrested and booked but not officially charged with a crime in a complaint. The charge is made in a criminal complaint filed by the district attorney, who has 48 hours to do this. If a criminal charge has been filed, the crime report will carry that fact. When a person is booked, you can write, 'Joseph Jones was arrested in connection with the armed robbery of. . . .' Do not write that he was charged with the crime unless the charge is filed."

"An essential part of effective crime coverage is gaining the trust of investigators and command personnel. Usually, a reporter can do this by carefully evaluating information before writing a story so as not to damage a case being investigated. Trust can also be attained by daily bull sessions with officers to try to get a feel for the stress, pressure and pace of their jobs."

"A good police reporter must know the penal code of the state, which can save a lot of time with routine reports. For example: By leafing through a standard crime report and looking at the upper left box for the penal code, a reporter can determine if he should dig deeper. Familiarity with the penal code can also help the reporter ferret out good stories from the constant chatter of the police and fire frequencies, which at times can become maddening. An alert ear will pick up a PC 211, PC 187, or a PC 261, and leave the other chatter alone.

"Throughout the morning as other deadlines approach, beat checks are made in an attempt to be as up-to-date as possible as each edition goes to press."

Despite all this, Carroll finds time to dig into stories on his beat. He respects good police work and will look into an arrest to find out how the investigating officers solved the crime.

Traditionally, police reporting concentrated on suspects and arrests—the criminal. Now, reporters take equal interest in the victim. The same emphasis has been developing in stories about accidents, which used to be stories about jarring collisions, careening vehicles and death and injury. Carroll says he tries to find out where the victims were going or where they had been when the accident occurred. A follow-up story would go into how the accident affected the lives of the families involved. For fire stories, Carroll tries to learn where those burned out will sleep and what they lost in addition to their home. Polished interviewing techniques are important to the police reporter.

Even suicides, long a taboo subject for newspapers and broadcast stations, and usually only briefly reported, are explored for human interest. (See "A 15-Year-Old's Suicide.")

By LARRY CARROLL
Bee Staff Writer

Fifteen-year-old Steven Ray Hendrix spoke often about joining his deceased father, but nobody seemed to take him seriously, nor did they interpret the telltale signs of his deep depression.

Steven, whose body was found beside his bicycle near Lake Washington in Roeding Park last week, was buried next to his father in El Paso, Tex., Wednesday.

Investigators say Steven probably died of an overdose of sleeping pills, taken because he could no longer cope with the loss of his father, who died last October of cancer at the age of 45. He came to Fresno to live with his mother after his dad died.

"Last Thursday he told me, 'Nobody knows how depressed I've been,' " said his mother, Mrs. Ruth Thompson.

She said she took home a pick-up camper she was thinking of buying, but said Steven showed no interest.

"So I returned it and when I came back, he was gone and I noticed my sleeping pills missing," she said.

Aware that Steven was deeply committed once he made up his mind, Mrs. Thompson called the sheriff's office and told about

Steven Ray Hendrix
. . . no one understood.

the sleeping pills and the possibility her son could be found in Roeding Park.

Officers told her they would check, but beyond that there was little they or she could do.

"He had no friends or any-

place to go," Mrs. Thompson said, "so I knew they would eventually find him."

The next morning, Mrs. Thompson said, there was a knock on the door. She opened it, and a coroner's deputy stood there. He gave her the bad news.

"Steven talked a lot about joining his father, but I couldn't understand him and told him not to talk that way," she said.

Stephen viewed his father as "God instead of man," Mrs. Thompson said, and could not understand how he could become weak and succumb to cancer instead of fighting off the disease.

The most painful part of the ordeal was Steven's gradual falling apart after his father died, Mrs. Thompson said.

"He was a straight A student before that, but just prior to his death his grades dropped to Bs and Cs and he no longer seemed interested," she said.

Steven talked often about studying nuclear physics at Massachusetts Institute of Technology and his tested IQ of 136 probably would have allowed him to do so, according to his mother.

After he moved to Fresno from Texas in January, Mrs. Thompson said, Steven's depression deepened and his interest in hobbies, school and God fluctuated from hot to cold.

"One day last week he looked at me and said, 'You know, Mom, we really are generations apart,' " Mrs. Thompson said. "I thought I knew what he was talking about, but I guess I didn't."

An Arrest Story The battered body of a 77-year-old man was discovered in his home at 11 p.m. by a neighbor who called the police. The neighbor said she saw two youths running from the scene. Police conducted an investigation and within five hours arrested the two, a 16-year-old and a 14-year-old. The two were charged with second degree murder and at their arraignment entered pleas of not guilty.

The reporter for the local afternoon newspaper learns all this on his 7 a.m. check. He calls the coroner to obtain information about the cause of death, and he questions the police about the murder weapon and the motivation. He also asks where the youths are being held and the precise time they were arrested. With the information on hand, he calls his desk to report what he has and the city editor tells him to give the story 200 to 250 words. The dead man was not prominent; he ran a fuel oil and coal company in a poor section of town.

The editor asks about the neighbor: Did she identify the youngsters, and if not how did they learn the identities of the youths? The reporter says the police will not comment about the neighbor. The story will have to be a straight murder-and-arrest piece. Here is how the reporter wrote it:

> Two Saratoga youths were arrested early today and charged with the murder of 77-year-old Anthony Hay, a local fuel oil and coal dealer, whose battered body was found last night in his home.
>
> Police identified the youths as Arthur Traynor, 16, of 61 Joshua Ave., and John Martinez, 14, of 15 Doten Ave. Police said a neighbor saw two youths fleeing from Hay's residence at 342 Nelson Ave. The arrests were made within five hours of the slaying.
>
> The youths entered pleas of not guilty at their arraignment this morning on charges of second degree murder and were being held in the county jail pending a preliminary hearing.
>
> Hay's body was found at 11 p.m. in the business office of his home. He was "badly beaten about the head and face and had a fractured skull," Coroner Clark Donaldson reported. Police said they recovered the death weapon, a three-foot wooden club. They declined to give any motive for the slaying.

Spot News

The police reporter spends much of his or her time thumbing through police reports and records. But now and then, the reporter speeds to the scene of a crime or some other activity involving the police. The police reports are usually fairly simple to handle. Reporting on the scene is often a challenge as it requires sorting out scores of details and putting order to the chaos of the event.

If the reporter is on deadline, one of the first tasks is to locate a telephone that probably will not be used by other reporters. Another early requirement is location—police lines are usually set up to keep any but officers from crossing. In this case, the reporter stations himself or herself near someone in authority or next to an officer handling the police communications system.

Catching the Drama. Close and direct observation of the event leads to better pictures and stories. For this picture of a suspected armed robber whose attempt to hold up a jewelry store went awry, Randy Piland of *The Macon Telegraph* edged through police lines. The man had threatened to shoot himself and held off police for 45 minutes before being talked into surrendering.

The police reporter must know the procedures involved in an arrest, and because on some smaller newspapers and on many radio and television stations the same reporter who covers an arrest might stay with the case through the trial, a knowledge of the criminal court process is necessary, too. Here, we will discuss the arrest process. In the next chapter, criminal court procedures are outlined.

A person may be arrested on sight or upon issuance of a warrant. Let us follow a case in which a merchant spots in his store a man he believes robbed him the previous week.

The store owner calls a patrolman who arrests the man. The suspect is searched on the scene and taken to a station house. The suspect is then searched again in front of the booking desk. His property is recorded and placed in a "property" envelope. The suspect's name and other identification and the alleged crime are recorded in a book known to old-time reporters as a blotter. (The blotter supposedly takes its name from the work of turn-of-the-century police sergeants who spilled considerable ink in their laborious efforts to transcribe information and then had to sop up the splotches with a blotter.)

The suspect will be told his constitutional rights, the Miranda warnings, at any one or at each of these first three steps—on the scene, in the patrol car, or at the booking desk. The police are required to tell a suspect at the time of arrest that he has the right to remain silent and to refuse to answer any questions. He also has the right to consult an attorney at any time and is told that if he cannot afford a lawyer one will be provided. Unless the suspect waives these rights, damaging statements obtained from him cannot be used against him at his trial.

The rights of those arrested grew out of a Supreme Court case involving Ernesto A. Miranda, an Arizona truck driver whose conviction for rape was reversed by the Court because Miranda's constitutional rights had been denied by the police. On arrest, police read these rights from a card, called a Miranda card. They are also often printed on arrest forms.

The arresting officer questions the suspect after reading him his rights and obtaining a signed waiver from him.

The signed waiver permits the police immediately to interrogate the suspect about his actions, background and whereabouts in connection with the crime. If he is a suspect in a homicide case, the usual practice is to call in an assistant prosecutor immediately to insure the admissibility of any admission or confession.

The officer then prepares an arrest report, which is written in the presence of the suspect who also supplies "pedigree information"—age, height, weight, date and place of birth and other details necessary for full identification. (See "Arrest Report.")

The suspect may then be photographed and fingerprinted and be allowed to make a telephone call. A record is made of the number and person called and the suspect is returned to a detention cell to await arraignment. The arresting officer goes to the complaint room to confer with the victim and an assistant district attorney so that a complaint can be drawn up. The police officer may ask the complainant to identify the suspect again in a line-up.

(Later, a defendant has the right to a so-called Wade Hearing—named after the Wade-Stovall cases before the Supreme Court. In the hearing the defendant can

Arrest Report

The form below is used by the New York City Police Department. In this arrest, the suspect, Roosevelt B. Thomson, a 19-year-old white male residing at 1870 Columbus Avenue, was arrested for assaulting a 22-year-old male, Haywood Clarke, with a knife in an empty apartment at 159 W. 105th St. The time was 3:30 a.m. The police have their own abbreviations:

n/a—not available
a/o—arresting officer
A/C—according to Complainant
T/p/o—time and place of occurrence.

Thomson is accused of stabbing Clarke in the back, face and right side. He is arrested with someone else, presumably Miguel Negron about whom we know nothing. Why Clarke was in the empty apartment and what Thomson's motive may have been are not described in the police report. The arresting officer would have to be interviewed. But it appears that Clarke did not know his assailant because his identification is based upon photos shown him by officer John Vance.

On deadline, with no interviews possible, here is how an early lead might go:

A 19-year-old unemployed plumber, described by police as an heroin addict, was accused today of the pre-dawn stabbing of a 22-year-old man apparently lured to an empty apartment on Manhattan's west side.

The victim, Haywood Clarke, stabbed in the back, face and side, was in serious condition at Logan Hospital. Police were interviewing Roosevelt B. Thomson and a companion, Miguel Negron, to try to establish a motive . . .

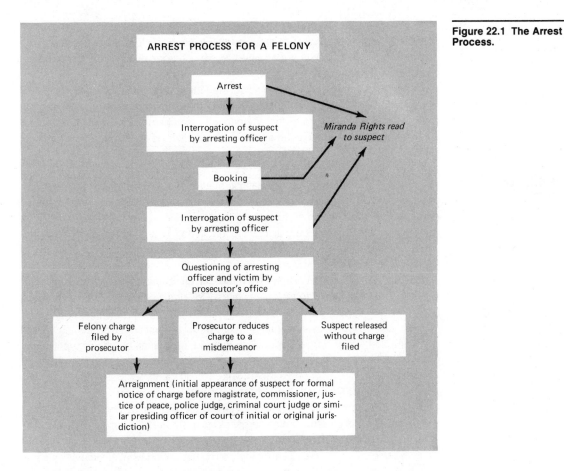

Figure 22.1 The Arrest Process.

ARREST PROCESS FOR A FELONY

Arrest

Interrogation of suspect by arresting officer

Miranda Rights read to suspect

Booking

Interrogation of suspect by arresting officer

Questioning of arresting officer and victim by prosecutor's office

Felony charge filed by prosecutor

Prosecutor reduces charge to a misdemeanor

Suspect released without charge filed

Arraignment (initial appearance of suspect for formal notice of charge before magistrate, commissioner, justice of peace, police judge, criminal court judge or similar presiding officer of court of initial or original jurisdiction)

challenge a prior, out-of-court identification of him by the victim on the ground that the line-up was unfairly composed, the procedure was suggestive, or a lawyer requested by him was not present at the line-up.)

The assistant district attorney has to decide whether the case is strong enough, the witness reliable, the offense worth prosecuting. The prosecutor must also determine whether to reduce a felony charge to a lesser felony or to a misdemeanor. He may reduce the charge if he feels the reduction would lead to a guilty plea.

The police officer may have to file additional reports. If he fired his weapon, he must file an "unusual incident report," as it is described in some jurisdictions, and if he shot someone he files an "inspector's report." Reporters should be familiar with all these records.

The fingerprints are checked in a central state agency to determine whether the suspect has a record, and the suspect's file is sent to the courts. The information is required before an arraignment can be conducted. The presiding judge uses it to determine whether bail should be set and the amount. A suspect with no record who is arrested for a minor crime may be released on his own recognizance, that is, without putting up bail.

In large cities, most of which have vast backlogs of untried cases and overcrowded detention facilities, suspects may be released on low bail or even paroled. Sometimes, these suspects are arrested on new charges even before the pending charges are disposed of.

Another procedure used to unclog the judicial system is plea bargaining, in which the defendant agrees to plead guilty to a lesser charge so the case can be disposed of then and there at the arraignment (see chapter 23). This situation has led to the description of the court system in these cities as revolving-door or turnstile justice.

Effect on Police

The winnowing process of plea bargaining may be the only way the judicial system can cope with an increasing crime load, but it can lead to a disillusioned police force. A suspect whose arrest may have involved investigative work and some risk becomes the subject of plea bargaining. Brought in on a charge of armed robbery, the suspect is out on the street the next day with a suspended sentence for petty theft. Eventually, police officers will spend less time on the crimes they know will lead to plea bargaining and light punishment. Worse, citizens sometimes engage in vigilante activities or take the law into their own hands. One of the consequences is the staggering number of handguns in the United States.

In some large cities, several types of nonviolent crimes have been, in effect, decriminalized. Minor drug violations are ignored. Few small burglaries are investigated. Car theft is infrequently investigated and rarely prosecuted in metropolitan areas. In New York City during a recent year, 105,000 automobiles were stolen. The police arrested 9,000 persons on a charge of grand larceny motor vehicle theft. Nine were sent to prison as felony offenders. In many large cities, 80 percent of all felony arrests are either dismissed or plea bargained to misdemeanors or low-level felonies. Few of those arrested serve time.

In some cities, the district attorney's office has set up what are known as early case assessment bureaus or career criminal tracking systems. These methods enable prosecutors to single out the defendants they consider the most dangerous and most likely to commit further crimes. These few cases are prosecuted fully.

In the case of the robbery suspect whose arrest we are following, the assistant district attorney would not agree to a plea bargain because, the store owner said, a gun was used and the defendant had a long criminal record.

The suspect then entered the next phase, which the police reporter may cover also, the preliminary hearing (see chapter 23 on courts).

Types of Felonies

There are seven types of felonies, which fall into two general categories, not including the so-called possessory felonies involving weapons and drugs.

Violent crime—murder, rape, robbery, aggravated assault.

Property crimes—burglary, larceny-theft, motor-vehicle theft.

The FBI keeps crime data according to these categories, as do local police departments. National figures over the years indicate that 10 percent of all felonies are violent and 90 percent are crimes against property.

Table 22.1 Crime Rate

	Metropolitan areas	Other cities	Rural
Murder	11.0	5.3	7.2
Forcible Rape	41.7	20.7	15.2
Robbery	322.5	60.5	20.9
Aggravated Assault	316.2	243.0	129.4
Burglary	1,858.4	1,208.9	786.6
Larceny-Theft	3,484.6	3,389.7	1,097.5
Motor Vehicle Theft	570.3	235.7	119.4

Rate per 100,000 inhabitants.
These figures are based on the number of reported crimes, taken from the FBI's Crime
Index of Offenses, 1981.

Crime Rate

The amount of crime is almost directly proportionate to the size of the city, FBI crime rate figures have revealed over the past several years. (See table 22.1.) In recent years, the FBI reports, serious crime is rising at a faster rate in the suburbs and rural areas than in large cities, although the crime rates are still highest in metropolitan areas. In the 58 core cities with populations of more than 250,000, the rape victim risk-rate was 81 per 100,000 females in the 1980s. In rural areas, the rate was 30.

As every reporter knows, the amount of crime has been growing. Over the past decade, violent crime increased 59 percent and property crime was up 62 percent. The population in that period increased about 5 percent. A violent crime is committed about once every 24 seconds, and a property crime once every three seconds.

Police reporters often write stories comparing the crime rates of their city and nearby suburban areas with the national data. The figures they use are taken from the annual report of the FBI, "Crime in the United States, (Year of Publication), Uniform Crime Reports," which is available from the Superintendent of Documents, U.S. Government Printing Office, Washington, D.C., 20402.

Every police reporter should have a copy. You should keep in mind, however, that the local police and the FBI record only those crimes that are reported. Because many people do not report crimes, the Census Bureau since 1973 has been asking samples of people whether they have been victims of crime.

The results of the sampling show far more crime occurs than is reported.

Newsworthy Crimes

Table 22.2 shows the 10 cities with the highest crime rates in metropolitan areas in the country. Sociologists say crime reflects social and economic conditions. The surge of crime in Florida revealed in these figures is said to have been the result of the vast amount of drugs that enter the country through the state and the social turmoil caused by the influx of large numbers of Haitians and Cubans.

The appearance of Atlantic City in two of the categories parallels the legalization of casino gambling, which is said to have attracted drifters and undesirables to this once staid resort community.

Table 22.2 The Most Dangerous Cities in the United States

Total crimes		Violent crimes		Property crimes	
Average for cities	**7,179**	**Average**	**752**	**Average**	**6,427**
1. Atlantic City	11,500	1. Miami	1,792	1. Atlantic City	10,475
2. Miami	10,820	2. New York	1,786	2. Las Vegas	9,112
3. Las Vegas	10,297	3. Los Angeles	1,301	3. Miami	9,028
4. W. Palm Beach/ Boca Raton, Fla.	9,761	4. Baltimore	1,210	4. Gainesville	8,592
5. Gainesville, Fla.	9,601	5. Las Vegas	1,185	5. W. Palm Beach/ Boca Raton	8,579
6. Sacramento	9,232	6. W. Palm Beach/ Boca Raton	1,182	6. Sacramento	8,505
7. Orlando, Fla.	9,100	7. Newark, N.J.	1,060	7. Odessa, Tex.	8,191
8. New York	9,034	8. Atlantic City	1,024	8. Tucson	8,122
9. Ft. Lauderdale/ Hollywood, Fla.	8,974	9. Gainesville	1,009	9. Orlando	8,107
10. Tucson	8,761	10. Orlando	994	10. Ft. Lauderdale/ Hollywood	8,020

These figures are based on the number of reported crimes per 100,000 inhabitants of the cities in the table. The figures are taken from the FBI's *Crime in the United States,* 1981.

Table 22.3 Murder and Non-Negligent Manslaughter

The first three cities in the homicide rate in 1982 were Odessa, Tex., 29.8; Miami, 29.7; and Houston, 28.2. Four Texas cities (Odessa, Houston, Longview-Marshall and San Antonio) were among the top 10 in homicides per 100,000 population in 1982.

Metropolitan areas		States	
Average	**11.0**	**Average**	**9.8**
Miami	34.5	Nevada	17.5
Albany, Ga.	25.9	Georgia	17.2
Savannah, Ga.	23.9	Texas	16.6
Las Vegas	23.6	Louisiana	15.6
New Orleans	23.5	Florida	15.0
Odessa, Tex.	22.5	Alaska	14.6
Pine Bluff, Ark.	21.9	California	13.0
Corpus Christi, Tex.	21.3	Mississippi	12.6
New York	20.7	New York	12.3
Los Angeles	19.6	Alabama	11.9
Bakersfield, Calif.	19.6		
Mobile, Ala.	18.8		
Jackson, Miss.	18.3		
Gary/Hammond, Ind.	17.7		
Dallas/Ft. Worth	16.4		

Rates per 100,000 inhabitants.

Table 22.4 Forcible Rape

Metropolitan areas		States	
Average	**41.7**	**Average**	**35.6**
Savannah, Ga.	94.6	Alaska	102.2
Memphis, Tenn.	84.9	Nevada	64.9
Las Vegas	78.1	California	56.2
Tacoma, Wash.	76.8	Florida	56.1
Tallahassee, Fla.	74.3	Washington	50.2
Gainesville, Fla.	73.2	Michigan	47.5
Lubbock, Tex.	73.2	New Mexico	47.3
Miami	68.4	Texas	46.2
Lawton, Okla.	68.3	Colorado	45.6
Reno	67.9	Georgia	42.4
Orlando, Fla.	66.9		
Bakersfield, Calif.	66.2		
Little Rock, Ark.	66.0		
Atlantic City	65.5		
Dallas/Ft. Worth	65.1		

Rates per 100,000 inhabitants.

Tables 22.3 and 22.4 show the 15 metropolitan areas and 10 states with the highest rates of murder and rape for 1981, according to figures compiled by the FBI, which defines a metropolitan area as "a core city or cities with a combined population of 50,000 or more inhabitants and the surrounding county or counties which share certain metropolitan characteristics."

Good local stories can be developed by comparing the FBI data in the three tables (22.2, 22.3 and 22.4) with the reporter's home area.

The consequence of this surge in crime is that definitions of newsworthy crime have changed. A robbery is no longer news in a large city, unless the victim happens to be a Justice of the Supreme Court of the United States. Even bank robberies, once good for major attention, now rate a few lines unless the amount is large or someone has been shot or killed.

Murder, once sure to rate newspaper and broadcast station coverage, is now a frequent occurrence in several metropolitan areas. Ten cities have more than one murder a day, and three metropolitan areas—Chicago, Los Angeles and New York—

have three or more murders a day. In these large cities, most homicides are disposed of in a few lines of type under a label headline:

From the Police Blotter

Lloyd Tatham, a retired policeman, was fatally shot by one of three men involved in a holdup at a tavern at 2326 Seventh Ave. Mr. Tatham, 57, lived at 1965 Lafayette Ave. in the Bronx.

A 26-year-old man was found stabbed to death, his hands tied behind his back, in his apartment at 194 Edgecombe Ave. A television set and a stereo were taken, the police said.

In most cities, police coverage concentrates on individual crimes. But there is an increasing tendency for police reporters to concentrate on patterns of crime, such as the growing amount of violence among young persons. Most violent crime is committed by those classified as post-adolescents, those from 16 to 25. A fifth of those arrested for violent crimes are under 18. Other patterns that can be examined include the sex of the suspect; the relationship of the suspect and the victim (race, family ties, age), time, date and location of crimes, percentage of those arrested who are charged with a crime, or percentage of those charged who plead guilty or are convicted.

Police Effectiveness

One measure of the effectiveness of a police force is the percentage of cases the prosecutor drops because of insufficient evidence or poor witness support. In Washington, D.C., the prosecutor drops about half of all arrests. Brian E. Forst, director of research for the Institute for Law and Social Research in Washington, says a major factor in these decisions is inadequate police work.

In Washington, a tenth of the police force accounted for half the convictions that followed arrests. "Clearly," Forst says, "some officers reveal a special skill in obtaining supportive witnesses, recovering evidence useful to the prosecutor, and in general making arrests with an eye to conviction. Most officers have no incentive for doing so, since police officers are not typically evaluated on the basis of what happens after arrest." In New York City, the police department engaged in a program to educate police officers to make quality arrests.

Reporters can learn about the situation in their communities through the Law Enforcement Assistance Administration, which has a computerized information system with data about police activities.

Another check of departmental activity can be made by examining the response to calls made to the police. A study of 2,000 calls to the St. Louis Police Department found that 25 percent of the calls were ignored. Of the 75 percent to which the police responded, arrests were made 50 percent of the time. Ten percent of those arrested went to trial, and 4 percent of those arrested were convicted.

Large-city reporters are especially interested in departmental accountability and integrity. The police have often operated in a world of their own. Increasingly, reporters have sought to penetrate this closed society to determine police effectiveness in crime prevention and control. Because of highly publicized inquiries into endemic police corruption in such cities as Albany, Boston, New York, Indianapolis and Denver, police reporters know that their editors and their readers expect them to dig into the subject.

Departmental Activity

A reporter may be required to learn a new vocabulary to understand the underworld of deals, bribes and corruption. Some police officers have an "organized pad," by which they mean a secret list of underworld figures who pay them for protection. Most often, a pad contains the names of drug dealers and suppliers, vice operators and gambling operators.

The "grass eaters" are corrupt police officers who take only small gratuities in connection with minor infractions, such as traffic violations, or who coerce small merchants into gifts and free meals. The "meat eaters" are the corrupt police who take payoffs to release suspects, or who deal in drugs or perjure themselves on the witness stand.

The Personal Equation

Studies of police activity in Boston, Chicago, and Washington, D. C., show that in 43 percent of the situations considered felonies, and in 52 percent of the incidents in which a misdemeanor charge could have been filed by the police, no arrests were made or charges filed. Clearly, the police officer applies the law as he or she sees fit. The officer has, in a sense, as much discretion in making arrests as the reporter has in selecting facts for a story.

James Q. Wilson, a political scientist and writer, says that police data reveal "that almost all disorder, tolerable or intolerable, occurs among persons who are likely to share common norms because they are acquainted or related." Police act on the basis of what they sense these norms to be, he continues. Thus, what may be an offense leading to arrest in a middle-class neighborhood will result in only a warning in a low-income neighborhood.

Albert Reiss, a sociologist and the author of *The Police and the Public,* (New Haven: Yale University Press, 1971), says the police live in a world with their own set of ethics and that some of their actions can be explained by their frustration over having their efforts undermined by politicians and judges and through plea bargaining. Most departmental rules, Reiss writes, are seen by the police officer as punitive and ultimately encourage the officer to establish elaborate procedures to circumvent them.

The Reporter

Police reporters sometimes take on the cynicism of the men and women on their beat, police and criminals. Things are seldom what they seem. The sobbing woman who claims she was badly beaten by an unknown intruder is covering for her boyfriend. The clerk who says a gunman cracked him over the head and took the insurance company payroll turns out to have taken the money himself.

A distraught mother tells police her 4-year-old daughter and 2-year-old son disappeared in a department store on Christmas Eve. Bloodhounds, a helicopter and many police, some off-duty, join in the search. A local newspaper carries a two-column picture of the children and quotes the mother's prayer that they are alive.

Watching the woman on television, a police reporter turns to a friend: "Something is phoney. That woman is carrying on too much. Most people in that situation are deadened, out of it."

Two days later, the newspaper story about the children begins:

> Two small Queens children whose mother had reported losing them in a crowded Flushing department store on Christmas Eve were found dead in a rubble-strewn lot in East Harlem last night, and the mother and a man with whom she lives were charged with the murders.

The children had been beaten to death, gasoline was poured over their bodies, and the bodies ignited. The boyfriend had complained that the children were bothering him.

Checklist: Crime—Homicide

____ Victim, identification.
____ Time, date, place of death.
____ Weapon used.
____ Official cause of death or authoritative comment.
____ Who discovered body.
____ Clues. Any identification of slayer.
____ Police comments. Motivation for crime.
____ Neighbors, friends comments.
____ Any police record for victim; any connection with criminal activity.
____ Consequences to victim's family, others.

Checklist: Arrest—Homicide

____ Name, identification of person arrested.
____ Victim's name; time, date, place of crime.
____ Exact charge.
____ Circumstances of arrest.
____ Motive.
____ Result of tip, investigation.
____ Officers involved in investigation, arrest.
____ Booking.
____ Arraignment.
____ Suspect's police record (in states where it is not illegal to publish such information).

Burglary (B) is a crime against property, usually involving a home, office, or store break-in. Robbery (R) is a crime against a person, involving the removal of the person's goods or money with force or threat of force and is categorized as a violent crime.

Checklist:
Crime—Burglary,
Robbery

____ Victim, identification.
____ Goods or money taken. Value of goods.
____ Date, time, location of crime.
____ (R) Weapon used.
____ (B) How entry made.
____ (R) Injuries, how caused.
____ Clues.
____ Unusual circumstances. (Overlooked valuables, frequency of crime in area or to victim, etc.)
____ Statements from victim, witness.

____ Name, identification of person arrested.
____ Details of crime.
____ Circumstances of arrest.

Checklist:
Arrest—Burglary,
Robbery

There are, of course, many more crimes than homicide, burglary and robbery. However, most of the other crimes are reported only if the circumstances of the offense or the arrest are unusual.

Garish details of rapes, homicides and assaults are considered unnecessary.

Cautions

Details essential to an investigation are not used, although there is no legal prohibition against using information obtained legally. Usually, police will not reveal too many details about an investigation that is underway. Nor will they usually give reporters: confessions, statements, admissions, or alibis by suspects; names of suspects or witnesses; details of sex crimes against women. (Publication of a confession or statement can jeopardize a defendant's rights.)

All names, addresses, occupations should be double-checked against the city directory, telephone book and any other available source.

Beware of sudden clean-up drives for vice, gambling. Usually, they are designed for public consumption.

When the police arrest a suspect, reporters ask for his or her arrest record or rap sheet. In many cities and states the record may be denied or only a portion of it released to the press for dissemination.

Sometimes the refusal to release the record is the result of state law. There has been a growing sensitivity among officials concerning the need to guarantee the accused a fair trial. Revelations about past crimes might compromise the defendant's rights.

Conviction data—information about a guilty plea, a conviction, or a plea of *nolo contendere*—usually can be used. But half the states make it illegal to use non-conviction data. Non-conviction material covers:

Acquittals
Dismissals
Information that a matter was not referred for prosecution or that proceeding have been indefinitely postponed
Records of arrests unaccompanied by dispositions that are more than a year old and in which no prosecution is actively pending.

Publication of arrests that did not lead to conviction could be considered an invasion of the individual's privacy. These state laws that seal arrest records take precedence over sunshine laws. In states where there are no explicit prohibitions against the use of such records, it is permissible to use them, whatever the disposition of the arrests.

Reporters can use non-conviction information that they find in public documents that are traditionally open to the press: court records of judicial proceedings, police blotters, published court opinions, wanted announcements, traffic records.

Juvenile records usually are sealed, and family court rules almost always prohibit press coverage. But there are few state laws that make it illegal to identify a juvenile as a suspect or that prohibit stories about a juvenile's conviction. Generally, the press has gone along with officials who contend that such publicity could make rehabilitation of the young offender more difficult.

When a nine-year-old boy turned himself in to the FBI as a bank robbery suspect, New York City newspapers and television stations gave the story huge play. The youngster took $118 from a teller in midtown Manhattan. The teller said the boy held what looked like a pistol.

The newspapers and stations that were unhappy about using the story said they had no recourse. It was "pointless" not to publish a picture of the youngster, said the metropolitan editor of *The New York Times*, that was already "on television all over town."

Fire Coverage

The police reporter sitting in his or her room at the police station monitors the police radio for reports of fires. If a fire is serious or involves a well-known building or downtown area, the reporter will drop what he or she is doing and take off to the scene. Importance can be determined by the number of units dispatched, usually expressed in the phrase one alarm, two alarm, etc. The larger the number, the more units sent to fight the fire. On large newspapers, general assignment reporters are assigned to fires.

When a fire broke out in a downtown tire store at noon, it was too late for the staff of *The Anniston* (Ala.) *Star* to cover it for that day's newspaper. The presses had already started to roll. Because of the intensive radio coverage of the fire, the

Entire block endangered by disabled butane truck too near flaming building

Heroes

By PAM NEWELL SOHN
Star Staff Writer

They talked like it was all in a day's work.

. . . like anyone would work on a disabled, half-filled butane truck a few feet from a building burning out of control.

. . . like the expectation the truck might explode and level the entire block was of no more consequence than answering a ringing phone.

Their apparent attitude: It had to be done. And the handful of men did it.

WHILE POLICE were evacuating about 100 spectators from the scene of a savage fire Thursday at Virgil Coker Tire Service on Noble Street, and while firemen were trying to tame the flames, four men ignored warnings and made fast, makeshift repairs on the tank truck. Then they half-drove, half-dragged it out of immediate danger.

The four men were Anniston Police Sgt. Mike Fincher, wrecker driver Kenneth Garrett and brothers Lamar Crosson and Buford Crosson, both employees of Virgil Coker Tire Service.

The Southern Butane Co. truck, carrying about 400 gallons of highly flammable gas, was parked for repairs near the rear of the building when a fire broke out there at about 11:20 a.m.

The front-end of the truck was near a telephone pole and could not be moved forward. Two rear wheels and the drive axle had been removed from the truck. The empty wheel space was on the side of the burning building. Coker employees said work on the truck had reached a standstill waiting for the delivery of a new wheel hub.

WHEN IT BECAME apparent that the fire could not be extinguished quickly, some firemen and the four men began contemplating how to move the disabled truck.

Lamar Crosson said he heard mention of pulling the truck away from the blaze just as it stood. "But the (gas) valve was right there on the bottom and it could have broke and burned," said Crosson.

Crosson said that at about that time, the new hub was delivered and he and his brother began to reassemble the wheel hub and mount the tire, working between the truck and the burning building. They were assisted by fireman Jimmy Crossley, fincher and Garrett.

The men said they had to work "on and off" because of the intense smoke from the fire. And at times, according to Garrett, flames were as close as 10 feet away. When the smoke wasn't blinding and choking them, they were being doused with water from a fire pumper truck spraying cooling water on the butane tank, they said.

FINALLY, the men were able to secure one

(See Truck, Page 12A)

reporter assigned to the story knew that her piece for the next day's newspaper would have to feature some aspect other than the basic facts. Pam Newell Sohn found a feature angle and put a delayed lead on her story:

On the jump page, Sohn wrapped up the details of the fire under this lead:

Virgil Coker Tire Service officials said today they are considering whether to rebuild a downtown Anniston warehouse blitzed by a spectacular fire Thursday.

If a fire is serious enough to merit a folo story, one of the possible themes is the progress of the investigation into the cause. Another may be the cost of replacing the destroyed structure. Here is the beginning of a folo that appeared three days after a longer piece about a horse barn fire:

> The cost to replace a privately owned horse barn next to the Fairmount Race Track near Collinsville may be as much as $200,000, authorities have been told. The barn burned Sunday night, killing 21 race horses.
>
> The horses were valued at about $80,000. Authorities believe the fire was deliberately set, but no suspects have been arrested. . . .
>
> —St. Louis Post-Dispatch

Checklist:
Fires

___ Deaths, injuries.
___ Location.
___ Cause.
___ When, where started.
___ How spread.
___ When brought under control.
___ Property loss: How much of structure damaged.
___ Estimated cost of damage.
___ Type of structure.
___ Measures taken to protect public safety.
___ If rescue involved, how carried out.
___ Who discovered fire.
___ Number fire companies, men assigned. (How much water used.)
___ Exact cause of deaths, injuries.
___ Where dead, injured taken.
___ Quotes from those routed. Effect on their lives.
___ Comments of neighbors, eyewitnesses.
___ Insurance coverage.
___ Arson suspected?
___ Any arrests.
___ Unusual aspects.

Sources

___ Fire chief, marshal, inspector.
___ Police department.
___ Hospital.
___ Morgue, mortuary.
___ Welfare agencies, rescue groups (Red Cross).
___ City building, fire inspection reports.

A New Jersey newspaper sent a young reporter to cover a fire in the business section. The fire had started in a hardware store, and the reporter asked one of the firemen about the cause. "Looks like he had naphtha in the place," the fireman replied, and the reporter wrote that. After the newspaper appeared, the store owner called the editor to complain that he never kept naphtha in the store. The point is that statements about causes should be carefully handled and that only the chief, a marshal, or the fire inspector should be quoted about the cause.

Many fires, because they last for some time, are covered first-hand, particularly by television since fires make dramatic film. The presence of television equipment brings out persons who are eager to provide colorful detail. Treat these sources with care. Look for the persons involved directly in the fire.

23 The Courts

Preview
    Coverage of the courts involves the reporter in handling:

■ Civil law—Actions initiated by an individual, usually a person suing another individual or an organization for damages.

■ Criminal law—Actions initiated by the government for violation of criminal statutes. The court reporter has to master the legal process that begins with the arraignment of the accused and concludes with dismissal, a not guilty verdict or sentencing after a conviction.

Ours is a litigious society, as law schools around the country have discovered. Their libraries have run out of shelf space trying to keep up with the opinions, orders and appeals that flow from the courts. The courts are overwhelmed. They are at the confluence of a rising tide of crime, an unceasing torrent of litigation and swelling numbers of new laws. The United States Constitution runs nine pages in the *World Almanac*. Any of several state constitutions would fill much of the thick volume.

Watching over all this, pencil poised, is the reporter. What a dramatic image. But the truth is that the courthouse reporter and his or her colleagues sent out on assignment to cover an arraignment, trial or hearing are in a constant struggle to keep from being engulfed. The only way these reporters maintain stability in this swelling tide of words—most of which are dense and arcane—is through knowledge of the judicial system, good sources and the ability to pick out the significant and interesting stories.

There are two basic judicial systems, state and federal. State systems differ in detail but are similar in essentials.

There are two kinds of law, criminal and civil. The distinction is that in criminal law the government is the accuser, and in civil law an individual or group usually initiates the action, although the government can bring an action in the civil courts. Because crime stories make dramatic reading, the criminal courts receive the most media attention. However, reporters do cover the civil courts for damage suits, restraining orders and court decisions on such issues as taxes, business operations and labor conflicts.

These criminal and civil proceedings take place in state courts with a variety of titles—district, circuit, superior, supreme. There are many lower-level courts of original jurisdiction at the city and county government levels—criminal, police, county, magistrate and the justice of the peace court. These lower courts handle misdemeanors, traffic violations and arraignments. The federal court system includes the federal district courts, the circuit courts of appeals and the Supreme Court, the highest court in the land.

The county courthouse or criminal courts reporter will handle state and local courts and the office of the district attorney. The reporter assigned to the federal courthouse will cover the federal attorney, the federal commissioner and the federal courts. A key source is the commissioner who arraigns those arrested on federal charges, sets bail and arranges trial dates.

In covering the courts, reporters must be certain to be accurate and specific. The reporter who confuses plaintiff and defendant is heading for a libel suit. The reporter who writes "federal court" instead of the specific "federal district court" may be taken off the beat for fear that that will be the first of many blunders.

There are special state and local courts, such as the domestic relations or family court, sometimes called children's court; small claims; surrogate's court (where wills are probated); and landlord-tenant court. There are others, depending upon the state. But the court reporter's major emphasis is on the civil and criminal proceedings in the state courts of superior jurisdiction—district, superior, circuit or supreme courts—and in the federal system.

Civil Law

Civil law is divided into two major divisions, actions at law and equity proceedings.

Actions at Law

These suits include recovery of property, damages for personal injury and breach of contract. They are usually filed in the county courthouse. The reporter who thumbs through the daily flow of suits singles out those in which large amounts in damages are sought and those with unusual, important or timely elements.

The following story is about a lawsuit involving unusual circumstances and a large damage claim:

OREGON CITY—A 13-year-old who broke both arms during a Little League baseball game has filed a $500,000 suit in Clackamas County Circuit Court through his guardian. It charges the Lake Oswego School District and Nordin-Schmitz, Inc., a private corporation, with negligence.

According to the suit, plaintiff Martin K. McCurdy was injured when he fell into a ditch on the boundary between the school district and Nordin-Schmitz property as he was chasing a ball during a Little League game May 16.

In a damage suit story by Ed Bean of *The Lexington Leader,* the unusual circumstances that led to the suit became the basis of a delayed lead. Here is the way the story begins:

A giant air bag was supposed to break the fall of stuntman A. J. Bakunas when he jumped from Kincaid Towers for a movie stunt in September 1978.

But the bag burst on impact and Bakunas, whose fall measured 315 feet, hit the concrete.

The 27-year-old stuntman, who had been working on the movie, *Steel,* died from his injuries the next day.

Now Bakunas' family is suing the manufacturer of the air bag in a product liability case in New Orleans.

Bakunas' five sisters and parents are asking for $1.5 million in damages—$500,000 for the one second of suffering he felt as he hit the ground and $1 million in additional damages, according to Harry Burglass, the New Orleans attorney who is representing the family.

Caution: Increasingly, lawyers are filing damage suits seeking vast sums. A $1 million lawsuit is commonplace in some jurisdictions. Most damage suits are settled for far less or tossed out of court. The careful reporter will examine the suit to see whether it has newsworthy elements in addition to the amount sought.

When a large award is made or a large settlement is reached, then the writer gives it full effort. Here is the beginning of a 17-paragraph story that moved on the AP wires in South Carolina:

```
    CHARLESTON--What probably is the "largest
wrongful death settlement" in state history
guarantees a 3-year-old Fayette County girl $5.95
million and assures her another $10.1 million if
she lives to be 79, according to a lawyer who
worked on the settlement.
    Jackie Rogers was 2 years old on May 4, 1980,
when the car in which she was riding with her
parents was involved in an accident that killed
both Charles and Barbara Rogers. . . .
```

Another AP story begins:

```
    DETROIT--A 7-year-old girl who was burned from
an overturned deep-fat fryer when she was 14
months old has been awarded a settlement of an
estimated $1.7 million, her lawyer said.
    U.S. District Judge Horace Gilmore gave his
approval Friday to the settlement between . . .
```

Notice in both these cases, settlement was reached out of court. The writers carefully point this out by using the word "settlement" in the lead, and they attribute to the lawyers information about the amounts awarded.

Equity Proceedings

The courts have the power to compel individuals and organizations to do something or to refrain from action. When such an order is requested, the complainant is said to seek equitable relief. Reporters most often come across these legal actions in the form of injunctions and restraining orders. Here is a story about a restraining order from the radio news wire of one of the press associations:

> PROVIDENCE, R.I.--A federal judge has issued a temporary order stopping efforts to put a reservist on active army duty because he refused to shave off his beard.
> District Judge Edward Day in Providence, R.I., yesterday gave the army 10 days to answer a suit filed Friday by the American Civil Liberties Union. . . .

Temporary injunctions, also known as preliminary injunctions, are issued before the case is heard on its merits in order to freeze the status quo until an emergency court hearing can be scheduled. Thus, it makes no sense to write that the petitioner has "won" an injunction in such a preliminary proceeding (which is also called an "*ex parte* proceeding") since a permanent injunction cannot be issued until an adversary hearing is held in which both sides are heard. The respondent in such an action is ordered to show cause at the hearing why the temporary injunction should not be made final or permanent.

The show cause order is signed by the judge when he or she grants the temporary injunction, and the respondent is given a week to two weeks—or a shorter time, if necessary, as in labor strike cases—to answer the show cause order. A typical show cause order reads like this:

> It is further ordered that (the respondents) appear before this court in the Bernalillo County Courthouse, Albuquerque, New Mexico, at the hour of 1:30 p.m. on the 7th day of November, 1983, and then and there show cause, if any there be, why they should not be restrained and enjoined from using the premises and buildings located at (address) for the purpose of lewdness and assignation and in such a manner to as to constitute a nuisance.

Equity proceedings can involve the request of a party to compel another party to take an action:

> The developers of a proposed shopping center and office complex at the intersection of Route 13 and West Trenton Ave. have asked Bucks County Court to order Falls Township to issue a building permit. . . .
> *—Bucks County Courier Times*

The courthouse reporter regularly checks court papers filed in the clerk's office. The material usually is privileged for use as soon as the clerk acknowledges receipt of the material by stamping it received. (By privileged, we mean that the reporter is free to use the material without fear of libel because it has been given official status.) Statements in court are privileged.

A complaint lists the cause of action, the parties to the action, and the relief sought. The defendant has several alternatives. He or she may file a motion seeking to delay, alter or halt the action. He or she can ask for a change of venue, a bill of particulars or file other motions. When the defendant is ready to contest the action, or if no motions to stop the action have been granted, he or she files an answer.

The case may then move to trial. Although the number of civil trials far exceeds the number of criminal trials, few civil trials are covered. Reporters usually rely on records and court personnel for information on civil trials. When a civil action is covered, stories are written on filing of the action and at the completion of the trial or at settlement.

Pretrial and Trial

Checklist: Civil Actions

____ Identification of person or organization filing action.
____ Background of plaintiff or petitioner.
____ Defendant; respondent.
____ Type of damage alleged.
____ Remedy sought.
____ Date of filing; court of jurisdiction.
____ Special motivation behind action, if any.
____ History of the conflict, disagreement.
____ Similar cases decided by courts.
____ Could suit lead to landmark decision? Is it a precedent?
____ Possibility of an out-of-court settlement.
____ Significance of action; effect on others.
____ Lawyers for both sides; types of firms they are associated with.
____ Date and presiding judge for trial, hearing.
____ Judge's reputation with similar cases.

This checklist is based on suggestions made by Art Carey of *The Philadelphia Inquirer* and Michael Hiltzik of the *Los Angeles Times*.

Should the reporter cover the trial, key points for reporting are: selection of the jury; relevant evidence; identification and expertise of witnesses; demeanor of witnesses on stand; judge's rulings; pertinent material from opening and closing statements of attorneys; the damages, if any are assessed; and whether the losing party intends to appeal.

Checklist: Verdict Stories

Here are the essentials of verdict stories for civil actions:

____ Verdict. Damages, if awarded. (Same, less, greater than those sought.)
____ Parties involved.
____ Judge's statement, if any. Deviations by judge from jury's findings.
____ Summary of allegations by plaintiff.
____ Key testimony and attorneys' points.
____ Length of jury deliberations.
____ Comment by jurors on deliberations, verdict.
____ Any appeals or motions.

This checklist was compiled by Jonathan Dedmon of the *Rocky Mountain News* of Denver, Colo.

Here are major sections from a story by Jonathan Dedmon in the *Rocky Mountain News* of Denver, Colo., that includes most of these essentials:

Former Jefferson County Commissioner Joe B. Lewis Friday won a $6,000 slander judgment in Golden District Court against a local businessman who called him a crook.

Lewis, 62, originally had asked for $155,000 from Joe W. Nimmo of 5500 McIntyre St., a private investor who served as his own attorney even though he had never been in a courtroom before.

He had no opening statement, no closing statement and barely cross-examined witnesses, asking at most one or two questions. His only evidence was his own brief testimony.

The suit, originally filed in August 1972, alleged Nimmo "embarked on a campaign to vilify, disgrace, degrade, shame, discredit, dishonor, humiliate and ridicule" Lewis by "unlawful, wrongful, malicious, false, deceitful, spurious and feigned utterances.". . .

Nimmo, who also collects antique horse-drawn buggies in addition to investing, said he had spoken only to Brid-well and said, "I think Joe Lewis is a crook. That's my crime."

In an hour-long display of courtroom oratory, Lewis' attorney, Frank Bruno, told the four-woman, two-man jury that Nimmo's statement was "just as venomous as the poison of a serpent. But when you're bitten by an asp, death comes soon and you don't have to face your accusers."

The jury spent 3½ hours deliberating before returning its judgment to Dist. Judge Winston Wolvington—$3,000 in actual damages and $3,000 in exemplary damages.

Bruno said that Lewis had been interested only in "vindicating his name."

Nimmo said he didn't think he had been able to get a fair trial in Jefferson County because of Lewis' popularity.

He said he didn't have an attorney because "I couldn't find one that suited me. I'm just funny I guess."

He said he planned to appeal the decision, but with an attorney.

Sources: Civil Actions

Private attorneys representing plaintiff and defendant; judges and their law clerks and clerks of the court; court stenographers; county courthouse clerk or assistant who is in charge of filing such actions. The clerk is usually the best source for tips on important cases that have been filed or are about to be filed.

Negotiations between the sides often will continue even after a trial begins, and the reporter should be aware of the possibility of a sudden settlement. In many damage suits, the plaintiff threatens to go to court to support his or her demand for a certain sum or other remedy. In turn, the defendant who is unwilling to accede appears to be unconcerned about the possibility of a court battle. In reality, neither side welcomes the time, inconvenience, tension, cost and unpredictability of a trial. The judge, too, is anxious for a settlement. The civil courts, like the criminal courts, are overwhelmed.

Attorneys for the losing side usually indicate an appeal will be filed. Do not overplay these assertions, but when an appeal is filed it can be a good story.

Criminal Law

Whether it is night court where the sweepings of the city streets are gathered, or a high-panelled district courtroom where a woman is on trial for the murder-for-hire death of her wealthy husband, the criminal courts offer endless opportunities for exciting coverage.

The assumption that underlies the criminal justice system is that an injury to the individual affects the general public. Crimes are therefore prosecuted in the name of the state as the representative of the people.

The public prosecutor is usually known as the district attorney, state's attorney, county attorney or people's attorney. In the federal system, the prosecutor is called the United States attorney.

Criminal Court Process

The criminal court system goes into operation shortly after the arrest. The system can be divided into two major divisions, pretrial and trial.

The pretrial period can be divided into four actions, which are taken in order. Usually, these are accomplished quickly, in line with the constitutional provision: "In all criminal prosecutions, the accused shall enjoy the right to a speedy and public trial. . . ." However, as the number of arrests has doubled and tripled during the past two decades in most cities, the system has stuttered in some areas and has almost halted in some others. This is the procedure for the pretrial process:

Arraignment

At his or her arraignment, the defendant is advised of the charges lodged and of his or her right to an attorney. If the defendant cannot afford a lawyer, he or she is assigned one by the court.

Arraignments are held in courts of original or least jurisdiction. These courts are empowered to try only misdemeanors and violations, such as gambling, prostitution, loitering and minor traffic offenses. In a felony case, the court will determine bail, if any. In some smaller cities, the defendant usually has no lawyer at the arraignment if the question of bail is reviewable at a higher court level. The prosecutor is present, and he or she may decide to dismiss or lower the charge. If a felony charge is lowered to a misdemeanor, with the defendant's agreement to a guilty plea, the case can be disposed of then and there.

The arraignment court, often called the criminal or city police court, acts like a fine-necked funnel, allowing only those crimes to pass through that the district attorney considers serious and that could lead to conviction. Others are reduced to violations and misdemeanors and handled forthwith. In New York, arraignment court is known as "the floor," a reference to the trading floor of the Stock Exchange, because of the rapid-fire, high-pressure plea bargaining that goes on there.

At the arraignment, the defendant may plead to the charge. If the defendant pleads guilty to a misdemeanor, the court will have jurisdiction and can sentence immediately. If the court lacks jurisdiction because the guilty plea is to a felony charge, the case is referred to another court for sentence.

If a plea of not guilty is entered, and the judge has jurisdiction, he or she can then conduct a trial or preliminary hearing. If the judge does not have jurisdiction over the offense he or she will refer the case to the appropriate court for a preliminary hearing. If the preliminary hearing is waived, the defendant is then bound over to the grand jury for action.

Here is an arraignment story:

Seven patrolmen and a civilian technician of the Police Department voluntarily appeared in City Court today and pleaded innocent when arraigned on second-degree assault charges.

All pleaded innocent and demanded an immediate hearing, finally set down for Wednesday, on the complaint by William A. Johnson Jr., 23, of 258 Loring Ave., who claimed he was beaten twice at the Genesee Station and once at Police Headquarters.

Johnson failed to appear for the arraignment, although Asst. Dist. Atty. Margaret Haggerty, who said she had anticipated the demand, had sought since last Thursday to assure his appearance and wrote him a letter. She said he telephoned today and said he couldn't appear, asking a postponement until Wednesday.

"He is not working. He could be here," attorney Adrian R. Weissfeld told Judge Honan. He asked that Judge Honan set the hearing, which is to determine if the defendants should be held for grand jury action, for 2 p.m. today and notification be sent to Johnson to appear. . . .

—*Buffalo Evening News*
(Buffalo, N.Y.)

**Checklist:
Arraignments**

____ Formal charge.

____ Plea.

____ Bail. (Higher, lower than requested?)

____ Behavior, statements of defendant.

____ Presentation, remarks of prosecutor, defense lawyer, judge.

____ Summary of crime.

Determination is made whether there are reasonable grounds, or probable cause, to believe the accused committed the offense and whether there is sufficient evidence for the case to be bound over to the grand jury for possible indictment. If the presiding judge considers the evidence insufficient, he or she can dismiss the charge. Also, bail can be increased, eliminated or reduced at the hearing.

Since the defendant is represented by an attorney, he or she has another opportunity to plea bargain. Many attorneys handling criminal cases prefer to have their clients plead guilty and receive probation or a light sentence rather than risk a trial and a lengthy sentence. Also, the bulk of crimes involve low-income defendants who are represented by public defenders, who cannot stay with a criminal case through the months and sometimes the years of the criminal court process, since they are overwhelmed by work. The prosecutor usually goes along with plea bargaining, but if the crime is serious, the defendant has a long record, or the presiding judge is convinced there is reason to believe a serious crime was committed, the case will be sent to a grand jury for action.

Here is the beginning of a story of a preliminary hearing in the federal system:

> BOSTON, Dec. 24—A Harvard Law School student, who allegedly enrolled under separate identities twice in the last seven years, was ordered yesterday bound over to a United States grand jury on charges that he had falsified a federal student loan application. . . .
>
> United States Magistrate Peter Princi found probable cause yesterday that the student falsified applications for $6,000 in federally insured loans, which helped to see him through 2½ years of law school. . . .

A jury of citizens, usually 23 (of which 16 is a quorum), decides whether the evidence is sufficient for a trial on the charges brought. If 12 jurors so decide, an indictment, known as a "true bill," is voted. If not, dismissal, known as a "no bill," is voted. Only the state's evidence is presented to the jury. Many states and the federal criminal justice system use the grand jury, but several states have a two-track felony prosecution system that permits the prosecutor either to file a felony "information" in the court without the interposition of a grand jury or to present the case to the grand jury. Following the filing of an information, the defendant is entitled to a preliminary hearing. In California, as the result of a state supreme court decision that grand juries are dominated by the prosecutor, defendants indicted by a grand jury are also entitled to a preliminary hearing. The result has been the near-abandonment of the grand jury indictment in California and the use of the information.

Preliminary Hearing

Grand Jury Action

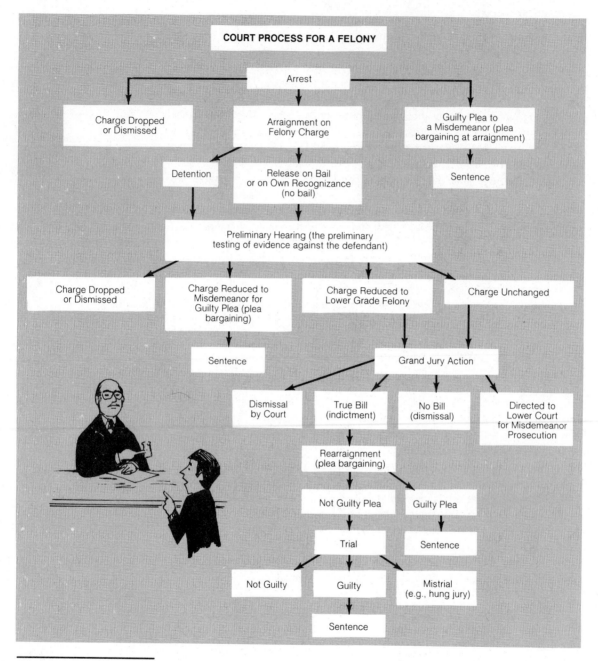

COURT PROCESS FOR A FELONY

Arrest

- Charge Dropped or Dismissed
- Arraignment on Felony Charge
- Guilty Plea to a Misdemeanor (plea bargaining at arraignment)

Arraignment on Felony Charge
- Detention
- Release on Bail or on Own Recognizance (no bail)

Guilty Plea to a Misdemeanor → Sentence

Preliminary Hearing (the preliminary testing of evidence against the defendant)
- Charge Dropped or Dismissed
- Charge Reduced to Misdemeanor for Guilty Plea (plea bargaining)
- Charge Reduced to Lower Grade Felony
- Charge Unchanged

Charge Reduced to Misdemeanor for Guilty Plea → Sentence

Grand Jury Action
- Dismissal by Court
- True Bill (indictment)
- No Bill (dismissal)
- Directed to Lower Court for Misdemeanor Prosecution

True Bill → Rearraignment (plea bargaining)
- Not Guilty Plea
- Guilty Plea

Guilty Plea → Sentence

Not Guilty Plea → Trial
- Not Guilty
- Guilty
- Mistrial (e.g., hung jury)

Guilty → Sentence

Figure 23.1

Following the grand jury indictment, the defendant is again arraigned, this time before a judge empowered to try felony cases. If he pleads not guilty, a date for trial is set.

For example:

Feb. 11 Trial Date Set In Slaying Of Coed

Superior Court Judge William T. Low yesterday set a Feb. 11 trial for Ellis Lee Handy Jr., 21, who is charged with murder in the death of San Diego State University coed Tanya Yvonne Gardini, 18.

Handy, a sailor from the helicopter carrier New Orleans, was arraigned on a grand jury indictment and pleaded innocent. He is represented by attorney Thomas Ryan.

On recommendation of Deputy Dist. Atty. Joseph Van Orshoven, Low ordered Handy held without bail. However, at Ryan's request, Low set a bail review for Dec. 30.

Miss Gardini's body was found in her dormitory suite Dec. 2 by her roommate. According to the coroner, she died from strangulation. Superficial stab wounds and bruises also were found and she had been sexually assaulted, a coroner's aide said.

—*The San Diego Union*

Plea bargaining continues at the rearraignment following grand jury indictment. Felonies, which usually are classified by degree—Class A, B, C, D and E—can be adjusted downward, a Class A felony moving down to a C or D, a Class C or D being negotiated down to a misdemeanor in the hope the defendant will plead guilty and help the state avoid the cost of further litigation. Of course, the lower the grade of the crime with which the defendant is charged, the lesser the scope of punishment available to the judge.

There are stories at each level of this procedure, although only the most serious crimes, or those involving prominent persons, will be thoroughly covered.

The key to obtaining records about a case, pending or completed, is the docket book. Under the defendant's name is the date of the arrest and the docket number of the case. With the docket number, various records may be obtained, such as: the police complaint, the affidavit filed by the complainant, the felony complaint, the disposition if a plea was made at the arraignment or preliminary hearing, the amount of bail. If there has been an indictment and a trial has been held, this may be kept in another file, again by docket number.

If every arrest were to be followed by a plea of not guilty and the accused granted the speedy trial promised by the Bill of Rights, the court system in every large city in the country would collapse. Simply put, the courts cannot handle the current rate of crime. The only way they can cope with the crush is to permit or to encourage arrangements whereby the defendant and the prosecutor agree that in return for a lowered charge the defendant will plead guilty.

Rearraignment

Court Records

Plea Bargaining

Prosecutors often will agree to reduce felony charges of assault to simple assault (a misdemeanor) if the incident involves a family quarrel or if the injury sustained by the victim was superficial or not inflicted with a weapon.

An employee charged with stealing from his boss may have his or her grand larceny charge reduced to petty larceny, a misdemeanor. Auto theft by juveniles without criminal records may be reduced to joy-riding, a misdemeanor.

The defendant goes along because in most cases he or she will be given a suspended sentence, probation or a short jail or prison sentence. The duration of the sentence is often explicitly promised by the judge as a condition to the defendant's agreement to plead guilty.

No reporter can cover the criminal justice system without understanding plea bargaining. In Milwaukee County, Wis., the district attorney estimated that 70 to 75 percent of the cases handled by his office involved plea bargaining.

The figures are even more startling for cities with high crime rates. In Manhattan, about 15 percent of those indicted and 3 percent of those charged with a felony go to trial.

Even serious crimes such as murder and rape are the subject of plea bargaining. In New York City, 80 percent of all murder arrests were plea bargained, and in Philadelphia the figure was 60 percent. Newspapers in both cities revealed many cases involving brutal slayings that were reduced to manslaughter, and in return for guilty pleas the killers were given three-, four-, and five-year prison terms. Prosecutors defend the practice by saying that plea bargaining is necessary to cut down on the backlog of cases in the courts. In Philadelphia, the backlog was cut from 20,000 to 13,000 through plea bargaining.

Plea bargaining also holds another inducement to prosecutors—bringing in a guilty plea and eliminating the risk of losing the case.

Plea bargaining is pervasive. It was used by Vice President Agnew, who was allowed to plead "no contest" to a single felony indictment, although federal officials released documents that showed kickbacks were made to Agnew.

Some critics of the judicial system say it has become administrative rather than adjudicative. In their defense, prosecutors say they are willing to plea bargain most cases so they have time for cases involving hard-core criminals. In several cities, the district attorneys have set up what they call career criminal tracking systems or early case assessment bureaus. When a felony arrest is made, the prosecutor decides whether to press for the maximum penalty on the basis of the findings of the system or bureau. If the defendant is a repeater, the prosecutor will not agree to plea bargain.

Pretrial Motions

After the defendant has been formally accused, several kinds of motions can be filed:

> *Motion to quash the indictment:* The defendant can challenge the legality of the indictment. If the motion to dismiss is granted, the indictment is quashed. The prosecutor can appeal the quashing. He can also draw up another

indictment if the grand jury again hands up a true bill, even if the first has been quashed because the constitutional protection against double jeopardy does not apply here.

Motion for a bill of particulars: When the defense attorney wants more details about the allegations against the accused, such a motion is filed.

Motion to suppress the evidence: Evidence shown to be seized or obtained illegally may not be used in the trial if the court grants such a motion.

Motion for a change of venue: A defendant who believes he or she cannot receive a fair trial in the city or judicial area where the crime took place may ask that it be transferred elsewhere. Such motions are also filed to avoid trials before a particular judge.

The Supreme Court has ruled that judges may close pretrial hearings if the material at the hearing could jeopardize the defendant's right to a fair trial.

Jury Selection

When a case emerges from the pretrial process on a not guilty plea and has been set for trial, a jury is usually empanelled. In some cases, a jury trial may be waived and the judge hears the evidence. Jurors are drawn from a wheel or jury box in which the names of all jurors on a jury list are placed. The list is made up of men and women drawn from the voting lists in the judicial area. Twelve jurors and several alternates are selected in a procedure during which the defense attorney and prosecutor are permitted to challenge the seating of jurors. There are two types of challenges: Peremptory, when no reason need be given for wanting a person off the jury; for cause, when a specific disqualification must be demonstrated. The number of peremptory challenges allotted each side is usually set by statute. A judge can set any number of challenges for cause, at his discretion.

"Most trials are won or lost in jury selection," says Larry Scalise, a trial lawyer who served as attorney general of Iowa. The attentive reporter can spot the strategy of the prosecution and the defense during the questioning of potential jurors. Jury selection is so important, it spawned an industry—jury consultancy. Behavioral consultants advise attorneys how to select sympathetic jurors and how to use psychological techniques to persuade juries.

During the selection of a jury for one of the Watergate defendants, defense lawyers asked potential jurors about their favorite movie actors and their religious preferences. Those who said they liked John Wayne and attended mass regularly were sought as jurors by the defense, which obviously wanted a God-fearing conservative jury that would be inclined to believe officials.

The Trial

A reporter cannot attend all the trials conducted in the courthouse he or she covers. Most trials are covered through interviews with the various persons involved in the trial. A reporter may sit through opening and closing statements and key testimony, but only the most celebrated cases are covered from opening statement to verdict and sentence.

Because the reporter is dependent on sources who often have a stake in the trial, court transcripts are often used if they can be obtained in time for publication. A friendly court stenographer can quickly run off key testimony in an emergency.

The trial procedure follows this pattern:

1. Opening statements by prosecuting attorney and the defense attorney on the case indicate the theory of the state's case, the defense or alibi of the defendant and give a general preview of the evidence. The statements acquaint the jurors with the case.
2. The prosecution presents its case through testimony of witnesses and evidence. At the end of the presentation, a judge can "direct a verdict" of acquittal if he or she finds that the state has not established what is called a *prima facie* case. This situation occurs when the state fails to present sufficient proof of each element of the crime that is charged. The questioning by the prosecutor of his or her witness is called direct examination.
3. The defense attorney may cross-examine the state's witnesses.

For example:

> The prime witness in the case against suspended Treasurer Bruce Knapp testified last night that in a routine audit he discovered Oakland had failed to pay the federal government taxes withheld from the paychecks of municipal employes.
>
> Joseph W. Davis, the borough auditor, itemized his findings as he was led by Borough Atty. William DeLorenzo through most of the 17 counts of financial irregularity charged against Knapp.
>
> Defense attorney Richard DeKorte later hammered away at Davis's testimony, chiefly by challenging his expertise in tax and accounting procedures. . . .
>
> —*The Record*
> (Hackensack, N.J.)

Direct examination

Cross-examination

4. Redirect examination is permitted the prosecutor should he want to re-establish the credibility of evidence or testimony that the defense's cross-examination has threatened.

5. The defense may make a motion for a directed verdict of acquittal or of dismissal based on its contention the state did not prove its case.
For example:

An Evergreen man charged with murdering his wife and setting her and his house on fire to disguise the crime was acquitted Tuesday in Golden District Court.

Jerome Joseph Downer, 38, was found innocent of second degree murder and first degree arson by Dist. Judge George C. Priest.

The decision came after the prosecution had rested its case in the week old trial and defense attorney Jay Gueck moved for acquittal by the judge.

In not allowing a jury verdict, Priest said Dist. Atty. Nolan Brown "didn't have much of a case."

He said the evidence presented "wasn't of sufficient quality and quantity to persuade a reasonable man the defendant is guilty beyond a reasonable doubt."

–Rocky Mountain News
(Denver, Colo.)

6. The defense may call witnesses to rebut the state's case. The defendant may or may not be called, depending on the defense attorney's strategy. The prosecutor is not permitted to comment on the defendant's failure to take the stand.
7. The prosecutor may cross-examine the defense witnesses.
8. Should the state seem to weaken the defense's case through its cross-examination, the defense may engage in redirect examination of its witnesses.
9. Rebuttals are offered on both sides. Witnesses may be recalled. New rebuttal witnesses may be called, but new witnesses ordinarily cannot be presented without the judge's permission after a side has rested its case.
10. Closing arguments are offered by the defense and the state in which the case is summarized for the jurors. These presentations, known as summations, provide reporters with considerable news. Attorneys often make dramatic summations before the jury.
11. The judge charges or instructs the jury before it retires for its deliberations. The judge may review the evidence, explain the law that should be applied to the facts of the case and explain the possible verdicts that can be reached. The jury must accept the judge's explanation of the law but is the sole judge of the facts in the case.
12. Jury deliberations may be short or extended. In important trials, the reporter may want to stay with the jury until deadline, because verdicts make headlines. A jury may ask for further instructions on the law, or it may wish to have certain material from the trial for review. Stories can be written speculating on the meaning of lengthy deliberations or the questions the jury asks the judge.

Note: At any time during the trial the defense may move for a mistrial, usually on the basis that some irregularity has made a fair verdict by the jury impossible. If the judge grants the motion, the jury is discharged and the trial is stopped. Since double jeopardy does not apply in such situations, the defendant can be tried again.

13. The verdict in criminal trials must be unanimous. After being discharged, jurors may report their discussions in the jury room to the press unless the judge gags the jurors. (In most states, the judge does not have the power to gag jurors, and the first amendment would seem to forbid its use anywhere.) A jury may return a verdict of guilty or not guilty. If the jury reports it is hopelessly deadlocked, the judge declares a mistrial because of the so-called hung jury. After a verdict of guilty, the defense may file to set aside the verdict, or it may make a motion for a new trial, which usually is denied but can be appealed.

   For example:

A Superior Court jury Friday acquitted Cheshire building contractor Guy E. Michaud, on trial for threatening two people with a pistol in an early-morning incident on a Lanesboro back road in January.

The jury deliberated less than two hours before returning at 12:10 p.m. with not-guilty verdicts on the two counts of assault with a dangerous weapon.

Michaud, 31, who lives in the Pine Valley Trailer Park, had been arrested Jan. 17 for the assault on Richard J. DeGroat and a passenger in his auto, Patricia A. MacHaffie, both of Pittsfield. . . .

—*The Berkshire Eagle*
(Pittsfield, Mass.)

Sentencing

14. The sentence may be pronounced immediately after the verdict or several days later, pending a probation report. The state laws usually set ranges—minimum and maximum sentences—that may be imposed. Convictions on more than one count can lead to concurrent or consecutive sentences. A judge may also issue a suspended sentence, place the defendant on probation, or levy a fine. Sometimes, the judge will comment at the sentencing, and this could be an important part of the story.

   For example:

The organizer of a forgery ring which cashed more than $16,000 in phony State of Colorado checks, is going to prison despite the pleas of several prominent Denver residents.

Judge Robert Fullerton of Denver District Court Thursday afternoon refused to grant probation to Ralph Brown George and indicated the court wasn't overly impressed by the testimony and letters of George's friends.

The friends, who urged that George be given another chance and placed on probation, included State Sen. George Brown, the Democratic candidate for lieutenant governor, and Elvin Caldwell, a Denver city councilman.

"Other people who come before me don't have the acquaintances you have," Fullerton said before ordering George to serve an indeterminate term, not to exceed 10 years, in the Colorado State Penitentiary in Canon City.

"For this reason, I can't give a great deal of weight to their comments.

". . . there also is the implication that people who have friends such as these will get better treatment. I don't want that implication left in this case." . . .

—*The Denver Post*

In a story about a sentencing that followed plea bargaining, John Katzenbach of *The Miami Herald* began with the sentence, gave the circumstances of the crime, and described the defendant as he heard his sentence of life in prison:

Emilio Cabrera, the accused killer of three—a suspected drug dealer, a man whose body he sawed into eight pieces, and his own son—pleaded no contest to murder charges Tuesday and was sentenced to life in prison.

Cabrera peered out from behind thick black-rimmed eyeglasses as Dade Circuit Judge Bruce Levy sentenced him to three concurrent life terms. The 47-year-old former owner-operator of La Union Cafeteria will serve a mandatory 25 years, according to the plea negotiated by Assistant State Attorneys Jeff Swartz and David Waksman and defense attorney John Thornton.

Cabrera showed little emotion. As part of the plea, the state reduced the charges from first-degree murder to second-degree murder in two cases: the deaths of alleged drug dealer Andres Doreuit, 48, last Feb. 14, and of his own son, Emilio Cabrera Jr., 24, a month later.

Cabrera then pleaded guilty to first-degree murder in the March 1981 death of Cecilio Hernandez, whose chopped and burned body was dumped into Biscayne Bay.

Later in the story, Katzenbach tells the reader why the prosecutors decided to plea bargain this heinous crime rather than try for conviction of first degree murder, which in Florida carries the death sentence.

The case, he writes "hinged on the testimony of the murdered son's common-law wife. . . . But the woman's testimony might have been excluded as hearsay by the trial judge. . . ."

He quotes one of the prosecutors as saying that they "ran the risk of not getting" their major witness to the stand and that might have resulted in "a directed verdict of acquittal." Katzenbach concludes his story:

Prosecutors said they offered Cabrera the plea out of fear they might lose the entire case. They said evidence on the murder of the son was weak, since his wounds were "contact" wounds, which could have been interpreted as suicide.

"With everything considered the jury could have found him not guilty," Swartz said. If convicted, however, Cabrera could have been sentenced to death.

In reporting a sentence, indicate along with the minimum and maximum terms when the defendant will be eligible for parole. In some states, in trials involving the possibility of a death sentence, the jury decides the sentence following conviction, or a new jury is empanelled to decide.

Many states are following the lead of California, Illinois, Indiana and Maine in turning away from the indefinite sentence to the definite or determinate sentence. Under the new system, sentences are fixed by law with no judicial latitude possible and no parole.

A follow-up to a sentencing can make a good story. Often, the victim of the crime is asked whether he or she thinks the sentence matches the severity of the crime. Here is a story from *The Miami Herald:*

Officer Decries Sentence for Man Who Shot Him
By John Katzenbach

His voice is thick; one bullet split his tongue. His right thumb, fractured by another slug, won't bend. His spleen is gone, surgically removed, along with 20 inches of intestines. He spends much of his time visiting doctors as he re-orders his life.

Metro Officer Richard Wentlandt's freedom has been curtailed, as much by the memory of his shooting as by his wounds.

Tuesday, Wentlandt watched the man who shot him lose his freedom.

Bernard Pratt, a 23-year-old Miami man, pleaded guilty to the attempted first-degree murder of Wentlandt and the kidnap-rape of a young woman. Pratt, who had been scheduled for trial when he entered the plea, was sentenced by Dade Circuit Judge Fredricka Smith to 90 years in prison. He must serve at least nine years before he can be considered for parole.

Wentlandt gripped his wife Wendy's hand tightly as Pratt stood before the judge.

The policeman was asked by the judge if he had anything to say. "I wish he would be in jail for a while," Wentlandt said.

He told the judge that after the May 29 shooting he spent eight days in Parkway Hospital. His life probably was saved by a bullet-proof vest he wore when he came upon Pratt and the woman victim in a car parked in a deserted area adjacent to Florida Memorial College.

When he ordered the pair from the rear seat of the car, Pratt came out shooting a .357 Magnum revolver, hitting Wentlandt in the jaw, back and hand.

Judge Smith also asked the rape victim if she had anything to say. Trembling with emotion, the young woman said: "He raped me. It affected my life. He should be locked up because he might do it to somebody else. I have a little daughter. He might do it to her."

The victim paused, then added in a barely audible voice, "He took away my pride."

Pratt, sitting next to defense attorney Jesse McCrary, didn't react. He seemed reluctant to make the plea—a plea that was offered by Judge Smith, not by prosecutors Rabin and Pat Ewing.

Pratt, a thin, wiry man with a scant black moustache and wispy beard, huddled with a half-dozen family members discussing the offer. At one moment he could be heard saying, "I don't want to do any time!"

But he faced a possible life term on each count, if convicted. When he finally agreed to the deal, he replied to Judge Smith's questions in a soft, monotonal voice.

Outside the courtroom, Wentlandt said that he wants to remain a police officer, but that he couldn't take working the streets again. He hopes to go into administration or teaching, he said. Considered disabled by the force, he said that more than five months after the shooting, he continues to see doctors.

"Maybe now we can get on about our lives," his wife said.

Asked about Pratt's sentence, Wentlandt said, "I feel it should be more time, but I know the way the system works. It should be a lot more time, but it can't be.

"Our system stinks."

A checklist for coverage of pre-trial and trial stories would run on and on. Jonathan Dedmon of the *Rocky Mountain News* suggests that a story written at any one of the 14 points in the process include: the charge, full identification of the defendant, the circumstances surrounding the charge, summary of the preceding developments.

In covering trials, Dedmon tries to find material that gives the trial individuality. It may be the personality of the defense attorney, the record of the prosecutor or unusual testimony. Drama is enhanced by describing the setting, the reactions of spectators and the behavior of the defendant and jurors. Stories about the examinations and cross-examinations can be written using the question-and-answer technique.

The reporter must evaluate testimony and from time to time give the public a sense of the trial's momentum. Good reporters understand the necessity of finding patterns of strategy and tactics during a trial. Every prosecutor has a plan, and every defense attorney keys his presentation to a theme. Each witness, every bit of evidence is presented with a purpose. It is the reporter's job to discover the design of each side in this adversary proceeding. This task can be accomplished by interviewing the attorneys on the case and through perceptive observation.

Strategy and tactics shift with the evidence, requiring the reporter to be alert during each day's testimony. The reporter should always ask himself or herself: What is the purpose of this line of questioning, this witness, this piece of evidence?

This kind of coverage gives the reader, listener, or viewer a sense of the movement and direction of the trial. All other coverage is episodic.

Private attorneys; prosecutor's office, which includes assistant prosecutors, investigators and bureau heads; legal aid attorneys; law clerks of the judges; clerks of the court; court stenographers; bailiffs and security guards; police officers; probation department; state parole office, and trial judges, many of whom, despite their image as wise and silent elders, like to chat with reporters. Clerks also can tip reporters to important motions, hearings and trial dates.

Sources

Stories About the System

Courthouse reporters are increasingly being asked to take an overview of their beats. Editors want stories about: trends in the handling of criminal cases, how Supreme Court decisions affect the local judicial system, plea bargaining, new investigative techniques by the prosecutor's office. Some editors want their reporters to do accountability pieces: Does the system work; are some judges giving unusually light sentences to mobsters or drug pushers; are white collar criminals being treated leniently? These stories call for the beat reporter's expertise and the investigative reporter's ability to probe and pry and to document tips and rumors, which permeate every courthouse in the nation.

Much of the public awareness of developments such as plea bargaining came from reporters who were sensitive to the underlying currents in the judicial system. Like any other beat reporter, the court reporter takes time each day to chat with sources, which range from the courthouse buffs—persons who hang around the courthouse and sit in on trials—to judges, defense attorneys and prosecutors.

Douglas Watson of *The Washington Post* became aware that during the five years of Gov. Marvin Mandel's administration he had appointed 12 of the 17 appellate judges serving on the two highest courts in Maryland. Most were Democrats, and many were liberal. Watson's idea was for a piece on a change in the personnel and the philosophy of the appellate courts.

After discussing the story with his editor, Watson decided on a lead and story that embraced both points. His story begins:

Maryland's appellate courts have been undergoing great changes in their complement of judges, legal responsibilities and judicial outlook.

Gov. Marvin Mandel has appointed 12 of the state's 17 appellate judges—five of the seven members of the Court of Appeals, the state's highest court, and seven of the 10 members of the Court of Special Appeals, its eight-year intermediary court. . . .

Random interviews with prominent lawyers in eight counties around the state reflect a belief among them that the judges appointed by Mandel have begun to gradually swing the generally conservative Court of Appeals toward a more moderate to liberal philosophy.

The Courts and Politics

Whether elected or appointed, the judiciary has a deep involvement in politics. Mayors, governors and the president reward friends and campaign supporters, despite their campaign promises of appointments to the bench "strictly on the basis of merit without any consideration of political aspect or influence," as Jimmy Carter put it during his campaign for the presidency in 1976.

But even before he was elected, according to *The Nation* magazine, Carter made a deal with Senator James Eastland, chairman of the Senate Judiciary Committee. "The administration would agree not to challenge senatorial patronage prerogatives for selection of district court judges and U.S. attorneys in exchange for the establishment of presidentially appointed panels to select circuit court judges," *The Nation* said.

This kind of trade-off is natural to the political system. The good reporter keeps his or her eyes on political reality. In many areas, the path to the bench begins with a political apprenticeship, either in a campaign or in a party post. Or it may be paved with contributions to a campaign. A vacancy on the Sixth Circuit, which includes Kentucky, Ohio, Michigan and Tennessee, was considered a Tennessee seat and priority was given to Sen. James Sasser of that state. He favored Gilbert Merritt, a contributor to Sasser's campaigns. (Three contributions of $1,000 each were made to Sasser's 1976 campaign by three of Merritt's children, the oldest 12 years of age.) Merritt was given the appointment as a federal judge.

When President John Kennedy wanted congressional action on some key legislation he found it bogged down in the senate, blocked by Sen. Robert Kerr. A Kennedy aide called Kerr and asked why, and Kerr answered, "Tell him to get his dumb (expletive) brother to quit opposing my friend Ross Bohannon for a federal judgeship in Oklahoma." (Kennedy's brother, Robert, was attorney general.) Kennedy thereupon called up his brother, Bohannon was confirmed as a federal judge and Kennedy soon had senate action on his bill.

The same politicking occurs in states and communities. Judgeships, with their long terms and prestige, are sought by lawyers tired of their practices, or by lawyers who seek to cap their practices with public service. Many political hacks have been elevated to the bench, but fine judges have come out of the political system also. Some of the great justices on the Supreme Court of the United States owed their appointments to political considerations. The reporter who examines the system of election and appointment to the bench whereby the insiders are favored must be careful not to predict performance.

The grand jury may initiate investigations as well as act on charges brought by a prosecutor. It can look into the administration of public institutions, the misconduct of local and state officials or initiate investigations into crimes of various kinds. In some states, grand juries must be empanelled to make periodic examinations of specific state institutions and official bodies.

The Grand Jury

Special grand juries can be appointed to look into certain matters, such as mistreatment of patients in a state hospital or a tie-in between the police vice squad and the Mafia. The district attorney or the attorney general's office directs the inquiry, although the governor in many states may appoint a special prosecutor to direct an investigation.

When a grand jury initiates action on its own and hands up a report on offenses, the report is known as a presentment. A presentment may be a statement of the jury's findings or it can charge a person with a crime.

Grand jury deliberations are secret and any publication of the deliberations is treated severely by the courts. However, reporters are free to write about the area of investigation, and witnesses can talk to the press about their testimony.

Reporters often will try to learn who is going into the grand jury by stationing themselves near the jury room. Knowing the identity of witnesses, reporters are free to speculate. But considerable controversy centers on the morality of publishing the names of witnesses or subjects of investigation, since the grand jury may question witnesses not directly involved in wrongdoing, and even those under suspicion are not to be considered guilty. One way reporters have learned about witnesses is by watching for any motions to dismiss subpoenas issued to require an appearance before the grand jury. Such motions are usually part of the public record and thereby provide the reporter with an official and revealing document that can be reported.

In covering grand jury matters, as any pretrial proceeding, the danger is that publicity may harm innocent persons or impair a defendant's right to a fair trial. Pretrial publicity has been held by the courts to be injurious, and several verdicts have been reversed because of newspaper and broadcast coverage. The reporter must balance the right of the individual with the right of the public to know what its official bodies are doing. Once the grand jury takes formal action, the report can be publicized.

Trouble Areas

Some reporters knowingly violate or skirt the laws in obtaining information about grand jury investigations and police inquiries. They act in the belief there will be no prosecution of their deeds. Sometimes they are mistaken, as the managing editor, city editor, and two reporters for *The Fresno Bee* learned after their newspaper published material from a sealed grand jury transcript. They refused to reveal their source and were charged with 73 contempt of court citations.

After serving two weeks on a prison farm, the journalists were released by a judge who said it was pointless to hold them longer as they steadfastly refused to identify their source.

Most often, the violations stem from ignorance of the law. Since the law in these areas is state law, the reporter should check the laws of his or her state, particularly when assigned to the police or court beats. Here are some actions reporters can take that violate the laws of many states:

- Publish confidential grand jury information leaked by someone in the prosecutor's office. (It is legal to use information provided by a witness as to what he has told the grand jury.)
- Use documents or property stolen from the police or an individual.
- Use confidential records transmitted or sold by the police.

In these instances, the reporter becomes an accomplice to a criminal act and can be prosecuted.

Court Terms

The judicial system has a language of its own that lawyers, judges and clerks use with exactitude. The beginning reporter should learn the appropriate terms and add to them through reading and experience.

Officers of the Court

attorneys Prosecutors and defense attorneys whose duties are to represent their clients; the attorney's role is partisan; he is an advocate; it is not unusual, therefore, for him to sell his case to the press and the press should be skeptical of statements outside the courtroom.

bailiff Keeps order in courtroom; takes charge of the jury; sees to it no one talks to jury.

court clerk Calls the court to order before each stage of the proceedings and administers the oath to witnesses; clerk's office contains records of all judicial proceedings. (This office is an excellent source of news.)

court reporter Records the courtroom proceedings; unless records are sealed, transcripts can be purchased but price varies from court to court and state to state.

judge Presides over trial, rules on points of law dealing with trial procedure, evidence and law; the jury determines the facts.

acquit A verdict of not guilty. The legal and formal certification of innocence of a person charged with a crime.

adjudicate To make a final determination through legal action.

adversary proceeding An action that is contested by opposing parties.

alibi Used in criminal law; to be elsewhere, in another place.

allegation The assertion, declaration or statement of a party to an action; an assertion of what is expected to be proved.

arraign In criminal practice, the formal calling of a prisoner to the bar of the court to answer charges in the indictment or to give information as to whether he is guilty or not guilty. Suspect is acquainted with charge against him following arrest; bail set at arraignment.

arrest The deprivation of a person's liberty by authority of the law.

autopsy The inspection and dissection of a body to learn the cause of death.

bail The security given for the release of a prisoner. Cash or a bond is placed in the court to guarantee that the person held in legal custody will appear at the time and the place the court sets. Defendants are usually entitled to be set at liberty on bail unless charged with an offense punishable by death, and even sometimes in these instances. The judge or magistrate sets bail. The Constitution prohibits excessive bail.

beneficiary One for whose benefit a trust is created.

booking The process whereby a suspect's name, address and purported crime are entered into a book in the police precinct or police headquarters.

bribery The receiving, offering or soliciting by or to any person whose profession or business involves the administration of public justice or has other official status in order to influence his or her behavior. Giving or taking a reward in connection with voting also constitutes bribery.

brief A written document prepared by counsel to serve as the basis for argument. It embodies the points of law that the counsel desires to establish.

burglary Breaking and entering the house of another with intention of committing a felony, whether the felony is committed or not. Burglary does not involve a crime against a person.

chambers The private room or office of a judge.

charge In criminal law, an accusation.

code A collection, compendium or revision of laws.

complainant A person who brings a criminal or civil action.

concurrent In a prison sentence, terms that are to be served together (not in succession). In judges' action or opinion, an agreement.

conspiracy In criminal law, the agreement between two or more persons for the purpose of committing some unlawful act.

contempt A willful disregard of public authority.

contract A promissory agreement between two or more persons that creates, modifies or destroys a legal relation.

cross-examination The practice whereby an opposing lawyer questions a witness at a hearing or trial.

de facto In fact or actually. Usually refers to a situation or an action that has the appearance of legality and is generally accepted as such but is actually illegal.

de jure Rightful, legitimate, legal.

defendant A person in a criminal or civil action who defends or denies the allegations.

dissent The explicit disagreement of one or more judges with the decision passed by the majority in a case before them.

eminent domain The power to take private property for public use by paying for it.

evidence Presented at trial through witnesses, records, documents, concrete objects for the purpose of inducing belief in the minds of the trial judge or jury.

exculpatory Clearing or tending to clear from alleged guilt.

extradition When one state (or nation) surrenders to another state an individual accused or convicted of a crime outside its territory.

felony A crime of a graver or more atrocious nature than one designated as a misdemeanor.

grand jury A jury of inquiry whose duty is to receive complaints and accusations in criminal cases, to hear the evidence presented by the state and to find bills of indictment when the jury is satisfied a trial ought to be held.

homicide The killing of any human being.

indictment An accusation handed up to the court by a grand jury.
indigent A poor person. In court, an indigent is usually defended by legal aid or an attorney in the public defender's office.
information A formal accusation of a crime by the appropriate public official such as the prosecuting attorney. In some states, accused persons may be brought to trial by an information—a sworn, written accusation that leads to an indictment without a grand jury investigation.

jury The court-approved individuals—twelve for criminal cases and six or eight for civil cases depending on the attorneys' stipulations—who decide the guilt or innocence of defendant(s) in a trial; their verdict in a criminal case must be unanimous. (Referred to as petit juries in criminal and civil cases.)

manslaughter The unlawful killing without malice of another human being.
misdemeanor Offenses lower than felonies and generally punishable by fine or imprisonment in other than a penitentiary.

nolo contendere "I will not contest it." The defendant does not contest the facts. The plea has the same legal effect as a plea of guilty, but it cannot be used as an admission of guilt elsewhere, as in a civil suit.

parole The conditional release of a prisoner from confinement. The condition usually is that if the prisoner meets the terms of the parole he or she will be given an absolute discharge from the remainder of the sentence. If not, the prisoner is returned to serve the unexpired term.
plea A response to the court made by the defendant himself or herself or his or her representative either answering the charges or showing why he or she should not be required to answer.

plea bargaining The arrangement between prosecutor and defendant whereby the state offers to reduce the charges against the defendant in return for a guilty plea.
preliminary hearing Follows arraignment; at a preliminary hearing, evidence is heard to determine if a crime has been committed. The judge may, at this point, dismiss the case if he feels the evidence against the suspect is insufficient or was illegally obtained. If he believes the evidence is sufficient, he will bind the case over to the grand jury for possible indictment. If an indictment ensues, the case is transferred to a higher court.
presentment The written action by a grand jury without an indictment; a presentment usually seeks to change the nature or operation of a particular institution, which, for one reason or another, permitted offenses against the public to take place.
probation Allowing a person convicted of a criminal offense to stay out of jail under a suspension of sentence during good behavior and generally under the supervision or guardianship of a probation officer.

search warrant A court order authorizing an officer or a citizen to search a specified house or other premises for evidence, stolen property or unlawful goods.
stay An action that stops or arrests a judicial proceeding by order of the court.
suspended sentence After conviction, a sentence may be withheld or postponed by the judge. In most cases, the suspension is indefinite and depends upon satisfactory probation reports.

term Used in some jurisdictions to denote the ordinary session of court.

unconstitutional An action, law that is contrary to the Constitution or to state constitutions. (Do not confuse with illegal.)

venue The place or county in which an injury or crime is said to have been committed.
voir dire The preliminary examination that the court or lawyers may make of a prospective juror to determine whether he or she is acceptable to decide a case as a juror.

24 Sports

Preview   Sports news is, second to the local news, the most heavily read section of the newspaper, and television coverage of baseball, basketball and football games draws millions of viewers. The nation is made up of fans, many of them experts on the sports they follow.

The sports reporter handles a variety of assignments:

- Game stories—Coverage of high school, college and professional sports. Game stories require score, key plays, effect of game on standings, turning point of game and locker-room interviews.

- Profiles—Personality stories on newly acquired players, athletes having outstanding seasons, game stars, owners of professional teams. Profiles require: Background of individual, plenty of quotations, examples and anecdotes of the person in action.

- Sports as business—The emergence of billion-dollar television contracts for baseball and similar big-money deals requires coverage of the financial aspects of sports.

Television, said the sages of journalism, will cause a drastic change in the way news-papers cover sports. Game coverage will shrink, they said. Why would anyone want to read about a game he or she had seen the day before on television? Sportswriters would emphasize investigative and feature articles on subsidies for college athletes, the stars' personal lives and the business aspect of professional sports.

A glance at the sports pages of any newspaper proves the prophets part right, part wrong. Depth coverage has increased in many papers, but radio and television seem to have whetted the appetite of readers for details of the game.

When Susan V. Hands went to her first reporting job to cover sports for *The Charlotte Observer* she was anxious to investigate the growth of participant sports, to explore a wide variety of games and activities and to promote the development of women's athletics. Hands, the *Observer's* first woman sports writer, quickly shifted gears.

"I learned that people buy the morning paper to find out what happened in last night's football or basketball game. And our readers would be angry if, instead of finding the highlights and statistics of yesterday's North Carolina State basketball game, there was an investigative piece on the lack of athletic training available to girls in Charlotte high schools," she says.

Readers do want to see the score, and they want to savor the key plays again, despite having seen them twice the day before—once as they unfolded, and once again, courtesy of instant replay.

"Games results sell newspapers," says Hands.

Prelude to a Fall. The so-called minor sports such as gymnastics, wrestling, swimming, track and field and others have fans as avid as the followers of basketball and football.

Expanded Coverage

It is true that the sports pages encompass more than they did a couple of decades ago—more analytical stories, more interviews with players. New areas of coverage have been developed, such as the commercial side of college and professional sports, women's sports activities, the increasing amount of international competition and the use of drugs by athletes.

Participant sports have grown enormously in this period, and they have received extensive coverage. Hunting and fishing columns are regular features in most newspapers, and the standing of the many bowling leagues in town spot the back

Big One. Newspapers are paying more attention to participant sports such as fishing, hunting, tennis and golf. Here, a couple on vacation land a good-sized Muskie on the French River in Ontario, Canada.

pages of most sports sections. Local tennis and golf tournaments attract local coverage as well as local participants. A young journalist who fancies a sportswriting career would be wise to learn about one or more of these sports.

Sports editors of nonmetropolitan newspapers have emphasized local high school and college coverage, leaving the intensive coverage of professional sports to the metropolitan dailies, television and radio. Editors have also opened their pages to the so-called minor sports such as swimming, wrestling, track and field, and others that usually have fewer fans than basketball and football.

Fans spend more time than ever watching sports on television, and then they turn to the sports pages to find out why the Syracuse coach pulled his quarterback in the second half, the strategy by which Missouri managed to hold Kansas State to seven points in the last six minutes of play, what happened to the Boston Bruins defenseman who was punched to the ice by a Philadelphia Flyers forward. They look for the explanations and facts that the broadcast—indeed their own attendance at the game—may not have revealed. Game stories must give the fan what happened and also how and why.

Checklist: Game Coverage

_____ Result: Final score, names of teams, type of sport (if necessary to explain that it is high school, college, professional). League (NFL, AFC, Big Eight, Ivy League, NHL).

_____ Where and when game took place.

_____ Turning point of game; winning play; key strategy.

_____ Outstanding players.

_____ Effect on standings, rankings, individual records.

_____ Scoring. (Details of important baskets, goals, runs, etc.; summaries of others.)

_____ Streaks involved, by team or player.

_____ Post-game comments.

_____ External factors; weather; spectators.

_____ Size of crowd.

_____ Injuries and subsequent condition of athlete.

_____ Statistics.

_____ Duration of game when relevant.

Sources

It is not difficult to find reliable sources for most professional sports. Since these sports thrive on newspaper and broadcast coverage, owners usually are generous to reporters, providing everything from athletes for interviews to statistics, ballpoint pens, hot dogs, and even full-course meals in the press boxes. Many colleges, which field highly professional teams despite their amateur status, are equally helpful.

High school sports coverage is another matter. Coaches often are busy with physical education classes and are inaccessible. Players are unavailable, except during and after games. There is little assistance in the high school press box, unlike the paid publicity personnel at college and professional games.

The sources for sports stories are as varied as the sports themselves. For participant sports, bowling lane managers and tennis and golf professionals are anxious to call in unusual scores and the results of tournaments and matches. Although these callers often are self-serving, they do turn in newsworthy material and reporters should encourage such calls.

One day, the _Times-Union_ of Rochester, N.Y., was called by the manager of a bowling center and told that a league bowler had bowled 299. An interview followed with the man, a plumber who was bowling on his day off. A 183-average bowler, his 299 had helped his team move into first place by two points. The human interest story was a switch from the usual sports page emphasis on games.

Metropolitan newspapers play up the exploits of the stars in the big leagues, but most medium- and small-size newspapers depend on local sports activities and use brief wire stories of the professional games. The sources for these local events must be cultivated by the local reporter. He or she should attend sports banquets, drop by the pro shops at the golf and tennis courts, chat with the unsung athletes on the high school swimming, soccer, wrestling and track teams.

The newspapers and broadcast stations that emphasize local coverage concentrate on the major spectator sports, but many are gradually recognizing the interest in the so-called minor sports. The high school and college athletes who may go through a season never playing before more than a handful of spectators are excellent sources for stories. Not many readers know why a youngster will run 10 to 20 miles a day to prepare for a cross-country meet, what it is like to engage in a noncontact sport in which the only adversary is the athlete's own mind and body. The runners, the javelin throwers, the swimmers, the fencers and the wrestlers should not be overwhelmed by the glut of basketball and football coverage.

On most newspapers, a reporter will cover several different sports. It pays to keep a list of key contacts who can supply background quickly and accurately on all the sports the newspaper or station handles. Usually, the first name on the reporter's list is the athletic director or the publicity director.

Know the Experts

Fans, especially the armchair expert who has made his avocation following one of the local teams, can be excellent sources. The "sports nut," as some reporters call this person, has at his fingertips records, statistics, standings going back years.

Ron Rapoport, sportswriter for the *Chicago Sun-Times*, says sports writers are probably closer to their sources than are other reporters.

Close and Too Close

"They cover the same people day after day, often travel with them and spend, on the whole, a huge amount of time with the people they write about. This can have both a good and a bad effect," he says.

"On the one hand, sportswriters get to know the people they're writing about quite well and this can be useful in writing about their personalities and in getting tips for other stories. How are you going to find out that Art Kusnyer, a reserve catcher for the Angels who hardly ever plays, amuses himself in the bullpen during games by talking about whips and chains and murder and torture? You hear it because Bill Singer happens to be talking about it at breakfast.

"The perils of such close proximity, however, must be guarded against. If age is finally catching up with perhaps the least-talented, but hardest-working man ever likely to be named to the Hall of Fame (as it did with Maury Wills in 1972), can the reporter keep the personal sadness out of his stories? If he's honest, he can.

"The team must not become 'we.' The player you had breakfast with must not have excuses made for his errors. It is impossible to spend so much time with a team and not have personal favorites. Political reporters have theirs, too. The sports reporter has to guard against letting his prejudices show, just as does the political reporter."

Carried Away. Sports fans root for their teams and celebrate their victories. But not the sports writer, who is expected to walk the line between total detachment and partisanship. This enthusiastic fan had to be carted off the field following a Tennessee-Alabama football game.

Partisanship

"Sportswriting has survived because of the guys who don't cheer," said Jimmy Cannon, a gifted New York sports columnist. He was friendly with some of the players whose teams he covered, but was never a cheerleader. In broadcasting, the premier announcer in radio's palmiest days was Red Barber, and his credo was nonpartisanship. In a warm southern drawl, he described the Brooklyn Dodgers with no greater affection than the visiting Giants or Cubs. His love was the game, not the team. His ability to call the shots impartially may have cost Barber his job when local sports coverage on television turned to the gee-whiz crowd and the rooters.

Reporters do cover local teams from the point of view of the home town fans, telling them how their teams have fared against their opponents. This is fair. But the reporter is not supposed to cross the line between reporter and rooter, as some journalists in Philadelphia did one summer.

Shortly before the 1980 All Star baseball game, the *Trenton Times* in southern New Jersey startled fans with a story that reported that several players for the Philadelphia Phillies were wanted for questioning in connection with a drug investigation. The story said that a doctor for the Phillies' farm team in Reading, Pa., had been under inquiry for supplying amphetamines (greenies) to players without an examination. The story, by J. Stryker Meyer, the crime reporter for the *Times,* said that among those wanted for questioning were Larry Bowa, Pete Rose, Greg Luzinski and Mike Schmidt—top players on the team.

Soon the *Reading Times* had its own story. It learned that three pitchers on the team were also being sought for questioning.

As the story developed, two situations emerged, one natural in the development of a news story, the other unique to situations in which supposedly unbiased observers become partisans.

The natural development was the changing nature of the story. First, a district attorney cleared Bowa and Schmidt of involvement. Next, officials said that the team doctor had issued prescriptions to Sheena Bowa and Jean Luzinski, wives of two of the players.

The unique development occurred fairly soon after the two newspapers had broken the story: The Philadelphia press attacked the bearer of the news, reporter Meyer. A columnist for the *Philadelphia Daily News* wrote that Meyer's story was "irresponsible reporting by a minor league investigative reporter for a minor league newspaper. . . ." Another reporter said that she had overheard sports reporters talking about Meyer. The "guys who cover the team were saying things like they were going to kill this summabitch," she said.

Four months after the story broke, the attorney general of Pennsylvania charged the doctor with 23 counts of prescribing amphetamine compounds beyond the scope of the doctor-patient relationship. Prescriptions, the official said, had been written for one of the pitchers and for Rose, Luzinski, Bowa and his wife and Tim McCarver, a former Phillie catcher. When the case went to court, several of those involved changed their testimony and the judge dismissed all the charges.

As the full story developed, several of those who had been critical of Meyer engaged in some self-examination.

Meyer's story, the editor of the *Philadelphia Daily News* wrote, was "dead, solid accurate." Another Philadelphia editor tried to explain why some of the local newspapers had ignored the story and some reporters had attacked Meyer personally instead of jumping on the story:

"We chose to ignore the *Trenton Times* story, probably because it involved the so-called heroes of the local baseball team. Subconsciously at least, we appeared to be more concerned about the welfare of the team than the truth," wrote Craig Ammerman, executive editor of the *Bulletin.*

Greenies and the Phillies

Sometimes the reporter turned rooter sees only the excitement and drama of the sport he or she is covering and ignores the cheap shots, the drug use, the sordid deals and the crass commercialism of the sport.

Going out Swinging

In the closing minutes of the 1979 Gator Bowl football game, Ohio State, which was losing 17–15, tried a pass. The Clemson nose guard intercepted the pass and was knocked out of bounds on the Ohio State sideline near the Buckeyes' coach, Woody Hayes.

Hayes, 65 and the Ohio State football coach for 28 years, knew that the interception meant the end of the game for his team. A tempestuous man who had been reprimanded often for a variety of incidents, including hitting a television cameraman the previous season during a losing game to Michigan, Hayes again lost his temper. Fists swinging, Hayes made for the Clemson player. An Ohio State player tried to restrain him and was punched in the face by Hayes. He managed to reach his target and hit the Clemson guard in the neck in the exposed area between the player's shoulder pads and face guard.

But the millions who were watching the game on ABC television caught only a glimpse of the action when the cameras followed the play to the sidelines. There was no replay. Nor was there any discussion of the incident by the announcers. ABC officials said there had been no tape of the incident. But that did not quiet critics who felt that the network had intentionally covered up for Hayes because it did not want to jeopardize its contract to telecast college football games.

Switchboards across the nation were flooded with protesting callers. "Others," wrote Gary Deeb, the television critic of the *Chicago Tribune,* "simply sat back and chalked up another triumph to the see-hear-and-speak-no-evil mentality of TV sports."

The Hayes incident seems to have taught television a lesson. During a game between the New York Jets and the Green Bay Packers, a Jets linebacker smashed his forearm into the neck of a Packers end and sent the player sprawling to the ground senseless. The announcers showed the infraction several times, and they commented that it was a brutal act.

Young reporters sooner or later have to decide how to handle sports, as entertainment or as news, and how to treat athletes. Stanley Woodward, sports editor of *The New York Herald Tribune,* used to shake his head at the veneration of athletes that seeped through copy. "Will you please stop godding up these ball players," he would tell his staff.

Red Smith, author of several books and columnist for *The New York Times,* was no hero worshipper, either. Although, like Cannon, he had many friends among the athletes, he wrote with distance and some bemusement about sports. "I've tried not to exaggerate the glory of athletes," he said.

The sports reporter who becomes too deeply involved in his or her coverage might take lessons from Smith. Or chat with the political reporter, who usually can provide ample evidence of what partisanship can do to a working journalist.

"Only politicians lie more than football coaches," Cannon once observed.

Involvement can lead to dislike as well as admiration, but sports writers usually manage to control these feelings. However, if the athlete is the beneficiary of often-unmerited admiration, perhaps the balance should be struck with an occasional insight into the reality of the athlete's life.

Here are the comments of a *New York Post* sports columnist about a New York Yankee third baseman:

> Graig Nettles doesn't like me even a little bit. The feeling is mutual. Just so I would know how he feels about me last week in St. Petersburg he decided to call me a "backstabbing Jew bleeper." He said it three times, so I would get the point.
>
> . . . Graig is too vicious for me. On two occasions he has treated official sources with whom he disagreed foully enough to make your stomach turn. . . .

Game stories can be difficult to handle because of the pressure to have the story in before deadline and because of the essential similarity of the stories—one team wins, the other loses. The reporter copes with deadline problems with careful preparations. This may mean arriving at a high school gym well ahead of the game to find a telephone that will be available late in the evening so that the story can be called in to the sports desk.

Coverage Preparation

Everyone prepares. The AP team assigned to a World Series between the New York Yankees and the Los Angeles Dodgers arrived at the Dodgers' ball park three hours before game time to check the telephones, the communications setup and, as Howard Smith, AP deputy sports editor, put it, "to get the lay of the land."

During the baseball season, Rapoport arrives at the ball park at least an hour before the game. "The more information you can gain before the game, the better off you're likely to be," he says. He recalls one payoff for an early check: "Clyde Wright, who pitched for the California Angels, had lost five straight games when a switchboard operator at Anaheim Stadium presented him with one of those yellow, 'Have a Nice Day' pins, complete with smiling face. Only on this pin, the smile had been changed to a frown, and the legend had been changed to include an obscenity.

"Wright stuck the pin on his uniform. Wearing it, he won that day. It was a nice angle for the lead."

Hands trades stories with local reporters when covering out-of-town teams. This practice turns up nicknames, team mascots and the detail that gives a story the little convincing touches.

Needed: Sharp Reporting

Readers of the sports pages want three ingredients in their stories: a capsule of what happened, details and entertainment. The first two demand accurate reporting, and the third requires good writing.

The sports reporter operates under greater pressure to report accurately than do his or her colleagues in most other departments. The reason is that there are several thousand experts out there scrutinizing the reporter's every word. They have seen the game on television or from the stands, and some can rattle off won-lost records, the weight of the largest bass caught in local waters last year and the basketball standings in the NBA, Big Eight and the state high school leagues. Sports fans are sticklers about facts.

Keeping Statistics

One way to avoid trouble about game facts is to keep statistics of the event. Let us watch Hands cover a high school football game.

When she gets to the stadium, she checks the program to make sure the numbers on the players' jerseys are the same as those on the program. Then she sets up her scoring sheet.

"Every sportswriter has developed his own method of keeping a play-by-play and statistics, and of course, each sport lends itself to a different method," she says. "It's a good idea for a beginner to check with his or her editors or other sports writers and to try a few out on radio or TV games before trying the first one at a game. It's necessary because you can't count on being able to remember the sequence of plays, and you'd better not count on anybody else keeping statistics.

"You have to keep all the statistics you can because you can never tell what's going to be important. The game may be decided by punting. It may be decided by return yardage (which is not included in total offense). The key to the game may be one player's ability to set up tackles.

"If you can bring along a friend to spot tackles while you keep offense, that's great. Sometimes you can trade off with another sports writer in the press box. I've never seen anybody who can keep offense and defense at the same time, but I'm told there are a couple.

"Use half-time to tally up. Sometimes it is surprising to see what the statistics reveal: They don't always match the appearances."

Hands says she does not mind doing most press box chores by herself. "That way, I'm never at the mercy of PR men. I'm glad to have them help me, but I don't have to count on it," she says.

Reporters hang on to these statistics and score cards. They come in handy. Rapoport was watching the Los Angeles Dodgers one evening when the game pattern began to seem familiar. Al Downing was pitching for the Dodgers and his infielders seemed to be booting as many grounders as they fielded. "It came to me that I had seen something like this before, and I began to flip through the pages in my score book," Rapoport says. "The last time Downing had pitched, the Dodgers had made several errors and he had lost. And twice before that as well.

"A quick recapitulation of those losing games along with the day's score and a wry quote from Downing made for a fairly decent start to an otherwise routine game story."

A survey of sports readers by the Sports Committee of the Associated Press Managing Editors Association indicated that readers depend on the newspaper for tabulated detail: box scores, racing entries and results, football summaries and the other data the fans take seriously. More than half the readers always read baseball box scores, and two-thirds always read the football summaries.

Not all figures are equal. Some can be dangerous if taken too seriously. Enter the computer.

Watch Out

Sports fans enjoy comparing the merits of one team with another, or their team against others in the league or conference. This has spawned the rankings business. As the season approaches, sports writers rank teams, and as the college football and basketball seasons continue, teams are ranked each week.

The rankings make good stories, especially since some have the aura of scientific certainty. That mysterious instrument—the computer—does the rankings for some of the media. Coaches and sports writers also rank teams. Good copy all right, but hardly reliable.

Week after week, the No. 1 or No. 2 team is battered by a lowly opponent. One week, Pittsburgh's football team was to play Notre Dame. Pittsburgh was ranked No. 1 by the AP, UPI and *The New York Times* computer. The Irish ranked No. 20, according to the UPI, and were unranked by the AP and the *Times*. Final score: Notre Dame over Pittsburgh 31–16.

Unless a game is exciting or important, Rapoport says he tends not to emphasize too much detail.

Game Details

"Usually a couple of paragraphs are enough to sum up the key plays and others can often be worked in naturally throughout the story. I prefer to use the space concentrating on one or two or three of the most interesting things that happened and telling what the players involved or the manager thought about them. And what I thought.

"Often, a game story will be built around somebody who had a large effect—positive or negative—on the outcome," Rapoport says. "It is almost mandatory that we hear from this key player and, though there are some spontaneous talkers who begin at the sight of a notebook, it is almost always better to have a question in mind. This sounds simple enough, but often takes some thought. The right question will often do wonders.

"I also like to listen to what's being said by the players—not to reporters—but to each other. They often have funny conversations when they've won, sympathetic ones when they've lost. Good dialogue can dress up a story."

The small moves, the unnoticed shift in position, a change in the way a guard plays his man—these small details that the observant reporter picks up often mean the difference between victory and defeat. Watch a center fielder play each batter differently. Keep an eye on the way a forward moves to the basket in the second period when all his shots missed or were blocked in the first period.

Take That. Pittsburgh Pirates third baseman Bill Madlock shows what he thinks of umpire Gerry Crawford's third-strike call. Photographer Robert Pavuchak caught this detail for *The Pittsburgh Press.* In covering sports, reporters and photographers are alert for the details that highlight the game.

Changes

Sports reporting, like any other kind of coverage, responds to changing situations. Two major changes have swept through sports in the past four decades: The increasingly important role of money in amateur as well as professional sports and the inclusion of blacks and women in activities that had been closed to them.

Sports is a commercial enterprise, whether the game is played in the Astrodome or on a small college football field. Once, says Gerald Eskenazi of *The New York Times,* "an athlete was revered by the American public, placed on the same pedestal reserved for generals, Medal of Honor winners, movie stars, aviators . . ." Today, the pedestal is gone, and alongside the athlete in the public's mind are agents, lawyers and financial advisers.

In the 1970s, the average baseball player earned $35,000 a year. A decade later, the average was $145,000. In the old days, players stayed with one team for their entire career. Now, they move to the call of the highest bidder, and teams are likely to trade away athletes with high salaries. Historian Henry Steele Commager noted the shifting about and commented, "We have nothing to be loyal to."

At the college level, football and basketball are million dollar enterprises, much of the fuel coming from booster clubs. A survey by the National Collegiate Athletics Association found that the average big-time sports school received $437,000 in gifts for the athletics department in 1981.

Here are amounts from booster clubs that some institutions received in 1981, as compiled by the *Omaha World-Herald:*

Big Eight

Oklahoma	$3,500,000
Oklahoma State	1,500,000
Kansas State	1,500,000
Missouri	1,500,000
Kansas	1,240,000
Iowa State	900,000
Colorado	662,000
Nebraska	462,000

Big Ten

Iowa	$1,900,000
Illinois	1,350,000
Indiana	1,350,000
Ohio State	1,250,000
Purdue	1,000,000
Michigan State	965,000
Minnesota	550,000
Michigan	400,000
Northwestern	300,000
Wisconsin	not available

Southeastern

Georgia	$2,700,000
Florida	1,750,000
Vanderbilt	1,500,000
Alabama	1,200,000
LSU	1,100,000
Kentucky	850,000
Mississippi	700,000
Mississippi State	600,000
Tennessee	not available
Auburn	not available

Independents

South Carolina	$2,300,000
Florida State	2,100,000
Penn State	1,470,000
West Virginia	1,140,000
Pittsburgh	657,000
Tulane	525,000
Notre Dame	not available

Atlantic Coast

Clemson	$3,140,000
North Carolina	3,000,000
N.C. State	1,900,000
Virginia	1,600,000
Wake Forest	1,500,000
Maryland	1,300,000
Duke	1,000,000
Georgia Tech	945,000

Pacific Ten

Stanford	$4,000,000
Washington	2,000,000
UC Berkeley	2,000,000
Southern Cal	1,600,000
Arizona State	1,200,000
Oregon State	965,000
Arizona	800,000
UCLA	800,000
Oregon	765,000
Washington State	602,000

Southwest

SMU	$1,900,000
Texas A & M	1,800,000
Houston	1,600,000
Arkansas	1,500,000
Texas Tech	1,200,000
Rice	575,000
Baylor	450,000
TCU	450,000
Texas	not available

Others

Wichita State	$1,000,000
Tulsa	625,000
Texas-El Paso	500,000
Brigham Young	500,000
Wyoming	450,000
Creighton	81,000
UN-Omaha	70,000

While these contributions have kept many schools from dropping deeply into the red in their athletic programs, they also have caused considerable turmoil on and off campus. Frederick C. Klein of *The Wall Street Journal* found that many "in college sports regard the necessity of raising large sums of money from boosters as unfortunate . . . ." One of the consequences is an increase in "the already-enormous pressure for victory in those 'revenue' sports. . . ."

Boosters are hard to control. Arizona State University was given a two-year NCAA football probation partly as the result of improper payments to athletes and coaches by a local booster club. The University of San Francisco dropped varsity basketball after it found it could not control student-aid violations by alumni. The situation has led to new kinds of stories. Hero worship has been replaced by exposé.

New Players

On April 15, 1947, Jackie Robinson played first base for the Brooklyn Dodgers. He became the first black in modern history to break the color line. Since then, blacks have been the dominant figures in professional sports.

In baseball, over a dozen years, 22 of the 24 National and American League stolen-base leaders were black, as were 16 of the 24 batting champions. Every rushing leader in the National Football League since 1963 has been black, and in the National Basketball Association only three white players have led the league in scoring since 1960 and only two in rebounding since 1957.

Hank Aaron, who hit more home runs than any player in history, says the black player changed baseball from a "one base, one run and waiting-for-the-big-hit" game to a more exciting chance-taking game. Basketball, players say, is now more competitive, more intense, harder played. The team concept is less emphasized.

Women are more recent entrants on the athletic field. They participate in big-money golf and tennis tournaments, and sports pages chronicle the games of women's college teams.

Sports coverage changed, too. The athlete became as much the center of coverage as the game, as did the financial backdrop against which all this was being played out. Add to this the lessons the New Journalism was teaching journalists.

The Chipmunks

In the 1960s, a new breed of reporter emerged that reflected the New Journalism's personal reporting. In sports reporting, the symbol of this new reporter was the chipmunk, a description coined by an old-style sports reporter who was appalled by the work of these eager young reporters. One of the best of the new lot had two prominent front teeth, hence the term chipmunk.

Although to some it was a derogatory term, to others, such as Al Silverman, former editor of *Sport* magazine, the chipmunks symbolized the opening up of sports journalism.

To the more critical, the chipmunk is accurately portrayed in an incident said to have occurred after the 1962 World Series in which Ralph Terry of the New York Yankees had beaten the San Francisco Giants twice. After the final game, Terry's wife called him in the Yankee dressing room to congratulate him and to tell him their new baby was doing well. Overhearing the call, a reporter asked Terry where his wife was.

"Feeding the baby," Terry said.

"Breast or bottle?" asked the reporter.

This story is related by Roger Kahn in *Esquire* with obvious distaste for the chipmunk style in which the meaning of the game is hidden under a barrage of irrelevant or hyped-up detail, he says.

Every editor, of course, wants reporters who can ask tough questions, reporters who can ask a coach why he followed a certain game strategy when it did not seem to be working.

"It's far from easy," says Frank Cardon, sports editor of the *Times-Union* of Rochester, N.Y. "Many athletes are big babies. Rich and pampered. They don't want the tough question. They have little regard for the underpaid and unknown newspaper reporter."

One of the reasons athletes ignore some reporters is that so many sports reporters fail to do their homework, Cardon says. "The result is a lot of stupid questions and the impatient athlete soon gets tired of it all."

An Overview

Clearly, Kahn—who wrote a fine book about baseball, *The Boys of Summer* (New York: Harper & Row, 1972)—has a basic approach to his reporting. Most good sportswriters do. Here, from one of Kahn's columns in *Esquire,* is how he describes his approach to his beat:

> Sports tells anyone who watches intelligently about the times in which we live: about managed news and corporate politics, about race and terror and what the process of aging does to strong men. If that sounds grim, there is courage and high humor, too. . . .
>
> . . . I find sport a better area than most to look for truth. A great hockey goalie, describing his life on ice, once said, "That puck comes so hard, it could take an eye. I've had 250 stiches and I don't like pain. I get so nervous before every game, I lose my lunch."
>
> "Some football players," I said to the goalie, whose name is Glenn Hall, "say that when they're badly scared they pray."
>
> Hall looked disgusted. "If there is a God," he said, "let's hope he's doing something more important than watching hockey games." Offhand I can't recall a better sermon.

Robert Lipsyte, author of books and articles on sports and a former sports columnist for *The New York Times,* says of sports coverage:

> A baseball game may be a pleasure or a bore, but it is not necessarily news, like a fire, nor is it an example of the durable purity of American Democracy. A baseball game is a staged entertainment, and baseball players are paid performers.
>
> And sportswriters are professional newsmen. Newsworthy things happen at sports events, and there are valid sociological implications to be found there, but if games are to be regularly covered at all, they should probably be treated as consumer products judged on value given; poor sightlines, bad hot dogs, unsafe restrooms, a centerfielder who dogs it, an owner who lies, a commissioner lobbying for special privileges are sportstyle rip-offs the best sportswriters have told us about.

Roger Angell, a sportswriter for *The New Yorker,* says that although sports does grip us because of the remarkable physical capacities of the athletes and the high stakes for which they play, sometimes "we stop cheering and look on in uneasy silence." The athlete we are watching, we realize, is only a man:

> The enormous alterations of professional sport in the past three decades, and especially the prodigious inflation of franchises and salaries, have made it evident even to the most thoughtless fan that the play he has come to see is serious indeed, and that the heart of the game is not physical but financial. Sport is no longer a release from the harsh everyday American business world but its continuation and apotheosis. Those of us (fans and players alike) who return to the ball park in the belief that the game and the rules are unchanged—merely a continuation of what we have known and loved in the past—are deluding ourselves, perhaps foolishly, perhaps tragically. . . .

Red Smith, who was writing his sports column for *The New York Times* until a few days before he died in 1982, said of sports:

> Sports is not really a play world. I think it's the real world. The people we're writing about in professional sports, they're suffering and living and dying and loving and trying to make their way through life just as the bricklayers and politicians are.
> This may sound defensive—I don't think it is—but I'm aware that games are a part of every culture we know anything about. And often taken seriously. It's no accident that of all the monuments left of the Greco-Roman culture, the biggest is the ball park, the Colosseum, the Yankee Stadium of ancient times. The man who reports on these games contributes his small bit to the history of his times.

Rapoport takes what he calls a practical view of sports coverage. "If you can't find something light or something that will make the reader smile or laugh, at least remember and try to show, in style or substance, that these are games these people are involved in, not foreign policy discussions," he says.

"However, dramatic things do happen and when they do the reporter shouldn't be afraid to haul out the heavy artillery. The day a young player left his career on a cyclone fence in the outfield, the lead was:

> Bobby Valentine sat in center field, facing the fence the ball had just gone over, staring down at the grotesque sight the broken bone was making beneath the skin, trying not to scream, not to think, not to do anything.

Wanted: Writers

A former wire service reporter who turned college sports public relations man and talks with dozens of sports writers a year, lists the basics of good sports coverage as: imagination, innovation, freshness, interesting details, good writing.

Significantly, writing is last. Sports fans tend to tolerate almost any kind of writing so long as they are given the correct scores, accurate details of the game, interesting anecdotes and inside information about teams and players.

Kahn, considered one of the best of the sportswriters, gives another hint as to why sportswriting may be, to quote the cliché about it that endures, "the best and the worst writing to be found in the American newspaper today." He says that at first glance "sports appears to be the shallow end of the American sea: puerile speeches at the letter club banquet, the hustling of transparent con men, simple adults pursuing childhood activities, amiable anecdotes repeated on old-timer's day. The same man who demands harsh film criticism and likes his political reporting merciless accepts a pablum view of sport. . . ."

But this is changing. The sports pages are no longer the exclusive reading of the sports nut whose consuming passion in life is the Dallas Cowboys or the Southeastern Conference basketball standings. Sports appeals to a wide range of readers and viewers, many of them seeking good writing as well as information.

Internal pressures also move sports reporters to work at their writing. Conscious of the criticism of sports writing as the slag heap of journalism, they can, and do, point out that some of the country's best writers graced the country's sports pages.

Sportswriters are heirs to a splendid writing heritage—Ring Lardner, Westbrook Pegler, Heywood Broun, Red Smith—and many, like Kahn, are serious guardians of that tradition.

When Smith was commenting in his column about an article that criticized sportswriting, he wrote that the story "started on the front page of the *Los Angeles Times* and ran through the paper for 26 miles, 385 yards." That is the distance of the marathon in the Olympics. Smith's metaphor is more appropriate to his topic—sports—than the adjective most of us would grasp at. Most of us probably would have written that the *Times* piece was "lengthy." But then, Smith was a writer.

With the new seriousness sportswriters take to their work, they must be able to resist the temptation to turn the colorful and exciting language of sports into the homogeneous prose that infects most newspaper and television writing. Russell Baker, a columnist for *The New York Times,* bemoaned the decline of baseball talk that, he wrote, once "crackled with terseness, vibrancy and metaphor." He had heard a television sportscaster say, "Ryan has good velocity and excellent location." He meant, wrote Baker, that Ryan "is throwing very fast and putting the ball where he wants to."

This kind of impoverished writing, while sports is flourishing, is the result of sports "going through a period of highbrow pretension, brought on perhaps by the hordes of college men cluttering up the locker rooms and the advent of high-falutin' sportswriters too self-conscious about their master's degrees in creative writing to risk playing a kid's game at the typewriter," Baker wrote.

The situation makes a sports fan long for Dizzy Dean, the St. Louis Cardinals pitcher and then sports announcer who was known for his picturesque language. Once he was struck on the toe while pitching and a doctor examined him on the mound. "This toe is fractured," the doctor said. To which Dean replied, "Fractured hell. The damn thing's broken."

Sports writers have written some memorable lines, such as this one about a midwestern quarterback who was a wizard on the field, a dunce in the classroom: "He could do anything with a football but autograph it."

The line came back to some sportswriters when they wrote about a football player at UCLA who was arrested for killing his drug dealer. The player, it turned out, could not read—the product of the win-at-any-price philosophy of big-time sports.

Red Smith was a master writer. Of a notorious spitball pitcher, he wrote that "papers needed three columns for his pitching record: "won, lost and relative humidity."

Look at this lead he wrote about Buck Leonard, a black first baseman whose career ended before baseball was integrated:

> Wearing a store suit, horn-rimmed glasses, and a smile that could light up Yankee Stadium, a sunny gentleman of 64 revisited his past yesterday and recalled what it was like to be the black Lou Gehrig on a food allowance of 60 cents a day.

The last few words chill an otherwise warm recollection. They sum up a period of American life in a phrase.

Anecdotes Good sports writers have memories that go back to the details of the first high school basketball game they covered, and further. They are insatiable collectors of anecdotes, to be stored away and used at the appropriate moment.

When an imaginative boxing promoter was trying to schedule a match between Muhammad Ali, who had made a friendly visit to Arab countries, and Mike Rossman, who carried the nicknames the Jewish Bomber and the Kosher Butcher, James Tuite of *The New York Times* recalled in his story a similar ethnic promotion. Some 60 years before, Irish Eddy Kelly and Benny Leonard, a Jewish fighter, were in the ring. Leonard was battering Kelly. Finally, in a clinch, Kelly whispered to Leonard, "Hub rachmones. (Yiddish for "take pity.") I'm really Bernie Schwartz."

Rossman, Tuite pointed out, was born Mike DePuano and took to wearing the Star of David on his trunks along with his new name to help sell tickets. The Ali-Rossman match was laughed out of the ring by pieces like Tuite's.

Common Writing Faults

Whatever the sports writer's overview of his or her job, most of the good writers agree that the sports journalist has greater writing freedom than any other member of the news staff, but does not use it when he or she:

- Uses the jargon of the trade—hoop, netminder, pigskin, split the uprights, gave it the big try, and the scores of others that infect sports pages.
- Plays the expert by using technical language to persuade the reader he or she is savvy.
- Follows formulas: _____ (passed, ran) for _____ touchdowns as _____ (outscored, manhandled, held off) _____ Saturday, _____ to _____ .
- Tries too hard.

Young sportswriters sometimes try too hard to write. They press language, reach for words and phrases. When this happens, the result is sawdust and shavings. Here is a lead from the Baltimore *News-American* that tries so hard to invest sports with some higher value that it is tasteless:

> Martin Luther King had a dream. John McKay, Sr., had a plan. Both men were persecuted in their attempts to overcome adversity. Only McKay lived to tell how difficult it was to succeed, but there were times when he, too, felt he was going to die. Coaching the Tampa Bay Buccaneers had not been easy.

Direct, slender, purposive prose flows naturally from the event. Sports lends itself easily to good writing, for it has built-in the essentials of drama—conflict, leading characters, dramatic resolution.

Opening day of the baseball season is usually dramatic, whatever the score. Baseball fans may have tuned in the Sunday professional football games on television, even managed to get down to a college basketball game or two, but all winter they drummed their fingers waiting for their sport to begin. Red Smith recognized that in his account of opening day at Yankee Stadium, and he had a good ball game to work with. Here's how his account begins:

> In the press box somebody asked who had been the last man to pitch a no-hitter on opening day. There had been only one, the guy was told, Bob Feller. Nobody knew for sure just when that had happened, but there would be time to look it up. It was still only the sixth inning. "Well," someone else said, "this will be the first by a left-hander. And the first perfect game ever on opening day."
>
> There were 52,719 cash customers in Yankee Stadium, and many of them must have been talking in the same vein, for every time Ron Guidry threw the ball the crowd responded with wild-animal cries. . . .

Smith then tells the story chronologically. "Five innings were gone and no Brewer had reached base by any means," he writes in the third paragraph. Then the sixteenth batter and a line-drive out to shortstop.

Now, every fan in town knew how Guidry had done on opening day. Yet Smith retells the tale, knowing full well how much we all love to relive the stories of triumph and disaster. The technique Smith uses works only for such events as opening day, the pennant-deciding playoff game, or similar big games, and it would not work at all for wire service sportswriters whose task is to give newspaper and broadcast station clients the outcome quickly, in the lead.

The Brewers make their first hit, a single by the seventeenth batter, and it is put in the fifth paragraph. Not until the sixth paragraph does Smith give the final score—a 5–1 Yankee loss.

Leads   Even the wire services try to introduce some interesting element in their leads along with the score:

> LOS ANGELES (AP)--San Diego fouled up on a bizarre variation of "who's on first?" Thursday when two men headed for the same bag in the ninth inning, but the Padres still scored to win their National League opener against the defending National League champions, the Los Angeles Dodgers, 4-3.

In writing a sports story, it is usually a good idea to find an interesting element to go along with the score in the lead. Compare these two leads, the first by a wire service, the second by a staff reporter, that appeared in the same newspaper one Sunday:

> LAWRENCE, Kan., Oct. 6--Joe Morris rushed for three touchdowns and a school-record 251 yards today to give Syracuse a 45-27 victory over Kansas.

> ANNAPOLIS, Md. Oct. 6—George Welsh, the 46-year-old head football coach at the Naval Academy, said, "I have trouble sleeping these days, and on the night before a game I don't sleep at all. Maybe it's because I'm getting old and this coaching is more and more a young man's job."

Advice From a Pro

Smith was always helpful to young writers. When a college student sent Smith columns he had written for his college newspaper, Smith replied:

> When I was a cub in Milwaukee I had a city editor who'd stroll over and read across a guy's shoulder when he was writing a lead. Sometimes he would approve and sometimes say gently, "Try again," and walk away.
> My best advice is, try again. And then again. If you're for this racket, and not many really are, then you've got an eternity of sweat and tears ahead. I don't mean just you; I mean anybody.

Charles McCabe of the San Francisco *Chronicle* wrote in a column shortly after Smith's death in which he said:

> Red was nearly always the last man to leave the press room. Like Westbrook Pegler, he was a bleeder. I well remember him at the Olympic Games in Squaw Valley in 1960. When everyone else left and was up at the bar, Red sat sweating, piles of rejected leads surrounding him. He hadn't really even started his story yet. But when the lead came he wrote fluently and always met his deadline.

Smith once remarked, "The English language, if handled with respect, scarcely ever poisoned the user."

Both reporters are trying to give their stories the added lift of an interesting piece of information to supplement the score. The wire service reporter cannot quite get away from the score. But in the piece from Annapolis, the writer does not mention the score until the third paragraph after describing how Welsh's sleeplessness may have been the result of Navy's four close wins in the season to date. The lead is appropriate because in its fifth game, the one the reporter was covering, "the Middies were forced to hang on for the remaining 50 minutes to beat Air Force, 13–9."

The news writer is always looking for that one incident or situation that makes this particular game different from scores of others that week. Stan Sutton of *The* Louisville *Courier-Journal* found the extra dimension in an action by an official, and he made this his lead—one of the few occasions in which an official finds his name anywhere but in the tiny type that accompanies a box score.

In this case, the official could not get out of the way of a touchdown pass. Here are Sutton's first seven paragraphs:

RICHMOND, Ky.—Burrell Crowell has slowed down a bit in recent years. His hairline is receding and he runs the 40 yards in something like 12.4 seconds. Yesterday he tried to run one yard in three seconds and couldn't make it in time.

Crowell, a football and basketball official from Manchester, Tenn., has a habit of adding controversy to the Eastern Kentucky-Western Kentucky rivalry. He and Ralph Stout were involved in a bitter controversy in the 1979 Ohio Valley Conference basketball tournament in which Eastern beat Western. Yesterday he found controversy again as Eastern defeated Western 19–11.

Leading only 9–3, Eastern was at Western's six-yard line on the first play of the fourth quarter. Facing a third down, tight end Tron Armstrong angled for the right side of the end zone and quarterback Chris Isaac lofted the ball toward him for a certain touchdown.

But Crowell, the umpire, was unable to react and was leveled by Armstrong an instant before the receiver could reach the ball. With the incompletion, Eastern had to settle for a 22-yard field goal by Jamie Lovett.

Although he is ineligible for OVC Defensive Player of the Week, Crowell's play assured the estimated 20,800 fans of a close game. In fact, Western was at the Eastern 35-yard line in the final minute with a chance to tie the game and utilize the league's new tiebreaker rule for the first time.

"I knew it had to be an open field. I thought maybe I'd run into a pole, or something," Armstrong said.

"Durn Burrell!," said Eastern coach Roy Kidd. "If we made that touchdown there's no way they're going to tie it. That's carelessness on his part. But I'm sure he didn't do it intentionally."

Stout realized that his readers undoubtedly knew how the game had come out since, as the story points out, the two teams have an old rivalry. So he concentrated on an important aspect of the game that most of those who followed it on radio or television may not have caught. Stout provides a bit of fun for the reader with his approach, though in the seventh paragraph he quotes the Eastern Kentucky coach about the seriousness of the official's action.

Covering a Baseball Game

Vinny DiTrani covers baseball for *The Bergen Record.* He covers a lot of games in a season, sometimes almost as many as the full schedule.

"In baseball, where there are 162 games each season, often the game itself can be submerged in favor of a personality piece, or an overall situation piece concerning a player or a team's status. In football, where there are only 16 games, I think more attention must be focused on the actual contest."

DiTrani was assigned to cover a game between the Minnesota Twins and the New York Yankees. The Twins pitcher was Jerry Koosman, who had pitched for the New York Mets for 11 years before being traded. It was clear to DiTrani that his story would have to focus on Koosman since many of his readers had followed the Mets and Koosman. He wanted to give the readers a "status report," he said.

"Luckily, in this case, the game result fits perfectly into the personality piece." When he was with the punchless Mets, Koosman lost many close games. Now, with the Twins, he was still losing them. Here's how DiTrani began his piece:

NEW YORK—Some things just never change for Jerry Koosman. He still gets a thrill when he sees the bright lights of New York City. He still can't get over the hustle and bustle that goes on beneath those bright lights. He still thinks of the whole New York scene as home.

And he still manages to lose one-run ball games.

"Those things happen to every pitcher at one time or another," rationalized the veteran lefthander, who nevertheless collected more than his share of wasted efforts while pitching for the Mets. Last night, however, it was the Twins who did the wasting, dropping a 3–2 decision to

the Yankees in Koosman's homecoming game.

It was the fourth straight setback for the 35-year-old Koosman, who started the year with a team-record seven consecutive victories. Three of the four losses have been by one run, and Koosman's earned run average has dwindled from 4.23 to 3.64 during that stretch.

"I'm throwing as well as I did in '76, when I won 21 games for the Mets," Koosman said. "The way this club comes back (three singles off Ron Guidry after two outs in the ninth to tie the game at 2–2) reminds me of the '69 Mets. These guys never quit, either."

DiTrani says that his major thought before writing a game story is, "What do the fans want to know about this game? In this case, I thought they most wanted to know about Koosman. In another, it may be the mechanics around a certain play, or the overall effect of the game on a team's outlook, its standing, and so on."

He described the game story as a "challenge, to create a story the reader will not pass over as just another of 162 installments."

Quick Learning

Since fans usually are experts in the sports they follow, the sports reporter has to know at least, and probably a bit more, than his or her readers or viewers. This takes work. When Andrea Sachs, a journalism student, was assigned to interview a jockey at a horse race track on Sunday, she was worried.

Sachs had never been to a track and, as she put it, "I did not know the difference between a horse and a goat at that point." She recalled:

"That night, I bought a copy of *The Daily Racing Form* and two track magazines at a newsstand. I asked the man behind the counter if he knew anything about racing. He suggested that I talk to the customer standing next to me.

"The customer was able to give me the names of the top jockeys at the track, and he explained a little about racing.

"I called the publicity office at the track and asked if I could speak to one of the apprentice jockeys. I made several other calls and worked out apointments.

"Before I went to the track, I read the racing section of the newspaper. I discovered that a race was being televised that Saturday and bought another *Racing Form* and watched the race. That provided me with background knowledge and some conversation openers for my interviews."

Youngster at the Big A.
Apprentice jockey Robbie
Davis on the way out of the
saddling enclosure to the
starting gate at the Aqueduct
Race Track in New York.

Sachs left early for the track in order to be able to watch the horses being exercised. She wandered around the track, chatting with jockeys and trainers, building up her knowledge. At the coffee stand, she asked a man to explain the betting system.

When the racing started, she followed the advice of one of her new-found friends and bet. "I lost $2," she said.

Finally, she was able to interview her jockey, Robbie Davis, a youngster from Pocatello, Idaho, who had just won the first race he rode in at the track.

"He was amazingly open and willing to answer any questions. I spoke to him several times during the afternoon."

Her article for her class assignment began:

Robbie Davis's first race at Belmont was a young jockey's dream.

The shy 21-year-old apprentice jockey from Pocatello, Idaho, had driven to New York a week earlier from Louisiana Downs, where he had been riding since May. After exercising horses for a few days at Aqueduct, Davis went to Belmont in early September for the first time.

He was to ride Comanche Brave in a mile-and-an-eighth claiming race with experienced jockeys such as Angel Cordero and George Martens.

Davis recalls his feelings: "I didn't know the track at all . . . it was the biggest track I'd ever seen."

Comanche Brave went off at 20–1 odds, on a muddy track. Davis, who was used to shorter tracks, said that he watched "real close, trying to save as much horse as I could, because I knew it was a long straightaway."

The strategy worked. The next thing he knew, Davis was sitting in the winner's circle. "I couldn't believe it."

Encouraged by her instructor, Sachs tried to sell the article to Davis's hometown newspaper, *The Idaho State Journal*. The newspaper bought it. (See "Tall in the Saddle" news story.)

Tall in the Saddle:

Pocatello Jockey Finds His Way to the Big Time

By ANDREA SACHS
Special to Enjoy

NEW YORK—Robbie Davis's first race at Belmont was a young jockey's dream.

The shy 21-year-old jockey from Pocatello had driven up to New York a week earlier from Louisiana Downs, where he had been riding since May. After exercising horses a few days at Aqueduct, Davis went to Belmont in early September for the first time.

He was to ride Commanche Brave in a mile-and-an-eighth claiming race with experienced jockeys like Angel Cordero and George Martens.

Davis recalls his feelings at the time. "I didn't know the track at all ... it was the biggest track I'd ever seen."

Commanche Brave went off at 20-1 odds, on a muddy track. Davis, who was used to shorter tracks, said that he "watched real close, trying to save as much horse as I could, because I knew it was a long straight-away."

The strategy worked. The next thing he knew, Davis was sitting in the winner's circle. "I couldn't belive it."

Neither could his new agent, Steve Adika. "I was a little bit surprised — it was like hitting a grand slam home run when you've come up from the minor leagues."

On a recent Sunday, Davis sat on a bench outside of the jockey's quarters at Belmont between races, watching Angel Cordero and Jorge Velasquez filing in and out of the room. He still could not believe that he was racing next to some of the best known jockeys in the country at one of the country's three major tracks. "I'm still in a daze," said Davis. "It's hard for me to accept that I'm riding with them. It's come too soon."

Unlike many apprentice jockeys — or "bug boys" as they are known at the track because of the asterisks that mark their names on the racing forms — Davis was not born to the saddle. Raised by his mother in Pocatello, Davis never rode a horse until he was 18 years old.

It was in 1980, when Davis was working at a bakery loading bread onto trucks, that a friend took him to the Pocatello Turf Club. Liking what he saw, Davis knew immediately that he wanted to become a jockey. A week later, he quit his job at the bakery, and took a job cleaning stalls at the track.

At first, the work was unnerving. "I was scared of the horses — I was afraid they were going to trample me," said the 5-foot-1, 105-pound jockey. "It took me a week to put a halter on a horse."

Davis' first ride, on "an old pony horse," was equally challenging. "I didn't know a horse's mouth at all," said Davis, explaining that the bit kept slipping. "I was determined to stay on." The horse was determined to throw him off, "raring and propping" for the whole two-mile ride. When he got off, Davis said, "I fell on the ground — my legs were too weak to stand up."

Davis persisted, and in October, 1980, a friend arranged a job for him at a horse breeding ranch in Victorville, Calif. It was the first time Davis had been away from home, and it meant leaving his girlfriend and car back in Pocatello. Of the 16-hour bus ride to California, Davis said, "I didn't know where I was going, or who was going to meet me or anything."

His job at the ranch was to gallop, or exercise, two dozen horses a day, for $400 a month, plus room and board. Despite the hard work, and a day that began at 6 a.m., Davis said that he loved his job. "The horses were so good — it was a challenge to get on them."

Davis went back to Pocatello in June, 1981, and began racing quarter horses on the fair circuit. According to Ed Madson, Racing Secretary for the Idaho Fair Circuit, Davis showed "a lot of ambition and prospect," winning leading rider awards in Burley, Rupert, and Blackfoot. Although he was riding quite a bit — "people wanted to put me on" — Davis longed to race thoroughbreds. In October, he moved his tack to Turf Paradise in Phoenix, Ariz.

In Phoenix, Davis discovered that he would have to change his riding style in order to race thoroughbreds. After coming in fourth in his first race on a horse named Irish Lick, Davis said, "I was super, super tired ... I was dead. I was riding him like a quarter horse." He started swimming to gain strength, as well as training with a jump rope.

From Phoenix, Davis moved on to Shreveport in May, 1982, to race at Louisiana Downs. There, his agent, Wendy Smith, recommended him to his current agent in New York, believing that Davis's style would be better suited to New York racing than the sprinting that dominated small race track racing.

It was. Davis has ridden 72 mounts at Belmont, winning five races, placing in five, and showing in seven.

New York race goers like the youngster. Recently, as Davis sat straight in the saddle while walking through the dirt walkway to the track, a fan shouted "You're a good rider, Davis."

He placed two times in his three races that day. Later, assessing the afternoon, Davis said "I feel good that I lit the board," but admitted, "I like to win — that's the best satisfaction."

For Davis, riding at a competitive track like Belmont has been a challenge. "This is such a big change from the other places that I've been," he said. "It's difficult to make the right judgments."

Davis and famed jockey Angel Cordero, at Aqueduct

Student Story. The *Idaho State Journal* used the story of Davis in its Sunday magazine section.

In her story, Sachs blended observations, direct quotations and background. The story was a convincing portrait of a young jockey who had realized his ambition to ride in the big time. The story that *The Idaho State Journal* published ended this way:

Some of those judgments involve other jockeys. "They want you to show them you're not wild, not a loose rider. I know that I have to show them consideration—don't bump them, don't bother them, don't cut them out."

Davis credits experienced jockeys like Jacinto Vasquez and Eddie Maple with having helped him by pointing out his mistakes during the replays of the races. For example, said Davis, he has learned about "rating a horse—saving it for the stretch." Lingering by the pictures on the walls of famous jockeys and horses who have ridden at Belmont, Davis admitted that he still has much to learn.

Now that Belmont has closed for the season, Davis has moved to Aqueduct and the Meadowlands for the winter. As an apprentice until May 28, Davis's goal is to be able to stay at Belmont—"I don't want to step down"—after he loses the weight allowance granted apprentices.

He knows the difficulty of attaining that goal. Of the 25 or so apprentice jockeys who have ridden at Belmont this year, it is unlikely that more than two or three of them will be able to continue past their apprentice year.

An apprentice is given a weight allowance of 10, 7, or 5 pounds, depending upon how many races he has won, which allows the horse that he is riding to carry that much less weight. This allowance makes good apprentice jockeys an attractive choice for owners and trainers.

After the apprentice year, though, a jockey loses his weight allowance, and must compete at full weight with both new apprentices and more experienced riders. Thus, unless they are exceptionally good riders, most apprentices here move on to other tracks at the end of their first year, or step into jobs as exercise boys or assistant trainers.

"I tell my agent to chew me out—be my father or whatever . . . get after me," said Davis. "This is my only chance."

High School Sports

Most beginners on the sports beat are assigned to local high school basketball and football coverage. To the young reporter who can quote the pass completion percentage of all the quarterbacks in the National Football League, being assigned to cover a Friday night high school football game may seem a comedown.

Richard H. Growald, the UPI's national reporter, noted that "despite the growth in popularity of such attractions as professional football, local high school sports remains a dominant civic factor. An American may not be too familiar with the workings of his city hall, but he knows his high school football team lineup."

High school sports is the major sports interest in most towns and cities because it is the only local spectator sport available to these fans. For every Ohio State enthusiast, there are a dozen high school fans in the state.

"It's not uncommon in North and South Carolina for 10,000 people to watch a regular season high school football game," Hands says. "And every one of those 10,000 is a potential reader of the sports page, if his or her hometown high school hero's name is in the paper."

In fact, Hands says, the most widely read stories in the *The Charlotte Observer* are high school sports. Hands was responsible for covering 116 high school teams in the Carolinas. She handled most of the coverage by telephone and covered one game a week.

In Danville, Ill., the *Commercial-News* covers two local high schools and 30 area high schools as well as a local junior college and Big Ten sports at the University of Illinois and Purdue. Fowler Connell, the sports editor, says that during the school year, "football and basketball on the local scene are king, although the other sports are covered also.

"We feel we are obligated to do more for our readers than any big-city paper can possibly do. Danville and our area towns belong to 'us' and, conversely, we like to think they want us in their homes," he says.

The paper covers all home and away games of the local teams and each of the other 30 high schools at least once. If an area team is in contention for the state playoffs, the newspaper will cover it several times.

"That means on a Friday night we will have four bylined stories by our regular staff and one from a part-timer at our Covington, Ind., bureau," says Connell.

The newspaper also runs roundups of the area teams Tuesdays, "Player of the Week" features during football and basketball seasons Wednesdays, pre-game advances and an area roundup of coming games on Thursdays. Illinois and Purdue are given the big play Fridays for their Saturday games. Friday nights the staff is out covering high school games, and Saturday's newspaper is dominated by the results of these games.

With demands such as these on his staff, everyone has to be able to cover several sports. "No one is wedded to any one team or any one sport," says Connell.

Women Sports Writers

"I think women belong in the kitchen," said the owner of the San Francisco 49ers football team, Edward DeBartolo Jr. He was commenting after a federal judge ruled that the National Football League team had to grant equal access to its locker room to a female sports reporter for *The Sacramento Bee.*

Characters like DeBartolo and his coach are rarities these days in professional sports. By now, women sports writers are an accepted part of the sports scene. The victory was hard won, however. Not until 1975 were women admitted to locker rooms of professional basketball and hockey teams for post-game interviews.

In 1976, a female reporter for *Sports Illustrated* was denied access to the Yankee Stadium clubhouse and filed suit in federal court. She won, and baseball teams opened their locker rooms and clubhouses.

Some resentment lingers, and some teams still make women sports writers uncomfortable. Jane Gross, a sports reporter for *The New York Times,* had trouble with the Cleveland Indians baseball team. She recalled gathering with reporters in the Indians' clubhouse after a game the Indians won against the Yankees. The reporters were interviewing the winning pitcher.

The Indians players singled Gross out for obscene and profane remarks. ''I make a point not to turn my head,'' she said, describing the scene.

''The abusive language continues, but now I am being pelted with french fries from the postgame meal. As I finish my interview, a baseball glances off my shoulder.''

Most athletes no longer care whether they are interviewed by a male or a female sports writer. The story is told about a female sports writer in the San Diego basketball team's locker room following a game. As Randy Smith started to pull off his uniform, a fellow player cautioned him, ''Randy, there's a lady in the room.'' Smith replied:

''That's no lady. That's only a writer.''

25

Business Journalism

Preview   Business news affects everybody. The business reporter handles:

■ Local spot news stories—Store openings and closings, company personnel changes, new construction, changes in the business climate, annual reports of local companies.

■ Features—New products developed by local enterprises, personality profiles of company officials and working people.

■ Interpretative stories—Effects of national and international developments on local business, the power of local businesses on municipal policies such as the tax structure.

Business reporters read widely for background—Business newspapers and magazines, books on business and economics and the wide array of pamphlets and reports put out by private and government groups.

The subject of business has become everybody's personal business. Most of us want to know about the cost of living, the possibilities for employment in certain fields, how high or low interest rates may go, whether layoffs are imminent in local industries and the value of a bond or stock that we or our parents own.

Our food, clothing and shelter are produced by business enterprises, and their quality and the prices we pay for them are largely the result of business decisions. Even the quality of the air we breathe and the water we drink are affected by decisions made by the business community. We have a large stake in those decisions, and we want to be informed of them and to know how they were made.

News about commerce is as old as the newspaper itself. The gazettes and newsletters of the 17th century were established in the business centers of Europe for the new commercial class that was emerging. Traditionally, business news has been aimed at this mercantile class. In recent years, a revolution has occurred in the coverage of business and economic news. Though it seems obvious that everyone would have a great interest in pocketbook news—news of the economy—editors came lately to the realization.

One of the causes of this awakening was the consumer movement in the 1970s that resulted in a new kind of coverage for television and for many newspapers— consumer journalism. Reacting to what appeared to be an attitude of *caveat emptor* (let the buyer beware) among U.S. businesses, newspapers and broadcast stations went out into the marketplace to find out why the quality of goods and services was declining while prices were steadily rising.

Curiosity, if not skepticism, about business was strong. Consumers were irritated by products that fell apart too soon and too often, and they were infuriated by the indifference of manufacturers, sellers, repairmen and mechanics.

The environmental movement also turned public attention, and then media attention, to the board rooms of corporations. An awareness of corporate responsibility developed "to a degree that was unheard of a decade or two ago," said Tom Johnson, publisher of the *Los Angeles Times*.

Johnson said that "the decisions of the business community . . . have become more important than ever in the past . . . business news has become page one news because of the emergence of highly controversial issues in which there is an obvious potential for conflict between the corporate and the public interest."

Johnson described some of the "complex and volatile issues" in recent years that intruded into the public consciousness:

> The safety and siting of nuclear power plants and the disposal of nuclear waste . . . proposals for off-shore oil drilling . . . demands for the opening of public lands to resource development . . . deregulation, safety in the work place . . . the inequities of the tax structure.

Public awareness of the world of business was also heightened by the increasing ownership of stocks and bonds by the public. AT&T alone has more than 3 million shareholders and General Motors has more than 1 million shareholders.

In this chapter, we will be looking at business journalism. The next chapter, 26, will discuss consumer journalism.

The Scope of Business News

Friday night, Mr. and Mrs. Ryan sit down after dinner to make a decision. The birth of their second child has made their apartment too small for comfort. They will need another bedroom, a larger dining area. They must decide whether to rent a larger apartment, to buy a cooperative, a condominium or a house.

They reread their local newspaper's business section about mortgage rates. The reporter who wrote the article has surveyed the savings and loan associations and describes the going interest rate for home loans. He also quotes local and federal officials on the prospect of a decline in the interest rate. The prospect, he writes, is good. Interest rates will probably go down slightly over the next six months. But they are still high. The Ryans decide to rent until the rate falls some more.

Interest rates also are a concern of the Goldensohn family. Robert, a high school senior, wants to attend a private college. The tuition is high and he must have a student loan. His father, whose income meets the necessities and not much more, says that Robert may have to borrow at least $5,000 a year.

If they cannot handle the loan, Robert will have to attend the local community college. Their newspaper carries a story on the latest information about student loans and interest rates. The Goldensohns decide Robert will attend the community college.

In homes in every part of the city, people look to business stories for information that affects their lives. Workers whose contracts are tied to the cost of living watch the papers and television to see how their paycheck will be affected by the latest figures from Washington.

Oxford reports record earnings

By Robin Schatz
Staff Writer

Because of continuing healthy sales growth for its recession-resistant, high-priced clothing lines, Atlanta-based Oxford Industries Inc. chalked up record sales and earnings for its first fiscal quarter ended Aug. 27.

The apparel manufacturer reported profits of $5.6 million, or $1.94 per share, up 50.7 percent from $3.7 million, or $1.27 per share, for the same quarter last year. Sales were $126.8 million, a 25.8 percent increase from $100.7 million last year.

However, the company said it is expecting the dramatic sales growth in such designer lines as Ralph Lauren for Girls, Polo for Boys and Merona sportswear to begin slowing in subsequent quarters. Meanwhile, the sluggish economy, while leaving sales of designer labels unscathed, has reduced sales of popularly priced merchandise and private-label lines.

Oxford president J. Hicks Lanier said the company was "extremely pleased" with its first quarter results. He said significant gains were recorded in premium priced brands and designer-label lines.

"During the first quarter last year, these (premium) lines were in the early stages of the dramatic growth which they recorded during the year. While we will continue to have sales increases in these lines, the quarter-to-quarter comparative percentage gains will begin to slow in the second and succeeding quarters," Lanier said.

R. William Lee Jr., vice president of finance and administration, said the designer lines are higher margin items typically purchased by middle and upper income people "whose buying patterns are less affected by the general economic situation."

Lee said the up-scale lines had a very strong third and fourth quarter last year.

Farmers follow the livestock and commodity markets. Vacationers search through the list of foreign exchange rates to see what the dollar is worth abroad before deciding where to spend their vacation. Residents north of the city hear that a new shopping center will be built there; they look through the business pages to find out more about it.

Just about everyone works for a living or depends on someone who does. All of us have a need to know about what is happening in the business world.

Quarterly Report. Readers want to know how local businesses are doing, and their quarterly and annual reports supply that information. Here the Atlanta *Constitution* gives its readers information about a local clothing manufacturer.

The Beat

The business reporter ranges widely. In the morning, he or she may be assigned to interview local service station dealers on a price war, and that afternoon the reporter will have to localize a story about the new prime rate or the failure of the coffee crop in Brazil.

Local stories include:

Store openings, expansions and closings.
Real estate transactions. New products from local enterprises. Construction
  projects planned.
Plants opened, expanded, closed. Labor-management relations. Union
  elections. Personnel changes, awards, retirements. Layoffs, bankruptcies.
Annual and quarterly business reports. Annual meetings.

In addition to these spot news stories, the business reporter is aware of trends and developments in the community and area. The business reporter has a sense of the relationship between, for example, the prime rate and the local housing market. The business reporter understands how the city's parking policies can help or hurt downtown merchants.

The more the newspaper or station stresses local news, the more detailed these stories will be. In small communities the line between news and free advertising is so narrow it approaches invisibility. A large department store that is opening in the center of town will be covered by the biggest newspapers. But a drug store opening will not. The smaller newspaper or station will probably carry the drug store opening, and might even run a story about the enlargement of a hardware store.

Merchants want news stories of this kind, and sometimes enthusiastic advertising sales people promise a new or regular advertiser a story about a store expansion or about the cashier who has spent 25 years behind the Hamburger Heaven

Two Types of Companies

Publicly held—Company owned by investors who bought its stock. Stock is traded on exchange or market where its price or market value is determined by what investers pay to own it. Must file documents with SEC and publish annual reports, which are sources of information for reporter.

Privately or closely held—Company is usually controlled by a small group or a family. Stock is not publicly traded on an exchange. Value is set by owners. Information is difficult to obtain. Company may be regulated by state or federal agency, which will have some information about it.

Tailor Frank Saporito opens shop on Fenn St.

By Bob McDonough

For 10 years, tailor Frank Saporito plied his trade with Davis & Norton Inc. on North Street here, where he was in charge of all alterations. When that business closed last month, Saporito was out of work — but not for long.

Saporito landed on his feet and decided to go into business for himself at 251 Fenn St., just across the street from the post office. He's been open there a little more than a week.

"I wanted to try it by myself," Saporito said. "I think it's a good move. I sure hope so."

Native of Sicily

A native of Gela, Sicily, Saporito spent two years studying in Rome, earning a diploma in design. "You need a diploma in Italy," Saporito said. "You've got to know how to make a suit,

not just alterations like here."

He opened his own shop in Gela in 1953 and operated it 10 years, employing six. In 1964, he came to this country with his wife, Angela, settling in Poughkeepsie, N.Y., where her brother lived. There, Saporito found work as a tailor with M. Shwartz & Co., a major clothing firm where he first met Warren A. Davis. When Davis was sent to Pittsfield in 1971 to run Shwartz's store here, Saporito also came. Davis and partner Thomas J. Norton bought the Shwartz store in 1973, and Saporito had been their head tailor ever since.

Machines were gift

When the store closed, Davis and Norton showed their appreciation for Saporito's dedication by giving him the machines and other fixtures he now uses in his new shop. That included several

thousand dollars worth of tables and machines that include a monogram machine, a blend stich machine and two sewing machines.

"This was my present because I worked very hard for these fine people," Saporito said.

Saporito said he had to do no major alteration to the office, which most recently housed the offices of chiropractors Henry J. Hogan and John J. Hunter. Saporito has his machines in the front of the office by the windows, and he has a fitting room and a storage room with a press in the back.

Likes the competition

Saporito said he realizes there are other tailors around, "But people see the difference in quality between my work and somebody else's — I love the competition." He is also counting on his loyal customers from

Davis & Norton days, plus an affiliation with local clothing stores who ship out their alteration assignments. Saporito said he will handle any alteration work on men's, women's and children's clothing.

Saporito and his wife have two daughters, Maria, a nursing student at Berkshire Community College, and Enza, a Pittsfield High senior.

Saporito's hours are Monday through Saturday from 8:30 a.m. to 5:30 p.m.

Store Opening. This three-column story about a new tailor shop ran in *The Berkshire Eagle*. Such local business stories are run frequently in small- and medium-sized newspapers.

checkout counter. When the publisher orders and the editor agrees to the story, the piece is known as a BOM (business office must). Even on larger newspapers or in stations, advertisers often put pressure on the news staff to run—or not to run—stories about them. News executives themselves, being important business people in the community, may order stories to be run because of their own interests.

Increasingly, media critics have condemned these stories as free advertising, and fewer and fewer newspapers are willing to risk censure. Still, it could be argued that some of these events can make good stories. The perceptive business reporter sent to interview the hardware merchant who is enlarging his store might find that the store owner is staking his last dime on this gamble to keep from losing business to the franchise hardware dealer in the big shopping center. And the cashier could become the human interest story of that day's newspaper or local news broadcast.

Yes, the business reporter also writes feature stories. And even the straight news story is increasingly being given a delayed lead in an attempt to featurize the news. The *Minneapolis Tribune's* story about the economic difficulties of International Harvester began this way:

> GLENCOE, Minn.—A year ago Kenneth and Byron Wacker decided it was time to circle the financial wagons.
> The farm economy was nose-diving, so they merged their International Harvester dealership in nearby Hutchinson, Minn., into the one they owned in Glencoe. . . .

Let's look at the kind of stories that appear on the business pages of newspapers:

The *Rockford* (Ill.) *Register Star*—New car sales for the first two months of the year in northern Illinois show a 29 percent drop from the preceding year.
The Des Moines Register—Despite widespread economic problems this spring, fewer Iowa farmers than normal have actually quit and sold out.
The New York Times—In a story from Kenosha, Wis., a staff correspondent reports American Motors is beginning production of a subcompact car in its final effort to remain a volume manufacturer of passenger cars.
Chicago Tribune—A profile of Charles T. Grant and the Fort Dearborn Paper Co., the $17 million-a-year paper converting firm Grant purchased through the Minority Enterprise Small Business Investment Companies Act. The firm is one of the 10 largest black-owned businesses in the United States.
The Nevada State Journal—Union Carbide's proposed Glad Bag plant in Stead will probably employ a large number of workers, but officials are not yet saying how many.
The Salt Lake Tribune—A comprehensive economic development plan is proposed to bring industry to Salt Lake City.

The Business Reporter

The business reporter is a specialist, which means that he or she has a detailed knowledge of a specific area or beat. Many business reporters prepared for their careers by studying economics and finance in college, and all have read in their field.

The business reporter feels at home with numbers and is not frightened off by lengthy reports and press releases, many of which contain rates, percentages, business and consumer indexes and the jargon of the business world.

The business reporter recognizes the power of business in society but has a healthy skepticism that keeps him or her from being in awe of the muscle and money that business power generates.

A Pro's Advice

Paul E. Steiger, financial editor of the *Los Angeles Times,* says that the business reporter's "central problem is that of steering the narrow path between talking down to our specialized readers and talking over the heads of our general ones." He offers the following principles as a guide to coping with this problem:

1. When in doubt, lean toward the general reader.
2. Avoid jargon, and explain that which is used.
3. Explain, but don't explain too much.
4. Page one stories require more explanation than those in the business section because page one stories are aimed at a wider audience.
5. Say what a trend or event means, as well as what it is.
6. Don't be afraid to translate and popularize. Even more than general assignment reporters, business and economic writers must use analogy, anecdote and personification to convey the essential reality of the subject they are covering.

Media and Business Elites

At first glance, the top men and women in journalism and business are alike. Many of the major companies are headed by white males from the northeast and north-central states. The media elite—those who work for the major newspapers, the three networks and the leading newsmagazines—is composed mainly of white males, most of whom are from northern industrial areas.

But here the similarities end, according to a study made by Professors S. Robert Lichter and Stanley Rothman, "Media and Business Elites," published in the October/November 1981 *Public Opinion.* The differences are often the cause of tension between the journalist and the business community.

Journalists are one of the best educated groups in the country; 93 percent have college degrees and 55 percent attended graduate school. Most were raised in upper-middle-class homes, and two of five are the children of professionals. On political, social and economic issues, journalists consider themselves liberals.

Business leaders, as might be expected, are considerably more conservative. In summing up their findings, Lichter said, "It's fair to say that you have more Horatio Alger stories in the boardroom than in the newsroom. They (business leaders) tend to come from less favored social backgrounds . . . they certainly tend to be politically more conservative, more likely to vote for Republican candidates, less critical of the American social system, less likely to reject traditional canons of morality, for example."

Given the liberalism of many journalists, it is not accidental that business leaders are wary of the journalist.

"In my mind, there's absolutely no question that there is bias," says Richard L. Lesher, president of the Chamber of Commerce of the United States. "I would also say that there's no question it's in a leftward direction, that it's a liberal bias, as opposed to a conservative bias when it comes to reporting business and economic news."

Lesher says he is convinced there is "an anti-business bias, and that may go back to the old adage that good news is not news, that we're always looking for something bad, something that we can be critical of."

Nevertheless, Lesher does not find the situation "absolutely terrible." He does not believe that there is "no balance whatsoever, ever, in the news."

The doubts that business people have about journalists are further compounded by the changing nature of business and economics coverage. Peter Kilborn, the former editor of the Sunday *New York Times* business section, says that in the past newspapers filled their business sections with stories about one corporation or businessman. "The stories tended to let the source tell the story," he says. "Now we go out and talk to the financial analysts and the competitors."

A. Kent MacDougall of the *Los Angeles Times* finds it ironic that the "business-press controversy is heating up at a time when some captains of industry and commerce, who were early, vocal critics of business news coverage, now credit journalists with increasing competence, sophistication and fairness."

MacDougall made an extensive examination of business complaints against the media for the *Times*. He found that newspaper and television coverage of business was often "simplistic, careless and cursory." But he found few cases of deliberate distortion and bias. In fact, he pointed out, business generally finds in the press an open conduit to the public, for business writers often use "a considerable amount of fluff supplied by businesses to promote food, fashions, travel, real estate, sports and stocks."

The business reporter has a harder job digging for information than most of his or her newsroom colleagues. Most reporters deal with public officials who live in a goldfish bowl—open to public scrutiny. Laws and a long tradition have made the public sector public.

The business world, however, is generally private, secretive and authoritarian. The head of a company can order his employees not to talk to reporters, and that's that. Since business people usually are in competition, secrecy is a natural part of business life. True, business is required to file many kinds of reports with various governmental agencies, and these are excellent sources of information. But in the day-to-day coverage of the beat, the business reporter must rely on human sources.

Human Sources

Good contacts and sources can be made among the following:

Bank officers, tellers.
Savings and loan officials.
Chamber of Commerce secretaries.
Union leaders.
Securities dealers.
Real estate brokers.
Trade organization officials.
Teachers of business, economics.
Transportation company officials.
Federal and state officials in agencies such as the Small Business
   Administration, Commerce Department, various regulatory agencies.

On first contact with a reporter, the business source is likely to be wary, says James L. Rowe Jr., New York financial correspondent of *The Washington Post.* "As a result, it is often difficult to gain the source's trust.

"But if the reporter does his or her homework, learns what motivates business people, is not afraid to ask the intelligent questions but doesn't have to ask the dumb one, more than enough sources will break down."

In developing these sources, the reporter will want to find men and women who can put events into perspective and who can clarify some of the complexities the reporter cannot fathom. Caution is important here. Not only must the sources be dependable, they must be independent of compromising connections and affiliations. Obviously, such sources are hard to find. The traditional independent source was the academician, the cloistered professor who had no financial stake in the matters he would comment about. But that has changed. Academicians now serve on the boards of banks, chemical companies and pesticide manufacturers. The alert reporter makes certain that background information from these sources is neither biased nor self-serving.

Sources are used in two ways—for quotations in the story and for background information. When quoting a source, note all of the person's business affiliations relevant to the story. In a banking story, it's not enough to say that Professor Thomas Graham teaches economics at the state university. His membership on the board of directors of the First National Bank should also be included.

The background source is rarely quoted, and so readers and viewers cannot assess the information in terms of the source's affiliations. Since background sources exercise great influence over reporters, providing perspective, the independence of these sources is essential. Good background sources can be found without leaving the office. The accountants, marketing people and the legal adviser to the newspaper or station can figure out some of the complexities of reports and documents. They also are close to the business community and know what is going on.

The business office has access to the local credit bureau and the facilities of Dun and Bradstreet, which can provide confidential information. These can be helpful in running a check on a local business.

Chris Welles, director of the Walter Bagehot Fellowship Program in Economics and Business Journalism at Columbia University, says that when he is assigned to do a story about a company he always lets the company know. Often, the public relations staff will set up interviews with the people he wants to reach.

"By far the most important sources on company stories are former executives," Welles writes in an article, "The Craft of the Business Reporter," that appeared in the May 1982 *Folio* magazine. "Unconstrained by the fear of being fired if word gets out that they talked to you, they can be extremely forthcoming about their former employer."

Welles is cautious about the information from these sources, which he says is mostly negative. He verifies all facts such sources give him. Opinions and comments are not too useful, he has found.

Competitors are another good source, as are suppliers, the managers of investment portfolios, bankers and others who are likely to know the company's financial situation.

In dealing with sources, Welles often confesses his problems in unearthing material. "Most people are predisposed to respond favorably to someone who, in a non-threatening way, asks for a little help." Wells says during interviews he listens "with great interest and sympathy." He says that "sources have a great deal of trouble terminating a conversation with someone who seems to be hanging on their every word."

Welles finds sources for company stories often request anonymity. He is willing to grant it, and he sticks to his word. Reporters who don't keep their word find their sources soon dry up.

Speak to a lot of people, he says. Look through as many documents as possible. In short, "Work your tail off."

Physical Sources

At the local level, reporters should know how to use city and county tax records. The assessor's office has the valuation of real property and of the physical plant and equipment—whatever is taxed. The sales tax can show how much business is being done by the firm that the reporter is checking. Many local governments issue business licenses on which the principals involved are named and other information is given.

State governments also issue business licenses. There are scores of state boards that license barbers, engineers, cosmetologists, doctors, morticians, lawyers, accountants and so on. These agencies usually keep basic information about the businesses they oversee.

The state corporation commission or the secretary of state will have the names, addresses and sometimes the stock held by directors of corporations incorporated in the state and firms that do a large amount of business in the state. The company's articles of incorporation and by-laws are also on file.

The state usually regulates banks, savings and loan institutions, insurance companies and public utilities. The state agencies handle rate applications and oversee operational procedures. Basic information about these businesses is available to the journalist.

Reporters also use the records and documents on file with the federal government.

Federal Records

For companies with $1 million in assets and at least 500 stockholders, the Securities and Exchange Commission requires regular reports. Some 10,000 companies file such reports, listed in the annual *Directory of Companies Required to File Annual Reports* (Superintendent of Documents, U.S. Government Printing Office, Washington, D.C., 20402; $4.75). To obtain the directory and other reports write: Public Reference Section, Securities and Exchange Commission, 450 Fifth St. N.W., Washington, D.C. 20549. For general information, call 202 272–2650.

Among the SEC reports available are the 10-K, which many reporters use because it includes the company's finances, ownership, major contracts, management history, salaries and other monies paid the major officers.

Welles, who has been writing about business and economics for 20 years, says that when he is to write about a company the first step he takes is to obtain three basic documents: The 10-K, the annual report and the proxy statement. Like the 10-K, the other two are available from the SEC.

Welles describes the annual report as "a kind of public relations version of the 10-K." Welles says that "no single body of information is more crucial to the understanding of a corporation than its financial statements." We will be looking at the annual report in detail later in this chapter.

The third must item on Welles's list is the proxy statement. This SEC-mandated document is sent to all stockholders before an annual meeting. It contains the salaries and stockholdings of most senior executives. The statement also lists any deals between the firm and its management or directors. Other useful documents are the 8-K, which is filed for important company activities such as a merger, and the 10-Q, a quarterly report with information like the annual 10-K.

Non-profit organizations must file Form 990 with the Internal Revenue Service. The report includes information on the income and expenses of officials of the organizations. The expenses can be illuminating. Often, a small part of the money raised by the organization is used for charity or for whatever other purpose the organization raises money.

SEC material can be obtained from regional SEC offices. Companies usually send on request their 10-K, proxy statement and annual report.

FOIA

Brian Donovan used the Freedom of Information Act to obtain a study made by the Department of Energy of gasoline company activities during the 1979 oil crisis. The study, which had not been released by the department, revealed that Mobil and Gulf had plenty of gasoline at a time they were saying they had short supplies.

Donovan investigated petroleum policies as an Alicia Patterson Fellow. (The fellowships are awarded to U.S. print journalists with five years of professional experience.) In his article in the Summer 1982 *APF Reporter* entitled "Cutting Back," Donovan writes:

WASHINGTON, D.C.—While motorists waited in lines during the 1979 oil crisis, Mobil and Gulf made sharp cuts in gasoline allocations that were not consistent with their ample stocks of gasoline and crude oil, an unpublished government study shows.

Department of Energy officials used a computer to analyze confidential company supply data and found that although Mobil and Gulf were not short of oil, they imposed gasoline allocation cutbacks similar to those of companies that were suffering shortages.

The study adds new information to the controversy over oil companies' role in the crisis, which started with a temporary halt in Iranian oil exports and resulted in a doubling of world oil prices. Although the study does not impute motives to the companies, its findings add support to the arguments of critics who contend that oil industry actions during the crisis helped prolong the market panic that encouraged the Organization of Petroleum Exporting Countries (OPEC) to keep raising its prices.

Gulf and Mobil spokesmen criticized the study, calling it misleading. . . .

Donovan's investigative work on the lessons of the 1979 oil crisis led to a special citation for financial reporting from the Deadline Club, the New York City chapter of the Society of Professional Journalists.

Daily reading of *The Wall Street Journal* is necessary for the business reporter. The student may want to study the *Journal's* style. Written for business people and those with some involvement in financial matters, the stories nevertheless are written in layman's language. The newspaper is both record-keeper for the business community and its watchdog. Its investigative reporting is among the best in the country.

Business Week, a weekly business news magazine, is staffed by journalists with a good command of business, finance and economics. The magazine concentrates on the major industries and companies. Its long articles are aimed at the men and women who are in executive posts in business, though, of course, it has many other kinds of readers.

Forbes is addressed to investors, people who own stock in companies. The *Journal, Business Week,* and *Forbes* are pro-business. Though they do go after the bad apples in the barrel, they never question the barrel, the system itself, as former *Journal* staffer Kent MacDougall puts it. The most pro-business publication is *Nation's Business,* which is published by the U.S. Chamber of Commerce and the National Association of Manufacturers.

There are a great variety of trade publications, magazines and newspapers that cover a particular business or trade. The reporter who specializes in one area will be a regular reader of the trade publications in his or her field.

Reading

"Because trade journalists write for people who know the industry," says Professor Warren Burkett of the University of Texas at Austin, "the facts, figures and quotations generally will be accurate. It's the interpretations of the material that you must watch out for. These often are given in light of what is best financially for most companies, as the editors see it.

"This does not invalidate the use of these publications as sources for the facts, figures and quotations."

References

A good local library or any business school library at a college or university will have the following references that business reporters find useful:

Dun and Bradstreet Directories—One covers companies with capital under $1 million; another is for those whose capital exceeds $1 million.
Who Owns Whom—To find the parent company of a firm you are checking.
Standard & Poor's Register of Corporations, Directors and Executives.
Moody's Manuals.

Regulatory Agencies

All levels of government regulate business. Local laws prescribe health, fire and safety regulations to which businesses must adhere. The city grants franchises and checks to see that the provisions are followed, such as those requiring public access to the local cable company. Regional and county governments set standards for factory emissions.

Note: Some of these agencies may take their cases to court. The business reporter should know how to use the documents in civil, criminal and bankruptcy courts.

At the state level, the licensing boards also regulate the trades and professions they license. Usually, they have the power to investigate complaints and to hold hearings. Although most of these boards are creatures of the fields they regulate, occasionally a board will act decisively. Of course, failure to take action is an even better story, as one reporter learned when the board regulating veterinarians failed to hold a hearing for a veterinarian who was the subject of a number of complaints by pet owners whose dogs and cats had died in his care.

Although most federal regulatory agencies are in Washington and too distant for personal checking, a local business reporter can ask the newspaper's Washington bureau or the AP or UPI to run something down. These agencies compile considerable material about companies and individuals seeking permission to operate interstate. Some agencies:

Interstate Commerce Commission (ICC)—regulates trucking companies, railroads, freight carriers, oil pipelines and express agencies.
Federal Communications Commission (FCC)—regulates radio and television stations. Ownership and stock information are available.
National Labor Relations Board (NLRB)—is concerned with labor disputes.

Business pumps out vast quantities of information for newspapers and broadcast stations, some of which is useful to the business and economics reporter. Naturally, much of the information is laudatory, and certainly it is narrow, focusing on the business or industry that sent out the release. The business reporter has to dig deeper and look more widely for news.

Don Moffitt, a veteran reporter with *The Wall Street Journal,* says that business reporters "should consider that they have a license to inquire into the nuts and bolts of how people make a living and secure their well-being.

"For a local paper, the fortunes of the community's barbers, auto mechanics, bankers and public servants are business stories. Business is how people survive."

Moffitt believes in personalizing the news about business and economic affairs.

"If people are falling behind in their mortgage payments, write about individuals in the community and show how and why they are falling behind, how they feel about it and what they're trying to do about it," he says.

"Local government financing and spending is, in part, a business story. Who's making money off the local bond issues, and why? Is the bank keeping the county's low-interest deposits and using the cash to buy the county's high-yielding paper? Who suffers when the township cuts the budget, or can't increase it? Show how they suffer."

The Wall Street Journal is an excellent model for journalists aspiring to cover business. Its longer stories usually stress the human angle, the consequences of events and decisions. In a story on the shortage of low-priced office space, the *Journal* began its piece this way:

> Paul Jones wasn't looking for anything plush, just 7,500 to 10,000 square feet of office space in New York's lower Manhattan financial district for his J. P. Sedlak Associates Inc. data processing firm.

The story went on to tell of Jones's fruitless search and the problems of others looking for office space they could afford.

Among the vast quantities of material the business reporter receives are the newsletters and reports from various trade associations. These can be good sources for enterprise stories.

James R. Toland developed an interesting story about beer consumption in California for the San Francisco *Chronicle* by picking up a trade association report. His story began this way:

> The race to win California's beer drinkers is tightening up.
> Adolph Coors is still leading the derby but Anheuser Busch is making steady gains to capture the No. 1 spot.

Jay Bryan, one of 10 business reporters at *The Gazette* in Montreal, received a brief press release from a copper company announcing the shutdown of its mine and smelter in Murdochville, about 100 miles outside the newspaper's major circulation area.

"Normally, such a story wouldn't merit much space at a time when major layoffs are common," Bryan said, especially when the event is outside the paper's readership area.

"What made the difference in this case was that the impact on the local community appeared to be devastating," he said. He made several telephone calls—to the mayor, company officials at the mine and others—and he developed a story that began:

> Canada's recession arrived in the small Gaspé town of Murdochville full force Wednesday when nearly half the workers at the only big company in town found out they were out of work for as long as it takes for the economy to recover.

Always go beyond the press release, business reporters say. When a $69 million dollar reconstruction job at a shopping center was announced, the developers sent out stacks of press releases. By asking why so much money was being spent, Bryan learned that sales at the center had sharply declined recently—a fact not mentioned in any of the releases.

Steve Lipson, business news writer for *The Times-News* in Twin Falls, Idaho, says he develops ideas for stories by a simple technique—keeping his eyes open.

"I read ads. I notice changes in the businesses where I shop. I count the number of cars in a car dealer's lot, and I look at what people wear, eat and drink," Lipson says.

He says that imagination is important, too. "I look for unique stories," he says. He did one on the growing popularity of potato-skin appetizers. "This big boost to potato consumption would land someone in the Idaho Hall of Fame if anyone knew who was responsible. Alas, my story found no one really knows why the dish suddenly became chic."

Lipson knows that local merchants usually put a good face on business conditions. "So I asked a team of Yellow Page ad salesmen for their summary of the local business mood after they finished a 10-week selling blitz in the area and had talked to virtually every retailer in town."

Here is the beginning of Lipson's story:

> TWIN FALLS—Before people can let their fingers do the walking, Mountain Bell sends salesmen through town selling those advertisements found in the Yellow Pages.
>
> The salesmen, instead of relying on their fingers, do most of their work by car, foot and phone. Yet by the time they finish, their fingers have a good feel for the local business pulse.
>
> The Mountain Bell directory sales crew spent about 10 weeks in Twin Falls during November, December and January. The salesmen visited more than 1,000 businesses while preparing the directory. What they found is that the pulse remains strong, although the patient is weaker.

Agri/Business

Building permits
Building permits for new homes issued by Twin Falls city or county officials.

Jobless rate
Seasonally adjusted unemployment rate for Twin Falls, Jerome and Gooding counties—Oct., 1981, to Sept., 1982. Dashed line is previous year's rate.

Farm price index
A Magic Valley commodity price index.

September 24, 1982 — 75.12%
September 25, 1981 — 85.33%
November 14, 1980 (base date — 100%)

Interest rates
Prevailing national prime interest rate and monthly average of maximum interest paid on $10,000 certificates of deposit.

Home sales
Homes sold by Realtors in Twin Falls County. Source: The Twin Falls Board of Realtors.

Utility activity
Net change during the quarter in the number of electric customers, active phone numbers and natural gas users in Twin Falls County. Source: Utilities.

Auto sales
New car and truck sales to Twin Falls County residents.

Help wanted ads
A measure of Times-News help wanted advertising.

Bank deposits
Total deposits in bank or savings and loan branches within Twin Falls city limits. Source: Financial institutions.

3rd quarter, 1982 — $361,378,454
3rd quarter, 1981 — $336,285,740

Market basket
An average cost of a basket of goods at three local markets.

$56.24 — 3rd quarter 1981
$60.28 — 3rd quarter 1982

Hints of an upturn during 3rd quarter

By STEVE LIPSON
Times-News writer

TWIN FALLS — An evil spell that gripped the local economy for three quarters may have been broken during the third quarter of this year.

A group of Times-News economic indicators show that high interest rates, low farm commodity prices and the national recession continue to constrain economic activity in the Magic Valley. But unlike the previous three quarters — when every indicator added another reason for doom, gloom and despair — some figures showed improvement during the most recent quarter.

The change in July, August and September could mark the bottom of the local recession. Or it might signal the first stirrings of a recovery. But it might also be a meaningless blip — a repeat of the third quarter of 1981, when the indicators showed similar mixed results, which proved to be only a pause in the downward course of the indicators and the local economy.

Perhaps it is fitting that there are three possible explanations for what happened in the third quarter, since the number "three" is important to this quarter's economic report for one more reason. The local economy's signs of strength came from three indicators.

The Times-News economic report

With these quarterly business reviews, the Times-News hopes to increase understanding of the local economy.

Analysis

Auto sales to Twin Falls County residents by the county's auto dealers grew almost 10 percent from the third quarter of 1981. County registration records show 837 sales for the 1982 quarter, compared with 763 during the same period last year.

This increase reverses the trend of the first six months of this year, which saw sales decline 16 percent, compared with the first six months of the previous year.

But sales for the year are still down compared with last year. In the first three quarters of this year, car sales are 8.4 percent behind sales in the comparable period of 1981.

The number of building permits issued by Twin Falls city and county officials for new homes jumped during the quarter, to 48 permits, compared with 19 during the same three months of 1981.

The estimated value of the new construction is slightly more than $2 million, which is slightly less than double the figure from the previous year. The cause of the building surge was a burst of low-cost federal money that was made available, nationwide, for new homes on a first-come, first-served basis for about a month, starting in the middle of August.

The third positive indicator during the past quarter comes from a group of three figures that summarize utility activity. But there was some devilment at work in this index. Several of the numbers showed sizable increases, but there was no ready explanation for the changes. Likewise, during the third quarter of 1981, utility activity seemed to increase without apparent reason. The records of the utilities fail to suggest what accounts for this seemingly seasonal surge.

One thing that did not cause it, however, was the increase in housing starts. All but a few of the homes were started too late in the quarter to be ready for utility service.

While the spell from the past may have been broken by these indicators, some skeletons from the economic closet remained during the third quarter.

Area unemployment stayed at near-record levels throughout the quarter. The

•See ECONOMY on Page D8

Commentators are, from left, Tom Courtney, Bill Babcock, Dick Converse, Mike Dolton and Bill Kyle

Optimism, caution combined in opinions of commentators

By STEVE LIPSON
Times-News writer

TWIN FALLS — No one would accuse the panel of commentators assembled to add their views to this quarterly economic report of being overly optimistic.

Despite projections for strong local growth from new industries and expansion of some local businesses, they were cautious. Their modest hope is that the economy will return to the employment levels and growth rates it had several years ago.

The obvious bright spot in the local economy is the E.F. Johnson Co. and his plans to manufacture cellular telephones in Twin Falls. Industry analysts say the new technology, mobile-communications systems could increase demand for mobile phones by 100 times before the end of the decade.

If those projections are accurate — and if E.F. Johnson gets the share of this market it expects — this growth will produce thousands of jobs in Twin Falls

during that time.

"Most of the projections indicate the equipment we will be making in Twin Falls won't really start to move until possibly late 1983," says Dick Converse, who will manage the company's Twin Falls plant.

Current plans call for production of other radio communications equipment to start in Twin Falls early in 1983. The company will employ about 60 people then. By the end of the year, when it begins production of the first cellular units in Twin Falls, it probably will employ about 120, Converse says.

The company expects to have 500 to 1,000 employees in Twin Falls within three to five years, and perhaps 2,000 by 1990.

And each of those jobs will create two or three additional jobs in the local economy, Converse says.

Some businesses that supply materials for E.F. Johnson may choose to start new operations in Twin Falls, he says. Conventional services, such as financial institutions, schools, travel services and more

probably will have to expand.

"If we bring 1,000 people in, that says there are going to be 2,000 to 3,000 other jobs created," he says. "A lot of the services that we need, a lot of them are existing services. It's difficult to project when they will become taxed to the extent that they have to be added to, at what point that becomes another schoolteacher, policeman or another clerk at City Hall."

While saying that E.F. Johnson is "the shot in the arm we've needed," Bill Babcock finds it hard to shrug off the problems he sees in other sectors of the local economy.

Babcock, the manager of one of Idaho First National Bank's branches in Twin Falls, says that deposit and loan growth have slowed in Twin Falls. And for the economy's mainstay, agriculture, times are about as tough as he can recall.

Magic Valley farmers produce diverse crops, which has always helped shield the economy in the past, he says. When the

•See PANEL on Page D3

Panel presents 'trick or treat' view of growth in Twin Falls

TWIN FALLS — In honor of Halloween, this quarter's panel of economic commentators could be called a "trick-or-treat" panel.

The panel members were picked to discuss the robust economic growth Twin Falls may be treated to in the near future because of such things as the recruitment of the E.F. Johnson Co. and the recent $835,000 economic-development grant awarded to the city.

E.F. Johnson forecasts say the company might hire 1,000 people here within four or five years. And the state-administered economic grant is expected to help provide 350 jobs by building roads, sewers, a railroad spur and other improvements on a 20-acre industrial site owned by the Twin Falls Chamber of Commerce.

But the trick, according to the panel members, is that the first few years of this projected growth will be needed simply to return the community to the level of business it enjoyed in the late 1970s.

The last few years have really been lean years as far as the number of jobs," said panel member Tom Courtney, the Twin Falls city manager. His job is to see that the city is prepared to supply services to new industries and the expanding population they can bring.

Another panel member made the same point when he said his profits peaked during 1977 and 1978. Bill Kyle, the owner of the McDonald's franchise in Twin Falls and Burley, looks forward to economic growth and the population growth it can

bring because that is the only way he can expect to see significant sales growth.

More months to feed would mean more Big Macs sold.

"It's just a numbers game," Kyle says.

Other panel members were:

• Mike Dolton, the executive director of the Twin Falls Chamber of Commerce, who helped lead the recruitment effort that brought E.F. Johnson to Twin Falls.

• Dick Converse, who will manage E.F. Johnson's subsidiary, U.S. Communications Corp., when it starts production in Twin Falls early next year.

• Bill Babcock, the manager of Idaho First National Bank's branch off Blue Lakes Boulevard North and a member of the chamber's board of directors.

Local Indicators. Business reporter Steve Lipson takes the pulse of the local economy every quarter. His survey includes 10 economic indicators and the comments of a panel of local people.

Lipson developed a local economic report that runs every three months. He put together 10 economic indicators "by examining various economic reports prepared by federal and state agencies and private forecasters, then by looking around the community to see what kind of figures were available locally. I talked with bankers and businessmen who were involved in any kind of forecasting to find out what indicators they liked to use."

His local data include building permits, farm price index, home sales, utility activity (changes in the number of electric, phone and natural gas users), auto sales, help wanted ads in *The Times-News* and deposits in local banks and savings institutions.

In a sidebar, he has a panel of business people talk about business conditions. The panel changes each quarter.

Consumer Price Index

Another resource that can be put to good use by the business reporter is the Consumer Price Index (CPI), a statistical measure of changes in prices of goods and services put together monthly by the Bureau of Labor Statistics. The index represents price changes for everything people buy and pay for—food, clothing, automobiles, rent, home furnishings, fuel and energy, recreational goods, fees to doctors, beauty shops and so on.

The Bureau calculates monthly indexes for the country and for five major areas. Bimonthly indexes are published for 23 areas. When the CPI goes up, it means that the dollar is buying less. In February, 1983, in the northeast, the index stood at 283.2, which meant that $28.32 was required to buy what $10 could purchase in February 1967, which is used as the base period. (1967 = 100.)

Honesty and Realism

In journalism's old days, newspapers turned away from unpleasant business news. The business news pages believed in boosterism. The credo was: If you can't boost, don't knock. But the professionalization of journalism has led journalists to give the same careful scrutiny to business as to other news.

When the recession of the 1980s hit many areas of the country, newspapers looked deeply at the consequences. The *Buffalo Evening News* decided to study the city's economic condition. "With declining neighborhoods, declining population, and all the attendant problems, we decided to look at the Buffalo of the future," said Murray Light, the editor. The view was not pleasant. But the newspaper did not shrink from facing up to reality. The first article of the five-part series began:

> Buffalo will never again be what it once was.

Light said that the newspaper "drew a good deal of heat" from the Chamber of Commerce and other local business boosters. But, he added, "it demonstrated to our readers that we cannot bury our heads in the sand and that it isn't all bad to be a smaller city."

Optimistic annual business surveys used to be the rule for the newspaper's year-end business section. No more. The *Akron* (Ohio) *Beacon Journal* produced an innovative 13-part series that compared the recession of the 1980s to Akron's boom period, 1910–1920, and to the Depression of the 1930s.

Many students are attracted to journalism because it is concerned with people and how they get along with each other. These students are interested in the qualitative aspect of life. Journalism, with its feature stories and its emphasis on human interest, can use the talents these students take to the job. But much of what we know about the world—and people—is derived from quantitative studies. We know something about why people vote from the polls we take. The introduction of the computer into the newsroom has allowed journalists to analyze complicated situations for news stories, for example, how judges treat defendants of different races and economic status.

The student who is thinking about a career in business journalism—and this is one area of journalism that never seems to have enough reporters and editors—cannot manage without some ability to deal with numbers. If business is the bottom line, then the student thinking of becoming a business reporter has to know what to make of the numbers on the line.

The ability to blend the qualitative and the quantitative is essential to the business journalist. Numbers alone do say a lot, but when these barometers are put alongside human beings, they take on dramatic significance. When home loan applications go down (quantitative), the reporter finds a family like the Ryans we met a while back and shows why this family decided against a home loan (qualitative).

Let's look at an example of a story the business reporter handles that is concerned primarily with figures. In our list of stories with which the business reporter deals we mentioned annual reports.

Numbers and More Numbers

The business reporter must be able to swim through a sea of figures toward the few pieces of essential information in the report. Annual reports are issued by companies that are public. Newspapers usually run a summary of the annual reports of industries and businesses in their readership area. Readers want to know the economic health of the companies that employ local people, and some may own stock in these firms. Many readers want to know about the status of the well-known firms that have large numbers of shares of stock distributed nationwide—IBM, Kodak, General Motors, Polaroid, AT&T, Ford, General Electric. These readers may be shareholders—more than half the adult population owns stock—or they may be planning to invest in stocks.

Annual Reports

What to Look For

First off, read the auditor's report, which is usually at the back. "Generally, if the Auditor's Report is two paragraphs long, the financial statements have been given a clean bill of health," says the American Institute of Certified Public Accountants. "Anything longer—an extra paragraph or so—and normally that's a red flag alerting you to look further."

Jane Bryant Quinn, CBS business commentator, suggests that annual report readers watch out for the words "subject to" in the auditor's report.

"They mean the financial report is clean *only* if you take the company's word about a particular piece of business, and the accountant isn't sure you should," she says.

The CPA Institute has a general caution about the auditor's report: "All it means is that the financial statements are fairly presented in conformity with generally accepted accounting principles." It doesn't mean that the company is in great financial shape, or even adequate condition. All it means is that the books are kept properly.

Next, skim through the footnotes, says Quinn. Sometimes they explain the figures that seem surprising, even alarming. Earnings might be down. But the footnote may explain that the company has applied a policy of accelerated depreciation on plants and other equipment. "This," says the CPA Institute, "could reduce earnings, while a slower depreciation rate could boost earnings."

Here, it is important to point out that the good story will compare the current annual report with previous reports. Trends can be spotted in the five- and ten-year financial summaries.

Next, look at the letter from the chairman or the president's report. This is in front of the annual report and usually is frank—that is, if it adheres to the standards set by the CPA Institute. Usually, the statement is a candid summary of the past year and of prospects.

The Figures

The figure in which most people are interested is "earnings per share," also called "net income per common share." This is the bottom line, a sign of the company's health. It is, in effect, the profit the company has made. It is computed by dividing the total earnings by the number of shares outstanding. The CPA Institute says that slight year-to-year changes can be ignored. Look for the trend in the five- and ten-year summaries. "If the EPS either remains unchanged or drops off, this may pinpoint trouble ahead," it says.

Be careful about net earnings per share. A sudden increase can come from selling a plant or cutting advertising or research, says Quinn. The footnotes will explain unusual increases if they have unusual causes. A sudden decrease can come from a change in the number of shares, a stock split or a new issue—which is also noted in the report.

Next, look for the figures on working capital. "This is regarded as an important index of a company's condition because it reports whether operations generate enough cash to meet payroll, buy raw materials and conduct all the other essential day-to-day operations of the company," says the CPA Institute.

Table 25.1 Net Income per Common Share

	1983	1982	% Change
Net sales from continuing operations	$671,227,000	$601,960,000	+ 11.5
Income from continuing operations..............	$36,031,000	$43,685,000	− 17.5
Income from discontinued operations..........	—	$1,112,000	—
Gain on sale of discontinued operations	$5,300,000	—	—
Net income..	$41,331,000	$44,797,000	− 7.7
Net income per common share Continuing operations..................................	$2.62	$3.18	− 17.6
Discontinued operations	—	$.08	—
Gain on sale of discontinued operations	$.39	—	—
Net income per common share	$3.01	$3.26	− 7.7
Dividends per common share.......................	$1.14	$1.03	+ 10.7
Cash dividends paid	$15,251,225	$13,736,454	+ 11.0
Capital expenditures...................................	$27,535,000	$20,722,000	+ 32.9
Stockholders' equity...................................	$259,668,000	$233,529,000	+ 11.2
Equity per common share at year end.........	$18.91	$17.02	+ 11.1
Outstanding common shares at year end ...	13,730,288	13,720,186	—

Net income per common share is a sign of the company's health. Business reporters look for this figure in annual reports.

Table 25.2 Consolidated Statements of Changes in Financial Position

	1983	1982
Continuing Operations: Net income	$36,030,608	$43,685,180
Depreciation	7,994,778	7,538,977
Deferred income taxes.................................	4,824,703	1,313,933
Total provided from continuing operations...........	48,850,094	52,538,090

After all the expenses have been met, the company uses part of its net income to pay dividends. These are paid from net working capital, and if this figure (net working capital) shrinks consistently from year to year, even quarter to quarter, it is a sign the company may "not be able to keep dividends growing rapidly," says Quinn.

Look over the record of dividends as well as the current dividend. Is there a trend? Here is a five-year period of dividends:

Dividends per common share	1983	1982	1981	1980	1979
	$1.14	$1.03	$1	$.99	$.91

This firm shows a steady climb in dividends over the past five years. However, the business reporter will note that although the 1983 dividend is larger than the previous year's dividend, the company's net earnings per share were down. (See table 25.1.) In other words, the company plowed less of its earnings back into the firm in 1983 than it did in 1982 in order to keep the dividends on an upward course.

The business reporter should write to companies in his or her area and ask to be placed on their mailing list for annual and quarterly reports. If these reports raise questions, call the company for clarification. If the report indicates the company is in trouble, it is necessary to obtain comments from company officials, the accountants, shareholders and any public agencies that may be involved.

A number of organizations study and rate companies and issue regular reports. Value Line, for example, keeps track of 1,700 companies. It summarizes on a single page the relevant financial data about each of these companies. Standard & Poor's and Moody's also publish investment advisories that are useful to the business reporter.

Some tips:

- Well-managed companies should have at least twice the amount in current assets as they have in current liabilities.
- Avoid advising readers to buy or sell any particular stock. This is called "touting," and to offer such advice you must be registered with the SEC, as some advisory services are. Some reporters who have given such advice have been fined.
- Be careful of press releases about new products or developments. These may be planted to drive up the price of a certain stock. After a while, says Warren Burkett, a business reporter learns which are the trustworthy and responsible sources and which are trying to use the media.

For further information about how to read an annual report, write the CPA Institute, 1211 Avenue of the Americas, New York City, N.Y., 10036, and ask for the booklet, "What Else Can Financial Statements Tell You?"

Stock Tables

The business reporter sometimes needs to check the current price or the dividend of a stock listed on one of the exchanges. Here are a few stocks listed on the New York Stock Exchange and a guide to understanding the symbols:

High	Low	Stock	Div.	Yld %	P-E Ratio	Sales 100s	High	Low	Close	Net Chg.
[1] **63¼**	**49**	[2] **ATT**	[3] **5.40**	8.8	7	10740	61½	60	61½	+1
53½	29½	Gannett	1.72	[4] **3.2**	[5] **16**	1833	53	51¼	53	+¼
45¼	36	GMot [6] **pf**	5	11	. . .	[7] **7**	45½	45	45	. . .
38½	24⅛	GulfOil	2.80	8.2	6	1190	**34¼** [8]	**33**	34⅛	+¼
10¼	6	Playboy	.12	1.5	. . .	158	8	7¾	**8** [9]	+⅛

1. The highest and the lowest price the stock has sold for in the the past 52 weeks.

2. Abbreviated name of the corporation that lists the stock. Stocks are common stocks unless an entry after the name indicates otherwise.

3. The rate of the annual dividend. When a letter follows the dividend, a box at the bottom of the stock table is consulted as a reference.

4. This is the dividend paid by the company expressed as a percentage of the current price of the stock. A stock that sells for $50 at the current market value and that is paying a dividend at the rate of $2 a year is said to return or to have a yield of 4 percent. In the example of Gannett above, the closing price of 53 divided by the dividend of $1.72 results in the yield percentage of 3.2.

5. P-E Ratio stands for the price-earnings ratio. The price of a share of stock is divided by the earnings per share over a 12-month period. A stock selling for $50 a share with annual earnings of $5 a share is selling at the price-earnings ratio of 10 to 1. The P-E ratio is 10.

6. pf following the name indicates a preferred stock. Usually, preferred stock entitles stockholders to a specified rate of dividends, here $5 a year. Holders of preferred stock are entitled to a claim on the company's earnings before dividends may be paid to holders of common stock.

7. The number of shares traded this day for the stock, listed in 100's. Here, 700 shares of General Motors preferred stock were sold.

8. The highest price paid for this stock during the day's trading was $34.25. The lowest price paid was $33.

9. The closing price, or the price of the stock on the last sale of the trading day. Here, the closing price was $8 a share. The closing price was up 12½ cents (1/8 of a dollar) from the closing price of the previous day.

Annual Meetings   The annual meetings of most companies are prosaic affairs. Often held in some out-of-the-way place to discourage small shareholders from asking embarrassing or troublesome questions, the big companies have well-programmed meetings. The news story is usually based on an announcement by the president, chairman or chief executive officer.

> DETROIT, May 13 (AP)—Philip Caldwell, chairman of the Ford Motor Company, told shareholders at today's annual meeting that he expected the No. 2 United States auto maker to turn a profit, but he stopped short of saying when he expected the return to black ink to occur.

President's announcement

> Ford lost $1.06 billiion last year and $355.4 million in the first quarter of this year. Sales are off 9.5 percent so far this year. Ford also has canceled dividends for the first two quarters of the year—for the first time since the company went public in 1956.

Background

> In his speech to shareholders, Caldwell cited Ford's plans to introduce 33 "all-new or substantially changed cars and trucks" worldwide between now and 1985 as reasons for his optimism on the company's future.

Elaboration of lead

> The chairman, however, said that Ford's improved performance would depend on the economy, declaring: "We can assure you that the second quarter will be substantially better than the first quarter but beyond that, how well we do depends on how well the economy does. There's no question that interest rates must come down—and the economy must turn around—before auto demand will improve much."
>
> Caldwell said that Ford would cut its budget by $1 billion this year, in addition to the $2.5 billion already cut over the past two years.

Additional information

Although these annual meetings are "carefully choreographed by management," says Jay Bryan of *The Gazette* in Montreal, it is "a good opportunity for a reporter to buttonhole senior executives who might otherwise be inaccessible behind a screen of secretaries and public relations people."

At annual meetings the attempts of one company to take over another are voted on. Also, dissident shareholders can voice their displeasures with the way the company is being run—which can give the observant reporter a good insight into the company.

Preparation is essential. Bryan usually has several questions he has drawn up from past experience and from reading about the firm.

The best kind of business reporting blends spot news with trend, depth and investigative reporting. Business journalism has emerged from the days of puffery and is no longer a handmaiden to every local merchant who seeks space. It has also done a good job exposing the bad apples in the business community. But it has not done so well examining the way business affects government (in the U.S. and abroad), how it prices its goods and services and the way business and government exchange personnel and the consequences.

The Founding Fathers were concerned about the dangers of a strong central government. They could not have imagined the power that business would acquire. International banks and the conglomerates exercise enormous influence over the lives of people everywhere, and this power is worthy of scrutiny by the press in its role as watchdog for the people.

Such examination starts at the local level. How much power does the local real estate business have over planning and zoning decisions? What role does money play in local, county and state elections, and where does it come from? Does local government really have to give businesses and developers tax write-offs and abatements as an incentive? Is the tax structure equitable, or does it fall too heavily on families, working people, home owners? In states with natural resources, is the severance tax properly balanced with other taxes, or are the extractive industries being given preferential treatment?

Business Terms

This material was prepared by Jim O'Shea for *The Des Moines Register*.

assets These are anything of value the company owns or has an interest in. Assets usually are expressed in dollar value.

balance sheet A financial statement that lists the company's assets, liabilities and stockholder's equity. It usually includes an *Earnings* or *Income Statement* that details the company's source of income and its expenses.

calendar or **fiscal year** Some companies report their income or do business on the regular calendar year. Others do it on a fiscal year that could run from any one month to the same month a year later. Always ask if the companies do business on a fiscal or calendar year. If the answer is fiscal, ask the dates and why. You might find out something unusual about the company.

capital expenditures This is the amount of money a company spends on major projects, such as plant expansions or capacity additions. It is important to the company and the community as well. If the company is expanding, include it in the story. Frequently, such plans are disclosed in stock prospectuses and other SEC reports long before the local paper gets its press release.

earnings Used synonymously with profit. Earnings can be expressed in dollar terms (XYZ earned $40) or on a per-share basis (XYZ earned $1 per share for each of its 40 shares of stock). When used as an earnings figure, always compare it to the earnings for the same period in the prior year. For example, if you want to say XYZ earned $1 a share during the first quarter, half or 9 months of 1983, compare that with the 50 cents per share the company earned in the first quarter, half or 9 months of 1982. That would be a 100 percent increase in profit.

liabilities These are any debts of any kind. There are two types of liabilities—short term and long term. Companies consider anything that has to be paid off within a year a short-term liability and anything over a year a long-term liability.

sales or **revenues** These terms are used synonymously in many companies. A bank, for example, doesn't have sales. It has revenues. But a manufacturer's sales and revenues frequently are the same thing, unless the company has some income from investments it made. Always include the company's sales in a story with its earnings. If you say a company earned $40 in 1983 compared to $30 in 1982, you also should tell the reader that the profit increase came as the company's sales went up 100 percent, from $100 in 1982 to $200 in 1983. Use sales and earnings figures together. Don't use one and not the other.

stockholder's equity This is the financial interest the stockholders have in the company once all of its debts are paid. For example, say XYZ company has assets of $1,000 and total debts of $600. The company's stockholder's equity is $400. If that figure is expressed on a per-share basis, it is called *book value*. (If XYZ had issued 40 shares of stock, each share would have a book value of $10.)

26 Consumer Reporting

Preview   Consumer reporting is concerned with anything that involves the expenditure of money. The reporter goes into the marketplace to report the price and quality of merchandise. The reporter also tells readers and listeners about business practices and the consequences of business decisions to consumers.

Consumer reporting falls into four categories:

■ Newsworthy events—Court decisions, health department regulations and findings, decisions of regulatory agencies.

■ Marketplace practices—Credit changes, illegal and deceptive business activities, pricing changes.

■ Service reporting—Consumer assistance in buying a product or service.

■ Critical reporting—Assessments of the products and services consumers use and buy.

In September 1899 the first recorded automobile fatality occurred. Over the next six decades, 1,125,000 people died and millions more were injured in traffic accidents. In 1957, congressional hearings were held to seek the reasons for this appalling toll. For the next six years, the committee held occasional hearings.

One of the major points witnesses made was that the automotive industry had the capacity to design cars that were far less dangerous than those moving off the assembly line.

Newspapers and broadcast stations paid little attention to the hearings. Not until 1965 with General Motors' attempts to stifle a critic of the automotive industry, Ralph Nader, did the press begin to report the importance of automotive design to safety. Without this reporting, says *Washington Post* reporter Morton Mintz, the Automobile Motor Vehicle Safety Act of 1966 would not have passed.

Although a few newspapers encouraged reporters to examine the quality of goods and services and their prices, most steered clear of consumer-oriented journalism—understandable in a business sensitive to those who pay most of the bills, the advertisers.

But the consumer movement in the late 1960s and the 1970s became too significant to ignore. Prices had risen to inflationary highs and the quality of goods and services had declined. Business seemed to be guided by the philosophy of *caveat emptor*—let the buyer beware. Buyers refused to remain passive, however, and the government responded with new laws and regulations.

The Press Responds

The press responded, too. It could not remain impassive to a report by the National Commission on Product Safety stating that 30,000 Americans are killed and 110,000 permanently disabled every year in the home by incidents connected with the use of consumer products.

In 1969, the commission held a hearing on the hazards of sliding doors fitted with cheap glass. Mintz says that the government had estimates that as many as 100,000 children a year had been injured, some fatally, by striking these doors, not knowing they were there. A Georgia couple testified that their nine-year-old daughter had run into a sliding glass door.

"She was severely cut," the child's mother testified. "Her jugular vein was cut. The glass went in her and penetrated her spinal column. She also had severe cuts on her leg and bled to death."

A Washington, D.C., policeman said his five-year-old son was helping the family move into a new apartment and walked into a sliding glass door. He was badly cut. "I took my hand and I put his nose back where it belonged," the boy's father testified.

The response of the press to stories such as these varied. Most stepped tentatively into consumer journalism. Some became strong consumer advocates. Some assigned reporters to investigate the fat content and bacterial counts of hamburgers sold by supermarkets. Some consumer reporters disconnected wires in automobiles and television sets to check on the honesty and competence of local repair shops. The coverage of the activities of consumer advocacy groups increased.

The Scope

At WMAL-TV in Washington, D.C., Melinda Nix began an action-line service that she hoped "would give the little guy a chance to fight back at local businesses and bureaucracies." Nix says she handled small stories at first—a man who missed three days of work waiting for a washing machine repairman to show up at his home; a secretarial student who was unable to have her typewriter repaired.

Gradually, she said, she enlarged her reporting to include the "industrial offenders." Some of the larger newspapers also scrutinized the large industrial and business giants. Some of this work involved investigative reporting, ferreting out records of various agencies that revealed interlocking directorships that kept prices up and other practices that were systematic abuses of public trust at the corporate level. Nursing homes, food processing plants and retail stores also were investigated.

Consumer reporters broke many business taboos. Defective automobiles were mentioned in newspapers by name, one of the many results of Nader's campaign for safe cars. Banks, long sacrosanct institutions, were treated like any other business. The *Los Angeles Times* jumped on Christmas advertisements of some California banks. The banks had told readers they could forget about paying the banks' credit card bill for that month. But the *Times* pointed out that the amnesty lasted only one month and that consumers would find on the following month's bill "the balance you were told to forget, plus an interest equal to 18 percent annually."

The *Pittsburgh Post-Gazette* examined the funeral industry and pointed out that membership in a burial society is one way to avoid the high cost of dying. The *National Observer* exposed a vast advertising program as misleading to automobile owners. The newspaper showed that the various gasoline additives advertised by different companies as having unique effects actually do the same thing—and not much at that. Even the student press ventured into consumer reporting to protect its readers from exploitation and danger. The *Indiana Daily Student* reported that water buffalo sandals, a favorite with college students, often caused foot rashes that spread to other parts of the body if not treated.

Comparison shopping by reporters listed prices at various local stores, and although some newspapers and broadcast stations pulled back from this and other consumer reporting when the business backlash developed, most continued to expand their consumer journalism.

Some reporters say that consumer reporters should be concerned with anything that involves the expenditure of money for a product or a service. Betty Furness, consumer reporter for a New York television station, puts it this way:

"The ideal consumer reporter would keep the public alerted to traps in the marketplace. The reporter would explain what consumer rights are—the right to look at your credit report, the right to know what a store's return policy is, the right to know what's happening at the FTC."

The editorial director of Consumers Union, Irwin Landau, says, "Everything that concerns the way business is conducted is within the domain of the consumer reporter." He and Furness are quoted in "Beyond Nader," by Denis M. Hurley, which appeared in the September, 1980 issue of *Quill*.

Landau says that all reporters should be consumer reporters. "I would tell my science reporter, 'You are a consumer reporter and I want you to be sophisticated about environmental things, about carcinogens, about the food supply. . . .' "

Growth and Decline

By 1974, it was estimated that there were 500 consumer reporters in the United States. Less than a decade later, the number was 200. The decline was the result of several factors: The most severe consumer abuses had been corrected; reporters on other beats became consumer-conscious, and the national mood had changed.

With the election of Ronald Reagan, enthusiasm for tough-minded consumer journalism waned. The 1980 Republican campaign stressed an easing of government regulations to give business a freer hand in the marketplace. The onset of the recession and Reagan's victory seemed to indicate to politicians that the fervor of the consumer movement had abated.

The media reaction to the new national mood and to the recession was mixed. Worried by declining advertising, some editors cut back on consumer stories. But there was no turning back completely to the old days of ignoring the consumer, as some congressmen learned.

Killing the Lemon Rule

Make a guess: What is the cause of the greatest number of consumer complaints? The answer: The automobile, especially used cars. Infuriated buyers write and call the government daily to ask for help.

In response, the Federal Trade Commission drafted a rule that would have required used car dealers to put a window sticker on their cars with a list of all known major defects in the vehicle. The rule was known as the "lemon rule."

But the FTC picked the wrong year. The political climate had changed. On the day in 1982 that the federal rule was to have taken effect, the House affirmed earlier Senate action and killed the rule.

The press did not hesitate to see a connection between the vote in the House and lobbying by the National Automobile Dealers Association. Here is how the AP described the relationship in its story:

> The rule was opposed vigorously by the National Automobile Dealers Association, which contributed money to candidates in the last congressional election. That provoked backers of the rule to complain that the vote was a return on the auto dealers' investment.

In addition to moving a long story on the vote, the AP sent out a long list of congressmen who had accepted campaign contributions from the automobile dealers association. Many newspapers localized the wire story by publishing the names of congressmen from their areas and how they had voted on the lemon rule. Here is how the Rochester, N.Y., *Democrat & Chronicle* ended its story on the vote:

> Area Republicans who voted against the rule and the amounts they received from the association: Frank Horton of Rochester, $1,500; Barber B. Conable of Alexander, $50; Jack Kemp of Buffalo, $2,500, and Gary Lee of Dryden, $3,500.
>
> Democrats who voted for the rule and the amounts they received: John LaFalce of Niagara Falls, $150, and Stanley Lundine of Jamestown, $200.

Post script: A Connecticut newspaper published a picture of the owner of a lemon picketing the local Ford dealer. The editor who approved the photo was fired for failing to give the dealer's side of the story.

Although many state and federal agencies involved with consumer protection lost personnel in the great budget slashings of the 1980s, many newspapers and stations continued to be alert and consumer groups stepped up their activities. These groups, which are excellent news sources, include Common Cause, Consumers Union and the various environmental organizations: the Sierra Club, Audubon Society, Friends of the Earth and others.

When the Highway Loss Data Institute distributed injury and collision data for 1979–1981 passenger cars, the press eagerly picked up the figures. The Institute, funded by insurance companies, showed wide variations in injuries and collision loss, though for the most part the loss experience of a car model was consistent in the three loss categories—overall injury results, severe injury results and collision results.

The best results, the Institute reported, were for station wagons and four-door models. The worst data involved two-door and sports models. The cars with the worst loss experience in all categories were Japanese imports.

In the following table, injury results are presented in terms of the frequency of claims listed under Personal Injury Protection Coverage for 1979–1981 models. Collision results are presented in terms of the average loss payment per insured vehicle year for 1980 and 1981 models. All results are stated in relative terms, with 100 representing the average for all cars.

Substantially Better than Average	<70
Better than Average	70–79
Average	80–120
Worse than Average	121–130
Substantially Worse than Average	>130

Table 26.1 Injury and Collision Loss Experience

Car	Injury		Collision
	Overall	Severe	
Volkswagen Rabbit*	98		114
Honda Accord	102	98	95
Plymouth Reliant*	105		89
Mercury Lynx*	106		95
Volkswagen Scirocco	108	111	200
Dodge Aries*	109		91
American Spirit	113	102	88
Ford Escort*	114	102	93
Mercury Capri	121	109	130
Toyota Celica	123	130	138
Chevrolet Chevette	124	113	88
Datsun 310	124	117	119
Dodge Colt	124	127	110
Ford Mustang	125	129	122

**Two-Door Models
Small Cars**

* 1981 Models Only

Table 26.1 Injury and Collision Loss Experience (Continued)

Car	Injury		Collision
	Overall	Severe	
Two-Door Models **Small Cars**			
Plymouth Horizon	127	114	133
Honda Civic	131	133	92
Plymouth Champ	132	123	108
Dodge Omni	134	122	131
Toyota Corolla Tercel**	134	126	108
Datsun 210*	136	145	129
Toyota Corolla*	138	133	133
Datsun 200 SX**	141	140	178
Plymouth Sapporo	148		145
Dodge Challenger	160		178
Four-Door Models **Small Cars**			
Dodge Aries*	86		65
Honda Accord	93	90	87
Plymouth Reliant*	94		72
Volkswagen Rabbit*	97		83
Dodge Omni	107	97	82
Plymouth Horizon	107	103	83
Chevrolet Chevette	112	102	79
Toyota Corolla*	118		112
Sports and Specialty Models **Small Cars**			
Chevrolet Corvette	90	106	255
Datsun 280 ZX 2+2	104		185
Datsun 280 ZX	111	125	235
Mazda RX-7	121	130	184
Honda Prelude	122	135	134
Fiat Spider 2000	123		193
Medium Cars			
Audi 5000	81	98	181
Pontiac Grand Prix	101	104	102
Ford Thunderbird**	104	121	114
Chevrolet Monte Carlo	107	114	97
Mercury Cougar XR-7**	110		119
Pontiac Firebird	111	118	162
Chevrolet Camaro	115	122	135
Toyota Celica Supra	129		185

* 1981 Models Only
** 1980 and 1981 Models Only

Francis Pollock, the editor of the now defunct monthly *Media & Consumer* that published the work of consumer journalists, says that consumer journalism falls into four major areas as follows:

1. *Reporting of newsworthy consumer events.* The major actions of regulatory agencies, significant court decisions affecting consumers and findings of generally respected consumer or business organizations. Health Department ratings of restaurant cleanliness come under this category, as do the findings of the Federal Trade Commission.
2. *Reporting on marketplace practices that may not seem newsworthy but which have a significant effect on consumers.* Changing credit practices, systematic auto repair abuses and shifting judicial interpretation of product liability law are types of stories in this category. Also included is the reporting of practices that may be technically legitimate but which are deceptive, questionable or debatable. It is illegal in some states to use pink or red lights to illuminate meat in a food store; in other states it is legal. But illegal or legal, common sense suggests the practice is questionable if not deceptive.
3. *Service reporting.* Assistance to the consumer in helping him or her to buy a product or service. In these stories, consumers are told what to look for. For example, package price is less important than unit price. Thus, a cake mix that sells for 47 cents a box is more expensive than the competitor that sells for 50 cents because the 47-cent mix contains 5.75 ounces and the 50-cent mix contains 6.25 ounces.
4. *Critical reporting.* Assessments of the products and services consumers purchase. Whereas movies, plays and books are regularly evaluated by the press, other kinds of consumer purchases usually are not—food, automobiles, homes, college education. Frances Cerra, a consumer reporter for *The New York Times,* made a consumer study of 24 automobile-repair shops. It appeared on page one under the headline: "11 of 24 Auto-Repair Shops Pass a Test on Honesty."

Pollock describes these four areas as the major components of a minimally competent consumer reporting effort. He adds other areas such as investigative consumer reporting, comparative evaluations of products and services and the so-called action-line reporting in which reporters help consumers with problems.

The press has been strongest in the first and second areas. Service and critical reporting require initiative and time. Joseph Carey of *The Daily News* had a good idea for a story about New York City's emergency rooms, and he took the time to develop it. In his story, he described the proper way to telephone for help, and he discussed the use of public and private ambulances. (Service reporting.) Then he went on to evaluate the emergency rooms in each of the city's major hospitals. (Critical reporting.)

Imaginative reporters can expand the areas of consumer coverage by reading widely. For example: A reporter read an article in *The Atlantic* magazine in which the authors blamed unimaginative children's books for the poor reading ability of many youngsters. ("Why Children Don't Like to Read," by Bruno Bettleheim and Karen Zelan, November 1981.)

The reporter then looked at readers used in city schools. He could see why the authors had concluded that the content was "nonsense" and "drivel," and he could understand why they stated that children are driven from reading by boring, repetitive textbooks. He quoted from the books in his story.

Although massive amounts of money are spent by schools on textbooks, few reporters have bothered to examine the textbook industry and its products. Since textbook publishers seek the widest possible use, their books often pass over what they consider to be controversial. Studies of textbooks have found that they have ignored women, handled the New Deal gingerly and are more critical of communism than fascism.

With a little initiative, highly readable and important stories can be turned out by the reporter that examine and evaluate a wide variety of the goods and services people use.

Checklist: Consumer Reports

—— Careful record keeping of purchases or services: time, date, place, amount, descriptive notes, names of salespersons, retention of sales slip or corroboration of transaction by another person.

—— Use of outside experts to evaluate results. (Choose carefully to avoid conflict of interest.)

—— Return to subjects of story for comments.

—— Comments by trade associations, industry groups, officials.

Sources

Bureau of Product Safety of the U.S. Food and Drug Administration; the Federal Trade Commission (which has a mailing list to which journalists can subscribe); U.S. Department of Agriculture; National Highway Transportation Safety Administration; state and local government agencies with regulatory responsibilities similar to the federal agencies; local and state testing laboratories; local and state consumer groups; the various Ralph Nader enterprises, including the Center for Auto Safety, Health Research Group, and state chapters of the Public Interest Research Group; the trade press—*Business Week, Supermarket News, Advertising Age* and others; local business and industrial organizations; Better Business Bureau; and communications from readers and listeners.

Before starting on a consumer project, consult experts to determine the proper method of conducting the inquiry. Check to determine whether the same type of story has been done elsewhere and whether the results were similar.

Consumer reporting should be unrushed, says Cerra, because haste leads to superficial stories based on misleading facts. All sources must be questioned, and the research of consumer groups should be examined carefully.

Some consumer stories can damage an individual or his or her business and thus come within the scope of libel. The usual precautions should be taken, and when there are doubts, the lawyer for the paper or station should be consulted. Libel is avoided when the story is accurate and all facts can be proved.

The Associated Press Managing Editors' Business-Economics Committee has suggested that all writers become consumer reporters. "First we need to train all our reporters to take normal stories from their beats and translate them into what it might mean to the consumer—who is, of course, any of us," the committee reported. "Consumer reporting is all around us. It is no longer something out of the ordinary, if indeed it ever was."

27 Covering Local Government

Preview   The local government reporter covers the actions of agencies and departments in ongoing municipal affairs, the interplay of special interest groups and government and the response of local officials to interest groups and public opinion. Some special areas of coverage are:

- Politics—The activities of candidates and elected officials.
- Budgets, taxes and bond issues.
- City planning and zoning.
- Education—The financing of the school system, curriculum decisions. (Often, newspapers make this a separate beat.)

"You told us it would happen, and we never believed you," the letter began. "I had to write a budget story my first week here. It made page one." The letter from a young reporter on *The White Plains* (N.Y.) *Reporter Dispatch* did not surprise her former journalism instructor. He had a collection of similar letters.

"Tax hikes, millages, assessed valuations and all that," a reporter for a Pennsylvania newspaper had written. "You warned us."

Covering local government—indeed, covering all levels of government—requires a knowledge of how money is raised and spent, how decisions are made and how the political process works. These are complicated matters, and usually the best reporters in the newsroom are assigned to city hall, county government, the statehouse and Washington.

Basic to the coverage of these beats is the ability to follow the dollar. In essence, this means understanding the budget process.

The expenditure of public funds is determined by the budget, which affects every member of the community, county, state and nation. The budget is a forecast or estimate of expenditures that a governmental unit will have to make during the year and the revenues needed to meet those expenses. It is, in short, a balance sheet. Budgets are made for the fiscal year, which may be the calendar year or may run from July 1 through June 30 or other dates. The budget is made by the executive branch (mayor, governor, president, school superintendent) and then submitted to the legislative body (city council, state legislature, Congress, board of education) for adoption.

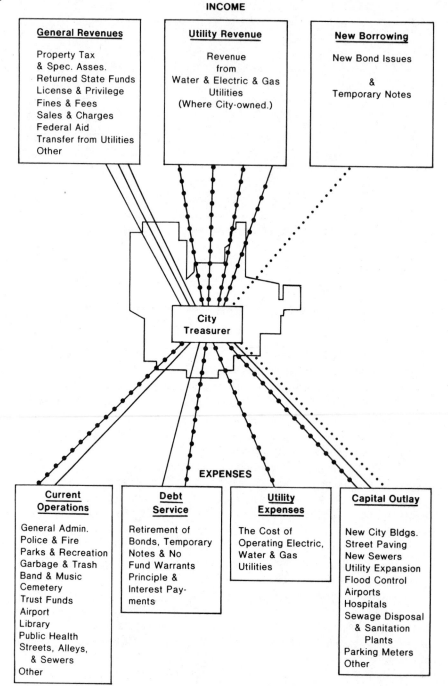

Figure 27.1 A City's Money Flow. Here are the major sources of revenue and the major areas of expenditures in an average city. Note the specific uses to which income may be put by following the lines to and from the city treasurer.

INCOME

General Revenues

Property Tax & Spec. Asses.
Returned State Funds
License & Privilege
Fines & Fees
Sales & Charges
Federal Aid
Transfer from Utilities
Other

Utility Revenue

Revenue from Water & Electric & Gas Utilities (Where City-owned.)

New Borrowing

New Bond Issues
&
Temporary Notes

City Treasurer

EXPENSES

Current Operations

General Admin.
Police & Fire
Parks & Recreation
Garbage & Trash
Band & Music
Cemetery
Trust Funds
Airport
Library
Public Health
Streets, Alleys, & Sewers
Other

Debt Service

Retirement of Bonds, Temporary Notes & No Fund Warrants Principle & Interest Payments

Utility Expenses

The Cost of Operating Electric, Water & Gas Utilities

Capital Outlay

New City Bldgs.
Street Paving
New Sewers
Utility Expansion
Flood Control
Airports
Hospitals
Sewage Disposal & Sanitation Plants
Parking Meters
Other

In the words of Aaron Wildavsky of the University of California at Berkeley, the budget is "a document containing words and figures, which proposes expenditures for certain items and purposes." It is the final resolution of the conflicting claims of individuals and groups to public monies. This means that the conscientious reporter watches the budgeting process as carefully as he or she examines the finished document.

Wildavsky, in *The Politics of the Budgetary Process* (Boston: Little, Brown and Co., 1947), describes the budget as "a series of goals with price tags attached." If it is followed, he says, things happen, certain policy objectives are accomplished.

The budget is hardly the impersonal document its figures would indicate. It is a sociological and political document. As Prime Minister William Ewart Gladstone of Britain remarked more than 100 years ago, the budget "in a thousand ways goes to the root of the prosperity of the individuals and relation of classes and the strength of kingdoms."

Appropriations in the budget can determine how long a pregnant woman waits to see a doctor in a well-baby clinic, how many children are in a grade school class, whether city workers will seek to defeat the mayor in the next election.

Here is the beginning of a budget story by Paul Rilling of *The Anniston* (Ala.) *Star:*

A city budget may look like a gray mass of dull and incomprehensible statistics, but it is the best guide there is to the plans and priorities of city government.

Rhetoric and promises aside, how the city council decides to spend available money says what it really sees as the city's top priorities.

Tuesday, the Anniston City Council will consider for formal adoption the proposed city budget for fiscal. . . .

City hall, education, county and legislative reporters handle budget stories on a regular basis. Reporters on these beats begin to write stories several months before the new fiscal year begins. In a six-week span, beginning in February, Bill Mertens, city hall reporter for *The Hawk Eye,* wrote more than a dozen stories. Here are the beginning paragraphs of three of them:

School crossing guards may be one of the programs lost if Burlington city councilmen intend to hold the new budget close to the existing one.

Nothing has been included for the service in the preliminary budget for the 1976–77 fiscal year beginning July 1. A final decision will await a meeting the council hopes to hold with the Burlington school board and school district officials next week. . . .

The city council has asked Burlington fire department heads to cut $30,000 from their 1976–77 budget request.

Council members say they want to make it clear to all departments that the requests should not show an increase from the existing budget. Finance commissioner Jack Waldhoff informed fire officials of the need for the cuts at the end of city budget talks Wednesday afternoon. . . .

> The 1976–77 fiscal year budget for Burlington will be "a couple of million dollars" less than the existing total, but that doesn't mean much except on paper.
>
> City residents shouldn't start counting on a corresponding drop in tax askings to ease the pain of increased property valuations.
>
> City officials have a rough budget estimate but won't give it out yet because, according to budget director Mike Darnall, the figures might be misleading. . . .

Most of the dozen-plus stories were enterprised by Mertens. Knowing the budget process and having cultivated sources, Mertens was able to keep a steady flow of interesting and important copy moving to the city desk. In his stories, Mertens was always conscious of the human consequences of the belt-tightening.

Types of Budgets

There are two types of governmental expenses that have to be budgeted—funds for daily expenses and funds for long-range projects. At the local governmental level, these expenses are included in two kinds of budgets:

Daily Expenses

1. *Expense or executive budget.* This budget covers costs of daily services, which include salaries, debt service and the purchase of goods and services. Expense budget revenues are gathered from three major sources:
   a. Taxes on real estate—the property tax—usually the single largest source of income.
   b. General fund receipts, which include revenues from fines, permits, licenses, and taxes such as the income, corporation, sales and luxury taxes. (States must give cities permission to levy taxes.)
   c. Grants-in-aid from the federal and state governments.

Long-Range Projects

2. *Capital or construction budget.* This budget covers the costs of capital projects to be built and major equipment and other long-range products to be purchased. The borrowing period is 10, 20 or 30 years. Capital budget funds are raised by borrowing, usually through the sale of bonds pledged against the assessed valuation of real estate in the governmental unit. Bonds are approved by the voters and then sold to security firms through bidding. The firms then offer them for public sale. The loan is paid back much like a homeowner's payments on his mortgage. Principal and interest are paid out of current revenues, and this item is listed in the expenditures column of the expense budget as "debt service," which should run under 10 percent of the total budget for the city to be on the safe side.

Budget session 7 tonight

A contingent from the League of Women Voters is expected to be among the crowd of objectors at tonight's public hearing on the Burlington city budget proposal. The hearings start at 7 p.m. on third floor of city hall, and is the only business on the agenda.

The questions are expected to be varied, but the League has a special interest in the budget decisions. Its members have followed the local use of general revenue sharing (GRS) in the past two years, and is interested in the planned use during the fiscal year beginning July 1.

In its monthly letter, "The Burlington Voter," the League has listed six objections to the planned use of the funds:

- No open meeting for citizen input was held.
- Most GRS monies have been and are being used for capital expenditures — machinery, etc. — or for general governmental expenditures.
- Funding for the Library has not been correctly reported.
- There are no provisions for "people" programs.
- The council ignored requests from groups that wanted to apply for funding.
- The material on Equal Employment Opportunity cannot be verified because the forms, due Dec. 31, 1975, have not been submitted to Washington.

In the existing budget, revenue sharing funds totaling $548,000 were earmarked for the following expenditures: operation of city-school swimming pool, $65,989; Port of Burlington, $75,000; ambulance operation, $49,928; city's share of county health operation, $65,823; Public Library, $160,580; and $42,000 for some costs in the property maintenance and vehicle maintenance departments.

The council has budgeted $237,000 of revenue sharing funds in the $10.6-million proposal for 1976-77 for operation of the city-school pool, the Library and the city summer recreation program.

The city only budgeted for funds to be received before the end of 1976, since renewal of revenue sharing has not been approved by Congress, although extension is expected. If so, the city would receive another $158,000 during the first of 1977, if funding levels remain the same.

Also, the city is proposing the transfer of $287,583 from the revenue sharing reserve to the general fund to meet working capital reserves needs for the first quarter of the new fiscal year. That would leave a balance of revenue sharing funds, as of June 31, at $70,837, according to city officials also.

Burlington has received more than $1 million through the program since its inception in 1972.

Most budgets are adopted in this series of steps:

1. Budget request forms go out to all department heads, who must decide on their priorities for the coming year and submit them to the budget officer, mayor or school superintendent.
2. Meetings are held between budget officer and department heads to adjust requests and formulate a single balanced program.

Making the Budget

3. Submission of the budget, sometimes accompanied by a "narrative" explaining the requests, to the city council or commission, the board of education or other legislative arm of the governmental unit.
4. Study by the legislative body and adoption of budget items for each department.
5. Public hearings. (See "Budget Session" news story.)
6. Adoption of the budget.

The reporter can do stories at each stage of this process. Good reporters describe the behind-the-scenes bickering, dickering and politicking as well as the formal activities of the various department heads, executives and the legislators. All sorts of pressures are brought to bear on the budget makers. Property owners and real estate interests want the budget held down, for increased expenditures usually mean higher property taxes. The business men and women who rely on selling goods and services to the city seek to keep the money flowing to the departments and agencies they serve. Inside government, employees want salary increases, more generous fringe benefits and more lines in the budget for promotions. Politicians seek to reward constituencies and to fulfill campaign promises in order to advance their careers and their party's future.

Checklist: Budget Adoption

____ Amount to be spent.
____ New or increased taxes, higher license and permit fees and other income that will be necessary for revenues.
____ Cuts, if any, to be made in such taxes, fees or fines.
____ Comparison with preceding year(s).
____ Justification for increases sought, cuts made.
____ Rate of current spending, under or over budget of previous year.
____ Patterns behind the submission and subsequent adjustments, such as political motives, pressure groups, history.
____ Consequences of budget for: agencies, departments, businesses, the public.

Checklist: Budget Follow-Up

____ Per-person comparison of costs for specific services with other cities or school districts of the same size.
____ Check of one or more departments to see how funds are used, whether all funds were necessary.

Sources

There are five major types of sources that constitute the interest groups that seek to influence the making of the budget:

1. *Government*—Chief executive, who submits the budget: mayor, governor, school superintendent, president; city manager; head of budget bureau or budget director; department heads; finance and taxation committees of the city council or commission; council members. (Party leaders outside government are sometimes helpful.)

2. *Money-providing constituencies*—Local real estate association; real estate or property owners association; chamber of commerce; taxpayer organizations; merchant and business groups; banks; savings and loan associations.
3. *Service-demanding groups*—Lobbyists for education, health, welfare and other services.
4. *Organized bureaucracies*—Public employees, municipal unions, civil service associations and the public employees' retirement fund manager.
5. *Independent groups*—League of Women Voters; National Municipal League; National League of Cities; U.S. Conference of Mayors; Advisory Commission on Intergovernmental Relations. (Addresses for most of these usually can be obtained from the state university's political science or government department, which itself may have a municipal study organization.)

Money is the source of great passion in the political marketplace, and politicians often seek to impress the public with promises of parsimony to avoid angering the money-providing constituencies.

Cautions

The truth is that many items in the budget are nontransferable or uncuttable. These monies are earmarked and mandated costs that no one can shift or eliminate. The mandated funds include salaries the city has contracted to pay, debt service, pensions, matching funds that localities must produce to meet state and federal grants, particularly for such services as health, welfare and education.

When the city accepts grants from the state or federal government, it must abide by the rules and regulations that often necessitate additional expenditures.

The actual maneuvering room in most budgets is not great, especially since salaries, which represent the largest single expense item, are set by contract in many cities. Only about 10 percent of the budgets for most large cities is discretionary because of mandated costs.

Costs can be reduced if salaries, pensions and commitments to the poor, the elderly and the ill are cut back. However, this would antagonize the service-demanding constituencies. Maneuvering room could be created by making earmarked funds general funds. Again, groups that benefit from the status quo would object.

The competition for existing free-floating funds is always intense, and the perceptive reporter will examine this contest during the budgetary process. In this competition, the administrator finds it necessary to trade off the demands of various groups. The tradeoffs make good stories.

A little skepticism helps in assessing requests. Departments and agencies usually exaggerate their requests, and pressure groups seek deeper cuts than are feasible. The reporter must realize that budget making is a give-and-take process and that despite the agonized pleas or the dire warnings of the participants, the city, state or nation usually survives.

Demands Exaggerated

Although most attention is directed at the increases and decreases proposed in the budget, the reporter should not neglect the major part of the budget, the large base that continues unchallenged year after year.

Hidden Motives   Some aspects of the process are hidden from view. The reporter must dig them out and learn the real constituencies involved, the actual motives of the participants. Are political debts being paid by building a school in one section of the city or by increasing salaries for a particular agency? Have cuts been made in the department of a critical or independent administrator?

The fiscal balance that the final budget represents is the result of a political as well as a financial balancing act—the adjustments between groups, organizations and classes that seek more money and services and those who resist the taxes and other costs necessary to meet these needs and demands. One of the few spectators of this balancing act is the reporter.

Budget Politics   During a legislative session, Gov. Malcolm Wilson of New York, a Republican, proposed a new formula for the distribution of state aid to local school districts that reflected the demands of big city school officials. A few days later, a group of Republican state senators and assemblymen from Long Island met with the governor, who was facing reelection. Following the meeting, the governor's aid formula was changed to give more aid to suburban school districts, especially to Long Island.

"What happened at the gathering," reported *The New York Times*, "was summed up later by Joseph M. Margiotta of Uniondale, the powerful Nassau County Republican leader, who related that the Long Island delegation had simply delivered to Mr. Wilson the stern message that without more state education aid, Long Island property taxes would skyrocket in September and Mr. Wilson's campaign would sink in October."

When Mayor John Lindsay of New York "dropped the broom and picked up the nightstick"—the graphic phrase the *Daily News* used to describe the shift in budget priorities from clean streets to public safety—it was widely interpreted as Lindsay's recognition that law and order would make a more attractive national issue than sanitation. Lindsay had presidential ambitions.

When President Carter tried to cut into deficits during his administration he decided to eliminate some runs of the national rail service, Amtrak. To achieve this, he had to move his proposal through Congress. Many lines were to be cut. But the administration was careful to give wide berth to service in western Massachusetts and Nevada. A senator from Nevada and a congressman from Massachusetts headed key transportation committees through which the Carter plan had to move before it could be acted on.

Budgeting, says Wildavsky, deals with the many and diverse purposes of man.

A Final Caution   Officials sometimes evade discussing higher taxes for fear of offending special-interest groups. The possibility of new taxes may have to be dug up by the reporter, who should know the sources of revenues.

The property tax is the largest single source of income for municipalities, counties **Property Tax**
and school systems and affects more people than any other local tax but the sales
tax. Much of the local, county and school budget coverage centers on the action of
the council, commission or board in setting the property tax. The reporter should
know the formula for figuring the property tax. The tax is formally known as the mill
levy. A mill is .1 cent (1/10¢), and the property tax technically is expressed in terms
of mills levied for each dollar of assessed valuation of property. Here is the formula:

Mill levy=(Taxes to be collected)÷(Assessed valuation)

Let us assume budget officials estimate that $1 million will have to be collected
from the property tax and that the assessed valuation of real estate in the city or
school district is $80 million; here is how the tax is figured:

Mill levy=($1 million)÷($80 million)

Mill levy=$1÷$80=$.0125

Mill levy=1.25 cents on each $1 of assessed valuation

Since mill levies are usually expressed against $100 or $1,000 in assessed
valuation, the levy in this community would be $1.25 for each $100 in valuation, or
$12.50 for each $1,000 in valuation.

Here is a paragraph from a reporter's story in which these figures are used to
describe the municipal budget in a medium-size Kansas community:

> Last year, the commission budgeted
> $1,161,313 of which $641,135.25 was to
> be raised from property taxes. These
> taxes, based on the assessed valuation of
> property, were based on a 20.91 mill levy,
> or $20.91 for each $1,000 property val-
> uation. The total assessed valuation was
> $30,661,583.

The beginning reporter might want to check his or her mathematical ability by
deriving the mill levy from the total property tax and the assessed valuation in the
preceding paragraph.

The property tax formula is handy for city hall and education reporters who
want to inform their readers of the consequences of proposed budgets. As we saw,
authorities are sometimes reluctant to talk about the taxes needed to finance their
requests until the budget is set. A reporter able to use the formula can do the job
himself or herself.

Reporters should always apply the mill levy to representative home values. But they must note that the mill levy is applied to assessed valuations, not to actual value as determined in the marketplace. Assessed value is usually a percentage of market value. The mill levy of $20.91 in the story from the Kansas newspaper made greater impact on readers because the reporter later noted that the property tax on a home with an assessed valuation of $10,000 would be $209.10. (The $20.91 multiplied by 10.)

Here is the beginning of a story on a school board budget by Art Carey:

The Pennsbury School Board adopted a $21.7 million budget last night which will cost residents another six mills in property taxes. . . .

The new budget means the tax rate in the Pennsbury School District stands at 108.5 mills. . . .

Those living in homes assessed at $5,000 can expect to pay $542; those living in $10,000 homes, $1,085; those living in $15,000 homes, $1,627; and those living in $20,000 homes, $2,170.

—*Bucks County Courier Times*
(Levittown, Pa.)

Since the property tax is levied against ownership of the property, the third paragraph would have been more accurate had it stated, "Those *owning* homes assessed at. . . ."

Remember that the property tax is a major source of revenue for several governmental units. When covering the action of one unit in setting a tax rate, it is necessary to inform the reader that this particular property tax is not the only one the property owner will pay. Often overlooked by reporters are the property taxes levied by special assessment districts, which can add a large chunk to the tax bill. These districts cover services in particular areas. If a neighborhood wants street paving or street lighting, it may form such a district. There are cemetery districts, weed control districts and scores of others, each with the power to levy taxes on property within the districts.

Property taxes are based on the assessed valuation of property. Valuations are made by the tax assessor and are public record. The tax rate is set each year, but valuations on individual pieces of property are not changed often. Total assessed valuation does change each year because of new construction and shutdowns that add to or subtract from the tax rolls. The taxing district must establish the total assessed valuation each year before a new tax rate can be set.

When the assessor does make new valuations, the intensity of feeling is considerable, as revealed in this story:

SPRING VALLEY, N.Y., Dec. 12— Listening to people here, a visitor would almost think that someone was stalking the streets, sowing horror and destruction.

But it is only the tax assessor, equipped with a collapsible 10-foot measuring stick, a set of appraisal cards,

a practiced eye that can tell the difference between a toilet and a water closet and experience that tells him which adds more value to a house.

This village of 22,450 persons, 2,219 dwellings and 109 commercial properties is nearing the end of a year-long reappraisal. . . .

The assessor sometimes is politically motivated in establishing assessments. In some cities, residential properties are consistently underassessed in order to placate homeowners. In Philadelphia, tax officials assessed residences at 40 percent of market value, whereas commercial property was assessed at 54 percent and industrial property at 59 percent. In the Chicago area, the political machine of Mayor Richard J. Daley underassessed large corporations and industries. At election time, these beneficiaries of the assessor could be counted on for large campaign contributions.

Borrowing

Few government institutions can meet their needs out of current revenues. Most cities need "seasonal" funds to tide them over while waiting for federal or state funds owed them. There is also a need for large amounts of money to finance major construction projects. Sometimes at the end of the fiscal year or during the year an emergency will come up and quick cash is needed.

There are two ways of coping with these needs for cash. For seasonal borrowing or for emergencies when small amounts are needed, the city may issue tax or revenue anticipation notes that the city sells to banks. Future tax collections and anticipated grants-in-aid are pledged as security. Usually, the state must approve.

Most large borrowing is done through the sale of bonds. Let us examine bonds first.

Bonds

The idea behind the sale of bonds is that the costs of such long-range projects as schools, hospitals, streets, sewage plants and mass transit should be borne by those who use them over the anticipated life of the project.

There are three major types of bonds. They differ as to the type of security pledged to repay them:

General Obligation: Most frequently issued. Security is the general taxing power of the city. Bonds are retired by taxes on all property owners in the city.

Special Improvement: For construction of streets, sidewalks, sewers and similar public works. Taxes are levied on the property owners who will benefit from the construction. Charges levied on the property are called special assessments. Special assessment districts are set up to levy and collect the taxes.

Revenue Bonds: To pay for the acquisition, construction, improvement of such properties as college dormitories and public utilities. Pledge is a lien on earnings, which are used to redeem the bonds. These earnings come from room charges in dormitories, water, gas and electric collections from utility customers, toll charges on bridges and highways. (See "Revenue Bonds" news story.)

For Capital Improvements

Water Bills Will Increase In City

By KURT VAN der DUSSEN

Water bills for Vincennes water users will be increased by 167 per cent on bills due in February following the Vincennes Water Board's acceptance of bids for a $4.470 million bond issue Thursday.

Three firms bid on the 20-year bonds. The lowest bid came from Dillon, Read Municipals of New York. The firm bid an interest rate of 6.9095 per cent on the bonds.

Goldman Sachs of Chicago bid 6.9236 per cent on the bonds and Trahb & Co. of Indianapolis bid 7.0777 interest.

Water department manager James Kerlin said the impact of the bonds would first be seen on bills sent out late in January and payable in February. The rates will increase 167 per cent so that a person paying $1.50 for water now will pay $4 in February.

The rate increase is the first for city consumers in 25 years, the last rate hike occurring in 1950.

The massive bond issue will support a couple of years' worth of expansion and modernization of the city's water system. Kerlin said contracts still have to be awarded, so that work won't get underway for two or three months.

When it does, the department will be laying 27.3 miles of new water mains around the city. Most of that total will be for 12-inch connectors in the older parts of the city and for a 12-inch main around the periphery of Eastgate, plus replacement of many old two-and three-inch mains in the city with new six-inch mains.

Also planned is construction of a new, one-million-gallon water storage reservoir on Hillcrest Road. Two new wells will be dug at the wellfield south of town and an emergency standby generator will be installed. Kerlin said a couple of months ago that the project will take place in three phases. First priority goes to the new wells and generator, the storage tank and the Eastgate mains.

Phase two will involve laying of several miles of mains along stretches of Willow Street, Old Decker Road, Ramsey Road, Niblack Road, Emison Street, Cloverdale Avenue, and Mentor, Wheeler, Bayou, 14th and 17th streets.

Phase three will involve replacement and addition of mains throughout the central city.

Kerlin said this summer that the present system provides "adequate" service, but that "you've got to keep upgrading all along or you're going to fall behind.

"This project is being designed to take care of the city's water needs to the year 2,000," he said.

Bonds are paid off in two ways:

Term Bond: The securities are retired at the end of the specified term, 10, 15, 20 years. Meanwhile, money is set aside regularly in a sinking fund and invested to be used to pay off at the end of the term.
Serial Bond: Most common. A portion is retired each year.

Here are the opening paragraphs from a *Wall Street Journal* story about the sale of a bond issue for a public works project:

NEW YORK—A $60 million package of Kentucky Turnpike Authority revenue bonds sold out after reaching the market yesterday through underwriters led by Dillon, Read & Co.

The toll road agency offered about $51 million of 7 3/8% term bonds, due 2010 and priced at 100, plus about $9 million of serial securities priced to yield from 5.30% for the 1974 maturities to 7.10% for bonds, due 1990. The 40-year securities attracted orders from casualty insurance companies, while the serial bonds were placed largely with banks. . . .

In writing bond stories, the reporter should make sure to include the cost of the bonds to taxpayers. Some readers will be astonished to learn how much a seemingly small rate of interest can amount to over 10 or 20 years.

Many units of government maintain bank accounts that draw little or no interest at the same time they issue bonds at rates higher than their savings are drawing. This incongruity can be the basis of excellent stories.

The other kind of borrowing that reporters should watch carefully is short-term low-interest borrowing to meet cash-flow problems. Reporters tend to ignore these notes, sometimes to their regret. There are three types of anticipation notes—revenue, tax and bond. All must be repaid in a year.

If we look at the sources of revenue for the expense budget we see that grants-in-aid are an important part of the governmental unit's income or revenue. But these federal and state payments for such items as education, welfare, health and other services usually do not arrive in time to meet the payroll or the demands of vendors to be paid for their goods and services. The city, county or school district may have to borrow money for a short time, then pay it back when the grants arrive. This borrowing is in the form of revenue anticipation notes (RANS) sold to banks.

Some local taxes are not collected until late in the year, and the anticipated income has to be made up for by short-term loans, which are made by issuing tax anticipation notes (TANS).

Bond anticipation notes (BANS) are sold in anticipation of revenue from the sale of bonds. Here is the beginning of a story from *The Daily Register* of Shrewsbury, N.J., about a school board borrowing money in anticipation of income from the sale of bonds:

> MONMOUTH BEACH—The Board of Education is borrowing another $150,000 at 5 1/2 percent interest from Colonial First National Bank to finance the Griffin St. school addition.
>
> The money is being borrowed against the $1,422,750 bond issue approved by voters in March. The board has been waiting for a favorable bond market before selling the bonds. . . .

New York City, faced with stable or declining revenues and increased demands for services, stepped into fiscal disaster by overusing these anticipation notes to finance the services that political leaders felt were politically and humanely necessary. Unlike other cities, New York City's anticipation notes anticipated no specific taxes or revenues. They were issued on a hope and a prayer that money would turn up. What turned up was a bright young lawyer for a bank who showed his superiors that the sale of $260 million in TANS—supposedly issued against taxes to be collected—was actually backed by taxes that had been collected and spent.

Although the practice contributed to New York City's crisis, the idea is so tempting other cities have flirted with it. Reporters should watch for this kind of borrowing. The city also shifted some operating expenses into the capital budget, which, one economist noted, was like a family taking out a 30-year note to pay its grocery bill. This kind of juggling should be watched by reporters.

City Government

The process leading to and including the adoption of the annual budget is usually the most important single story the city hall reporter will cover. It is also one of the most important functions of local government. There are, of course, other essential activities carried out by municipal government that the reporter must scrutinize:

1. Authorization of public improvements, such as streets, new buildings, bridges, viaducts.
2. Submission to the public of bond issues to finance these improvements.
3. Adoption of various codes, such as building, sanitation, zoning.
4. Issuance of regulations affecting public health, welfare and safety. Traffic regulations come under this category.
5. Consideration of appeals from planning and zoning bodies.
6. Appointment and removal of city officials.
7. Authorization of land purchases and sales.
8. Awarding of franchises.

Many of the city government's decisions are routine. But a significant number affect large numbers of city residents and businesses. The city government sets the direction and pace of growth and expansion. It is a major buyer of goods and services, and usually one of the city's largest employers. Its decisions can enrich some businesses as the beginning of this story by Josh Getlin of the *Los Angeles Times* indicates:

> During the last year, Los Angeles Councilman Howard Finn and his wife enjoyed a free weekend in Newport Beach and Councilwoman Peggy Stevenson was wined and dined at some of New York's finer restaurants.
>
> In both cases, Group W Cable TV officials were wooing council members to round up votes for the East San Fernando Valley franchise that could be worth $75 million.
>
> Lavish entertaining is just part of a multimillion dollar campaign by six firms to win the city's last major cable franchise. . . .

In order to cover these activities, the local government reporter must have a sure understanding of how city government works. The starting point in understanding municipal government is the fact that the city is the creature of the state. The state assigns certain of its powers to the city, enabling the city to govern itself. The city has the three traditional branches of government: a judicial system, an executive and the legislative arm. These vary considerably from city to city. In some cities, the executive is a powerful mayor who has control over much of the municipal machinery. In others, the mayor's job is largely ceremonial and the mayor may not even have a vote on the city council.

Legislative branches differ, too. But for the most part the city council or commission has the power to act in the eight areas outlined previously.

The council or commission takes action in the form of resolutions and ordinances. A resolution indicates the intention or the opinion of the legislative branch. Or it may grant permission to take an action. An ordinance is a law. An ordinance is *enacted* and a resolution is *adopted*.

Cable Talk. Josh Getlin of the *Los Angeles Times* interviews the deputy of a Los Angeles city councilman about the wining and dining of council members by cable companies seeking a lucrative franchise.

The city council-mayor system is the most common form of local government. In large cities, the mayor is usually a powerful figure in city government, the centerpiece of what is called the strong mayor system of local government. In this system, the mayor appoints the heads of departments and all other officials not directly elected by the people. The system enables the mayor to select the people he or she wants to carry out executive policies.

Forms of Local Government

One way to classify local government is by the strength of the office of the mayor, the power the chief executive has to initiate and carry out programs and policies. The two systems have variations:

Weak Mayor
Commission
Commission-manager
Council-manager

Strong Mayor
Council-mayor
Mayor-manager

The weak mayor systems and the creation of the post of city manager were reactions to the misuse of power by strong mayors and their inability to manage the bureaucracy. To be elected and to hold office, the mayor must be an astute politician, not necessarily an able administrator. The wheelings and dealings of the strong mayors—exposed by such muckrakers as Lincoln Steffens—caused a reaction, a repulsion from the system that some critics saw as permitting unchecked corruption. A movement toward less-politicized and more efficient local government developed early in the 20th century. It took the form of the council-manager system.

The manager, who is hired by the council, is a professionally trained public administrator. He or she attends to the technical tasks of running the city government—preparing the budget, hiring personnel, administering the many departments and agencies. While the manager unquestionably does increase the managerial efficiency of local government, the system has been criticized as insulating government from the electorate by dispersing responsibility and accountability. Several cities have returned to the strong mayor system in an effort to place responsibility in an identifiable, elected official.

An offshoot of the council-manager system has been the mayor-manager plan. This combines the strong mayor, politically responsive to the electorate, with the trained technician who carries out executive policies and handles day-to-day governmental activities.

The council-manager and the mayor-manager systems are the most prevalent in the country. The commission system, once strong in cities of less than 500,000 population, appears to be giving way to the commission-manager.

In weak-mayor systems, elected commissioners serve as the legislative branch and the executive branch. The commissioners are legislators and also head various municipal departments—finance, public works, public safety, planning, personnel. Often, the commissioner of public safety also serves as mayor, a largely ceremonial post in this system.

The commission form has been criticized for blurring the separation of powers between the legislative and executive branches. In the commission system, there is no single official that the electorate can hold responsible for the conduct of local affairs.

Figures 27.2(a) and 27.2(b) show how the two major forms of local government are organized:

MAYOR-MANAGER FORM

(A strong mayor system)

The mayor appoints most department and agency heads and the City Manager who is responsible for day-to-day operations.

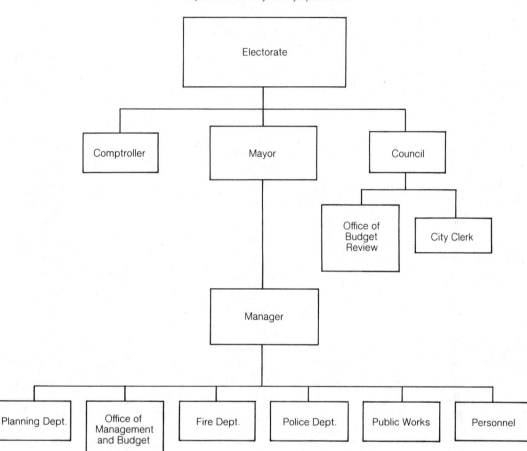

Figure 27.2(a) A Strong Mayor System.

Figure 27.2(b) A Weak Mayor
System.

COUNCIL-MANAGER FORM

(A weak mayor system)

The mayor, who is separately elected, serves as
a member of the City Council. The mayor's
powers are mostly ceremonial. Major
appointments are made by the council.

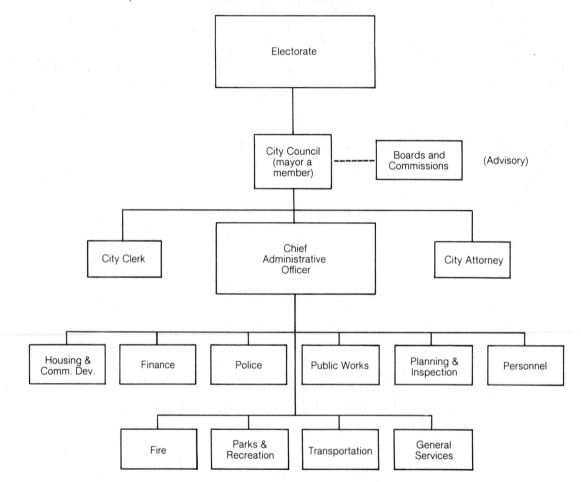

As we saw, the city manager plan was initiated during a period of reform as a means of taking politics out of local government. Other means have been advanced: The nonpartisan ballot, extension of the merit system and the career services to protect city jobs from being used for patronage, the payment of low salaries to mayors and council or commission members to take the "profit" out of public service.

Many cities have been the battleground between the good government groups and their opponents, who disdainfully describe the good government people as the goo-goos. The clean government people have been most successful in small cities. Many cities of less than 100,000 population have commission government and low salaries for their council and commission members. In Odessa, Tex., neither the mayor nor the council members are paid. The city manager is salaried. In DeKalb, Ill., which adopted the managerial form of government in 1960, being mayor is a part-time job paying $1,200 a year. The mayor's tasks include presiding at council meetings and attending to ceremonial functions.

The theory that the removal of partisan politics makes local government cleaner, more efficient and more accountable has been under fire lately. The critics say that the actual result of taking power from party leaders and elected officials is its transfer to nongovernmental groups and the bureaucracies. A city hall reporter must discern who these interest groups may be and cover them.

There are few identifiable public interests that most people agree upon. There can be a public consensus on such matters as public safety and national defense. But the great majority of issues resolve into a contest among differing special interests. The political process involves much more than the nomination and election of candidates. We can define the political process as the daily interaction of government, interest groups and the citizenry.

Professors Wallace S. Sayre of Columbia University and Herbert Kaufman of Yale put the political process in graphic terms useful to the government reporter. They describe the participants as actors in a contest for a rich variety of goals, stakes, rewards and prizes. The police officer on the beat whose union is seeking to fend off reductions in the police force is an actor in the contest, as is the mother of three who is urging her school's Parents Association to speak out for more crossing guards at the elementary school. They are just as much a part of the political process as the mayor when he or she journeys to the state capital to seek a larger slice of the state's funds for welfare and health, or when he decides to seek reelection and lines up backing from unions and ethnic groups.

We can group the participants in the city's political process as follows:

The political party leaders—The leaders and their organizations have a strong hand in the nominating process, but the other participants have increased their power and influence recently, while the party has declined in importance. Insurgents sometimes capture nominations, and the leaders must compromise their choices for the highest offices in the interest of finding a candidate who can win.

Elected and appointed officials—The mayor, members of the city council or commission and their appointed administrators occupy key roles in governing the city. As the party has declined in importance, the mayor and the visible elected and appointed officials have become independent decision makers.

Interest (pressure) groups—Every aspect of city policy making is watched by one or more of the political interest groups. Business groups are especially interested in the budget process: real estate interests will want a low property tax rate but usually will seek larger or more efficient police and fire departments; the banks scrutinize debt policies since they are the buyers of bonds and notes; contractors urge public improvements. The bar associations watch the law enforcement agencies and the legal department as well as the judiciary.

Religious groups and educational organizations are interested in the education department. Medical and health professions examine the activities of the health department. The nominating process and the election campaigns attract ethnic and labor groups as well as the good government groups.

Interest groups compete with each other to influence the city leadership and its bureaucracy, and this limits their influence. Sometimes, however, an interest group may control the decision making of a department or agency, as when, for example, the real estate interests take over the planning and zoning department or the banks and bond market have a powerful voice in an authority and thus control decisions about the sale of bonds.

Organized and professional bureaucracies—City employees have become independent of the party organization as patronage has declined and the merit system, unionization and the professionalization of city service have increased. Police, firemen and teachers have been among the most active in seeking to influence the political process.

Other governments—The city government is in daily contact with a variety of other governmental units: the county, the state, the federal government, public authorities and special assessment districts. These governments are linked by a complex web of legal and financial involvements. State approval is often necessary for certain actions by the city. State and federal governments appropriate large amounts of funds for such city services as education, health and welfare. City officials are almost always bargaining with other governmental units, as are the other participants in the city's political process.

The press—"The communication media provide the larger stage upon which the other participants in the city's political contest play their parts with the general public as an audience," says Prof. Kaufman. But, he continues, the media "do more than merely provide the public stage." They also take a direct part in the process. Having its own values, emphasis, stereotypes and preoccupations, the press is not an exact mirror or reporter, he says.

He finds the press shortsighted in its governmental coverage. The media highlight personalities, are fond of exposés, are prone to fall for stories about new public works, are too zealous in looking for stories about patronage crumbs—and are too skeptical of officials and party leaders.

Prof. Kaufman says all of this is useful, especially as it keeps officials alert. It does raise the level of behavior of the participants in the political process, he concedes. But it omits important aspects of the process, and it contributes to the caution, timidity and delay of the participants in decision making.

In most medium and small cities the city clerk is a key official. The clerk is usually a career public official who knows local government inside and out. In Fresno, Calif., the present city clerk took office in 1963. Her predecessor held office for 25 years. Through changes in administration and even changes in governmental systems, the city clerk serves as the one permanent official handling the thousand-and-one matters that keep government functioning despite the changes.

City Clerk

The city clerk, who usually is appointed by the council or commission, serves as secretary to the legislative branch, issues city licenses, keeps all records and statistics and registers voters. The city clerk draws up the agenda for the council or commission, records ordinances and resolutions and keeps the minutes of the meetings. But most important, a good city clerk who has been in office for a while can be one of the reporter's major sources. Remember: The clerk is viewed as nonpartisan, which means that inside information sometimes has to be treated with care so as not to compromise the clerk.

Reporters who cover city, county and state governments master the ways money flows into and out of government. One of the checkpoints is the office where vouchers and purchase orders are stored. These documents must be approved before any purchase of goods or services can be made. They are usually kept in the auditor's or comptroller's office.

Checking Vouchers

When a governmental unit wants to buy something, it sends a purchase order to the comptroller or auditor's office. The office checks to see whether the agency has the funds to make the purchase and whether the purchase has been made legitimately through bids or negotiated purchase. The order is given approval and sent to the vendor. Records are kept by the number of the purchase order, the agency involved and often by the name of the vendor.

When the goods or services are delivered, a voucher is made up with the accompanying bill, and this starts the payment to the vendor. The payment is made in the form of a check, which is called a warrant.

When Christopher Scanlan of *The* Providence *Journal* was examining vouchers of the Providence Housing Authority he came upon recent payments of $3,319.59 made to restaurants in Providence and Warwick for "authority meetings." On checking, he learned that members of the authority had been meeting over meals for years.

"The restaurant tabs were paid from authority funds, the majority of which are derived from rents paid by low income tenants at the city's 14 public housing projects and from federal subsidies," Scanlan wrote. After the story ran, the authority members agreed to hold meetings in the housing projects it manages.

An examination of vouchers and warrants enabled George Thiem, a reporter for *The Chicago Daily News,* to expose a multi-million dollar corruption scheme by the Illinois state treasurer. Thiem could see that a number of checks were signed by typewriter. Interviewing some of those who supposedly were paid by these checks for work done for the state, he learned that the persons listed on the checks had never done state work; nor had they received the checks. The treasurer went to prison as a result of Thiem's investigation.

A key official for any government reporter is the auditor or comptroller. This official conducts pre-audits of purchase orders and vouches for their regularity. The auditor checks: Are there certified receipts for the delivered goods; does the contract show competitive bidding when necessary by law; are the prices reasonable? Increasingly, auditors and comptrollers are doing performance audits, which check the efficiency of the services, the quality of the goods and the necessity for purchasing them.

Pre-audit example: A state official claims travel reimbursement for an official trip between Boulder and Denver. The auditor will determine whether the 39 miles claimed on the official's expense account attached to a pay order is the actual distance and will see whether the 19 cents a mile is the standard state payment.

Performance audit example: The comptroller has decided to make a check of welfare rolls to see whether money is going out to ineligible persons. The office makes a computer check of the welfare rolls against a) death lists; b) marriage certificates (if a person receiving aid to dependent children has married, the working spouse is obligated to support the children); c) children in foster care homes still listed as at the residence; d) city and state payrolls to determine if any employed persons are receiving welfare.

Zoning and Planning

For centuries, the mentally ill had been locked up, away from family and friends. The reasons seemed logical: Isolated, the mentally ill could be healed more rapidly; free in society, their conditions worsened, they menaced others and they were a danger to themselves. Gradually, the truth seeped out of these institutions. They were, as journalists showed, snake pits where the patients were treated inhumanely. Few were cured of their ailments. With the development of tranquilizing drugs and other treatment, it became possible to return many persons to society and to offer them outpatient care. But there had to be a transition, a halfway house to help the patient adjust after his or her institutionalization.

In New Jersey, the Catholic Diocese of Trenton decided to administer several such houses. The state was going through de-institutionalization of its mental patients, and the Diocese sought to help. In one community, Willingboro, the Diocese found a structure that fit its needs. But it needed permission from the zoning board to use the building for a halfway house since it was in a residential area.

The Willingboro zoning board, like thousands of other such boards, is the agency that carries out the community's planning goals, which are usually set by the planning commission. The zoning boards divide an area into zones or districts and designate them residential, commercial or industrial. The boards then grant building and construction permits consistent with these designations.

The boards also regulate the use of land and buildings within these zones. They regulate the height of buildings, lot size, yard dimensions and other aspects of construction. The city council adopts the ordinances that the zoning board enforces.

The growth and development of the community is planned by the planning commission or board, which was the outgrowth of the haphazard way in which cities developed. Slaughterhouses were built next to churches, congested roads were laid out near schools, and in recent years fast-food concerns, junkyards, auto showrooms and garages lined major roads into and out of cities, marring the countryside.

The planning commission or board is required to make and adopt a master plan. Although such plans have traditionally been concerned with land use, planning bodies today consider social as well as economic purposes in their plans. The planning body is usually headed by a career planner or engineer.

Planning is concerned with the layout of the community, the delivery of essential services and facilities, the protection of natural assets and the accommodation of anticipated population and economic changes. In Willingboro, the area that the Diocese of Trenton sought to use for its halfway house had been designated in the master plan as a residential area, and it was the zoning board's responsibility to examine any request for a variance from this zoning pattern.

Laura King, who covered Willingboro on her suburban beat, had picked up the zoning board agenda and noticed the item. Checking with the board's attorney, she learned there was community resistance to the request. King made some calls to verify this and to get background. She says that because planning and zoning matters can be technical, such advance checking usually is necessary.

"At the meeting, I was struck by the suspicion and hostility of the crowd and by the number of people opposing the house," she said. "That was the story, I felt, rather than just the fact that the variance had been requested and heard on first reading." Her story began this way:

WILLINGBORO — A proposal by the Catholic Diocese of Trenton to put a halfway house here for former mental health patients met with opposition last night from township residents.

About 75 persons filled the council chambers to hear and react to details of the proposal, the first of its kind for this 17-year-old bedroom community.

"I believe in helping the sick, mental, all of that," said one of the most outspoken residents, Robert E. Conklin. "But I don't believe in putting this house in my neighborhood. My house will depreciate to half what it's worth now."

Several times during the four-hour session of the zoning board, Conklin and others in the audience got into shouting matches with Howard Stevenson, acting zoning board chairman, particularly during the presentation by Victor Friedman, lawyer for the Catholic diocese.

A month later, after a second hearing, the request came to a vote and King was there. Her story began:

WILLINGBORO — The zoning board last night told the Catholic Welfare Bureau to take its proposed home for former mental patients somewhere else besides this town.

On a 4–1 vote, members denied the bureau's request for a variance to put nine former patients and one supervisor into a white Colonial home in Somerset Park.

The vote followed two heated board meetings where Somerset residents had expressed fears of possible property depreciation and what "these kinds of people" might do to their children.

King says that in many cases zoning is restrictive, a way of keeping someone out of an area. Zoning can be positive, she says, but it can also be morally indefensible. For example: By requiring that new construction be of single-residence homes on one-acre lots, a zoning regulation will effectively keep out of the area all but the well-to-do. When the New Jersey Supreme Court ruled that Mount Laurel must provide its "fair share" of low- and moderate-income housing and must change its zoning ordinances to provide for that kind of housing, King wrote a feature that began:

March 24, 1975 may well go down as the day the carefully built walls of such upper class suburban meccas as Mount Laurel and Moorestown began to crumble.

It was the day the New Jersey State Supreme Court struck down exclusionary zoning practices in the sprawling bedroom community of Mount Laurel.

And it was a victory not just for low-income people but for as much as 60 percent of the present South Jersey population, according to Carl Bisgaier, attorney for the successful plaintiffs in the Mount Laurel case.

"The number of people who cannot afford conventional housing built under existing zoning has greatly increased since our original case in 1971," Bisgaier, now deputy director of the N.J. Public Interest Advocate's office, says.

Eight years later, the New Jersey Supreme Court reaffirmed its decision in the Mount Laurel case. The court struck down restrictions on lot sizes, density and mobile homes that prevented low- and moderate-income housing from being built in six New Jersey communities. The court said that suburban areas are obligated to encourage the development of housing for the poor.

Reporters have developed interesting stories by looking at the availability of low- and moderate-income housing in the suburbs.

Covering the Schools

Communities spend more money on public education than on any other single tax-supported activity. The cost is borne by all in the community, whether the individual has children in the public school or not. The reason was given succinctly by Thaddeus Stevens to the Pennsylvania state legislature in 1835 when some legislators objected to the general financing of the schools.

"Many complain of the school tax," Stevens said, "not so much on account of its amount, as because it is for the benefit of others and not themselves. This is a mistake. It is for their own benefit, inasmuch as it perpetuates the government and ensures the due administration of the laws under which they live, and by which their lives and property are protected."

The faith in education as the underpinning of democracy is a constant theme in American life, along with the belief that it paves the way for upward mobility. At the more mundane level, education pervades the life of most families because they have children in school.

The good education reporter is conscious of this range of interest.

The school system is based in school districts that are usually contiguous with city boundaries. The schools are independent of municipal government and are subject to state regulations. School boards, usually with five to seven members, are elected in nonpartisan elections, though in some cities board members are appointed by the mayor. The board hires a superintendent of schools who is responsible to the board.

Structure of the System

Reporters covering the education beat tend to center their attention on the administration of the system. Stories from the board and the superintendent's office involve such subjects as changes in the curriculum, hiring and firing of teachers, teacher contracts, the purchase of new equipment, aid to education, teacher certification, school dates for opening, closing and holidays and the vast area of school financing that includes budgeting and the issuance of bonds.

The school administration can provide material for assessing the performance of the system and its schools. Excellent records are kept of the results of standardized tests, and the reporter can compare the community-wide scores with those of other cities. Comparisons can also be made of schools within the system. The good beat reporter may want to compare districts: Do the students in the low-scoring schools come from economically depressed areas with serious social and economic problems? Is there a correlation between these factors? Historical comparisons can also be made: Are students in a relatively stable school district doing as well as or worse than their parents did in reading and writing?

A check of high school graduates would indicate what percentage are going to college from each school. Interviews with the students may uncover information just as revealing as the students' test scores. This takes us to the primary responsibility of the education reporter.

Education reporters walk the corridors of high schools and sit in the classrooms of junior high schools. They visit the cafeterias and playgrounds of the elementary schools.

In the Classroom

The education reporter's responsibility is to hold the school system accountable to parents and to the community. The United States has committed itself to an educational system that will turn out large numbers of people educated beyond the level that the country demanded only of its educated elite a century ago. How well is it doing this?

The only way to find out is to visit the classroom, to look at what is happening day after day and to check these observations against test scores and the assessments of parents and educators. When Bob Frazier of the *Register-Guard* in Eugene, Ore., covered education he would fold his 6'4" frame into a grade schooler's chair and sit in class. The stories he wrote were much more significant than any release from the superintendent's office.

Gregor W. Pinney of the *Minneapolis Tribune* also visits classrooms to get the feel for what and who he is writing about. (See news story on next page.)

Students Find There's More
to Art Than Meets the Eye

By Gregor W. Pinney

At 10:30 one morning, Roy Larson lugged two boxes of gray clay into a fourth-grade classroom for a lesson on pottery-making. But the youngsters didn't get their hands on the clay until 30 minutes later because Larson had something else to teach them first.

Larson, an art specialist in the White Bear Lake schools, is one of a new breed of art teachers who want to do more than just teach youngsters how to produce art. He wants to impart some knowledge about it—its history, its concepts, its value, its connection with the lives of the students.

"Who were the first people to use clay?" asked Larson, as he looked out over a class at Golfview Elementary School.

"The Babylonians," replied a boy.

"Who was the first man—ah, person—to live on earth?" asked Larson, still looking for the correct answer.

"Cave people," a girl said.

"Right," exclaimed Larson. But he still was not certain he had their attention.

"Living in caves was easy," he went on. "Whenever they wanted anything to eat or wear, all they had to do was go about a block to the local store and buy it."

Education reporters who are doing this in the 1980s are learning that the educational system is passing through still another crisis, one brought about by social and economic factors affecting students and teachers. Teachers expect less of their students, some taking a patronizing view toward minority children who increasingly are making up the bulk of students within large urban school systems. Teachers suffer from what they consider society's undervaluing their occupation. Students arrive in the classroom "unfit for the presuppositions of a classroom," according to Neil Postman, a professor of media ecology at New York University. They cannot adjust to the orderly and structured experience that underlies education.

Some of the results are disorder in the classroom, declining scores on standardized tests, high truancy rates, many dropouts, increasing failures throughout the elementary and high school years.

There are other issues the education reporter examines: integration of the schools and the teaching force, drug use, racial tensions in the classroom and on school grounds, bilingualism, church-state confrontations, conflicts over the curriculum. These arouse passions and generate acrimony in the community. Intelligent reporting can aid in the resolution of some of them. The parroting of press releases and handouts is insufficient response to the importance of the beat.

Most of these issues are argued and resolved, sometimes only temporarily, within a political context.

Some Suggestions for Visiting Elementary Schools

1. Adults are bigger than children. As soon as you enter a classroom, sit in a chair; better still, with young children, kneel so that you can talk to them comfortably and look them in the eye.
2. Let children come to you. Most children are shy, but almost all are curious enough to come over to you eventually to ask what you are doing in their room. Letting them take the initiative will create a more natural atmosphere.
3. Don't patronize children. Don't laugh at what they say because you consider it cute. Children usually want to be taken seriously. Treat them like intelligent human beings and you will get the story you seek.

Rachel Theilheimer, who made these recommendations, has taught in grade schools and directed a day care center. She says principals are often uncomfortable about allowing reporters into schools, fearing they might "get a bad impression." She suggests reporters go to a teacher and have the teacher convince the principal to allow a visit.

Making Eye Contact. A youngster is comfortable talking to someone at eye level rather than looking up, especially when the child is being asked a lot of questions. Beth Hughes of the San Francisco *Examiner* kneels to interview a little girl.

Politics and Education

The conventional wisdom is that education is "above politics." The proof: The administration of the schools is separated from city government and placed in an independent board whose members are chosen without regard to party affiliation, usually in elections separated from the partisan campaigning of the regular local election.

The truth is that education is inextricably bound up with politics. "There is no comprehending the forces that move American education apart from more general political considerations," says Lawrence A. Cremin, the president of Teachers College at Columbia University. Politics enters the scene because, to put it simply, people differ in their notions of how youth should be trained, who should pay for it, who should control it. These differences are resolved in a political context. The conflict and its resolution should be at the heart of much of the reporter's coverage.

To take one example, financing: Since the 1940s, the pattern of school financing has changed drastically, moving away from local sources to the states and the federal government in Washington, D.C. The local property tax, under attack as unconstitutional at the one end and as regressive and burdensome at the other, can no longer sustain the schools. Fifty years ago, the local taxpayers provided 70 percent of the money for running the public schools. Today, the federal and state governments provide the majority of the funding.

The financing of the schools is made by politicians subject to the pressures of interest groups in a charged political atmosphere. Classic confrontations result: taxpayers anxious to hold the property tax down versus teachers worried about salaries during an inflationary period; state legislators and congressmen concerned over budget deficits facing up to the powerful teachers' unions, parents' organizations and the vested interest of the educational establishment; parents pressuring school administrators and public officials to introduce prayer in the classroom and instruction in creationism in the curriculum.

Although reporters tend to stress the financial conflicts, there are other issues just as important. Administrative decisions about how the schools are to be run are always in flux. Debate is intense among school and parent groups about the curriculum. The relationship of church and state, its roots deep in western history, is always in tension. (Cremin says the church-state conflict may never be resolved.) In many communities, the school system is a major source of jobs, and politicians seek to use it for patronage and to reward businessmen and merchants. In big cities, where many middle-class white families have fled from the city core, school authorities face serious problems integrating classes and schools. There simply are not enough white children remaining, and the solution—busing—has aroused intense feelings that are worked out in a political setting.

School board meetings are often political battlegrounds where various interest groups confront one another. Here is a guide to covering board meetings.

Financing the Schools

One measure of a school's effectiveness is its financial support from the community. Here are some average figures. The first column is for a bedroom community, the suburban town that relies almost completely on taxes from homeowners rather than from the business section. The second column is for cities with a large number of stores and other businesses:

	Suburb	City
Tax rate per $1,000 valuation	$30.35	$19.50
Property value per student	$54,300	$215,500
Amount spent per pupil	$3,215	$4,815

Information to have in mind before meeting:

_____ Names of board members and areas they represent if elected by subdistricts.

_____ Names of superintendent and top aides.

_____ Number of students in district, geographical area it covers. Demographic data on school district, if relevant.

For story about meeting:

_____ Exact wording of actions taken.

_____ How each member voted. If there is no formal vote but an informal consensus, get nods of heads or any other signs of approval or disapproval. Ask if uncertain.

_____ The size and makeup of audience.

_____ Reaction of audience to proposal(s).

_____ Position of groups or organizations with a position on the issue. (Obtain beforehand if possible.)

_____ Arguments on all sides.

_____ Statements from those for and against proposal on what the decision of the board means.

**Checklist:
Board of Education
Meeting**

Here is the beginning of a story Pinney wrote about a short meeting of the Minneapolis school board. His familiarity with the school system and the persons in it enable him to blend interpretation with straight, Level I reporting.

Civic Coalition Demands
Long-Range Plan on Schools

By Gregor W. Pinney

Frustrated by the response they have received so far, three community groups have joined forces and demanded Tuesday night that the Minneapolis school board take action on recommendations they have made this year for changes in the school system.

They were supported by a fourth group that has made similar recommendations in recent years and also has expressed frustration.

Primarily, the groups want the board to draw up a long-range plan so the community will know where the school system is headed on school closings, student achievement, involvement of parents and evaluation of teachers and administrators.

But they got no more response from the board last night than they have in the past.

The encounter took place at a board meeting at North High School, and it lasted only a few minutes. But it indicated a growing estrangement between the board and civic organizations that pride themselves on support of the school system. The groups say they want more stability in the school system so that more families will stay in the city.

The situation could change somewhat in January, however, when Judy Farmer and Joy Davis join the board. They were elected last week after making long-range planning the chief issue in their campaigns. They will not be able to make any changes on their own because they will hold only two of the seven seats, but they clearly are receptive to the groups that are calling for changes in management.

The three groups are the Minneapolis Urban Coalition, the League of Women Voters and the Educational Planning Steering Committee, a group appointed last year by the school board as required by law. The three have joined forces in something they call the "Coalition for Public Schools. . . ."

Many meetings of school boards are concerned with new programs. Here is a checklist of items for the reporter:

Checklist: a New Educational Program

These checklists are based on suggestions made by Gregor W. Pinney, education editor for the *Minneapolis Tribune.*

_____ Source of the idea.

_____ The superiority to the present program as claimed by sponsors.

_____ The cost and the source of funding the program.

_____ The basic philosophy or idea of the program.

_____ Other places it has been tried and the results there. (Make an independent check of this, if possible. How well is it working there; its cost.)

_____ Whether it has been tried before and discarded.

_____ How does it fit in with what the system is doing now. How it fits with trends in the area, state, nation.

_____ If someone is suggested to head it, who the person will be.

_____ Arguments pro and con, naming those involved.

The reporter who covers political campaigns must make a number of assumptions in order to do the job. Despite appearances, campaigns are carefully planned. This is assumption number one. From it, a reporter can infer that, as Ralph Whitehead at the University of Massachusetts says, "It is possible to read a campaign.

"Assume every decision is made for a reason. Hence, a campaign can be decoded. A reporter's job is to do this decoding. For example, for the week before the 1976 presidential primary in Florida, Jimmy Carter fairly leapt off the stage to plunge into the crowds. A competent reporter would try to read this maneuver. One possibility is that Carter was trying to dramatize vigor, to contrast his health with that of his major opponent in the south, George Wallace." Wallace, bound to a wheelchair by an assailant's bullet, was hurt by the health issue, an NBC poll found after the primary.

Just as an attorney enters a trial with a plan to defend his client or a quarterback goes into a game planning to exploit the opposition's vulnerability to the pass, so does a candidate enter a campaign. The plan is rarely divulged. But unless a reporter identifies the plan, it is impossible for him to put the campaign into a meaningful perspective.

David Broder, who covers politics for *The Washington Post,* says, "It is the job of the political reporter to cull from the thousands of words and the hundreds of incidents that comprise each day on the road with a presidential contender those few words, incidents and impressions that convey the flavor, the mood and the significance of what occurred." This means selectivity, Broder says, "the essence of all contemporary journalism. And selectivity implies criteria. Criteria depend on value judgments, which is a fancy term for opinions, preconceptions and prejudices. There is no neutral journalism."

Among the judgments reporters make in covering pre-election activities is who among the possible candidates to cover and then, in a primary, to whom to devote attention. In essence, "the political reporter not only puts some men forward, he rather ruthlessly bars the door to advancement for other men," says Broder. This is an awesome responsibility for the few people making the decisions—reporters and their editors.

Another task the political reporter takes on is that of "race caller or handicapper," Broder says. People want to know who's ahead, who will win or lose. And that, says Broder, is a question no reporter can answer with any confidence. Polls help (see chapter 4). But they make no pretense to exactitude in prediction. Reporters often fall back on the "feel" of a campaign. That is, they make their own judgments.

Broder sees another role for the reporter covering election campaigns, that of public defender. Reporters often make assessments of the men and women they cover. Sometimes the reporter overdoes this and becomes "an arbiter of the outcome of the election," Broder says. But the reporter can use this instinct to protect the public by holding candidates accountable for what they say, by asking for details on ambiguous and ambitious programs, by inserting background that reveals the actual dimensions of the candidates' promises.

Some Tips

Campaigns are confusing at best, no matter how ably run. The nature of politics is such that no one can predict their form and shape from day to day. A political reporter needs some general steering points.

Candidates go where the votes are. This is applicable to candidates for local and state offices, less so to candidates for the major national offices since television takes their campaigns into homes everywhere. The reporter covering a mayoral or gubernatorial campaign who watches the candidates' schedules for the week can make some informed conclusions, says Whitehead.

Where does the candidate go, how often and on what terms? When a Jewish candidate spends most of his time in the Catholic areas of town, one conclusion may be drawn. If he gives a large part of his time to appearances at synagogues and Jewish organizations, another conclusion may be drawn. When a Republican candidate for governor of New Mexico devoted 75 percent of his time to campaigning in Democratic strongholds, few reporters drew the obvious inference: The Republicans felt the Democratic candidate was highly vulnerable in areas Democrats took for granted. Not only did reporters fail to perceive the strategy—neither did the Democrats. In that election, the Democrats lost the statehouse for the first time in 20 years when the Republican candidate picked up almost half of the registered Democratic vote and 80 percent of the much smaller Republican vote. Reporters were surprised by the result.

Another tip: Watch the campaign's media purchases. If it is buying television spots near daytime soap operas, it is looking for the homebound female.

Whitehead suggests a rule of thumb: "The larger the electorate, the more likely a candidate will run a rational and intelligent campaign." The larger the electorate, the more money a candidate is allowed to raise and spend, and the skilled professionals in the campaign management business are attracted to the big spenders. When a small-town candidate runs a skilled and well-financed campaign, chances are that a foundation is being built for future campaigns for higher office.

Most candidates run to win, but sometimes a candidate runs to raise an issue, or is being used as a strawman or stalking horse for other interests. If an Irish candidate is running against a candidate of Polish descent, the Irishman may field another candidate of Polish descent to split the Polish vote. The subsidized candidate is known as a stalking horse.

Reporting the Issues

All of these suggestions are aimed at making the reporter competent at digging beneath the handout and the press release, the prepared text and the vapid television appearance. The purpose of a reporter's coverage should be to learn precisely what the candidate is trying to do and to reveal that to the electorate. There is another purpose to political reporting: To hold the candidate to the relevant issues.

If voters are to cast ballots intelligently rather than on the basis of paid television spots—which surveys indicate are an important basis of voting behavior—then reporters must direct their questions and coverage to what they consider the issues candidates should speak to. This is nothing unusual for the journalist. Every reporter who goes out on a story draws up questions for sources. The political reporter is no different. He or she has a sense of the important matters facing the community, state or nation, and these become the substance of questions directed to the candidates. Their answers can provide the voters with more tangible evidence for voting than the source-originated handout or speech. Reporters have a role in setting the political agenda.

Too many reporters have more interest in the politics of government than in its substance. The result is that many reporters are unable to make judgments about substantive matters and must rely on the so-called experts, some of whom have vested interests in the issues. James Fallows, the Washington editor of *The Atlantic* and a contributing editor of *The Washington Monthly,* says that emphasizing "the business of winning elections and gaining points in the polls" does readers and viewers a disservice. In his article, "The President and the Press" in the October 1979 *Washington Monthly,* Fallows says, "We all love a horserace. All they (reporters) leave out is the *what*—what he's saying, what happened when that approach was tried before, what effect this proposal will have on the permanent culture of the government or the national culture outside.

"The *what* is missing because most reporters still lack either the interest or the confidence to judge the substance of government as acutely as they judge politics."

The banner across the window of campaign headquarters read, "Your congressman is there when you need him." The theme was repeated in the congressman's campaign for re-election. No one bothered to ask what it meant. Emboldened by the acceptance of slogans and generalities, politicians and office-seekers generate empty catch-phrases by the bushel.

The political reporter should see through these slogans. They are substitutes for the specific. They are the calculated devices by which the candidate or the official avoids taking a position. It is impossible to hold a public official accountable for his resounding promise: "I pledge to work for you." Nor is the public a whit more informed after being told the candidate "cares" and intends to "listen to you."

The political reporter must bring the high-flying orator back to earth by asking questions about issues. The reporter should not shun the task of moving political discourse to the confrontation of relevant issues before the public. The alternative is to permit the candidates to trivialize the campaign.

Cutting Through the Rhetoric

Reporters who cover government are so trained to find the malfunctions and the excesses and failures that they become cynical about government. They forget that the tasks of government often reflect the demands citizens make on government. They join a skeptical public in what Felix Frankfurter, a distinguished former justice of the Supreme Court of the United States, has described as "the paradox of both distrusting and burdening government." He said that this state of mind "reveals the lack of a conscious philosophy of politics."

Cynicism

The Many Tasks of Government. Local governments collect trash, build and maintain roads, clean graffiti off public buildings and attend to the hundreds of other tasks citizens ask of their city officials, who often have limited funds. A major job of the reporter is to present clearly the unlimited demands on government and its limited resources.

A reporter needs to define for himself or herself some approach to the job of covering the interaction between those who govern and those who are governed. Cynicism disables the reporter in his or her task of helping the public to articulate its demands on its officials. The cynic believes that the process is futile or the actors in it are hopelessly corrupt or so inefficient that nothing can work. The concept of the reporter as stenographer to officialdom is equally useless since it deprives the public of the informed intelligence of the reporter in helping to set the agenda for public debate. The reporter must understand that for individuals to lead fruitful lives there must be systematized cooperation between the governed and those who govern and that the journalist helps to bring this about by pointing to the necessity for interdependence of all the actors in the public drama.

Government has a role to play, just as does the independent press. Both can be powerful and positive forces in articulating the demands of the public.

Terms

budget Two kinds, capital and expense. Capital is for construction and long-range projects. Expense is for salaries and other daily expenses.

budget gap The difference between expenditures and revenues. Cities are required by law to balance their budgets.

cost-benefit analysis To analyze a proposed policy or to justify an expenditure, a cost-benefit analysis may be made. This analytic tool examines the impacts of a proposal and assigns values to these impacts. An analysis may be made of the short-term and long-range costs and benefits of an expenditure. The examination may be made by the executive in scrutinizing budget requests from departments and agencies, or it may be made by a governmental unit in order to justify a proposal to the public such as a bond issue.

debt limit Maximum amount city can borrow. In many cities, the limit is 10 percent of full valuation of real estate averaged over last five years. The debt limit does not apply to revenue-producing ventures, sewage disposal or water supply.

debt service Funds set aside in expense budget to cover the costs of borrowing money in capital budget.

grants The federal government allocates vast sums of money to state and city governments in the form of grants. The reporter of local and state governments should be familiar with these types:

matching grants must be matched by the city or state receiving the money. For example: Urban renewal project grants usually carry a provision requiring the recipient to put up one-third the cost of construction in matching funds.

categorical grants must be used for specific purposes stipulated in the federal enacting legislation and are tied to narrowly defined federal goals. Local communities found categorical grants too confining and as a result block grants were devised.

block grants can be used by the recipients for a variety of purposes so long as they meet open-end federal goals such as the alleviation of poverty or improvement of educational levels.

formula grants are allocated according to formulas that take into account prescribed numerical factors—numbers of poor, young, aged, etc.

project grants are appropriated for assistance for particular projects or proposals submitted by the state or local government.

These definitions were made available by Jeanette M. Gougeon.

line budget A schedule of spending that lists the position and salary of each city employee. A specific line is listed in the budget for each position, and exceptions can be made only with permission of the city budget officer.

program budget Also known as performance budget. Sums are appropriated to agencies to carry out programs, and the agencies are free to allocate the funds for these programs. Less restrictive than the line budget.

revenue sharing Federal funds are allocated to large cities and states under a "three-factor formula" that takes into account population, per capita income and effort in collecting local and state taxes. This formula is sometimes altered to include the number of people in urban areas and local tax revenues and then is known as the "five-factor formula." Usually, two-thirds of the appropriation is passed on to local governments by the states. Local authorities are given the leeway to spend their appropriations on basic necessities, such as police and fire protection and mass transit.

uncuttables Expense budget items that cannot be reduced, including money for pensions and debt service.

zero-based budgeting Proposed budget items must be justified completely, that is, starting from zero. Agency heads must justify all proposals, new and old. The concept works best at state and municipal levels. Each department breaks its request into decision packages and the packages are presented with analysis of purpose, costs, measures of performance, benefits, alternative courses of action and consequences of rejection of proposed expenditure. Packages are then rated in order of priority for final decision.

Stylebook

The purpose of the stylebook is to set standards of consistency for abbreviations, capitalization, punctuation and other usage on which there may be differences of opinion. The stylebook makes the rules. This brief stylebook is based on common practices adopted by the AP and UPI for their stylebooks.

Addresses, months, states and titles are often abbreviated.

Abbreviations

Addresses Abbreviate Avenue, Boulevard, Street with specific address—1314 Kentucky St. Spell out without specific address—Kentucky Street, Fifth Avenue.

Months Abbreviate month with specific date—Jan. 25, 1927. Spell out when month stands alone or is followed by a year—January 1927.

States Abbreviate all states but the following when used with a city, in a dateline, or with party affiliation—Alaska, Hawaii, Idaho, Iowa, Maine, Ohio, Utah. Do not use Postal Service abbreviations. Spell out all states when standing alone.

Ala.	Fla.	Md.	Neb.	N.D.	Tenn.	Wyo.
Ariz.	Ga.	Mass.	Nev.	Okla.	Tex.	
Ark.	Ill.	Mich.	N.H.	Ore.	Vt.	
Calif.	Ind.	Minn.	N.J.	Pa.	Va.	
Colo.	Kan.	Miss.	N.M.	R.I.	Wash.	
Conn.	Ky.	Mo.	N.Y.	S.C.	W. Va.	
Del.	La.	Mont.	N.C.	S.D.	Wis.	

Titles Abbreviate titles before a name. When standing alone, spell out—The governor vetoed the bill.

Addresses Use figures for the address number—3 Third Ave.; 45 Main St. Spell out numbers under 10 as street names—21 Fourth Ave.; 450 11th St.

Age **Infant** Under one year of age.

Child The period between infancy and youth, ages one to 13.

Youth 13–18.

Man, Woman Over 18.

Adult Over 18, unless used in specific legal context for crimes such as drinking.

Middle-aged 35–55.

Elderly Over 65. Avoid when describing individuals.

Capitalization Generally, follow a down style.

Proper nouns Use capitals for names of persons, places, trademarks; titles when used with names; nicknames of persons, states, teams; titles of books, plays, movies.

President Make it a capital when it precedes the name; lowercase in all other uses—President Hoover. The president.

False titles Generally avoid false titles—right fielder Tommy Jones; television star Babs Buchin. Put such titles after person's name within commas—Tommy Jones, right fielder, struck out. Lowercase the title if used to precede name.

Contractions Avoid unless used in direct quotes or to set an informal tone to story.

Miss, Mrs., Ms., Mr. are usually not used on first reference with the full name. Use **Courtesy Titles**
Mrs. on first reference for clarity when a woman requests that her husband's first
name be used or her own first name cannot be ascertained—Mrs. Bruce Berning.
On first reference, use the woman's first name. Do not use Mr. in any reference.

Many newspapers use the courtesy title for a woman on second reference,
following the woman's preference: If married, use Mrs. unless she prefers Ms. If married and she prefers to be known by her maiden name, use Miss or Ms. If unmarried,
use Miss on second reference unless the woman prefers Ms. For divorced women
or women whose husbands have died, use Mrs. on second reference unless the
woman prefers Ms.

A number of newspapers drop Mrs., Miss and Ms. as well as Mr. on second
reference: "A Norfolk woman, Frances Savage, accused the judge of running a 'three-
ring circus.' Savage made her charges in a letter to the editor." This practice may
become more prevalent as newspapers continue to eliminate sexism in their news
stories.

Punctuation July 6, 1957, was her birth date. (Use commas.) She was born in July **Dates**
1957. (No comma between month and year.)

Abbreviations Abbreviate month with specific date—Feb. 19. Spell out all months
when standing alone. With dates, use abbreviations: Jan., Feb., Aug., Sept., Oct.,
Nov., Dec.; spell out March, April, May, June, July.

Spell out one through nine; use figures for 10 and above. **Numerals**

Spell out a number when it begins a sentence—Fifteen members voted against
the bill. Use figures when a year begins a sentence—1980 began auspiciously.

Use figures for percentages and percents.

For amounts of $1 million and more, use the $ sign and figures up to two dec-
imal places with the million, billion, trillion spelled out—$1.65 million. Exact amounts
are given in figures—$1,650,398.

When spelling out large numbers, separate figure ending in "y" from next number with a hyphen—Seventy-nine; one hundred seventy-nine.

A pronoun should agree with its antecedent in number, person and gender. The most **Pronouns**
common fault is a shift in (1) number or (2) person.

1. The organization added basketball and hockey to their winter program.
   (Wrong.)
   The organization added basketball and hockey to its winter program.
   (Right.)
2. When one wants to ski, you have to buy good equipment. (Wrong.)
   When one wants to ski, he or she has to buy good equipment. (Right.)

If the antecedent is singular, it is referred to with a singular pronoun. A singular pronoun is preferred with these antecedents: each, every, either, neither, someone, somebody, anyone, anything, anybody, everyone, no one, nobody.

A common error is to give teams, groups and organizations the plural pronoun:

The team played their best shortstop. (Wrong.)
The team played its best shortstop. (Right.)

The Police Department wants recruits. They need 1,500 applicants. (Wrong.)
The Police Department wants recruits. It needs 1,500 applicants. (Right.)

The nouns in the above examples are called collective nouns. If the noun is plural in idea, use the plural pronoun:

The family enjoyed their vacations.

Punctuation

Keep a good grammar book handy. No stylebook can adequately cover the complexities of the 13 punctuation marks: apostrophe, brackets, colon, comma, dash, ellipsis, exclamation point, hyphen, parenthesis, period, question mark, quotation marks, semicolon. The following is a guide to frequent problems and usages:

Apostrophe Use for (1) possessives, (2) to indicate omitted figures or letters and (3) to form some plurals.

1. *Possessives:* Add apostrophe and "s" ('s) to the end of singular and plural nouns or the indefinite pronoun unless it has an s or z sound:
   The woman's coat. The women's coats.
   The child's toy. The children's toys.
   Someone's pistol. One's hopes.
   If the word is plural and ends in an s or z sound, add apostrophe only:
   Boys' books. Joneses' farm.
   If the word is singular and ends in an s or z sound and has one syllable, add apostrophe and "s."
   James's hat. Jones's application.
   If the word is singular, has more than one syllable and ends in an s or z sound, add apostrophe only:
   Stevens' invention. Velazquez' paintings.
   Note: if the second s or z sound is necessary for broadcast purposes, then add the apostrophe and "s."
   The hostess's gown.
2. *Omitted figures or letters:* Use in contractions—Don't, can't. Put in place of omitted figure—Class of '86.
3. *To form some plurals:* When figures, letters, symbols and words are referred to as words, use the apostrophe and "s."

   - Figures: She skated perfect 8's.
   - Letters: He received all A's in his finals.
   - Symbols: Journalists never use &'s to substitute for the ands in their copy.

Caution: The pronouns ours, yours, theirs, his, hers, whose do not take the apostrophe. Its is the possessive pronoun. It's is the contraction of it is.

Note: Compound words and nouns in joint possession use the possessive in the last word:

- Everybody else's homes.
- His sister-in-law's book.
- Mondale and Kennedy's party.

If there is separate possession, each noun takes the possessive form:

Carter's and Kennedy's opinions differ.

Brackets Check whether the newspaper can set them. The wire services cannot transmit brackets. Use to enclose a word or words within a quote that the writer inserts—"Happiness [his note read] is a state of mind." Use for paragraph(s) within a story that refer to an event separate from the datelined material.

Colon The colon is usually used at the end of a sentence to call attention to what follows. It introduces lists, tabulations, texts and quotations of more than one sentence.

It can also be used to mark a full stop before a dramatic word or statement— She had only one goal in life: work. The colon is used in time of day, 7:45 p.m.; elapsed time of an event, 4:01.1, and in dialogue in question and answer, as from a trial.

Comma The best general guide for the use of the comma is the human voice as it pauses, stops and varies in tone. The comma marks the pause, the short stop:

1. He looked into the hospital room, but he was unable to find the patient.
2. Although he continued his search on the floor for another 20 minutes, he was unable to find anyone to help him.
3. He decided that he would go downstairs, ask at the desk and then telephone the police.
4. If that also failed, he thought to himself, he would have to give up the search.

Note that when reading these sentences aloud, the commas are natural resting points for pauses. The four sentences also illustrate the four principles governing the use of commas:

1. The comma is used to separate main clauses when they are joined by a coordinating conjunction. (The coordinating conjunctions are: for, nor, and, but, or.) The comma can be eliminated if the main clauses are short—He looked into the room and he froze.
2. Use the comma after an introductory element: a clause, long phrase, transitional expression or interjection.

3. Use the comma to separate words, phrases or clauses in a series. Also, use it in a series of coordinate adjectives—He was wearing a long, full cape.
4. Set off nonessential material in a sentence with comma(s). When the parenthetical or interrupting nonrestrictive clauses and phrases are in the middle of a sentence two commas are needed—The country, he was told, needed his assistance.

Other uses of the comma:

Use a comma with full sentence quotes, not with partial quotes—He asked, "Where are you going?" The man replied that he was "blindly groping" his way home.

To separate city and county, city and state. In place of the word "of" between a name and city—Jimmy Carter, Plains, Ga.

To set off a person's age—Orville Sterb, 19, of Fullerton, Calif.

In dates—March 19, 1940, was the date he entered the army.

In party affiliations—Bill Bradley, D-N.J., spoke.

Caution: The comma is frequently misused by placing it between two main clauses instead of using the period or semicolon. This is called comma splice:

- The typewriter was jammed, he could not type his theme. (Wrong.)
- The typewriter was jammed. He could not type his theme. The typewriter was jammed; he could not type his theme. (Right.)

Dash Use a dash (1) to indicate a sudden or dramatic shift in thought within a sentence, (2) to set off a series of words that contains commas and (3) to introduce sections of a list or a summary.

The dash is a call for a short pause, just as are the comma and the parenthesis. The comma is the most often used and is the least dramatic of the separators. The parenthesis sets off unimportant elements. The dash tends to emphasize material. It has this quality because it is used sparingly.

1. He stared at the picture—and he was startled to find himself thinking of her face.
   The man stood up—painfully and awkwardly—and extended his hand in greeting.
2. There were three persons watching them—an elderly woman, a youth with a crutch at his side and a young woman in jeans holding a paperback— and he pulled her aside out of their view.
3. He gave her his reasons for being there:
   —He wanted to apologize;
   —He needed to give her some material;
   —He was leaving on a long trip.
   (*Note:* This third form should be used infrequently, usually when the listing will be followed by an elaboration.)

The dash is also used in datelines.

Ellipsis Use the ellipsis to indicate material omitted from a quoted passage from a text, transcript, play, etc.—The minutes stated that Breen had asked, "How many gallons of paint . . . were used in the project?" Put one space before and one space after each of the three periods. If the omission ends with a period, use four periods, one to mark the end of the sentence (without space, as a regular period), three more for the ellipsis.

The ellipsis is also used by some columnists to separate short items in a paragraph.

Do not use to mark pauses, shifts in thought, or for emphasis.

Exclamation point Much overused. There are reporters who have gone through a lifetime of writing and have never used the exclamation point, except when copying material in which it is used. The exclamation point is used to indicate powerful feelings, surprise, wonderment. Most good writers prefer to let the material move the reader to provide his or her own exclamation.

When using, do not use a comma or period after the exclamation point. Place inside quotation marks if it is part of the quoted material.

Hyphen The hyphen is used (1) to join words to express a single idea or (2) to avoid confusion or ambiguity.

1. Use the hyphen to join two or more words that serve as a single adjective before a noun—A well-known movie is on television tonight. He had a know-it-all expression.
   Caution: Do not use the hyphen when the first word of the compound ends in "ly" or when the words follow the noun—He is an easily recognized person. Her hair was blonde black.
2. (a) Avoid ambiguity or (b) an awkward joining of letters or syllables by putting a hyphen between prefixes or suffixes and the root word.
   a. He recovered the chair. He re-covered the chair.
   b. Re-enter, macro-economics, shell-like.

Parenthesis Generally, avoid. They may be necessary for the insertion of background or to set off supplementary or illustrative material.

Use period inside closing parenthesis if the matter begins with a capital letter.

Period Use the period at the end of declarative sentences, indirect questions, most imperative sentences and most abbreviations.

The period is placed inside quotation marks.

Question mark The question mark is used for direct questions, not indirect questions.

> Direct: Where are you going?
> Indirect: He asked where she was going.

The question mark goes inside quotation marks if it applies to the quoted material—He asked, "Have you seen the movie?" Put it outside if it applies to the entire sentence—Have you seen "Guys and Dolls"?

Quotation marks Quotation marks set off (1) direct quotations, (2) some titles and nicknames and (3) words used in a special way.

1. Set off the exact words of the speaker— "He walked like a duck," she said. He replied that he walked "more like an alley cat on the prowl."
2. Use for book and movie titles, titles of short stories, poems, songs, articles from magazines and plays. Some nicknames take quotation marks. Do not use for nicknames of sports figures.
3. For words used in a special sense—An "Indian giver" is someone who gives something to another and then takes it back.

Punctuation with quotation marks:

> *The comma*—Use it outside the quotation marks when setting off the speaker at the beginning of a sentence—He said, "You care too much for money." Use inside the quotation marks when the speaker ends the sentence— "I just want to be safe," she replied.
> *The colon and semicolon*—Always place outside the quotation marks—He mentioned her "incredible desire for work"; he meant her "insatiable desire for work."
> *The dash, question mark and exclamation point*—inside when they apply to quoted matter only; outside when they refer to the whole sentence—She asked, "How do you know so much?" He asked himself, what's the meaning of "know so much"?

For quotes within quotes, use single quote mark (the apostrophe on typewriter) for the inner quotation—"Have you read 'War and Peace'?" he asked. Note, no comma is used after the question mark.

Semicolon Usually overused by beginning reporters. Unless there is a special reason to use the semicolon, use the period.

Use the semicolon to separate a series of equal elements when the individual segments contain material that is set off by commas. This makes for clarity in the series—He suggested that she spend her allowance on the new series at the opera, "Operas of the Present"; books of plays by Shaw, Ibsen and Aristophanes; and novels by Tolstoy, Dickens and F. Scott Fitzgerald.

Avoid stereotyping women or men. Be conscious of equality in treatment of both **Sexism**
sexes.

In writing of careers and jobs, avoid presuming that the wage earner is a man
and that the woman is a homemaker.

> The average worker with a wife and three children . . . (Wrong.)
> The average family of five . . . (Right.)

Avoid physical descriptions of women or men when not absolutely relevant to
the story.

Use parallel references to both sexes—the men and the women, not the men
and the ladies; husband and wife, not man and wife.

Do not use nouns and pronouns to indicate sex unless the sex difference is
basic to understanding or there is no suitable substitute. One way to avoid such
subtle sexism is to change the noun to the plural, eliminating the masculine pronoun:
Drivers should have their licenses.

Personal appearance and marital and family relationships should be used only
when relevant to the story.

When in doubt about spelling, consult an accepted dictionary. Use the first spelling **Spelling**
listed. If the word is not listed, do not use it unless it is in a direct quote.

Exact times are often unnecessary. Last night and this morning are acceptable sub- **Time**
stitutes for yesterday and today, if appropriate. Use exact time when pertinent, but
avoid redundancies—8 a.m. this morning should be 8 a.m. today or 8 o'clock this
morning.

Use figures except for noon and midnight.

Separate hours from minutes with a colon—3:15 p.m.

Glossary

These definitions were provided by the press associations and working reporters and editors. Most of the brief entries are from the *New England Daily Newspaper Study,* an examination of 105 daily newspapers, edited by Loren Ghiglione (Southbridge, Mass.: Southbridge Evening News Inc., 1973).

add An addition to a story already written or in the process of being written.

assignment Instruction to a reporter to cover an event. An editor keeps an assignment book that contains notations for reporters such as the following:

Jacobs—10 a.m.: Health officials tour new sewage treatment plant.

Klaren—11 a.m.: Interview Ben Wastersen, possible Democratic congressional candidate.

Mannen—Noon: Rotary Club luncheon speaker, Horlan, the numerologist. A feature?

attribution Designation of the person being quoted. Also, the source of information in a story. Sometimes, information is given on a not-for-attribution basis.

background Material in a story that gives the circumstances surrounding or preceding the event.

banger An exclamation point. Avoid. Let the reader do the exclaiming.

banner Headline across or near the top of all or most of a newspaper page. Also called a line, ribbon, streamer, screamer.

B copy Bottom section of a story written ahead of an event that will occur too close to deadline for the entire story to be processed. The B copy usually consists of background material.

beat Area assigned to a reporter for regular coverage; for example, police or city hall. Also, an exclusive story.

body type Type in which most of a newspaper is set, usually 8 or 9 point type.

Print Terms

boldface Heavy, black typeface; type that is blacker than the text with which it is used. Abbreviated bf.

break When a news development becomes known and available. Also, the point of interruption in a story continued from one page to another.

bright Short, amusing story.

bulldog Early edition, usually the first of a newspaper.

byline Name of the reporter who wrote the story, placed atop the published article. An old-timer comments on the current use of bylines: "In the old days, a reporter was given a byline if he or she personally covered an important or unusual story, or the story was an exclusive. Sometimes if the writing was superior, a byline was given. Nowadays, everyone gets a byline, even if the story is a rewrite and the reporter never saw the event described in the story."

caps Capital letters; same as upper case.

caps and lower case Initial capital in a word followed by small letters. See lower case.

clip News story clipped from a newspaper, usually for future reference.

cold type In composition, type set photographically or by pasting up letters and pictures on acetate or paper.

column The vertical division of the news page. A standard-size newspaper is divided into five to eight columns. Also, a signed article of opinion or strong personal expression, frequently by an authority or expert—a sports column, a medical column, political or social commentary, and the like.

copy Written form in which a news story or other material is prepared.

copy flow After a reporter finishes a story it moves to the city desk where the city editor reads it for major errors or problems. If it does not need further work, the story is moved to the copy desk for final editing and a headline. It then moves to the mechanical department.

correction Errors that reach publication are retracted or corrected if they are serious or someone demands a correction. Libelous matter is always corrected immediately, often in a separate news story rather than in the standard box assigned to corrections.

correspondent Reporter who sends news from outside a newspaper office. On smaller papers often not a regular full-time staff member.

crony journalism Reporting that ignores or treats lightly negative news about friends of a reporter. Beat reporters sometimes have a tendency to protect their informants in order to retain them as sources.

crop To cut or mask the unwanted portions, usually of a photograph.

cut Printed picture or illustration. Also, to eliminate material from a story. See trim.

cutline Any descriptive or explanatory material under a picture.

dateline Name of the city or town and sometimes the date at the start of a story that is not of local origin.

deadline Time at which the copy for an edition must be ready.

edition One version of a newspaper. Some papers have one edition a day, some several. Not to be confused with issue, which usually refers to all editions under a single date.

editorial Article of comment or opinion usually on the editorial page.

editorial material All material in the newspaper that is not advertising.

enterprise copy Story, often initiated by a reporter, that digs deeper than the usual news story.

exclusive Story one reporter has obtained to the exclusion of the competition. A beat. Popularly known as a scoop, a term never used in the newsroom.

feature Story emphasizing the human or entertaining aspects of a situation. A news story or other material differentiated from straight news. As a verb, it means to give prominence to a story.

file To send a story to the office, usually by wire or telephone, or to put news service stories on the wire.

filler Material used to fill space. Small items used to fill out columns where needed. Also called column closers and shorts.

flag Printed title of a newspaper on page one. Also known as logotype or nameplate.

folo Story that follows up on a theme in a news story. When a fire destroyed a parochial school in Chicago, newspapers followed up the fire coverage with stories about fire safety precautions in the Chicago schools.

free advertising Use of the names of businesses and products not essential to the story. Instead of the brand name, use the broad term camera for Leica or Kodak.

futures calendar Date book in which story ideas, meetings and activities scheduled for a later occurrence are listed. Also known as a futures book. Kept by city and assignment editors and by careful reporters.

good night Before leaving for the day, beat reporters check in with the desk and are given a good night, which means there is nothing further for the reporter from the desk for the day. On some newspapers, the call is made for the lunch break, too. Desks need to know where their reporters are in case of breaking stories.

graf Abbreviation for paragraph.

Guild Newspaper Guild, an international union to which reporters and other newspaper workers belong. Newspapers that have contracts with the Guild are said to be "organized."

handout Term for written publicity or special-interest news sent to a newspaper for publication.

hard news Spot news; live and current news in contrast to features.

head or headline The display type over a printed news story.

head shot Picture featuring little more than the head and shoulders of the person shown.

HFR Abbreviation for "hold for release." Material that cannot be used until it is released by the source or at a designated time. Also known as embargoed material.

insert Material placed between copy in a story. Usually, a paragraph or more to be placed in material already sent to the desk.

investigative reporting Technique used to unearth information that sources often want hidden. This type of reporting involves examination of documents and records, the cultivation of informants, painstaking and extended research. Investigative reporting usually seeks to expose wrongdoing and has concentrated on public officials and their activities. In recent years, industry and business have been scrutinized. Some journalists contend that the term is redundant, that all good reporting is investigative, that behind every surface fact is the real story that a resourceful, curious and persistent reporter can dig up.

italics Type in which letters and characters slant to the right.

jump Continuation of a story from one page to another. As a verb, to continue material. Also called runover.

kill To delete a section from copy or to discard the entire story; also, to spike a story.

lead (pronounced leed) First paragraph in a news story. In a direct or straight news lead it summarizes the main facts. In a delayed lead, usually used on feature stories, it evokes a scene or sets a mood.
Also used to refer to the main idea of a story: An editor will ask a reporter "What's the lead on the piece?" expecting a quick summary of the main facts.
Also: A tip on a story; an idea for a story. A source will tell a reporter, "I have a lead on a story for you."

localize Emphasizing the names of persons from the local community who are involved in events outside the city or region: A local couple rescued in a Paris hotel fire; the city police chief who speaks at a national conference.

lower case Small letters, as contrasted to capitals.

LTK Designation on copy for "lead to come." Usually placed after the slug. Indicates the written material will be given a lead later.

makeup Layout or design. The arrangement of body type, headlines and illustrations into pages.

masthead Formal statement of a newspaper's name, officers, place of publication and other descriptive information, usually on the editorial page. Sometimes confused with flag or nameplate.

morgue Newspaper library.

mug shot See head shot.

new lead See running story.

news hole Space in a newspaper allotted to news, illustrations and other nonadvertising material.

obituary Account of a person's death; also called obit.

offset Printing process in which an image is transferred from a printing plate to a rubber roller and then set off on paper.

off the record Material offered the reporter in confidence. If the reporter accepts the material with this understanding, it cannot be used except as general background in a later story. Some reporters never accept off-the-record material. Some reporters will accept the material with the provision that if they can obtain the information elsewhere they will use it. Reporters who learn of off-the-record material from other than the original source can use it.
No public, official meeting can be off the record, and almost all official documents (court records, police information) are public information. Private groups can ask that their meetings be kept off the record, but reporters frequently ignore such requests when the meeting is public or large numbers of persons are present.

op-ed page Abbreviation for the page opposite the editorial page. The page is frequently devoted to opinion columns and related illustrations.

overnight Story usually written late at night for the afternoon newspapers of the next day. Most often used by the press services. The overnight, or overnighter, usually has little new information in it but is cleverly written so that the reader thinks the story is new. Also known as second-day stories.

play Emphasis given to a news story or picture—size and place in the newspaper of the story; typeface and size of headline.

P.M. Afternoon or evening newspaper.

pool Arrangement whereby limited numbers of reporters and photographers are selected to represent all those assigned to the story. Pooling is adopted when a large number of persons would overwhelm the event or alter its nature. The news and film are shared with the rest of the press corps.

precede Story written prior to an event; also, the section of a story preceding the lead, sometimes set in italic.

press release Publicity handout, or a story given to the news media for publication.

proof Reproduction of type on paper for the purpose of making corrections or alterations.

puff or puffery Publicity story or a story that contains unwarranted superlatives.

quotes Quotation marks; also a part of a story in which someone is directly quoted.

rewrite To write for a second time to strengthen a story or to condense it.

rewrite man Person who takes the facts of stories over the telephone and then puts them together into a story and who may rewrite reporters' stories.

roundup A story that joins two or more events with a common theme such as traffic accidents, weather, police reports. When the events occur in different cities and are wrapped up in one story, the story is known as an "undated roundup."

rowback A story that attempts to correct a previous story without indicating that the prior story had been in error or without taking responsibility for the error.

running story Event that develops and is covered over a period of time. For an event covered in subsequent editions of a newspaper or on a single cycle of a wire service, additional material is handled as follows: new lead— Important new information; adds and inserts—Less important information; sub—Material that replaces dated material, which is removed.

scanner Electronic device that reads prepared copy for the generation of tape that can be fed into a photocomposition machine or for entering material into the system for subsequent processing.

sell Presentation a reporter makes to impress the editor with the importance of his or her story; also, editors sell stories to their superiors at news conferences.

shirt tail Short, related story added to the end of a longer one.

short Filler, generally of some current news value.

sidebar Story that emphasizes one part of another nearby story.

situationer Story that pulls together a continuing event for the reader who may not have kept track as it unfolded. The situationer is helpful with complex or technical developments or on stories with varied datelines and participants.

slant To write a story so as to influence the reader's thinking. To editorialize, to color or misrepresent.

slug Word or words placed on all copy to identify the story.

source Person, record, document or event that provides the information for the story.

source book Alphabetical listing, by name and by title, of the addresses and the office and home telephone numbers of persons on the reporter's beat and some general numbers—FBI agent in charge in town, police and fire department spokesmen, hospital information, weather bureau.

split page Front page of an inside section; also known as the break page, second front page.

stringer Correspondent, not a regular staff member, who is paid by the story or by the number of words written.

style Rules for capitalization, punctuation and spelling that standardize usage so that the material presented is uniform. Most newspapers and stations have stylebooks. The most frequently used is the common stylebook of the United Press International and the Associated Press. Some newspapers stress the "down" or "lower case" style, by which is meant that most titles are lower case. Some newspapers capitalize (upper case) frequently. Also, the unique characteristics of a reporter's writing or news delivery.

stylebook Specific listing of the conventions of spelling, abbreviation, punctuation, capitalization used by a particular newspaper, wire service. Broadcast stylebooks include pronunciations.

sub See running story.

subhead One-line and sometimes two-line head (usually in boldface body type) inserted in a long story at intervals for emphasis or to break up a long column of type.

text Verbatim report of a speech or public statement.

thumbnail Half column-wide cut or portrait.

tight Full, too full. Also refers to a paper so crowded with ads that the news space must be reduced. It is the opposite of the wide open paper.

tip Information passed to a reporter, often in confidence. The material usually requires further fact gathering. Occasionally, verification is impossible and the reporter must decide whether to go with the tip on the strength of the insider's knowledge. Sometimes the reporter will not want to seek confirmation for fear of alerting sources who will alter the situation or release the information to the competition. Tips often lead to exclusives.

titles Mr., Mrs., Miss, Ms., Secretary of State, Police Chief, Senator are formal designations and may be used before the person's name. Usage depends upon the station's or newspaper's policy. False titles—Vietnam war hero, actress, left fielder—are properly used after the name: For instance, Nate Thurmond, the center . . . instead of Center Nate Thurmond . . .

trim To reduce or condense copy carefully.

update Story that brings the reader up to date on a situation or personality previously in the news. If the state legislature appropriated additional funds for five new criminal court judges to meet the increased number of cases in the courts an update might be written some months later to see how many more cases were handled after the judges went to work. An update usually has no hard news angle.

VDT Video display terminal; a part of the electronic system used in news and advertising departments that eliminates typewriters. Copy is written on typewriter-like keyboards and words appear on attached television screens rather than on paper. The story is stored on a disc in a computer. Editing is done on the terminals.

verification Determination of the truth of the material the reporter gathers or is given. The assertions, sometimes even the actual observation, do not necessarily mean the information is accurate or true. Some of the basic tools of verification are: the telephone book, for names and addresses; the city directory, for occupations; *Who's Who,* for biographical information. For verification of more complex material, the procedure of Thucydides, the Greek historian and author of the *History of the Peloponnesian War,* is good advice for the journalist: "As to the deeds done in the war, I have not thought myself at liberty to record them on hearsay from the first informant or on arbitrary conjecture. My account rests either on personal knowledge or on the closest possible scrutiny of each statement made by others. The process of research was laborious, because the conflicting accounts were given by those who had witnessed the several events, as partiality swayed or memory served them."

wire services Synonym for press associations, the Associated Press and United Press International. There are foreign-owned press services to which some newspapers subscribe: Reuters, Tass, Agence France Presse.

actuality An on-the-scene report.
audio Sound.

closeup Shot of the face of the subject that dominates the frame so that little background is visible.
cover shot A long shot usually cut in at the beginning of a sequence to establish place or location.
cue A signal in script or by word or gesture to begin or to stop. Two types: incue and outcue.
cut Quick transition from one type of picture to another. Radio: A portion of an actuality on tape used on broadcast.
cutaway Transition shot—usually short—from one theme to another; used to avoid jump cut. Often, a shot of the interviewer listening.

dissolve Smooth fading of one picture for another. As the second shot becomes distinct, the first slowly disappears.
dolly Camera platform. Dolly-in: Move platform toward subject. Dolly-out: Move platform away.
dub The transfer of one video tape to another.

establishing shot Frequently a wide shot; used to give the viewer a sense of the scene of action.

FI or fade in A scene that begins without full brilliance and gradually assumes full brightness. **FO** or **fade out** is the opposite.
freeze frame A single frame that is frozen into position.

graphics All visual displays, such as art work, maps, charts and still photos.

jump cut Transition from one subject to a different subject in an abrupt manner. Avoided with cutaway shot between the scenes.

lead-in Introductory statements to film or tape of actual event. The lead-in sets up the actuality by giving the context of the event.

lead-out Copy that comes immediately after tape or film of an actuality. The lead-out identifies the newsmaker again so listeners and viewers will know whom they just heard or saw. Used more often in radio. Also known as tag lines.
long shot Framing that takes in the scene of the event.

medium shot Framing of one person from head to waist or of small group seated at table. Known as MS.
mix Combining two or more sound elements into one.
montage A series of brief shots of various subjects to give a single impression or communicate one idea.

O/C On camera. A reporter delivering copy directly to the camera without covering pictures.
outtakes Scenes that are discarded for the final story.

panning or pan shot Moving the camera from left to right or right to left.

remote A taped or live broadcast from a location outside the studio; also, the unit that originates such a broadcast.

segué An uninterrupted transition from one sound to another; a sound dissolve. (Pronounced seg-way.)
SOF Sound on film. Recorded simultaneously with the picture.
SOT Sound on tape. Recorded simultaneously with picture on tape.

trim To eliminate material.

V/O Reporter's voice over pictures.
VTR Video tape recording.

zooming Use of a variable focus lens to take closeups and wide angle shots from a stationary position. By using a zoom lens an impression can be given of moving closer or farther away from the subject.

Broadcast Terms

Index